KU-204-562

to change rapidly, especially in shops and restaurants. If prices vary wildly from those we've quoted, ask whether there's a good reason, and then please email us to let us know. We aim to give the best and most up-to-date advice, and we always want to know if you've been badly treated or overcharged.

THE LIE OF THE LAND
While the various individual neighbourhoods and cities that make up Los Angeles are fairly easy to navigate, the metropolitan area as a whole is daunting for the first-time visitor. To help ease the stress, we've provided detailed driving directions for all establishments listed in the book, giving not only their address and cross street but also instructions on how to reach them from the most convenient freeway or major road. (The exit given might not be the nearest, but is the most straightforward.) For a primer on LA's layout, *see pp68-70*.

LA's neighbourhoods have very distinct characters, but the boundaries that separate them are often fuzzy. We've generally used the most commonly accepted demarcations; for a

map that defines them, *see p336*. The back of this book also includes street maps of the most commonly visited parts of LA, along with a comprehensive street index. The street maps start on page 326, and pinpoint the locations of hotels (❶), restaurants (❶), coffeehouses (❶), and bars (❶) featured elsewhere in the guide. For all addresses throughout the book, we've given both a cross-street and a map reference, so finding your way around should be simple.

TELEPHONE NUMBERS
The LA region has numerous phone codes. All local phone numbers in this guide are prefaced by a 1 and an area code: for example, 1-310 123 4567. Always dial the 11-digit number as listed, even if you're calling from a phone in the same area code. For more, *see p311*.

ESSENTIAL INFORMATION
For practical information on the city, including visa, customs and immigration information, disabled access, emergency phone numbers, useful websites and the local transport network, see the Directory (*pp302-314*).

LET US KNOW WHAT YOU THINK
We hope you enjoy *Time Out Los Angeles*, and we'd like to know what you think of it. We welcome tips for places that you believe we should include in future editions and appreciate your feedback on our choices. Please email us at guides@timeout.com.

There is an online version of this guide, along with guides to more than 50 other international cities, at **www.timeout.com**.

Up to 20%
Time Out
discount

▶ **California driving**

Time Out readers renting with Alamo across the USA enjoy up to 20% discount off our fully inclusive rates.

Plus, we're offering you free additional driver cover, saving you up to $70 per week, per driver.

■ Choice of cars including convertibles and SUVs
■ Locations throughout LA and California
■ Free one-ways
■ Great value

Click on the latest Alamo deals at
www.alamo.co.uk/offer/timeout
or call 0870 400 4565 quoting TIMEOUT

Los Angeles

timeout.com/losangeles

917 . 9494

Published by Time Out Guides Ltd, a wholly owned subsidiary of Time Out Group Ltd.
Time Out and the Time Out logo are trademarks of Time Out Group Ltd.

© **Time Out Group Ltd 2008**
Previous editions 1997, 1999, 2001, 2004, 2006.

10 9 8 7 6 5 4 3 2 1

This edition first published in Great Britain in 2008 by Ebury Publishing
A Random House Group Company
20 Vauxhall Bridge Road, London SW1V 2SA

Random House UK Limited Reg. No. 954009

Random House Australia Pty Limited 20 Alfred Street, Milsons Point, Sydney, New South Wales 2061, Australia
Random House New Zealand Limited 18 Poland Road, Glenfield, Auckland 10, New Zealand
Random House South Africa (Pty) Limited Isle of Houghton, Corner Boundary Road & Carse O'Gowrie,
Houghton 2198, South Africa

Distributed in the US by Publishers Group West
Distributed in Canada by Publishers Group Canada

For further distribution details, see www.timeout.com

ISBN: 978-1-84670-062-0

A CIP catalogue record for this book is available from the British Library.

Printed and bound by Firmengruppe APPL, aprinta druck, Wemding, Germany.

The Random House Group Limited supports The Forest Stewardship Council (FSC), the leading international
forest certification organisation. All our titles that are printed on Greenpeace approved FSC certified paper carry
the FSC logo. Our paper procurement policy can be found at www.rbooks.co.uk/environment.

Time Out carbon-offsets all its flights with Trees for Cities (www.treesforcities.org).

Time Out Guides Limited
Universal House
251 Tottenham Court Road
London W1T 7AB
Tel + 44 (0)20 7813 3000
Fax + 44 (0)20 7813 6001
Email guides@timeout.com
www.timeout.com

Editorial

Editor Will Fulford-Jones
Consultant Editor Rebecca Epstein
Copy Editors Holly Pick, Edoardo Albert,
Charlie Godfrey-Faussett
Listings Editor Miranda Morton
Proofreader Patrick Mulkern
Indexer Anna Norman

Managing Director Peter Fiennes
Financial Director Gareth Garner
Editorial Director Ruth Jarvis
Deputy Series Editor Dominic Earle
Editorial Manager Holly Pick
Assistant Management Accountant Ija Krasnikova

Design

Art Director Scott Moore
Art Editor Pinelope Kourmouzoglou
Senior Designer Henry Elphick
Graphic Designers Gemma Doyle, Kei Ishimaru
Studio Intern Tamarin Wilkinson
Advertising Designer Jodi Sher

Picture Desk

Picture Editor Jael Marschner
Deputy Picture Editor Katie Morris
Picture Researcher Gemma Walters
Picture Desk Assistant Marzena Zoladz

Advertising

Commercial Director Mark Phillips
International Advertising Manager Kasimir Berger
International Sales Executive Charlie Sokol
Advertising Assistant Kate Staddon

Marketing

Marketing Manager Yvonne Poon
Sales & Marketing Director, North America Lisa Levinson
Senior Publishing Brand Manager Luthfa Begum
Marketing Designers Anthony Huggins, Nicola Wilson

Production

Group Production Director Mark Lamond
Production Manager Brendan McKeown
Production Controller Damian Bennett
Production Coordinator Julie Pallot

Time Out Group

Chairman Tony Elliott
Group General Manager/Director Nichola Coulthard
Time Out Communications Ltd MD David Pepper
Time Out International Ltd MD Cathy Runciman
Group IT Director Simon Chappell
Head of Marketing Catherine Demajo

Contributors

Introduction Will Fulford-Jones. **History** Will Fulford-Jones (*Man about town* Kim Cooper). **Los Angeles Today** Frances Anderton. **Architecture** Frances Anderton. **On the Road** Will Fulford-Jones. **Eternal Fame** Lesley McCave. **The Natural World** Frances Anderton. **Where to Stay** Will Fulford-Jones, Allison Milionis (*Spa for a day* Lesley McCave). **Sightseeing** Will Fulford-Jones (*Sex on the beach*, *The great escape* Miranda Morton; *The secret gardens*, *Fruit for thought*, *Days of the dead* Kim Cooper; *Ghouls' paradise* Lesley McCave; *The great white way forward*, *Grow your own* Allison Milionis). **Restaurants** Richard Foss (*Life is sweets*, *Vintage vittles* Kim Cooper). **Coffeehouses** Katherine Spiers. **Bars** Julianne Gorman (*Top ten: Happy hours* Miranda Morton). **Shops & Services** Lesley McCave, Will Fulford-Jones (*It's easy being green* Allison Milionis; *Take a letter* Julianne Gorman). **Festivals & Events** Shana Nys Dambrot. **Children** Frances Anderton (*Bob's your uncle* Kim Cooper). **Comedy** Libby Molyneaux. **Film & TV** Jason Jude Chan (*Caught on camera* Matthew Duersten). **Galleries** Shana Nys Dambrot (*Trains of thought* Allison Milionis). **Gay & Lesbian** Julian Hooper. **Music** Natalie Nichols, Will Fulford-Jones (*Mix and match* Natalie Nichols). **Nightlife** Dennis Romero (*High spirits* Will Fulford-Jones). **Sports & Fitness** Isaac Davis (*Two wheels good* Allison Milionis; *Them's the breaks* Dennis Romero). **Theatre & Dance** Don Shirley. **Trips Out of Town** Will Fulford-Jones (*Mountain high* Kim Cooper; *Hollywood and vines* Richard Foss). **Directory** Will Fulford-Jones.

Maps john@jsgraphics.co.uk, except p335 used by kind permission of the Los Angeles Country Metropolitan Transit Authority.

Photography Sarah Hadley, except: pages 4, 285, 290, 294 Heloise Bergman; pages 7, 293 RW Sims; pages 9, 25, 32, 75, 82, 83, 90, 115, 126, 170, 214, 220, 229, 230, 272 Amanda C Edwards; page 15 Autry National Center; page 17 Associated Press; pages 18, 22, 38, 39, 44, 77, 78, 80, 96, 98, 112, 122, 124, 125, 136, 165, 189, 218, 219, 276 Max Malandrino; page 21, 40 Getty Images; page 24 AFP/Getty Images; pages 26, 36, 56, 65, 85, 86, 105, 106, 109, 111, 118, 139, 253, 288, 296, 298, 299 Will Fulford-Jones; page 29 Peer Eschenbach; page 34 Luca Babini/CORBIS; page 107 Olivia Rutherford; page 153 Oliver Knight; page 225 Rex Features; page 233 Faces Distributing Corporation/Photofest; page 250 Los Angeles Philharmonic; page 268 Angels Baseball; page 274 Elan Fleisher; page 277 Craig Schwartz; page 278 Ed Will; page 281 John Luker. The following image was provided by the featured establishment/artist: page 60.

The Editor would like to thank Dan Epstein; Robin McClain, Michael McDowell, Bill Karz and Kiyomi Emi at LA Inc; Gayle Anderson at the MTA; and all contributors to previous editions of *Time Out Los Angeles*, whose work forms the basis for parts of this book.

Contents

Limerick
County Library

Introduction	**6**

In Context — **9**

History	**10**
Los Angeles Today	**22**
Architecture	**25**
On the Road	**34**
Eternal Fame	**37**
The Natural World	**40**

Where to Stay — **43**

Where to Stay	**44**

Sightseeing — **67**

Introduction	**68**
Santa Monica & the Beach Towns	**74**
Brentwood to Beverly Hills	**84**
West Hollywood, Hollywood & Midtown	**92**
Los Feliz to Echo Park	**104**
Downtown	**110**
East Los Angeles	**120**
South Los Angeles	**123**
The Valleys	**129**
Heading South	**136**

Eat, Drink, Shop — **143**

Restaurants	**144**
Coffeehouses	**170**
Bars	**175**
Shops & Services	**187**

Arts & Entertainment — **211**

Festivals & Events	**212**
Children	**217**
Comedy	**223**
Film & TV	**227**
Galleries	**235**
Gay & Lesbian	**242**
Music	**250**
Nightclubs	**261**
Sports & Fitness	**268**
Theatre & Dance	**277**

Trips Out of Town — **283**

Getting Started	**284**
North to Santa Barbara	**285**
The Deserts	**287**
South to San Diego	**295**

Directory — **301**

Getting Around	**302**
Resources A-Z	**306**
Further Reference	**313**
Index	**315**
Advertisers' Index	**322**

Maps — **323**

Los Angeles Overview	**324**
Santa Monica & Venice	**326**
Beverly Hills & Around	**327**
West Hollywood & Around	**328**
Hollywood & Midtown	**329**
East of Hollywood	**330**
Downtown	**331**
Street Index	**332**
Metro Rail Network	**335**
Los Angeles by Area	**336**

Introduction

These are interesting times in Los Angeles. First settled in the late 1700s, the city really began to grow about 100 years later when the railroad arrived, and was allowed to expand more or less unchecked throughout the last century. However, the wild growth it enjoyed has come at a cost. And the result, at least in recent years, has been a small but potentially profound change in the way LA manages the further expansion that now seems inevitable.

With space at a premium, architects are building upwards rather than outwards for the first time, with condo towers now starting to look down over the single-family homes that constitute the city's infamous sprawl. And with traffic almost at a standstill, the city's Metro rail network is at last being extended beyond its previously limited reach.

The fact that this new urbanism has been greeted in several quarters by derision and resentment – a number of residents have actively campaigned against the expansion of the Metro network into their neighbourhoods – is indicative of how deeply wedded some Angelenos are to the lifestyle that brought many of them to the city in the first place. Over the years, countless people from countless cultures have headed here in search of the year-round sunshine and wide-open boulevards of popular legends. So many, in fact, that the year-round sun is now often wrapped in a blanket of smog caused, in part, by the volume of traffic.

Up to a point, then, Los Angeles has been a victim of its own success. However, despite problems with its infrastructure, a success it remains. At the turn of the 20th century, this was a city built on hard work and outlandish dreams. One hundred years later, the same is still true. LA began to grow almost as part of a social experiment, an attempt to inhabit a region that appeared uninhabitable. And despite the heat, the earthquakes and, before William Mulholland piped it in, the lack of water, the experiment succeeded.

And although it appears unmanageable at first glance, LA's spreadeagled immensity is ultimately its greatest asset. Without it, the variety that spices life here would not be anything like as rich. Honeypot attractions such as the Getty Center and Disneyland are balanced by unassuming neighbourhoods rich with history and community spirit; the natural appeal of the Pacific coast stands in rugged, bemused opposition to the skyscrapers of Downtown and Century City; and the manicured, star-packed likes of Beverly Hills and Bel Air provide a thick contrast to poorer, livelier locales dominated by Thais and Mexicans, African Americans and Japanese Americans. These are interesting times in Los Angeles. But it was ever thus.

ABOUT TIME OUT CITY GUIDES

This is the sixth edition of *Time Out Los Angeles*, one of an expanding series of more than 50 Time Out guides produced by the people behind the successful listings magazines in London, New York, Chicago and a variety of other cities around the globe. Our guides are all written by resident experts who have striven to provide you with all the most up-to-date information you'll need to explore the city or read up on its background, whether you're a local or a first-time visitor.

THE LOWDOWN ON THE LISTINGS

We've tried to make this book as useful as possible. Addresses, telephone numbers, websites, transport information, opening times, admission prices and credit card details have all been included in the listings, as are details of selected other facilities and services. All were checked and correct at press time. However,

business owners and managers can change their arrangements at any time, and with little notice. Before you go out of your way, we strongly advise you to phone ahead and check opening times and other relevant particulars. While every effort has been made to ensure the accuracy of the information in this guide, the publishers cannot accept responsibility for any errors it may contain.

PRICES AND PAYMENT

Our listings detail which of the five major credit cards – American Express (AmEx), Diners Club (DC), Discover (Disc), MasterCard (MC) and Visa (V) – are accepted at each venue. Many businesses will also accept other cards, as well as travellers' cheques issued by a major financial institution.

The prices we've listed in this guide should be treated as guidelines, not gospel. Fluctuating exchange rates and inflation can cause prices

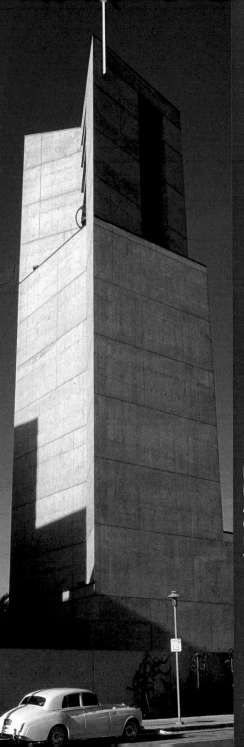

In Context

History	10
LA Today	22
Architecture	25
On the Road	34
Eternal Fame	37
The Natural World	40

Features

Man about town	15
Gold in them hills	18
Googie	27
Y viva España	29
Perfectly Frank	32

Cathedral of Our Lady of the Angels.
See p31.

The Hollywood Freeway, under construction in the '50s. *See p19.*

History

Films and freeways, invention and tension.

Given the city's recent developmental history, perhaps it's appropriate that settlement in Los Angeles began with a series of single-family suburbs scattered haphazardly across its landscape. Prior to the arrival of Spanish colonists in the latter part of the 18th century, what is now metropolitan Los Angeles was populated by 30,000 Native Americans. But they weren't farmers: instead, they relied on hunting and native plants for food. And, unlike the Iroquois and other tribes in North America, they hadn't yet organised themselves into strong political confederations. Instead, they lived in small settlements surrounding the area's few rivers, each group adopting a separate identity.

Backed by military muscle, the Spanish arrived and began to establish a string of

Franciscan missions along the coast. The first was established in San Diego during 1769; two years later, the San Gabriel Mission marked the initial Spanish foray into what would later become Los Angeles County. The missionaries' supposed ambition was to spread the Christian faith, but life on their new missions proved feudal and even brutal. The reluctant Native American converts were rounded up from their small settlements and virtually enslaved by the Franciscans. Thousands died, leading the missionaries to head deep into the surrounding countryside in search of more 'converts'.

The history of Los Angeles as a city begins in 1781, the year the British surrendered to George Washington in Virginia and effectively ended the War of Independence, when the

Spaniards decided that they needed a settlement (or pueblo) in Southern California to serve as a way-station for the military. At a site nine miles east of the San Gabriel Mission, where the Los Angeles River widened, governor Felipe de Neve laid out a plaza measuring 275 feet by 180 feet (84 metres by 55 metres). Around it were marked a series of lots, each with a 55-foot (17-metre) frontage on the plaza.

De Neve commissioned his aides to recruit 24 settlers and their families from Sonora, more than 350 miles north. On 18 August 1781, after a forced march of 100 days through desert heat, the 12 men, 11 women and 21 children who survived the trip arrived at the plaza. Thus did El Pueblo de Nuestra Señora la Reina de Los Angeles de Porciúncula begin as it has always since grown: not with a hardy band of motivated settlers, but with a real estate agent looking for customers. (The remains of this early settlement stand just north of modern-day Downtown LA, on now-touristy Olvera Street. They were designated a Califoria State Historic Landmark in 1953.)

Although other missions were established in and near the region, among them San Buenaventura, San Fernando and San Juan Capistrano, De Neve's new settlement remained, literally, a dusty cow town for decades: the population in 1800 was made up of 315 people and 12,500 cows. However, after Mexico declared itself independent from Spain in 1821 and annexed California during the following year, the Spanish-born priests were ordered out of the area. The mission system soon broke down, and powerful local families, eager to exploit mission land, received dozens of large land grants from the Mexican government. Most of these *ranchos*, which were typically several thousand acres in size, were recognised as valid claims of title when California entered the United States in 1850. Many remained intact into the 20th century, one of many factors that allowed large-scale, mass-production land development to occur in the region.

Americans had been informally colonising Los Angeles throughout the era of Mexican rule, as wandering opportunists arrived in the town, married into prominent 'Spanish' families and renamed themselves 'Don Otto' or 'Don Bill'. The transfer of the cow town into US hands occurred during the forcible annexation of California that triggered the Mexican-American war of 1846-48. On 13 August 1846, Commodore RF Stockton landed at San Pedro with 500 marines and started his march to the pueblo. With political support from the 'Dons', he captured the settlement without firing a shot. The US-Mexican treaty of 1848 confirmed US dominion over

California; on 9 September 1850, it officially became the 31st state of the Union.

BOOMS AND BUSTS

Los Angeles grew steadily but somewhat unspectacularly over the next 20 years, becoming a centre of California's 'hide and tallow' trade: farmers would raise cattle, then sell the hides for coats and the fat for candle-tallow to trading companies from the East Coast and Europe. Richard Henry Dana's *Two Years Before the Mast* (1840), California's first literary masterpiece, includes memorable descriptions of the author trudging through the shallow waters of San Pedro harbour with cowhides on his back. But when the gold rush hit Northern California, the cattle barons of Los Angeles discovered they could sell the cows for beef at $30 a head to the gold fields, rather than at $3 a head to the traders.

'Nothing captures a sense of LA's primal energy during the 1920s like the rampant oil business.'

In 1883, the transcontinental railroad from New Orleans to Los Angeles was finally completed, bringing with it the long-expected boom. A price war broke out among the railroads, and the cost of a one-way ticket to LA dropped from $125 to a mere dollar. Naturally enough, more and more people took the westbound railroad: in 1887, the Southern Pacific Railroad transported 120,000 people to LA, at the time a city of just 10,000 residents. The instability of the local economy meant that the real estate boom didn't last: one of the reasons that LA's population had grown so dramatically was that many immigrants simply couldn't afford to leave. But despite the crash, the 1880s transformed Los Angeles from a cow town into a fast-growing hustlers' paradise.

After the short-lived prosperity of the 1880s, the land barons and real estate operators who came to dominate LA became determined to lay more solid foundations for the city's expansion. Forming the Los Angeles Chamber of Commerce in 1888, they took the unprecedented step of embarking on a nationwide campaign to attract new immigrants to the region, sending advertisements, brochures and even quasi-evangelical speakers to spread the word of the Golden State in the Midwest. It was this commercial offensive that led journalist Morrow Mayo to conclude that LA was not a city but 'a commodity; something to be advertised and sold to the people of the United States like automobiles, cigarettes and mouthwashes.'

Joy Ride

For shopping, dining and simply loving life, there's no place like it. Experience the magic of the one and only, **The Grove.**

T H E
G R O V E

189 The Grove Drive,
Los Angeles, CA 90036
323.900.8080
thegrovela.com

Life. Style. Caruso.

Custo Barcelona	The Cheesecake Factory
Crate & Barrel	Tracy Allen Fine Jewelry
Michael Kors	Barneys New York CO-OP
Nordstrom	Kiehl's since 1851
Abercrombie & Fitch	Bistro The Farm of Beverly Hills
American Girl Café	Morels French Steakhouse & Bistro
Pottery Barn Kids	Theodore
Coach	*partial listing*

The Icon of Style

The ultimate in shopping, dining, entertainment and hotel-style living. Introducing luxury apartments and condominiums. **The Americana at Brand.**

Gilly Hicks	Barneys New York CO-OP
Calvin Klein	Barnes & Noble
Michael Stars	Kitson
Stuart Weitzman	Katsuya
Paperchase	Cole Haan
Tiffany & Co.	Peek, Aren't You Curious
Ruehl	Frida Mexican Cuisine
Puma	BCBGMAXAZRIA
Caffe Primo	*partial listing*

Still, the charm offensive had a tangible effect. As commodity prices rose in the first decade of the 20th century, thousands of Midwestern farmers sold up, moved west and set in motion the wheels of a new boom. Encouraged by the influx of new residents, the city's land barons soon pulled off one of the most audacious and duplicitous schemes ever devised to ensure a city's greatness.

WATER, WATER EVERYWHERE

In 1904, former Los Angeles mayor Fred Eaton travelled to the Owens Valley, a high-desert region 230 miles north of Los Angeles. Claiming that he was working on a dam project for the federal government, Eaton began purchasing land along the Owens River. But after he'd bought huge swathes of the area, Eaton revealed his true purpose: to divert the Owens River through an aqueduct to LA.

Whipped into a frenzy by trumped-up fears of a drought in 1905, Los Angeles voters approved a bond issue that called for the construction of an aqueduct from the Owens Valley to the city. LA had enough water to serve the population at the time, but not enough to enable its growth. As William Mulholland, the city's water engineer, put it: 'If we don't get it, we won't need it.' Mulholland, a self-taught Irish immigrant, went on to direct one of the great engineering feats in US history. A century after its completion, his 230-mile aqueduct still operates without electrical power, entirely on a gravity system. 'There it is,' Mulholland told the people of LA when the floodway opened in 1913. 'Take it.' The aqueduct didn't actually come to the heart of Los Angeles: it went only as far as the San Fernando Valley, an adjacent farming region. But in the last and perhaps most masterful part of the scam, it turned out that LA's land barons had secretly bought the valley on the cheap, annexed it to the city and then splashed irrigating Owens Valley water on it, all in a successful attempt to increase its value. Today, the San Fernando Valley, population 1.5 million, is the prototypical US suburb, and its people chafe under the Los Angeles city controls that brought water to their valley in the first place.

MOTORS AND MOVIES

With its water supply in place, Los Angeles boomed in the 1910s and 1920s like no other American city. The expansion was partly dependent on real-estate speculation, but it was also due to the rise of three new industries: petroleum, aircraft and movies. With little natural wood and almost no coal, the city suffered regular fuel crises that, in some cases, were as severe as its water problem. However,

the discovery of oil in metropolitan LA between 1900 and 1925, particularly around the La Brea Tar Pits, in Huntington Beach and at Santa Fe Springs, put an end to the troubles. The result was a plentiful supply of oil that enriched the region and helped to fuel the city's growing love affair with the automobile.

Its residents scattered far and wide, Los Angeles took to the car more readily than any city except Detroit. Car sales were high: the city soon developed its own thriving oil, automobile and tyre industries, each with its own monuments. In 1928, Adolph Schleicher, president of the Samson Tire & Rubber Co, constructed an $8-million tyre plant modelled after a royal palace once built by the king of Assyria. The plant (5675 Telegraph Road, City of Commerce) has since been reborn as a shopping mecca.

Movies and aircraft came to Los Angeles during the 1910s for the same reasons as its incoming residents: temperate weather, low rainfall and cheap land, the last of these providing the wide open spaces that both industries needed in order to operate. In 1921, Donald Douglas founded his aircraft company, a predecessor to McDonnell-Douglas, at Clover Field in Santa Monica (now Santa Monica Municipal Airport); the Lockheed brothers moved their business from Santa Barbara to LA in 1926; and Jack Northrop, who had worked with both Douglas and the Lockheeds, started his own company in Burbank in 1928. Together, the three firms later formed the foundation of the US's 'military-industrial' complex.

Filming began in Los Angeles around 1910, moving to Hollywood in 1911 when the Blondeau Tavern at Gower Street and Sunset Boulevard was turned into a movie studio. At the time, Hollywood was being marketed as a pious and sedate suburb, and the intrusion of the film industry was resented. The business was never really centred on the neighbourhood: Culver City and Burbank, both home to a number of studios, have stronger claims on the title of the industry's capital. Nevertheless, Hollywood became the financial and social centre of the film world, as the area's population grew from 4,000 in 1910 to 30,000 in 1920 and 235,000 in 1930. The wealth that defined the period is still visible in the magnificent commercial architecture along Hollywood Boulevard between Cahuenga and Highland Avenues. However, the town's earliest movie palaces were built not in Hollywood but on Broadway in Downtown LA.

PROGRESS OF SORTS

During the 1920s, a decade that saw the population of Los Angeles double, the city became a kind of national suburb, where the

Man about town

Charles Fletcher Lummis is today chiefly remembered, if he's remembered at all, as the founder of the Southwest Museum. However, the New England-born, Harvard-educated Lummis was one of early LA's most colourful characters, a corduroy-clad literary adventurer who helped shape the city simply because he could never sit still.

Lummis's Californian adventure began in 1884 when, while working as a reporter in Cincinnati, he was offered a job with the *Los Angeles Times*. He left his home, his job and his tolerant physician bride Dorothea and began a 143-day solo tramp across the country, submitting weekly reports on his misadventures to the *Los Angeles Times*. Harrison Gray Otis, the paper's owner, put him to work as its city editor on the morning after he finally arrived in LA; Lum didn't sleep for more than two hours nightly until three years later, when he woke up partly paralysed after a stroke.

Recalling his happy travels through the pueblos of the Southwest, Lum moved to New Mexico, where he willed himself well while learning the local lore and language. Although recuperating, he continued to write, and soon made powerful enemies through his investigative journalism. One man was even moved to shoot at Lummis: he would have died but for a well-timed yawn, which left him with only a minor wound rather than a shattered jaw. Lum also risked death journeying south in an attempt to photograph the secret rites of a mysterious local Catholic cult as they reenacted Christ's Crucifixion, but he escaped unharmed and eventually returned to Los Angeles.

Back home, Lum turned his hand to construction and built El Alisal (*see p109*), a rough-hewn home made from Arroyo river rock and a great deal of sweat. As if that didn't take enough of his time, he founded a literary magazine, took a job as the city's official librarian (burning his personal brand into the top edge of the rarer books), collected Indian artefacts, founded the Landmarks Club in a bid to save the deteriorating missions and built the city's first true museum on the hill above his Highland Park home (*see p109*). And after Theodore Roosevelt, his Harvard classmate, became president, he used his influence to advocate for Native American rights.

Lum was made of sturdy stuff, but not even he could continue to expend such energy. As he aged, Lum suffered physical and emotional trials, and eventually became estranged from his second wife, Eva, after she objected to the young 'secretaries' he kept on hand at all times. His final years were spent at a much diminished El Alisal, with infrequent visitors. But upon his death in 1928, at the age of 69, Lummis left a legacy of respect for native peoples and traditional mores that places him among the most influential figures in the Southwest. His home and museum still stand as symbols of his abiding love for the region.

middle classes sought refuge from the teeming immigrant groups so prevalent in other large metropolises. Civic leaders worked hard to build the type of edifices and institutions that they thought a big city deserved: the Biltmore Hotel and the adjacent Los Angeles Central Library, Los Angeles City Hall, the Los Angeles Coliseum, the University of Southern California and Exposition Park. And with the creation of the Los Angeles Stock Exchange (now the Pacific Stock Exchange), LA became the financial capital of the West Coast.

However, this process of making Los Angeles the great 'white' city served to marginalise the minority groups that had long been a part of local life. The Mexican and Mexican American population, which had grown rapidly and had provided the city with a much-needed labour force, was pushed out of Downtown into what is now the East LA barrio. And the African Americans, who had previously lived all over the city, found themselves confined to an area south of Downtown straddling Central Avenue, which became known as South Central. Both of these mini-migrations laid the foundation for serious social unrest in later decades.

Despite these problems, Los Angeles in the 1920s had an irrepressible energy. The arrival of so many newcomers created a rootlessness that manifested itself in a thousand different ways. Those in need of companionship were drawn to the city's many cafeterias (invented in LA), which served as incubators of random social activity. Those in need of a restored faith had, and still have, their choice of any number of faith healers. And those searching for a quick profit were drawn to the tantalising claims of local oil companies in search of investors. Indeed, nothing captures a sense of LA's primal energy during the 1920s like the rampant oil business.

With a steady supply of gushers, often in residential areas, oil promoters had a ready-made set of samples with which to promote their products. And with an endless stream of equity-rich farm refugees from the Midwest, they also had a ready-made pool of gullible investors. The most skilled promoter was a Canadian named CC Julian, who attracted millions of dollars to his oil company with a string of newspaper ads that had the narrative drive of a soap opera. When it became clear that he couldn't deliver on his promises, he was elbowed out of his own firm by other swindlers who continued the scam, issuing millions of bogus shares and bribing the district attorney in a bid to stay out of trouble. The end came in 1931, when a defrauded investor opened fire in an LA courtroom on

a banker who had been involved in the scam. The failed investor had ten cents to his name when he was arrested. The crooked banker's pockets held $63,000.

GROWING UP

As was the case elsewhere in the US, the 1930s proved rather more sober than the roaring '20s in Los Angeles. With the boom over and the Depression in full swing, the city's growth slowed, and the city's new arrivals were very different from their predecessors. Instead of greeting wealthy Midwestern farmers, LA now attracted poor white refugees from the Dust Bowl of Oklahoma and Texas, the 'Okies' made famous in John Steinbeck's novel *The Grapes of Wrath*. These unskilled workers wound up as farm labourers and hangers-on in the margins of society.

Dealing with these newcomers proved difficult for Los Angeles, but the problem was intertwined with another conundrum: how to handle the equally poor and unskilled Mexican and Mexican American population. After farm owners chose to hire Okies over Mexicans, LA County became overwhelmed by the cost of public relief. The authorities resorted to repatriating even those Mexicans who were born and raised in Los Angeles.

The arrival of the Okies and other hobos caused a nasty public backlash. But it also built a liberal political mood among the have-nots, which culminated in the near-election of reformer and novelist Upton Sinclair as California's governor. In the early '30s, Sinclair wrote a diatribe called *I, Governor of California, and How I Ended Poverty*, before going on to found the End Poverty in California (EPIC) movement and eventually winning the Democratic gubernatorial nomination for the 1934 elections. Only a concerted effort by reactionary political forces, aided by movie-house propaganda from the film industry, defeated his bid. After his failure, Sinclair followed his original pamphlet with a book entitled *I, Governor of California, and How I Got Licked*.

The region also had other problems with which to contend: the 1933 Long Beach earthquake, for example, the first major tremor to hit the city after its expansion. But optimism gradually returned, with a handful of developments lending the locals some new-found pride. Held at the Coliseum, the 1932 Olympics saw the expansion and aesthetic redevelopment of 10th Street: the street was renamed Olympic Boulevard and lined with palm trees, thus setting the fashion for palms in LA. Seven years later, the first local freeway was built: the Arroyo Seco Parkway, now the Pasadena Freeway. And in 1941, a new aqueduct brought water from the Hoover Dam along the Colorado River, helping to cater for the city's continued growth.

World War II caused the single biggest upheaval Los Angeles had seen to that point, laying the foundations for the modern metropolis it went on to become. Already at the forefront of aviation, the city rapidly grew industrialised during the war, becoming both a major military manufacturing centre and

a staging ground for the American fight against Japan in the Pacific. More than 5,000 new manufacturing plants were built in LA during the war, mostly in outlying locations. Dormitory communities sprang up to accommodate the workers, many of them 'model' towns sponsored by industrialists or the military. These new settlements helped to establish the sprawling pattern of urban development that came to characterise LA in the post-war years.

Controversial **Dodger Stadium**. *See p19.*

Gold in them hills

It seems wholly appropriate that the most famous landmark in Los Angeles wasn't built out of civic pride or in an attempt to improve the environment, but as a wildly ostentatious piece of advertising. Stuck for ideas as to how best to promote their new real-estate development in the Hollywood Hills, *Los Angeles Times* publisher Harry Chandler and Keystone Cops creator Mack Sennett hit upon an idea that was devastating in its simplicity. Some 50 feet tall, 450 feet wide and lit by 4,000 lightbulbs, their unmissable HOLLYWOODLAND sign was unveiled on 13 July 1923 and served its purpose brilliantly.

The sign was meant to stand for just 18 months, but it remained long after Chandler and Sennett had sold their properties. It briefly returned to the news in 1932, when 24-year-old British-born actress Peg Entwistle threw herself off the top of the 'H' after her dreams of stardom collapsed around her. But the sign was otherwise left to rot: into the late 1930s, when vandals laid waste to its lights, and the mid 1940s, when ownership of the land (and, it follows, the sign) slipped into the hands of the local government.

Only when the 'H' collapsed in 1949 did the authorities start to realise that they had to do something about the sign's decay. Some lobbied to get rid of it, while others campaigned to keep it. In the end, a compromise of sorts was reached: the last four letters were removed, but the first nine were given a refurbishment (albeit without their lights). HOLLYWOODLAND was dead; hooray, instead, for HOLLYWOOD. Still, the decline was stemmed only temporarily: despite being granted landmark status in 1973, no effort was made to protect the

sign. Graffiti was scratched on it, some parts of it were stolen, and, in 1977, an arsonist tried to torch the second 'L'.

It took an unlikely figure to restore a little star power to the landmark. When the Hollywood Chamber of Commerce estimated that a new sign would cost $250,000, Hugh Hefner hosted a fundraising gala at which individual letters were sponsored, to the tune of $27,700, by the likes of Gene Autry (the second 'L'), Andy Williams (the 'W') and Alice Cooper (the middle 'O', which he dedicated to Groucho Marx). The old sign came down in 1978, whereupon it was sold to a nightclub promoter named Hank Berger for $10,000. Three months later, the new version, its letters 45 feet tall and between 31 and 39 feet wide, was unveiled to much fanfare. It's this incarnation that still looks down over LA, protected by a security system following several unauthorised alterations: supporters of Oliver North covered the initial 'H' during the 1987 Iran-Contra hearings, two years after punk band the Raffeys had managed to adapt it so it read RAFFEYSOD.

In November 2005, the sign received its first all-over refurbishment in a decade. A San Diego-based firm sent 300 gallons of paint in a shade they named 'Hollywood White'; another company then moved in to do the five-week job, stripping back both the fronts and backs of the letters before giving them a fresh coat. In the same month, a gentleman named Dan Bliss put the original sign up for sale on eBay, having bought it from Berger two years earlier. The sale netted $450,400, roughly 20 times what the sign had cost to build 82 years earlier. Bliss's reason for selling? He needed to raise funds to invest in a movie.

COLOUR CLASH

The population of Los Angeles diversified still further during the '40s. During the war, more than 200,000 African Americans moved to the city, mostly from Louisiana and Texas, to take advantage of the job opportunities. But the restrictive property laws meant that the South Central ghetto didn't expand geographically in order to accommodate these new arrivals, and the area became seriously overcrowded. It wasn't until 1948, when the Supreme Court threw out restrictive covenants and paved the way for an exodus of middle-class blacks west into the Crenshaw district, that the South Central's burden began to ease.

> **'In the decade after the war, the entire LA region devoted itself to building anything and everything.'**

In desperate need of labourers, Los Angeles welcomed the return of the Mexicans and Mexican Americans who had been pushed out a decade earlier. However, tensions between white Angelenos and Mexicans were widespread and constantly threatened to boil over. In 1942, roughly 600 Mexican Americans were arrested in connection with a murder in the city. No fewer than 22 were charged, and, in January 1943, 17 were eventually convicted following a trial thick with racial epithets. The worst, though, was still to come.

When a white sailor on shore leave was injured during a group brawl with a number of Mexican Americans in May 1943, more than 100 sailors left their ships and stampeded into East LA in search of Latinos. A number of Mexicans were injured in the ensuing skirmishes, which became known as the Zoot Suit Riots after the baggy suits favoured by Mexican American men at the time. A national civil rights outcry ensued and a committee was set up to investigate the trouble. However, no punishment was ever meted out to the sailors, and some sections of the local press even praised their actions. On 2 October 1944, the 17 Mexican Americans found guilty at the 1943 murder trial each had their convictions quietly quashed at appeal, but the tensions nonetheless remained.

Discrimination against LA's growing Japanese community was even more pronounced. Most Japanese Americans on the West Coast were interned in camps by the federal government during World War II, no matter how patriotic their attitude to their new home. (Indeed, in a supreme irony, some young men were permitted to leave the internment camps to join the US armed forces, which many did enthusiastically.) Most Japanese lost their property during these years, much of it concentrated in the Little Tokyo area of LA just east of City Hall. It took decades for the neighbourhood to return to prosperity.

When the African Americans, Latinos and Japanese who fought for the US during the war returned to continued housing discrimination, police brutality and the general Angeleno attitude that they were not 'real Americans', their sense of alienation grew further. But because Los Angeles was a highly segregated city, most whites were able to ignore the race problem – especially after the war, when the city reaped the benefits of industrialisation and a new suburban boom began.

AFTER THE WAR

The post-war era in Los Angeles is often recalled as an idyllic spell of prosperity and harmony. In fact, it was an unsettled period during which the city struggled to keep up with the demands of massive growth. Taxes rose in order to fund new facilities and heavily oversubscribed schools went on 'double-sessions', teaching two classes in the same classroom.

In the decade after the war, the entire LA region devoted itself to building anything and everything. Freeway construction (*photo p10*), which had been stymied by the war, exploded in 1947 after California imposed an additional petrol tax to pay for a new road network. Over the next two decades, virtually the entire freeway system was constructed, a marvel of modern engineering and the driving force behind the city's unstoppable expansion. The new road network opened up vast tracts of land for urban development in outlying areas: chief among them were the San Fernando Valley and Orange County, linked to Los Angeles by the I-5 (aka the Golden State Freeway). A crucial event in the success of this suburbanisation was the opening, in 1955, of Disneyland, the world's first theme park.

Other leisure attractions helped to establish Los Angeles as a major city during the same period. In 1958, the city achieved 'major league' status by luring New York's Brooklyn Dodgers baseball team to the West Coast. But, as so often in LA's history, even this event was marred by racial tensions. In order to attract the Dodgers, the city gave them a spectacular site in Chavez Ravine, overlooking Downtown LA. Located in a low-income Latino neighbourhood, the site had been earmarked for use as a public housing project. The project, though, was never built; Dodger Stadium (*photo p17*) still stands today.

As suburbanisation continued in the 1950s and '60s, some areas prospered but others were left behind. On a hot summer night in 1965, the pent-up frustrations of the black ghetto exploded into one of the first and most destructive of the US's urban disturbances. The Watts Riots began after an African American man was pulled over on a drink-driving charge. By the time they were over, dozens of locals had been killed and hundreds of buildings had been destroyed; some estimates pinned the cost at around $40 million, a huge figure for the time. For many Angelenos living in their comfortable suburbs, the riots were the first indication that all was not well in their metropolis.

ONWARDS AND OUTWARDS

After the Watts Riots, Los Angeles began to struggle with its image problem, as national newspapers and magazines began to proclaim the end of the California Dream. Under a series of hard-line chiefs, the Los Angeles Police Department continued to treat minority neighbourhoods as if they were occupied territories. As they did so, a violent gang culture gradually began to develop in pockets of South Central LA.

'At the beginning of the 1990s, racial tensions turned Los Angeles into a social tinderbox.'

In 1966, despite having no previous political experience, former actor Ronald Reagan was elected as the state governor on a law-and-order platform. But despite his efforts, the city continued to grab the national headlines in a number of undesirable ways. Three years after Reagan's election, the Charles Manson cult killed actress Sharon Tate and others at a home in Benedict Canyon, disturbing the sense of tranquillity that permeated the high-end Beverly Hills suburb. And in 1971, the city suffered its worst earthquake in 38 years, escaping a high death toll only because the quake struck at the early hour of 6am. Out of this troubled period, however, emerged a towering political figure: Tom Bradley, an African American police captain who had grown up in the segregated world of Central Avenue and who later held his own in such white-dominated enclaves as UCLA and the LAPD.

While at the LAPD in the '50s, Bradley was assigned to improve relations with beleaguered Jewish shopkeepers in black neighbourhoods, an opportunity he used to help forge a cross-racial political alliance that sustained him for years. After retiring from the police, Bradley was elected to the City Council and, with strong support in South Central and the largely Jewish West Side, ran for mayor. He lost in 1969 but won four years later, becoming the first African American mayor of a predominantly white city (according to the 2000 census, the black population of the City of Los Angeles is only 12 per cent, and that of Los Angeles County a mere 10.5 per cent). By moving into the mayor's mansion, Bradley helped desegregate the Hancock Park neighbourhood, which had violently resisted the arrival of Nat 'King' Cole some years before.

A low-key man with a calming personality, Bradley successfully ruled the city for 20 years through the power of persuasion. During the 1970s, he sought to heal the city's long-open racial wounds. And in the early 1980s, he turned his attention to development, reviving Downtown and courting international business: the 1984 Olympics were to prove his greatest triumph. Bradley's efforts also benefited from a huge flow of Japanese capital into Los Angeles real estate in the 1980s. However, his popularity levels fell in the early 1990s, due in part to his handling of the Rodney King affair, and he was replaced as mayor by Richard Riordan in 1993 after deciding not to seek a sixth term in office. He died five years later.

TROUBLED TIMES

For all the optimism engendered by Bradley's work, the period during which he led the city offered only a partial respite from LA's chronic social and racial tensions. Public opinion in the region became more polarised in the 1970s, as affluent whites grew more conservative and found little in common with the immigrants who were turning LA into a melting pot. The decline of agriculture in Latin America made the city a magnet for immigrants from rural Mexico and elsewhere, both legal and illegal, while political strife in Central America led to the arrival of thousands more new arrivals. The city's position on the edge of the burgeoning Pacific Rim also attracted people (and capital) from Korea, the Philippines, Taiwan and Hong Kong.

The vast central areas of Los Angeles were re-energised by these newcomers. Tourism, trade and the garment industry boomed, as did the rapidly expanding Koreatown. But as the neighbourhoods changed, so friction grew. Latin American immigrants began crowding into historically black South Central, creating a culture clash with middle- and working-class home-owners. African Americans, in particular, felt more alienated than ever.

These tensions turned Los Angeles into a social tinderbox at the beginning of the 1990s.

The arrest and beating of black motorist Rodney King by four LAPD officers in 1991, captured on tape by a home video enthusiast, proved to be the turning point. When a jury acquitted the officers of assault in 1992, it touched off a three-day riot during which 50 people died and 1,000 buildings were destroyed by fire and looting. The events were more widespread and destructive than the Watts disturbances of 1965: indeed, it was the worst urban riot in US history. Then, in 1995, the arrest and trial of OJ Simpson, an African American football star accused of killing his white ex-wife and another man, gripped the city. Simpson's acquittal stunned white residents, but reassured doubting black locals that the legal system could be on their side.

INVENTING THE FUTURE

Yet despite racial tensions, an economic renaissance that began in the mid 1990s brought new life to LA. As the aerospace industry declined, so the entertainment industry rapidly expanded. In 1997, house prices started to rocket once more, just as they had in the 1970s and '80s. Meanwhile, the Latino community grew into the dominant racial group in Los Angeles County, a dramatic demographic change that affected everything from shopping malls to city government. Latinos are now the pivotal voting group in the city: for evidence, look no further than the triumph of Antonio Villaragoisa in the mayoral elections of 2005. By defeating incumbent candidate James Hahn in a run-off election, Villaragoisa became the city's first Latino mayor in more than a century.

Regardless, Los Angeles continues to face the political tumult typical of a big American city, something only amplified by the preponderance of different governments. Although it's hard to imagine anything could top the events of 2003, which saw California's governor Gray Davis turfed out of office in the middle of his term and replaced by actor-bodybuilder Arnold Schwarzenegger, scandal never seems far away. As LA edges into the 21st century, it faces the substantial challenge of finding ways to harness its formidable multicultural strengths.

MAR. 3 1991

Rodney King falls victim to the LAPD in 1991.

Slow going on the freeway...

LA Today

Frances Anderton wonders how the City of Angels will face a future that's no longer as bright as the midday sun.

On the surface, Los Angeles is an unusual place: sunshine in July and December, the effects of plastic surgery lining the faces of everyone from waitresses to doctors, freeways snaking in every direction. But beneath its surface image lie a number of other, subtler ways in which LA is different from your average East Coast metropolis. Locals here aren't woken by sounds typical to other cities: a rumbling subway, a diesel-belching bus, chiming church bells. If you're drunk and need a ride home, you can't stand at the side of the road and hail a cab. Although there's plenty of water and a port, there's no river running through the heart of the city. And those people in suits you see heading to work at 8am are probably earning less than the casually dressed men sitting idly outside Starbucks at 11am.

This is how Los Angeles has been for much of its existence. Urban in a very anti-urban way, the city is an alternate universe that inspires love and hate but rarely indifference: it's repellent to those who feel at home in London or Paris or New York, but hugely attractive to

those who are desperate to shake off the weight and the *mode de vie* of old cities. Or, at least, it has been until now. For LA is suffering through what can only be described as an identity crisis.

GROWING PAINS

For decades, Angelenos knew their home town was considered unusual and even weird by outsiders. Although they were hooked on the lifestyle it offered, they often felt insecure – some locals even aspired to the culture and the old-world prestige attached to cities on the East Coast and out in Europe. Eventually, Los Angeles became established in its own right, the grande dame of the sunbelt cities. But it's now starting to lose the very qualities that helped make it so different.

The space for constant reinvention once offered by Los Angeles is now harder than ever to find. The city has traditionally favoured single-family residences over apartment blocks and high-rises: as far back as 1930, an astonishing 93.7 per cent of LA's residential properties were single-family homes. However, as the city struggles to cope with its ever-growing population, urban planners have been forced to consider building not outwards but upwards, gradually turning LA from a horizontal city to a vertical one.

In the 12-month period after Antonio Villaraigosa was voted into office as the city's mayor in 2005, 86 per cent of the 16,874 housing units built in Los Angeles were multi-family properties. Some were just a few floors tall; others were towers with more than 30 storeys. Many analysts have seen this trend as the inevitable solution to the problems caused by the city's abundance of low-density housing. But this shift in LA's urban planning ideal hasn't come without its controversies: especially on the West Side, the most congested part of LA. Some residents were so angry at councilman Jack Weiss for supporting new high-rises in his district that they even tried to recall him from office.

Running hand in hand with these issues surrounding population density is the dreadful traffic that's now blighting a city once defined by its freewheeling, car-based culture. Built for the automobile, Los Angeles has also been ruined by it, as the ceaseless influx of people wanting to live in this paradise has made the lifestyle untenable. Day after day, citizens sit seething on clogged freeways and surface streets, commuting for hours between home and work. The issue has only been exacerbated by the lack of affordable housing: many Angelenos face lengthy commutes from outlying suburbs simply because they can't afford to live nearer their workplaces. The frustration sometimes snaps into road rage-inspired shootings: there were two separate incidents during the week that this essay was written.

The pro-growthers have justified their enthusiasm for new residential construction by promising new public transit systems for the affected areas in order to ease the burden on the roads. A number of new subway lines and rapid bus services have indeed opened during the last decade, but many other proposed additions to the public transportation system have not yet been built; the city is getting denser without welcoming any of density's advantages. Most notable among these unrealised plans is the long-mooted extension to the subway network's Purple Line that would, if it's eventually built, connect Downtown with Santa Monica.

However, many longtime Angelenos don't even want an expanded public transport network because they don't want LA to change; or, to be precise, they don't want it to *progress*. Essentially, they want to turn back the clock to the good old days: they want the people to disappear, the traffic to start moving and life

to return to the way it was before, back when you could sail 25 miles along an open freeway just to meet a friend for dinner. And, just as pertinently, public transit plans have also become a locus for LA's racial tensions: some residents of the city's nicer neighbourhoods essentially prefer to keep the city segregated.

IT'S NOT EASY BEING GREEN

This sense that LA's car-based lifestyle is under assault has been intensified by the aggravations of rising gas prices and the increasing awareness of global warming. The point of Los Angeles has always been consumption: large houses, oversized cars, ever-running air-conditioning, giant lawns drinking gallons of water channeled from outside the city. But the energy-inefficient lifestyle that the locals have long taken for granted has not only become congested but expensive and, worse, guilt-inducing.

Paradoxically, some of the more imaginative green design is being created here, and many leaders of the current American environmental movement are wealthy Angelenos. California governor Arnold Schwarzenegger owns five Hummers and flies a private jet back and forth almost daily to Sacramento. However, by backing green legislation, he's managed to position himself as the local poster boy for saving the planet. Many others in the entertainment industry have pulled the same sleight of hand, making public displays of their greenness by driving the kids to school in biodiesel-fuelled cars or adding solar panels to their 6,000-square-foot homes.

ENTERTAINMENT TONIGHT

The entertainment business has also suffered a hit to its confidence. In February 2008, the industry struggled to get back on its feet at the end of a 100-day writers' strike that put paid to most TV and movie production in the city. But the following month, the two leading unions representing TV and movie actors split in acrimonious fashion. Rather than presenting a united front in their own contract discussions with television and movie producers, the Screen Actors Guild (SAG) and the American Federation of Television & Radio Artists (AFTRA) ended up negotiating separately, causing yet more strife within an already troubled industry.

One result of the writers' strike was that the industry's creatives found they weren't quite as indispensable as they perhaps believed. During the strike, a number of prime-time TV shows went off the air, but many viewers seemed happy to pick from reruns and other cheaply produced programming spread across hundreds of cable channels, while others turned to

YouTube for their entertainment. At the same time, on a more general level video games and the internet have stolen the attentions of potential younger viewers, throwing a further spanner in the works of the entertainment business. While certainly not yet out, the industry is nonetheless down. Like the newspaper world, it knows the business is changing, but nobody understands exactly how.

NEIGHBOURHOOD WATCH

One quietly significant marker that points to the possible demise of LA's oddball soul is the emergence of Historic Preservation Overlay Zones, ordinances designed to protect historic neighbourhoods from alteration or demolition. The first HPOZ, covering the Victorian-era properties in Angelino Heights, was established in 1983. Today, the city of Los Angeles has 22 in total, with 16 others under consideration. Because HPOZs outlaw the demolition of buildings within their boundaries, and because they subject property owners to strict design reviews, they're the source of huge contention. The ordinances pit preservationists and house-proud home-owners against residents who wish to expand or change their properties and developers who might wish to eradicate them.

On one hand, it's a relief to know that after decades during which much of the city's heritage was destroyed, the survival of some historic properties has effectively been guaranteed. But one of the things that made and continues to make Los Angeles special is its lack of hindsight, its capacity to live in the present and continue reinventing itself. In previous decades, LA was an architects' paradise, resulting in a vast and varied canvas of buildings. HPOZs represent an aspiration towards good taste and social control, both of which seem deeply un-Angeleno. Many of the creative minds who moved here to take advantage of the regions' freedoms are now starting to look for new frontiers.

Los Angeles has never been a static city. A constant flow of new residents has maintained an exciting and dynamic state of flux. However, some aspects of immigration have had a destabilising effect. Perhaps most notable among them has been the arrival of huge numbers of Latin American immigrants (chiefly from Mexico) into neighbourhoods traditionally dominated by African Americans.

As more Latinos have arrived in the city, black Angelenos have found their communities transformed in ways they weren't anticipating, and their concerns haven't been helped by the anti-black prejudices held by some members of these new Latino communities. At the same time, black politicians have been left frustrated as they've lost ground to rising Latino political power; and on the streets, black gangs have found themselves outnumbered and outgunned – literally, in the case of numerous racially tinged shootings – by Latino tribes. This simmering anger hasn't been helped by other deprivations that have affected many corners of LA, regardless of race: terrible public schools, for instance, and limited job opportunities. These long simmering tensions have led even the most idealistic activists to warn of an explosion on the streets as bad as the 1992 Rodney King riots.

Los Angeles historians would confirm that immigration and real estate development are the engine of the region: there's never been a time when people weren't complaining about the negative by-products of one, the other or both. However, at the moment, it does feel as if the area is undergoing a seismic shift in lifestyle. Only time will tell how the city copes with the adjustment. But in the meantime, you can rest assured that, at least for the foreseeable future, the sunshine, the plastic surgery and the freeway network will all remain as tangible as ever.
● *Frances Anderton is the host of* DNA: Design and Architecture *and the producer of* To the Point, *both on KCRW 89.9 FM.*

... as the Governator hops into his Hummer.

Architecture

In terms of its buildings, variety really is LA's spice of life.

Los Angeles was founded and repeatedly reinvented by adventurers and fortune-seekers. Some showed up with 'nothing to declare but my genius', as Oscar Wilde once famously told a US customs officer. However, many others came laden with cultural baggage and the desire to carve a piece of their past into their future. The presence of these outsiders helps explain why much of LA's architectural landscape is a chaotic mishmash of borrowed styles, often executed with little finesse or imagination. But ever since the arrival of the transcontinental railroad in 1883 turned a dusty cow town into a forward-thinking metropolis, originality has flourished.

For the most part, LA appears bewilderingly vast: featureless and horizontal, at least from the freeways. And although there's been a spurt of noteworthy civic building in the last decade or so, the city boasts relatively few major public buildings or landmark corporate structures. To discover LA's architectural diversity, it's necessary to explore its residential districts. Topography offers a clue: much of the best work is tucked away in the hills, clinging to

'unbuildable' sites that appeal to clients with budgets to match their ambitions. As it did all those decades ago, Los Angeles continues to reward the explorer.

A CITY IS BORN

Little remains of the original 18th-century settlement of El Pueblo de Nuestra Señora la Reina de los Angeles de Porciúncula, and the newer buildings that have attempted to follow in its tradition are largely unmemorable. Misty-eyed preservationists often blather on about the city's roots and the adobe tradition, but the evidence is unconvincing: dull, provincial buildings, rebuilt or prettified.

Just north of today's Downtown, the **Olvera Street** district was the city's original hub, and today serves as a low-key, Mexican-themed tourist attraction. A handful of 19th-century

> **Chemosphere** (*p28*) Troy McClure lives in a cartoon version of Lautner's dazzling structure in a 1994 episode of *The Simpsons*

Bradbury Building.

buildings remain in place, many of them standing on or around an appealing, compact square that hosts regular markets and sporadic festivities. Among the more notable structures is the Italianate **Pico House**: built in 1870, it was the city's first hotel with indoor plumbing.

Other neighbourhoods hold a rich legacy of residential buildings that went up during the land boom of the late 1880s. In Echo Park, not far north of Downtown, stand a number of handsome houses built in the Queen Anne and Eastlake styles: the most impressive are located on the 1300 block of **Carroll Avenue**, between Douglas Street and Edgeware Road. And to the north-east, at the foot of the San Gabriel Mountains, **Pasadena** is home to many handsome bungalows built during the same period in the Craftsman style, an offshoot of the Victorian Arts & Crafts movement. The standout is Charles and Henry Greene's 1908 **Gamble House** (4 Westmoreland Place; *see p132*), a marvel of polished mahogany and Tiffany glass.

The most remarkable Victorian structure in LA, though, is south of Olvera Street in Downtown and explicitly not designed for residential use. The brick façade of the **Bradbury Building** (304 S Broadway; *see p117*), constructed as a garment factory by George Wyman in 1893 and now used as offices, is perfectly handsome, but it offers no hint of the astonishing interior: pass through the main doors (the building is open to the public) and you'll be greeted by a stunning sky-lit atrium, ringed by tiled galleries and ornamented with polished wood balustrades and open-cage lifts. The design was reputedly inspired by Edward Bellamy's science-fiction novel *Looking Backward*; appropriate, then, that it featured prominently in *Blade Runner*.

BETWEEN THE WARS

During the 1920s, Southern California embraced Mediterranean and Spanish-style traditions (*see p29* **Y viva España**). Local architects erected a panoply of pocket haciendas, Churrigueresque car showrooms and abstracted Andalucian farmhouses, and LA developed an insatiable and discriminate appetite for all things foreign and exotic. George Washington Smith and Wallace Neff set the pace: the town of **San Marino** contains several examples of their Spanish revivalist tendencies. However, all Beaux Arts-trained architects were masters of period style, and every builder could run up a mosque, a medieval castle or an Egyptian tomb. The movies emerging from Hollywood legitimised this eclecticism; the impulse came from newcomers who flocked to LA, dreaming of fortune or an easy life in the sun.

The city's favourite fantasy house sits, perhaps appropriately, in Beverly Hills. The **Spadena House** (Walden Drive, at Carmelita Avenue, Beverly Hills; *see p90*), commonly known as the Witch's House and the Hansel & Gretel House, was built as a movie set by Henry Oliver in 1921; five years later, it was moved to its present location and converted into a private residence. LA's greatest personal fantasy, though, is not a cinematic creation or a rich man's folly. Built between 1921 and 1954 with dogged, irrational but ultimately heroic persistence by an Italian tilesetter named Simon Rodia, the **Watts Towers** (1727 & 1765 E 107th Street, Watts; *see p126*) have assumed landmark status in the last half-century.

The city's yen for fantasy found a grander and more public outlet in a parade of exotic movie palaces built during the '20s. Hollywood Boulevard boasts a trio of classics, all still open: **Grauman's Chinese Theatre** (No.6925; *see p230*), built in 1927; the **El Capitan Theatre** (No.6838), completed a year earlier and returned to its former glory by a 1991 renovation; and the **Egyptian Theatre** (No.6712; *see p231*), part of Sid Grauman's empire when it opened in 1922 and now home to the American Cinematheque. Other cinemas from the '20s and '30s have found new specialities in later life: the **Pantages Theatre** (6233 Hollywood Boulevard, Hollywood; *see p278*) stages theatrical blockbusters, while the **Wiltern Theatre** (3790 Wilshire Boulevard, Koreatown; *see p255*) is now a rock venue.

Architecture in '20s LA wasn't only about such flights of fantasy: many Downtown buildings of the period were driven by a more cultured Beaux Arts sensibility. Bertram Goodhue's **Central Library** (630 W 5th Street, Downtown; *see p116*) includes spirited murals and lofty inscriptions; likewise, the vast, pyramid-capped 1928 **City Hall** (200 N Spring Street, Downtown; *see p114; photo p25*) was intended to impress to the point of pomposity. Its commercial counterpart, completed in the same year, was **Bullocks Wilshire** (3050 Wilshire Boulevard, near Koreatown), the grandest of the old department stores. Now a law school, its art deco façades still survive.

During the same period, LA's architectural eclecticism extended to residential construction. Frank Lloyd Wright designed several buildings in LA, among them the **Hollyhock House** (4800 Hollywood Boulevard, Los Feliz; *see p104*) and the currently closed **Ennis-Brown House** (2655 Glendower Avenue, Los Feliz; *see p104*), before two Austrian-born protégés of Wright made their first marks on the city. Rudolph Schindler's notable buildings include his own live-work space, now the **MAK Center for Art & Architecture** (835 N Kings Road, West Hollywood; *see p94*), and, in Orange County, the concrete-frame **Lovell Beach House** (13th Street, at Beach Walk, Balboa Island). Among Richard Neutra's finest residences, meanwhile, are the 1929 **Lovell House** (4616 Dundee Drive, Griffith Park; *see p104*), designed for the same clients as Schindler's abovementioned house, and the **Strathmore Apartments** (11005 Strathmore Drive), stacked up a Westwood hillside and completed in 1937. Lloyd Wright, Frank's son, also got in on the act, building a number of private residences around the city during the '20s and '30s.

The Los Angeles area fared better than most American cities during the Depression. However, the old extravagance vanished, and a New World streamline moderne style replaced the European models. One classic example of the idiom is Robert Derrah's **Coca-Cola Bottling Plant** (1334 Central Avenue, Downtown), an ocean liner moored amid warehouses since 1937. **Union Station** (800 N Alameda Street; *see p112*), completed two years later as the last of the great US passenger terminals, successfully fuses streamline moderne styling with old-fashioned Spanish revivalism. But as so often in LA, the sublime was accompanied by the ridiculous.

IN THE VERNACULAR

As automotive travel became a central part of Angeleno existence in the '20s and '30s, local entrepreneurs quickly grew to understand the value of eye-catching roadside advertising. Untroubled by zoning laws or good taste – this was a city whose hottest dining spot was the hat-shaped Brown Derby, now painted dark pink and perched atop a mini-mall in Koreatown – they built an array of cartoonish roadside buildings that effectively served both to advertise and describe themselves. You could buy ice-cream from a towering ice-cream cone, grab a ham sandwich from the mouth of a whale-sized pig, or even buy silk stockings inside a colossal leg.

These buildings weren't built to last. And those whose plaster-and-chicken-wire façades didn't crumble with age typically fell victim to the march of progress. However, a few remain. The most striking is **Randy's Donuts** (805 W Manchester Boulevard, Inglewood), built in the '50s and one of three donut-shaped donut shops in the city. But there's also the tamale-shaped

Googie

After the Depression and World War II, a mood of optimism and faith in technology swept America. Cars were designed to look like jet fighters, while coffeehouses and car washes strove to look as though they were moving at warp speed. Lloyd Wright (Frank's son) and LA-based architect John Lautner led the charge; in 1949, Lautner designed an angular wood-and-glass coffeehouse called Googie's on the Sunset Strip. Googie's has long since vanished, replaced by a pastel shopping-and-cinema complex, but the name lives on as shorthand for the single-storey, neon-topped coffeehouses epitomised by the futuristic drive-by design of the 1950s and '60s: slick and angular, their furnishings a mix of cosy and gee-whizz (Naugahyde booths and space-age lamps).

The best of the survivors may be **Pann's** (still open at 6710 La Tijera Boulevard, Inglewood) and **Ship's Culver City** (now a Starbucks; 10705 W Washington Boulevard, Culver City); the earliest surviving **McDonald's** (10207 Lakewood Boulevard, Downey), built in 1953, also shares the aesthetic. But although Googie itself didn't last long, it briefly influenced handful of LA architects in the '90s: check out Stephen Ehrlich's **Robertson Library** (1719 S Robertson Boulevard, Beverly Hills), for example, or the vibrant primary colours of Kanner Architects' **In-n-Out Burger** (922 Gayley Avenue, Westwood).

former tamale stand (now a beauty parlour) at 6421 Whittier Boulevard in East LA; Hollywood's **Capitol Records Building** (1750 N Vine Street), reputedly built to resemble a stack of 45s on a spindle; and the **Crossroads of the World** mall (6671 Sunset Boulevard), with an 'international' flavour reflected by an ocean liner-like centrepiece and its European-themed bungalows. What's more, hopes remain that the **Tail-o'-the-Pup** hot dog stand will return: built in 1938, but uprooted in 2005, the owners apparently still hope to re-locate it.

POST-WAR GROWTH

The population of Southern California exploded in the 1950s. New suburbs obliterated fields and citrus orchards, extending, with the freeways, into the desert. Business interests spurred the renewal of Downtown, razing the decaying Victorian mansions atop Bunker Hill and creating, from the early '60s, a corridor of office towers. But thanks to clogged freeways and abysmal public transport, Downtown LA never took off. Instead, Century City and other new commercial hubs began to serve the increasingly fragmented metropolis.

'A succession of recessions, riots, earthquakes and floods jolted the city into a sense of civic responsibility.'

Between 1945 and 1962, influential magazine *Arts + Architecture* sponsored the Case Study House programme, a visionary project with a mission to create prototypical low-cost houses using new prefabricated materials and building methods. Although they never achieved mass popularity, the houses stand as icons of Southern Californian design, characterised by the use of glass walls and doors – to make the exterior landscape flow into the interior, and vice versa – and open-plan glass-and-steel volumes. One of the best is the steel-framed **Eames House** (203 Chautauqua Boulevard, Pacific Palisades; *see p74*), a fusion of poetry and technology by famed husband-and-wife design team Charles and Ray Eames.

Several post-war LA architects were heavily influenced by Frank Lloyd Wright's organic modern tradition. When John Lautner first came to LA in 1939 in order to supervise construction of Wright's **Sturges House** (441 Skyeway Road, Brentwood), he was sickened by the

> **Capitol Records Building** (*p95*)
> Destroyed by a tornado in
> *The Day After Tomorrow*

ugliness of the city. But it occurred to him, as it had to Wright in the 1920s, that he could realise his vision here as he never could in the tradition-bound East and Midwest. Among his more daring properties were the 1960 **Chemosphere** (7776 Torreyson Drive, north of Mount Olympus), now home to publisher Benedikt Taschen, and, in Palm Springs, the **Elrod House** (*see p290*), later famous as a location in *Diamonds Are Forever*. However, Lautner did no more than scrape a living, and achieved widespread fame only in the few years before his death in 1994.

THIS IS THE MODERN WORLD

Leaving aside the short-lived trend for Googie in the '50s and '60s (*see p27*), the decades after the war produced little architecture of note in LA. The 1980s, though, saw Morphosis and Eric Owen Moss develop a recognisable local aesthetic, their whimsical designs characterised by skewed planes, contorted structures and elaborate details. You can get a taste of this style at the **Hayden Tract**, a collection of converted warehouses designed by Moss for maverick development company Samitaur Constructs in Culver City (*see p86*). (Moss's influence is now wider than ever: he's a director of SCI-Arc, the Southern California Institute of Architecture in Downtown LA.)

Around this time, LA began to change dramatically, as a bewildering succession of recessions, riots, earthquakes and floods jolted the city into a sense of civic responsibility. With tremendous zeal, local architects organised seminars and community workshops, out of which came numerous well-intentioned plans for LA. Most of them never got further than the drawing board, and many areas that had been devastated by economic and natural disasters were eventually rebuilt by developers and politicians in the most expedient way possible. However, this brief period of reflection did produce some notable legacies: designed by Frank Gehry alumnus Michael Maltzan, **Inner-City Arts** (720 S Kohler Street, Downtown) quickly came to life in a converted car repair shop after a post-riot rush of donations. Later, it bore fruit in new schools and libraries.

As LA started to emerge from recession in the early 1990s, the town's most powerful industry decided to revitalise itself with a host of new projects. All the major movie studios embarked on expansion plans, developing restaurants, leisure centres and themed entertainment/retail destinations. There's no greater example of the trend than **Universal CityWalk**, an artificial street of noise and colour at Universal City (*see p131*) built by the Jerde Partnership International in 1992.

Y viva España

Among architects in LA, belief in modernism is so strong that you'd be forgiven for thinking everybody wants to live in industrial-looking buildings with large windows, tons of light and no applied decoration. But the reality is that by far the favoured residential style among Angelenos is Spanish revival. From Santa Barbara to San Diego, Southern California is covered with residential properties boasting red-tiled roofs, arched doorways and fake adobe walls.

Most of these houses, especially the more recent examples of the style, are kitschy descendants of the Spanish revival style that flourished from the 1920s to the 1940s. It grew out of the Mission revival style of the late 19th century, itself very popular. Architects of the time drew their inspiration from the early Spanish missions in California and from Helen Hunt Jackson's *Ramona*, a hugely popular 1884 novel that romanticised Spanish Californian society.

Some marvellous civic structures emerged from the early fashion for Spanish revival architecture. **Scripps College** in Claremont remains very handsome more than 80 years after its construction, and **Union Station** (*see p112*) is still in good shape. But the Spanish revival aesthetic became most prevalent in residential neighbourhoods, as architects such as Richard Requa, George Washington Smith, Wallace Neff, Lillian Rice and Paul Williams built detached houses for well-to-do

clients. A typical Spanish revival house of the time features a picturesque combination of white-stuccoed arches, towers, balconies and terraces, with colourful tiling, wrought-iron window grilles and heavy wooden doors.

The style was and is seen by many as nostalgic and romantic. But according to Los Angeles writer DJ Waldie, co-author with Diane Keaton of a coffee-table book about classic Spanish-style houses in Los Angeles, the style was also forward-thinking. The houses contained the most modern conveniences of the era; and, unlike the Victorian architecture imported from the east, they were also tailored to the climate and light of Southern California. They had, wrote Waldie, such 'astonishing sympathy and presence that they continue to be the common memory of what many Californians call home'.

Many of the classic Spanish-style houses have been torn down, and those that survive tend to be in private hands and hence difficult to visit. However, a few are open to the public. Designed by Mark Daniels and completed in 1928, **Villa Aurora** in Pacific Palisades periodically opens for lectures (www.villa-aurora.org). The Carl Lindbom-designed **Casa Romantica** in San Clemente is a cultural centre (www.casaromantica.org). Further south, in Carlsbad, near San Diego, stands **Rancho de los Quiotes**, designed by actor Leo Carillo (www.carrillo-ranch.org).

Villa Aurora.

The Morphosis-designed **Caltrans District 7 Headquarters** in Downtown LA. *See p33.*

As it did in buzzing cities the world over, the hotel sector soon became a driving force behind forward-thinking design in LA. However, many of the more interesting developments actually came not through new construction but within the frameworks of existing buildings: old hotels, apartment blocks and even retirement homes that were renovated, remodelled and, in some cases, partly rebuilt. The most notable conversions have been the **Mondrian** (8440 Sunset Boulevard, West Hollywood; *see p58*), a 1959 apartment building redesigned by Philippe Starck; and the cheap, chic interiors created by Shawn Hausman for the **Standard Hotel** properties in West Hollywood (8300 Sunset Boulevard; *see p60*) and Downtown (550 S Flower Street; *see p63*). And then there are the hotels restored by designer Kelly Wearstler: the mid-century modern **Avalon** (9400 W Olympic Boulevard, Beverly Hills; *see p54*); the Chinoiserie-inspired **Maison 140** (140 S Lasky Drive, Beverly Hills; *see p57*); and the **Viceroy** (1819 Ocean Avenue, Santa Monica; *see p48*), where English country-house meets the future.

A very different colour of money paid for perhaps the most exciting architectural commission in LA's recent history. Although its lengthy genesis meant that it eventually opened a year after his crisp **Paley Center for Media** opened in 1996 (465 N Beverly Drive, Beverly Hills; *see p91*), it was the long-awaited completion of the **Getty Center** (1200 Getty Center Drive, Brentwood; *see p84*) that really introduced Richard Meier's brand of cool international modernism to LA. Some visitors found the buildings a little too cool, but the outdoor areas, including a main garden designed by artist Robert Irwin, are a real catch. Unsurprisingly, it didn't come cheap: total construction costs topped $1 billion.

The Getty Center and the Museum of Television & Radio have been supplemented by several other notable museum projects in recent years. The original Getty Museum, a replica Roman villa in Pacific Palisades now known as the **Getty Villa** (17985 Pacific Coast Highway; *see p75*) was beautifully restored and remodelled in 2006 by Machado & Silvetti Associates as a centre for classical antiquities and comparative archaeology. And 2008 saw the opening of the **Broad Contemporary Art Museum** (aka BCAM) at the Los Angeles County Museum of Art (5905 Wilshire Boulevard; *see p100*). A simple travertine box designed by Renzo Piano after Rem Koolhaas's plans for a more substantial renovation of

LACMA were rejected, the building doesn't have the chutzpah of Piano's famed Pompidou Center in Paris. However, the bright red exterior escalator does afford stunning views to the Hollywood Hills.

GOING DOWNTOWN
After the spread of the freeway network helped decentralise the city in the '50s, Downtown LA went into steep decline. It remained the seat of local government, but many of the area's gracious early 20th-century office buildings fell into disrepair, and the only people seen at night were the growing army of homeless people centred on the city's infamous Skid Row.

By the mid-1990s, Downtown had begun to stir. Some commentators have pinned Frank Gehry's **Disney Hall** (*see p32* **Perfectly Frank**), completed in 2003, as the spur for this re-emergence. However, the roots of the area's new lease of life lie with a slew of other public buildings conceived and completed in the '80s and '90s. Four years after Gehry had completed his 1983 remodelling of an old hardware store into the **Geffen Contemporary** (152 N Central Avenue; *see p112*), Japanese architect Arata Isozaki built the **Museum of Contemporary Art** (250 S Grand Avenue; *see p112*), a complex of geometric solids and sky-lit galleries. And the revival was later helped by the arrival of Rafael Moneo's austere Catholic **Cathedral of Our Lady of the Angels** (555 Temple Street; *see p115*), completed in 2002, which sits at the opposite end of Downtown to Pei Cobb Freed's soaring extension for the **Los Angeles Convention Center** (1201 S Figueroa Street; *see p119*).

Construction work on other major public projects continues today. Adjacent to the Staples Center stands **LA Live** (*see p119*), a partially completed entertainment hub; to the north, near Disney Hall, work is scheduled to begin on the **Grand Avenue Project**, plans for which call for cinemas, shops, offices and even a new park. But Downtown's continuing revival would have been impossible without the explosion of residential development in the neighbourhood's old commercial buildings, which has been mirrored by the but related arrival of new independent bars, restaurants and galleries. For the first time in years, the district has a moneyed local community that doesn't desert the area at 6pm.

During the late 1990s, the city's growing population began to find property prices too high in much of the Los Angeles basin. Around the same time, the LA Conservancy helped bring about a change in the law that allowed commercial buildings to be converted into residential properties. As a result of this new legislation, more than 100 commercial buildings dating from the turn of the century to the 1970s, a few of them genuine Downtown treasures, have been transformed: the century-old structures around **4th and Spring Streets**; the **General Petroleum Building** (612 S Flower Street), designed by celebrated LA architect Welton Becket and now the Pegasus Apartments; and Claude Beelman's **Eastern Columbia Building** (849 S Broadway), an eyecatching zig-zag moderne building built in 1930. The trend has even reached the streets east of Little Tokyo, with the conversions of a 1924 warehouse into the **Toy Factory** apartment complex (1855 Industrial Street) and a former Nabisco factory into the **Biscuit Company Lofts** (673 Mateo Street).

ONWARDS AND UPWARDS
With historic, convertable buildings now in shorter supply than they were a decade ago, developers have begun to erect new residential high-rises in Downtown. The most concentrated developments have been in South Park, near the Staples Center and LA Live. The Johnson Fain-designed **Metlofts** (1050 S Flower Street) come complete with an exterior digital light display that's activated by people walking into the building. And close by, at 11th Street and Grand Avenue, stand the **Elleven**, **Luma** and **Evo** condo buildings. This trio are the work of the South Group, whose commitment to sustainable design even extended to widening the sidewalks and adding bike racks.

'LA is being transformed from a suburban city to a semi-urban one.'

Whether in converted commercial buildings or new structures, this fresh wave of residential buildings shares a common influence: the boutique hotels mentioned above. Most of the new condo developments include high-design lobbies, shared lounges and computer rooms. A number also feature high-rise roof gardens with open-air pools and cabanas, providing residents with even greater exclusivity than even the Standard Downtown can offer at their famously fashionable rooftop pool parties.

The high-end condo trend has become so popular that today's hottest architects have

Los Angeles Herald-Examiner Building (*p119*) The police station in *The Usual Suspects*

Perfectly Frank

Walt Disney Concert Hall.

Just as Frank Lloyd Wright inspired the first generation of modernists in Southern California, so Frank Gehry – born in Toronto, but resident in LA since childhood – has the free-spirited architects of today. Although it took until 1997, and the opening of the Guggenheim Museum in Bilbao, Spain, for him to attain worldwide fame, Gehry has been known to Angelenos for years.

Of his early work, perhaps the most notable is the 1964 **Danziger Studio/Residence** (7001 Melrose Avenue, Hollywood), two bold, simple cubic structures. Soon, though, Gehry began to grow more experimental, drawing inspiration from artists rather than architects. Witness his 1978 remodelling of his own home (1002 22nd Street, Santa Monica), a collage of chainlink fencing, plywood and exposed structure. Must-see examples from the 1980s and early 1990s include the **Loyola Law School** (1441 W Olympic Boulevard, Downtown); the **Edgemar Center for the Arts** (2437 Main Street, Santa Monica); **Santa Monica Place** (Broadway & 4th Street, Santa Monica), famous for its layered chainlink façade on the garage, visible from 2nd Street to the south; and the former **TBWA Chiat/Day office** (340 Main Street, Venice), with its eye-catching binoculars portico designed by Claes Oldenburg and Coosje van Bruggen.

In the 1990s, Gehry's work moved from raw, makeshift construction to complex, sensuous structures clad in rich materials and designed with the aid of sophisticated computer programmes. Two buildings in Anaheim – the **Team Disney** administration building (800 W Ball Road), with its undulating yellow façade, and the muscular **Disney Ice Arena** (300 W Lincoln Avenue) – inspired and amazed. But even these eye-catching structures pale in comparison with the LA building, finally completed in 2003, for which Gehry will surely be best remembered.

The **Walt Disney Concert Hall** (135 N Grand Avenue, Downtown; *see p251*) was actually commissioned and designed a decade before the Guggenheim Museum in Bilbao, but years of financial problems and construction delays nearly killed it. Its undulating aluminium exterior is similar to that of the Guggenheim (where the exterior is titanium), but the interior of the Disney Hall is arguably superior. The highlight is the auditorium, with warm wooden surfaces, a curved ceiling and marvellous acoustics.

Gehry's influence runs far and wide across LA, and there are several must-see buildings by architects working under his influence. The finest are in Culver City, where Eric Owen Moss has remodelled a succession of warehouses into cutting-edge workspaces on land known as the Hayden Tract. Among them are the **Box** (8520 National Boulevard) and **Samitaur** (3457 S La Cienega Boulevard). For more, *see p86*.

got in on the act. Frank Gehry has been tapped to create a residential high-rise as part of the Grand Avenue Project; and Morphosis have designed two new residential towers for the **Los Angeles Herald-Examiner Building** (1111 S Broadway), a Mission-revival structure designed by Hearst Castle architect Julia Morgan in 1912 and due to be converted into offices and shops by Brenda Levin. However, the sub-prime mortgage crisis in the US has left some developments in doubt. Levin's Herald-Examiner renovation and Morphosis's accompanying towers are currently on hold.

THE LEARNING ZONES

In recent years, architects have turned their attention to the city's educational system. The list of architecturally notable new schools in and around LA include the **Accelerated Charter School** (116 E Martin Luther King Boulevard, Exposition Park) by Marmol Radziner & Associates, known mostly for restorations of mid-century modern classics; **West Adams Preparatory High School** (500 W Washington Boulevard, Harvard Heights), designed by Robert Mangurian and Mary-Ann Ray of Studio Works; and the Morphosis-designed **Science Center School** in the north-east corner of Exposition Park (*see p123*), an old Armoury remodelled to include a bamboo garden and a classroom building. Further west, Morphosis were commissioned by the Pomona School District to create **Diamond Ranch High School** (100 Diamond Ranch Road, Pomona), a striking sculptural building built high on a hill for a shoestring budget. More recently, the firm was also responsible for the **Caltrans District 7 Headquarters** in Downtown LA (100 S Main Street; *photo p30*).

But in truth, these schools have been exceptions to the rule. The massive programme of construction undertaken by the Los Angeles Unified School District has built in great quantity but not great quality, in stark contrast to the string of fine small buildings built over the last eight years as part of the Los Angeles Public Library network. Perhaps the finest of them is the **Miriam Matthews Branch Library** (2205 Florence Avenue, Hyde Park): it was designed by the firm Hodgetts + Fung, responsible for the most recent remodelling of the **Hollywood Bowl** (*see p251*).

HOMES AT LAST

Los Angeles is gradually being transformed from a suburban city to a semi-urban one, as politicians, planners and architects struggle to provide for the rising population while facing the twin challenges of growing traffic and no comprehensive public transport system. 'Smart growth' is the buzz phrase of the moment. The mayor and city planners have designated certain parts of town, typically located near major transit connections, as ripe for denser residential redevelopment through the addition of multi-family apartment or condo buildings. Several residential high-rises have been proposed for Century City; in other areas, residential streets have been re-zoned to allow the construction of multi-family properties in place of single-family residences.

The formerly shambling beach town of Venice has seen an explosion of such structures: check out Abbot Kinney Boulevard between Main Street and W Washington Boulevard, and, running parallel to it, Electric Avenue. Both West Hollywood and Hollywood also have their share of very stylish multi-family apartment and condo buildings: Lorcan O'Herlihy, designer of the **Lexton-MacCarthy House** in Silver Lake (3228 Fernwood Avenue) and his own **Vertical House** (116 Pacific Avenue, Venice), designed both the very striking **Habitat 825** (825 N Kings Road, next door to the MAK Center) and **Gardner 1050** (1050 N Gardner Street). The spread of such multi-family buildings has outraged many owners of single-family homes, but the trend has proved to be a great source of work for local architects.

Another recent phenomenon has been the emergence of a sustainable design sensibility, as designers try to integrate solar power and energy-efficient technologies into clean, modern buildings. One of the more worthwhile examples is **Colorado Court** (502 Colorado Avenue, Santa Monica), a complex of affordable apartments with a wall of solar panels. Pugh Scarpa architects, who designed it, were also responsible for Larry Scarpa's own home in Venice: the **Solar Umbrella House** (615 Woodlawn Avenue), at which solar panels form a canopy over the house and wrap the southern side. Another proponent of green building is David Hertz, designer of his own **McKinley Residence** (2420 McKinley Avenue, Venice).

LA's most interesting architecture continues to be residential, then, but the innovation that characterised the city's best housing in the 20th century has come up against some hurdles of late. Most visible are the ghastly, oversized McMansions that dominate parts of the region, but architectural invention is also being challenged by the emergence of militant design review boards that are becoming increasingly protectionist and dictatorial about how new homeowners can build. This preservationism is testament to the maturation of LA, but it's also made the city less of a design frontier. The Angeleno creative architecture spirit lives on, but within tighter parameters than of yore.

On the Road

How Los Angeles learned to love the automobile.

Los Angeles wasn't entirely built around automobile travel. Not quite. The city had started to boom long before Henry Ford's Model T made car travel something other than a luxury for many Americans. Indeed, without the arrival of the transcontinental railroad in 1886 to what was then a dusty cow town, it's arguable that Los Angeles wouldn't have expanded to anything like the size that it has.

However, the city has since grown up around the possibilities of the motor car. As early as 1920, Los Angeles had more automobiles than any other US city. Four years later, despite a decent public transit network, more than half the commuters to what is now Downtown arrived by car. In a bid to discourage automobile use, the city council decided to outlaw street parking in the area between 11am and 6.15pm. After a massive outcry, the ban was revoked just 19 days later; it was the last time for several decades that local residents were dissuaded from driving.

LA's love affair with the car resulted in the sprawl that's now come to characterise it: the mile-wide boulevards and avenues, the low-rise, low-density tract homes that cover the suburbs and exurbs, the drive-up and drive-thru consumer culture, and the wild, tentacular network of freeways. But how did it all come to pass?

LAND OF THE FREEWAY

Sections of Los Angeles were once traversed by a network of streetcars and trolleys. Founded in 1901, the Pacific Electric Railroad linked Downtown LA with such disparate points as San Bernardino, Hollywood, Santa Monica and Long Beach. Ridership began to fall four decades before its closure in 1961, albeit with a huge spike in demand during World War II after gasoline was rationed and car production more or less ceased: in 1944, an astonishing 109 million people rode the network. Roughly 40 years after this halcyon time, construction began on an underground rail network that's still expanding today. However, it was what happened in between that has really defined modern-day LA.

By the late 1930s, the public were clamouring for major improvements in the road network. In 1940, with the opening of the much-heralded Arroyo Seco Parkway, they got them. Linking Downtown LA to Pasadena, the four-lane, crossing-free, 45mph-limit highway was modelled in part on the prettified parkways of New York, but with elements of modernity included in its design. An immediate hit, it proved the prototype for a network of roads that changed the very infrastructure of Los Angeles. (Aside from the conversion of the hard shoulders into traffic lanes, the stretch of road remains largely unchanged today; it's now called the Pasadena Freeway.)

The success of the Arroyo Seco Parkway inspired the local authorities to explore further the possibility of a citywide network of freeways. Various plans were brought to the table, and construction commenced in earnest soon after the end of World War II. The eight-lane Hollywood Freeway, linking Downtown to Hollywood and the San Fernando Valley, was the first major road to be constructed, and set the tone for the rest of the network. Construction of the road razed 2,000 buildings; all attempts at aesthetically pleasing landscape design, along the lines of that found on the Arroyo Seco Parkway, were eradicated between the drawing board and the building site. This was a purely functional road, and Heaven help anyone standing in its way.

By the time President Eisenhower signed the Federal-Aid Highway Act of 1956, setting into motion the construction of the US-wide Interstate network, LA was well on the way towards building its own web of freeways. Over the following 15 years, more than 200 miles of them were constructed in LA, development that scarred the city while simultaneously opening it up. There's been little freeway construction since the mid 1970s, but the landscape of the city has changed beyond all recognition.

PASSING TRADE

On the maps, between La Brea and Fairfax Avenues, it's plain old Wilshire Boulevard. Its nickname, though, is the Miracle Mile, a moniker for which we owe thanks to a forward-thinking developer named AW Ross. When Ross bought this patch of land in 1920, there was virtually nothing there; the road itself wasn't even paved, and the land on either side was mostly given over to farming fields. Ross, though, not only predicted the increasing popularity of the car, but designed the entire road to suit it.

New buildings – department stores, mostly – were set tight against the roadside in order to attract passing traffic. At their sides, a revolutionary development, stood huge parking lots. By the 1930s, the mile-long stretch of road had become a sensation, attracting thousands of shoppers each day and revealing to Americans the true commercial possibilities of automotive travel. The country in general, and Southern California in particular, might have grown up in a very different way without it.

'There's an increasing sense in Los Angeles that the city's overarching reliance on the car is unsustainable.'

One of Ross's theories was that buildings should be as attention-grabbing as possible: strong, bold and immediately appealing when seen from the driver's seat. It was this theory that eventually led architect John Lautner to table an extraordinary set of designs for a new coffee shop on Sunset Boulevard, to be called Googies. When it opened in 1949, its sharp angles, plate-glass frontage and exotic signage were unlike anything ever seen in the city, and customers flocked to it. The space-age structure moved from novelty to craze in months; the style became known as Googie architecture after Lautner's revolutionary design.

Googies has long since been demolished, but one imitator remains on the Miracle Mile. Built as Romeo's Times Square in 1955, Johnie's (6101 Wilshire Boulevard) served its last cup of joe in 2000. However, it still stands as a monument to the '50s boom in LA's automotive culture, and often appears in movies. Bulbs ripple on and off beneath a red neon sign designed to draw the eye of the passing motorist; inside, a handful of dim fingerspots pick out the counter and a handful of booths.

Other landmarks of roadside design remain from this era. Pann's (6710 La Tijera Boulevard, Inglewood), which dates from 1956, may be the finest piece of Googie architecture in the city, its prominent lot helping it draw passing trade. Randy's Donuts (805 W Manchester Avenue, Inglewood) is a shambling 1952 shack topped with a 22-foot doughnut that can't help but catch the eye. And Bob's Big Boy (4211 Riverside Drive, Burbank; *photo p36*), built to Wayne McAllister's design in 1949, is a dazzling affair, unmissable from the main road on which it sits.

Today, in a tribute to its early days, Bob's Big Boy offers car-hop service: waiters flit from auto to auto, taking orders and delivering food through the open windows. However, it was by no means the first place in LA to offer such convenience. Opening in Los Feliz in 1921, the same year Ross began developing what would become the Miracle Mile, Montgomery's Country Inn (later the Tam O'Shanter) opened as the first drive-in restaurant on the West Coast, a visionary move that took into account both the growing prevalence of the automobile and the sunny Southern Californian climate.

Imitators followed all over the country, but nowhere was the trend more prevalent than LA. Countless similar enterprises opened in the 1920s, '30s and '40s (a story told, with copious photographs, in Jim Heimann's book *Car Hops and Curb Service*), and have continued to open. However, where once such businesses were a novelty, they're now part of everyday life; entrepreneurs don't need to work so hard to attract attention, since the public is already expecting them to be there. Ringing Bob's Big Boy are innumerable drive-thru eateries, pharmacies, even banks. Not even their staff could tell you anything about their appearance.

THE FUTURE
The Los Angeles area is continuing to grow. The city's borders seem to edge further out each year, and the population is still on the rise. But for many locals, Los Angeles is shrinking. The traffic has grown so bad in recent years that residents are reluctant to travel any more than

strictly necessary, and are spending more time than ever in their home neighbourhoods. In many regards, this is welcome: long-tired or neglected corners of the city are at last developing a genuine sense of community. But it also speaks ill of the city at large, gridlocked into submission. Just over a decade ago in LA-set thriller *Speed*, a bomb on board Sandra Bullock's bus was set up to activate itself as soon as the vehicle exceeded 50mph. There's little danger of that happening here today.

There's an increasing sense in Los Angeles that the city's overarching reliance on the car is unsustainable. Long the poor relation of LA's car culture, the public transportation network is improving and growing for the first time since the glory days of the Pacific Electric Railroad: the Metro system is currently being expanded in several directions, and there are hopes that it may eventually reach the coast. To combat the city's awful smog, some drivers run their vehicles on sustainable fuels such as biodiesel or vegetable oil: if you see an old Mercedes with a 'Lovecraft Bio-Fuels' sticker, you've found one more driver who's kicked the petrol habit. And the fast-rising trend for urban living, especially Downtown, may yet see a decline in automotive commuting. Granted, you can't unring a bell: LA will always be a drivers' town. But something needs to be done, simply to get the city moving once more.

Eternal Fame

Welcome to the celebrity capital of the world.

It's a typically hot afternoon on Robertson Boulevard in West Hollywood, as a black SUV with tinted windows drives up to the sidewalk. A figure emerges from the anonymity of the car and is immediately bundled into a nearby store by two burly bodyguards. A commotion ensues, quickly followed by the whirring of camera shutters (digital, naturally). Shoppers stop to gawp at the scene. Within seconds, half of them have pulled out their cellphones and started to take their own photographs.

But of whom? Madonna? Brangelina? J-Lo? George Clooney? Could be. But it's just as likely to be a near-unknown whose face looks only vaguely familiar, whose name rings just a distant bell, and who, if it wasn't for the SUV and the bodyguards, would have slipped into the store unnoticed. Welcome to 21st-century Los Angeles, where celebrity – or, at least, the impression of celebrity – remains the most valuable currency of all.

The entertainment industry is a global concern these days. However, as the city where it all began, and the city in which most of the major deals are still inked, Los Angeles remains its epicentre. In some ways, the business is much as it was in its early days: it still comes down to stars and studios with something to sell. But much has changed in the century since the motion-picture studios were founded here, not least the ways in which celebrities interact with their public.

Once upon a time, the media had to rely on carefully edited publicity shots of Hollywood's latest and greatest. Any nascent scandals were swept under the carpet by the efficient studio-run publicity machine – major stars were not free agents, as they are today, but tied to individual studios. When stars did get caught with their trousers down, as happened most infamously with silent screen star Fatty Arbuckle in the early '20s, it was huge news, but such misdemeanours were the exception rather than the rule. Indeed, celebrities were rarely even seen out on the town; when they were spotted having dinner or at a premiere, it was a big deal. (As far back as 1952, the movie *Singin' in the Rain* had great fun satirising this state of affairs.)

This aura of untouchability has long since evaporated. In the 21st century, anyone – and we mean *anyone* – can become a celebrity in Los Angeles. Lindsay Lohan's mum, Charlie Sheen's ex-wife and Jerry Springer's bouncer all have their own reality shows, and the public clamours equally over Kevin Spacey and Kevin Federline. A flick through a typical night's TV schedule brings up such horrors as *Celebrity Rehab with Dr Drew*, *Pussycat Dolls 2: Girlicious*, *Celebrity Circus* and *Date My Ex: Jo & Slade*, a spin-off from something called *The Real Housewives of Orange County*. Where *E! True Hollywood Story* used to profile the Kennedys, now the show concentrates on the family of OJ Simpson's dead attorney Robert Kardashian (who, naturally, also have their own show, *Keeping Up with the Kardashians*). Each week brings a new nadir of banality.

THE PRESS GANG
At the forefront of Hollywood's starmaking machine, as they have been for decades, are the American gossip magazines, which continue to track every move of more or less every celebrity in the US. In the last week of June 2008, a pretty average week in gossip terms, the magazines were dominated by such headlines as 'Dr Phil's Wife Kicks Him Out!' (*National Enquirer*), 'Inside Heather's Breakdown' (*People*), 'Jake Moves In!' (*Us Weekly*), '39 Best & Worst Beach Bodies' (*In Touch Weekly*), 'Jamie Lynn: Delivery Room Drama!' (*Star*) and even 'Camilla Collapses After Charles Tells Her "It's Over"' (*National Examiner*). Inane polls on the ensuing pages plumb new depths: 'Who Would You Want to Go to a Fourth of July Barbecue With?: Tom and Katie, Jess and Tony, Reese and Jake or Will and Jada. Vote Now!'

However, it's now gone far beyond the point at which people are famous simply for being famous. Even people who blog about the famous are now stars. Case in point:

Mario Armando Lavandeira, Jr, aka Perez Hilton. Best known for his gossip website (www.perezhilton.com), Lavandeira now also has his own TV and radio shows, plus, incredibly, his own clothing line (didn't anyone look at him before signing him up?).

> **'Products are launched almost daily on the back of some celebrity or other; magazines pay millions for shots of stars or their offspring.'**

The success of Hilton's often vindictive blog proves not just that the day-to-day lives of celebrities are of interest to the average Joe, but that those same celebrities are now considered fair game for a thorough kicking. Schadenfreude is alive and well in Los Angeles, presumably because it makes ordinary citizens feel better about their own problems. After all, if so-and-so isn't happy in the glamorous surroundings of Los Angeles, maybe our own dreary lives ain't so bad.

The gossip magazines are now just the tip of the iceberg. Alongside Hilton's blog and the likes of TMZ (www.tmz.com), a fearsomely catty website run by entertainment behemoth Time Warner that's also spawned its own television spin-off show, every major news website from the BBC to CNN has a dedicated 'Entertainment' section. The UK tabloids even have their own gossip queens in situ in LA, ready for action. At the height of Beckham mania in 2007, the *Mirror* sent one of its 3AM Girls out to the city to cover the story. She's still here.

This appetite for celebrity demands – what else? – more celebrities. Over and above the mothers, brothers and daughters, reality shows feature celebrities that few people recognised at the height of their fame, let alone 15 years later. TMZ's site proudly shows off 'then' and 'now' photos of celebrities on its 'Memba Them?' pages, zeroing in on every frown line, balding head and sagging gut with glee.

At the heart of it all, of course, is money. The corporate world has been predictably quick to capitalise on the public's obsession with fame, with new products launched almost daily on the back of some celebrity or other.

Magazines pay millions for shots of stars or their offspring, knowing that sales for that particular week will soar. Celebrity endorsements also bring in huge bucks, from those where the link between star and product is tangible (Tiger Woods and Nike, say) to those that it's difficult to believe even made it past the first meeting (Carlos Santana sandals? A body lotion marketed by Alan Cumming called Cumming All Over?). Fashion lines send free clothing and jewellery to celebrities in the hope that they'll be seen wearing it in public, preferably at the Oscars or the Golden Globes. And the presence of a celebrity can make – or, in some cases, break – a venue. One particular West Hollywood nightclub was a hot spot until shots of a 76-year-old Elizabeth Taylor being wheeled in and out of the venue made it into the tabloids.

YOU CAN LOOK BUT YOU'D BETTER NOT TOUCH

Until just a few years ago, the closest any tourist got to spotting a celebrity in Los Angeles was on a guided tour of Beverly Hills, where, if they were extremely lucky, they'd catch a glimpse of their favourite star through the gate at the end of their driveway. More often than not, that hazy figure turned out to be a security guard or a housemaid, but at least it kept up the illusion of exclusivity. Nowadays, though, there's no unique allure. Everyone can afford not just to visit Los Angeles but also to stay in the hotels and restaurants frequented by the stars. Aside from the celebrities' own homes (and even that's debatable, thanks to reality TV), very few places are truly private.

The city's hot spots seem to change by the week, but spend just a short amount of time here and you're likely to run into someone famous. LA eateries with good star-spotting opportunities include the new Nobu in West Hollywood, STK, longtime favourites Koi and Katsuya, and Beso, which gets extra points for being co-owned by actress Eva Longoria. (Murphy's law has it that by the time you eventually secure a reservation, none of these restaurants will be flavour of the month.)

The Ivy's star has waned to some degree, certainly, but at least the patio is a nice place to hang.

Clubs and hotel bars are top celeb magnets. The watering holes at the Thompson and Hollywood Roosevelt hotels are both 'in' – or, at least, they were at the time of writing. The list of hot clubs is volatile; but in late 2008, it included the likes of Villa and Foxtail. Beware the velvet rope – if you can't get on the guest list, call ahead for pricey bottle service. And always dress to the nines if you want to stand a good chance of getting in.

If you're the athletic type, head for the jogging trail of Runyon Canyon; if you prefer to watch your sport rather than take part in it, catch a Lakers game, where superstar superfan Jack Nicholson can invariably be seen cheering from the sidelines, or an LA Galaxy football match, the team for which David Beckham plays. And if you like to shop while you stalk, forget Rodeo Drive and instead try the Grove, located next to a branch of the celebrity-friendly Whole Foods supermarket. For fashion, Kitson on Robertson Boulevard and Fred Segal on Melrose Avenue are both good bets, and you're more likely to gain access to either of them than to the number of 'exclusive' shops that maintain their aura by placing a velvet rope outside.

As a rule, mornings rather than afternoons are a better time to catch celebrities, but don't bother on Mondays or weekends. And don't expect said celeb to pose for photos or sign autographs. Some will: if they're down the pecking order, they may be glad of the attention. But some won't. Orange County-based *Autograph* magazine produces a list of the 'best' and 'worst' signers (Johnny Depp and Will Ferrell in 2007).

Above all, don't get too close without permission. The gossip columnists and the paparazzi may be annoying to celebs, but they haven't crossed the line into stalker territory. Yet.

The Natural World

Earth, wind and fire: how LA struggles with its surroundings.

More than most other cities in the US, Los Angeles retains a close connection to nature. Mountain ranges bisect the region, which is bracketed by the ocean on the west and by desert to the east. Benignly sunny most of the time, the Southland is nonetheless regularly riven by earthquakes, battered by flash floods and whipped into fateful fires by the Santa Ana winds. As Mike Davis wrote in *Ecology of Fear: Los Angeles and the Imagination of Disaster*, the city 'has deliberately put itself in harm's way... Historic wildfire corridors have been turned into view-lot suburbs, wetland liquefaction zones into marinas, and floodplains into industrial districts and housing tracts.'

Whether despite or because of its connection to its natural surroundings, alternately barren and wild, Los Angeles has been manicured to within an inch of its life. Trees of every species can be found shading the streets in affluent neighbourhoods, with unnaturally green lawns providing a welcoming carpet outside their million-dollar homes. The city is covered in public and private gardens that have proved to be playgrounds for their designers: almost anything can be made to grow here, at least

if it's irrigated by water channelled from outside the naturally semi-arid terrain.

At first glance, Los Angeles seems like the triumph of engineering over wilderness. However, Angelenos know that nature can, and often does, bite back...

SANTA ANA WINDS

Also sometimes known as the Santanas, LA's famed Santa Ana winds form in the Great Basin of the western United States as a result of increased air pressure. When the winds blow towards Los Angeles, reaching speeds of up to 80 miles an hour through canyons and passes, the air gets drier and hotter as it falls in altitude and compresses. And by the time the Santa Anas reach LA, usually between September and March, they've become 'devil winds': hot, dry and dangerous gusts that can blow for up to four days at a time. At best, the Santa Anas turn your lips dry and leave your hair crispy. At worst, they help fuel major fires across the region.

The Santa Anas loom large in LA culture. Steely Dan ('Babylon Sisters') and Randy Newman ('I Love LA') have both paid homage to them in song, and Raymond Chandler even titled a short story after another of their nicknames. In 'Red Wind', Chandler described the Santa Anas as 'those hot dry [winds] that come down through the mountain passes and curl your hair and make your nerves jump and your skin itch. On nights like that, every booze party ends in a fight. Meek little wives feel the edge of the carving knife and study their husbands' necks. Anything can happen.'

FIRES

Centuries ago, the Gabrieleño Native American tribes learned that the glorious canyons which snake through Southern California's mountain ranges are essentially chimneys, funnelling the hillside fires that occur when tinder-dry chaparral is set aflame. Before the area was urbanised, these hills would naturally combust every few years: chaparral produces seeds that germinate only after they catch fire. However, the blazes these days are typically started by human hands, whether by design or by accident, and are then fanned into huge, terrifying and destructive fires by the aforementioned Santa Ana winds. The problems are exacerbated by temperatures topping 100°F and humidity levels of almost zero.

> **'Angelenos have tried to engineer the region to act against its nature.'**

October 2007 saw Southern California torched by some of the most dramatic fires in the region's history. Between Santa Barbara County and the border with Mexico, at least 1,500 homes were destroyed, and more than 500,000 acres of land burned; nine people died, and 85 others were injured. The flames themselves weren't visible from the centre of LA. However, the city's skies were cloaked in smoke for weeks, and the quality of the already smoggy air fell to appalling levels.

Several of these fires were triggered by power lines that had been damaged by the high winds. Others were thought to be the work of arsonists, and one occurred by accident after a young boy played with matches. But according to many fire and planning experts, the primary source of the blazes was, in simple terms, construction. If people no longer built in the canyons, runs their theory, the fires would occur naturally and then simply burn out without any great damage. However, there's not a politician in the region that would dare to try to regulate development in what is, despite the inherent dangers, some of the most sought-after residential real-estate in the Southland.

Whenever major fires occur in the region, the same cycle of events takes place. TV news shows have a field day, especially when celebrities lose their Malibu mansions. Politicians garner brownie points by showing sympathy and declaring states of emergency. The majority of locals who don't live in fire zones complain about how a disproportionate percentage of their tax dollars is being diverted towards firefighting resources and disaster relief. And then, once the smoke has dissipated, the rebuilding begins, ensuring that there'll be something to burn when the chaparral next catches fire.

FLOODS AND MUDSLIDES

Los Angeles doesn't get much rain. But when the rainstorms arrive, usually between January and March, they can be torrential. And when they follow serious fires, the rain pounds down on land so bare and non-absorbent that it triggers mudslides, a common problem for Angelenos who live on or near the hills.

Many locals try to take the mudslides in their stride. As *Los Angeles Times* reporter Al Martinez wrote in 1996, reporting on one major mudslide: 'As always, the residents of Malibu, both famous and not famous, emerged from the muck proclaiming they would not live anywhere else in the world… [They] sang as they shovelled the gluck from their living rooms.' They're the lucky ones. In 2005, a mudslide collapsed on to La Conchita, a small town that sits in a precarious hillside position about an hour up the coast from Santa Monica. Roughly 20 per cent of the town's houses were left uninhabitable, and ten of the town's residents were effectively buried alive.

Again, Angelenos have tried to engineer the region to act against its nature. Before it was settled, the land that now makes up Los Angeles was a flood plain. When the annual rains fell and the alluvial Los Angeles River burst its banks (as, for that matter, did other unstable tributaries), the land was drenched. Three years after the torrential three-day storms of 1938 that killed more than 100 people and destroyed more than 5,000 homes, US Congress passed the Flood Control Act of 1941; out of it came a new network of flood control channels and storm drains. But while these engineering marvels have prevented large-scale flooding, they haven't stopped the mudslides. And nor have they stopped the mini-inundations on LA's surface streets that occur when the storm drains fail to cope with sudden rain. The resulting images of floating cars and desperate drivers provide yet more fodder for local TV news networks.

EARTHQUAKES

From the Malibu Coast Fault on the west to the infamous San Andreas Fault that passes through Riverside County, Los Angeles is lined with tectonic faults. There are at least 20 under LA, all primed to split at any moment. 'We live under a tectonic death sentence called the Big One,' wrote Bill Moseley in *Glue* magazine back in 1998, 'and by golly, that's exciting. Not just anybody can happily go about their business knowing that today's cosy Craftsman cottage could be tomorrow's gaping hole.'

Indeed, most people do tend to carry on blithely despite fears of a quake. The biggest tremor in recent memory was the Northridge Earthquake of 1994, a 6.7-magnitude rumble that caused so much damage – 70 deaths, more than 11,000 injuries and an estimated $12 billion of structural destruction – that thousands of people left town. But many soon returned, settling back into their pleasant Southern California lifestyles. Many of them probably even forgot to stock an earthquake kit to aid their survival in the event that the Big One should ever hit the city.

In 2008, the US Geological Survey reported that a powerful earthquake 'capable of causing widespread destruction' is 99 per cent certain to hit California within the next 30 years. The most likely source is the San Andreas Fault, which they described as 'ten months pregnant' and fit to burst. The fault has generally spawned a large earthquake every 150 years or so, but it's already been 300 years since its last major tremor. You, and they, have been warned.

TREES

When Los Angeles was settled in the 19th century, new arrivals found a landscape lined with chaparral and other scrub plants but, away from the mountains and with few water courses, largely devoid of trees. Less than 200 years later, one of the city's most distinctive sights is the array of greenery that towers over the region's single-storey houses. In Beverly Hills, for instance, each street north of Santa Monica Boulevard boasts a beautiful canopy created from a different species of tree. But although LA is now far more forested than nature intended, it still contains less tree cover than the average American city. In poorer southern and eastern neighbourhoods, trees shade only five per cent of the urban environment, six times below the national average.

The palm tree is now a Los Angeles icon, but it's not native to the city. Palms were first planted here in the late 19th century by developers looking to sell the city as a sun-soaked paradise; 30,000 Mexican palms, still the most common variety, were imported as part of a beautification project tied to the 1932

Olympics. A fuss ensued in 2007 after a rumour spread that some of these palms were to be uprooted by the city, but it proved a false alarm. As part of his Million Trees LA project, mayor Antonio Villaraigosa had simply made plans to introduce other, shadier trees to less leafy parts of the city, in an attempt to alleviate the 'urban heat island effect' that blights LA. Elsewhere, the palms will remain; or, at least, they will if they survive *fusarium wilt*, a deadly fungus native to LA that has killed hundreds of palms around the city during the last decade or so.

But Villaraigosa's trend is being bucked by the city council in Santa Monica, which has announced plans to uproot 53 of its own iconic, shade-giving ficus trees in an effort to make its streets sunnier. A group of angry activists, calling themselves the Treesavers, have announced that they'll tie themselves to each of their beloved trees until they can get a court order forcing the council to reverse its decision.

WILDLIFE

Still just a few degrees of separation from its natural past, the Los Angeles area remains home to a number of wild creatures. Possums, squirrels and rats dwell in the lowlands; bobcats and coyotes live in the mountains. Coyotes regularly wander into the gardens of houses in the foothills, gobbling up pets if they have been foolishly left outside. In 2008, a swimmer in San Diego was bitten to death by a great white shark, which is thought to have confused the wetsuit-clad man for a seal. And back on the land, between 4,000 and 6,000 cougars (mountain lions) reside in the mountains across the state of California, many of them not far from Los Angeles. Although cougars rarely kill humans, a cyclist in Orange County's Whiting Ranch Wilderness Park was devoured by one in 2003; another cyclist was literally pulled from the same animal's jaws by a brave friend.

In November 2007, pupils at a school in the California town of Redlands were surprised to see two mountain lions perched in a nearby tree. The Associated Press reported that wardens shot tranquilliser darts at the lions, while children at the school shouted at them to stop. Zoologists believe that such encounters result from man-made development encroaching on the wilderness, and dry conditions that force the animals to look for prey outside of their normal habitats.

In the unlikely event that you encounter a mountain lion while in the region, don't approach it, don't run away, and don't crouch down: to the animal, you'll resemble four-legged prey. Instead, you're supposed to stand and face the creature, waving your arms slowly and speaking firmly and loudly. That should scare it away. If only the same tactic worked on reality-show celebrities.

Where to Stay

Where to Stay   44

Features
The best Hotels   45
The chain gang   47
Spa for a day   53
Carry on camping   57

Thompson Beverly Hills. *See p57*.

Where to Stay

Welcome to the Hotel California.

You only need to close the **Shutters on the Beach** when the sun sets. *See p48*.

If the American economy really is heading downhill, someone needs to tell LA's hoteliers. The last few years have seen a slew of new hotels open in the city, the majority at the high end of the market. At the same time, a number of existing hotels have embarked on redesigns and renovations in a bid to keep pace with their shiny new rivals. However, despite this activity, one problem remains: there's still a profound lack of decent affordable accommodation.

When deciding on a hotel, you'll first need to decide on a location. Where you choose to stay will greatly affect your time here, and will also affect how much you pay. Even basic hotels can charge a premium if they're near the beach; conversely, a room in a business-friendly

❶ Green numbers given in this chapter correspond to the location of each hotel on the street maps. *See pp326-331*.

Downtown property can be had for a song on weekends. Assuming a similar standard of service, one basic rule holds true: the closer to the Pacific, the pricier the room.

LA's history might be short, but a number of hotels make great play of their own past. The **Beverly Hills Hotel & Bungalows** (*see p54*), the **Hotel Bel-Air** (*see p54*) and the **Chateau Marmont** (*see p58*) all tap into their Hollywood heritage in a variety of ways, while the **Millennium Biltmore** (*see p63*) prides itself on its old-money feel. Standing in stylish opposition to them is a new breed of fashion-friendly operations, the likes of the **Viceroy** (*see p48*) and the **Shade** (*see p65*). Some hotels, such as the **Hollywood Roosevelt** (*see p61*) and the **Avalon** (*see p54*), have a foot in both camps, trading off both past and present. And on the other end of the scale are the chains that dot the region, providing characterless but reliable lodgings; *see p47* **The chain gang**.

INFORMATION AND PRICES

Room rates vary wildly, both from hotel to hotel and within a single property: public holidays, big conventions and awards shows are just three events that affect rates. Obtained from the hotels, the prices listed here reflect that disparity. The rates listed are for double rooms.

Rates can be high, but the hidden extras are the real killer. Quoted room rates will exclude a gasp-inducing 14 per cent room tax. And while parking is free in a few hotels, most charge heavily for the privilege: we've included nightly parking rates in our listings, but you can expect to pay $25-$30 in many properties. So, in other words, a double room with a quoted rate of $300 will probably set you back $375 with tax and parking – effectively, a 25 per cent mark-up.

When making a reservation, first call the hotel or, better still, go to the hotel's website: many properties offer internet-only specials that can shave as much as $50 from the rates. It's also worth visiting sites such as www.priceline.com, www.lastminute.com and www.expedia.com: they may have better deals, though be sure to check the small print as add-ons vary. And always check cancellation policies: many hotels won't charge you if you cancel more than 24 hours ahead, but you might not be eligible for a refund if you book through an outside website.

We've listed a selection of services for each hotel at the end of its review, from pools (all are outdoors unless stated) to entertainment (all hotels have in-room TVs unless stated). For internet access, 'wireless' denotes Wi-Fi, while 'high-speed' is used where high-speed access is available only via a cable. California law requires all hotels to provide non-smoking rooms and facilities for disabled visitors.

Santa Monica & the Beach Towns

Malibu

Expensive

Malibu Beach Inn

22878 Pacific Coast Highway, between Malibu Pier & Carbon Canyon, Malibu, CA 90265 (1-800 462 5428/1-310 456 6444/www.malibubeachinn.com). Bus 534/I-10, exit PCH north. **Rates** $325-$825. **Rooms** 47. **Credit** AmEx, DC, MC, V.

Completed in 2007, a $10-million renovation added a number of deluxe amenities to this contemporary-style beachfront hotel: custom-stocked bars, very private balconies, Dean & DeLuca snacks (a nod to the hotel's New York guests) and even in-room wine

cellars featuring local varietals. Bathers may be disappointed to learn that all the tubs have been removed to make guests feel at home on Carbon Beach. *Bar. Internet (free wireless in lobby & high-speed in rooms). Parking ($23). Restaurant. Room service. TV: DVD & pay movies.*

Moderate

Casa Malibu Inn on the Beach

22752 Pacific Coast Highway, between Malibu Pier & Carbon Canyon, Malibu, CA 90265 (1-800 831 0858/1-310 456 2219). Bus 534/I-10, exit PCH north. **Rates** $169-$499. **Rooms** 21. **Credit** AmEx, DC, MC, V.

Located on the sand, Casa Malibu is the only hotel on this stretch that has its own beach for exclusive use of guests. Malibu Colony is within walking distance; so is Malibu Pier, where fabulous breaks provide some of the best longboard surfing in Southern California. The inn offers four types of room, including two mini-suites with king-size beds, fireplaces and kitchens. The beachfront and ocean-view rooms are coveted, but all have private decks and some include adjacent rooms for families. Considering the location and amenities, rates are very reasonable. *Gym. Internet (free wireless). Parking (free). Room service. TV: DVD.*

Santa Monica

Expensive

Casa del Mar

1910 Ocean Way, at Pico Boulevard, Santa Monica, CA 90405 (1-800 898 6999/1-310 581 5533/www. hotelcasadelmar.com). Bus 33, 333, SM1, SM7,

 Hotels

For history, LA style
Sunset Tower. See p61.

For 90 years of star power
Beverly Hills Hotel & Bungalows. See p54.

For beachside chic
Viceroy. See p48.

For Britain with better weather
London West Hollywood. See p58.

For a Downtown bargain
Hotel Figueroa. See p64.

Amsterdam 2009

Barcelona 2009

Berlin

Cyprus

Dubai

Dubrovnik

Edinburgh

Florence

Las Vegas

London

Malta

Manchester

Marrakech

New York 2009

Nice & Cannes

Paris

Prague 2009

Rome 2009

San Francisco

Sydney

Tokyo

Venice

- **Pocket-sized guides**
- **What's on, month by month**
- **Full colour fold-out maps**

SM10/I-10, exit 4th-5th Street south. **Rates** $475-$875. **Rooms** 129. **Credit** AmEx, DC, Disc, MC, V. **Map** p326 A3 ❶

Located on the sand, close to Santa Monica's shops and restaurants, this elegant and architecturally significant hotel is a local landmark. Most of the plush rooms and suites offer ocean and coastline views; for a really opulent stay, reserve one of the two-storey penthouse suites or the super-deluxe presidential suite. An afternoon at the spa is a vacation in itself; salon services can be enjoyed in one of five Mediterranean-style treatment rooms or, better yet, under a cabana on the fifth-floor pool deck. The bar in the ornate and well-furnished lobby is a popular meeting spot for the bronzed and beautiful locals. *Bars (2). Business centre. Concierge. Gym. Internet ($12 wireless). Parking ($35). Pool. Restaurants (2). Room service. Spa. TV: DVD & pay movies.*

Fairmont Miramar

101 Wilshire Boulevard, at Ocean Avenue, Santa Monica, CA 90401 (1-800 441 1414/1-310 576 7777/www.fairmont.com). Bus 20, 534, 720, SM1, SM7/I-10, exit 4th-5th Street north. **Rates** $309-$1,429. **Rooms** 300. **Credit** AmEx, DC, Disc, MC, V. **Map** p326 A2 ❷

The Miramar has been pampering the glamorous and the powerful in California for nearly a century: past guests have included everyone from Greta Garbo to Bill Clinton. Built in 1924, the hotel has undergone several tasteful renovations; the most recent encompassed a remodel of the lobby and the Grille. Families clamour for the 32 bungalows with private patios surrounded by lush tropical landscaping, but the rooms boast the ocean and city views. *Bar. Business centre. Concierge. Gym. Internet ($13.95 wireless in lobby & high-speed in rooms). Parking ($33). Restaurant. Room service. Spa. TV: pay movies.*

Hotel Oceana

849 Ocean Avenue, at Montana Avenue, Santa Monica, CA 90403 (1-800 777 0758/1-310 393 0486/www.hoteloceanasantamonica.com). Bus 534, SM4/I-10, exit 4th-5th Street north. **Rates** $350-$750. **Rooms** 70. **Credit** AmEx, DC, Disc, MC, V. **Map** p326 A2 ❸

A recent multi-million-dollar renovation catapulted this boutique into chic status. Designer Chris Barrett fine-tuned the interior spaces, but managed to retain the warm ambience that has long characterised the property. While the Oceana is a destination hotel for holidaymakers, business travellers and aspiring screenwriters will find nice touches throughout: rooms have exec-size desks and there's Wi-Fi throughout the hotel, including poolside. The Ocean Lounge serves gourmet cooking and fine wines. *Concierge. Gym. Pool. Internet (free wirelesss). Parking ($28). Restaurant. Room service. TV.*

Huntley Hotel

1111 2nd Street, at California Avenue, Santa Monica, CA 90401 (1-310 394 5454/www.the huntleyhotel.com). Bus 4, 20, 534, 704, 720, SM1,

SM7, SM8, SM10/I-10, exit 4th-5th street north. **Rates** $369-$469. **Rooms** 209. **Credit** AmEx, DC, Disc, MC, V. **Map** p326 A2 ❹

There's something of the W chain about this operation, located in the building that previously housed a branch of the unremarkable Radisson chain. The design of the public areas makes the most of the sunlight that so often illuminates Santa Monica: the occasional shiny surface and lots of light colours, including a daring amount of white that must have the cleaners working overtime. The most memorable space is the Penthouse, a handsome, airy and altogether quite impressive bar/restaurant that affords dramatic views over the Pacific. Many of the rooms also look out towards the ocean. There's no pool, but the beach is a mere pebble's throw away. *Photo p48. Bar. Business centre. Concierge. Gym. Internet ($9.95 wireless). Parking ($30). Restaurants (2). Room service. Smoking rooms. TV: DVD & pay movies.*

Loews Santa Monica Beach Hotel

1700 Ocean Avenue, between Colorado Avenue & Pico Boulevard, Santa Monica, CA 90401 (1-800 235 6397/1-310 458 6700/www.loewshotels.com). Bus 33, 333, 534, SM1, SM7, SM10/I-10, exit 4th-5th Street south. **Rates** $300-$489. **Rooms** 342. **Credit** AmEx, DC, Disc, MC, V. **Map** p326 A3 ❺

This is pretty much a quintessential corporate-Californian property: light and airy, warm and beachy, casual but elegant in an almost entirely non-descript way. Although the pool area is pretty nice, the most eye-catching part of the property is the

The chain gang

The following hotel chains all have branches in and around LA.

Moderate

Hilton *1-800 445 8667/www.hilton.com.*
Hyatt *1-888 591 1234/www.hyatt.com.*
Marriott *1-888 236 2427/ www.marriott.com.*
Radisson *1-888 201 1718/ www.radisson.com.*
Sheraton *1-800 325 3535/ www.starwoodhotels.com/sheraton.*

Budget

Best Western *1-800 780 7234/ www.bestwestern.com.*
Comfort Inn *1-877 424 6423/ www.comfortinn.com.*
Hampton Inn *1-800 426 7866/ http://hamptoninn.hilton.com.*
Holiday Inn *1-800 465 4329/ www.holiday-inn.com.*
Motel 6 *1-800 466 8356/ www.motel6.com.*

Take in the sun at **Huntley Hotel**. *See p47.*

four-storey glass atrium. Except, that is, for the inevitable ocean views: the location is its main selling point. The spa contains four treatment rooms and runs Pilates classes; there's food at Ocean & Vine and drinks in the smartish Papillon lounge.
Bars (2). Business centre. Concierge. Gym. Internet ($9.95 wireless & high-speed). Parking ($28). Pool. Restaurants (3). Room service. Smoking rooms. Spa. TV: pay movies.

Le Merigot

1740 Ocean Avenue, between Colorado Avenue & Pico Boulevard, Santa Monica, CA 90401 (1-888 539 7899/1-310 395 9700/www.lemerigothotel.com). Bus 33, 333, 534, SM1, SM7, SM10/I-10, exit 4th-5th Street south. **Rates** $300-$850. **Rooms** 175. **Credit** AmEx, DC, Disc, MC, V. **Map** p326 A3 **❻**
Sure, there are trendier and swankier properties in the area, but Le Merigot has a lot going for it, not least its low-key vibe. The rooms have a slightly corporate feel – the hotel attracts the business brigade – but with comforts such as 37in LCD TVs and Cloud Nine beds (which live up to their name), it's also popular with vacationers. Other draws include an outdoor pool, a high-tech gym and a serene spa with eucalyptus steam room and cedar wood sauna. Check the website for interesting packages that include sports-car rentals and surfing lessons.
Bar. Business centre. Concierge. Gym. Internet ($9.95 wireless & high-speed). Parking ($29.50). Pool. Restaurant. Room service. TV: DVD & pay movies.

Shutters on the Beach

1 Pico Boulevard, at Ocean Avenue, Santa Monica, CA 90405 (1-800 334 9000/1-310 458 0030/www. shuttersonthebeach.com). Bus 33, 333, SM1, SM7, SM10/I-10, exit 4th-5th Street south. **Rates** $495-$875. **Rooms** 198. **Credit** AmEx, DC, Disc, MC, V. **Map** p326 A3 **❼**
Formerly a cool retreat for hot Hollywood stars and now a sister to Casa del Mar (*see p45*), Shutters has a relaxed but decidedly upscale style. Filled with comfortable sofas, club chairs and prints by modern masters such as David Hockney, the lobby mirrors the beach-cottage ambience of the rooms and suites, which in turn feature lovely, dark hardwood floors and the hotel's signature white shutters. Guests who prefer gentle pampering to the myriad outdoor beach activities can spend a day at the spa or sit poolside sipping wine and taking in the ocean views. The luxury is low-key, but it's luxury all the same. *Photo p44. Bars (2). Business centre. Concierge. Gym. Internet ($12 wireless). Parking ($33). Pool. Restaurants (2). Room service. Spa. TV: DVD & pay movies.*

Viceroy

1819 Ocean Avenue, at Pico Boulevard, Santa Monica, CA 90401 (1-800 622 8711/1-310 260 7500/www.viceroysantamonica.com). Bus 33, 333, 534, SM1, SM7, SM10/I-10, exit 4th-5th Street south. **Rates** $399-$559. **Rooms** 163. **Credit** AmEx, DC, Disc, MC, V. **Map** p326 A3 **❽**
Several years on from its 2002 opening, the Viceroy remains the hippest hotel on the west side. More crucially, though, it's also its most stylish and impressive operation. Interiors diva Kelly Wearstler is behind the design: sleek and chic yet quietly playful, with modern amenities set amid an overall look that nods both to a camped-up British country-house aesthetic and the hotel's history (it was built in 1969). The bar hums with activity, though many drinkers take their cocktails to the bijou pool area out back; Whist restaurant provides sustenance. Light sleepers should note that the oceanside rooms are a tad louder than those on the other side of the building.
Bar. Business centre. Concierge. Gym. Internet ($10.95 wireless). Parking ($29). Pool. Restaurant. Room service. TV: DVD & pay movies.

Moderate

Ambrose

1225 20th Street, between Wilshire Boulevard & Arizona Avenue, Santa Monica, CA 90404 (1-877 262 7673/1-310 315 1555/www.ambrosehotel.com). Bus 20, 720, SM2/I-10, exit 4th-5th Street north. **Rates** $229-$279. **Credit** AmEx, DC, Disc, MC, V. **Map** p326 C2 **❾**
This boutique avoids the stereotypical super-sunny decor prevalent in so many Santa Monica hotels, preferring a cultured mixture of sturdy Craftsman tradition and Asian chic. The latter influence extends to the faintly Asian-inspired garden; however, the stately rooms, some of which come with terraces and fireplaces, are more tangibly American in style. The

hotel is currently talking up its environmental friendliness, which covers everything from energy-efficient LED signs and low-flow toilets to a limo service in a London cab that runs on biodiesel. *Concierge. Gym. Internet (free wireless & high-speed) Parking (free). Room service. TV: DVD & pay movies.*

Georgian Hotel
1415 Ocean Avenue, at Santa Monica Boulevard, Santa Monica, CA 90401 (1-800 538 8147/1-310 395 9945/www.georgianhotel.com). Bus 4, 534, 704, SM1, SM7, SM8, SM10/I-10, exit 4th-5th Street north. **Rates** $250-$479. **Rooms** 84. **Credit** AmEx, DC, Disc, MC, V. **Map** p326 A3 ⑩
Built in 1933 during the peak period of California coastal expansion, the Georgian Hotel is a finely conceived amalgamation of Romanesque revival and art deco styles, and a 2007 renovation brought out the building's most flattering assets. The rooms are elegantly modern yet maintain some original features, such as exposed water pipes and solid wood doors; the old-school elevator won't get you there in a hurry but will get you there in style. One of the hotel's best attributes is the lovely veranda on which guests can take their morning coffee or evening cocktail. *Bar. Business centre. Concierge. Gym. Internet (free wireless). Parking ($21). Restaurant. Room service. TV: DVD & pay movies.*

Hotel California
1670 Ocean Avenue, between Pico Boulevard & Colorado Avenue, Santa Monica, CA 90401 (1-866 571 0000/1-310 393 2363/www.hotelca.com). Bus 33, 333, SM1, SM7, SM10/I-10, exit 4th-5th Street south. **Rates** $209-$309. **Rooms** 26. **Credit** AmEx, DC, Disc, MC, V. **Map** p326 A3 ⑪
It might be just next to the Loews *(see p47)*, but this jaunty motel offers its guests a different type of Californian experience. Surfboards hanging from the façade underline the location; surfers even get a 10% discount if they turn up with board. The decor is homey rather than stylish, old-fashioned rather than old-school. But prices are good. Like the song says, some guests never leave: there are eight long-stay apartments, with monthly rental from $2,450. *Concierge. Internet (free wireless). Parking ($18). Room service.*

Hotel Shangri-La
1301 Ocean Avenue, at Arizona Avenue, Santa Monica, CA 90401 (1-800 345 7829/1-310 394 2791/www.shangrila-hotel.com). Bus 20, 534, 720, SM1, SM7, SM8, SM10/I-10, exit 4th-5th Street north. **Rates** call for details. **Rooms** call for details. **Credit** call for details. **Map** p326 A2 ⑫
Scheduled for completion in late 2008, a $25-million renovation at this Santa Monica favourite will thankfully preserve the streamline moderne exterior that has been delighting locals since 1939. However, Marc Smith's designs for the interior should reflect a more contemporary aesthetic with a cool Hollywood edge. The additions to the property will include a much-needed pool, a rooftop bar, a restaurant, as well as a

number of new rooms and suites. Updated rates weren't available at the time this guide went to press; call or check online for further information. *Call for details of hotel services.*

Sheraton Delfina
530 W Pico Boulevard, between 4th & 7th Streets, Santa Monica, CA 90405 (1-888 627 8532/1-310 399 9344/www.sheratonsantamonica.com). Bus 33, 333, SM1, SM7, SM10/I-10, exit 4th-5th Street south. **Rates** $269-$549. **Rooms** 310. **Credit** AmEx, DC, Disc, MC, V. **Map** p326 B3 ⑬
Down the road from the beach, the Delfina was designed by the über-stylish Kor Group for the über-corporate Sheraton chain. A little of both approaches is evident throughout the property: the design is handsome and modern but also overfamiliar, as if those behind it were perhaps wary of frightening the horses. Still, the amenities are excellent, the rooms are in good nick (some have balconies and ocean views), and the service is as reliable as you'd expect. A nice alternative for travellers who want a bit of the Viceroy's style without worrying about whether they're wearing the right label jeans in the bar. *Bar. Business centre. Concierge. Gym. Internet (free wireless in lobby, $11.95 high-speed in rooms). Parking ($28). Pool. TV: pay movies.*

Budget

Bayside Hotel
2001 Ocean Avenue, at Bay Street, Santa Monica, CA 90405 (1-310 396 6000/www.baysidehotel.com). Bus 33, 333, SM1, SM7, SM10/I-10, exit 4th-5th Street south. **Rates** $109-$269. **Rooms** 45. **Credit** AmEx, DC, Disc, MC, V. **Map** p326 A3 ⑭
This unpretentious hotel underwent decorative renovations recently. Although it's still modestly furnished, it offers something most other Santa Monica hotels don't: free parking. Rates are reasonable, and advance reservations will secure a clean, comfortable room with an ocean view. One appealing feature is the retro blade sign on the corner, which harks back to the days when Santa Monica truly was a laid-back beach town at the end of Route 66. *Concierge. Internet ($9.95 wireless). Parking free.*

HI-Santa Monica
1436 2nd Street, between Santa Monica Boulevard & Broadway, Santa Monica, CA 90401 (1-888 464 4872 ext 137/1-310 393 9913/www.hilosangeles. org). Bus 4, 20, 534, 704, 720, SM1, SM7, SM8, SM10/I-10, exit 4th-5th street north. **Rates** $32 dorm bed. **Beds** 260. **Credit** AmEx, DC, MC, V. **Map** p326 A3 ⑮
Book far in advance for this four-floor, 260-bed Santa Monica hostel: the location ensures that demand is always high. The rooms more than cover the basics: the dorms sleep between six and ten. There's a café for breakfast, video games, TV and movie rooms, a kitchen, a courtyard and all the other budget-travel basics you could possibly want. *Internet (free wireless). Parking ($21).*

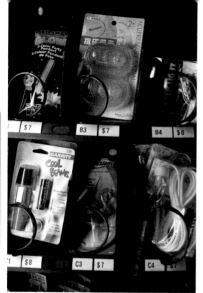

Custom Hotel.

Hotel Carmel

201 Broadway, at 2nd Street, Santa Monica, CA 90401 (1-800 445 8695/1-310 451 2469/www. hotelcarmel.com). Bus 4, 20, 534, 704, 720, SM1, SM7, SM8, SM10/I-10, exit 4th-5th street north. **Rates** $165-$255. **Rooms** 100. **Credit** AmEx, DC, Disc, MC, V. **Map** p326 A3 ⑯

Founded in 1929, the Carmel has been spruced up of late. Although it's by no means luxurious, the rooms and suites are at least pretty spacious, with decor that's most flatteringly described as contemporary craftsman. Some of the suites have ocean views, and a complimentary breakfast is offered each morning. Valet parking is available, although the hotel is within walking distance of all Santa Monica's attractions. *Internet ($9.95 wireless). Parking ($12).*

Venice

Budget

Cadillac Hotel

8 Dudley Avenue, at Speedway Street & Ocean Front Walk, Venice, CA 91291 (1-310 399 8876/www.thecadillachotel.com). Bus 33, 333, C1, SM1, SM2/I-10, exit 4th-5th Street south. **Rates** $129-$179. **Rooms** 47. **Credit** AmEx, DC, MC, V. **Map** p326 A5 ⑰

After a long run as a budget beach hostel, the pink Cadillac has been transformed into a boutique hotel by a new team. All the rooms, the lobby and the lounge have been renovated and the exterior has been given a fresh coat of paint; works of art and decorative objects created by local artisans will also be put on display in due course. However, although the management is working to change the hotel's image, they do aim to keep the 'Venice vibe alive'. *Internet ($7 wireless). Parking ($10).*

Venice Beach House

15 30th Avenue, at Speedway Street, Venice, CA 90291 (1-310 823 1966/www.venicebeachhouse. com). Bus 108, 358, C1/I-10, exit 4th-5th Street south. **Rates** $145-$235. **Rooms** 9. **Credit** AmEx, MC, V. **Map** p326 A6 ⑱

This craftsman-style inn was built in 1911 by Warren Wilson, the owner of the now-defunct *Los Angeles Daily Journal.* Now on the National Register of Historic Places, it's been faithfully restored and furnished with exceptional antique pieces; many of the rooms are named after characters with ties to the area (Venice founder Abbot Kinney, sometime local Charlie Chaplin). Each of the nine rooms has its own character and amenities, though four share a common bath. The more extravagant suites offer an ocean view, a fireplace, a patio or a private entrance. *Internet (free wireless). Parking ($12).*

Marina del Rey to LAX

Expensive

Ritz-Carlton, Marina del Rey

4375 Admiralty Way, between Bali & Promenade Ways, Marina del Rey, CA 90292 (1-310 823 1700/www.ritzcarlton.com). Bus 108/Hwy 90, exit Mindanao Way west. **Rates** $299-$489. **Rooms** 304. **Credit** AmEx, Disc, DC, MC, V.

Marina del Rey's best hotel is every bit as smart as you'd hope a Ritz-Carlton to be. However, it's not as traditional: a recent renovation was designed to bring a hint of Hollywood style to the hotel, without importing any of the Hollywood attitude. The rooms are traditional without being stuffy; many have views over the marina. Downstairs, it's a little more modern but still ritzy, with an excellent take on

Californian food served in the Jer-Ne restaurant and some indulgent treatments offered in the new spa. Another nice local touch is the addition of yoga and spinning classes by the pool at weekends, run by the renowned YAS centre in Venice (*see p276*).
Bar. Business centre. Concierge. Gym. Internet ($9.95 wireless). Parking ($31). Pool. Restaurants (2). Room service. Spa. TV: DVD & pay movies.

Sheraton Gateway

6101 W Century Boulevard, between Airport & S Sepulveda Boulevards, Los Angeles, CA 90045 (1-888 544 8983/1-310 642 1111/www.sheraton.com). Bus 117, 439/I-405, exit Century Boulevard west. **Rates** $389-$499. **Rooms** 802. **Credit** AmEx, DC, Disc, MC.
Presumably in an attempt to differentiate the property from the cluster of over-familiar hotels that ring LAX, Sheraton engaged the services of the fashion-friendly Kor Hotel Group to sprinkle their magic dust on this place a few years ago. The result is the most handsome hotel in the airport's immediate shadow, albeit one that doesn't match the likes of the Viceroy (another Kor property) in the style stakes. On the other hand, it doesn't try to: the Sheraton Gateway offers instead a slightly bland but generally likeable interpretation on modern boutique decor. Unusually for an airport hotel, amenities include an outdoor pool.
Bar. Business centre. Concierge. Gym. Internet ($10.95 wireless). Parking ($13-$20). Pool. Restaurant. Room service. TV: pay movies.

Moderate

Custom Hotel

8639 Lincoln Boulevard, at W Manchester Avenue & Fordham Road, Playa del Rey, CA 90045 (1-877 287 8601/1-310 645 0400/www.customhotel.com).
Bus 115/I-405, exit Jefferson Boulevard west. **Rates** $170-$250. **Rooms** 250. **Credit** AmEx, DC, Disc, MC, V.
You can't miss this new arrival as you drive up from LAX or Marina del Rey: topped with a glowing neon sign announcing its name, it's the only all-black building on the horizon. Things are more colourful inside, but no less stylish: the lobby opens out into a sleek but playful bar area (say hello to the sheep), and there's also a restaurant (Bistrotek) and a beautifully designed pool area at the back (the Hopscotch Pool Bar & Grill). The rooms are lovely, comfortable beds supplemented by quirky design touches and all mod cons. There's not much in the vicinity, but you'd be forgiven if you didn't want to leave the hotel.
Bars (2). Business centre. Concierge. Gym. Internet (free wireless). Parking ($22). Restaurants (2). Room service. TV: DVD & pay movies.

Inn at Playa del Rey

435 Culver Boulevard, at Pershing Drive, Playa del Rey, CA 90293 (1-310 574 1920/www.innat playadelrey.com). Bus 220, 625/I-405, exit Culver Boulevard west. **Rates** $175-$425. **Rooms** 21. **Credit** AmEx, DC, MC, V.
The Inn at Playa del Rey has the rare distinction of being minutes from LAX and yet also within easy walking distance from the beach. The standard rooms are decorated individually; all are comfortable and have a homey ambience. Some rooms offer views of the marina, while others look out over the nearby wildlife habitat. Parents with children in tow will be relieved to find that there are also two-bedroom family suites available. The hotel offers complimentary bike rentals to guests and, for a nominal fee, skateboards and in-line skates.
Internet (free wireless & shared terminal). Parking (free). TV.

Time Out
Travel Guides

USA

Written by local experts

**Available at all good bookshops
and at timeout.com/shop**

**Time Out
Guides**

Brentwood to Beverly Hills

Westwood

Expensive

W
*930 Hilgard Avenue, at Le Conte Avenue, Westwood,
CA 90024 (reservations 1-800 421 2317/1-310 208
8765/www.whotels.com/losangeles). Bus 2, 302, 305,
720, SM1, SM2, SM3, SM8/I-405, exit Wilshire
Boulevard east.* **Rooms** 258.
Credit AmEx, Disc, DC, MC, V.
Westwood is a wonderful place to walk, eat and
attend university, but it's not really a thrill-a-minute
urban hub. As such, the W has become essential to
the area: located on a sidestreet lined with apartment
complexes, the hotel offers a sleek environment in
which locals and outsiders can indulge their inner
hipster. Rooms are unsurprising but well conceived;
the public areas tend to be dark and rather drab, but
Thom Filicia (*Queer Eye for the Straight Guy*) has
redesigned many of the spaces, including the poolside restaurant and courtyard. Intriguingly, pets
under 40lbs are welcome for an additional fee, and
are given their own bed and dishes. Woof!
*Bar. Business centre. Concierge. Gym. Internet
($14.95 high-speed). Parking ($31). Pool. Restaurants
(3). Room service. Smoking rooms. Spa. TV:
DVD & pay movies.*

Moderate

Angeleno
*170 N Church Lane, at W Sunset Boulevard, Los
Angeles, CA 90049 (1-866 264 3536/1-310 476
6411/www.hotelangeleno.com). Bus 2, 302, 761/
I-405, exit Sunset Boulevard west.* **Rooms** 208. **Credit** AmEx, DC, Disc, MC, V.
The Bay Area-based Joie de Vivre Group's first
entry in the Los Angeles market is an eye-catching,
custom-built circular tower overlooking I-405 (happily, there's no traffic noise) and within reach of the
Getty Center in the hills above. The amenities on
offer include a slightly underwhelming pool area,
and the often-buzzing West bar and restaurant on
the top floor. The rooms themselves are decorated
plainly but attractively; each has its own small balcony. However, perhaps the hotel's best amenity is
the variety of views available from the upper rooms,
down I-405 and out across the city.
*Bar. Business centre. Gym. Internet (free wireless).
Parking ($18). Pool. Restaurants. Room service.
TV: pay movies.*

Hotel Palomar
*10740 Wilshire Boulevard, at Selby Avenue, Los
Angeles, CA 90024 (1-800 472 8556/1-310 475
8711/www.hotelpalomar-lawestwood.com). Bus 20,*

Spa for a day

OK, so the rooms at the five-stars may be
beyond your budget… but surely you can
treat yourself to a facial? There's a spa
around every corner in LA, and the crème
de la (face) crème are found at hotels.
All of them cater to visitors as well as
hotel guests, and many have become
destinations in their own right.

At the clinic-style Bliss spa at the
beyond-cool **W** hotel (*see left*), whale
music is replaced by Stevie Wonder,
and the lounge provides not dried fruit
but brownies. The experts (we recommend
Kathryn) aim at getting results, yet the
vibe is still relaxing: despite including
extractions, the signature Triple Oxygen
Treatment ($160/85 minutes) will
send you straight to sleep.

Unsurprisingly, many hotels in Beverly
Hills boast raved-about spas. However,
the best is at the **Beverly Hills Hotel &
Bungalows** (*see p54*), where La Prairie
Spa showcases the luxe Swiss skincare
brand (splurge on the legendary Caviar
Firming facial, $290/90 minutes). Some
treatments can be taken in private
cabanas by the pool; you even get
to choose the music.

When it comes to post-shopping
indulgence, LeSpa at the **Sofitel** (*see
p58*) couldn't be better located. And for
sheer sophistication, it's hard to top.
As you sip herbal tea, your feet will be
soaked in a bowl of warm water and petals
– and that's before you even get to the
candle-lit therapy rooms. During awards
season, demand soars for the Carita
Ageless Beauty facial ($280/90 minutes).

Location is also a prime draw at the
beautiful, Michael Smith-designed One
spa at **Shutters on the Beach** (*see p48*).
The brevity of the menu works in its favour,
with a well-edited selection of therapies
using products by facialist-to-the-stars
Ole Henriksen. Even the pedicures are
memorable: try Surf's Up ($110/80
minutes), and request Traci Harris.

Superbly set on a bluff overlooking
the ocean, Spa Montage at the **Montage
Laguna Beach** (*see p66*) is known for
its 'Surrender' experiences (from $450/
120 minutes), but it also does more
straightforward fare: Swedish massages,
for example. So surrender to the rub.

720/I-405, exit Wilshire Boulevard east. **Rates**
$199-$369. **Rooms** 268. **Credit** AmEx, DC, Disc,
MC, V. **Map** p327 A4 ⑲

Just a couple of years after the successful Joie de
Vivre hotel group brought its Bay Area sensibility
south to LA for the first time, San Francisco rivals
Kimpton Hotels followed them down the coast and
into Westwood. While JdV built their own hotel in
the shape of the Angeleno, Kimpton settled on this
former Doubletree property, sprucing it up so that
it's more or less unrecognisable from its previous
incarnation. The style throughout is handsome and
pleasingly muted, and the in-room technological
amenities are impressive (massive TVs, free Wi-Fi).
Kimpton's long-held reputation for excellent service
is another selling point at this welcome newcomer.
*Bar. Business centre. Concierge. Gym. Internet (free
wireless). Parking ($30). Pool. Restaurant. Room
service. TV: pay movies.*

Bel Air

Expensive

Hotel Bel-Air

*701 Stone Canyon Road, at Bellagio Road, Bel Air,
CA 90077 (1-800 648 4097/1-310 472 1211/www.
hotelbelair.com). I-405, exit Sunset Boulevard east.*
Rates $395-$4,500. **Rooms** 91. **Credit** AmEx, DC,
Disc, MC, V.

Hardly hip but by no means uncool either, this elite
and quietly decadent Mission-style '20s hotel is a
dreamy getaway on 12 fairytale acres of lush landscaping: hidden from the traffic and frenetic energy
of Los Angeles, it almost feels like a country retreat.
Guests can choose to spend long afternoons by the
pool eating chilled grapes, relaxing in one of 91 individually decorated rooms, meandering through the
gardens or subtly trying to spot which Hollywood
player is sitting at the next table in the Restaurant
(yes, that's its name). A new day spa is scheduled to
open in January 2009; the pampering it offers will
almost certainly be out of this world.
*Bar. Business centre. Concierge. Internet (free high-
speed). Gym. Parking ($30). Pool. Restaurant. Room
service. TV: pay movies.*

Century City

Moderate

Hyatt Regency Century Plaza

*2025 Avenue of the Stars, between Constellation &
W Olympic Boulevards, Century City, CA 90067
(1-877 787 3452/1-310 277 2000/www.hyatt.com).
Bus 4, 28, 316, SM5/I-405, exit Santa Monica
Boulevard east.* **Rates** $275-$500. **Rooms** 726.
Credit AmEx, DC, Disc, MC, V. **Map** p327 B4 ⑳

No surprises: this is simply a comfortable and efficient hotel that offers a lot of services designed to
please the Hyatt's legions of business travellers. The
architecture is rather corporate (the views from the

building are more appealing than the views of it) and
the interior is predictable. Still, there's something to
be said for the convenience, the reliability and the
sheer size of the place. Round-the-clock room service
is a plus, as are the capacious fitness centre and the
spa (which features 27 treatment rooms).
*Bar. Business centre. Concierge. Gym. Internet
($9.95 wireless & high-speed). Parking ($31). Pool.
Restaurant. Room service. Smoking rooms. Spa.
TV: pay movies.*

Beverly Hills

Expensive

Avalon

*9400 W Olympic Boulevard, at S Canon Drive,
Beverly Hills, CA 90212 (1-800 670 6138/1-310 277
5221/www.avalonbeverlyhills.com). Bus 28/I-10, exit
Robertson Boulevard north.* **Rates** $309-$389. **Rooms**
84. **Credit** AmEx, DC, Disc, MC, V. **Map** p327 D4 ㉑

Opened as the Beverly Carlton in the 1940s, this
streetside property was renovated and regenerated
by the Kor Hotel Group in 1999, setting the tone for
the boutique-hotels-in-old-buildings schtick later
brought to something approaching perfection by the
company at the Viceroy in Santa Monica (*see p48*).
Through the lobby, hidden behind a fabulous
boomerang façade and a cluster of trees, is a kidney-
shaped pool that provides a focal point for a buzzy
bar scene (and, thus, rarely seems to welcome any
actual swimmers). The rooms are retro-handsome
but slightly worn; scheduled for 2008, a property-
wide renovation should spruce things up a little.
*Bar. Business centre. Concierge. Gym. Internet ($10.95
wireless). Parking ($28). Pool. Restaurant. Room
service. Smoking rooms. TV: DVD & pay movies.*

Beverly Hills Hotel & Bungalows

*9641 Sunset Boulevard, at N Crescent Drive, Beverly
Hills, CA 90210 (1-800 283 8885/1-310 276 2251/
www.thebeverlyhillshotel.com). Bus 2, 302/I-405, exit
Sunset Boulevard east.* **Rates** $485-$635. **Rooms** 204.
Credit AmEx, DC, Disc, MC, V. **Map** p327 B2 ㉒

The famous pink stucco façade, the manicured
grounds and the sumptuous rooms of the Beverly
Hills Hotel look as fresh and fanciful as they did on
opening day more than 90 years ago. It oozes exclusivity: every screen legend from Valentino to Arnie
has slept in this fabled hideaway or held court in its
still-popular Polo Lounge. The biggest draw are the
bungalows, where Liz Taylor spent six of her honey-
moons: No.5 has its own pool; No.7 is decorated
to Marilyn's taste. Take the time to hit backhands
with the tennis pro (1959 Wimbledon champ Alex
Olmedo) before hitting the suitably extravagant spa.

> **Beverly Hills Hotel &
> Bungalows** (*p54*) Richard
> Gere takes his dates here
> in *American Gigolo*

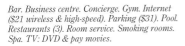

Thompson Beverly Hills. *See p57.*

Bar. Business centre. Concierge. Gym. Internet ($21 wireless & high-speed). Parking ($31). Pool. Restaurants (3). Room service. Smoking rooms. Spa. TV: DVD & pay movies.

Beverly Hilton

9876 Wilshire Boulevard, between Santa Monica Boulevard & Whittier Drive, Beverly Hills, CA 90210 (1-310 274 7777/www.beverlyhilton.com). Bus 16, 20, 316, 720/I-405, exit Wilshire Boulevard east. **Rates** $295-$475. **Rooms** 570. **Credit** AmEx, DC, Disc, MC, V. **Map** p327 C3 ㉓

For years, this hotel was a dowdy property famous only as the home of the Golden Globes. However, a 2007-08 refit has spruced the place up no end. The rather tired decor has been replaced by a look that's both comfortable and handsome, classic but not wedged in the past. The Aqua Star Spa offers a string of upscale treatments; unusually for a hotel in this part of town, the heated pool is big enough to swim in. Dining and drinking options are provided by Circa55 and tiki lounge Trader Vic's; up in the rooms, all mod cons are present and correct. *Bars (2). Business centre. Concierge. Gym. Internet ($9.95 wireless & high-speed). Parking ($32). Pool. Restaurant. Room service. Smoking rooms. Spa. TV: pay movies.*

Beverly Wilshire

9500 Wilshire Boulevard, at S Rodeo Drive, Beverly Hills, CA 90212 (1-800 427 4354/1-310 275 5200/ www.fourseasons.com/beverlywilshire). Bus 4, 14, 16, 20, 316, 704, 720/I-405, exit Wilshire Boulevard east. **Rates** $445-$700. **Rooms** 395. **Credit** AmEx, DC, Disc, MC, V. **Map** p327 D3 ㉔

The ornate detailing on this Four Seasons-operated gem, famous for its role in *Pretty Woman*, recalls 19th-century French splendour, but recent additions such as a Richard Meier-designed restaurant add 21st-century sophistication. The new spa is worth a peek: the staff are gracious and the treatment rooms are blissful. The proximity to Rodeo Drive ensures a wealthy and occasionally sniffy crowd, but there's still something warm about the place. If the room rates are out of your range, stop by and relax with a coffee or a cocktail at Blvd, a lovely sidewalk café. *Bar (2). Business centre. Concierge. Gym. Internet ($15 wireless & high-speed). Parking ($35). Pool. Restaurants (3). Room service. Spa. TV: DVD.*

Four Seasons Los Angeles at Beverly Hills

300 S Doheny Drive, at Gregory Way, Beverly Hills, CA 90048 (1-800 332 3442/1-310 273 2222/www. fourseasons.com). Bus 20, 28/I-10, exit Robertson Boulevard north. **Rates** $425-$615. **Rooms** 285. **Credit** AmEx, DC, Disc, MC, V. **Map** p327 D3 ㉕

The Four Seasons pampers its guests something silly. From the fragrant, flower-filled lobby to the immaculate rooms, every detail is calculated to spoil visitors. Free cellphones and limos to Rodeo Drive are standard; on the rooftop terrace, cabanas come with TVs, phones and fully stocked refrigerators.

Chamberlain. *See p58.*

Downstairs, the high-tech rooms feature balconies, marble-topped desks and Frette linens.

If the hotel's fully booked, don't worry: similar luxury should be available at the unrelated **Montage** (225 N Canon Drive, 1-310 860 7800, www.montage beverlyhills.com), due to open in late 2008.
Bar. Business centre. Concierge. Gym. Internet ($10 wireless & high-speed). Parking ($32). Pool. Restaurants (2). Room service. Spa. TV: pay movies.

Luxe Hotel Rodeo Drive
360 N Rodeo Drive, between Brighton & Dayton Ways, Beverly Hills, CA 90210 (1-866 589 3411/ 1-310 273 0300/www.luxehotels.com). Bus 14, 16, 20, 316, 720/I-405, exit Wilshire Boulevard east.
Rates $309-$359. **Rooms** 88. **Credit** AmEx, DC, Disc, MC, V. **Map** p327 C3
The design of this hotel is an exercise in restraint. Located on Rodeo Drive (it's the only hotel on Beverly Hills' most famous street), the Luxe has an intimate lobby defined by its monochromatic palette and sleek decor, and 88 rooms and suites that share an equally polished aesthetic. The high-priced luxury is tangible in the quality of the linens, the generous amenities and the professional service. The hotel is alluring for Hollywood movers and shakers, but it's also a good option for families.
Bar. Business centre. Concierge. Internet (free wireless & high-speed). Parking ($28). Restaurant. Room service. TV: pay movies.

Mosaic
125 S Spalding Drive, between Wilshire & Charleville Boulevards, Beverly Hills, CA 90212 (1-310 278 0303/www.mosaichotel.com). Bus 4, 16, 20, 316, 704, 720/I-405, exit Wilshire Boulevard east.
Rates $325-$470. **Rooms** 49. **Credit** AmEx, DC, Disc, MC, V. **Map** p327 C3
The old Beverly Hills Inn was brought into the 21st century with some style in 2003, and it remains an impressive operation. The luxury here is all in the best possible taste: the earth-toned rooms come complete with wonderful linens, immense shower-heads and free high-speed internet access, with the one- and two-bedroom suites simply continuing the theme on a larger scale. With only 49 rooms, the Mosaic has the feel of a boutique hotel, a welcome change from some of its more impersonal neighbours. Rodeo Drive is a short stroll from the door.
Bar. Business centre. Concierge. Gym. Internet (free wireless & high-speed). Parking ($25). Pool. Restaurant. Room service. TV: pay movies.

Peninsula Beverly Hills
9882 Santa Monica Boulevard, between Wilshire & Charleville Boulevards, Beverly Hills, CA 90212 (1-800 462 7899/1-310 551 2888/www.peninsula.com). Bus 4, 16, 20, 316, 704, 720/I-405, exit Santa Monica Boulevard east. **Rates** $525-$725. **Rooms** 194.
Credit AmEx, DC, Disc, MC, V. **Map** p327 C3
Designed to look and feel like a private estate, the Peninsula exudes opulence. There are 193 rooms, suites and private villas situated on the lushly landscaped grounds, along with a fitness centre, a spa, a rooftop garden and a lap pool. Just off the lobby, the gorgeous Club Bar offers entertainment on most nights. The Belvedere, which serves classic American cuisine such as macaroni cheese with a gourmet twist, is considered one of LA's favourite top-class restaurants. White-glove service throughout only adds to the high-end appeal.
Bar. Business centre. Concierge. Gym. Internet (free wireless & high-speed). Parking ($28). Pool. Restaurants (2). Room service. Spa. TV: DVD & pay movies.

SLS Los Angeles
465 S La Cienega Boulevard, at Clifton Way, Beverly Hills, CA 90048 (1-310 247 0400/ www.slshotels.com). Bus 28, 105, 328/I-10, exit

La Cienega Boulevard north. **Rates** call for details. **Rooms** 297. **Credit** AmEx, DC, Disc, MC, V. **Map** p328 B3 🆉

On the very edge of Beverly Hills, this property was part of the luxurious Le Méridien chain until 2008, when management of the operation was taken over by restaurateur, nightlife promoter and all-round powerful guy Sam Nazarian. In a press release announcing the takeover, Nazarian suggested that 'the name [SLS] will become synonymous with timeless elegance, intelligence, humanity, discovery and a completely novel guest experience'. If his nightlife ventures are anything to go by, that ought to translate to high-concept luxury (the hotel's look has been designed by Philippe Starck), high-maintenance guests (his clubs have long attracted A-list celebs) and some soaringly high prices. The hotel was scheduled to open in autumn 2008.
Call for details of hotel services.

Thompson Beverly Hills

9360 Wilshire Boulevard, at S Crescent Drive, Beverly Hills, CA 90212 (1-310 273 1400/www. thompsonhotels.com). Bus 4, 14, 16, 20, 316, 704, 720/I-405, exit Wilshire Boulevard east. **Rates** $299-$379. **Rooms** 107. **Credit** AmEx, DC, Disc, MC, V. **Map** p327 D3 🆉

The latest offering from the company behind the regeneration of the Hollywood Roosevelt (*see p61*), the Thompson is a brighter, airier property than its sister operation. Designed by Dodd Mitchell and open since 2008, it's a real looker, from the BondSt sushi restaurant to the rooftop pool area and the handsome, understated lobby. Other points of interest include a number of works by New York artist Steven Klein. *Photo p55.*
Bars (3). Concierge. Gym. Internet (free wireless & high-speed). Parking ($28). Pool. Restaurants. Room service. Smoking rooms. TV: DVD & pay movies.

Moderate

Crescent

403 N Crescent Drive, off Santa Monica Boulevard, at Brighton Way, Beverly Hills, CA 90210 (1-310 247 0505/www.crescentbh.com). Bus 4, 14, 16, 20,

316, 704, 720/I-405, exit Wilshire Boulevard east. **Rates** $175-$325. **Rooms** 35. **Credit** AmEx, DC, Disc, MC, V. **Map** p327 D2 🆉

Hotelier Gregory Peck (no relation) and designer *du jour* Dodd Mitchell reworked this handsome 1926 building into a boutique hotel in 2003. Its best feature is Boé: it's a mellow spot during the day (the Beverly Hills power-lunchers prefer other spots in the neighbourhood), but it thrives at night, drinkers spilling out on to the deck as they join the scene with a cocktail or a glass of white in hand. The rooms aren't huge – indeed, some are tiny – but they are comfortable.
Bar. Concierge. Internet (free wireless). Parking ($26). Restaurant. Room service. TV: DVD.

Maison 140

140 S Lasky Drive, at Charleville Boulevard, Beverly Hills, CA 90212 (1-800 432 5444/1-310 281 4000/ www.maison140beverlyhills.com). Bus 4, 14, 16, 20, 316, 704, 720/I-405, exit Santa Monica Boulevard east. **Rates** $229-$319. **Rooms** 43. **Credit** AmEx, DC, Disc, MC, V. **Map** p327 C3 🆉

The rather small rooms at this bijou Kor Hotel Group property seem designed to prove that form is more important than function. The Kelly Wearstler decor in the individually decorated rooms, a chic return to 18th-century Paris with a few contemporary Asian twists, is every bit as glamorous a look as you'd hope to find in a building that was once owned by Lillian Gish. Bar Noir provides guests with somewhere to unwind in a neighbourhood that's strangely short on nightlife. There's no pool, but guests are welcome to use the facilities at the nearby Avalon (*see p54*).
Bar. Business centre. Concierge. Gym. Internet ($10.95 wireless & high-speed, free shared terminal in lobby). Parking ($24). Room service. TV: DVD.

Budget

Hotel Beverly Terrace

469 N Doheny Drive, at Santa Monica Boulevard, Beverly Hills, CA 90210 (1-800 842 6401/1-310 274 8141/www.beverlyterracehotel.com). Bus 4, 14, 16, 20, 316, 704, 720/I-405, exit Wilshire Boulevard east. **Rates** $149-$209. **Rooms** 39. **Credit** AmEx, DC, Disc, MC, V. **Map** p327 D2 🆉

Carry on camping

Perhaps the most scenic camping in LA is found at **Malibu Creek State Park** (four miles south of US 101 on Las Virgenes/Malibu Canyon Road). The park offers 4,000 acres for hiking, fishing and horseback riding, as well as 15 miles of stream-side trails. Not far away in Malibu is **Leo Carrillo State Beach** (35000 PCH, Malibu), which has 1.5 miles of beach for swimming, surfing and fishing. Reservations for both parks –

staff recommend booking six months ahead for summer – can be made on 1-800 444 7275; see www.parks.ca.gov for more.

Private campsites tend to be less scenic than their state counterparts, but offer more amenities. **Malibu Beach RV Park** (25801 PCH, 1-800 622 6052, 1-310 456 6052, www.maliburv.com) has 50 tent sites, priced from $20 to $56 depending on the view and the time of year.

The rooms at the Beverly Terrace are smaller and less luxurious than other Beverly Hills hotels, but this mid-century spot does offer one of the best deals to be found in the area. Teak furniture and planted palms hint playfully towards a tropical getaway, though the decor in the rooms themselves (which aren't huge) is retro and minimal. Continental breakfast is included in the rates; Trattoria Amici, the hotel's restaurant, offers Cal-Italian cooking. There's also a small garden and a nice little pool. *Internet (free wireless). Parking (free). Pool. Restaurant. TV.*

West Hollywood, Hollywood & Midtown

West Hollywood

Expensive

Chamberlain

1000 Westmount Drive, at W Knoll Drive, West Hollywood, CA 90069 (1-800 201 9652/1-310 657 7400/www.chamberlainwesthollywood.com). Bus 2, 302/I-10, exit La Cienega Boulevard north. **Rates** $309-$399. **Rooms** 114. **Credit** AmEx, DC, Disc, MC, V. **Map** p328 B2 ㉞

Open only since 2005, the most discreet of all the Kor Hotel Group's properties is also one of its most appealing. Tucked away in a quiet West Hollywood sidestreet, the Chamberlain is less buzzy than the Viceroy (*see p48*) and subtler than the Avalon (*see p54*), but the understated look is perfect for the location and part of the property's appeal. The rooms are a reasonable size and decorated in homely yet stylish fashion, and all of them come with several mod cons (DVD players, large desks). Still, don't be surprised if you spend a lot of your time with cocktail in hand up in the atmospheric pool area. *Photo p56. Bar. Business centre. Concierge. Gym. Internet ($9.95 wireless & high-speed). Parking ($27). Pool. Restaurant. Room service. Smoking rooms. TV: DVD & pay movies.*

Chateau Marmont

8221 Sunset Boulevard, between N Harper Avenue & Havenhurst Drive, West Hollywood, CA 90046 (1-800 242 8328/1-323 656 1010/www.chateaumarmont.com). Bus 2, 302/I-10, exit La Cienega Boulevard north. **Rates** $370-$480. **Rooms** 63. **Credit** AmEx, DC, Disc, MC, V. **Map** p328 B1 ㉟

One of the many beautiful things about this Hollywood Hills fixture is that it's barely changed over the decades. The hotel still attracts the brazen and the beautiful (everyone from Led Zeppelin to Lindsay Lohan has stayed here; John Belushi OD-ed in bungalow 3); it still offers a quintessentially glamorous LA experience; and it still promises its guests absolute discretion. The only dramatic change in recent years has been the arrival in the kitchen of chef Carolynn Spence; however, while the menu has changed, regulars will be glad to know that the classic Bar Marmont vibe remains intact (*see p180*). *Bar. Business centre. Concierge. Gym. Internet (free wireless). Parking ($28). Pool. Restaurant (2). Room service. Smoking rooms. TV: DVD & pay movies.*

London West Hollywood

1020 N San Vicente Boulevard, at Holloway Drive, West Hollywood, CA 90069 (1-866 282 4560/1-310 854 1111/www.thelondonwesthollywood.com). Bus 4, 105, 220, 305, 550, 704/I-10, exit La Cienega Boulevard north. **Rates** $279-$629 suite. **Rooms** 200. **Credit** AmEx, DC, Disc, MC, V. **Map** p328 A2 ㊱

Formerly the Bel Age, this hotel reopened in spring 2008 following a total makeover by design guru David Collins. All 200 rooms are generous suites, featuring subtle sage and tan palettes, Italian linens and luxurious white bathrooms. Each has a private deck or a balcony with decent views; for truly extraordinary panoramic vistas, especially at dusk, head upwards to the rooftop pool deck. The off-Sunset location makes it a popular location with leisure-seekers, who'll also be lured by the spa (set to open in 2009); businessfolk enjoy complimentary Wi-Fi and free telephone calls to London. Even without the bonus of a Gordon Ramsay restaurant (*see p154*), this place would be a knockout. *Bar. Business centre. Concierge. Gym. Internet (free wireless & high-speed). Parking ($30). Pool. Restaurant. Smoking rooms. Spa. Room service. TV: pay movies.*

Mondrian

8440 W Sunset Boulevard, at N Olive Drive, West Hollywood, CA 90069 (1-800 525 8029/1-323 650 8999/www.mondrianhotel.com). Bus 2, 302, LDHWH/I-10, exit La Cienega Boulevard north. **Rates** $445-$495. **Rooms** 237. **Credit** AmEx, DC, Disc, MC, V. **Map** p328 B1 ㊲

Built as an apartment block in the 1950s, this tower was converted into a hotel by businessman Ian Schrager and designer Philippe Starck in the mid '90s, and immediately became the hottest spot in the city. It still carries a certain amount of star quality, but changes are afoot: Schrager left the company (Morgans Hotel Group) a few years ago, and Starck's designs are being replaced in late 2008 by those of Benjamin Noriega-Ortiz, whose work is generally more homely and less minimalist. Expect the celeb-friendly Skybar and luxurious Agua Spa to remain, and the hotel to continue drawing a starry crowd. *Bars (2). Business centre. Concierge. Gym Internet ($10 wireless & high-speed). Parking ($29). Pool. Restaurants (2). Smoking rooms. Spa. Room service. TV: DVD & pay movies.*

Sofitel Los Angeles

8555 Beverly Boulevard, at N La Cienega Boulevard, West Hollywood, CA 90069 (1-800 521 7772/1-310 278 5444/www.sofitel.com). Bus 14, 16, 105, 316, LDF, LDHWH/I-10, exit La Cienega Boulevard north. **Rates** $300-$385. **Rooms** 295. **Credit** AmEx, DC, Disc, MC, V. **Map** p328 B3 ㊳

A shopper's paradise but a driver's nightmare – that's the best way to describe the location of this hotel, close to the Beverly Center in the heart of one of the most congested areas in LA. The good news, though, is that there are countless shops, restaurants and bars just a short walk from here. And once you've made it through the traffic, you'll find a very impressive hotel operation: smart, reliable and also, thanks to the presence of the Simon LA restaurant (run by star chef Kerry Simon) and the Stone Rose Lounge, surprisingly fashionable.
Bar. Business centre. Concierge. Gym. Internet ($9.95 wireless). Parking ($29). Pool. Restaurant. Room service. Smoking rooms. TV: pay movies.

Sunset Marquis Hotel & Villas

1200 N Alta Loma Road, between W Sunset Boulevard & Holloway Drive, West Hollywood, CA 90069 (1-800 858 9758/1-310 657 1333/ www.sunsetmarquishotel.com). Bus 2, 302/I-10, exit La Cienega Boulevard north. **Rates** $385-$650 suite. **Rooms** 154. **Credit** AmEx, DC, Disc, MC, V. **Map** p328 B1 ③
Since its opening in 1963, the Sunset Marquis has attracted a steady stream of A-listers to its discreet surroundings. Some of the amenities are aimed at a niche audience: for example, it's unlikely that many guests will want to avail themselves of the on-site, state-of-the-art recording studio. However, the pair of outdoor pools and the divine Bar 1200 have wider appeal. A property-wide renovation in 2007 added 40 new villas to the existing 12, and updated the hotel's suites into a casually cosy style.

If you're here for a longer stay, consider the unrelated but not entirely dissimilar **Palihouse** a stone's throw from here (8465 Holloway Drive, 1-323 656 4100, www.palihouse.com), which offers capacious and upscale rooms with a seven-night minimum.
Bar. Business centre. Concierge. Gym. Internet ($12 wireless & high-speed). Parking ($30). Pools (2). Restaurant. Room service. TV: pay movies.

Moderate

Élan

8435 Beverly Boulevard, at N Croft Avenue, Los Angeles, CA 90048 (1-888 611 0398/1-323 658 6663/www.elanhotel.com). Bus 14, 16, 105, 316, LDF, LDHWH/I-10, exit La Cienega Boulevard north. **Rates** $189-$269. **Rooms** 49. **Credit** AmEx, DC, Disc, MC, V. **Map** p328 B3 ④
The simplicity of the Élan's unabashedly modernist architecture, especially its concrete and plate glass façade, continues inside the 50-room property: the lobby area is crisp and welcoming, and a 2008 renovation updated the formerly slightly drab rooms with a slightly sharper look. Unusually, there's no pool, restaurant or bar, but the reasonable rates do include continental breakfast.
Business centre. Concierge. Internet (free wireless & shared terminal). Parking ($19). Room service. TV.

Grafton on Sunset

8462 W Sunset Boulevard, between N Olive Drive & N La Cienega Boulevard, West Hollywood, CA 90069 (1-800 821 3660/1-323 654 4600/

Sunset Tower: 'Where every scandal that ever happened happened,' said Capote. *See p61.*

Renaissance Hollywood.

www.graftononsunset.com). Bus 2, 302, LDHWH/I-10, exit La Cienega Boulevard north. **Rates** *$209-$249.* **Rooms** 108. **Credit** AmEx, DC, Disc, MC, V. **Map** p328 B1 ④

Formerly a speakeasy and then a rather seedy hotel, the Grafton was given a huge makeover prior to its reopening in 2000. It's now pretty modern, but its four suites pay homage to Hollywood troublemakers of yore: the Rat Pack is (or attempts to be) a swingin' bachelor pad, while the Jane is dressed with come-hither satin sheets. The other rooms are decorated with an eye on the funseeking hipsters who constitute the target audience. The Mediterranean-inspired garden area is a real boon, and the salt-water pool is another attractive feature.

Bar. Business centre. Concierge. Gym. Internet ($3.99 wireless, free shared terminal). Parking ($26). Pool. Restaurant. Room service. Smoking rooms. TV: pay movies.

Le Montrose Suite Hotel

900 Hammond Street, at Cynthia Street, off W Sunset Boulevard, West Hollywood, CA 90069 (1-800 776 0666/1-310 855 1115/www.lemontrose.com). Bus 2, 105, 302/I-405, exit Santa Monica Boulevard east. **Rates** *$225-$369 suites.* **Rooms** 173. **Credit** AmEx, DC, Disc, MC, V. **Map** p328 A2 ④

Conveniently close to the action on the Sunset Strip but far enough from it to feel like a retreat, this all-suites property is located on a quiet residential street. Some of the large suites come with fireplaces; unusually, the restaurant and bar is open exclusively to hotel guests. The refurbished rooftop pool deck offers decent city views; active guests can play tennis on the hotel's courts, rent a bicycle or hit the state-of-the-art equipment at the fitness centre.

Bar. Business centre. Concierge. Gym. Internet ($4.50 high-speed). Parking ($26). Pool. Restaurant. Room service. TV: DVD & pay movies.

Orlando

8384 W 3rd Street, at Orlando Avenue, CA 90048 (1-800 624 6835/1-323 658 6600/www.theorlando.com). Bus 16/I-10, exit La Cienega Boulevard north. **Rates** *$249-$329.* **Rooms** 98. **Credit** AmEx, DC, Disc, MC, V. **Map** p328 B3 ④

The $5m renovation lavished on the Orlando in 2005 brought a tasteful, straightforward aesthetic and cultured amenities. Done out in crisp white linens, with clutter conspicuous by its absence, the rooms aren't massive but they're not pokey either; stand-out features include comfortable beds and iPod speaker systems (the latter in some rooms only). The property also boasts a sparkling saltwater rooftop pool and a high-quality restaurant, Gino Angelini's La Terza. And the location is excellent too, slap on pedestrian-friendly W 3rd Street, lined with independent shops and restaurants, and within walking distance of the Farmers Market and the Grove.

Bar. Business centre. Concierge. Internet ($10.95 wireless). Parking ($26). Pool. Restaurant. Room service. Spa. TV: pay movies.

Standard Hollywood

8300 W Sunset Boulevard, at N Sweetzer Avenue, West Hollywood, CA 90069 (1-323 650 9090/www.standardhotel.com). Bus 2, 302/I-10, exit La Cienega Boulevard north. **Rates** *$160-$325.* **Rooms** 139. **Credit** AmEx, DC, Disc, MC, V. **Map** p328 B1 ④

In 1998, at the height of *Austin Powers* mania, the Standard was converted from a '60s retirement home to a tongue-in-chic shag pad: the bright bedrooms come with minibars peddling condoms, and the space-age influence extends to the groovy lobby carpeting and the furniture. The schtick is looking a little weary these days, but the poolside lounge remains popular with a see-and-be-seen scene and the staff are more welcoming than you might expect at a property where image is so crucial. For the Standard Downtown, see p63.

Bars (2). Business centre. Concierge. Internet (free wireless). Parking ($27). Pool. Restaurant. Room service. Smoking rooms. TV: DVD & pay movies.

Sunset Tower

8358 Sunset Boulevard, at N Sweetzer Avenue, West Hollywood, CA 90069 (1-800 225 2637/1-323 654 7100/www.sunsettowerhotel.com). Bus 2, 302/ I-10, exit La Cienega Boulevard north. **Rates** $295-$395. **Rooms** 73. **Credit** AmEx, DC, Disc, MC, V. **Map** p328 B1 ⓮

One of the most memorable buildings on the Sunset Strip (it's on the National Register of Historic Places), this beautiful tower opened in 1931 as an apartment block, but it's been a hotel for years. These days, the decor is a fine-tuned balance of old Hollywood charm and contemporary chic, and service is excellent. The elevated pool and lounge afford wonderful views of the city below, although equally breathtaking vistas can be enjoyed through floor-to-ceiling windows in the nicely sized rooms and suites.

Bar. Business centre. Concierge. Gym. Internet (free wireless). Parking ($32). Pool. Restaurant. Room service. Spa. TV: DVD & pay movies.

Budget

Secret Garden B&B

8039 Selma Avenue, at Laurel Canyon Boulevard, West Hollywood, CA 90046 (1-877 732 4736/1-323 656 3888/www.secretgardenbnb.com). Bus 28, 302, LDHWH/I-10, exit Fairfax Avenue north. **Rates** $145-$170. **Rooms** 5. **Credit** AmEx, DC, MC, V. **Map** p328 C1 ⓯

Close to the Sunset Strip and yet enviably, surprisingly serene, the Secret Garden is one of LA's relatively few B&Bs. The operation changed hands a couple of years ago, but it remains a charming little place. The main house holds five individually decorated rooms in a lovely garden setting; in addition, there's the very private cottage guest house, which features a large tub with body-pulsing water jets. Mornings begin with a full organic breakfast.

Internet (free wireless in lobby). Parking (free). TV: DVD.

Hollywood

Moderate

Hollywood Roosevelt

7000 Hollywood Boulevard, at N Orange Drive, Los Angeles, CA 90028 (1-800 950 7667/1-323 466 7000/www.hollywoodroosevelt.com). Metro Hollywood-Highland/bus 163, 180, 181, 210, 212, 217, 312, 363, 780, LDH/US 101, exit Hollywood Boulevard west. **Rates** $239-$499. **Rooms** 300. **Credit** AmEx, DC, Disc MC, V. **Map** p329 A1 ⓱

After a 2003 restoration by designer Dodd Mitchell, this 1927 landmark, a beautiful example of Spanish colonial design, once more welcomed the A-listers who frequented it during Hollywood's heyday. The hotel is at its most dramatic downstairs: in the Dakota steakhouse, at the discreet Library Bar, and around the pool, which boasts a restored underwater mural by David Hockney and an often-buzzing bar scene at the poolside lounge. The rooms are sleek, dark and, in places, showing a few signs of wear and tear. Look out for the occasional subtly placed photographic nod to the starry location.

Bars (3). Business centre. Concierge. Gym. Internet (free wireless). Parking ($28). Pool. Restaurants (3). Room service. Smoking rooms. TV: pay movies.

Magic Castle Hotel

7025 Franklin Avenue, between N Sycamore Avenue & N Orange Drive, Hollywood, CA 90028 (1-800 741 4915/1-323 851 0800/www.magiccastle hotel.com). Metro Hollywood-Highland/bus 163, 180, 181, 210, 212, 217, 312, 363, 780, LDH/US 101, exit Hollywood Boulevard west. **Rates** $164-$329. **Rooms** 40. **Credit** AmEx, Disc, DC, MC, V. **Map** p329 A1 ⓲

This unusual property is connected to the Academy of Magical Arts, an exclusive organisation made up of roughly 2,500 American magicians; guests have access to the otherwise private Magic Castle, where AMA members perform nightly for clued-up crowds. However, the hotel itself is no illusion. Of the 40 units, three-quarters are apartment-style suites with kitchenettes and living areas; some have balconies overlooking the pool. Amenities include continental breakfasts with baked goods from Susina, one of LA's best bakeries.

If you're looking for a room with a view, try the Hollywood Hills Hotel, the Magic Castle's sister (1-323 874 5089, www.hollywoodhillshotel.com). Although not as nice, the 40 rooms have good views.

Concierge. Internet (free wireless). Parking ($10). Pool. TV: DVD.

Renaissance Hollywood

1755 N Highland Avenue, at Yucca Street, Los Angeles, CA 90028 (1-800 769 4774/1-323 856 1200/www.renaissancehollywood.com). Metro Hollywood-Highland/bus 163, 180, 181, 210, 212, 217, 312, 363, 780, LDH/US 101, exit Hollywood Boulevard west. **Rates** $279-$349. **Rooms** 632. **Credit** AmEx, DC, MC, V. **Map** p329 A1 ⓳

Hollywood Roosevelt (*p61*)
Masquerading as the Tropicana Motel, it's one of the places at which Leonardo DiCaprio narrowly avoids pursuing FBI agent Tom Hanks in Steven Spielberg's caper movie *Catch Me If You Can*

By no means the blandly corporate operation you might expect given the branding, this was the first Marriott to make the cover of *Architectural Digest*. No wonder: its designers took the 'no brass, marble or beige' mandate to heart. The atrium lobby is a showy array of primary colours and retro furnishings; a grand staircase leads to the Hollywood & Highland mall. The rooms aren't as interesting, but they're crisp, colourful, nicely sized and well maintained. Not the most fashionable hotel in Hollywood, but a very decent option. *Photo p60.*
Bar. Business centre. Concierge. Gym. Internet ($9.95 wireless & high-speed). Parking ($29). Pool. Restaurant. Room service. Spa. TV: pay movies.

Budget

Banana Bungalow Hollywood

5920 Hollywood Boulevard, at N Bronson Avenue, Los Angeles, CA 90028 (1-877 977 5077/1-323 469 2500/www.bananabungalow.com). Metro Hollywood-Vine/bus 2, 302/US 101, exit Hollywood Boulevard west. **Rates** $55-$85 double; $18-$27 dorm bed. **Credit** AmEx, DC, MC, V. **Map** p329 C1 ⑤⓪
See below **Banana Bungalow West Hollywood**. *Internet (free wireless & shared terminal).*

Highland Gardens Hotel

7047 Franklin Avenue, at N Sycamore Avenue, Los Angeles, CA 90028 (1-800 404 5472/1-323 850 0536/www.highlandgardenshotel.com). Metro Hollywood-Highland/bus 163, 180, 181, 210, 212, 217, 312, 363, 780, LDH/US 101, exit Hollywood Boulevard west. **Rates** $109-$129. **Rooms** 72. **Credit** AmEx, DC, MC, V. **Map** p329 A1 ⑤①
This hotel opened as the Hollywood Landmark hotel in the 1950s; while it's been renovated since, it still feels pretty old-fashioned both inside and out. The mid-century post-and-beam architecture and courtyard pool with mature tropical landscaping are memorable assets, but the rooms are forgettable. Still, if you plan on spending most of your time at the many sights within a short distance of the hotel, you'll get from it what you need: a place to sleep, a place to shower and a safe place to store your bags. *Internet ($8.99 wireless, free high-speed). Parking (free). Pool. TV: DVD & pay movies.*

Fairfax District

Moderate

Farmer's Daughter

115 S Fairfax Avenue, at W 1st Street, Los Angeles, CA 90036 (1-800 334 1658/1-323 937 3930/www.farmersdaughterhotel.com). Bus 217, 218, LDF/I-10, exit Fairfax Avenue north. **Rates** $165-$220. **Rooms** 66. **Credit** AmEx, MC, V. **Map** p328 C3 ⑤②
You can tell instantly that this was once a basic motel. It's a credit to the new owners of the gingham-giddy Farmer's Daughter that it feels pretty fresh. The rooms have been duded up in blue and yellow checks and denim bedspreads; farm and barnyard

humour abounds. Other amenities include a DVD library at the front desk, a small pool and Tart, which serves good ol' country cooking for breakfast and lunch. The rates are higher than they should be given the amenities. However, you could say the same about countless other hotels in the city, including many with far worse locations: this one is right by the Farmers Market and the Grove.
Bar. Internet ($9.95 wireless & high-speed). Parking ($14). Pool. Restaurant. TV: DVD.

Budget

Banana Bungalow West Hollywood

603 N Fairfax Avenue, at Clinton Street, Los Angeles, CA 90036 (1-877 666 2002/1-323 655 2002/www.bananabungalow.com). Bus 10, 217, 218, LDF/I-10, exit Fairfax Avenue north. **Rates** $69-$79 double; $22-$27 dorm bed. **Credit** AmEx, DC, MC, V. **Map** p328 C2 ⑤③
The name of this cheap but very cheerful hostel is slightly naughty, since it's not in West Hollywood at all. Still, the location is nonetheless excellent: close to both WeHo and Hollywood, within a short walk from the Farmers Market and the Melrose shopping strip. The dormitories have six beds per room; however, there are also a number of private rooms, great value given the location. There are several separate communal areas, including a courtyard on which barbecues are sometimes held. Call for details of the free shuttle from LAX. And for the other Banana Bungalow in LA, *see above.*
Internet (free wireless & shared terminal).

Beverly Laurel

8018 Beverly Boulevard, between S Laurel & S Edinburgh Avenues, Los Angeles, CA 90048 (1-800 962 3824/1-323 651 2441). Bus 14, 217, 218, LDF/I-10, exit La Cienega Boulevard north. **Rates** $109-$150. **Rooms** 52. **Credit** AmEx, DC, MC, V. **Map** p328 C3 ⑤④

The story of **O**.

This '50s motel is one of the best buys on Beverly, its location and attitude making it popular with younger movers and shakers who either don't have the cash to splash on an updated Kor Group property of the same vintage or would rather save their money. Luxury is conspicuous by its absence: the rooms are unashamedly basic, and the pool area is about as plain as you'll ever find. Still, the funkiness is all part of the appeal, the hotel's diner (Swingers) is a real winner, and the price is most definitely right. *Internet ($5.95 wireless). Parking (free). Pool. Restaurant. TV.*

Downtown

Moderate

Millennium Biltmore

506 S Grand Avenue, at W 5th Street, Los Angeles, CA 90071 (1-800 245 8673/1-213 624 1011/www. thebiltmore.com). Metro Pershing Square/bus 14, 37, 70, 71, 76, 78, 79, 96/I-110, exit 6th Street east. **Rates** $159-$375. **Rooms** 683. **Credit** AmEx, DC, Disc, MC, V. **Map** p331 B3 ⑤⑤
Built in 1923, the Biltmore retains the Italian-Spanish renaissance elegance that once enticed such dignitaries as Winston Churchill and JFK. The ground level is striking, one gorgeous room after another peeling off the exquisite lobby; a number of them, such as the Crystal Ballroom and the Gold Room, are available only for private hire, but if there's no event being staged and you ask nicely at reception, someone will show you around. Next to such extravagance, the rooms can hardly compete, but they're comfortable in an old-fashioned way.
Bars (3). Business centre. Concierge. Gym. Internet ($9.95 high-speed & wireless). Parking ($40). Pool (indoor). Restaurants (3). Room service. TV: pay movies.

O
819 S Flower Street, between W 8th & W 9th Street, Los Angeles, CA 90017 (1-213 623 9904/www. ohotelgroup.com). Metro 7th Street-Metro Center/bus 16, 18, 55, 62/I-110, exit 6th Street east. **Rates** $149-$219. **Rooms** 68. **Credit** AmEx, DC, Disc, MC, V. **Map** p331 B4 ⑤⑥
This understatedly named hotel is pretty much the poster child for the ongoing regeneration of LA's Downtown. Until a few years ago, this was a down-market residential hotel housing low-income tenants. However, it was transformed during 2007 into a sleek boutique hotel, a slicker and less rowdy competitor of sorts to the established Standard up the road. The lobby area opens out into a stylish lounge and split-level restaurant; a six-room spa is due to open in late 2008. Upstairs, the rooms are pretty small, but they are crisp and comfortable.
Bar. Business centre. Concierge. Gym. Internet (free wireless & high-speed). Parking ($22). Pool. Restaurant. Room service. Smoking rooms. Spa. TV.

Omni Los Angeles

California Plaza, 251 S Olive Street, between W 2nd & W 3rd Streets, Los Angeles, CA 90012 (1-800 442 5251/1-213 617 3300/www.omnihotels.com). Metro Civic Center/bus 16, 18, 55, 62/I-110, exit 4th Street east. **Rates** $139-$539. **Rooms** 453. **Credit** AmEx, DC, Disc, MC, V. **Map** p331 C2 ⑤⑦
Located close to Downtown's growing cultural district, the Omni offers theatre and concert packages for those wanting to come here and catch a show or attend a party. However, this is chiefly a business hotel, and an efficient one. Decorated in slightly gloomy shades of taupe and olive, the bedrooms are comfortable; 'club level' guests get butler service, free breakfasts and cocktails. Other amenities include a smallish pool and a largeish exercise room.
Bar. Business centre. Concierge. Gym. Internet ($9.95 wireless & high-speed). Parking ($30). Pool. Restaurants (2). Room service. Smoking rooms. Spa. TV: pay movies.

Standard Downtown

550 S Flower Street, between W 5th & W 6th Street, Los Angeles, CA 90071 (1-213 892 8080/www. standardhotel.com). Metro 7th Street-Metro Center/bus 16, 18, 55, 62/I-110, exit 6th Street east. **Rates** $225-$525. **Rooms** 207. **Credit** AmEx, DC, Disc, MC, V. **Map** p331 B3 ⑤⑧
The Downtown version of the Sunset Strip shag pad (*see p60*) pokes fun at jet-setting '60s bachelors, with the lobby setting the tone. The swinger-style rooms come equipped with platform beds, tubs for two and peek-a-boo showers. Complete with DJs, vibrating waterbeds and views, the rooftop pool bar can be a tough ticket on weekends for non-guests; you'd do as well to hang out in the ground-level bar. In case you're wondering about the artefacts in the lobby, the hotel was once the HQ of Superior Oil.
Bars (2). Business centre. Concierge. Gym. Internet (free wireless). Parking ($28). Pool. Restaurant. Room service. Smoking rooms. TV: DVD & pay movies.

Westin Bonaventure

*404 S Figueroa Street, at W 4th Street, Los Angeles,
CA 90071 (1-800 937 8461/1-213 624 1000/
www.starwoodhotels.com). Metro 7th Street-Metro
Center/bus 16, 18, 55, 62/I-110, exit 6th Street east.*
Rates $249-$339. **Rooms** 1,460. **Credit** AmEx, DC,
Disc, MC, V. **Map** p331 B3 ⑤⑨

In the bizarre absence of a hotel near the Los Angeles
Convention Center (a state of affairs that will change
in late 2009 with the arrival of a Marriott/Ritz-Carlton
tower at LA Live; *see p119*), this five-tower, 35-
storey, 1,400-room monster does decent business.
Certainly, it looks the part: the huge lobby features
a central bar that specialises in coffee during office
hours and alcohol when day turns to night. Several
restaurants provide other opportunities for visitors
to fill up their expense accounts. The rooms are unremarkable but comfortable; needless to say, the views
are terrific the higher your room. The pool's a good
size, though you'll need a map to locate it.
*Bar (2). Business centre. Concierge. Gym. Internet
($12.95 wireless & high-speed). Parking ($42). Pool
(2: 1 indoor). Restaurants (7). Room service. Spa.
TV: pay movies.*

Budget

Hotel Figueroa

*939 S Figueroa Street, between W 9th Street & W
Olympic Boulevard, Los Angeles, CA 90015 (1-800
421 9092/1-213 627 8971/www.figueroahotel.com).
Metro 7th Street-Metro Center/bus 16, 18, 55, 62/
I-110, exit 9th Street east.* **Rates** $134-$194. **Rooms**
285. **Credit** AmEx, DC, MC, V. **Map** p331 B4 ⑥⓪

This striking hotel is a dramatic mix of Morocco and
Mexico, and oozes the kind of charisma after which
boutique hotel designers flail but so often fail to
achieve. Built in 1925 as a YWCA, the Figueroa is
now more exotic, but it's still an absolute bargain.
The hotel's airy lobby is a pot-pourri of Moroccan
chandeliers, huge cacti and woven rugs; towards the
back, there's a low-key bar and a lovely pool area
that's at its atmospheric best after dark. The rooms,
which vary in size, are done out in funky casbah chic
with Mexican-tiled bathrooms. Mod cons are few
and far between, but they're not really the point.
*Bar. Concierge. Internet ($8 wireless). Parking ($12).
Pool. Restaurant. TV.*

Inn at 657

*657 W 23rd Street, at S Figueroa Street, Los
Angeles, CA 90007 (1-800 347 7512/1-213 741
2200/www.patsysinn657.com). Bus 81, 381/I-110,*

exit Adams Boulevard west. **Rates** $135-$250.
Rooms 5. **Credit** MC, V.

The individually designed rooms at this European-
style B&B vary in size and character; the room rates
all include parking and a full breakfast prepared by
innkeeper/cook Patsy Carter. The pleasant, landscaped courtyard with café tables is another nice
touch. The location is good, too: it's just south of
Downtown but within walking distance of the convention centre and LA Live to the north, and USC
and Exposition Park to the south.
*Internet (free wireless & shared terminal).
Parking (free).*

Ritz Milner

*813 S Flower Street, at W 8th Street, Los Angeles,
CA 90017 (1-877 645 6377/1-213 627 6981/www.
milner-hotels.com). Metro 7th Street-Metro Center/
bus 16, 18, 55, 62/I-110, exit 9th Street east.*
Rates $89-$99. **Rooms** 137. **Credit** AmEx, DC,
Disc, MC, V. **Map** p331 B4 ⑥①

Once a luxury inn and later a Skid Row-esque slum,
the decidedly un-ritzy Ritz was overhauled in 2003
and now rather optimistically sells itself as a low-
budget 'boutique'. The hotel's 135 rooms are safe,
but they're small and won't win any design awards.
The hotel's main selling point is the location: the
hotel is within a few blocks of LA Live and the convention centre, in one of Downtown's safer pockets.
The restaurant next door serves brunch and lunch.
*Bar. Concierge. Internet (free high-speed). Parking
($10). Restaurant. Smoking rooms. TV.*

The Valleys

San Fernando Valley

Moderate

Sportsmen's Lodge

*12825 Ventura Boulevard, at Coldwater Canyon
Avenue, Studio City, CA 91604 (1-800 821 8511/
1-818 769 4700/www.slhotel.com). Bus 150, 167,
240, 750/US 101, exit Coldwater Canyon Avenue
south.* **Rates** $179-$245. **Rooms** 199. **Credit**
AmEx, DC, Disc, MC, V.

The unusual country-manor theme of this 1960s-era
hotel is actually appropriate when you consider the
location: it wasn't that long ago that this whole area
was, at least in Los Angeles terms, relatively rural.
Some of the rooms overlook an inviting pool, and
there's also a café and a bar, but the amenities are
generally somewhat limited. The draw, perhaps surprisingly, is in fact the location: families will appreciate its proximity to Universal Studios; outdoorsy
types will find amazing hiking trails in the nearby
Santa Monica Mountains; and for everyone else, the
101 freeway to LA is close at hand.
*Bar. Business centre. Gym. Internet ($9.95 wireless),
Parking ($10). Pool. Restaurant. Room service.
Smoking rooms. TV: pay movies.*

San Gabriel Valley

Expensive

Langham Huntington Hotel & Spa Pasadena

1401 S Oak Knoll Avenue, at Wentworth Avenue, Pasadena, CA 91106 (1-800 241 3333/1-626 568 3900/http://pasadena.langhamhotels.com). I-110, exit Glenarm Street east. **Rates** $299-$419. **Rooms** 380. **Credit** AmEx, DC, Disc, MC, V.

Formerly a Ritz-Carlton, this grand old-money hotel changed hands in 2008. The new owners intend to preserve the heritage of the elegant 100-year-old property, referring to their planned upgrades as 'gentle'. Still, some $25 million worth of freshening up is scheduled for the cottages, the spa, the dining room, the terrace restaurant and the landscaping, so guests can expect to see tangible improvements to the property over the next few years.

Bar. Business centre. Concierge. Gym. Internet ($9.95 wireless & high-speed), Parking ($25). Pool. Restaurants (2). Room service. Spa. TV: pay movies.

Heading South

Manhattan Beach

Moderate

Shade

1221 N Valley Drive, at Manhattan Beach Boulevard, Manhattan Beach, CA 90266 (1-310 546 4995/www.shadehotel.com). Bus 126/I-405, exit Manhattan Beach Boulevard. **Rates** $295-$395. **Rooms** 38. **Credit** AmEx, DC, Disc, MC, V.

This sparkling property hasn't been solely responsible for the regeneration of Manhattan Beach, but its influence has been huge. It's a small property but pretty perfectly formed: slick yet approachable, stylish yet not without a sense of humour. The 38 guestrooms make great use of the space: multi-purpose tables can be rolled back and forth over the beds for breakfast or for use as a desk, while all rooms have vast spa-baths, DVD players and colour-adjustable lighting. Downstairs is a big central courtyard and

Hotel Figueroa offers vintage style at vintage prices.

the slick Zinc lounge; upstairs is the handsome Skydeck, complete with a bijou pool. Still, if you stay in the penthouse suite, you'll need neither: it has a beer tap in its kitchenette. An impressive spot.

Bars (2). Business centre. Concierge. Gym. Internet (free wireless). Parking ($15). Pool. Restaurant. Room service. TV: DVD.

Long Beach

Moderate

Queen Mary

1126 Queens Highway, Long Beach, CA 90802 (1-800 437 2934/1-562 435 3511/www.queenmary. com). Metro Transit Mall/I-405, then I-710 south. **Rates** $119-$189. **Rooms** 307. **Credit** AmEx, DC, Disc, MC, V.

This grand cruise ship hasn't sailed since the 1960s; these days, it multitasks as a rather muddled tourist attraction (*see p138*), an eating and drinking spot (the bar is a wonderful art deco glory) and, of course, a hotel. Unsurprisingly, given the boat's age (it was built in 1936), the guest cabins aren't huge, and nor are they stocked with modern amenities. Still, that's hardly the point: they're handsome, historic and nicely maintained. An intriguing novelty.

Bar. Business centre. Concierge. Gym. Internet ($9.99 wireless & high-speed). Parking ($15). Restaurants (3). Room service. Spa. TV: pay movies.

Orange County

Expensive

Disney's Grand Californian Hotel & Spa

1600 S Disneyland Drive, between Ball Road & Katella Avenue, Anaheim, CA 92802 (1-714 635 2300/www.disney.com). I-5, exit Disneyland Drive south. **Rates** $405-$505. **Rooms** 745. **Credit** AmEx, DC, Disc, MC, V.

This Disney hotel aims to blur the lines between luxury and fantasy: the 745-room property is effectively an extension to Disney's California Adventure, so much so that guests even have their own entrance to the park. Grown-ups may take to the Mandara Spa, a suitably peaceful escape from the theme-park chaos mere yards away; kids, on the other hand, will probably prefer the slides in the Redwood Pool or the activities in Pinocchio's Workshop. A getaway for children and their parents, albeit a pricey one.

Bar. Business centre. Concierge. Gym. Internet (free high-speed). Parking ($17). Pools (3). Restaurants (3). Room service. TV: DVD.

Montage Laguna Beach

30801 South Coast Highway, Laguna Beach, CA 92651 (1-888 715 6700/1-949 715 6000/www. montagelagunabeach.com). I-405, exit PCH south. **Rates** $595-$995. **Rooms** 250. **Credit** AmEx, DC, Disc, MC, V.

Consuming 30 acres of land at the top of a bluff overlooking the Pacific, the Montage was designed to be a self-contained village of luxury. There are four dining and drinking venues, a massive indoor/outdoor spa and no fewer than three outdoor pools, all set in immaculately landscaped grounds that overlook a beautiful stretch of beach. Accommodation ranges from spacious doubles to a vast suite; all include floor-to-ceiling windows with views of the Pacific.

Bars (4). Business centre. Concierge. Gym. Internet ($15.95 wireless & high-speed). Parking ($30). Pools (2). Restaurants (3). Room service. Spa. TV: DVD & pay movies.

St Regis Monarch Beach Resort

1 Monarch Beach Resort, at Niguel Road, Dana Point, CA 92629 (1-800 722 1543/1-714 234 3200/ www.stregismonarchbeach.com). I-5, exit Crown Valley Parkway west. **Rates** $425-$900. **Rooms** 400. **Credit** AmEx, DC, Disc, MC, V.

Part of the none-more-swanky St Regis chain, this Tuscan-inspired resort is an Orange County icon. Although it's not a beachfront property, the resort does afford picturesque views of the coastline, and even runs a shuttle to carry sunbathers to and from the sand. Still, you might not actually want to leave the property, what with the on-site spa and salon, the 18-hole golf course and the three outdoor pools.

Bars (2). Business centre. Concierge. Gym. Internet ($12.99 high-speed, free wireless in lobby). Parking ($30). Pools (3). Restaurants (5). Room service. Spa. TV: DVD & pay movies.

Moderate

Disneyland hotels

Disneyland Hotel *1150 W Magic Way, between Ball Road & Katella Avenue, Anaheim, CA 92802 (1-714 520 5005/1-714 778 6600/fax 1-714 956 6597).* **Rates** $240-$320.
Disney's Paradise Pier Hotel *1717 Disneyland Drive, at Katella Avenue, Anaheim, CA 92802 (1-714 999 0990/fax 1-714 776 5763).* **Rates** $215-$295. **Credit** AmEx, DC, Disc, MC, V.
Both *www.disney.com. I-5, exit Disneyland Drive.* **Credit** AmEx, DC, Disc, MC, V.

The **Disneyland Hotel** is the original, classic property adjacent to the Disney Downtown entrance. It's very big and very Disney. The huge pool with a water slide is great for parents and kids. **Paradise Pier**, meanwhile, has different amenities – a rooftop pool, fitness centre, Japanese restaurant – and is considerably smaller than its counterpart. However, service is as slick as you'd expect from a Disney hotel.

If you'd rather not stay so close to Disneyland during your visit, it's worth looking into Disney's 32 'Good Neighbor' hotels, dotted throughout the Anaheim area. Prices and quality vary, but there are many reputable chains among the options. If you'd prefer a hotel with its own identity, consider the recently revived **Candy Cane Inn** (1747 S Harbor Boulevard, Anaheim, 1-714 774 5284, www.candy-caneinn.net), handily close to the parks.

Sightseeing

Introduction	68
Santa Monica & the Beach Towns	74
Brentwood to Beverly Hills	84
West Hollywood, Hollywood & Midtown	92
Los Feliz to Echo Park	104
Downtown	110
East Los Angeles	120
South Los Angeles	123
The Valleys	129
Heading South	136

Features

The best Attractions	69
Street talk	71
Sex on the beach	81
LA's best beaches	82
Walk UCLA campus	88
The secret gardens	93
Streets of glory	96
The great escape	99
Ghouls' paradise	102
Fruit for thought	107
Public art	114
The great white way forward	118
Days of the dead	121
Towers of strength	126
Grow your own	128

BCAM at Los Angeles County
Museum of Art. *See p100.*

Introduction

Welcome to Los Angeles.

Sightseeing

Greater Los Angeles is a sprawling, amorphous agglomeration, spread over a huge flood basin, subdivided by freeways and bound by ocean and hills: on its western edge, by 160 miles of Pacific coastline, and then, clockwise, by the Santa Monica, San Gabriel, San Bernardino, San Jacinto and Santa Ana Mountains. Laid over this landscape is a dizzying variety of cities and neighbourhoods. Precisely what constitutes Los Angeles is a matter for interpretation.

As you drive, you may be confused by signs pointing to 'Los Angeles'. They're here because the city of Los Angeles is a distinct settlement within Los Angeles County. Together with Riverside, Ventura, Orange and San Bernardino Counties, Los Angeles County is part of the Greater Los Angeles metropolitan region, a daunting aggregation of 34,000 square miles and 15 million people.

Los Angeles County contains 88 incorporated cities, each with its own jurisdiction; among them are Santa Monica, Beverly Hills, Culver City, Pasadena and Los Angeles itself. To add to the confusion, some areas – for example, East LA and Marina del Rey – are unincorporated, under the jurisdiction of Los Angeles County but not the city. While West Hollywood is an independent city, Hollywood is just one of many neighbourhoods in the city of Los Angeles. And matters are muddled still further by other broad area titles such as the Westside (which, confusingly, contains a separate area called West LA) and South LA (home to many black and Latino cities and neighbourhoods).

To make exploring this megalopolis easier, we've split it into a variety of different area groupings, which we've used not just in this Sightseeing section but throughout the book. We've summarised the areas over the next couple of pages and on a map on page *p336*; for more on how to get around, *see pp302-305*.

SANTA MONICA AND THE BEACH TOWNS
North to south along the coast, affluent **Malibu** (*p74*), desirable **Pacific Palisades** (*p74*), comfortable **Santa Monica** (*p76*), arty **Venice** (*p79*) and tidy **Marina del Rey** (*p80*) all have their own distinct characters. The area isn't at its best in late spring and early summer, when they're swathed in morning cloud known as June Gloom. For more on the beaches themselves, *see pp82-83* **LA's best beaches**.

BRENTWOOD TO BEVERLY HILLS
Moving inland, LA soon reveals itself to be the glamorous city of popular legend, though you'll have to pass likeable **Culver City** (*p86*), dull **West LA** and office-dominated **Century City** (*p89*) to find it. Wealthy **Brentwood** (*p84*) adjoins, to the west, university-dominated **Westwood** (*p87*) and, to the north, moneyed **Bel Air** (*p89*). To the east, **Beverly Hills** (*p90*) lives up to its upscale reputation.

WEST HOLLYWOOD, HOLLYWOOD AND MIDTOWN
Separated from Beverly Hills by Doheny Drive, parts of **West Hollywood** (*p92*) are nearly as swanky as its neighbour, but Beverly Hills doesn't have the nightlife to compete with WeHo's Sunset Strip. Due east is resurgent **Hollywood** (*p94*); to the south are the shops and eateries of the **Fairfax District** (*p98*); the museums of the **Miracle Mile** (*p99*); stately **Hancock Park** (*p102*); shiny **Koreatown** (*p103*); and just-waking **Westlake** (*p103*).

LOS FELIZ TO ECHO PARK
North-east of Hollywood, **Los Feliz** (*p104*) is home to funky shops and restaurants, and is the main entrance into vast Griffith Park. Further east, **Silver Lake** (*p108*) is artier, while neighbouring **Echo Park** (*p108*) is characterfully down-at-heel but rapidly gentrifying. North across the Los Angeles River, between Downtown LA and Pasadena, lie unsung but interesting districts, among them **Mt Washington** and **Highland Park** (*p109*).

DOWNTOWN
Stretching south from the eastern end of Sunset Boulevard, **Downtown** (*p110*) is the site of original city and home to most of LA's political and financial institutions. Wealth (the Financial District) sits side by side with extreme poverty (Skid Row); modern skyscrapers loom over old theatres. Also here are **Little Tokyo** (*p112*), Latino-dominated **Olvera Street** (*p111*) and a small-ish **Chinatown** (*p110*).

EAST LOS ANGELES
East LA (*p120*) has traditionally been the heartland of LA's Latino communities. It remains that way, but things are changing, as people with varied backgrounds move to the area in search of affordable housing.

SOUTH LOS ANGELES

Officially renamed from South Central by a city anxious to rescue its image, South LA is a jumble of neighbourhoods. While popular cliché about the area holds true in places (chiefly in long-troubled **Watts**; *p127*), it's blown out of the water in neighbourhoods such as affluent **Crenshaw** (*p127*) and cultured **Leimert Park** (*p127*). At the area's north-eastern tip, close to Downtown, is the cultural hub of **Exposition Park** (*p123*) and the USC campus.

THE VALLEYS

The **San Fernando Valley** (*p129*), north-west of LA, and the **San Gabriel Valley** (*p131*), to the north-east, are often mocked for embodying the hot and smoggy horrors of West Coast suburbia. The cliché holds largely true in the former, but several of the San Gabriel Valley's neighbourhoods, chief among them **Pasadena** and **Claremont**, are actually quite charming.

HEADING SOUTH

When Angelenos speak of the South Bay, they're usually referring to the coast-hugging cities south of LAX: **El Segundo**, **Manhattan Beach**, **Hermosa Beach** and **Redondo Beach** (*p136*). Across the Vincent Thomas Bridge from **San Pedro** (*p136*) is **Long Beach** (*p137*). And to the south-east, **Orange County** (*p139*) attracts 40 million visitors a year, many heading directly to Disneyland.

Sightseeing

When sightseeing in LA, it doesn't necessarily pay to get up at the crack of dawn. Certainly, you should aim to arrive at the big theme parks (**Universal Studios**, **Disneyland** and **Six Flags**) as early as possible to beat the worst of the crowds. But otherwise, unless the museum or attraction you're hoping to visit is close to your hotel and can be easily reached without recourse to the freeway system, you may just end up stuck in horrendous rush-hour traffic.

If you're planning to visit a number of attractions, it may be worth investing in a CityPass. These small booklets grant decent discounts on admissions, and also allow pass-holders to jump the queues. The **Hollywood CityPass** ($49.95, or $39 for 3-11s), includes admission to the **Hollywood Wax Museum** (*see p96*), a **Red Line** walking tour (*see p73*), a **Starline** tour (*see p73*) and either a tour of the **Kodak Theatre** (*see p96*) or entrance to the **Hollywood Museum** (*see p96*). The Southern California CityPass ($247, or $199 for 3-9s) includes a three-day pass to both **Disneyland** parks (*see p140*), admission to **Universal Studios** (*see p131*) and, in San Diego, passes

The best Attractions

The beaches
Some suit surfers, others attract hordes of gay men, while still others draw families out to play. Take your pick... *See pp82-83.*

Broad Contemporary Art Museum at LACMA
The ongoing renovations at the Los Angeles County Museum of Art (*see p100*) have paid immediate dividends with BCAM, a new gallery that contains a starry collection of modern works. Art-lovers should also seek out the Getty Center (*see p84*) and the Norton Simon Museum (*see p134*).

Disneyland
Whatever your hopes and fears, Southern California's most famous attraction lives up to them. *See p140.*

A walk around Downtown
LA's most pedestrian-friendly district offers a wealth of interesting sights, from Broadway's old theatres to the shiny glamour of Disney Hall. *See pp110-119.*

Grauman's Chinese Theatre
Hollywood history at its most outlandishly kitsch. *See p230.*

Griffith Observatory
Reopened at last, and as glorious as ever. *See p105.*

Huntington Library, Art Collections & Botanical Gardens
The library is terrific and the art strong, but the gardens at Henry Huntington's old estate are exceptional. *See p132.*

Insider tours
Los Angeles Conservancy's architectural walks, Esotouric's journeys into the underground and Red Line's tours of LA history all offer wonderful insights into this immense city. *See pp71-73.*

Mulholland Drive
The most interesting road in a city full of them. *See p97.*

Museum of Jurassic Technology
Truth melds with the imagination and dreams collide with nightmares at David Wilson's mesmerising museum. *See p87.*

Sightseeing

to **SeaWorld** and either the **San Diego Zoo** or the zoo's separate **Wild Animal Park** (*see pp296-298*). You can buy a CityPass from any participating attraction, or at www.citypass.com.

Guided tours

In addition to the tours listed below, **Pasadena Heritage** (1-626 441 6333, www.pasadena heritage.org) runs quarterly tours of Old Town Pasadena; the **City of Beverly Hills** run year-round trolley tours and occasional walking tours (1-310 285 2442, www.beverlyhills.org); and the **Friends of the LA River** (1-323 223 0585, www.folar.org) offers regular walks along and around the river. For the **Sierra Club**, which organises hikes in Griffith Park and elsewhere in LA, *see p273*.

Children's Nature Institute Family Walks

1-310 860 9484/www.childrensnatureinstitute.org. **Tours** vary. **Rates** *Suggested donation* $7 family. The CNI organises walks for under-8s in the Santa Monica Mountains and other areas near LA, introducing families to the outdoors while instilling respect for nature. Most are pushchair-accessible.

Esotouric

1-323 223 2767/www.esotouric.com. **Tours** most Sat; other days vary. **Rates** $55. The excellent Esotouric go where most other tour companies fear to tread, operating a range of coach

Street talk

LA is subdivided by freeways and a loose grid of large arteries, the boulevards and avenues (aka surface streets). Boulevards typically (but not exclusively) go east to west; avenues usually run north to south.

For street-numbering purposes, LA's ground zero is at the corner of 1st and Main Streets in Downtown. Addresses on east–west boulevards are numbered according to how many blocks east or west of Main Street they sit; the same is true of north–south avenues and 1st Street. These thoroughfares also determine the prefixes of some roads: North, South, East or West, abbreviated throughout this guide as N, S, E and W. For example, Fairfax Avenue is known as N Fairfax Avenue north of 1st Street and S Fairfax Avenue to the south of it. To confuse matters further, the numbering of some streets restarts at every city boundary; N Robertson Boulevard, for example, changes its numbering three times. Always check which stretch of road you need, and watch the numbering carefully.

When planning a journey, find the nearest cross-street: for example, Hollywood and Highland, or Sunset and San Vicente. If you're taking the freeway, find the exit nearest to your destination. Always double-check the specific city, as the same street names do occur in different cities: 3rd Street in LA, for example, bears no relationship to 3rd Street in Santa Monica. Throughout this book, we've included cross-streets and a freeway exit for every listed establishment, though do be aware that many venues are easily accessible from more than one freeway.

In the central portion of LA County, **I-10** traverses LA from west to east and separates

Hollywood, Beverly Hills and Midtown from South LA. **I-405** runs north–south on the west side of the City of Los Angeles, partitioning the affluent coastal and inland cities from the rest of LA. **I-110/Hwy 110** runs north–south, just west of Downtown. **US 101** and **I-5** head north-west from Downtown into the Valleys.

The freeways also have names, and it helps to know both names and numbers. The following are among the most widely used:

I-5 Golden State Freeway/
 Santa Ana Freeway
I-10 Santa Monica Freeway/
 San Bernadino Freeway
US 101 Hollywood Freeway/
 Ventura Freeway
I-110/Hwy 110 Harbor Freeway/
 Pasadena Freeway
Hwy 134 Ventura Freeway
I-210 Foothill Freeway
I-405 San Diego Freeway
I-710 Long Beach Freeway

The coast road, **Highway 1**, is also known as the Pacific Coast Highway (aka PCH), becoming Lincoln Boulevard and Sepulveda Boulevard when it moves inland. Similarly, **Highway 2**, aka the Glendale Freeway, becomes Santa Monica Boulevard when it moves through the Westside.

An essential aid is *The Thomas Guide: Los Angeles County Street Guide*, an easy-to-use, annually updated map to the region published by Rand McNally. For traffic updates, call the California Department of Transportation's information line on 1-800 427 7623 or see www.dot.ca.gov. For websites providing traffic reports and route planning, *see p314*.

Sightseeing

Airline flights are one of the biggest producers of the global warming gas CO_2. But with **The CarbonNeutral Company** you can make your travel a little greener.

Go to **www.carbonneutral.com** to calculate your flight emissions then 'neutralise' them through international projects which save exactly the same amount of carbon dioxide.

Contact us at **shop@carbonneutral.com** or call into the office on **0870 199 99 88** for more details.

CarbonNeutral®flights

tours that take in an array of grittily fascinating sights and themes: the unsolved Black Dahlia murder, Raymond Chandler's Los Angeles, the city's rock music heritage and so on. The majority of coach tours run for around five hours, and early reservations are recommended.

Los Angeles Conservancy Walking Tours

Information 1-213 430 4219/reservations 1-213 623 2489/www.laconservancy.org. **Tours** Sat, times and routes vary. **Rates** $10.

This praiseworthy organisation works to preserve and revitalise LA's urban architectural heritage, and then to educate the public about it. The Conservancy runs a wide variety of tours, taking in everything from Downtown's historic theatres (weekly) to architecture in San Pedro (bi-monthly). Reservations are required for many of the tours: they're understandably popular.

MONA Neon Cruises

1-213 489 9918/www.neonmona.org. **Tours** *June-Nov* 7.30pm Sat. **Rates** $55.

For six months a year, the **Museum of Neon Art** (*see p113*) runs nighttime tours in an open-top double-decker bus, taking in neon signs both old and new along with movie-theatre marquees and other related landmarks. Book ahead.

Red Line Tours

1-323 402 1074/www.redlinetours.com.

Tours *Hollywood: Behind the Scenes* 10am, noon, 2pm, 4pm daily. *Inside Contemporary Downtown LA* noon daily. *Inside Historic Downtown LA* 9.45am daily. **Rates** $20; $15-$18 discounts.

Red Line's two Downtown walking tours start at the Bradbury Building (304 S Broadway) and cover much of Downtown's interesting architecture; the Hollywood tour, which leaves from the Stella Adler Academy (6773 Hollywood Boulevard), visits many major Hollywood landmarks. Participants are given headphones and a small FM receiver tuned to pick up the guide, who speaks into a small transmitter; it's an inspired idea, perfect for blotting out the omnipresent roar of traffic. Early reservations are recommended.

Starline Tours

1-800 959 3131/1-323 463 3333/www.starlinetours. com. **Tours** check online. **Rates** $18-$450.

Starline run a broad range of tours around Los Angeles, from one-hour trolley rides to day-long excursions. Their most popular tour is a 2hr loop around the homes of Hollywood stars; it leaves **Grauman's Chinese Theatre** (*see p230*) every half-hour. However, at $37 (plus a tip for the driver), it's not cheap: to be honest, you might be better off buying a 'Star Map' from one of the vendors on Hollywood Boulevard or in Beverly Hills and guiding yourself. **LA Tours** (1-323 937 0999, www.la-tours.com) offers a similar range of excursions, and at pretty similar prices.

Urban Shopping Adventures

1-213 683 9715/www.urbanshopping adventures.com. **Tours** call for details. **Rates** $36-$54.

Enthusiastic, knowledgeable shopaholic Christine Silvestri offers tours of the Melrose Heights boutiques and Downtown's Fashion District, sorting the wheat from the chaff and showing customers where to find the area's best bargains. The most popular are the walking tours, though there are also a variety of coach tours available. Call ahead to book.

Studio tours

The most famous studio tour in the US is at **Universal Studios** (*see p131*), but a number of other major studios also offer the public a few brief glimpses behind the scenes.

NBC Studios

3000 W Alameda Avenue, at W Olive Avenue, Burbank (1-818 840 3537). **Tours** 9am-3pm Mon-Fri. **Rates** $8.50; $5-$6.25 discounts; free under-5s.

The cheapest way to get behind the scenes in Los Angeles (legally, at least), this 70-minute walking tour takes in the set of *The Tonight Show* (for show tickets, *see p234*) and a few other TV sound stages. Reservations aren't required.

Paramount Studios

5555 Melrose Avenue, at N Gower Street, Hollywood (1-323 956 1777/www.paramount.com). **Tours** hourly, 10am-2pm Mon-Fri. **Rates** $35. **Map** p329 C3.

The only studio in Hollywood is once again welcoming visitors. The tours take roughly two hours, and reservations are required.

Sony Pictures Studios

10202 W Washington Boulevard, at Jasmine Avenue, Culver City (1-323 244 8687/www.sony picturesstudios.com). **Tours** *Mid June-Sept* 9.30am, 10.30am, 1.30pm, 2.30pm, 6.30pm Mon-Fri. *Oct-mid June* 9.30am, 10.30am, 1.30pm, 2.30pm Mon-Fri. **Rates** $28. *Parking* free.

Low-key walking tours, open only to over-12s, are offered during the week at this storied lot. Movies such as *The Wizard of Oz* were shot here in decades gone by; these days, it's used for both TV and film. Reservations are recommended.

Warner Brothers Studios

3400 Riverside Drive, at W Olive Avenue, Burbank (1-818 972 8687/www2.warnerbros.com/vipstudio tour). **Tours** *VIP* regular intervals, 8.30am-4.30pm Mon-Fri. *Deluxe* 10.30am Mon-Fri. **Rates** *VIP* $45. *Deluxe* $150. *Parking* $5.

The 2¼-hour VIP tour of Warners' Burbank studios takes in a goodly portion of the facility before ending at a small museum. The Deluxe tours last five hours and go even further behind the scenes; reservations are recommended. Bring ID for both tours, and leave under-8s at home.

Santa Monica & the Beach Towns

LA's sunshine coast.

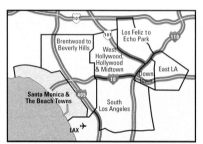

Malibu

Although it was officially incorporated as a city in 1990, Malibu is not a place so much as a 27-mile stretch of the Pacific Coast Highway that winds through some of Southern California's most magnificent coastal terrain. Parts of it are lined, on the ocean side, by beach houses of varying sizes and styles, with largely mediocre commercial buildings on the inland side nestling against the Santa Monica Mountains.

Malibu is such a desirable spot that its wildly wealthy locals, including privacy-hungry stars and publicity-shy industry moguls, are willing to live with the threat of fires and floods, and have formed a group dedicated to preventing new development from marring their lifestyle. Homeowners with properties backing on to Broad Beach and Carbon Beach have long tried to prevent the public from playing on the sandbar, but public protests have resulted in increased access.

Leaving aside **Adamson House** (*see below*) and the reservation-only garden tours at the 22-acre **Ramirez Canyon Park** (5750 Ramirez Canyon Road, 1-310 589 2850), donated to the Santa Monica Mountains Conservancy by Barbra Streisand, Malibu has no tourist attractions. Its treats lie in its beaches and canyons: within yards of the entrance to one of the many trails, you can be out of view of the city and communing with coyotes and red-tailed hawks. You can also access **Topanga** from here; *see p99* **The great escape**.

Adamson House

23200 Pacific Coast Highway (1-310 456 8432/ www.adamsonhouse.org). Bus 434/I-10, exit PCH north. **Open** *Tours* 11am-2pm Wed-Sat. **Admission** $5; $2 discounts; free under-6s. *Parking* free. **No credit cards**.

This striking 1929 Spanish-style building sits, along with the Malibu Lagoon Museum, inside the confines of Malibu Lagoon State Park. The major attraction at Adamson House is the array of decorative tiles manufactured at the once-celebrated but now-closed Malibu Tile Works. The guided tours allow visitors access to much of the property.

Malibu Chamber of Commerce

Suite 100, 23805 Stuart Ranch Road, at Civic Center Way, Malibu (1-310 456 9025/www.malibu.org). I-10, exit PCH north. **Open** 10am-4pm Mon-Fri.

Pacific Palisades

Between Malibu and Santa Monica lies Pacific Palisades, a small, rich community with a lower profile than its neighbours. The immaculate green lawns and large bungalows are straight out of *Leave It to Beaver*, but contained within its Santa Monica Mountains location are some wonderful, rugged places; among them are **Rustic Canyon Park** (1-310 454 5734), **Temescal Canyon Park** (1-310 454 1395) and **Will Rogers State Historic Park** (*see p75*). Nearby are the **Self-Realization Fellowship Lake Shrine** (*see p75*) and **Will Rogers State Beach**, a gay-friendly spot (*see p232* **Gay beaches**). However, the highlight for visitors is the newly revived **Getty Villa**, open to visitors who book ahead.

Eames House

203 Chautauqua Boulevard, off PCH (1-310 459 9663/www.eamesfoundation.org). Bus 434/I-10, exit PCH north. **Open** *Exterior tours, by arrangement only* 10am-4pm Mon-Fri; 10am-3pm Sat. **Admission** *Suggested donation* $5. *Parking* free on Corona del Mar, north of the house; no parking at house itself.

Charles and Ray Eames' landmark experiment in home design, built in 1949, is still used as a private residence by the Eames family. However, interested visitors are welcome to take a self-guided tour of the exterior on an appointment-only basis by booking at least 48 hours in advance.

Getty Villa

17985 Pacific Coast Highway (1-310 440 7300/ www.getty.edu). Bus 434/I-10, exit PCH north. **Open** 10am-5pm Mon, Thur-Sun; reservations essential. **Admission** free. *Parking* $8. **No credit cards.**

In 1974, oil magnate J Paul Getty opened a museum of his holdings in a faux villa in Malibu, based on the remains of the Villa dei Papiri in Herculaneum. Derision from critics and ridicule from art experts followed, but no matter – the Getty grew into a beloved local attraction. In 1997, the decorative arts and paintings were moved to the Getty Center (*see p84*), and the villa was closed for conversion into a museum for Getty's collection of Mediterranean antiquities. When it reopened in 2006, part-restored and part-transformed by architects Jorge Silvetti and Rodolfo Machado, the press were rather kinder.

There are roughly 1,200 artefacts on display at any one time, dating from between 6,500 BC and 500 AD, and organised under such themes as Gods and Goddesses and Stories of the Trojan War. If you're a novice, start in the Timescape room (numbered as room 113), where a wall-mounted frieze maps the different civilisations along with the art and statuary they created.

You could easily spend a few hours idly wandering through the galleries, but some exhibits really stand out. In room 101C, look for an amazing Greek perfume container that dates back to around 400 BC: it's incredibly elegant and, despite its age, entirely intact. Room 101 holds a collection of disparate items relating to Greek gods, among them a 2,500-year-old monumental statue of Aphrodite in limestone and marble, and some delicate painted oil jars. The outlandish, stag-spouted drinking horn in room 105 is gloriously absurd. And in room 108 stands a 1,900-year-old statue of Hercules, a real alpha-male figure that reputedly inspired Getty to built the museum in the design of a Roman villa.

Upstairs, room 217 holds an eerie limestone statue of a Cypriot fertility goddess from around 3,000 BC, her six toes implying superhuman qualities. In room 213, there's a vivid table support depicting two griffins going head to head as they devour a fallen doe. But the highlight is room 212, where you'll find some intricate Roman gems and coins alongside an unnerving miniature skeleton cast in bronze.

The site also holds conservation laboratories, seminar rooms and a research library, plus temporary exhibitions. Note, though, that you'll need to book a timed ticket (free) in order to visit the museum: walk-ins aren't accepted. At peak times, be sure to book well in advance; and try and book your ticket for early in the morning in order to beat the crowds.

Self-Realization Fellowship Lake Shrine

17190 Sunset Boulevard, at Pacific Coast Highway (1-310 454 4114/www.lakeshrine.org). Bus 434/I-10, exit PCH north. **Open** *Gardens* 9am-4.30pm Tue-Sat; noon-4.30pm Sun. *Visitors' centre* 9am-4pm Tue-Sat; 12.15-4pm Sun. **Admission** free.
See p93 **The secret gardens**.

Will Rogers State Historic Park

1501 Will Rogers State Park Road, at Sunset Boulevard (1-310 454 8212/www.parks.ca.gov). Bus 2, 302, 476/I-405, exit Sunset Boulevard west. **Open** *House tours* 11am, 1pm, 2pm Tue-Sun. **Admission** free. *Parking* free.

The former home of writer, cowboy philosopher, trick-roper and the first honorary mayor of Beverly Hills has been maintained as it was in the 1930s. The 186-acre grounds give access to some good hikes; one path takes you to Inspiration Point, from where you get a breathtaking view of mountains and sea. Polo matches are held on weekends (www.willrogers polo.org), and you can also take horse-riding lessons: call or check online for details.

Adamson House.

Santa Monica

Map p326

It's easy to see how people get drawn to Santa Monica, and why it's become the hub of LA's West Side. With the Santa Monica Mountains to the north and the shimmering Pacific to the west, the palm tree-lined cliffs and year-round sun tempered by ocean breezes, its natural surroundings couldn't be bettered. The roads, buildings and gardens that have grown up around it are immaculate: clean, tidy and easy on the eye. Outside of the frequent fogs, the living is easy in Santa Monica, especially if you've money in your pocket.

The area was inhabited for centuries by the Gabrieleno Native Americans, then by Spanish settlers who named the city and many of its major streets. Acquired by Anglo pioneers in the late 19th century, it soon snowballed from a small holiday resort into today's city, with a population of 84,000. Sunseeking Brits abound in Santa Monica, mixing with Iranians, retirees, health fiends, beach bums, families, young-free-and-singles, entertainment industry titans and entertainment industry wannabes.

Surprisingly, you'll also find plenty of homeless Angelenos ambling along its streets and beaches. The city's government has long taken a humanitarian approach to the issue of homelessness, part of a famously benevolent attitude to social problems. Indeed, the self-satisfied, bleeding-hearted, middle-class Santa Monica liberal has become a familiar political trope across both the region and the country, oft cited both by supporters and enemies.

As well as the tourist-oriented beaches and the strings of shops, Santa Monica also boasts some excellent, daring modern architecture. Much of Frank Gehry's work is here, including his own house, but Santa Monica also contains art deco landmarks such as the **Shangri-La** hotel (*see p49*) and some fine 1950s buildings. The **Stick House** at 1911 La Mesa Drive, which falls into the latter category, is the only home in the country designed by Oscar Niemeyer, albeit from a distance: the architect never set foot in the US.

What you won't find in Santa Monica is a cutting edge. The nightlife here is all white bread and mayo; outside of the galleries at Bergamot Station, the cultural scene is deeply indifferent; and while there are good places to eat here, too many of the restaurants promise more than they deliver. Still, such trifling issues don't seem to worry the locals, who seem convinced that they've found a suburban paradise by the Pacific. And you know what? They might be right.

Montana Avenue

Four blocks north of Wilshire Boulevard, Santa Monica's main east–west artery, **Montana Avenue** is situated towards the northern end of Santa Monica, bordering on the Santa Monica Canyons. A drab commercial strip during the 1970s, the street has since morphed into the Rodeo Drive of the coast, although conspicuous consumption here comes with a little more subtlety and a lot less flash. Designer stores sit alongside small boutiques and the sort of clean-cut restaurants favoured by casually clad ladies who lunch. It's a very agreeable street.

North of Montana, the streets get wider, the houses get broader and the gardens get more manicured. The four lanes of **San Vicente Boulevard** are separated by a grass verge lined with coral trees, which all but eliminates the impression that this is just another four-lane rat-run. The locale looks less like Santa Monica than Brentwood; which is, to the east at 26th Street, what it eventually becomes.

Third Street Promenade

Drifting south from Montana Avenue, Santa Monica gets steadily more commercial until you reach traffic-soaked Wilshire Boulevard and, eventually, the **Third Street Promenade**. A four-block pedestrianised stretch that runs down 3rd Street from Wilshire to Colorado Avenue, it's a pleasant but bland parade of mostly familiar names (Gap, Starbucks et al).

However, there are beacons of individuality: **Arcana** (No.1229, 1-310 458 1499, www.arcana books.com), which deals in rare books on art and design, and **Puzzle Zoo** (No.1413; *see p202*), which charms all and sundry with its engaging array of child-pleasing toys. The restaurants are ordinary , but the Wednesday-morning farmers' market makes up for it. At the Promenade's southern end is the Santa Monica Place mall, designed by Frank Gehry but due for demolition by the end of 2008.

Santa Monica Historical Society Museum

Santa Monica Public Library, 1350 7th Street, at Santa Monica Boulevard (1-310 395 2290/www. santamonicahistory.org). Bus 4, 20, 33, 333, 704, 720, SM1, SM5, SM7, SM8, SM10/I-10, exit Lincoln Boulevard north. **Open** from April 2009. **Admission** call for details. **Map** p326 B3.

Founded in the 1970s, the SMHS contains a variety of holdings relating to the intriguing history of this coastal town. The museum is currently closed, but it's due to reopen in 2009 at a new site in the Santa Monica Public Library building just a few blocks from the Third Street Promenade. Call in advance before setting out.

Santa Monica Beach

For a different perspective, head a block north and a block west from the Third Street Promenade to the Penthouse bar and restaurant at the **Huntley Hotel** (1111 2nd Street; *see p47*). On a clear day, you can see to Santa Catalina Island and the endless lizard's back of the jagged San Bernardino Mountain peaks.

Continuing a couple of blocks west will bring you to hotel-lined Ocean Avenue and, across the road, **Santa Monica Beach**. The focal point is **Santa Monica Pier** (at Colorado Avenue); on it is **Pacific Park** (free; www.pacpark.com), a traditional set-up stocked with a shiny new Ferris wheel, fairground games and cotton-candy stands. On warm weekends, the stretch is busy with families, beach bums and gym bunnies, who work out in public at the original **Muscle Beach** just south of the pier. Those who'd rather not get sand between their toes hole up at the posh terrace bar at **Shutters on the Beach**, before adjourning to the **Viceroy** to sup cosmopolitans with the beautiful people. For both, *see p48*.

Santa Monica Pier Aquarium

1600 Ocean Front Walk, at Colorado Avenue (1-310 393 6149/www.healthebay.org/smpa). Bus 33, 333, SM1, SM4, SM7, SM8, SM10/I-10, exit 4th-5th Street north. **Open** 2-6pm Tue-Fri; 12.30-6pm Sat, Sun. **Admission** $2-$5; free under-12s. **Credit** MC, V. **Map** p326 A3.

Santa Monica Pier.

Sightseeing

Run by environmental charity Heal the Bay and located underneath the pier, the Santa Monica Pier Aquarium takes an educational tack; indeed, it's closed during the morning to allow for school field trips. It's a low-key place, a galaxy away from the likes of SeaWorld, but there's fun here for youngsters in the form of touch tanks full of crabs, snails and the like. A good option for parents who can't bear the raucous atmosphere on the pier.

Ocean Park & Main Street

Beginning at the bottom of the Third Street Promenade, **Main Street** leads drivers past the conflicting designs of the '30s-era **Santa Monica City Hall** (No.1685) and the '50s-era **Santa Monica Civic Auditorium** before ending in the heart of Venice. However, its most interesting stretch runs between Pico Boulevard and Rose Avenue. This is the hilly locale of **Ocean Park**, immortalised often in paintings by local artist Richard Diebenkorn.

The third of Santa Monica's three main commercial drags (after Montana Avenue and the Third Street Promenade), Main Street is an upmarket strip, and the stretch between Ocean Park Avenue and Marine Street is the most charming part of Ocean Park. Dating from the early 20th century, its buildings are populated by a range of largely independent coffeehouses, restaurants and gift shops. Also here is the **California Heritage Museum** (*see below*) and the **Edgemar Center for the Arts** (No.2437, www.edgemarcenter.org), a Frank Gehry-designed cultural mall that hosts theatrical performances and classes.

California Heritage Museum

2612 Main Street, at Ocean Park Boulevard (1-310 392 8537/www.californiaheritagemuseum.org). Bus 33, 333, SM1, SM2, SM8, SM10/I-10, exit 4th-5th Street south. Open 11am-4pm Wed-Sun. Admission $5; $3 discounts; free under-12s. Parking free. Credit DC, MC, V. Map p326 A3.

This is an engaging, enthusiastically run operation, housed in an 1894 house and largely devoted to the decorative arts. The exhibits take the shape of rooms decorated in period style, among them a Victorian-era dining room and a 1930s kitchen. This permanent collection is supplemented by temporary displays; past shows have been devoted to everything from surfboards to old fruit-box labels. The museum is at its busiest on Sundays, though only outside: it hosts a hugely popular farmers' market every Sunday morning, for which *see p203*.

Santa Monica Visitor Center

1920 Main Street, at Pico Boulevard (1-310 393 7593/www.santamonica.com). Bus 33, 333, SM1, SM4, SM7, SM8, SM10/I-10, exit 4th-5th Street south. Open 9am-6pm daily. Map p326 A3.

Inland Santa Monica

Although inland Santa Monica is chiefly residential, it does hold pockets of interest for the visitor. Chief among them is **Bergamot Station**, a complex of art galleries created at a former Red Trolley terminus (2525 Michigan Avenue, at Cloverfield Boulevard). Its most famous tenant is the **Santa Monica Museum of Art**, but many of its other galleries merit attention; *see pp235-236*. The other major museum is the currently-closed **Museum of Flying** at the **Santa Monica Airport**, itself home to an antiques market (*see p207*) and the well-regarded **Typhoon** restaurant (*see p147*).

Museum of Flying

Santa Monica Airport (1-310 392 8822/www. museumofflying.com). Bus SM8/I-10, exit Bundy Drive south. Open call for details. Admission call for details. Credit AmEx, MC, V. Map p326 D5.

Dedicated to the history of aviation, this small museum closed in 2004 to move into new premises. The process has proven more time-consuming than the museum anticipated, but it hoped to move into new facilities at Santa Monica Airport by the end of 2009. Call or check online before setting out.

Santa Monica Museum of Art

Building G1, Bergamot Station, 2525 Michigan Avenue, at Cloverfield Boulevard (1-310 586 6488/ www.smmoa.org). Bus SM7/I-10, exit Cloverfield Boulevard north. **Open** 11am-6pm Tue-Fri; 11am-8pm Sat. **Admission** *Suggested donation* $5. **No credit cards. Map** p326 D3.

The West Side's art scene continues to offer plenty of interesting shows, with new galleries cropping up at regular intervals. However, this contemporary art gallery is the most prestigious of the lot. Housed in a former trolley stop on the LA–Santa Monica red line (**Bergamot Station**; *see also pp235-236*), the Santa Monica Museum of Art attracts sizeable crowds to its openings, which herald lively temporary exhibitions by local and international artists. Keep an eye out for the sporadic special events (lectures, discussions, family-oriented days and the like) that accompany the shows.

Venice

Map p326

Despite gentrification in and around the area, its continued popularity with tourists, and the fact that its name long ago passed into cliché as a byword for hippydom, Venice retains its edge. However, things are changing, and fast. The artists and dropouts who've long defined the area remain, but they're being usurped by young creatives in search of a countercultural edge, and by families driven down from their ideal-world home of Santa Monica by spiralling property prices. The uneasy mix is completed by low-income black and Latino communities in the troubled but improving Oakwood area, bounded by Lincoln and Venice Boulevards and Sunset and Electric Avenues.

Venice owes its existence to entrepreneur Abbot Kinney, who founded the city at the start of the 20th century in the hope that it would become the hub of an American cultural renaissance. The lagoon, the mock-Italian buildings and the canals were all his doing, as were the two dozen gondoliers imported from Italy. The cultural rebirth never quite happened, but Kinney's creation did grow into a lively and successful resort that was known, in its heyday, as the 'Playland of the Pacific'.

It wasn't until later, after many of its canals were tarmacked, that Venice became a cultural hotbed. Artists and writers have been attracted to the area for decades, drawn by the sense of community and cheap rents. If you're here in May, look out for the annual **Venice Artwalk** (*see p236*), a fundraiser for the Venice Family Clinic that offers visitors the opportunity to tour more than 60 artists' studios. Year-round, though, keep your eyes peeled for the public art. Jonathan Borofsky's *Ballerina Clown*, on the

corner of Main Street and Rose Avenue (*photo p80*), is the most striking, but Ocean Front Walk and its surrounding streets are home to more examples, including many murals.

In the 1980s, that Venice became a hive of architectural activity. The locale punches well above its weight with regard to the design of its buildings, and an enjoyable few hours can be spent touring its more notable spots. Frank Gehry's **Norton** and **Spiller Houses** (2509 Ocean Front Walk and 39 Horizon Avenue) are overshadowed only by his **Chiat/Day Building** (340 Main Street), its entrance marked by a gigantic pair of Claes Oldenburg-designed binoculars. Among other striking buildings are the **Sedlak** and **2-4-6-8 Houses** by Morphosis (Superba Court, Amoroso Court); Brian Murphy's **Hopper House** (326 Indiana Avenue); and several new apartment buildings by such notable local architects as Stephen Ehrlich (the **Venice Beach Lofts**, 25 Brooks Avenue), Koning Eizenberg (the **Electric ArtBlock**, 499 Santa Clara Avenue) and Mark Mack (the **Abbot Kinney Lofts**, 1200 Abbot Kinney Boulevard).

Abbot Kinney Boulevard

Venice's founder is commemorated in the name of its main thoroughfare, the increasingly chichi **Abbot Kinney Boulevard**. Not long ago, this was a ragged stretch of road that struggled to leave much of a lasting impression on locals or visitors. How times change. These days, at least between Broadway and California Avenues, Abbot Kinney is one of the nicest shopping streets in the entire LA region, lined on both sides with small stores, bars and restaurants.

Abbot Kinney has mostly resisted the chains that crop up elsewhere in LA. However, the big brands are circling, and **Venice Unchained** (www.veniceunchained.org) is determined to stop them. When organic frozen yoghurt chain Pinkberry opened a store on Abbot Kinney in 2007, Venice Unchained encouraged shoppers to boycott it. And talk that Starbucks might worm its way in to a new development on the corner of Venice Boulevard has had locals concerned that the area may become too homogeneous.

With the support of the local Chamber of Commerce, Venice Unchained have petitioned Venice's Planning & Land Use Committee to bring in an ordinance banning 'formula retail' from the area. Similar laws have been enacted in other arty communities up and down the coast, Carmel being the first to implement such a law back in the mid '80s. Is this NIMBYism? Dawn Hollier and Melissa Bechtel, the founders of Venice Unchained, admit that they shop at chains on Lincoln Boulevard, and claim they

Sightseeing

Jonathan Borofsky's **Ballerina Clown**.

the Hollywood Walk of Fame – the henna tattooists, abysmal performers and chips-cheap stalls recall nothing so much as Greenwich Village or Camden Market under the sun.

But for all its tackiness and exaggerated attempts at eccentricity, the Boardwalk continues to entertain. From skateboarders to radical pamphleteers, from romancing couples to steroid-stuffed bodybuilders at **Muscle Beach** (just north of Venice Boulevard), the people-watching is tremendous. And while the goods and services on offer are largely junk (cheap sunglasses, cheaper T-shirts, inedible snacks), there are a few beacons of civility along here. Snag some lunch at **Figtree's Café** (429 Ocean Front Walk, 1-310 392 4937, www.figtreescafe.com) before scanning the shelves at the excellent **Small World Books** (1407 Ocean Front Walk; see p190).

It's worth diving off the beach and exploring the so-called 'walk-streets' that join the main road to the beach. These skinny little alleys are lined on either side with houses and apartments, an implausibly cosy arrangement that depends on community spirit for its success. Luckily, Venice has such spirit in spades, and houses along here remain highly sought after properties. There's a more extensive network of walk-streets further inland, just west of Lincoln Boulevard; if anything, it's even more appealing.

don't have anything against chains in general. They just feel that bringing in a 'community character' zone of some sort is necessary to preserve the character of Venice. Only time will tell if this little grassroots organisation can stare down the big boys.

For now, though, the businesses are proud of their independence. At one end stands **Equator Books** (see p190), offering a hand-picked selection of esoteric tomes alongside regular exhibitions and a stash of vintage vinyl. At the other is the **Farmacy**, which sells what its sign carefully describes as 'Global organic medicine'. And in between stand stores selling designer duds and hand-made toys, salons offering haircuts and pedicures, and restaurants serving upscale American fare and downmarket barbecue. It's well worth a wander.

Venice Beach

While affluent new Venice can be seen in all its glory along Abbot Kinney Boulevard, shambolic old Venice remains in evidence along **Venice Beach** (see pp81-82 **LA's best beaches**). It's long been known as a mecca for kooky California culture and, up to a point, it remains so; repeated efforts by the authorities to rein in the vendors and entertainers have so far come to nothing. However, in the 21st century, it's as much of a tourist attraction as

The canals

Many of Venice's original canals were filled in during the 1920s by authorities unwilling to maintain them. However, a handful remain intact, offering a charming window into the way this neighbourhood must once have looked. Located south-east of the intersection of Venice Boulevard and Pacific Avenue, this small network of waterways is almost idyllic, a world away from the brashness of the beach.

It's worth spending a while idling along these waterways and bridges, nosily sneaking a peek into the homes and gardens of the lucky locals. You won't for one second believe that you're in Italy, but that doesn't matter – this neighbourhood has a character all its own.

Marina del Rey & around

Considering that Los Angeles is located next to the largest area of open water on the planet, it's slightly strange that more attention isn't paid to its community of sailors. However, while the city's surfers get all the fame, many other Angelenos keep boats at **Marina del Rey Harbor**, a resort and residential complex just south of Venice. Conceived a century ago but only completed in 1965, the marina consists of an artificial harbour with eight basins named to evoke the South Seas (Tahiti Way, Bora Bora Way) and filled with bobbing yachts, motor boats and flashy cruisers.

Like many similar resorts around the world, it's not a handsome place on land. Indeed, with the possible exception of Fisherman's Village, a cheesy recreation of a New England fishing town, it's actually pretty ugly. The marina is surrounded by unbecoming apartment blocks and bland hotels – it's almost as if the locals have made the area dreary simply in order to encourage themselves to hit the water. Still, in fairness, you'd no more visit Marina del Rey for the stunning architecture than you'd visit Downtown LA for the surfing – it's really missing the point.

The Marina's attractions are all recreational. Picnic, jog and cycle (the Marina is a link in the 21-mile coastal bike path) in **Burton W Chace Park** and **Admiralty Park** at the northern end; fish from a dock at the west end of Chace Park or rent a boat to go ocean-fishing at **Fisherman's Village**; or join whale-watching excursions run during winter by any number of charter companies. But otherwise, save your money: the shopping is touristy, and most eateries are more to be recommended for their waterside charm rather than their food.

Playa del Rey & Playa Vista

Playa del Rey is separated from Marina del Rey only by the skinny little Ballona Creek, but it feels like a very different place. Small and unfancy, it's more down to earth than its neighbour – although there's a small hotel (the **Inn at Playa del Rey**; *see p51*), Playa del Rey as a whole seems unenthusiastic about attracting tourists. There's a curious variety of buildings on the stretch of **Vista del Mar** that sits just north of Culver Boulevard: look out, in particular for the unexpectedly wonky green property at No.6672, designed by Eric Owen Moss in 1977. And there's a sweet little beach, too. But otherwise, there's not that much to see in the heart of what's basically a seaside village.

Hugging Ballona Creek are the **Ballona Wetlands**. This nature reserve once stretched to 2,000 acres, but years of over-construction (including Marina del Rey) have reduced it to just a tenth of that size. Despite the intrusion, more than 200 species of birds can still be seen here throughout the year, amid the variety of different habitats. See www.ballonafriends.org for details of tours and other events.

Developers have been trying to get their hands on the remaining stretch of the Ballona Wetlands for years, so far without success.

And if the rather sterile new residential neighbourhood of **Playa Vista** on the other side of Lincoln Boulevard is any indication of the kind of construction that might conceivably take its place, it's a good job that the area remains untamed. This huge development has been dogged by controversy since its inception, and there may well still be courtroom battles to be fought about proposed additions to the site in future years.

Sex on the beach

Three or four nights after full and new moons between March and September, a strange but entrancing event takes place along the coast in Southern California. On the beach under the moonlight, hundreds of locals with torches gather and look out to sea. They're waiting for thousands of grunion, small silver fish that beach themselves on the shore in a strange mating ritual. This is the Grunion Run, one of the oddest spectator sports in the state.

Female fish start the mating dance by riding a wave to the shore, wiggling their tails until they're half-buried in the wet sand. Up to seven or eight males then wrap themselves around each female, fertilising the eggs that she's laid under the sand. (It's estimated that a single female will lay as many as 18,000 over a season.) The eggs remain in the sand for about ten days until the next high tides, at which point the eggs hatch and the baby grunion are carried out to sea.

The ritual has piqued the interest of local residents and keen fishermen for decades. Most people are there simply to watch the show, but some 'Grunion Greeters' are there on semi-official business, observing the spawning runs and then filing reports. Others, meanwhile, are there to catch their dinner. During April and May, the season's peak months, fishing is banned. However, at other times, you can pick up as many as you like provided you have a fishing licence (*see p273*). The easiest time to catch a grunion is just after mating, when they're briefly stranded until the next wave comes to wash them back to sea. Typically grilled or sautéed, they taste similar to smelt.

For information on the timing of grunion runs, www.grunion.org. And for more, see the Department of Fish & Game's website, at www.dfg.ca.gov/marine/gruschd.asp.

LA's best beaches

Ever since Vasco Núñez de Balboa laid eyes on the Pacific Ocean in 1513, the world has gazed upon the Southern California coastline with wonder. With its gorgeous interface of sea and sky against a chiselled mountain backdrop, the 30-mile stretch of beaches along LA County's coastline – from Malibu in the north, through Santa Monica and Venice, and on to the South Bay – is incomparable.

Despite LA's surf city reputation, the Pacific is chillingly cold for nine months of the year. But in July and August, when oceanside temperatures hover around 90°F (32°C), the water can reach 70°F (21°C). The further you are from Santa Monica Bay, where waste is pumped into the ocean, the cleaner the water. That said, even the water in Santa Monica has improved under the auspices of **Heal the Bay** (1-310 451 1500, www.healthe bay.org), an environmental outfit devoted to monitoring pollution. Swimming is permitted on all beaches in LA County, but strong currents and pounding waves make it difficult.

Beaches officially open at 7am and close at 10pm. Many have space and rental gear for in-line skating, roller-hockey, cycling, surfing and volleyball, as well as refreshment stands, showers and toilets. Alcohol, pets and nudity are prohibited; bonfires are permitted only at Dockweiler State Beach in Vista del Mar and

Cabrillo Beach in San Pedro, and then only in designated fire rings. Lifeguards are on duty year round. Occasionally, due to rough rip tides, shark sightings and pollution, beaches may be closed by lifeguard crews, but such occurrences are rare. In summer, check the *LA Times* for ratings of all the local beaches.

Though there is limited free parking on the Pacific Coast Highway, parking can be difficult and expensive. Still, it's better to pay for a space than have your vehicle towed. For more information on beaches in LA, check the Department of Beaches & Harbors website at http://beaches.co.la.ca.us. The following are the pick of LA's beaches, from north to south.

El Matador State Beach
Around 32350 Pacific Coast Highway.
Small, beautiful and dominated by rocky outcrops, El Matador looks not unlike a European beach. Six miles north of Malibu and 25 miles from Santa Monica, it's just past Zuma Beach (*see below*), accessible via a steep gravelly path. Wear shoes and don't bring too much heavy gear. There are no lifeguards or other facilities, so you should be able to find some privacy on the beach; spread your towel in the cupped hands of the rocks. Arriving early or staying late should reward you with a memorable dawn or sunset.

El Matador and nearby **El Pescador** and **La Piedra** beaches collectively form the **Robert H Meyer Memorial Beaches**. All three are worth a visit.

Zuma Beach

Around 30000 Pacific Coast Highway.
The four-mile sprawl of immaculate sand that makes up family-friendly Zuma Beach is ideal for surfing, swimming, volleyball, sunbathing and long walks; the water is clean and the sand soft beneath your feet. Zuma can get crowded, and getting there along the traffic-congested PCH can be a challenge at weekends. There are lifeguards, toilets and showers. You can buy food from stands, but packing a picnic basket is a better idea.

Malibu

Surfrider Beach: around 23050 Pacific Coast Highway. For Malibu, see p74.
The public are legally allowed access to all beaches in Malibu, but finding the routes to them can be difficult: many of the houses that back on to them are owned by privacy-hungry celebrities. The public beaches are nothing out of the ordinary but are popular for swimming, sunning and watching the do-or-die surfers at Surfrider Beach. There are also tidepools, a marine preserve, and volleyball and picnic areas. Drive out towards Point Dume to see the opulent houses of the rich and famous, some sitting precariously on the edge of rocky bluffs.

Santa Monica State Beach

For Santa Monica, see p76.
This big beach, which effectively runs the length of Santa Monica itself, is usually crowded and has a festive, summer-holiday feel to it. The big attraction is Santa Monica Pier (on a level with Colorado Avenue), roughly three city blocks in length and packed with typical and endearingly low-tech distractions: pier fishing, video arcades, free twilight dance concerts in summer, fortune tellers, fairground games, rides and a shiny new Ferris wheel.

Venice Beach

For Venice, see p79.
People-watching is the raison d'être at Venice Beach, which effectively continues from the southern end of Santa Monica Beach without a break. Jump into the flow of the winding Venice Boardwalk, where you can skate or cycle, watch or play volleyball or basketball, and check out the pumped-up gym bunnies who work out at Muscle Beach. Street parking is usually jammed, but there are several beachside lots – try the end of Rose Avenue or Windward Avenue, off Pacific Avenue.

Manhattan Beach

For Manhattan Beach, see p136.
South of LAX, Manhattan Beach is right out of a Southern California postcard, offering clean water, sand that stretches out of sight, small piers and all kinds of activities: volleyball (there's an annual Volleyball Open each August), sailing and ocean-front paths for walking, cycling and in-line skating. The charm is the local flavour; visitors can swim, picnic and bask in the sun alongside residents and local fishermen. The surf isn't bad either.

Huntington State Beach

For Huntington Beach, see p139.
Essentially, more of the above, just further south (Huntington Beach is about 15 miles south of Long Beach). Its chief attraction is its surfing: Huntington Beach picks up swells from a variety of directions, which makes for good waves, and the water is often less crowded than at Malibu's Surfrider Beach.

Brentwood to Beverly Hills

Money, money, money…

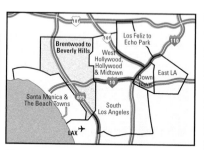

Brentwood

Brentwood consisted of farms and fields until 1915, when a real-estate agent named Bundy saw its potential. Landscape architects were asked to create 'flora, arbor and artistic park attractions'; everything that suggested a formal city was avoided. As such, Brentwood resembles a small town; **San Vicente Boulevard**, the area's main road, has running down its centre a line of coral trees, the official tree of the city.

Today, as ever, Brentwood is a leafy, largely residential neighbourhood; cruise up **Kenter Avenue** and **Bonhill Road** for a peek through the keyhole. There are numerous notable buildings: designed by Frank Lloyd Wright, the **Sturges House** (449 Skyeviay Road) is wedged dramatically on to a hill; and Eric Owen Moss's work in Culver City (*see p28*) finds a small but scintillating echo in the building he designed at **167 S Westgate Avenue**. However, there's also plenty of grandiose architectural mediocrity and an awful lot of tall, paparazzi-proof hedges.

Brentwood has always drawn the wealthy and the famous: Raymond Chandler wrote *High Window* while living at 12216 Shetland Place, and Marilyn Monroe died a lonely death at 12305 5th Helena Drive. However, it was another star who really put the area on the global map, although the exact parts he put on it are no longer there. The condo of murdered Nicole Brown Simpson (formerly 875 S Bundy Drive) has been relandscaped to deter sightseers, while OJ Simpson's house (formerly 360 N Rockingham Avenue) was bulldozed in summer 1998.

Getty Center

1200 Getty Center Drive, at I-405 (1-310 440 7300/www.getty.edu). Bus 761/I-405, exit Getty Center Drive. **Open** 10am-6pm Tue-Thur, Sun; 10am-9pm Fri, Sat. **Admission** free. *Parking* $8.
Los Angeles's acropolis occupies the top of a hill on land once destined to be the site of a co-operative housing development. The complex was conceived as a home for the hitherto disparate entities of the J Paul Getty Trust, but that's the only straightforward thing about it. Architect Richard Meier was hired to build the museum in 1984, but it took 13 years, several additional designers (to work on the interior and the landscaping) and $1 billion to complete. The end result is a remarkable complex of travertine and white metal-clad pavilions that resembles a kind of monastic retreat designed for James Bond. Its relative inaccessibility is more than compensated for by the panoramic views, from the hills and the ocean in the west all the way around to Downtown in the east.

Once you've parked at the bottom and taken the electric tram ride up the hill, one thing becomes apparent: it's a big place. To the west of the plaza is a café, a restaurant (*see p149*) and the circular **Research Institute**, which houses a private scholarly centre and a roster of public exhibits. Beyond it is the **Central Garden**, designed by Robert Irwin. North are the other institutes (some off-limits to the public) and the **Harold M Williams Auditorium**, where lectures and symposia alternate with concerts and film screenings. And to the south, up a grand Spanish Steps-style stairway, is the museum lobby, an airy, luminous rotunda that opens to a fountain-filled courtyard surrounded by six pavilions housing the permanent collection and temporary shows.

Collections

The Getty's budget is the envy of museums the world over, but it was a Johnny-come-lately to European art; until, say, the Vatican has a fire sale, the collections won't match the museums of the Old World. Still, that's not to write off its holdings. Certain aspects – post-Renaissance decorative arts, the expanding photography selection – are magnificent, and others are fast improving. The museum is constantly adding to its contemporary art collection, and recently acquired the excellent video-art holdings of the Long Beach Museum of Art (*see p138*).

The collections are spread over four two-level pavilions, all linked on both levels by walkways. The art is displayed more or less chronologically: the **North**

Pavilion contains pieces from prior to 1600; the **East** and **South Pavilions** feature works from the 17th and 18th centuries; and the **West Pavilion** runs from 1800 to the present day. The plaza level of each pavilion contains sculpture and decorative arts, along with temporary exhibits in other disciplines; the first floors are given over to paintings.

On the ground floor of the North Pavilion, room N104 contains an eye-catching array of glass objects dating from the 15th century, while N105 is home to a rotating series of small-scale displays drawn from the Getty's collection of illuminated manuscripts. Upstairs is dominated by Italian religious painting from the 15th and 16th centuries; highlights include a vast altarpiece by Bartolomeo Vivarini (N202) and a scintillating *Venus & Adonis* believed to have come from Titian's workshop (N205).

The East Pavilion is heavy on the Dutch and Flemish masters. Notable pieces include Gerrit van Honthorst's *Christ Crowned with Thorns* (E201); several works by Rubens, among them *The Entombment* (E202); and Gerrit Dou's intensely detailed *Astronomer by Candlelight* (E205).

One of the museum's strengths is the collection of 17th- and 18th-century decorative arts, most of it French, that monopolises the ground-floor galleries in the South Pavilion. Some rooms contain individual exhibits (seek out the bed in S109); others are virtual reconstructions of French drawing rooms, complete with original panelling. Next to this opulent array, the galleries upstairs can't compete, but they do contain two Gainsboroughs (S204) and Odilon Redon's *Baronne de Domecy*, a dream-like

piece that overshadows the rest of the pastels and watercolours in S206.

The ground-floor galleries in the West Pavilion are given over to European sculpture and decorative arts from the late 18th and 19th centuries plus, in W104-W107, changing exhibits from the Getty's drawings collection. Upstairs is a strong-ish selection of paintings, mostly from the 19th century. Room W201 contains a seascape by Turner entitled *Van Tromp, Going About to Please His Masters*, but the key exhibits are in W204: several Monet pieces, a Cézanne still life, a delightfully raffish Renoir portrait of composer Albert Cahen d'Anvers, and Van Gogh's *Irises*.

Elsewhere, look out for the rotating displays culled from the museum's world-class photography holdings. And don't miss the fine new sculpture gardens at the museum's entrance and by the West Pavilion, home to works by (among others) Miró and Moore.

Skirball Cultural Center

2701 N Sepulveda Boulevard, at I-405 (1-310 440 4500/www.skirball.org). Bus 761/I-405, exit Skirball Center/Mulholland Drive north. **Open** noon-5pm Tue, Wed, Fri; noon-9pm Thur; 10am-5pm Sat, Sun. **Admission** $10; $5-$7 discounts; free under-12s. Free to all Thur. *Parking* free. **Credit** DC, MC, V.

Something of a local powerhouse, the Skirball is a cultural centre as distinct from a museum, and aims to look at connections between 4,000 years of Jewish heritage and different communities around LA. Those with an interest in Jewish history will get the most from some of the exhibits (the 30,000-object collection is one of the largest holdings of Judaica in the US), but

Robert Irwin's beautiful gardens at the **Getty Center**.

this is an egalitarian enterprise that should interest most visitors with a sense of cultural adventure.

Visions & Values: Jewish Life from Antiquity to America, the central exhibit, offers a lengthy but interesting trawl through Jewish history and culture, taking in everything from Jewish holidays to the Holocaust. It's been joined recently by Noah's Ark, a wonderful kid-oriented exhibit that explores cultural differences through a retelling of the old animals-two-by-two tale. Folk art-esque animals hang from the ceilings and peer out from a mock-ark; hands-on inter-action is encouraged as part of what's the most enjoy-able family-friendly exhibit in the LA region.

These two headline-grabbing permanent exhibits are supplemented by a decent café and a pleasing gar-den; a lively programme of temporary exhibitions on everything from teenage immigration to Bob Dylan; talks and discussions, many related to ongoing dis-plays; and an unexpectedly rich schedule of concerts and other performances. The Skirball might be off the beaten tourist track, but it's well worth the diversion.

Culver City

Forget Hollywood: Culver City was once the cradle of the American movie industry. Many major motion-picture studios conducted their business from these streets, among them MGM and RKO; films of the calibre of *Citizen Kane* and *The Wizard of Oz* were shot here, at a time when the town produced more than half of all the movies shot in America. The entertainment industry retains a presence in the area: **Sony**

Pictures are squeezed in on part of the old MGM lot between W Washington and Culver Boulevards, just east of Overland Avenue (for tours, *see p73*). But there's more to the area than mere nostalgia for some long-lost cinematic golden age. Culver City, possibly for the first time in its existence, is hip.

After years as little more than a suburban adjunct to the more engaging neighbourhoods to the west and north, Culver City has spent the last decade or so turning itself around. The town's focal point is the downtown intersection of **Main Street** and **Culver Boulevard**, around which sit a low-key but lively collection of galleries (*see pp236-237*), shops and restaurants (*see p150*). Already popular, this area is also soon to get busier: new buildings, slated to house shops and restaurants, are scheduled for completion in 2010, adding more appeal to an area that's already bucking the downward economic trends elsewhere in LA.

For all its cultural appeal, the area doesn't really offer much for the sightseer. At the junction of Culver Boulevard and Irving Place, **Town Plaza** is surely the only block in the city with two fountain sculptures: Eric Orr's untitled triangular granite pole, and Douglas Olmsted Freeman's more eye-catching *Lion's Fountain*. A few yards to the west are a couple of historic structures: the **Culver Hotel**, built in the '20s, and the **Kirk Douglas Theatre** (*see p279*), an old '40s cinema topped by an iconic neon-lit tower. And north of here, across Culver

Skirball Cultural Center. *See p85.*

Boulevard, is the fabulous **Museum of Jurassic Technology** (*see below*).

However, Culver City's renaissance is best symnbolised by an 11-acre complex of buildings located at the corner of Venice Boulevard and Helms Avenue. Local bakers Helms baked their last loaf here in 1969, but its old premises have been spared the wrecking ball by forward-thinking local preservationists. Its glorious neon sign now fully restored, the **Helms Bakery** (www.helmsbakerydistrict. com) now houses an array of galleries, furniture shops and the **Jazz Bakery** (*see p260*).

Not far from here, on the 3500 block of Hayden Avenue near the junction with National Boulevard, is perhaps the most eye-catching architectural project in LA. In the '40s and '50s, the **Hayden Tract** was a thriving industrial area, but by the '80s the businesses had largely moved out. Enter Frederick Smith, an entrepreneur with a vision of how to regenerate the area, and Eric Owen Moss, the experimental architect he chose to give it life. Some of the old factories remain, but others have been replaced by Moss's odd yet dazzling office buildings.

Park outside the daunting black hulk of the **Stealth Building** (3528 Hayden Avenue); walk under it and into the parking lot to see Moss's singular style in full effect. In one corner stands the **Umbrella** (No.3542), its crazed exterior staircase leading nowhere; across the way is another building with a frontage that leans precariously forward, echoing the angles of the Stealth building. Back on the main road sits the demented façade of **3535 Hayden Avenue**, all spiky wood and awkward concrete. Just around the corner on National Boulevard are **8522 National**, a complex of five renovated warehouses, and the **Box**, whose meeting room sticks out like a sore (and square) thumb. And over on La Cienega Boulevard sits the strangely graceful **Samitaur Building** (No.3457).

Museum of Jurassic Technology

9341 Venice Boulevard, at Bagley Avenue (1-310 836 6131/www.mjt.org). Bus 33, 333, C1, C5, C7/ I-10, exit Robertson Boulevard south. **Open** 2-8pm Thur; noon-6pm Fri-Sun. **Admission** *Suggested donation* $5; $2-$3 discounts. **No credit cards.**
Don't be fooled by the name: this is not some kind of Spielbergian dinosaurland. It's far more interesting than that. Hidden behind an unassuming, windowless storefront, David Wilson's Museum of Jurassic Technology presents itself as a repository of curiosities (opera singer Madelena Delani, who suffered from terrible memory failings), scientific wonders (a bat that can fly through walls) and artistic miracles (the so-called 'microminiatures' of Soviet-Armenian refugee Hagop Sandaldjian, who painted impossibly tiny sculptures that fit within the eye of a needle with plenty of room to spare).

Fact is mixed with the fantastical, through the elaborate and beautiful treatment (dramatically lit vitrines, audio-visual displays) accorded to everything from the history of trailer parks to 17th-century Renaissance man Athanasius Kircher. Which exhibits, if any, are bona fide? Which, if any, are satirical? And, most crucially of all, does it matter? A subversive, witty and brilliant enterprise, Museum of Jurassic Technology challenges the very nature of what a museum is or should be, while also taking its place as one of the most fascinating attractions in the entire city. Wholly unique and unreservedly recommended.

Star Eco Station

10101 W Jefferson Boulevard, between Overland & Duquesne Avenues, Culver City (1-310 842 8060/ www.ecostation.org). Bus C3, C4/I-10, exit Overland Avenue south. **Open** *July, Aug* 1-5pm Mon-Fri; 10am-4pm Sat, Sun. *Sept-Jun* 1-5pm Fri; 10am-4pm Sat, Sun. **Admission** $8; $6-$7 discounts; free infants. *Parking* free. **No credit cards.**
Part-wildlife rescue centre, part-educational facility, this very family-friendly enterprise in Culver City practises what it preaches in terms of environmental awareness – it was even built from recycled materials. Staff provide care for unwanted exotic animals, many of which have either been donated by the public or confiscated by governmental agencies: families are welcome to pet an alligator or stroke a snake as they learn about endangered species, environmental concerns and how kids can make a change. A number of other exhibits add further context; call or check online for details of special events.

Westwood & around

The Westwood neighbourhood is dominated by the University of California, Los Angeles, better known by its abbreviated name of **UCLA**. The handsome and suitably cultured 400-acre campus makes for an agreeable diversion (*see p88* **Walk**). To reach it, drive up Westwood Boulevard and follow the right-hand fork as it turns into Westwood Plaza.

South of UCLA, centred around Westwood Boulevard and Broxton Avenue, Westwood's commercial district is walkable but not hugely inspiring. There's less to buy but more to see at the **UCLA Hammer Museum** (*see p88*) and **Westwood Memorial Park** (1218 Glendon Avenue, at Wilshire Boulevard, 1-310 474 1579), the final resting place of Marilyn Monroe, Billy Wilder and, in an unmarked grave next to actor Lew Ayres, Frank Zappa.

Walk UCLA campus

As befits one of America's most highly regarded academic institutions, the campus of UCLA is a grand place. It's a pleasant way to spend an hour or two, diverse architectural styles and noteworthy public art blending in beautifully landscaped grounds that highlight the school's huge wealth and influence. Before you stroll, pick up a campus map and a daily parking permit ($8) from the booth on **Westwood Plaza**: parking tickets are dispensed here with alarming enthusiasm.

Once you've parked, walk north from the information booth past the Ackerman Student Union Building and you'll come to **Bruin Plaza**, a buzzing spot for most of the day. Political and social groups campaign here, under the gaze of the fearsome **Bruin Bear** statue. There's more activity further north past the **Ashe Center** (named in honour of Arthur Ashe, a Davis Cup player while still a student here), but of a very different kind: in fine weather, **Wilson Plaza** is covered with students playing football, tossing Frisbees or flicking through textbooks.

Tucked in the north-east corner of Wilson Plaza is the **Fowler Museum of Cultural History** (1-310 825 4361, www.fowler.ucla. edu), which presents temporary exhibitions on diverse ethnographic themes. Although the subjects can be a little esoteric, they're presented in an approachable way. The one permanent display is of 250 pieces from the Francis Fowler silver collection.

From here, make your way up the **Janss Steps**, but be careful: a long-held superstition

runs that treading on the sixth step dooms the walker to bad luck and, perhaps, an extra year in college. At the top is **Dickson Terrace**, a handsome patch of green named for Edward Dickson, the university's founding father. To your right is **Royce Hall**, which hosts events in the university's excellent UCLA Live series. And on your left is the **Powell Library**, handsome from the outside and beautiful within. Both buildings were completed in 1929 and modelled, to some degree, after Italian churches: Royce Hall on the Basilica Sant'Ambrogio in Milan, and the Powell Library after the Basilica di San Zeno in Verona. Along with the **Humanities Building** and **Haines Hall**, which also flank Dickson Terrace, they're the oldest buildings on campus.

Continue past the flagpole and turn left past **Dodd Hall** and the **LuValle Commons** building (stop here for a snack if you're hungry), and skip quickly past the horrible **School of Public Affairs Building** on your right. You're now in the **Franklin D Murphy Sculpture Garden**, which holds works by the likes of Barbara Hepworth (*Elegy III*), Joan Miró (*Mère Ubu*) and Henry Moore (*Two-Piece Reclining Figure*). Don't be alarmed if you see a few students talking expansively to themselves: they're probably theatre students rehearsing for plays to be staged in one of two theatres in **MacGowan Hall**. To the north-east corner of the garden sits the new **Eli & Edythe Broad Art Center**, designed by Getty Center architect Richard Meier.

South of here, the area rather peters out. Wilshire Boulevard is dominated by drab skyscrapers; below it, Westwood Boulevard contains a few ethnic restaurants but not much else. The most powerful presence in the area is the **Mormon Temple** (10777 Santa Monica Boulevard, at Overland Avenue), topped by a 257-foot (84-metre) tower that's itself crowned with a gold-leaf statue of the angel Moroni. The temple, the largest Mormon house of worship outside Salt Lake City, is open only to church members, but the manicured lawn and white stone building are an awe-inspiring sight even if you're not Mormonically inclined. Similarly expansive but less impressive is the **Westside Pavilion**, a classic '80s mall that was spruced up a few years ago. It's still a pretty ugly sight, but it is now home to the **Landmark** (*see p228*), a comfortable, state-of-the-art cineplex.

UCLA Hammer Museum

10899 Wilshire Boulevard, at Westwood Boulevard (1-310 443 7000/www.hammer.ucla.edu). Bus 20, 720/I-405, exit Wilshire Boulevard east. **Open** 11am-7pm Tue, Wed, Fri, Sat; 11am-9pm Thur; 11am-5pm Sun. **Admission** $5; $3 discounts; free under-17s. Free to all Thur. *Parking* $3 first 3hrs with validation. **Credit** AmEx, DC, MC, V. **Map** p327 A4.
Industrialist Armand Hammer founded this museum, primarily to house his own collection. Now, under the ownership of UCLA, the Hammer stages fascinating themed shows of modern art, photography and design. The former have included everything from video installations to American comic art; the latter are often drawn from UCLA's Grunwald collection of graphic arts. The shows are supplemented by the Hammer Projects series, focused on emerging artists; works from Hammer's collections; and an excellent, largely free events programme that takes in music, films, symposia and so on.

Walk down Charles E Young Drive East and you'll come to the **Founders Rock**, a 75-ton boulder dragged here from Perris Valley (halfway between LA and San Diego) and dedicated in 1946 on the 20th anniversary of the founding of UCLA. Head past **Murphy Hall**, outside which are sculptures by Gordon Newell and Fritz Koenig, then go south to **Schoenberg Hall**; it's named in honour of exiled German composer Arnold Schoenberg, who served as professor here. To the west of the building is a model for Robert Graham's **Duke Ellington Memorial** in New York, Duke at the piano balanced on the heads of nine nude muses. And just south is perhaps the most striking piece of public art on the campus: Jere Hazlett's **Inverted Fountain**, inspired by the hot springs of Yellowstone.

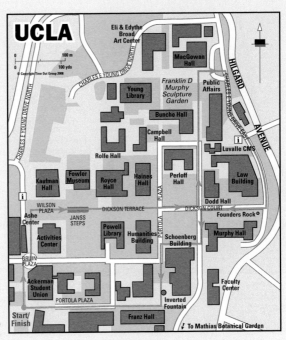

From here, you could wander south to the seven-acre **Mildred E Mathias Botanical Garden** (1-310 825 1260, www.botgard.ucla. edu). Alternatively, cut back through the campus, where your car awaits.

Bel Air

After it was developed by Alphonzo E Bell in the early 1920s, this sleepy hillside community north of Westwood, became a favoured location among stars who wanted to have privacy as well as fantastic views. Celebrities still abound, but there's not a great deal for the outsider to see along the winding roads. The **Hotel Bel-Air** on Stone Canyon Road (see p54) mirrors the tranquil, dripping-with-money locale, with its beautifully manicured gardens and luxuriant lake. Also here is the UCLA-run **Hannah Carter Japanese Garden** (1-310 794 0320, www.japanesegarden.ucla.edu; see p95 **The secret gardens**), open only by reservation three days a week. An address and directions will be provided when you book.

Century City

Century City was once a movie backlot, where Tom Mix filmed his Westerns. It's still home to Fox Studios, but it's also now characterised by a skyline-dominating overabundance of high-rise buildings. Most are nondescript, but there are a couple of exceptions, both by Minoru Yamasaki: the triangular **Century Plaza Towers** and the **Century Plaza Hotel** (now the **Hyatt Regency Century Plaza**; see p54), a huge, high-rise ellipse. Several other cloudbusters are being built, including two apartment complexes: the 24-storey Carlyle (10776 Wilshire Boulevard) and the 42-storey Century (next to the Hyatt Regency). However, business dominates, and the main attraction is the **Westfield Century City** mall (see p190).

Bedford Drive in Beverly Hills.

Beverly Hills

Map p327

There is Big Money in many corners of LA. However, nowhere is the local wealth displayed with quite such panache as it is in Beverly Hills. Its commercial thoroughfares are lined with high-end shops and eateries, its residential streets are immaculately manicured, and both foot and motor traffic are pristine. It is, in other words, the Los Angeles of popular imagination.

The area has been a star magnet for decades. Douglas Fairbanks and Mary Pickford were the first to move here in 1920, to a Wallace Neff-designed mansion at 1143 Summit Drive they called Pickfair (later demolished by Pia Zadora), and the celeb power remains strong. You'll occasionally see streetside vendors selling 'star maps', fold-out sheets that purport to pinpoint the homes of Hollywood bigwigs. It probably goes without saying that they're about as reliable as, say, Lindsay Lohan.

North of Santa Monica Boulevard

The best way to introduce yourself to Beverly Hills is to drive the residential streets in the area bounded by **Sunset Boulevard**, **Doheny Drive**, **Santa Monica Boulevard** and **Walden Drive**. There's an eerie quiet throughout: traffic is sparse, and the only

people on foot are gardeners. If you get the feeling you're being watched, you probably are: as tiny signs on almost every fencepost detail, security firms patrol these streets.

The area is anything but homogeneous. When you have as much money as the folks around here, you don't just buy a house: you build your own. And, of course, you build it exactly as you please, which might not be in anything like the same way as your neighbours. As a result, the architecture is a wild blend of styles: everything from squat modernist boxes to palatial mansions and Spanish villas, often all on the same street. Still, nothing is quite as wild as the fairytale folly of the 1921 **Spadena House**, also known as the Witch's House (516 N Walden Drive, at Carmelita Avenue). Built in Culver City to house a movie studio's offices, the fantastical structure was moved here in 1934. It's currently in poor shape, but a long-awaited renovation is hopefully close at hand.

At the north-eastern junction of Santa Monica and Wilshire Boulevards sits another slice of old Beverly Hills. Harnessing **Beverly Gardens**, a pleasant but unremarkable stretch of greenery, stands the **Electric Fountain**, built by architect Ralph Flewelling and sculptor Merrell Gage. Upon completion in 1931, the dramatic water displays and neon lighting stopped traffic. These days the traffic doesn't need any extra slowing down, but the fountain is still a fine sight. Its focal point is a Native American praying for rain.

Two landmarks sit north on Sunset Boulevard, by the junction with Beverly Drive. Known as the 'Pink Palace', the **Beverly Hills Hotel & Bungalows** (No.9641; see p54) was one of the first buildings to be constructed in the city. Close by is **Will Rogers Memorial Park**; it was here, in the park's public toilets, that George Michael was arrested in 1998.

The houses north of here, around **Benedict** and **Coldwater Canyons**, are grander than those south of Sunset, none more so than the **Greystone Mansion** (905 Loma Vista Drive, 1-310 550 4796, www.greystonemansion.org). Built in 1927 by oil millionaire Edward L Doheny for his son, who was shot dead within weeks of moving in, this 55-room Tudor-style home has featured in films such as *The Witches of Eastwick* and *Indecent Proposal*. The house is closed to the public (apart from for occasional special events), but its 18 acres of landscaped gardens are open 10am-5pm daily.

South of Santa Monica Boulevard

If the streets north of Santa Monica Boulevard are where the locals live, the roads south of it are where they spend their money. The pocket bounded by Wilshire Boulevard, Canon Drive and Little Santa Monica Boulevard, which includes Rodeo Drive, Dayton Way and Brighton Way, is known as the **Golden Triangle**. A few more prosaic chains have arrived in recent years, but the pedestrian-friendly area is still famous for the array of high-end fashion designers with shops here. **Two Rodeo**, a $200-million ersatz European cobbled walkway, is always busy with window-shopping tourists and serious spenders. Close by is **Anderton Court** (322 N Rodeo Drive), the only shopping mall designed by Frank Lloyd Wright.

Signs of wealth abound along **Little Santa Monica Boulevard**. The **Peninsula Beverly Hills** (No.9882, at Charleville Boulevard; *see p56*) is a good place for celebrity-spotting. And next door (9830 Wilshire Boulevard) stands a stunning building designed by IM Pei for über-agent Michael Ovitz's Creative Artists Agency, all white marble and cantilevered glass. (CAA moved to Century City in 2007, but the building remains.) **Beverly Hills Rent-A-Car** (9732 Little Santa Monica Boulevard, at S Linden Drive) deals not in Fords and Chevys but Porsches and Ferraris, while **Sprinkles** (9635 Little Santa Monica Boulevard, at S Bedford Drive, 1-310 274 8765) sells delicious $3.25 cupcakes to Hillbillies who are watching their figure only *so* closely. Other women sit in shop windows getting their hair coiffed. And at Little Santa Monica Boulevard and Rexford Drive sits the Spanish baroque-style **Civic Center**, as carefully maintained as any film set.

But for all the glamour, numerous remnants of old Beverly Hills have survived intact. **Nate 'n Al's** (414 N Beverly Drive, at Brighton Way; *see p164*) is a too-Jewish-to-be-true deli that draws a mixed crowd of young bucks and ancient ladies who lunch; south, the stretch of Beverly Drive between Wilshire and Pico Boulevards is a great example of classic LA 1950s architecture. Close by Civic Center, the **Union 76** gas station on the corner of Little Santa Monica Boulevard and Rexford Drive boasts a 1950s cantilevered concrete canopy. And a few blocks west is tobacconist **Al Kramer's** (9531 Little Santa Monica Boulevard) – in modern-day LA, there's nothing quite as old fashioned as smoking.

Beverly Hills Conference & Visitors Bureau

239 S Beverly Drive, between Charleville Boulevard & Gregory Way (1-800 345 2210/www.beverlyhills behere.com). Bus 20, 720/I-10, exit Beverly Drive north. **Open** 8.30am-5pm Mon-Fri. **Map** p327 D3.

Museum of Tolerance

Simon Wiesenthal Plaza, 9786 W Pico Boulevard, at Roxbury Drive (1-310 553 8403/www.museumof tolerance.com). Bus SM7, SM13/I-10, exit Overland

Avenue north. **Open** *Apr-Oct* 10am-5pm Mon-Fri; 11am-5pm Sun. *Nov-Mar* 10am-5pm Mon-Thur; 10am-3pm Fri; 11am-5pm Sun. **Admission** $13; $10-$11 discounts; free under-5s. *Parking* free. **Credit** AmEx, DC, MC, V. **Map** p327 C4.
Founded in 1993 by the Simon Wiesenthal Center, a Jewish organisation named after the famous Nazi-hunter and devoted to combating anti-semitism and other forms of prejudice, the Museum of Tolerance was seen as a daring enterprise: a museum devoted to an abstract concept rather than a specific type of artefact. However, while it's an adventurous conceit, it's also extremely enlightening, not least because the museum's set-up is careful to leave it to the visitor to come up with their own definition of the word.

The main exhibit is an involving hour-long walk-through on the Holocaust, which blends taped narration with photos, film footage, personal testimonies, dioramas and World War II artefacts. At the start of the exhibit, you're given a 'passport' with a child's photograph; their fate is revealed to you at the end of the tour. You can explore the subject further on the computers in the Multimedia Center (the material is online at http://motlc.wiesenthal.com), via displays of other Holocaust documents, and in conversation with a number of World War II survivors, who regularly visit the museum to give talks and host discussions.

Elsewhere in the museum, the Tolerancenter is an interactive exhibit that aims to spur visitors into thinking about their own prejudices. As well as attracting members of the public, it's used as an educational aid by local schools, and as a part of LAPD officer training. The newest of the three major exhibits is Finding Our Families, Finding Ourselves, in which the likes of Carlos Santana, Maya Angelou and Billy Crystal tell of their heritage as immigrants and children of immigrants. Call or check online for details of special exhibits, talks and discussions.

Paley Center for Media

465 N Beverly Drive, at Santa Monica Boulevard (1-310 786 1000/www.paleycenter.org). Bus 4, 14, 16, 704/I-10, exit Robertson Boulevard north. **Open** noon-5pm Wed-Sun. **Admission** *Suggested donation* $10 $10; $5-$8 discounts. *Parking* free first 2hrs, then $1 every additional 30mins. **No credit cards. Map** p327 C3.
Formerly the Museum of Television & Radio but now renamed after its co-founder, former CBS president William S Paley, the Paley Center boasts a permanent collection of more than 140,000 TV and radio programmes. The collection is accessible to the public for on-site viewing (search the database and request a tape); the museum, designed by Getty Villa architect Richard Meier, also organises regular screenings, seminars and discussions in its theatre.

City Hall (450 N Crescent Drive, Beverly Hills) The police station in *Beverly Hills Cop*; Harrison University in *Old School*

Sightseeing

West Hollywood, Hollywood & Midtown

Movie stars are absent, but Hollywood and its neighbours retain their glamour.

Sightseeing

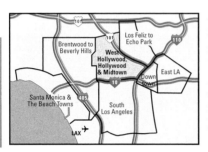

West Hollywood

Map p328

An independent city since 1984, West Hollywood is three bustling communities in one. Most famously, the tiny city – a little under two square miles – is the epicentre of gay and lesbian life in LA, with Santa Monica Boulevard as its main strip (*see pp243-247*). However, it's also home to the straight nightclubs of the fabled Sunset Strip, and, in the east, a community of immigrant Russians.

Sunset Strip, the stretch of W Sunset Boulevard that runs from Doheny Drive to Laurel Canyon, was developed in 1924. By the 1930s, it was Hollywood's playground: at the Trocadero and Ciro's, singers such as Lena Horne belted out sets for celebs, businessmen and mobsters. However, it was a very different type of nightlife that gave the Sunset Strip something approaching iconic status. Located at 8901 W Sunset, the **Whisky a Go-Go** (*see p258*) became the first discothèque on the West Coast when it opened in 1964, and was a hit almost from the moment it opened. Other clubs followed, and the area became the centre of LA youth culture during the 1960s, with everyone from the Byrds to the Doors playing regularly.

The area still has its nightlife, though it's all a bit forlorn these days. The **Comedy Store**, on the site where once stood Ciro's (No.8433; *see p224*), helped to break stars such as Robin Williams, but these days offers a less notable roster of comics. The venerable **Roxy** (No.9009;

see p258) and the younger **House of Blues** (No.8430; *see p254*) continue to host fine acts, but the Whisky long ago lost its spark. The Strip is otherwise kept alive by hotels such as the **Chateau Marmont** (No.8221; *see p58*).

West Hollywood's main points of interest during daylight hours are the eye-catchingly massive advertising billboards, some as big as the buildings to which they're attached. However, not all of those buildings catch the eye for the right reasons. West Hollywood is blighted by vast, ugly buildings that add little to the landscape except a profound sense of self-importance. The copper-coloured **Directors Guild of America** building (7920 W Sunset Boulevard, at Crescent Heights Boulevard), the blockish **Chrysalis Music Group** offices (8500 Melrose Avenue, at N La Cienega Boulevard) and the immense **Beverly Center** mall (8500 Beverly Boulevard; *see p188*) all dominate their respective horizons, but don't particularly impress with anything except their scale.

For all the hulking ghastliness of that trio of buildings, they're dwarfed by César Pelli's **Pacific Design Center** (8687 Melrose Avenue, at San Vicente Boulevard, 1-310 657 0800, www.pacificdesigncenter.com), a monstrous glass shed that's been generously nicknamed 'the Blue Whale'. A third new building is scheduled to join the existing blue and green behemoths in 2009, adding offices, a conference hall and two restaurants, but it's unlikely to redeem the centre's aesthetic. Built to house outlets for the interior design trade, the PDC is underused for its size, although **MoCA** (*see p116*; 1-310 289 5223) does leave its Downtown base to stage exhibitions here.

Away from the area's main roads, it's a different story. The residential streets of West Hollywood are cosy, densely packed and pleasingly free of pretence. A quick detour on wheels or on foot (as evidenced by the numerous dog-walkers, this is a pedestrian-friendly area) is an agreeable way to spend a half-hour or so. You might need a car to climb up steep **Sunset Plaza Drive**, but it's worth the effort simply to see how the other half live.

The secret gardens

One great surprise that LA holds for first-time visitors is its greenness. Some of the city's many iconic palm trees produce dates, the favourite food of the wild green parrots that can be heard screeching above Hollywood and points east. And those parrots know that LA is dotted with dozens of gardens, many of them the treasured retreats of locals.

Although it's run by UCLA, the **Hannah Carter Japanese Garden** (*see p89*) is not in Westwood but on a quiet street in nearby Bel Air. Through the heavy gate, you'll enter into a quiet world of exquisite, traditional Japanese landscaping. Paths meander over bridges and by waterfalls, with views of wooden tea houses, ancient statues and fat koi in cool ponds. Access to this amazingly peaceful spot is free to all who call ahead – visitor numbers are capped due to limited parking.

Just inland from the Pacific Coast Highway and easy to miss when you're rushing to catch the sunset, the mystical, mysterious **Self-Realization Fellowship Lake Shrine** (*see p75*) is run by a non-denominational order that welcomes visitors but doesn't proselytise to them. Set on a ten-acre site that was used as a film set during the silent era, the lovely gardens evoke old Hollywood: look out for the Dutch windmill chapel, the Mississippi

houseboat and a number of gliding swans. The East, meanwhile, is represented by a gilded lotus gate enclosing a shrine that contains some of Gandhi's ashes.

Few visitors to Frank Gehry's crumpled **Walt Disney Concert Hall** (*see p115 and p251*) realise that atop the structure stands a charming roof garden that affords views over the city. Designed by Melinda Taylor as a tribute to flower-loving patroness Lillian Disney, Walt's wife, it's stocked with seasonally flowering trees and colourful shrubbery, its meandering paths leading to a lotus-shaped Delftware mosaic fountain. A visit to the gardens reveals the surprisingly intimate core of a grand civic structure.

Not all of LA's secret gardens are open to just anyone. To tour Beachwood Canyon's unusual **Garden of Oz** (on Ledgewood Drive, not far from the Hollywood sign), you'll need to make friends with one of the select group of neighbours who hold a key, or be lucky enough to drop by when someone is already inside. Created by Gail Cottman with the help of a number of artists, the hilly site is so comprehensively covered with mosaic paths, sculptures, doll parts and loving messages that even peeking over the wall is a delightful sight.

Self-Realization Fellowship Lake Shrine.

Several small buildings are notable. The angular **Lloyd Wright Home & Studio** (858 N Doheny Drive) was designed by Frank's eldest son; it remains closed to the public. But the real gem, one of the city's best buildings, is at 835 N Kings Road: built as a live-work space by Rudolf Schindler, the extraordinary, secluded structure now houses the **MAK Center for Art & Architecture** (*see below*).

Given the MAK Center's architectural importance, it was hardly surprising when plans for a condo complex next door caused controversy when they were revealed in 2003. However, Lorcan O'Herlihy's sensitive designs gained planning approval, and **Habitat 825** (825 N Kings Road) was completed to great acclaim in 2007. O'Herlihy's also responsible for the more cocksure apartment complex at 1050 N Gardner Street, about a mile east of here.

MAK Center for Art & Architecture

Schindler House, 835 N Kings Road, between Waring & Willoughby Avenues (1-323 651 1510/ www.makcenter.com). Bus 10, 105/I-10, exit La Cienega Boulevard north. **Open** 11am-6pm Wed-Sun. *Tours* hourly 11.30am-2.30pm Sat, Sun. **Admission** $7; $6 discounts; free under-12s. Free to all 4-6pm Fri. **Map** p328 B2.
Constructed in 1922 by radical Austrian architect Rudolf Schindler, this landmark is a dazzling combination of concrete walls, redwood partitions, rooftop 'sleeping baskets' and outdoor living rooms. Tours of the modest house are offered on weekends, but, in keeping with Schindler's adventurousness, the building also hosts a variety of exhibitions, talks and concerts based on decidedly non-mainstream themes.

West Hollywood Convention & Visitors Bureau

Pacific Design Center, 8687 Melrose Avenue, at N San Vicente Boulevard (1-800 368 6020/1-310 289 2525/www.visitwesthollywood.com). **Open** 8.30am-5.30pm Mon-Fri. **Map** p328 A2.

Hollywood

Map p329

For years, tourists arrived in Hollywood expecting to walk on to a movie set: camera crews on every corner, paparazzi crowding the sidewalks. What they found was a shabby, glamour-free shambles. Granted, the floodlit paradise of filmic immortality conjured up by the name was the creation of imaginative press officers: movies haven't been filmed here for decades, and the continued use of its name as

shorthand for the movie industry is misleading. Still, few visitors were prepared for what they found. Word spread; people stopped coming.

Things have changed. Since the late 1990s, the city has made an effort to restore a little glitter to the area, and both tourists and locals have returned in their thousands. The regeneration has been without its critics – essentially, LA has done to parts of Hollywood what New York did to Times Square in the '90s. But the gripers have been outnumbered by moneyed night owls, savvy entrepreneurs, tourists and, tellingly, construction workers. Condo towers are springing up all over the area, as sure a sign as you'll find that Hollywood's resurgence is more than just a flash in the pan.

Hollywood Boulevard

The stretch of Hollywood Boulevard between La Brea Avenue and Vine Street was one of the city's seamier thoroughfares by the mid '90s, a decaying parade of adult theatres, souvenir stores and ne'er-do-wells. But now, re-dubbed the Hollywood Entertainment District after a makeover, it's once more a family-friendly tourist attraction with plenty of appeal.

The centrepiece of the regeneration is the four-storey **Hollywood & Highland** centre, an awkwardly designed but popular complex that's home to 40-plus high-end mall favourites (*see p189*), an upscale bowling alley (**Lucky Strike Lanes**; *see p272*), a vast nightclub (**Highlands**; *see p265*), the **Hollywood Pop Academy** (www.hollywoodpopacademy.com), the **Kodak Theatre** (*see p96*) and, connected at the rear, the **Renaissance Hollywood** hotel (*see p61*). However, perhaps the mall's greatest asset is its multi-level parking garage; the entrance to it is on Highland Avenue.

Hollywood & Highland is slick and modern. But for evidence of glamour, you'll need to head next door to the world-famous **Grauman's Chinese Theatre** (*see below and p230*). Indeed, the Hollywood buildings that exude the most star quality are the old cinemas: **El Capitan**, opposite Grauman's (No.6838), and the historic **Egyptian Theatre** (No.6712; *see p231*), home to the American Cinematheque. The **Hollywood Museum** (*see p96*) adds context, with extra glitz coming courtesy of the resurgent **Hollywood Roosevelt** (No.7000; *see p61*): built in 1927 and the host of the first Oscars, the hotel is once again a hot hangout. Continuing west, you'll find a trio of great old neon signs just past La Brea, with a pair of hotels (the **Hollywood Studio Inn & Suites** at No.7160 and the **Saharan Motor Hotel** at No.7212) sandwiching a strip club (the **Seventh Veil** at No.7180).

There's less glamour on Hollywood Boulevard to the east of Highland Avenue, where dull attractions (the **Hollywood Wax Museum** and **Ripley's Believe it or Not!**; *see pp96-97*) jostle for attention with souvenir shops, an adult theatre (the **Hollywood Cabaret** at No.6315) and a vast scientology centre. However, even this stretch is improving, with restaurants such as the **Geisha House** (No.6633) and bar-clubs including **Cinespace** (No.6356; *see p263*) joining 80-year-old restaurant **Musso & Frank Grill** (No.6667; *see p157*) and the vintage **Pantages Theatre** (No.6233; *see p278*). And on **Cahuenga Boulevard** between Hollywood and Sunset Boulevards, you'll find a string of pricey and, in some cases, exclusive new bars, restaurants and nightclubs. The Cahuenga Corridor, as it's known, has quickly become one of the most compact and popular nightlife districts in LA.

The area's resurgence as a residential quarter is most apparent at the corner of **Hollywood and Vine**, dominated by building work at present. Construction is well under way on a vast complex that will, when completed in 2009, hold a 300-room W Hotel, 500 condos and an array of shops. The 1929 **Equitable** office building, at the north-east corner of the intersection, and the former **Broadway** department store, at the south-west corner, are also being converted into apartments, and work has also started on a Palihouse hotel just north up Vine Street. Expect the construction teams to remain in residence until 2010.

All these new and newly converted buildings haven't quite overshadowed the 13-storey **Capitol Records Building** (1750 N Vine Street, just north of Hollywood Boulevard), a genuine Hollywood icon since it was completed in 1956. Instantly recognisable, it's shaped like a stack of records and topped with a stylus, reputedly the idea of songwriter Johnny Mercer and singer Nat 'King' Cole. EMI sold the building in 2006 but remain in residence; fears that it may be demolished or redeveloped have so far proven unfounded.

Grauman's Chinese Theatre

6925 Hollywood Boulevard, between N Orange Drive & N McCadden Place, Hollywood (1-323 464 8111/www.manntheatres.com). Metro Hollywood-Highland/bus 210, 212, 217, 310, LDHWH/US 101, exit Highland Avenue south. **Tickets** $11.25; $8.25-$9 discounts. **Credit** AmEx, Disc, DC, MC, V. **Map** p329 A1.

It's still a great place to catch a movie (*see p230*), but most people come to the Chinese Theatre for the hand and/or foot imprints of around 200 Hollywood stars. As legend has it, Norma Talmadge accidentally stepped into the wet cement outside the new building during construction; in response, theatre owner Sid Grauman fetched Mary Pickford and Douglas Fairbanks to repeat the 'mistake' with their feet and hands, beginning the tradition. The courtyard is usually choked with snap-happy tourists measuring their own extremities against the likes of John Wayne and Judy Garland; it's just a pity that its appeal is tempered by the tour hawkers and the ticket agents who clutter the forecourt.

The **Musso & Frank Grill**, Hollywood's oldest restaurant.

Streets of glory

From Bud 'Who's on first?' Abbott to bearded Texan bluesmen ZZ Top, more than 2,000 figures from the world of entertainment have been immortalised on the **Hollywood Walk of Fame** since actress Joanne Woodward received the first honour in 1960. Made of pink terrazzo inset with gold lettering and one of five symbols that denote the recipient's profession (film, TV, radio, music or stage), the stars line Hollywood Boulevard, between La Brea Avenue and Gower Street, and a stretch of Vine Street.

Stars are awarded by a mysterious committee convened through the Hollywood Chamber of Commerce; if your nomination is successful, you (or, more likely, your movie producers, TV network or record label) must stump up $25,000. Alongside huge names such as Paul Newman and Matt Damon sit a parade of forgotten actors, a wrestling promoter (Vince MacMahon, honoured in 2008), three dogs (Lassie, Rin Tin Tin and Strongheart, the latter solely remembered for stumbling into a hot studio light and dying in 1929) and a murderer (western swing musician Spade Cooley, who beat his wife to death in 1961).

Despite its quirks, the Hollywood Walk of Fame is one of LA's great glories, and precisely the landmark that Hollywood deserves. It is dazzling and bewildering, laughable and sentimental. But also, perhaps most pertinently, it is far, far too big, and offers the most blatant illustration of a truth that's dominated Hollywood for a century. If you're lucky, talent will take you to the top of your profession. But a big pile of cash, a bulging contacts book and a great agent will get you there quicker.

Hollywood Museum

1660 N Highland Avenue, between Hawthorn Avenue & Hollywood Boulevard (1-323 464 7776/ www.thehollywoodmuseum.com). Metro Hollywood-Highland/bus 210, 212, 217, 310, LDHWH/US 101, exit Highland Avenue south. **Open** 10am-5pm Thur-Sun. **Admission** $15; $12 discounts. **Credit** AmEx, DC, MC, V. **Map** p329 A2.

Designed as the Hollywood Fire & Safe Building in 1914, this building was converted in 1928 into a beauty salon by Max Factor. A refurbishment by Factor seven years later turned it into an art deco classic; it's now a museum dedicated to the movies. The ground floor has been decorated to resemble the original Factor shop, its walls lined with memorabilia related to stars of the 1930s, '40s and '50s. Out the back sits Cary Grant's gleaming 1965 Rolls-Royce. The top two floors bring things closer to the present day (Stallone's boxing gloves, Streisand-related goodies), while the basement holds a mock-up of Hannibal Lecter's cell from *The Silence of the Lambs*.

Hollywood Wax Museum

6767 Hollywood Boulevard, at N Highland Avenue (1-323 462 8860/www.hollywoodwax.com). Metro Hollywood-Highland/bus 210, 212, 217, 310, LDHWH/US 101, exit Highland Avenue south. **Open** 10am-midnight daily. **Admission** $15.95; $6.95-$13.95 discounts; free under-6s. *Joint ticket with Guinness World of Records* $17.95; $8.95 discounts; free under-6s. **Credit** AmEx, DC, Disc, MC, V. **Map** p329 A1.

Hollywood is pushing itself into the 21st century with vigour, but some attractions remain stuck in the past. The Hollywood Wax Museum harks back to days long past, when a poorly proportioned wax model of someone famous was liable to draw gasps of astonishment from fun-starved crowds. There's fun to be had trying to recognise the stars, but perhaps not 16 bucks' worth. Combined tickets are available with the **Guinness World of Records Museum** (No.6764, 1-323 462 5991) across the street.

Kodak Theatre

Hollywood & Highland, 6801 Hollywood Boulevard, at N Highland Avenue (1-323 308 6300/www.kodak theatre.com). Metro Hollywood-Highland/bus 210, 212, 217, 310, LDHWH/US 101, exit Highland Avenue south. **Open** Tours every 30mins *June-Aug* 10.30am-4pm daily. *Sept-May* 10.30am-2.30pm daily. **Admission** $15; $10 discounts; free under-5s. **Credit** AmEx, DC, MC, V. **Map** p329 A1.

The 3,300-seat home of the Academy Awards is a slick building that's under-used for the other 11 months of the year. That'll change in 2010, when the theatre is due to start hosting a year-round Cirque du Soleil show. In the meantime, it's open for pricey half-hour tours. Call ahead or check online before making the trip: on performance days, the theatre may not run its normal tour schedule.

Ripley's Believe it or Not!

6780 Hollywood Boulevard, at N Highland Avenue (1-323 466 6335/www.ripleys.com). Metro Hollywood-Highland/bus 210, 212, 217, 310, LDHWH/US 101, exit Highland Avenue south. **Open** *Summer* 10am-11pm Mon-Thur, Sun; 10am-midnight Fri, Sat. *Winter* 10am-10pm Mon-Thur, Sun; 10am-11pm Fri, Sat. **Admission** $12.99; $8.99 discounts; free under-5s. **Credit** AmEx, DC, MC, V. **Map** p329 A1.

This is one of many Ripley's museums around the US, and if you've been to any of the others, you can skip this. Indeed, even if you haven't been to any of the others, you can skip this, a gurning parade of bizarre 'facts' that stretches the definition of the word 'museum' to breaking point.

South of Hollywood Boulevard

Few visitors leave Hollywood Boulevard during their visit to Hollywood; few locals blame them. Still, though there's less obvious tourist appeal away from the main drag, it's a relief to escape the throngs and get into a neighbourhood with a little more dirt under its fingernails.

Walking two blocks south on Vine Street will take you to **Sunset Boulevard**, a formerly sleazy road (Hugh Grant met Divine Brown on the corner of Sunset and Courtney Avenue) that's a little nicer these days. The main attraction isn't even on Sunset: rather, it's the view from the intersection with Bronson Avenue, one of the best vantage points from which to see the **Hollywood sign** (*see p18*). South is the **Hollywood Forever Cemetery** (*see below*); nearby is **Paramount Studios**, the only working studio in Hollywood (*see p73*).

Back on Sunset, and heading west, the attractions are largely commercial. While the tourists wander Hollywood & Highland hoping to see a star, the in-the-know celeb-hunters are at the **ArcLight** cinemas (No.6360; *see p228*). A few blocks west sits the **Crossroads of the World** (No.6671), a formerly charming outdoor shopping plaza (now offices) built in 1936 that pre-dates LA's strip mall explosion by 50 years. Too bad its successors couldn't follow the example of its eye-catching mixture of English, French, Moorish and Spanish architecture.

There's more peculiar architecture a block south of Sunset at **1416 N La Brea Avenue**: these incongruous Tudor-style buildings now provide a home for Henson Productions, but for years were A&M Studios. Among the thousands of acts that recorded here down the decades are the Rolling Stones and the Carpenters, but its musical history is equalled

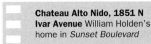

Chateau Alto Nido, 1851 N Ivar Avenue William Holden's home in *Sunset Boulevard*

by its cinematic past: its core was built in 1918 by Charlie Chaplin, who used it as his movie studio and whose footprints are (allegedly) visible in concrete outside Studio 3.

Hollywood Forever Cemetery

6000 Santa Monica Boulevard, between N Gower Street & N Van Ness Avenue (1-323 469 1181/www.hollywoodforever.com). Bus 4, 704/US 101, exit Santa Monica Boulevard west. **Open** *Summer* 8am-7pm daily. *Winter* 8am-6pm daily. **Admission** free. *Parking* free. **Map** p329 C2.

The owners of Hollywood Forever have come in for criticism for promoting the place as a tourist attraction, but any place that houses the remains of such celluloid luminaries as Cecil B DeMille and Jayne Mansfield would probably become one regardless. It's also the resting place of Rudolph Valentino; legend has it that a mysterious 'Woman in Black' still stalks the cemetery, mourning the demise of Hollywood's original lover man. Mel Blanc's headstone says 'That's All, Folks!'; Douglas Fairbanks Sr and Jr are in a huge tomb in front of a lake guarded by a fountain and three black swans. William Andrews Clark Jr, founder of the LA Philharmonic, has an even bigger mausoleum in the middle of a lake. For film screenings here, *see p234. Photo p98.*

The Hollywood Hills

For perspective on the **Hollywood Hills**, the fag-end of the Santa Monica Mountains that divide LA from the San Fernando Valley, take a ride along soaring, precarious **Mulholland Drive**. A mix of Hollywood-style spectacle and wild rural bramble that offers views in every direction, the road springs to life above the Hollywood Bowl (there's an amazing overlook at this eastern end), follows the crest of the hills and the mountains, and ends in Malibu, with a seven-mile stretch in the middle that's closed to traffic (Dirt Mulholland). Along its length, buildings are wedged into hillsides or perched on slopes, all the better to enjoy the amazing sunrises and sunsets. Scenic overlooks dot the roadside, offering fresh perspectives on the city and its suburbs. But Mulholland Drive is at its most mysterious after dark, with no street lights to guide the way and the city shimmering below like the treasure at the bottom of the ocean. It's LA's most spectacular road.

North of the West Hollywood strip, **Runyon Canyon Park** is a strip of canyon wilderness running from Mulholland Drive to Franklin Avenue (entrances on Fuller Avenue and Vista Street; www.laparks.org). As well as coyote

Sightseeing

Hollywood Forever Cemetery. *See p97.*

and deer, it contains the foundations of a Frank Lloyd Wright pool house and the recumbent but intact Outpost sign, sister real-estate billboard to the Hollywood sign. Trails of varying lengths and difficulty lead to 360-degree viewpoints.

Between Runyon Canyon and US 101 is the architecturally affecting **Hollywood Bowl** (*see below and p251*), best experienced at a concert but open year-round. Across US 101, the Hollywood Reservoir provides a chance to muse on LA's debt to William Mulholland. To the east are the hills of **Griffith Park** (*see pp105-107*); one way to access them is to hire a horse from **Sunset Ranch** (*see p273*).

Hollywood Bowl Museum

2301 N Highland Avenue, at US 101 (1-323 850 2058/www.hollywoodbowl.com). Bus 156/US 101, exit Highland Avenue north. **Open** *Mid June-mid Sept* 10am-showtime Tue-Sat; 4pm-showtime Sun. *Mid Sept-mid June* 10am-5pm Tue-Fri. **Admission** free. *Parking* free.
This fine little museum presents a lively account of the Hollywood Bowl's history, through archival film footage, audio clips, photography and all manner of other memorabilia. Rock + Bowl, a new exhibit, tracks the history of rock music at the venue.

Hollywood Reservoir & Dog Park

Lake Hollywood Drive, Hollywood Hills. Bus 156/ US 101, exit Barham Boulevard north.

Formed in 1924 when the Mulholland Dam was built, the Hollywood Reservoir was a landmark piece of engineering. Holding 2.5 billion US gallons, it provided the drinking water to facilitate the city's spread, piped in from 300 miles away through the Owens River Aqueduct system. Now most of its water storage is underground, but the pretty lake attracts runners, walkers and the occasional cyclist to its waterside trails, which offer a fantastic view of the Hollywood sign. Tucked behind the reservoir up Beachwood Canyon is the Hollywood Dog Park.

Fairfax District

Map p328

Although LA's first major Jewish community settled in Boyle Heights, the stretch of **Fairfax Avenue** between Beverly Boulevard and Melrose Avenue has been the city's main Jewish drag since the '40s. Grocers, butcher's shops, restaurants and bakeries line the street, nicknamed the 'Kosher Canyon'; all are excellent, and, naturally, almost all are closed on Saturdays. Open 24-7, however, is the legendary **Canter's Deli** (No.419; *see p158*), a decades-old kosher restaurant, deli and bakery.

Just south of the Beverly-Fairfax intersection lies **CBS Television City**, a studio complex built in 1952 and still in use today. Looking at it, you'd never guess the site once held a major sporting stadium: built in 1939, Gilmore Field was home to the minor-league Hollywood Stars baseball team until their demise in 1957, when CBS bought the lot and razed the ballpark. Next door, at the junction of W 3rd Street and Fairfax Avenue, is the tag-team retail experience of the **Grove** (*see p189*) and the **Farmers Market** (*see p159*).

One of LA's most popular malls, the Grove is dominated by all the usual chains. However, its spacey, open-air layout helps make it one of the most pleasant shopping centres in the city. The Farmers Market, meanwhile, predates the Grove by more than 60 years. Although the farmers who set up here in 1934 have long since moved on (*see p203*), food still dominates this wonderfully old-fashioned commercial corner. Some of the stalls here sell fruit, fudge and sundry temptations; others are full-service food counters, hawking everything from pizza to gumbo to cheerily ravenous crowds.

There's plenty of excellent shopping nearby. To the north, the stretch of **Melrose Avenue** around Fairfax Avenue is lined with small independent stores, with fashion dominating the landscape. And to the south, the stretch of W 3rd Street between Fairfax and the Beverly Center (*see p188*) holds several dozen small retailers selling everything from travel books to pet toys. For more, *see p192* **Who's on 3rd?**

Miracle Mile & Midtown

Map p328

Stretching along Wilshire Boulevard between Fairfax and La Brea Avenues, the **Miracle Mile** got its nickname from its astonishing commercial growth during the 1920s (*see p35*). Although many of the old buildings remain, including some real art deco glories, the street doesn't live up to its old moniker any more. The department stores that made its nickname have long since closed, as have smaller landmarks such as iconic Googie diner **Johnie's** (No.6101).

Still, the Miracle Mile is far from deserted, and is even making something of a comeback. The main attraction is the **Los Angeles County Museum of Art** (*see p100*), currently enjoying a deserved popularity spike after the 2008 opening of a new contemporary art wing; it's been pinned in recent years by a number of small commercial galleries, including several in the building at 6150 Wilshire Boulevard (*see p238*). Also here are four other very different museums: the **Petersen Automotive Museum** (*see p101*), the **Craft & Folk Art Museum** (*see below*), the **A+D Museum** (*see below*) and, best of all, the **Page Museum at the La Brea Tar Pits** (*see p101*), which explores the area's unexpected natural quirks.

A+D Museum

5900 Wilshire Boulevard, at S Spaulding Avenue (1-310 659 2445/http://aplusd.org). Bus 20, 217, 218, 720/I-10, exit Fairfax Avenue north. **Open** call for details. **Admission** $5; $2.50 discounts. **No credit cards.** **Map** p328 C4.

Having spent several years bouncing around the city, the A+D Museum – 'A' for architecture, 'D' for design – is now permanently ensconced at this building on the Miracle Mile. Although the location seems permanent, exhibitions are held far from regularly (always call or check online before setting out). However, they're generally interesting as and when they do occur.

Craft & Folk Art Museum

5814 Wilshire Boulevard, between S Curson & S Stanley Avenues (1-323 937 4230/www.cafam.org). Bus 20, 217, 218, 720/I-10, exit Fairfax Avenue north. **Open** 11am-5pm Tue, Wed, Fri; 11am-7pm Thur; noon-6pm Sat, Sun. **Admission** $5; $3 discounts; free under-12s. Free 1st Wed of mth. **Credit** AmEx, DC, MC, V. **Map** p328 C4.

Since being saved from oblivion by the city, which took it over in 1998 after financial troubles, LA's only public showcase devoted to functional and informal art has broadened its programming. Shows could take in anything from Venetian glassmaking to American printmaking, the circus-themed dioramas of Sonny King to a retrospective of work by Hungarian designer Eva Zeisel.

The great escape

A mere 25 minutes from the billboards and bright lights of Tinseltown sits a community that feels like it's a world away. Tucked into the Santa Monica Mountains, **Topanga** feels more like a forgotten rural outpost than a suburb of a major city. For decades, the canyon's calmness and natural beauty has attracted city residents looking for a more peaceful existence. In recent years, increasing property prices have moulded a community that's an interesting juxtaposition of modern money and old hippie values.

On the east side of the canyon is the 11,000-acre Topanga State Park, where you'll find 36 miles of trails and, on Sundays, free guided nature walks (Jan-June only; www.tc-docents.org). On days when the marine layer hangs over the West Side, Topanga basks in sunshine; the views from the top, across the Pacific, are magnificent. But even outside the park, Topanga doesn't feel like LA. The shops and restaurants, notably the well-established **Inn of the Seventh Ray** (*see p145*), are relaxed, mellow and free of velvet ropes.

Topanga has long been a haven for stars wanting to escape the Hollywood spotlight. In the '50s, Will Geer (Grandpa in *The Waltons*) sought refuge here after being victimised by the McCarthy blacklistings. Woody Guthrie formed an artists' colony here. And in the '60s, musicians including Neil Young and Gram Parsons called the area home.

Spring and summer offer a spread of culture. Over Memorial Day weekend (end of May), **Topanga Days** (www.topangadays.com) offers music and art; June's **Topanga Canyon Studio Tour** (www.topangacanyongallery.com) showcases 40 local artists; August's **Topanga Film Festival** (www.topangafilm festival.com) offers two days of shorts; and the open-air **Will Geer Theatricum Botanicum** stages plays from June to October (*see p280*).

Only one road runs through the area: Topanga Canyon Boulevard, which connects with Mulholland Drive in Calabases and then runs through Topanga to Pacific Palisades. This relative isolation, though, is just how the locals like it.

Los Angeles County Museum of Art

*5905 Wilshire Boulevard, at S Spaulding Avenue
(1-323 857 6000/www.lacma.org). Bus 20, 217, 218,
720/I-10, exit Fairfax Avenue north.* **Open** noon-
8pm Mon, Tue, Thur; noon-9pm Fri; 11am-8pm Sat,
Sun. **Admission** *General admission* $12; $8
discounts; free under-17s. Pay what you wish after
5pm daily. Free to all 2nd Tue of mth. *Special
exhibitions* prices vary. *Parking* $7. **Credit** AmEx,
DC, MC, V. **Map** p328 C4.

While LACMA's collections have long been the most
impressive in the city, the 20-acre complex of buildings in which they've been housed has been quite
the reverse. A bewildering jumble of architectural
styles blighted still further by abysmally poor signage, they never really did the artworks justice.

At last, though, things have improved. Funding
difficulties and public outrage forced the museum
to abandon Rem Koolhaas's original plans to rebuild
almost the entire complex from scratch in 2002.
However, Renzo Piano's subsequent blueprint for
a less dramatic and less expensive redevelopment
of the museum did get the go-ahead, and has already
yielded dividends. In 2008, phase one of the renovations were at last completed, and the museum is
already a lot more visitor-friendly.

It all starts with the new entrance: the **BP Grand
Pavilion**, which at last gives the museum a proper
focal point. The new entrance included the installation of Chris Burden's *Urban Light*, a piece made up
of 202 cast-iron street lamps gathered from around
LA, restored to working order and then installed in
a grid network.

But the most exciting development is the newly
constructed **Broad Contemporary Art Museum**
(widely known as BCAM), funded by LA philanthropists Eli and Edythe Broad and now home to a
dazzling selection of modern work. Spread over
three floors, the selection of pieces on display is
strong on American artists – there's a very impressive Richard Serra piece on the first floor; Cindy
Sherman and Jenny Holzer are among the artists represented on the second floor; and the third floor,
enlightened by a glass ceiling, holds classic pieces
by Andy Warhol, Robert Rauschenberg, Jasper
Johns and local artist Ed Ruscha.

The **Ahmanson Building** has also been spruced
up as part of the renovation work, and the collections reorganised. The modern collection on the
ground floor holds works by the likes of Picasso,
Mondrian, Klee and Kandinsky; upstairs, the Greek
and Roman art collections are now housed in a space
that benefits from huge picture windows and, thus,
lots of natural light. The American art collection has
also been reinstalled on the second floor of the Art
of the Americas building, where you'll also find the
Latin American collection.

Despite all this activity, the work is far from complete. Phase two of the transformation calls for the
renovation of **LACMA West**, housed in the old
May Co department store building at the corner of
Wilshire and Fairfax but strangely underused over
the last few years, and the construction of a new,
single-storey building behind BCAM that will house
temporary exhibits. And phase three provisionally
calls for the renovation of the galleries untouched
by phases one and two, which at present contain an
array of European art (including Impressionist and
post-Impressionist pieces by the likes of Cézanne,
Gauguin and Degas), a world-renowned collection
of Islamic art, plenty of pieces from Africa and, in
the **Japanese Art Pavilion**, all manner of delightful pieces from the far east. The precise plans for

phase three have yet to be finalised and may require the temporary closure of some galleries – call ahead if your interest is limited to a particular area.

The permanent collections are supplemented by some excellent temporary shows and a very strong programme of events, among them film screenings and plenty of free music. Full details of all events, including the variety of daily tours, are available on the museum's website

Page Museum at the La Brea Tar Pits

5801 Wilshire Boulevard, between S Stanley & S Curson Avenues (1-323 934 7243/www.tarpits.org). Bus 20, 217, 218, 720/I-10, exit Fairfax Avenue north. **Open** 9.30am-5pm Mon-Fri; 10am-5pm Sat, Sun. **Admission** $7; $2-$4.50 discounts; free under-5s. Free 1st Tue of mth. *Parking* $6 with validation. **Credit** AmEx, DC, Disc, MC, V. **Map** p328 C4.

Back in 1875, a group of amateur palaeontologists discovered animal remains in the pits at Rancho La Brea, which bubbled with asphalt from a petroleum lake under what is now Hancock Park. Some 130 years later, the pros are still at work here, having dragged more than 3.5 million fossils from the mire in the intervening years. Some are up to 40,000 years old; the museum estimates that about 10,000 animals, dipping their heads in search of water before becoming trapped in the sticky asphalt that bubbles from the ground, met their deaths here.

Many of these specimens are now on display in this delightfully old-fashioned museum, which can't have changed much since it opened in 1972. Interactivity is limited to several windows on to the labs where scientists work on bone preservation; the bulk of the museum is made up of simple, instructive displays of items found in the pits. Most are bones – of jackrabbits, gophers, a 160lb bison, skunks and a 15,000lb Columbian mammoth, plus an extraordinary wall of 400 wolf skulls – though there are also early cave drawings and human accoutrements such as bowls and hair pins. Outside, the pits still bubble with black goo; in summer, you can watch palaeontologists at work in the excavation of Pit 91 and inhale the nasty tang of tar in the air.

Petersen Automotive Museum

6060 Wilshire Boulevard, at N Fairfax Avenue (1-323 964 6315/1-323 930 2277/www.petersen.org). Bus 20, 217, 218, 720/I-10, exit Fairfax Avenue north. **Open** 10am-6pm Tue-Sun. **Admission** $10; $3-$5 discounts; free under-5s. *Parking* $8. **Credit** AmEx, DC, MC, V. **Map** p328 C4.

The Miracle Mile was the first commercial development in LA designed expressly for the benefit of drivers, and so this former department store makes an apt home for this museum of automobile culture. The story of how LA – and much of the west coast – was built around the needs of drivers is a fascinating and instructive tale. Unfortunately, the Petersen Museum doesn't tell it in any great detail, preferring instead to dazzle visitors with an admittedly impressive collection of autos from the last century.

Some of the vehicles wear their history with pride: a maroon 1942 Lincoln Continental, a delivery truck from Culver City's iconic Helms Bakery, even an old Vincent motorcycle. Others look ahead: Batmobiles from both the original TV series and the Tim Burton movies, a taxi designed by Syd Mead for *Blade Runner*. While the life-size dioramas of garages and diners evoke the early days of the US car obsession, the museum misses its chance to tell a story that really warrants telling. But the cars are lovely, and the themed temporary exhibitions are often a treat.

Works by (from left) Lichtenstein, Burden, Warhol and Koons at **LACMA**.

Hancock Park

Map p329

A handsome residential neighbourhood dating back to 1910 (and not to be confused with the park of the same name, west on Wilshire Boulevard), **Hancock Park** is home to some of LA's most palatial mansions, at least outside Beverly Hills and Bel Air. Historically an Anglo enclave, Hancock Park excluded blacks and Jews (who moved west) until 1948, when Nat 'King' Cole became the first African American to move to the neighbourhood. He wasn't to be the last, but Hancock Park remains a bastion of wealthy middle-class Anglo values and attitudes.

Bounded by Wilshire Boulevard and Van Ness, Highland and Melrose Avenues, the area is at its best at Christmas, when homeowners try to outdo each other with decorative displays of festive jollity. Some are delightful, subtle strings of fairy-lights highlighting the perfect geometry of these expensive homes. Others, though, are more demonstrative, such as **Youngwood Court** (south-east corner of W 3rd Street and S Muirfield Road). The 20-plus replicas of Michelangelo's *David*, arranged in a semi-circle around the front lawn, catch the eye year-round. But at Christmas, when the home is covered in lights and the statues are topped with Santa hats, it's a preposterous sight.

The area's main commercial drag is **Larchmont Boulevard**, between Beverly

Ghouls' paradise

On the whole, LA is safer than many other big US cities. But when it comes to violent celebrity deaths, it's off the radar. Over the decades, dozens of stars have expired in the city, but it's the murders that have the public clamouring for every detail. Murder happens on a grand scale here: you live big, you die big. And, in many cases, you die young.

Probably the most famous murders in LA history occurred on the night of 8 August 1969, when five people – including actress **Sharon Tate**, wife of film director Roman Polanski – were slain by hippie followers of self-styled guru Charles Manson. The house where the murders took place, at 10050 Cielo Drive (off Benedict Canyon Drive, north of Beverly Hills), was demolished in 1994; the property that now stands on the site is numbered 10066. The following night, Leno and Rosemary LaBianca were murdered by members of Manson's 'Family' at their home at 3301 Waverly Drive, Los Feliz (later renumbered 3311). Their connection to Manson? Simply that, a year earlier, he'd attended a party at the house next door.

A quarter of a century later, another brutal murder made headlines. This time, though, the celebrity was not the victim but the accused. On the night of 12 June 1994, Nicole Brown Simpson and her friend Ronald Goldman were stabbed to death at Simpson's house at 875 (now 879) S Bundy Drive in Brentwood. Five days later, football star, actor and Nicole's ex-husband **OJ Simpson** was arrested and then charged with their murders. Simpson was found not guilty in 1995, but was later deemed liable in a civil trial.

As well as the famous, there are the forgotten. *Rebel Without A Cause* star **Sal Mineo** was knifed to death during a botched robbery in his garage at 8563 Holloway Drive, just off the Sunset Strip, on 12 February 1976. Two decades later, actor **Haing S Ngor** – who survived life under the Khmer Rouge in Cambodia, and later won an Oscar for his performance in 1995's *The Killing Fields* – was murdered in an apparent robbery-gone-wrong outside his home at 945 N Beaudry Avenue, Chinatown, on 25 February 1996.

Some of LA's most notorious murders remain unsolved. Case in point: the drive-by shooting of rapper **Biggie Smalls**, aka the Notorious BIG, outside the Petersen Automotive Museum (*see p101*) on 9 March 1997. In 2007, Smalls' relatives filed a wrongful death suit against the City of Los Angeles, claiming they deliberately concealed the identity of – and failed to pursue – the killers. And then, of course, there's legendary record producer **Phil Spector**, accused of murdering waitress and B-movie actress Lana Clarkson at his 'Pyrenees Castle' in Alhambra (1700 Grand View Drive) on 3 February 2003. Spector was brought to court in 2007, but proceedings ended in a mistrial; a second trial was due to begin in late 2008.

Deaths such as these continue to generate both intrigue and revenue. Books roll off the presses, conspiracy theories swirl the internet, and guided tours of famous death sites have become a major tourist attraction. Perhaps the city's aspiring stars should take note: you might well end up more famous in death than in life.

Boulevard and W 1st Street and informally known as **Larchmont Village**. A little snatch of Main Street middle America in the heart of Los Angeles, the two-block stretch is lined with bijou restaurants, antique shops and the like. Some are chains but most are independently owned, and many are housed in handsome buildings that date back to the 1920s.

Koreatown & around

Map p329 & p330

Roughly bordered by Wilshire and Pico Boulevards, and N Western and N Vermont Avenues, **Koreatown** has made a comeback since being torched in the riots of 1992. Tensions between the Korean and African American communities (and, to a lesser extent, the area's Central American population) haven't entirely abated. However, an accord of sorts seems to have been reached, especially as blacks are perhaps now more concerned with their grievances against Latinos.

Korean businesses are still visible: some predating the riots, others established only in the last decade. Banks, men's clubs and shop-front grocers abound along Pico and Olympic Boulevards, and the area is dotted with Korean restaurants such as **Soot Bull Jeep** (3136 W 8th Street; see p161). However, despite its name, the district's character comes more from the Latin Americans who now outnumber the Koreans by around four to one. Among Anglos, **El Cholo** (1121 S Western Avenue) is the most popular Mexican restaurant, but you'll find more authentic food at colourful **Guelaguetza** (3337½ W 8th Street); for both, see p161.

Wilshire Boulevard and N Western Avenue, Koreatown's north-western corner, is dominated by the **Wiltern Center**. A green art deco pile built in 1931, it lingered in a state of advanced decay during much of the 1970s and '80s before being rescued and turned into a performing arts and commercial centre. The **Wiltern** (see p255) hosts rock shows and club nights; fans meet before or after for 'food and grog' at the **HMS Bounty** (3357 Wilshire Boulevard; see p183), a convivial gathering place for local soaks.

Across the street from the Bounty sits the site of the old Ambassador Hotel (No.3400, www.theambassadorhotel.com), a once-glamorous resort built in the 1920s but known to most as the site of Robert F Kennedy's

assassination. Despite numerous protests, the hotel was demolished in 2006 to make way for a new high school. However, another landmark has survived the wrecking ball: **Bullocks Wilshire** (No.3050), one of the first department stores to open outside Downtown (in 1929), has been transformed into a law school.

This area is slowly growing more residential, as prospective homebuyers look for bargains within easy reach of expensive Downtown. At the north-eastern corner of Wilshire and Vermont stands a vast new apartment complex, complete with all mod cons on the inside but something of an eyesore from the street. Unremarkable save for its slanted edges, it's a deeply inelegant block.

Westlake

Map p330

Two parks anchor the down-at-heel area of Westlake just west of Downtown: **Lafayette Park** (on Wilshire Boulevard, by the junction of S Hoover Street), and its larger neighbour, **MacArthur Park** (also on Wilshire, between S Alvarado and S Park View Streets). For years populated chiefly by gang members, drug dealers and the homeless, MacArthur Park is safer now than it's been for a while. Its former grandeur is only fleetingly apparent, even after the restoration of its lake and 500-foot (150-metre) high water spout, but it's still not difficult to see how the park could have inspired Jimmy Webb to pen his epic (if, to be honest, somewhat nonsensical) song in its honour.

If you'd like to leave a cake out in the rain here, your best bet is to head to **Langer's Delicatessen** (704 S Alvarado Street, 1-213 483 8050): considered by many to have the best pastrami sandwich in town, it also has a kerbside takeaway service for customers too scared to park their cars on the surrounding mean streets. Burger fans should seek out **Cassell's** (3266 W 6th Street; see p160).

Grier Musser Museum

403 S Bonnie Brae Street, between W 4th & W 5th Streets (1-213 413 1814/www.griermussermuseum. com). Metro Westlake-MacArthur/bus 18, 200/US 101, exit Alvarado Street south. **Open** noon-4pm Wed-Sat; reservations required. **Admission** $10; $5-$7 discounts. *Parking* free. **No credit cards.** Map p330 C6.

This Victorian house, located on an unremarkable residential street just north-east of MacArthur Park, has been maintained to reflect its origins, and is thus stuffed almost to bursting with antique fix-tures, fittings and general ephemera. Special events, including annual presentations at Hallowe'en and Christmas, keep things ticking over.

510 S Lucerne Boulevard, Hancock Park The eventual home of Samantha and Darrin in the film version of *Bewitched*

Los Feliz to Echo Park

The heart of LA's East Side continues to move up in the world.

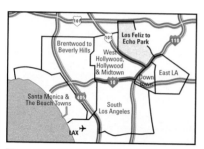

Los Feliz

Map p330

Desirable but never flashy, cool rather than fashionable, Los Feliz is a fluid melding of yuppie demand, hipster distinction and immigrant influence. Drive around the blocks leading to Griffith Park and you'll find huge mansions, luscious flora and fauna and signs from the local fire department directing you not to indulge in cigarettes while 'in the hills'. Life moves at a mellower pace here, and not solely due to the multitude of speed bumps.

Los Feliz is named in honour of José Feliz, a soldier who claimed the area in the 19th century and whose family held on to the district until they lost it 50 years later in a legal snafu. The area housed a number of film studios in the silent era: a set for DW Griffith's *Intolerance* stood at the Sunset Boulevard and Hillhurst Avenue site now occupied by the single-screen, Egyptian-flavoured **Vista** cinema. Walking north-west from here up Hollywood Boulevard will lead you past a scattering of shops towards **Barnsdall Art Park** (*see below*).

The stretch of **Vermont Avenue** that runs north of here, between bustling Hollywood Boulevard and bucolic Franklin Avenue, is one of Los Feliz's two main streets. It's a very pedestrian-friendly area, its hipster boutiques and eateries best approached on foot. Shops include fashion favourites **SquaresVille** (No.1800; *see p198*) and **Y-Que** (No.1770), and 'fiercely independent' (their words) bookstore

4616 Greenwood Place, Los Feliz Otherwise known as *Melrose Place*

Skylight (No.1818; *see p190*); the pick of the eating options is **Fred 62** (No.1850; *see p162*); and there's entertainment of sorts at the **Dresden Room** (No.1760; *see p183*), where you'll find ultra-campy lounge duo Marty and Elayne. The arty vibe is completed by the **Los Feliz 3 Cinemas** (No.1822, 1-323 664 2169).

Parallel to Vermont Avenue lies **Hillhurst Avenue**, a similarly wanderable stretch of road dotted with pleasing shops and approachable eateries, such as Carol Young's smart, handsome and all-organic **Undesigned** clothing boutique (No.1953½, 1-323 663 0088, www.undesigned. com), the **Alcove Café & Bakery** (No.1929, 1-323 644 0100, www.alcovecafe.com) and the smart **Vinoteca Farfalla** (No.1968, 1-323 661 8070, www.viontecafarfalla.com).

The residential streets in Los Feliz are almost all handsome, but a few properties stand out. One is Frank Lloyd Wright's **Ennis-Brown House** (2655 Glendower Avenue, north-east of Vermont Avenue, www.ennishouse.org), a boxily exotic concrete construction from 1924 that suffered horrible damage in the 1994 earthquake. Not far away but in rather better shape, Richard Neutra's International Modern **Lovell House** (4616 Dundee Drive) was built in 1929, but it's most famous for its starring role 70 years later in *LA Confidential*. Slightly further east, at **4053 Woking Way**, the fairytale structure just visible behind high walls and greenery was the home of Walt Disney from 1932 until 1949.

Barnsdall Art Park & Hollyhock House

4800 Hollywood Boulevard, between Edgemont Street & Vermont Avenue (Barnsdall Art Park www.barnsdallartpark.com/Hollyhock House 1-323 644 6269, www.hollyhockhouse.net). Metro Sunset-Vermont/bus 26, 204, 754, LDH/US 101, exit Sunset Boulevard east. **Open** *Hollyhock House tours* hourly, 12.30-3.30pm Wed-Sun. **Admission** *Hollyhock House tours* $7; $3 discounts; free under-12s. **No credit cards. Map** p330 A2.

After philanthropist Aline Barnsdall bought this cute little hill during World War I, she engaged Frank Lloyd Wright to build her a group of buildings at its summit. The complex was designed to include a cinema, a theatre and an array of artists' studios alongside Hollyhock House, Barnsdall's proposed home, but it was never completed. Judging by the speed with which Barnsdall moved elsewhere (she left the house in 1927, just four years after moving in), she was no great fan of Wright's work.

When she left Hollyhock House, Barnsdall gave the buildings and the land to the city on the premise that they be used as a public art park. More than eight decades later, the site still fulfils that role, with exhibitions in a variety of different gallery spaces. And following renovation work earlier in the decade, tours of the house are now offered five days a week. Reservations aren't required unless you're travelling in a group of ten or more people.

Griffith Park

Back in 1896, mining tycoon Griffith J Griffith donated 3,015 acres (five square miles) of land to the city for use as a public park. Expanded down the decades with other land donations and purchases, **Griffith Park** (*photo p218*) is now the largest city-run park in the US (five times the size of New York's Central Park), its vastness separating Los Feliz and the Hollywood Hills from Glendale and Burbank.

It's an immense, dramatic place. Some patches are flat, packed on warm weekends with picnickers, football-tossers, drumming circles and Frisbee-throwers. Other sections have been civilised by golf courses, tennis courts, soccer pitches and even the occasional museum. However, despite much-criticised plans to develop parts of Griffith Park with aerial tramways, multi-level parking garages and an array of commercial activity, supported by controversial local city councilman Tom LaBonge, it remains wild, rugged and untamed. The downside? It's prone to occasional but potentially destructive wildfires: in 2007, a major blaze devastated roughly one-quarter of the park. But such incidents are mercifully rare.

Despite the recent fires, the 53 miles of hiking trails offer far more variety than you'd expect from an urban park. One of the most popular trails is the half-hour schlep from Griffith Observatory to the 1,625-foot (495-metre) peak of Mount Hollywood, and not without good reason: the views from the top are awesome, the city spreadeagled around you in all its hazy majesty. Details of the park's trails can be obtained from the **Ranger Station** in the park's south-east corner (4730 Crystal Springs Drive), but be warned: the current hiking maps are poor. You might be better off joining one of the **Sierra Club**'s evening walks around the park (*see p272*), which run year-round and are especially wonderful under moonlit skies.

Away from the trails, the park's man-made attractions include the **Los Angeles Zoo**, the **Griffith Observatory**, the **Museum of the American West** and the open-air **Greek Theatre** (*see p253*). The gorgeous 1926 **Merry-Go-Round**, between the Los Feliz entrance and the zoo, is open daily in summer and weekends in winter (1-323 665 3051). The opening hours of the other attractions mentioned above vary; see the reviews below for individual details. However, regardless of the season, Griffith Park itself is open from 6am to 10pm every day. For more information, call 1-323 913 4688 or see www.laparks.org.

Griffith Observatory. *See p106.*

Go ape at **Los Angeles Zoo**.

Autry National Center: Museum of the American West

4700 Western Heritage Way, opposite LA Zoo, Griffith Park (1-323 667 2000/www.autrynational center.org). Bus 96/I-5, exit Zoo Drive west. **Open** 10am-5pm Tue-Sun. **Admission** $9; $3-$5 discounts; free under-3s. *Parking* free. **Credit** AmEx, DC, MC, V.

You might expect this Griffith Park museum to be a kitschy exploration of the life and works of the famous singing cowboy. However, though there's often some sort of Autry memorabilia on display in the foyer, it's actually a very engaging exploration of the western US, outlining its history and detailing the myths that came to surround it.

The museum is bigger than it looks, spread over two floors with permanent exhibits on the right and temporary shows on the left. The ground-floor galleries offer a collection of iconographic cowboy art, plus ephemera from the golden age of the western. And the downstairs galleries tell the story of Western migration by different communities, with illuminating exhibits on how they lived, what they hunted, where they settled and the like. Due homage is paid to the Spanish *vaqueros*, the original pioneering cowboys of the Old West whom Hollywood

> **Cave at Bronson Canyon, Griffith Park** In the 1960s TV series, the Batcave

largely wrote out of the history books. However, fans of Western myth and legend will enjoy catching sight of Doc Holliday's revolver from the shootout at the OK Corral, John Wesley Hardin's business card (complete with imitation bulletholes) and the 200-strong Colt Firearms Collection.

However, the next few years may see a slew of changes at the site. The Autry board has announced plans to expand the museum's floor space by 70 per cent as part of a $100-million programme of redevelopments, creating room for a selection of the Native American artefacts that were formerly displayed at the now-closed Southwest Museum of the American Indian in Mount Washington. If the plans get the go-ahead, part or all of the museum may close temporarily during the construction work: call or check online before setting out. The new galleries are provisionally scheduled to open in 2011.

Griffith Observatory

2800 E Observatory Road (1-213 473 0800/ www.griffithobs.org). Bus 180, 181, 380, then a long walk/I-5, exit Los Feliz Boulevard west. **Open** *Observatory* noon-10pm Tue-Fri; 10am-10pm Sat, Sun. *Planetarium* 8 shows, 12.45-8.45pm Tue-Fri; 10 shows, 10.45am-8.45pm Sat, Sun. **Admission** *Observatory* free. *Planetarium* $7; $3-$5 discounts; free under-5s (only admitted to 1st show daily). *Parking* free. **Map** p330 A1.

'If every person could look through that telescope,' declared Griffith J Griffith, 'it would revolutionise the world.' More than 70 years after this iconic building opened, the world remains unrevolutionised, and the city smog means that the views are not as crystal-clear as they were in Griffith's day. However, after a five-year programme of renovations at the observatory, the 12in (30.5cm) Zeiss refracting telescope is once again open to the public, providing the crowning glory for this wonderful old landmark.

You could comfortably spend a few hours here just taking in the exhibits and the shows. The ground floor holds the Hall of the Sky and Hall of the Eye, a pair of complementary displays that focus on humans' relationship to the stars; a Foucault pendulum, directly under Hugo Ballin's famed mural on the central rotunda; and the handsome, high-tech Samuel Oschin Planetarium. And downstairs, accessible via the campy displays of space-slanted jewellery in the Cosmic Connection Corridor, you'll find a number of other new exhibits. At the Leonard Nimoy Event Horizon Theater, you can see a short film about the history and resurgence of the observatory. Pieces of the Sky documents, brightly and informatively, the impact made on Earth by meteorites and other falling debris. The Gunther Depths of Space contains crisp descriptions of the planets, a bronze of Albert Einstein and a vast, 2.46-gigapixel image of the night sky taken from the Palomar Observatory in San Diego County. And there are above-par snacks in the Café at the End of the World.

However, the star attraction remains the building itself, both inside and out. Famous for its appearances in movies both acclaimed (*Rebel Without a Cause*) and

Sightseeing

disdained (*Lawnmower Man 2: Beyond Cyberspace*), this longtime Los Angeles icon has been returned to its former glory, and is once again one of the city's must-see attractions. *Photo p106*.

Los Angeles Zoo

5333 Zoo Drive (1-323 644 4200/www.lazoo.org). Bus 96/I-5, exit Zoo Drive west. **Open** 10am-5pm daily. Last entry 1hr before closing. **Admission** $12; $7-$9 discounts; free under-2s. *Parking* free. **Credit** AmEx, DC, Disc, MC, V.

The LA Zoo's greatest asset is its location, in the isolated hills of Griffith Park. It's a pretty popular place, but the zoo's size – 80 acres, plus a huge parking lot – means that, like the park itself, it rarely feels busy.

The list of the zoo's highlights is headed by the new Campo Gorilla Reserve, which opened in November 2007 and now serves as a home for six great apes, and the rather smaller Spider City, which comes with an agreeable schlock-horror theme and suitably dim lighting. Elsewhere, a herd of flamingos flop and flutter in a pond close to the entrance, while a nearby meerkat stands guard over proceedings. Sea lions slither and swim, an Indian rhino named Clara carries herself with hilariously little grace, and a snoozy jaguar takes another nap. Still, as a visitor attraction,

it's all a bit forlorn; you can't question the motives of the staff, but this is a slightly despondent place.

If you do want to visit, it's worth bearing in mind that some of the larger animals may seek shady refuge from the extreme heat on warm summer days, and by no means all of them will be visible. Also, some of the animals are led inside from 4pm.

Travel Town Museum

5200 Zoo Drive (1-323 662 5874/http://traveltown. org). Bus 96, CE549/Hwy 134, exit Forest Lawn Drive. **Open** *Summer (during DST)* 10am-5pm Mon-Fri; 10am-6pm Sat, Sun. *Winter* 10am-4pm Mon-Fri; 10am-5pm Sat, Sun. **Admission** *Museum* free. *Travel Town rides* $2.50; $2 discounts. *Parking* free. **No credit cards**.

This endearing outdoor museum in Griffith Park's north-west corner is made up of restored railroad cars from the Union Pacific, Atchison and Santa Fe lines, an early 20th-century milk delivery truck, and more than a dozen steam and diesel locomotives.

Adjacent to Travel Town is the **Los Angeles Live Steamers** (1-323 662 8030, www.lals.org), a club of rail enthusiasts that constructs and runs scale replicas of diesel, steam and electric engines. Free rides are offered every Sunday from 11am to 3pm.

Fruit for thought

When, during the 19th century, the railways promoted California tourism in an attempt to boost winter ticket sales, they used images of pretty Spanish señoritas holding fat, juicy oranges, and grapes hanging from the vine. The orange groves and vineyards have long gone, replaced by suburbs and shopping centres, but LA's gentle climate fosters fruit without the help of farmers. Wild edibles grow all over the city: on steep hillsides and in people's yards, alongside freeways, even between cracks in the sidewalks. Legally, anything found growing on public property is ripe for the taking, including fruit on branches hanging over garden fences on to the street.

Created by artist-activists Dave Burns and Austin Young and writer Matias Viegener, www.fallenfruit.org maps the locations and growing seasons of urban edibles in LA. Printable maps, some with photographs, reveal where you can find seasonal guavas, figs, prickly pears, bananas, passionfruit, avocados, nectarines, apples, grapes, elderberries, loquats, persimmons, olives, walnuts, pomegranates and – yes – fat, juicy oranges. It's a tasty excuse to take a leisurely stroll around some neighbourhoods you might not otherwise have visited, so grab a sack and get picking...

Silver Lake

Map p330

Gang activity still nibbles at its edges, and the clothes on sale in its boutiques won't confuse anyone into thinking they're on Rodeo Drive. But not even *Vanity Fair* tagging Silver Lake as the 'coolest neighbourhood in LA' several years ago has stopped its rise. Its blend of art school types, left-of-centre industry folk and immigrant communities has managed to stave off the chain stores. Instead, Silver Lake is dominated by bijou shops, restaurants and bars.

The convergence of W Sunset Boulevard and Santa Monica Boulevard – known as **Sunset Junction** – is the axis of Silver Lake. Between here and the junction of Silver Lake Boulevard, Sunset Boulevard is dotted with small shops: the majority sell quirky gifts (try **Serifos** at No.3814, 1-323 660 7467) or fashion items (at No.3938, **Kicks** hawks the kind of sneakers you don't wear to the gym), while **Lovecraft** (No.4000, 1-323 644 9072) converts old diesel cars to run on biofuel. To see the locale in all its glory, visit the **Sunset Junction Street Fair** in August (*see p214*).

The neighbourhood's namesake boulevard is worth driving if only for the curves around Silver Lake itself (it's actually a reservoir), glittery at night and enveloped by some of the area's nicest homes. This is a residential neighbourhood, pure and simple, and a bastion of refined old LA glamour: some of the city's finest architects worked here in the 1920s and 1930s. The many RM Schindler properties include the **Droste** and **Walker Houses** at 2025 and 2100 Kenilworth Avenue, and the daunting **Olive House** at 2236 Micheltorena Street. Also on Micheltorena are two buildings by John Lautner: **Silvertop** (No.2138) and **Lautner's own residence** (No.2007). Austrian-born architect Richard Neutra is represented by a cluster of buildings on Silver Lake Boulevard and on Neutra Place.

Echo Park

Map p330

In the early 1900s, a suburb called Edendale became a film industry hotbed, attracting movie-makers with its bright sun and clear days. Now known as **Echo Park**, the area is still a draw,

1345 Carroll Avenue, Angelino Heights The main house in Michael Jackson's video for 'Thriller'

albeit for different reasons: it's the gateway neighbourhood to LA's predominantly Latino east side, but is also home to a major-league baseball stadium, two parks and some delightfully preserved century-old buildings.

The neighbourhood of Echo Park is often defined as the area to the north of US 101 and east of Alvarado Street, but many locals mark the border with the giant 'Foot Clinic' sign at Benton Street and W Sunset Boulevard. This area, with Alvarado and Sunset as its nucleus, supports many of Echo Park's best cafés and shops, plus the **Echo Park Film Center** (No.1200; *see p234*). Beyond here, most of Echo Park is quietly, contentedly residential.

To the south-east of the junction of Sunset and Alvarado sits the green space from which the neighbourhood takes its name. **Echo Park** looks to be more water than land, the park's green space ringing a long, thin lake centred on a large fountain. The park was laid out in the 1890s by architect Joseph Henry Taylor to resemble an English garden. Take a paddle-boat ride through the blossoming lotuses in the lake, celebrated at July's **Lotus Festival** (*see p214*).

Emerging on the west side of Echo Park will lead you into **Angelino Heights**, a residential enclave famous for its Victorian mansions. There's scarcely an ugly building within its confines (it's loosely bordered by W Sunset Boulevard, Boylston Street, US 101 and Echo Park), but the 1300 block of Carroll Avenue is especially attractive. North-east is **Dodger Stadium**, the handsome home of the Los Angeles Dodgers baseball team (*see p269*). Owner Frank McCourt announced plans in 2008 for a $500-million renovation.

Beyond the outfield lies the vast **Elysian Park**, a sprawling jumble of nature and development, less scenic than Griffith Park, but not without worthwhile trails and picnic spots. **Bishops Canyon** hosts Little League baseball games; slightly further along the same road, **Angels Point** affords views of Dodger Stadium (though you can see only spectators, not players) and the Downtown skyline from Peter Shire's eyecatching Glass-Simons Memorial. Unexpectedly, it also features the **Los Angeles Police Academy** (1880 N Academy Drive), established in the 1920s as a shooting club for LAPD officers.

North-east of Elysian Park, the Echo Park neighbourhood is at its cosiest. The roads are skinny and the houses are packed together, exaggerated by the dramatic hills. The likes of **Ewing Street** and **Avon Street** are almost San Franciscan in their peaks and troughs: pray that your brakes don't fail on the way down. And with a gradient of 33 per cent, **Fargo Street** is said to be the steepest road in California. For 30 years, the LA Wheelmen cycling club (www.la

wheelmen.org) has organised a ride up it, usually in March; barely half the riders make the top.

Scattered throughout the neighbourhood are a number of quaint stairways – some from the 19th century, others reconstructed – that provide access from the streets. A couple are especially notable: at 232 steps, the **Baxter Steps** (at Baxter and Avon Streets) are believed to be the city's tallest, while at **923-927 N Vendome Street** are the steps up which Laurel and Hardy drag a piano in their 1932 film *The Music Box*.

The **Glass-Simons Memorial** in Echo Park.

Mt Washington to Eagle Rock

North-east of Echo Park, on the other side of I-5 and the Los Angeles River, sit a handful of interesting residential neighbourhoods. They're quieter than their neighbours to the south-west, but all are more desirable and, thus, more expensive than they were a decade ago, and the sort of hipster- and family-friendly sensibility of Echo Park and Silver Lake is taking hold here.

Just past the slightly sketchy neighbourhood of **Cypress Park** sits **Mt Washington**, formerly an artists' colony of sorts and still an independent-minded community. You can get a glimpse of the area's character by heading north up winding Mount Washington Drive to San Rafael Avenue; however, the only real attraction is, or was, the currently-closed **Southwest Museum of the American Indian** (234 Museum Drive, at Marmion Way, 1-323 221 2164, www.swmfuture.org). Founded in 1907 by Charles Fletcher Lummis (*see p15*), the museum and its collection of 250,000 Native American artefacts were bought in 2003 by the Autry National Center. Locals hoped that the deal would safeguard the museum's future; however, the Autry board have now announced hugely controversial plans to move its holdings to Griffith Park (*see p105*) and redevelop this site.

Highland Park

Just north-east of here, more or less between Mt Washington and the rapidly gentrifying area of **Eagle Rock**, sits the historic neighbourhood of **Highland Park**. Popular with LA's artistic community in the late 19th and early 20th centuries, it's not been without its problems of late: Latino gang violence remains a concern. But what trouble there is here is easily avoided.

Roughly halfway between Downtown Los Angeles and Pasadena, Highland Park is often described as LA's first suburb. Certainly, it's more attractive than the 'burbs that followed: its streets are dotted with grand old residences that have been well maintained. Notable buildings

include **Judson Studios** (200 S Avenue 66, at York Boulevard, 1-323 255 0131, www.judson studios.com), originally the home of the Los Angeles College of Fine Arts and now a stained-glass studio and gallery; and the residences on S Avenue 59 south of Figueroa Street.

El Alisal

*200 E Avenue 43, at N Figueroa Street (1-323 222 0546/www.socalhistory.org). Metro Southwest Museum/bus 81, 83, 252/Hwy 110, exit Avenue 43 west. **Open** Tours noon-4pm Fri-Sun. **Admission** free. Parking free. **No credit cards**.*
Built at the turn of the century by adventurous jack-of-all-trades Charles Fletcher Lummis (*see p15* **Man about town**), this eye-catchingly strange but admirable building is now open for low-key tours at weekends. Reservations aren't required.

Heritage Square

*3800 Homer Street, at E Avenue 43 (1-323 225 2700 /www.heritagesquare.org). Metro Southwest Museum /bus 81, 83, 252/Hwy 110, exit Avenue 43 west. **Open** Apr-Oct noon-5pm Fri-Sun. Nov-Mar 11.30am-4.30pm Fri-Sun. **Admission** $10; $5-$8 discounts; free under-6s. Parking free. **No credit cards**.*
Preservation, LA-style. The buildings that together make up this open-air museum were all moved here from other locations: a railroad station from Century City, a church from Pasadena, and a variety of formerly private residences from across the city.

Downtown

After years of neglect, LA's urban core is thriving again.

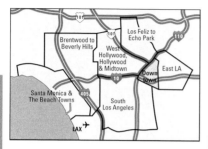

Map p331

By day, Downtown LA is many things: a crisp political district, a bustling centre of finance and commerce, a Mexican shopping mall, a convention hub, a multi-million-dollar fashion market and more. But by night, at least until a few years ago, it wasn't much at all. Few people lived here, and nightlife outside of the major hotels was limited to a few sketchy bars and some curiosities in Little Tokyo. Only Skid Row's sizeable homeless population prevented the locale from becoming a ghost town between 7pm and 7am.

However, the last few years have seen Downtown transformed in dramatic fashion, energised both by a wealth of new construction and by the radical redevelopment of many older buildings. The Staples Center and Disney Hall have helped lure outsiders back to the area; a number of smart new restaurants and bars have superseded the once-divey nightlife scene; and the low-key emergence of a small local arts district has added a little grass-roots culture.

But it's the re-emergence of Downtown as a residential sector that has been the biggest change. The last few years have seen a string of commercial buildings adapted for residential use, an unusually urban development in a city built on suburban principles. The trend has proved so successful that a second wave of construction has begun, this time in the shape of brand new apartment blocks. The residential population has been forecast to hit 40,000 by the end of 2008, a rise of 65% in just three years. And these are the kind of residents that developers and politicians adore: young, educated and with plenty of disposable income.

For all the recent improvements, Downtown isn't there yet. Parts of it remain edgy at night –

despite the new additions, the streets hardly thrum with activity after dark – and the sub-prime mortgage crisis has resulted in several developments being put on hold, as economic caution wins out over gold-rush optimism. Nonetheless, it might just be the most fascinating neighbourhood in Los Angeles: an uneasy collision between affluence and poverty; between culture and commerce; between Anglos and Latinos, Chinese and Japanese; and, most tangibly, between past, present and future.

Chinatown

LA's original Chinatown sprang up in the 1850s around Alameda Street. A thriving area at the turn of the 20th century, it began to fade soon after, and the land that held it was redeveloped as Union Station in the 1930s. (One remaining building from the original Chinatown holds the **Chinese American Museum**; *see p112*.)

However, although the Chinese community leaders had failed to secure a future for their neighbourhood, their children soon managed to establish a second Chinatown in an area just north-west of Union Station in what was once Little Italy. These pioneers set about building a neighbourhood that would serve the local Chinese American community while also appealing to tourists. In June 1938, Chinatown's Central Plaza, an inauthentic yet strangely exotic confection, opened to the public.

Almost 70 years later, Central Plaza is still the focal point of Chinatown, but Chinatown is no longer the focal point of LA's Chinese American communities: that role falls to Monterey Park, north-east of here. The small district feels a little forlorn these days, the streets often quiet outside of **Chinese New Year** (*see p216*). However, it has undergone a small revival of late, a cluster of galleries and bars making an interesting juxtaposition with the dusty old Chinese-owned bric-a-brac stores. For additional context, follow the excellent self-guided walking tour detailed on 16 panels throughout the area; it starts at Chinatown station but you can pick it up at any point.

N Broadway and, to a lesser extent, **N Spring Street** are the main roads, home to banks, grocers, bakeries (try the Phoenix, at 969 N Broadway) and a Metro station. However, the heart of Chinatown remains **Central Plaza**

(947 N Broadway), one of the nation's first pedestrian malls. These days, its businesses are a mix of old-fashioned restaurants and bars, tacky souvenir shops on Gin Ling Way, and new businesses such as hipster-friendly Asian eaterie **Café Via** (451 Gin Ling Way, 1-213 617 1481). A statue of Republic of China founder Dr Sun Yat-Sen sternly oversees proceedings.

North of Central Plaza, the volunteer-run **Chinese Historical Society** (411 Bernard Street, 1-323 222 0856, www.chssc.org, closed Mon, Tue & Sun) contains information on Chinatown's past. A block further north stand **St Peter's Church** and the **Casa Italiana** (1051 N Broadway, www.casaitaliana.org), two extant reminders of the Italian community that lived here before the Chinese arrived; there's another at the corner of Broadway and College Street in the shape of **Little Joe's**, established in 1908 but closed for a decade.

To the west of Broadway, **Hill Street** holds more Chinese businesses. On Thursdays from 4pm to 8pm, a farmers' market is held in the parking lot adjacent to No.727. Close by, in the lot at No.735, sits a string of 13 white letters spelling out 'CHINATOWNLAND'; created by local artist Andre Yi with more than a passing nod to the Hollywood sign, it's been here since 2002. But perhaps the area's most interesting street is

skinny **Chung King Road**, just behind it. Some of its old Chinese shops remain, but others have been taken over by Anglos and converted into tiny galleries. Among them are the Happy Lion (No.963) and Black Dragon Society (No.961); for details, *see p241*.

Olvera Street & the Plaza

Just across Cesar E Chavez Avenue from Chinatown is **El Pueblo de Los Angeles Historical Monument**, a restored 44-acre historic park that purports to be on the site of the original settlement of LA. In fact, the first settlement was half a mile from here, but no trace of it remains; LA's official birthday is 4 September 1781, the day that the first Spanish settlers began farming and building ranches.

It's a curious jumble of buildings, most built in the late 19th and early 20th centuries and used today for all manner of purposes. Your first stop should be to collect a map from **Sepulveda House** on the east side of N Main Street (No.622, 1-213 628 1274, www.lacity.org/elp), a 19th-century house that's now a visitors' centre. Alternatively, join one of the family-friendly free tours run by Las Angelitas del Pueblo (www.lasangelitas.org), which depart from the Las Angelitas office on the south side

'Forget it, Jake. It's **Chinatown**.'

of the Plaza at 10am, 11am and noon every day except Monday. Booking isn't required unless you're travelling with a large group.

Right by Sepulveda House, running east of Main Street, is **Olvera Street**, a narrow, pedestrianised thoroughfare. Renovated in 1930 as a Mexican marketplace, it's now just a tourist trap, albeit a generally enjoyable one. In between the odiferous taco stands and the stalls hawking colourful hats and shirts, keep an eye out for **Avila Adobe**, the oldest house in LA. Built in 1818, this small ranch-style home has been restored, and now operates as a museum.

At the southern end of Olvera Street sits the circular **Plaza**, the bustling focal point of El Pueblo. South of the Plaza is a cluster of old and not-so-old buildings; one, a 19th-century fire station, houses a diverting collection of old firefighting equipment. And just across Main Street from the Plaza are more historic buildings, including the oldest Catholic church in LA: Our Lady, Queen of the Angels, commonly known as **La Placita**.

Visible from the Plaza is **Union Station** (800 N Alameda Street). Opened in 1939 on the site of the original Chinatown, it was the last of the great American rail stations to be built, at a cost at the time of $11 million. By 1971, just seven passenger trains a day were running here; however, it's a bit busier today, and its Mission-style exterior, marble floors, high ceilings and decorative tiles make it a handsome place. However, don't confuse it with the Spanish colonial post officethat stands next to it.

Chinese American Museum

425 N Los Angeles Street, at Arcadia Street (1-213 485 8567/www.camla.org). Metro Chinatown/ bus 76/US 101, exit Los Angeles Street south. **Open** 10am-3pm Wed-Sat. **Admission** $3; $2 discounts. **No credit cards**. **Map** p327 C1.
While CAM's address in El Pueblo might seem a little incongruous, its location is actually very appropriate. This was LA's original Chinatown, and the Garnier building, in which part of the museum sits, is the most historic Chinese structure in the area: built in 1890, when Chinese immigrants dominated in this part of town, it's been home to a number of community organisations. Exhibits spotlight the history of LA's Chinatown and the more general experience of Chinese Americans in the US.

Little Tokyo to Skid Row

Head south down Alameda Street, past Temple Street to Central Avenue, and you'll reach the **Geffen Contemporary** wing of the **Museum of Contemporary Art** (*see p116*), housed in a former warehouse converted by Frank Gehry. Right by the museum, Roger Yanagita's *Go for Broke Monument* commemorates the Japanese American soldiers who fought in World War II, experiences dramatised in the 1951 movie *Go for Broke*. Further down Central Avenue is the **Japanese American National Museum** (*see p113*). Opposite, partly housed in the 1925 Nishi Hongwanji Buddhist Temple, is the JANM's **National Center for the Preservation of Democracy**. And due to open in late 2009 is a new Metro station as part of the Gold line extension, which is due to run from Union Station out into East LA.

It's at this corner that Little Tokyo really begins. Just across the road, running between 1st Street and 2nd Streets just west of Central Avenue, is the **Japanese Village Plaza**, a scruffy mini-mall with restaurants, shops and karaoke bars. Across from the Japanese Village Plaza is the **James Irvine Garden**, a lovely, romantic example of a traditional Japanese garden. The gardens are accessible by taking an elevator to the basement of the **Japanese American Cultural & Community Center** (244 S San Pedro Street, 1-213 628 2725, www.jaccc.org).

There's more to see to the east of Japanese Village Plaza. **Astronaut Ellison S Onizuka Street**, which runs diagonally south between 1st Street and the corner of 2nd and San Pedro Streets, is named for one of the astronauts who died in the *Challenger* crash in 1986; a model of the shuttle commemorates his life. A little further west is the 19th-century St Vibiana's Cathedral (210 S Main Street), renovated in 2005 and now a private-hire party and events venue. West stands the **Higashi Honganji Buddhist Temple** (505 E 3rd Street), which blends neatly and sweetly into its otherwise Western locale. And to the south is Block 8, a new residential development on a parking lot hemmed in by Los Angeles, San Pedro, 2nd and 3rd Streets.

South of Block 8 is a jolly little shopping district centred on Wall Street between 3rd and 5th Streets. Crammed together, dozens of shops and stalls sell everything to crowds of Asian and Latino customers. Signs read 'Wholesale only'; however, most shopkeepers don't seem fussy, and bargains abound.

Walking further south will bring you to LA's infamous **Skid Row**, centred on 5th Street between Main and Alameda Streets. The homeless have long congregated here, but the area has also become both a magnet for lowlifes and troubled souls of every stripe. Creeping gentrification at the area's western extremity has lifted the area, but even these changes have had their critics – some observers have claimed that a number of transients have been unlawfully forced from residential hotels by developers anxious to convert the buildings to swanky apartments. The battle for the soul of the area looks set to continue for a while.

Japanese American National Museum

369 E 1st Street, at N Central Avenue (1-213 625 0414/www.janm.org). Metro Union Station/bus 30, 31, 40, 42/US 101, exit Alameda Street south. **Open** 11am-5pm Tue, Wed, Fri-Sun; 11am-8pm Thur. **Admission** $8; $4-$5 discounts; free under-5s. Free to all 3rd Thur of mth & 5-8pm all other Thurs. **Credit** AmEx, DC, MC, V. **Map** p327 C2.

The story of Japanese immigration to the US really begins in 1882, when bosses were barred from importing cheap Chinese labour by the Chinese Exclusion Act. Thousands of Japanese arrived to take their place; many settled in the San Joaquin Valley and became farmers. But the Japanese were then excluded from American life in much the same way as the Chinese had suffered before them: prevented from owning land in 1913, banned from immigrating in 1924 and sent to brutal internment camps during World War II. Only in 1952 were people born in Japan allowed to become American citizens.

This museum, one of the city's best, tells the story of Japanese immigration to the US in lucid, engaging fashion. Even if you've no prior interest in the subject, you'll be drawn in to it by the perfectly pitched displays. Aside from the permanent exhibition, the museum stages an engaging roster of documentary and art exhibitions, including a wrenching yet beautiful display of images and artefacts from the aforementioned internment camps. To cap it all off, there's a lovely gift shop.

In 2006, the JANM opened the National Center for the Preservation of Democracy (111 N Central Avenue, 1-213 830 1880, www.ncdemocracy.org), an educational institute aimed at preserving and promoting democracy in the US. It's open only for group tours (by appointment only) during the week, but it's open to the public 11am-2pm on Saturdays.

Museum of Neon Art

136 W 4th Street, between S Spring & S Main Streets (1-213 489 9918/www.neonmona.org). Metro Pershing Square/bus 33, 55, 83, 92/US 101, exit Main Street south. **Open** noon-7pm Thur-Sat; noon-5pm Sun. **Admission** $7; $3-$5 discounts; free under-5s. **Credit** AmEx, DC, MC, V. **Map** p331 B4.

Recently relocated to the edge of Skid Row, the Museum of Neon Art mixes displays of fabulous vintage neon signs (soda-pop signs, restaurant displays and the like) with a grab-bag of modern neon art. The premises are only temporary, though, and the museum continues to look for a permanent location – call or check online before setting out. Regardless of the museum's location, it will continue to stage its Neon Cruises, evening-long tours of the city's best neon signs. For details, *see p73*.

Civic Center & around

Civic Center

Just north-east of Little Tokyo, there's a neat intersection of immigrant communities: **Judge John Aiso Street**, named for the highest-ranking *nisei* to serve for the Allies during World War II, connects to Temple Street at the

City Hall (*p114*) Blown up by Martians in *The War of the Worlds*

Edward R Roybal Federal Building (255 E Temple Street), named after California's first Mexican American congressman. Outside the latter is Jonathan Borofsky's sculpture *Molecule Man*, a quartet of huge metal figures.

The majority of LA's administrative and political institutions are based in this area, known as Civic Center. Just north of the Federal Building, at Aliso and Los Angeles Streets, is the **Metropolitan Detention Center**, LA's newest prison. Designed to blend in with the office blocks around it, the building looks nothing like a conventional jail; legend has it that a group of Japanese tourists once tried to check in, thinking it was a hotel.

To the east is the art deco-styled **City Hall** (200 N Spring Street, *photo p25*), built in 1928 and LA's tallest building until 1957. Free tours of the handsome old building are offered at 10am and 11am from Monday to Friday; you'll need to book in advance by calling 1-213 978 1995. However, you don't need to join a tour in order to visit the little-used observation deck, one of the best-kept secrets in Downtown. Simply ask for a free pass at the reception desk (9am-5pm daily) and then head up to the 27th floor, where you'll get some fabulous views of the city.

Back across 1st Street stands the 1930s **Times-Mirror Building** (202 W 1st Street), still home to the rather beleaguered *Los Angeles Times*. It's overshadowed by its neighbours, but it's worth popping into the lobby – enter on 1st Street, south-west of the intersection with Spring Street. A series of displays traces the history of the paper; in the centre, a rotating globe is set into a marbled plinth and ringed by a Hugo Ballin mural. Two quotations take pride of place: one by religious reformer Henry Ward Beecher. 'The newspaper,' wrote Beecher, rather piously, 'is a greater treasure to the people than uncounted millions of gold.' Needless to say, Beecher lived and died in the 19th century.

Two other buildings stand just east of here along Main Street, both of them new. Hemmed in by Spring, Main, 1st and 2nd Streets, the DMJM-designed **LAPD Headquarters** are due for completion in late 2008. When it's finished, the building should provide a suitably dramatic neighbour for Thom Mayne's amazing new **Caltrans District 7 Headquarters** , which occupies the whole of the next block to the east at Main and 1st Streets. In its vast, flat dimensions and enormous scale, it resembles nothing so much as a huge, shiny ocean liner. Appropriate, then, that it should stand close to a sign, at the north-east corner of 1st and Main, that points pedestrians in the direction of LA's sister cities. Among them are Bordeaux (5,755 miles away), Jakarta (8,977 miles) and, most unexpectedly, Beirut (7,449 miles).

Public art

The one characteristic that links every part of Downtown LA is the preponderance of public art: outside skyscrapers, on the walls of public buildings, even in the form of bicycle racks. Ruth Wallach's Public Art in LA website (www.publicartinla.com), is an unbeatable resource to the hundreds of works in the area; here are five of the best.

Hammering Man
Jonathan Borofsky (1988)
California Market Center, 110 E 9th Street, at S Main Street
This hulking, hammering silhouette is one of three Borofsky works in Downtown. The others are *Molecule Man*, outside the Federal Building (*see p113*); and *I Dreamed I Could Fly*, six figures suspended above the platform at Civic Center station.

Mind, Body and Spirit
Gidon Graetz (1986)
SW corner of 4th & Hope Streets
This twisty horn, made from stainless steel and bronze, forms part of a sculpture garden outside the YMCA. Other works here include two sports-themed pieces by Milton Hebald and a gymnast cast in bronze by Michael Zapponi.

Source Figure
Robert Graham (1991)
Hope Place, between 4th & 5th Streets
This three-foot bronze nude stands proudly atop a column in a fountain halfway up the Bunker Hill Steps. The 'source' is a nod to the water that flows from the pool towards the Central Library.

Friendship Knot
Shinkichi Tajiri (1972)
2nd & San Pedro Streets
LA-born, Netherlands-based Tajiri has long favoured knots in his works, which include sculptures such as this towering fibreglass object in Little Tokyo.

Bicycle Rack
Randall Wilson (1998)
corner of College & Yale Streets
Wilson's pair of inverted hearts are one of ten bike racks designed by students at the Southern California Institute of Architecture; others stand in Pershing Square, outside the Geffen Contemporary and by the Times-Mirror Building.

Sightseeing

Disney Hall & around

Though Downtown contains a surprising number of historic buildings, it's best known for two of its newest. The **Cathedral of Our Lady of the Angels** (555 W Temple Street) has had a number of nicknames pinned to it since its dedication in 2002: perhaps the most memorable is 'Our Lady of the 101', after the freeway from which it can clearly be seen.

It's a fine structure, but it's overshadowed by its neighbour. The **Walt Disney Concert Hall** (111 S Grand Avenue; *see p251*) opened in 2003 after an odyssey of promises, delays, starts, stops, shutdowns, ego battles, funding problems and structural concerns. But it was all worth it: bold, brash yet also sensual in its reflective glory, Frank Gehry's building sits like a reclining steel butterfly, its wings fanning languidly atop Bunker Hill. It's just as wonderful inside: the acoustic of the hall is said to be the best in the US.

Facing each other across 1st Street, Disney Hall and the buildings that comprise the **Music Center** (home to the **Dorothy Chandler Pavilion**, the **Ahmanson Theatre** and the **Mark Taper Forum**; *see p277*) are wildly different structures borne of different eras and of very different approaches to the same task. They don't gel as a unit at all, but it's daft to hold Gehry responsible for the architectural failings of earlier generations. Better, perhaps, to associate Disney Hall not with the Chandler Pavilion but with the gleaming modernity of the Downtown skyline to its south, or with the shimmering moat that surrounds the bold, blockish **Department of Water & Power Building** (111 N Hope Street).

This area looks set to change dramatically in the next few years thanks to the government-backed Grand Avenue Project, which calls for the construction of a 16-acre park between the DWP Building and City Hall, several condo buildings, a Mandarin Oriental hotel (designed by Gehry), various entertainment venues and a shopping mall. The whole development will come at a cost of between $2 billion and $3 billion, though it's far from certain that the project will go ahead and even less certain when it will be completed. For updates, see www.grandavenuecommittee.org.

The Financial District & Bunker Hill

South of Disney Hall, art meets commerce. At Grand Avenue and 3rd Street sits the **Museum of Contemporary Art** (*see p116*), part of the billion-dollar California Plaza. The museum

Cathedral of Our Lady of the Angels.

itself is unmissable – look for the huge Swiss Army knife, designed by Claes Oldenburg – but the plaza is by no means unmemorable, whether for the computer-operated fountain spraying 40-foot geysers or the daily concerts in summer. Across the road, meanwhile, sits the **Wells Fargo Center** (333 S Grand Avenue); as well as being a banking powerhouse, it's home to the **Wells Fargo History Museum** (1-213 253 7166), which tells the story of the bank founded in the heyday of the Gold Rush.

Known as **Bunker Hill**, this was where LA's wealthiest citizens built their houses a century ago: grand Victorian mansions, powerful illustrations of their owners' riches. However, after the once-exclusive area began to decay in the '40s and '50s, the mansions were razed. Eventually, a slew of shiny but architecturally unremarkable skyscrapers were built in their place, and Bunker Hill began to enjoy a second life as LA's financial district.

The only surviving remnant of the old Bunker Hill is **Angels Flight** (Hill Street, between 3rd & 4th Streets). Built in 1901 to ferry citizens to their hilltop homes, closed in 1969, reopened 27 years later and then shut down again after a fatal accident in 2001, it's the world's shortest railway. However, a small window into old Bunker Hill is still available at nearby **Angelus Plaza** (255 S Hill Street, 1-213 623 4352, www.angelusplaza.org): here, you'll find a collection of 50-year-old paintings of the locale, created by artist Kay Martin shortly before demolition work began. Angelus Plaza is actually a private retirement home; however, if you ask nicely at the front desk or call ahead on the above number, you should be allowed to peek at the evocative pictures.

A couple of blocks south sits **Pershing Square**. A public meeting place since 1866, it was renamed in 1918 after the commander of the US Army in World War I. It's now a restful place, hosting concerts in summer and an ice rink in winter. Dominating its edge is the **Millennium Biltmore** (see p63), built in 1923 and still one of the grandest hotels in Los Angeles. Another art deco prize sits just south of Pershing Square in the shape of the **Oviatt Building** (617 S Olive Street), designed in 1928 to house an exclusive men's haberdashery.

Continue directly south from Pershing Square down Olive or Hill Streets and you'll immediately find yourself in the **Jewelry District**, six square blocks bounded by 6th Street, Broadway (see p117), 8th Street and Olive Street. There are some 5,000 businesses here, set up in individual stores or in sprawling indoor marketplaces, and the area is a polyglot's delight: expect to hear anything from Hebrew to Armenian as the stallholders and repairers go about their exotic business.

A little west of Pershing Square is the **Richard J Riordan Central Library** (see below), a striking beaux arts building from 1926. After a fire in the 1980s, it was refurbished with money stumped up by the developers of **US Bank Tower** (formerly Library Tower, 633 W 5th Street); built by IM Pei in 1990 and towering 1,018 feet (310 metres) into the Downtown sky, it's the tallest building in LA. In front of the library is the oasis of the **Robert F Maguire Gardens**; the wide, graceful sweep of the 103 Bunker Hill Steps, linking 5th and Hope Streets.

Heading west from here along 5th Street will bring you within range of two major hotels. The hip **Standard** (550 S Flower Street; see p63) is housed in Claude Beelman's sturdy old Standard Oil Building, but it's overshadowed by the five-tower, business-oriented **Westin Bonaventure** (404 S Figueroa Street; see p64). Built by John Portman in the '70s, it still looks futuristic from the outside, though the dreary and abysmally signposted interior is another

matter entirely. These streets have also been resettled in recent years by moneyed twenty- and thirtysomethings hungry for an urban lifestyle: the **Pegasus Lofts** (Flower Street, between 6th Street and Wilshire Boulevard) is one such typical conversion.

Heading south down Figueroa Street will bring you to the Downtown Farmers' Market (S Figueroa & W 9th Streets), held here from 10am until 4pm on Thursday, Friday and Saturday. No matter which day you wander here, though, you'll see one of LA's best-known sculptures: Terry Allen's *Corporate Head*, a lifesize effigy of a corporate executive with its head disappearing into the side of the Citicorp office building (725 S Figueroa Street). It's the highlight of **Poet's Walk**, an assortment of verse inscriptions and public art.

Museum of Contemporary Art & Geffen Contemporary

MOCA *250 S Grand Avenue, at 3rd Street. Metro Civic Center/bus 16, 18, 55, 62/I-110, exit 4th Street east.* **Map** p331 B2.
Geffen Contemporary *152 N Central Avenue, at 1st Street. Metro Union Station/bus 30, 31, 40, 42/ US 101, exit Alameda Street south.* **Map** p331 C2.
Both *1-213 626 6222/www.moca.org.* **Open** 11am-5pm Mon, Fri; 11am-8pm Thur; 11am-6pm Sat, Sun. **Admission** *Combined ticket* $10; $5 discounts; free under-12s. Free to all 5-8pm Thur. **Credit** AmEx, DC, MC, V.
The city's premier showcase for post-war art, MoCA started life in a humongous busy barn on the edge of Little Tokyo. It's now the Geffen Contemporary, its spacious, raw interior designed by Frank Gehry in the 1980s; it's considered by some to be one of his gutsiest spaces. When MoCA's main building, designed by Japan's Arata Isozaki, was completed a block from the Civic Center, the museum was able simultaneously to mount ambitious survey exhibitions and to showcase items from its fine permanent collection, which includes pieces by Rauschenberg, Rothko, Twombly, Mondrian and Pollock.

Up to half a dozen shows can be viewed at any single time between the two galleries. MoCA stages the more mainstream exhibits (although such terms are relative; 'mainstream' here means the likes of Louise Bourgeois), leaving the Geffen Contemporary to concentrate on more esoteric artists. A programme of talks and performance events round out the scene.

Richard J Riordan Central Library

630 W 5th Street, between S Grand Avenue & S Flower Street (1-213 228 7000/www.lapl.org/central). Metro 7th Street-Metro Center/bus 16, 18, 55, 62/ I-110, exit 6th Street east. **Open** 10am-8pm Mon-Thur; 10am-6pm Fri, Sat; 1-5pm Sun. **Admission** free. **Map** p331 B3.
Designed by Bertram Goodhue, completed in 1926 and renamed after the city's former mayor in 2001, LA's main library is worth a look even if you've no interest in borrowing books. The exterior is a beaux

Bradbury Building
Rutger Hauer tracks Harrison Ford in *Blade Runner*

The best views of Downtown are found by looking up.

arts beauty, topped with a dramatic, tiled pyramid tower and decorated with bas-reliefs by Lee Lawrie, but there's also plenty to see inside. The main lobby is topped with an unexpectedly colourful ceiling mural by Venice artist Renée Petropoulos; other highlights include a frieze that retells Walter Scott's *Ivanhoe* (International Languages Department) and a series of murals dedicated to California history (Children's Literature Department). The Annenberg Gallery shows rare LA-related pieces from the library's collection; the Getty Gallery stages temporary shows; and there's a fine programme of lectures and discussions in the Mark Taper Auditorium (for details, see www.lfla.org/aloud).

Broadway

Between 1st Street and Olympic Boulevard (effectively 10th Street), Downtown's liveliest road is an intoxicating blend of LA history, Latino culture, old-world trade and modern-day wealth. Classic '20s theatres stand shoulder to shoulder with Hispanic markets and street traders; jewellers look out from shop windows at Downtown's wandering homeless. Even the scruffier buildings carry with them a grandeur bestowed by simple survival; the street life is the stuff of photographers' dreams.

Start at 1st and Broadway and wander south. After a quick detour east down 3rd Street to see Eloy Torrez's mammoth mural of Mexican American actor Anthony Quinn, arms spread wide as he looks down over a parking lot on the north side of 3rd between Broadway and Spring Street, you'll reach the magnificent **Bradbury Building** (304 S Broadway; *see p26*). Designed by otherwise unknown architect George Wyman in 1893, it's an extraordinary building, defined by its ornate cast-iron fittings and the

natural light that floods it. It's used as offices these days (with, dispiritingly, a branch of Subway on the ground level). However, visitors are welcome to take a look around the lobby and wander up the stairwell to the first landing.

Across the street from the Bradbury Building sits the enclosed Grand Central Market, a perpetually busy Mexican-style market with stalls selling everything from fresh meat to fruit smoothies. And just nearby is the **Million Dollar Theatre** (No.307), where Sid Grauman launched his West Coast operations. For more on the theatre and on the others that once constituted LA's Little White Way, *see p118* **The great white way forward**.

After several blocks dominated by Latino retailers, ancient theatres and, between 6th and 8th Streets, jewellers (this is the edge of the Jewelry District; *see p116*), you'll reach a key link between old and new Downtown. Designed by Claude Beelman and completed in 1929, the 13-storey **Eastern Columbia Building** (at the north-west corner of Broadway and 9th Street) is a gorgeous, turquoise art deco pile that's recently been dragged back to life after a period of irrelevance – it's been converted into loft apartments by the Kor Group, also responsible for a slew of fashionable hotels across LA.

The Fashion District & the Flower District

East of the Jewelry District are two other bustling commercial hubs. Centred on 8th and Wall Streets, the **Flower District** (www.la flowerdistrict.com) and the **Los Angeles Flower Market** are at their liveliest at the start of the day. Get here pre-dawn for a

The great white way forward

As lively as Broadway is in the 21st century, it was livelier in the '20s, when it was home to the largest theatre district west of the Mississippi. The grand theatres on the street, some a century old, have lain dormant for years. However, a group of locals has plans to return Broadway to its former glory.

Broadway went through several identities before becoming LA's theatrical centre in the early 20th century, its venues offering both live performances (Harry Houdini, WC Fields) and silent movies. Among the popular theatres and nickelodeons were the **Cameo** at No.528, completed in 1910 as Clunes Broadway, and the **Palace** at No.630, which opened in the following year as the Orpheum.

For all its popularity, Broadway remained a pretty low-rent part of town until one man arrived with a vision and the cash to make it happen. Built by Sid Grauman in 1918 for a then-outrageous seven-figure sum, the extravagant **Million Dollar Theatre** (No.307) was the first truly grand theatre to open

Downtown. Staging a spread of shows and movies, it single-handedly elevated Broadway above its low-rent vaudeville origins.

Inspired by Grauman, other promoters followed suit. The Rialto was joined on Broadway's 800 block by the **Orpheum** (No.842), which opened in 1926 as a vaudeville palace, and the **Tower** (No.802), a movie theatre completed in 1927. The same year saw the arrival of the **United Artists Theatre** (No.933), built by the UA studio to screen its own movies. And in 1931, the plush **Los Angeles Theatre** (No.615) was built in just 90 days at a cost of $1 million.

The party didn't last. As Downtown gave way to the suburbs in the years following World War II, its theatres fell on hard times. A resurgence during the 1960s was brief, and the remaining theatres fell into decrepitude or closed their doors for good.

Happily, however, most miraculously survived. Not all are in decent shape: the lobbies of several, including the Cameo

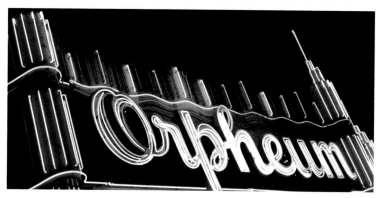

colourful riot of activity, as wholesalers unload truckloads of lilies, roses, orchids and tulips.

Close by, the roads around Los Angeles Street south of 7th Street received a rebranding in the '80s when real estate owners attempted to modernise the area. It seems to have worked: formerly the Garment District, a workaday name for a workaday area, the rechristened **Fashion District** (www.fashiondistrict.org) now pulses with activity. Clothes are still made here in decades-old warehouses, but many more are brought in from elsewhere and sold: the area does $7 billion a year in wholesale trade,

with a further $1 billion in retail to the public.

The four main market centres are all grouped together; spread over three 13-storey buildings housing 1,000 showrooms, the **California Market Center** (110 E 9th Street, www. californiamarketcenter.com) is the biggest. However, outside of the ground-floor fashion bookstore and Jonathan Borofsky's sculpture *Hammering Man*, or unless you're here for one of the sample sales (held on the last Friday of most months), there's not much to see. Instead, start pounding the pavements in search of bargains at the 150-plus shops around the area

and the **Rialto** (No.820), are home to a sad agglomeration of stalls, while the UA Theatre is now a church. However, a 20-year effort by the LA Conservancy, the city's loudest advocate for the preservation of the city's cultural monuments, has helped bring about a change.

In 2008, councilman José Huizar, with support from Mayor Antonio Villaraigosa and local property owners, announced **Bringing Back Broadway**, a public-private initiative designed to return vitality and splendour to the street. The ambitious group wants to complete the renovation of each of the 13 theatres that still exist, while also introducing other forms of entertainment, attracting big retail names and even reviving the old tram network.

While it sounds like a great plan (read more at www.bringingbackbroadway.com), there are many hurdles to overcome. But the rehabilitation of the theatres is already under way. After restoration, the Orpheum is once again staging concerts (*see p255*); the Palace and the Los Angeles Theatre are both used for filming (www.losangeles theatre.com); and the Million Dollar Theatre reopened in early 2008 after renovations that ran to, yes, a million dollars (www.milliondollartheater.com).

Access to most of the theatres is limited to tours run by the LA Conservancy every Saturday at 10am. But visitors to LA in May and June have the chance to watch a classic film in one of the old palaces as part of the Conservancy's **Last Remaining Seats** event, which offers modern day moviegoers a glimpse of the glamour of yesteryear. Booking ahead is essential; for more on the tours and Last Remaining Seats, see www.laconservancy.org.

that mix wholesale and retail trade. Chaotic **Santee Alley**, between Maple Avenue and Santee Street, deals mostly in cheap knock-offs, but there's nicer stuff elsewhere, much of it at extremely nice prices. For an insider's guide, take one of the regular tours with **Urban Shopping Adventures** (*see p73*).

The south-western edge of the Fashion District is marked by the **Coca-Cola Building** (1334 S Central Avenue). Built in 1937, it was designed by Robert Derrah to resemble an ocean liner. Further west, meanwhile, stand a few other notable buildings. The **Los Angeles**

Herald-Examiner Building (1111 S Broadway) was built in the Mission revival style in 1912 by Julia Morgan, who went on to build Hearst Castle. It was due for a major renovation in 2008, but the nationwide financial crisis resulted in the work being put on hold. A block from here stands the **Mayan Theatre** (1038 S Hill Street), complete with bizarre bas-relief warriors designed by Mexican artist Francisco Cornejo.

South Park & LA Live

Edging out cautiously from around the intersection of the Harbor Freeway and the Santa Monica Freeway (I-110 and I-10), **South Park** isn't actually a park at all but a rather drab locale that's been slowly resuscitated by a number of big-money developments. First to arrive was the **Los Angeles Convention Center** (*see p306*), open since 1971 and expanded 22 years later. Next to arrive, in 1999, was the 20,000-capacity, $400-million **Staples Center** (*see p269*) which was built next door, providing Downtown with a major venue for shows and sporting events. However, both the LACC and the Staples Center are about to be overshadowed by a major new arrival, just a stone's throw away.

Hemmed in by Olympic Boulevard, Figueroa Street, 11th Street and the Harbor Freeway, the $2.5-billion **LA Live** development is being billed by those behind it as 'Times Square West', an adult playground aimed at attracting moneyed suburbanites back to LA's urban core. It's being built in three phases, the first of which saw the opening in 2007 of the 7,000-capacity Nokia Theatre. Late 2008 will deliver several clubs (including the **Conga Room**; *see p263*), the West Coast headquarters of sports network ESPN, the **Grammy Museum** (www.grammymuseum.org) and a dozen restaurants. And phase three, due for early 2010, will see the arrival of a 14-screen cineplex and two major hotels.

It seems more likely than not that LA Live will be a financial success for AEG (Anschutz Entertainment Group), its powerhouse developers. But it's anyone's guess what it will mean in the long term for Downtown. The best-case scenario will see its visitors linger in and around the area, helping connect the isolated new development with the rest of Downtown LA. However, it's difficult not to suspect that LA Live will stand apart from the rest of the neighbourhood as a sanitised and self-contained theme park of sorts, a little bit of Downtown Disney in Downtown LA, and the streets around it will remain largely unchanged. It'll be interesting to see how it all unfolds.

Sightseeing

East Los Angeles

¿Usted habla español?

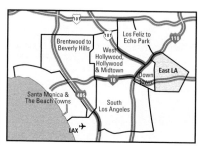

Many non-Anglo immigrant groups settled in East Los Angeles when they first arrived in the city. In the early 20th century, there was a sizeable Jewish community here; the Jews were then followed by Asians, blacks, Italians and, eventually, Mexicans, who have dominated the area for more than four years.

Officially, the unincorporated area of East LA takes Indiana Avenue as its western boundary. However, in modern-day shorthand, it also includes hilly **Boyle Heights** (part of the City of LA), which separates Downtown and East LA and takes the Los Angeles River and Indiana Avenue as its western and eastern borders. And some have argued that East LA's true spiritual starting point is **Olvera Street**, just across the river in Downtown (*see p111*).

Back in the '60s, East LA's political clout was so negligible that the area was torn asunder by freeway construction. However, it remains a lively area with a strong sense of Latino identity. And with Latinos now wielding more political power than at any point in the LA's history (in 2005, Boyle Heights native Antonio Villaraigosa became the city's first Hispanic mayor in more than 130 years), the future is as bright here as it's been for some time. It'll be interesting to see whether the arrival of the Metro network in East LA will affect the area: scheduled for late 2009, an extension to the Gold line will connect this downtrodden part of the city to its newly thriving Downtown core.

Commercial activity in East LA is centred on César E Chávez Avenue, 1st Street and Whittier Boulevard, three parallel east–west streets. Still, for all its points of cultural interest, the area is visually and architecturally undistinguished. Aside from a few handsome Victorian homes and a number of newer murals, which provide some interesting eye candy for the passing visitor, the charisma of East LA comes from the people rather than the buildings, which are mostly bland and unremarkable.

Boyle Heights

Named after the founder and former president of the United Farm Workers union, **César E Chávez Avenue** is actually a continuation of Sunset Boulevard, running from north of Downtown through Boyle Heights into East LA. The commercial activity begins just east of I-10, and is at its liveliest along Chávez Avenue between N Cummings and N Fickett Street. This stretch of road, the heart of Boyle Heights, is lined with earthy restaurants, basic-looking shops stocked with cheap clothing and other inessentials, street vendors hawking everything from papayas to bargain jewellery, and even strolling musicians, who will play a romantic bolero or two on their well-worn guitars for a reasonable fee as you dine at **La Parrilla** (2126 E César E Chávez Avenue; *see p165*). At the intersection of Chávez and Soto Street, look out for several murals by local artists.

Compared to Chávez Avenue, 1st Avenue (two blocks to the south) is pretty mellow. The main point of interest is at 1st Street and Boyle Avenue, just east of the 101 freeway: **Mariachi Plaza**, one of the largest congregations of freelance mariachi musicians outside Mexico City's Garibaldi Square. Sporting traditional black ranchero outfits, the musicians gather here and wait for passing drivers to hire them to play at social and family events. The square is charmingly scruffy at the moment, but it may not remain so for long: developers are planning to redevelop the square with new residential and commercial buildings, which will doubtless assume a higher value when the Gold line reaches here in 2009. Also under threat is the historic but dilapidated Boyle Hotel, a permanent home for many of the musicians.

Most of the other attractions along 1st Street are culinary; chief among them is **La Serenata de Garibaldi** (No.1842; *see p166*), which offers Mexican haute cuisine. Further east is **El Mercado** (No.3425, at Cheesebroughs Lane), a multi-level market reminiscent of those found in Mexican cities. Upstairs, you'll find restaurants with duelling mariachi bands, each seeking to

Days of the dead

When Los Angeles was settled, it kept its graveyards inside the Mission walls or over the rise. But as the population grew and land became more precious, those memorial plots started to look like a waste of good frontage. At the end of the 19th century, bodies were disinterred and reburied in two new graveyards east of the river, where ex-citizens could repose without impeding commerce. Both contain numerous beautiful monuments to celebrated Angelenos; both also continue to serve their communities as active burial sites.

Founded in 1877 and located on a hill in Boyle Heights, **Evergreen Cemetery** (204 N Evergreen Avenue, at E Cesar Chavez Avenue, 1-323 268 6714) affords views out to the snow-capped San Gabriel Mountains. Its meandering lanes are tightly packed with age-stained urns draped in mourning cloth, sad angels and an obelisk honoring the Van Nuys and Lankershim clans. Other monuments include a pink marble tiger marking the Pacific Coast Showman's Association plot, where circus folks received dignified send-offs; the Van Caster family's polished stone sphere; and the graves of supermarket magnate George A Ralphs and attorney Earl Rogers, LA's real-life Perry Mason. The newer graves are decorated with balloons, bottles of hooch and stuffed animals, reflecting the deep connection the Chicano community feels to their dead. Sadly, gang tags disfigure some crypts, suggesting that these feelings don't extend to the old Anglo burials.

Established 19 years after Evergreen Cemetery in unincorporated East LA, **Calvary Cemetery** (4201 Whittier Boulevard, at S Downey Road, 1-323 261 3106, www.calvarymortuary.com) is a driving cemetery. The broad avenues of this Catholic burial ground are lined with polychromed statues of the stations of the cross, tucked under glass to keep them crisp. Of the monuments, angels and saviours are particularly popular. Calvary's crown jewel is the Italian Romanesque Revival chapel, which comes

complete with a dramatic angel-lined entry court that would have done Cecil B De Mille proud (even though the director would never have tolerated a crow building her nest between the wings of one of his angels). The cool interior features pink striped marble walls, ram's head banisters and fine stained glass, and makes a suitably impressive resting place for oil magnate Edward Doheny and comic Lou Costello.

The blinding sun that you might face as you leave the chapel is a blessing. The view from the chapel's steps takes in the unfortunate new mausoleum, which resembles nothing so much as a parking garage at a suburban mall. More interesting is the nearby **Home of Peace** (4334 Whittier Boulevard, at S Eastern Avenue, 1-323 261 6135), a Jewish cemetery founded in 1902 and the final resting place for two of the Three Stooges and three of the four Warner Brothers.

Calvary Cemetery.

lure clientele from the others; downstairs teems with stalls selling all manner of clothes, food and consumer goods. It's tremendous fun.

Elsewhere, Boyle Heights and its surrounding streets boast three very pleasant parks, the largest of them just north of the I-10 on the cusp of Lincoln Heights. Among the attractions in **Lincoln Park** are some statues of Mexican revolutionary heroes and the Plaza de la Raza, a popular arts centre in a converted boathouse by the lake that offers art classes to children after school. The area's other parks include **Hollenbeck Park** (at 4th and Cummings Streets), built to an English model,

Mariachi Plaza. *See p120.*

and the heart-shaped **Prospect Park** (off Chávez Avenue at Echandia Street), a legacy of the local Jewish community.

East Los Angeles

Indiana Avenue serves as the eastern boundary of both Boyle Heights and the City of Los Angeles. Beyond it lies an unincorporated area officially known as **East Los Angeles**, which itself borders Monterey Park to the north (*see p135*), Montebello to the east and City of Commerce to the south. For the most part, this area is similar in character and appearance to Boyle Heights: both neighbourhoods are dominated by Latin Americans, both are slightly deprived and they both retain a tangible pride in their local identities.

As it does in Boyle Heights, Chávez Avenue contains a number of approachable eateries, but it's also home to one of East LA's best-known arts institutions. Founded in the early 1970s, the **Self-Help Graphics & Art** cultural centre (No.3802, at N Gage Avenue, 1-323 881 6444, www.selfhelpgraphics.com) runs community art workshops, stages sporadic sales and exhibits work by established and up-and-coming Latino artists. However, it's most famous for its annual **Día de Los Muertos** (Day of the Dead) celebrations each autumn (*see p215*). An East LA tradition, the event presents the cream of Latino counterculture; it's a must-be-seen-at event for local hipsters.

South of Highway 60 and **Calvary Cemetery** (one of two big local graveyards; *see p121* **Days of the dead**) is **Whittier Boulevard**, which is to East LA what Chávez Avenue is to Boyle Heights. Between Eastern Avenue and Atlantic Boulevard, Whittier is just as busy as Chávez, if not more so: the road is lined with clothes shops, restaurants, *botánicas* (selling herbs and incense), bakeries, nightclubs and bars, and traffic can be tough. Still, if the muffler on your car gives way, help is at hand in the shape of **El Pedorrero** (4101 Whittier Boulevard, at S Record Avenue), which must surely be the most exuberantly decorated car repair shop in North America.

Whittier Boulevard was once the main drag for locals who wanted to display their low-rider hot rods, until the local police eventually put a stop to the tradition. However, East LA remains the LA capital of hot rod design. If you're lucky, you'll see a spectacular example cruising the street while you wait in the traffic. Look out, too, for customised low-rider motorbikes.

On 29 August 1970, the Boulevard was the scene of a 'police riot' when a Chicano anti-war demonstration was attacked by police. During the disturbances, Chicano journalist Ruben Salazar was killed in the Silver Dollar bar (No.4945, at S La Verne Avenue, but long since closed) by a police tear-gas pellet to the head. The death of Salazar, a reporter for the *Los Angeles Times*, was thought by some to be retribution for his criticism of the sheriff's department's abusive behaviour towards people of colour. Back west along Whittier, a couple of blocks from the border with Indiana Avenue, a small green space has been renamed **Salazar Park** in his honour, and stands as a symbol of the 1970s Chicano Movement.

The culture of East Los Angeles spills over into its north-eastern neighbour, the city of Monterey Park. **Luminarias** (E 3500 Ramona Boulevard, at W Newmark Avenue, 1-323 268 4177, www.luminariasrestaurant.com), one of several Latino restaurants, offers an array of Mexican favourites. And nearby, the **Vincent Price Art Museum** at East Los Angeles College (1301 Avenida César Chávez, 1-323 265 8650) takes its name from the horror film icon and art enthusiast who donated more than 2,000 works of art from his personal collection (including many Latino pieces); because, as he put it, 'this is where it's needed'. However, the neighbourhood as a whole is dominated not by Latinos but by Asians; for more, *see p135*.

> **Boyle Heights** Plays the starring role in 2008 thriller *The Take*

South Los Angeles

Is its new name helping to give South Central a new lease of life?

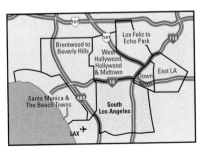

South Los Angeles owes its black identity to the era of restrictive covenants. Instituted in the early 20th century and finally repealed in 1948, these segregationist laws effectively determined the racial make-up of various residential districts in LA. As well as restricting Jews, Chinese and Mexicans to certain areas of the city, the regulations confined African Americans to a tight area around Central Avenue.

South Central LA, as it was then known, enjoyed a cultural boom during the jazz age. However, after the restrictive covenants were lifted, black Angelenos gradually moved west, making the Crenshaw district their cultural and commercial centre. In the past two decades, African Americans have vacated the area in growing numbers and headed to the suburbs. Into their homes have moved Latino families, who've made their mark in the form of a vibrant sidewalk culture.

Between the mid 1970s and the LA Riots of 1992, South Central developed an unenviable reputation as one of the most deprived and violent areas in the US. Gang warfare was rife, and it sometimes felt as though the drugs trade was the area's biggest employer. South Central LA had developed such a bad name that, in 2003, the city council passed an ordinance that officially changed it to South Los Angeles in a bid to help the area shed its appalling image. However, the name hasn't really caught on: many Angelenos, and most outsiders, still refer to the area by its more infamous moniker.

Whichever name you use, the area is not necessarily dangerous, and it's unlikely you'll get caught in the crossfire between the rival gangs that riddle the area. However, it can be bleak. Some of the homes and gardens in the area are quite pretty, but others are shambolic. Parkland and public landscaping are both limited: unrelieved by hills or sea, South LA appears as nothing but relentless flatlands of concrete and asphalt. Appealing shops and noteworthy restaurants are conspicuous by their absence: streets such as Western Avenue and Vernon Avenue are dotted with failed businesses, everything from ice-cream parlours to clothing boutiques. The only thriving storefronts seem to be liquor stores and barbers, which tells its own story.

Exposition Park & around

Los Angeles' love affair with farmers' markets has blossomed in recent years. However, it's actually been present since the late 19th century, when farmers sold food and plants in an open-air market at Agricultural Park to the south of Downtown LA.

By 1910, the park had crumbled into a shadow of its former self, attracting not farmers but deadbeats, gamblers and prostitutes. Help arrived in the shape of local attorney William C Bowers, who began a campaign to reclaim the land and build on it a public park and educational centre. In 1913, Bowers' vision became reality with the opening of the renovated and renamed Exposition Park, and his ideal remains tangible almost a century later. The park will soon be blessed with a Metro station as part of the new Expo line that's set to connect Downtown with Culver City; work on this extension to the rail network is scheduled for completion in 2010.

If you approach Exposition Park from Downtown along Figueroa Avenue, you may be alarmed by the sight of a large plane directly in front of you, seemingly in the middle of the road. Don't worry: the decommissioned DC-8 is merely the frontage of the **California ScienCenter's Air & Space Exhibits** (*see p124*). Close by is the **Californian African American Museum** (*see p124*); the park's northern frontier, meanwhile, is home to the seven-acre **Rose Garden**, home to around 100 varieties of rose and close to 10,000 individual plants. However, the park's main attraction is also its oldest: the **Natural History Museum of Los Angeles County** (*see p125*).

The south side of the park is dominated by the hulking **Los Angeles Memorial Coliseum**, built in 1923 and the main stadium for the Olympics of both 1932 and 1984. The Coliseum suffered major damage in the 1994 earthquake, just months before the Los Angeles Raiders NFL team, who had been using it as their home for a dozen years, moved back to Oakland. These days, it's used in autumn by the University of Southern California's Trojans football team (*see p270*); indeed, USC signed a new 25-year lease on the property in 2008, and have promised to assist with restoration work.

California African American Museum

Exposition Park, 600 State Drive, between S Figueroa Street & S Vermont Avenue (1-213 744 7432/www.caamuseum.org). Bus 40, 42, 81, 102, 381, 550/I-110, exit Exposition Boulevard west. **Open** 10am-5pm Tue-Sat; 11am-5pm Sun. **Admission** free; donations requested. *Parking* $6.

Bigger than it looks from the outside, this handsome museum and research library focuses on the artistic and historical achievements of African Americans. The small but tidy permanent exhibit loosely tells the story of African Americans' journey from Africa, through emancipation and into the 20th century, using an assortment of paintings, textiles, photographs, ceremonial objects, personal testimonies and other memorabilia. Included among the exhibits are substantial displays on Ella Fitzgerald, former LA mayor Tom Bradley and William Spiller, the first African American admitted into the PGA. The museum's other galleries host engaging temporary exhibits, some historical and some artistic, supplemented by a programme of talks, screenings and even the occasional concert.

California ScienCenter

Exposition Park, 700 State Drive, between S Figueroa Street & S Vermont Avenue (1-323 724 3623/IMAX 1-213 744 7400/www.casciencectr.org). Bus 40, 42, 81, 102, 381, 550/I-110, exit Exposition Boulevard west. **Open** 10am-5pm daily. **Admission** *Museum* free. *IMAX* $8; $4.75-$5.75 discounts. *Temporary exhibits* prices vary. *Parking* $6. **Credit** *IMAX* DC, MC, V.

A fusion of two longstanding prior facilities, the California ScienCenter opened in 1998 in a bright, airy building directly in front of the Rose Garden in Exposition Park. The main building is split into two loosely themed wings: Creative World, which focuses on technology (and has a little catching up to do), and World of Life, an engaging if sometimes slightly queasy selection of exhibits on all manner of living things. The top floor also features a Science Court, a fairly disparate jumble of interactive playthings, and the ever-popular High-Wire Bicycle, which allows the brave and the trusting to ride a bike along a one-inch wire some 43 feet above the ground in order to demonstrate the power of gravity. Next door, in a hulking, Frank Gehry-designed building, the Air & Space Exhibits include a replica of a Wright Brothers glider, a decommissioned police helicopter, and *Explorer 1*, the first American spacecraft to orbit the earth.

A supplementary permanent exhibit, World of Ecology, is scheduled to open in 2010, with Worlds Beyond due to follow at a currently unspecified date in the future. In the meantime, further entertainment is provided by a roster of temporary exhibits (CSI: The Experience will be here during 2009) and an IMAX cinema, screening the usual array of dazzling, quasi-educative, nature-slanted films. Entrance to the museum's permanent exhibits is free, which might explain why the main attraction on the ground floor is an enormous shop.

California ScienCenter.

effect, although the major work is still to come: the most eyecatching additions will be two new dinosaur halls, scheduled for completion in 2011. The museum staff hope to keep disruption to a minimum during the renovations. However, if you're heading here in the hope of seeing a particular exhibit, it's worth calling or checking online to confirm it's open before making a special trip. The website also has details of special events; among them is the First Friday programme held on the first Friday-night of the month, which features tours, lectures, music from hipster-friendly acts such as the Mountain Goats and even DJs.

University of Southern California (USC) & around

Fans of the aforementioned USC Trojans don't have far to travel for home games. The University of Southern California itself is just north of Exposition Park, bounded by Figueroa Street, Exposition Boulevard, Vermont Avenue and Jefferson Boulevard.

Established here in 1880, USC's campus is tidy but unspectacular when compared with the sculpture-studded home of **UCLA** (*see p88* **Walk**). However, several corners of the campus are worth exploration, whether alone (maps are available from www.usc.edu or at the campus entrances) or as part of the free 50-minute tours that leave on the hour between 10am and 3pm from the Admission Center in Trojan Hall, just off Figueroa Street at Child's Way. Chief among the attractions is the handsome **Doheny Memorial Library** (1-213 740 2924), where the first-floor Treasure Room offers an interesting roster of free exhibitions. Meanwhile, across campus, the **Fisher Museum of Art** (1-213 740 4561, http://uscfishermuseumofart.org) stages regular temporary shows, some of which feature the work of USC students.

Directly north of USC sits the 6,300-capacity **Shrine Auditorium** (665 W Jefferson Boulevard, at Royal Street). Built in 1926, this huge, Moorish structure is most famous for its role as the host of several of Hollywood's major annual awards shows. However, now that the Oscars have relocated to the Kodak Theatre in Hollywood and the Emmys have decamped to the new Nokia Theatre, questions have been raised about the theatre's future.

Natural History Museum of Los Angeles County

Exposition Park, 900 Exposition Boulevard, between S Figueroa Street & S Vermont Avenue (1-213 763 3466/www.nhm.org). Bus 40, 42, 81, 102, 381, 550/I-110, exit Exposition Boulevard west. **Open** 9.30am-5pm Mon-Fri; 10am-5pm Sat, Sun. **Admission** $9; $2-$6.50 concessions; free under-5s. *Parking* $6. **Credit** AmEx, DC, Disc, MC, V.

Housed in a handsome Spanish-Renaissance building that opened with Exposition Park itself back in 1913, and containing an amazing 33 million exhibits (not all of them are on display at any one time), the Natural History Museum of Los Angeles County claims to be the largest museum of natural history in the US. That may be true, but both the description and the name of the museum are somewhat misleading: the institution's remit stretches beyond the natural world.

It's an immense place, so it's well worth planning your visit. Those with only a little time to spare should head directly to the truly dazzling collections in the Hall of Gems & Minerals, where the exhibits include a 4,644-carat topaz, a 2,200-carat opal sphere and a quartz crystal ball which, with a diameter of 10.9in and a weight of 65lb, is one of the biggest on earth. Other highlights include the small but fascinating exhibit on chaparral, which includes an artful film about how fire regenerates landscapes; the effectively creepy and dauntingly crawly Insect Zoo; and the Ancient Latin America Hall, which is easily the most interesting of the anthropological exhibits.

Some of the exhibits here have been showing their age of late, but things will hopefully be a little brighter when a four-year, $84-million programme of renovations is finally completed. The wonderful skylight that crowns the museum's rotunda has already been restored to beautiful

Sightseeing

Towers of strength

When Italian-born tilesetter Simon Rodia moved to Watts, the neighbourhood was ethnically mixed. Three decades later, when he left, it was predominantly black and Latino, widely seen as the heart of LA's African-American community. In the intervening years, though, Rodia had constructed its single iconic structure, an extraordinary piece of folk art that's one of only a handful of National Historic Landmarks in Los Angeles.

Rodia started work on constructing what have become known as the **Watts Towers** shortly after purchasing a triangular lot in the area and moving on to the site in 1921. Using nothing but found objects (salvaged metal rods, cast-off pipe structures, broken bed frames), Rodia sent his towers inching gradually skywards over more than three decades, reinforcing them with steel and cement to prevent interference from both neighbours and the authorities.

Scaling the towers on a window-washer's belt and bucket, Rodia gradually decorated his towers with a patchwork of yet more found materials that inadvertently act as a reliquary of early and mid 20th-century consumer objects. The glass is mostly green and comes from bottles of 7-Up or Canada Dry; the tiles came from Malibu Pottery, where Rodia was employed in the late 1920s. Other objects clearly visible on the towers' coarse, gaudy 'skin' include jewellery, marble and an estimated 25,000 seashells.

The towers' construction, by a single pair of hands over a 33-year span, are part of their legend. But so is their wan, spectral beauty. Like skeletal echoes of Antoni Gaudí's voluptuous Barcelona church steeples, the towers reach for the sky in an elaborate network of spindly, curved tendrils, connected with equally playful, decorous webs. There are 17 of them in all, the tallest stretching 99 feet into the Los Angeles sky.

The locals, though, were never especially supportive of his endeavours. Miscreant kids regularly smashed the towers' glass and tiling; during the war, a rumour even started that Rodia was sending classified information to the Japanese through the towers, which didn't endear him to his neighbours. In 1954, after years of abuse and vandalism, the 75-year-old Rodia abruptly gave the land to a neighbour and moved away, apparently not caring what happened to the towers he'd spent 34 years constructing.

After Rodia's departure, the towers changed hands several times, but were issued with a demolition in 1957 on the basis that they were structurally unsound. A public outcry ensued, and two years later the city agreed to run stress tests on the towers to test their stability. A stress load of 10,000 pounds was applied to the towers, but they didn't budge an inch… Unlike the crane applying the stress, which buckled under the strain. The future of the towers was finally assured.

It's not all been plain sailing. The towers gradually deteriorated over the years, and were damaged in the 1994 earthquake. However, after a decade-long programme of renovations, they're now in great shape. For details of tours, call 1-213 847 4646.

Central Avenue

Between the 1920s and the '50s, the stretch of **Central Avenue** between Washington Boulevard and Vernon Avenue was home to some of the first financial enterprises, theatres, churches and social institutions established exclusively to serve blacks. This was the hub of LA's African American community, a vital and vibrant street that provided a beleaguered people with a social and commercial focal point. Read Walter Mosley's Easy Rawlins detective mysteries to get a flavour of the street, perhaps the single most important landmark in the history of black Los Angeles.

At the time, the road found a measure of nationwide fame for the music that boomed out of its bars and nightclubs: jazz at first, then R&B. In *On the Road*, Jack Kerouac eulogised it as 'a wild place… with chickenshacks barely big enough to house a jukebox'; more than half a century later, Wynton Marsalis perceptively tagged it as 'the 52nd Street of Los Angeles'. This musical heritage is celebrated every summer with the **Central Avenue Jazz Festival**, but modern-day Central Avenue is a rather sad and unalluring place. Many of its buildings and businesses have seen better days, and the African American influence has been partly usurped by Latino culture. Still, a few landmarks remain: the **Dunbar Hotel** (4225 S Central Avenue) was the first hotel built by and for African Americans, and still stands as a complex of low-income residential units.

The streets around Central Avenue seem trapped by a similar malaise, but a few sights stand out. Formerly the focal point of the city's gritty boxing-gym culture documented in the movie *Million Dollar Baby*, the city of **Vernon** to the east contains a couple of very handsome old streamline moderne buildings: the Owens-Illinois Pacific Building at the corner of S Soto Street and Fruitland Avenue, and the Lane-Wells Company Building to the south. And directly to the south is the city of **Huntington Park**, home to the humming Latino shopping street of Pacific Boulevard. Between Gage and Florence Avenues, the storefront windows are lined with cowboy hats and knock-off fashions, as accordion music echoes from the cranked-up speakers.

Watts

After the jazz era, blacks continued migrating south along Central Avenue towards Watts. The district is notorious for the riots of 1965 and 1992, but it also contains an LA landmark, the **Watts Towers** (*see p126*. The **Watts Towers Arts Center** (1727 E 107th Street, 1-213 847 4646) hosts exhibitions, festivals and concerts.

Though much of the area is still neglected, Watts is re-emerging as a focal point for black pride, a development embodied by the **Watts Labor Community Action Committee** (10950 S Central Avenue, 1-323 563 5639, www.wlcac.org). The centre was destroyed during the riots in 1965 and 1992, but it has been rebuilt as a social and cultural centre. The centre's *The Mother of Humanity* is the world's largest bronze sculpture of a black woman, and the building's main façade is the setting for *Mudtown Flats*, a mural showing historic sites on Central Avenue.

Leimert Park

Leimert (pronounced 'Luh-murt') Park is LA's most appealing black neighbourhood. Anchored by the park itself and Degnan Boulevard, the area has undergone a cultural renaissance in recent years, with art galleries, jazz clubs, speciality shops and restaurants springing up all over the place. Simultaneously, property prices have soared: wander up Degnan Boulevard just north of Stocker Street for a glimpse at the affluent side of the area.

Leimert Park Village, a pedestrianised area bordered by Crenshaw Boulevard, 43rd Street, Leimert Boulevard and Vernon Avenue, is the cultural centre of African American life in LA. There's live music nightly, whether it's blues at **Babe's & Ricky's Inn** (*see p259*) or uncompromising jazz at **World Stage** (*see p260*). On the food front, try **Café Soul** (33472 43rd Place, 1-323 299 7797). Also off Degnan is the famous **Phillips Barbecue** (4307 Leimert Boulevard, 1-323 292 7613): prepare to queue for a take-out order of some of the best ribs in town.

Crenshaw & around

Crenshaw, the area surrounding the boulevard of the same name south of I-10 to Florence Avenue, is today one of the few mainly black communities in LA County. But the site of the 1932 Olympic Village and LA's first airport had a different profile after World War II, when many Japanese returning from internment camps settled here and established themselves as landscape gardeners. Their legacy is still visible today: this is a handsome neighbourhood.

The Hills (Baldwin Hills, Windsor Hills, Fox Hills, View Park and Ladera Heights), which lie west of Crenshaw Boulevard around

Clyde Woodworth Elementary School, 3200 W 104th Street, Inglewood Where young Tré Styles goes to school in *Boyz n the Hood*

Grow your own

If you were to ask an Angeleno for their impressions of South LA, you'd hear the word 'dangerous' more than any other. The neighbourhoods that spread south-west of Downtown are rich in culture, history and civic pride, but the area's least appealing characteristics are the ones that seem to attract the most media attention. The Watts Riots and the Rodney King uprising were significant political and social revolutions, but it was the violence that defines them in the history books.

In 2006, another uprising took place in South LA that catapulted the beleaguered area back into the limelight. However, unlike the revolts of the past, this event was non-violent and focused on a 14-acre urban garden at the corner of E 41st and S Alameda Streets on the edge of Vernon. For nearly 15 years, the **South Central Farm** had been a presence in this industrial zone, and its vegetables, fruits and herbs provided fresh food for the hundreds of low-income families who worked the plots at this community garden. But then in June 2006, police descended on the farm and evicted its occupants. Three weeks later, the site was bulldozed.

Prior to the LAPD and the county sheriff department descending on the farm, there had been several years of lawsuits and haggling between City Hall and the site's developer, who hoped to erect a new condominium development on the site. Caught in the middle of the disputes, the farmers at first practiced diplomacy, but eventually resorted to civil disobedience in a doomed attempt to save their plots.

Only one positive emerged from the whole mess: a new groundswell of appreciation for community gardens, not just in South LA but throughout the city. Suddenly, the notion of growing one's own vegetables as part of a small community took on a new appeal, and more Angelenos have begun to seek out plots of land for their own agricultural interests.

Slauson Avenue, are home to some of LA's most prominent upper middle-class and professional blacks; indeed, the five connected neighbourhoods are said to have the highest concentration of black wealth in the US. Balancing this affluence at the base of these hills is an area known as the Jungle: the name derived from the neighbourhood's lush tropical plantings, but it's better known these days as a haven for drug dealing and other illicit activities.

In the 1940s, the first shopping plaza in the US was built at the intersection of Martin Luther King Jr (aka 'King') and Crenshaw Boulevards. Now transformed into the **Baldwin Hills Crenshaw Plaza** (www.crenshawplaza.com), it's the centre of the Crenshaw community, which finds a cultural anchor in the shape of the **Magic Johnson Theaters** (4020 Marlton Avenue). Part-owned by the former NBA great, the cinemas have some of the friendliest staff in LA, and some of the rowdiest crowds.

For a rousing religious experience, visit the **West Angeles Church of God in Christ** (3600 Crenshaw Boulevard, 1-323 733 8300, www.westa.org). Presided over by bishop Charles Blake, it's one of the city's most popular black Pentecostal churches. With the help of huge donations from Denzel Washington and Magic Johnson, both members of the church, Blake built this $40 million cathedral, which hosts services every Sunday at 8am and 11am.

On the far west side of Crenshaw, between La Cienega Boulevard and La Brea Avenue, is the **Kenneth Hahn State Recreation Area** (1-323 298 3660). Named after a popular former city councilman, it's a huge, delightful place, with a fishing pond, swans, a Japanese bridge over a waterfall, undulating hills and basketball courts. North of the park is the historic **West Adams** district (formerly known as 'Sugar Hill', extending from Figueroa Street to Crenshaw Boulevard and from Venice to Jefferson Boulevards), a lovingly preserved collection of Victorian, Craftsman and Colonial Revival houses laid out after the 1880s.

Inglewood

Although it's located outside the city limits, Inglewood is often considered part of South LA. It's best known as the home of two local institutions: the **Great Western Forum**, where the LA Lakers basketball team and LA Kings hockey team played before they moved to the Staples Center, and **Randy's Donuts** (*see p27*), an architectural classic of the 1950s. South of the Forum is the **Hollywood Park Race Track & Casino** (*see p270*), which features horse-racing and, each weekend, live music. East of Inglewood, in Hyde Park, sits the intersection of Florence and Normandie Avenues, the flashpoint for the 1992 riots.

The Valleys

There are treasures in LA's endless suburbs, if you know where to look.

San Fernando Valley

Located directly north of the Hollywood Hills, the San Fernando Valley is most famous for its girls. The gum-popping, air-headed Valley Girl, immortalised by the Frank Zappa song and the Martha Coolidge movie of the same name, is a quintessential 1980s phenomenon, but the local porn industry both pre- and post-dates it. While *The Brady Bunch* was being filmed in a split-level 1960s ranch house, other San Fernando backyards found girls in curls and guys in tight polyester trousers doing a lot more than playing ball. Paul Thomas Anderson fictionalised this sordid past (and present) in *Boogie Nights*.

The San Fernando Valley's two main cities sit more or less side by side, north of Griffith Park. Crisply pressed **Glendale** is larger and more charismatic than tidy **Burbank**. Still, both are ultimately pretty bland places that bring to mind Mark Twain's quote that 'Los Angeles is a great place to live, but I wouldn't want to visit': they're perfect spots in which to bring up 2.4 children, but not so perfect if you're in town with 2.4 thrill-seeking children to entertain. Indeed, Glendale's main attraction is a cemetery: the **Forest Lawn Memorial Park** (1712 S Glendale Avenue, 1-323 254 3131, www.forestlawn.com), the final resting place of celebrities such as Walt Disney, Errol Flynn, Spencer Tracy, Nat 'King' Cole and Clark Gable.

The film industry's influence runs so deep in Burbank that it was used as the last name for Jim Carrey's character in *The Truman Show*. **Warner Brothers** (*see p73*), NBC and Disney have studios here, with Disney's impossible to miss; the animation building, designed by postmodernist Robert Stern, is topped by a two-storey wizard's hat similar to the one worn by Mickey Mouse in *Fantasia*'s Sorcerer's Apprentice sequence, and the word 'animation' spelt out in 14-foot letters. However, aside from iconic drive-in **Bob's Big Boy** (4211 Riverside Drive), there's not much to see. Better, perhaps, to drive to **Universal Studios** (*see p131*).

Things don't get much more interesting elsewhere. North-west of Burbank sit Mission Hills and the **Mission San Fernando Rey de España** (15151 San Fernando Mission Boulevard, 1-818 361 0186), founded in 1797 and rebuilt after the 1971 earthquake; Sylmar boasts the two **Nethercutt Collection**

museums (*see below*); and, a short ride up I-5, Santa Clarita is home to the ever-popular **Six Flags** park (*see p130*). To the west sit **Sherman Oaks**, once Valley Girl Central but now considerably more diverse; **Tarzana**, where you'll find fabulously scruffy rock club **Paladino's** (6101 Reseda Boulevard); **Northridge**, most notable for the Googie-style **First Lutheran Church of Northridge** (18355 Roscoe Boulevard), aka the 'First Church of Elroy Jetson'; and Simi Valley, home of the **Ronald W Reagan Presidential Library & Museum** (*see p130*).

Suburbia aside, the San Fernando Valley is the gateway to the wonderful **Santa Monica Mountains**, one of the country's most beautiful and environmentally fragile urban mountain ranges. Separating the valley from the city basin and the ocean, the mountains are dotted with hiking and biking trails, and contain many ranches that once belonged to movie stars and the studios that employed them: there's the **Paramount Ranch** (2813 Cornell Road, off Kanan Road, Agoura) which has stood in for Tombstone and Dodge City, and was used for the TV series *Dr Quinn, Medicine Woman*. For more on the area, contact the **Santa Monica Mountains National Recreation Area** (1-805 370 2301, www.nps.gov/samo).

Nethercutt Collection

Nethercutt Museum *15151 Bledsoe Street, at San Fernando Road, Sylmar.* **Open** 9am-4.30pm Tue-Sat.
San Sylmar *15200 Bledsoe Street, at San Fernando Road, Sylmar.* **Open** *Tours* 10am, 1.30pm Thur-Sat. Booking essential.
Both *1-818 364 6464/www.nethercuttcollection.org. Bus 94, 394/I-5, exit Roxford Street east.*
Admission free. *Parking* free.
The collection of eccentric cosmetics heirs and philanthropists Dorothy and JB Nethercutt makes for a striking pair of museums. The San Sylmar site is home to a collection of old, fancy but functional objects, all in working order: everything from gorgeous old cars and Steuben Glass hood ornaments to French furniture and automated musical instruments. Among the sporadic events are recitals on the Mighty Wurlitzer theatre organ. Shorts and jeans are prohibited out of respect for the fancy merchandise. The Nethercutt Museum, meanwhile, provides a handsome home for 100 of the Nethercutts' 230-plus classic cars: Daimlers, Lincolns, Packards and Duesenbergs, all kept in immaculate order.

Lose yourself in the gardens at the **Huntington Library**. *See p132.*

Ronald W Reagan Presidential Library & Museum

40 Presidential Drive, at Madera Road, Simi Valley (1-800 410 8354/www.reaganlibrary.net). Hwy 118, exit Madera Road south. **Open** 10am-5pm daily. **Admission** $12; $3-$9 discounts; free under-11s. *Parking* free. **No credit cards.**

This place is great for fans of the Gipper, but liberals will probably see red. The museum contains an array of exhibits detailing Reagan's Illinois childhood and his years in office; the displays are supplemented by some more general displays covering American history. Ronnie is even buried here.

San Fernando Valley Conference & Visitors Bureau

Suite 200, 5121 Van Nuys Boulevard, between Magnolia Boulevard & Otsego Street, Sherman Oaks (1-818 379 7000/www.valleyofthestars.org). Bus 183, 233, 237, 761/US 101, exit Van Nuys Boulevard north. **Open** 8.30am-5pm Mon-Fri.

Six Flags California

Magic Mountain Parkway, off I-5, Valencia (Magic Mountain 1-661 255 4000/Hurricane Harbor 1-661 255 4527/www.sixflags.com). I-5, exit Magic Mountain Parkway. **Open** Hours vary by day: call or check online for full details, incl closing times. *Magic Mountain: Summer* usually from 10.30am Mon-Fri; from 10am Sat, Sun. *Winter* usually from 10.30am Fri; from 10am Sat, Sun. Hours vary by day: call or check online for closing times. *Hurricane Harbor:*

Summer usually from 10.30am Mon-Fri; from 10am Sat, Sun. *Winter* from 10am Sat, Sun. Call or check online for closing times. **Admission** *Magic Mountain* $59.99; $29.99 discounts; free under-2s. *Hurricane Harbor* $29.99; $20.99 discounts; free under-2s. *Combined ticket* $69.99. *Parking* $15. **Credit** AmEx, DC, Disc, MC, V.

Comprising Magic Mountain and newer watery cousin Hurricane Harbor, Six Flags delivers thrills for all but the most joyless and crowdphobic holidaymakers. The park offers rollercoasters and water rides for every level of screamer: while there are some gentle rides here, the park is most famous for the ones that'll push your heart into your mouth and your lunch on to the person sitting in front of you. It's a raucous place, both on the rides and off them: if you've got very young kids in tow, Disneyland and Universal Studios are both better bets.

Although a few of the rides at Magic Mountain come with Hollywood themes, such diversions are incidental to the excitement of the riding experience. Perhaps the most terrifying of all the park's rides is the Riddler's Revenge, the world's tallest, longest and fastest stand-up rollercoaster. However, it's got stiff competition. Other highlights include the Colossus, billed as 'the tallest and fastest wooden coaster in the West'; the ludicrous Viper, which soars 188ft (56m) in the air; the floorless Scream! 'coaster, hugely popular since its 2003 opening; and X2, revamped during 2008 in a bid to increase the terror levels still further. Happily, there are a number of activities that are suitable for riders of a nervous disposition, among them the gentler-than-it-sounds Canyon Blaster and the Log Jammer flume ride.

Hurricane Harbor is Magic Mountain's smaller, watery cousin. As you might expect, the rides here are a little milder, but there are still thrills to be had: try Tornado, billed as a 'six-storey funnel of fear'.

The parks' opening hours vary almost daily: check online for a detailed calendar, and for further information on the full range of admission-fee packages (including tickets covering both parks). Note that many rides have height restrictions, starting at around 48in (1.22m).

Universal Studios & CityWalk
100 Universal City Plaza, Universal City (1-800 864 8377/www.universalstudioshollywood.com/ www.citywalkhollywood.com). Metro Universal City/ bus 96, 156, 166/US 101, exit Universal Center Drive. **Open** *Hours vary by day: call or check online for full details, incl closing times. Universal Studios: Summer usually from 9am daily. Winter usually 10am-6pm daily. Citywalk 11am-9pm Mon-Thur, Sun; 11am-11pm Fri, Sat.* **Admission** *Universal Studios $64; $54 discounts; under-3s free. Call or check online for details of other combination tickets. Citywalk free. Parking $11.* **Credit** *AmEx, DC, Disc, MC, V.*

More than any of its Southern California competitors, Universal Studios is a theme park with a capital 'T'. The theme here, of course, is the movies. The park offers a necessarily selective ramble through the studio's hits and even one or two of its misses; it's difficult to know whether the park is here to promote the movies or vice versa. Either way, it's hard to shake the feeling that you've bought tickets to a colossal marketing exercise.

The rides aren't as exciting as you might expect: certainly, they lack both Disneyland's charm and the sheer terror inspired by Six Flags Magic Mountain. You're here for the illusion of glamour, the silver-screen memories brought back by the rides rather than the rides themselves. Adults will enjoy going back to the past on the *Back to the Future*-themed stomach-churner, young teenagers may enjoy the Jurassic Park River Adventure, and kids of all ages should be tickled by the new ride based on *The Simpsons*. Other films brought to something approaching life include *Terminator 2, The Mummy, Backdraft* and, bizarrely, *Waterworld*. However, the pick of the themed attractions, for both grown-ups and kids, is the cheeky *Shrek 4-D* movie.

Similarly, the studio tour itself is more about association than excitement. Despite all the hype boasting of how you're being let behind the scenes, the closest you'll likely get to seeing some actual action is spying the occasional spark's car parked behind an otherwise faceless sound stage. Still, once you've resigned yourself (and your kids) to a star-free afternoon, there's a great deal to enjoy, from old movie sets seemingly left lying around by careless stagehands, to the cheesily compiled set pieces and a dazzling chase sequence inspired by the Vin Diesel movie *The Fast and the Furious*.

Most attractions have the decency to save their souvenir shops until the end. Not here. You can't reach Universal Studios without strolling down CityWalk, a loud, colourful and oppressive pedestrianised street crammed with souvenir hawkers and junk-food retailers. If you've got children, don't be too surprised to find your finances severely depleted before you've even reached the gates of the studios.

Note that the prices detailed above are for basic admission only. A large variety of queue-jumping tickets are also available, starting at $99 for an off-season 'Front of Line' pass to $199 for a VIP ticket. Check online for a full list of ticket options and for detailed opening hours, which vary by the season and sometimes by the day.

San Gabriel Valley

Though crowded with suburban development and often choked with traffic, the San Gabriel Valley at least boasts a picturesque location, set against the striking San Gabriel Mountains to the north. Unlike the San Fernando Valley, the San Gabriel Valley is not part of the City of Los Angeles, an independence that's reflected in its neighbourhoods: it's a more charming place than its neighbour, more ethnically diverse and less architecturally homogeneous.

Pasadena & around

Pasadena is one of the most attractive towns in the region, and one of the few parts of Southern California where the term 'old money' still means something. It was developed in the 1870s and became popular with Midwesterners over the subsequent two decades; indeed, the famous **Tournament of Roses Parade** (*see p216*) was founded in 1890 as a marketing exercise, an attempt by the city fathers to show off Pasadena's immaculate climate to outsiders. More than a century later, the locals remain immensely proud of their city. And key to the area's continued appeal is its sense of history, and the locals' enthusiasm for preserving it.

The focal point is **Old Town Pasadena**, centred on Colorado Boulevard and bounded by Arroyo Parkway, De Lacey Avenue and Holly and Green Streets. And within this area, at the corner of Colorado and Fair Oaks Avenue, stands **One Colorado**, a perfect example of the way in which Pasadena fuses tradition with the

> **Toluca Lake United Methodist Church, 4301 Cahuenga Boulevard, North Hollywood**
> Where, in Tim Burton's biopic, *Ed Wood* goes in search of funding

21st century. As recently as the mid '80s, this was a sorry, rundown picture of boarded-up dereliction. Today, though, packs of teenagers mingle with families and couples in a tidy mix of restored old buildings and new construction. Unfortunately, chains dominate. A number of independent stores and eateries do thrive in Old Town Pasadena though, and the district's approachable streetscape is a world away from the Valley mall culture of myth and legend.

This keen preservationist instinct carries over into other parts of Pasadena, both in civic structures such as the grand old **Pasadena City Hall** (corner of N Garfield Avenue and E Holly Street) and in the handsome houses that line the city's residential corners. Charles and Henry Greene's **Gamble House** (*see below*) is deservedly the most famous; however, the streets around it, especially **Arroyo Terrace** (designed by the Greenes) and **Grand Avenue**, are lined with similarly delightful century-old homes. A self-guided tour of the area is available from the Gamble House's shop. Other notable residential districts include **Oak Knoll**, especially Hillcrest and Wentworth Avenues, and the **Bungalow Heaven** district, hemmed in by Washington Boulevard, Hill Avenue, Orange Grove Boulevard and Lake Street.

Pasadena also distinguishes itself with its array of visitor attractions, more interesting and varied than any other town in the valley. Among its museums are the **Norton Simon Museum** (*see p134*), the **Pacific Asia Museum** (*see p135*), the **Pasadena Museum of California Art** (*see p135*) and **Kidspace** (*see p133*) – all are worth a peek. The **Tournament House** (*see p135*) offers another window on the area's past; elsewhere, NASA's **Jet Propulsion Laboratory** (*see p133*) and the **Mount Wilson Observatory** (north of Pasadena; *see p134*) can provide unexpected glimpses of things very far beyond the San Gabriel Valley.

Two pleasant communities adjoin Pasadena. North-west is the picturesque hillside town of **La Cañada Flintridge**, home of the peaceful **Descanso Gardens** (*see below*) is open to the public: highlights include a world-class collection of books and manuscripts, and some of the most astonishingly beautiful and well-maintained gardens in America.

Gamble House The home of 'Doc' Emmett Brown in *Back to the Future*

Descanso Gardens

1418 Descanso Drive, at Oakwood Avenue & Knight Way, La Cañada Flintridge (1-818 949 4200/www. descansogardens.org). I-210, exit Gould Avenue north. **Open** 9am-5pm daily. **Admission** $7; $2-$5 discounts; free under-5s. *Parking* free. **Credit** AmEx, DC, MC, V.

This delightful tribute to the horticultural magic of Southern California includes more than 600 varieties of camellia (these are best seen between the middle of February and early May, when there are around 34,000 of the plants in bloom) and some five acres of roses. There are also lilac, orchid, fern and California native plant areas, as well as an oriental tea house donated by the Japanese-American community. The gardens host yoga classes amid the greenery.

Gamble House

4 Westmoreland Place, at Walnut Street, Pasadena (1-626 793 3334/www.gamblehouse.org). Bus 177, 267/Hwy 110 to Pasadena (hwy ends at Colorado Boulevard). **Open** *Tours* hourly, noon-3pm Thur-Sun. **Admission** $10-$12; $7 discounts; free under-12s. *Parking* free. **No credit cards**.

When brothers Charles and Henry Greene moved to Pasadena from Cincinnati in 1893, the Arts & Crafts movement had yet to take hold in California. By the time they built this house in 1908 for the Gamble family (as in Proctor & Gamble), their influence had travelled far and wide. This handsome house, on a leafy Pasadena street, is perhaps the leading example of Southern California's 'Craftsman' bungalow style, influenced – in typical fashion – by both Japanese and Swiss architecture. The house was almost sold by Gamble's daughter-in-law in 1962, but when she overheard the prospective buyers discussing their plans to paint everything white, she immediately pulled the home off the market. It's now in the hands of USC.

Highlights of the informative daily tours include the nature-themed frieze made from California redwood; Emil Lange's stunning glass doors; and the unexpected presence in the kitchen of the same tiling that was then used on the New York subway. Add in Tiffany lamps and Greene-designed furniture, and it's easy to see how the cost of the home escalated to $60,000 at a time when the average house in the area cost a mere $1,200. The bookshop is strong on architecture, and also offers a sheet detailing many other notable houses in the neighbourhood. Reservations are accepted only for the 2pm tours.

Huntington Library, Art Collections & Botanical Gardens

1151 Oxford Road, off Huntington Drive, San Marino (1-626 405 2100/www.huntington.org). Bus 79/Hwy 110 to Pasadena (hwy ends at Colorado Boulevard). **Open** *Memorial Day-Labor Day* 10.30am-4.30pm Mon, Wed-Sun. *Labor Day-Memorial Day* noon-4.30pm Mon, Wed-Fri; 10.30am-4.30pm Sat, Sun. **Admission** $15-$20; $10-$12 discounts; free under-5s. Free to all 1st Thur of mth (tickets required; call 1-800 838 3006). *Parking* free. **Credit** DC, MC, V.

Norton Simon Museum. *See p134.*

The bequest of entrepreneur Henry E Huntington is now one of the most enjoyable attractions in the Los Angeles region. It's also not a destination that you should attempt to explore in full during a single day: between the art, the library holdings and the spread-eagled outdoor spaces, there's plenty to see, and most of it is best enjoyed at lingering leisure rather than as part of a mad day-long dash.

Once you've paid your admission, you'll be close to the main library, which holds more than six million items and is open only to researchers (apply for credentials in advance of your visit). However, some of its most notable holdings, among them a Gutenberg Bible and the earliest known edition of Chaucer's *The Canterbury Tales*, are always on display in the adjoining exhibition hall, alongside regular themed temporary shows. The art collection is almost as notable as the library's collection. Built in 1910 and now open again after an extensive three-year renovation, the main house is home to a very impressive collection of British art, which includes Gainsborough's *The Blue Boy* alongside works by Blake, Reynolds and Turner. And over in the newer Scott and Erburu Galleries, you'll find a selection of American paintings.

However, despite all these cultural glories, the Huntington's highlights are outdoors in its vast jigsaw of botanical gardens, arguably the most glorious in the entire Los Angeles region. The 207 acres of gardens, 120 acres of which are open to the public, are divided into a variety of themes: the Desert Garden, now a century old, is packed with cacti and other succulents; the Shakespeare Garden evokes a kind of Englishness rarely seen in England these days; the Children's Garden is a delightful mix of educational features and entertaining diversions; and the Japanese garden is quietly, unassumingly magical. Most recent is the Chinese-themed Garden of Flowing Fragrance, a delicate environment built in part by Chinese artisans that was unveiled in early 2008 to great acclaim. Like much of this fabulous place, it's best approached in slow motion. *Photo p130.*

Jet Propulsion Laboratory

4800 Oak Grove Drive, north of Foothill Boulevard (1-818 354 9314/www.jpl.nasa.gov). Bus 177, 268/ Hwy 110 to Pasadena (hwy ends at Colorado Boulevard). **Open** *Tours call for details.* **Admission** free. *Parking* free.

Employing 5,000 people, and equipped with an annual budget of $1.4 billion, the JPL designed, built and now operates NASA's Deep Space Network; it was also responsible for the *Mars Pathfinder* and the *Spirit* rover's mission to Mars. Roughly once a week, the lab opens its doors to the public; the 2- to 2.5-hour tour begins with a multimedia overview of the set-up, after which the public are shown around the Space Flight Operations Facility and the Spacecraft Assembly Facility. Demand is high and booking well ahead is essential; security concerns dictate that US citizens need to bring a passport or driver's licence, while citizens of other countries must declare their nationality prior to booking and bring a passport and/or green card on the day. For full security and booking details, check the website.

Decide for yourself at the **Pasadena Museum of California Art**.

Kidspace Children's Museum

Brookside Park, 480 N Arroyo Boulevard, at W Holly Street, Pasadena (1-626 449 9144/www.kidspace museum.org). Bus 177, 267/Hwy 110 to Pasadena (hwy ends at Colorado Boulevard). **Open** *Sept-May 9.30am-5pm Tue-Sun. June-Aug 9.30am-5pm daily.* **Admission** $8; free under-1s. *Parking* free. **Credit** AmEx, DC, Disc, MC, V.

Housed for two decades in a school gym, this popular interactive children's museum moved to a new site in 2004 after an $18-million funding drive. There's a wide variety of exhibits and entertainments, from the Kaleidoscope entrance to the educational gardens and the Splash Dance water feature in the central courtyard, the perfect way to cool down on a baking valley afternoon. Pasadena's young 'uns are lucky to have it on their doorstep.

Mount Wilson Observatory

Mount Wilson Road, north of La Cañada Flintridge (1-626 449 6840/www.mtwilson.edu). Route 2 to Red Box Road. **Open** *Apr-Nov 10am-4pm daily.* **Admission** free. *Parking* free.

High up in the San Gabriel Mountains, the Mount Wilson Observatory affords terrific views of the surrounding region. If you're travelling with a group, you can book an after-dark session on the observatory's 60-inch telescope. Admission is free, but you'll need to buy a Forest Service Adventure Pass in order to visit the site as it's located within the Angeles National Forest; see the website for full details.

Norton Simon Museum

411 W Colorado Boulevard, between N Orange Grove Boulevard & N St John Avenue, Pasadena (1-626 449 6840/www.nortonsimon.org). Bus 177, 180, 181, 256, 380/Hwy 110 to Pasadena (hwy ends at Colorado Boulevard). **Open** noon-6pm Mon, Wed, Thur, Sat, Sun; noon-9pm Fri. **Admission** $8; $4 discounts; free students, under-18s. *Parking* free. **No credit cards**.

The Norton Simon's Gehry-helmed makeover in the late 1990s raised the museum's profile. But it also helped it expand the range of its collection, giving it more space and creating a calm, simple environment in which to display it. And this is a beautifully designed museum, its collection sympathetically mounted and immaculately captioned.

The museum is still best known for its impressive collection of Old Masters, notably pieces by 17th-century Dutch painters such as Rembrandt (a particularly rakish self-portrait), Brueghel and Frans Hals. The French impressionists are represented by, among others, Monet, Manet and Renoir. Other valuable holdings include a generous array of Degas's under-appreciated ballerina bronzes, some excellent modern works – including a haunting Modigliani portrait of his wife, some Diego Rivera paintings, and plenty of works by the so-called Blue Four (Feininger, Jawlensky, Klee and Kandinsky), and large collections of European prints, Far Eastern art and Buddhist artefacts. After you've checked out the temporary shows, head into the excellent sculpture garden. All told, a terrific museum. *Photo p133.*

Pacific Asia Museum

46 N Los Robles Avenue, at E Colorado Boulevard West, Pasadena (1-626 449 2742/www.pacificasia museum.org). Metro Memorial Park/bus 180, 181, 267, 687/Hwy 110 to Pasadena (hwy ends at Colorado Boulevard). **Open** 10am-6pm Wed-Sun. **Admission** $7; $5 discounts. Free to all 4th Fri of mth. Half-price if you've visited the Pasadena Museum of California Art on same day. *Parking* free. **No credit cards.**

Art and artefacts from Asia and the Pacific Rim are displayed in the historic Grace Nicholson Building, a re-creation of a northern Chinese palace with a charming Chinese Garden Court to match. Taken from the museum's collection of 14,000 items, the permanent displays include both contemporary and traditional Asian arts; they're supplemented by temporary shows, which tend to run for roughly four months at a time. Look out for special events.

Pasadena Convention & Visitors Bureau

171 S Los Robles Avenue, at Cordova Street, Pasadena (1-626 795 9311/www.pasadenacal.com/ visitors.htm). Metro Del Mar/bus 180, 181, 267, 687/Hwy 110 to Pasadena (hwy ends at Colorado Boulevard). **Open** 8am-5pm Mon-Fri; 10am-4pm Sat.

Pasadena Museum of California Art

497 E Colorado Boulevard, between S Los Robles & S Lake Avenues, Pasadena (1-626 568 3665/www. pmcaonline.org). Metro Memorial Park/bus 180, 181, 267, 687/Hwy 110 to Pasadena (hwy ends at Colorado Boulevard). **Open** noon-5pm Wed-Sun. **Admission** $6; $4 discounts. Free to all 1st Fri of mth. Half-price if you've visited the Pacific Asia Museum on same day. *Parking* free. **Credit** AmEx, DC, MC, V.

An open-air staircase beautified by moody lightplay from an oculus above it creates a striking entrance into this three-storey facility. The museum is dedicated to California art and design from the last 150 years, and often runs several temporary exhibitions simultaneously in its straightforward gallery spaces: you might find a collection of paintings by Pasadena Impressionist Benjamin Chambers Brown alongside a show devoted to toy culture. (One admission price covers all shows.) The PMCA also runs the California Design Biennial, featuring the best design emanating from the state; the next is scheduled for 2009.

Tournament House & the Wrigley Gardens

391 S Orange Grove Boulevard, between W Del mar & W California Boulevards, Pasadena (1-626 449 4100/www.tournamentofroses.com). Metro Memorial Park/bus 180, 181, 267, 687/Hwy 110 to Pasadena (hwy ends at Colorado Boulevard). **Open** Tours, Feb-Aug 2pm, 3pm Thur. **Admission** free. *Parking* free.

Formerly owned by chewing gum magnate William Wrigley, Jr, this grand old mansion is now home to the offices of the Tournament of Roses Parade. It's open for tours for six months of the year, and is worth a look as much for its stately gardens as for its handsome and occasionally stunning interior.

Heading east

As you head inland from Pasadena, points of interest become fewer and further between. In Arcadia sits an elegant 1930s racetrack, **Santa Anita Park** (*see p270*), and the **Los Angeles County Arboretum & Botanical Garden** (*see below*). Beyond are acres of suburbia, enlivened only by a handful of older foothill communities along the Foothill Freeway. Both Sierra Madre and Monrovia, which lie in the shadow of the San Gabriel Mountains, have charming early 20th-century downtown areas.

Continuing east on I-210, you'll eventually reach **Claremont** and the Claremont Colleges, a collection of six educational institutions near East Foothill Boulevard. The campus offers shady streets and an academic vibe reminiscent of East Coast Ivy League schools. The town's 'Village' (east of Indian Hill Boulevard, between 1st and 4th Streets) is another delightful downtown area, featuring buildings from the 1920s. South-east of Claremont is **Pomona**, home to another college (California State Polytechnic University) and, each autumn, the two-week **LA County Fair** (*see p215*). The area remains an important agricultural centre; you'll see the same giant vegetables and prize-winning pigs as you would in the Midwest.

The area south of Pasadena holds greater variety. The bustling suburbs of **Monterey Park**, **Alhambra** and **San Gabriel** have largely Chinese and Chinese American populations, many of them immigrants from Taiwan and Hong Kong. Forget Chinatown, just north of Downtown LA: this is one of the largest Chinese settlements in America. The strips of Atlantic Boulevard and Garfield Avenue contain Chinese restaurants of every sort, as well as groceries, bakeries and chemists.

Los Angeles County Arboretum & Botanical Garden

301 N Baldwin Avenue, between W Colorado Boulevard & Campus Drive, Arcadia (1-626 821 3222/www.arboretum.org). Bus 79, 264, 268/I-210, exit Baldwin Avenue south. **Open** 9am-5pm daily. **Admission** $7; $2.50-$5 concessions; free under-5s. *Parking* free. **Credit** AmEx, DC, MC, V.

These gorgeous grounds in Arcadia, very close to the Santa Anita racetrack, have been designed as an educational facility (the plants are mostly arranged by region, and tours are available), but many people simply come here for a little peace and quiet. You could wander these gardens for hours; many do, taking in tropical forests and waterfalls, trees and fish.

Weingart Stadium, East Los Angeles College, Monterey Park 'Run, Forrest! Run!'

Heading South

Bays, beaches and big round ears.

South Coast Botanic Garden

The South Bay & Long Beach

The South Bay

El Segundo to Redondo Beach

Getting to the South Bay is half the fun. The beachside Vista del Mar road starts about a mile south of **Marina del Rey**, off Culver Avenue at Dockweiler State Beach. Zip past LAX and you're in the district of **El Segundo**. The best non-aquatic attraction here is an old-fashioned cinema: the fabulous **Old Town Music Hall** (140 Richmond Street, 1-310 322 2592, www.otmh.org), open weekends only, features pre-1960s movies and organ concerts.

Continue south on Vista del Mar (which becomes Highland Avenue) until you reach Manhattan Beach Boulevard and then make a right towards the ocean. This is the heart of

Manhattan Beach, formerly a low-key, quasi-bohemian town that's been transformed over the last half-decade into an affluent, casually fashionable pocket of LA. The pedestrianised shopping streets hold more than their share of independent stores, but no business better epitomises modernised Manhattan Beach than the **Shade Hotel** (1221 N Valley Drive; *see p65*), an unexpectedly sleek boutique. The beach itself is less eccentric than Venice but also less people-crazed than Santa Monica; its fame is drawn from its status as the spiritual home of beach volleyball.

The surfside flavour continues south into nearby **Hermosa Beach** and **Redondo Beach**, the latter with one of the area's most developed piers in the shape of King Harbor (at the end of Portofino Way). Purists might find its shops, restaurants, fish markets and marina rather cheesy, but Redondo is the most family-oriented of the South Bay's beaches.

Palos Verdes & San Pedro

One of the best drives in Southern California is the loop around the scenic Palos Verdes Peninsula. Take the Pacific Coast Highway (Highway 1, aka the PCH) south to Palos Verdes Boulevard, go south again to Palos Verdes Drive West, along Paseo del Mar and then to Palos Verdes Drive South. On the way, stop at the lovely glass-and-stone **Wayfarer's Chapel** (5755 Palos Verdes Drive South, 1-310 377 1650, www.wayfarerschapel.org), the most visited building by architect Lloyd Wright (Frank's son), and the **South Coast Botanic Garden** (26300 Crenshaw Boulevard, 1-310 544 6815, www.southcoastbotanicgarden.org); both are open until 5pm every day.

And ritzy Palos Verdes shares the peninsula with one of LA's most colourful working-class communities: **San Pedro**, traditionally the home of fishermen, dockers, Navy staff, immigrants and the massive Port of Los Angeles. It's a surprisingly charismatic little place, proudly awash with reminders of its history (the LA Conservancy run regular guided walks; *see p73*) but also possessed of a quietly tangible ambition to smarten itself up a little: witness the handsome mock-vintage tram cars that run along the waterfront (Fri-Mon only; an all-day fare is $1).

Downtown San Pedro is centred on 6th Street between Pacific Avenue and Harbour Boulevard, dotted with cute independent shops and restaurants, but the highlight is the **Warner Grand Theatre** (478 W 6th Street, 1-310 548 7672, www.warnergrand.org), a restored 1931 movie palace that screens classic films and stages occasional concerts. Close at hand, just on the waterfront, is the **Los Angeles Maritime Museum** (*see below*).

Head south from Downtown along S Gaffey Street and you'll eventually reach **Angels Gate Park**. The views from the top are fantastic, arching out eastwards over industrial San Pedro, the harbour, the broad sweep of **Cabrillo Beach**, the Frank Gehry-designed **Cabrillo Marine Aquarium** (*see below*) and the isolated **Angels Gate Lighthouse**. Some of the best views to the south, meanwhile, are accessed from the **Friendship Bell**: presented by Korea to the United States on the occasion of the latter's bicentennial in 1776, it's housed in a traditional Korean pavilion.

Across the park is **Fort McArthur**, a slightly bedraggled and dissociated collection of buildings that are mostly closed to the public (many of the buildings house air force personnel who work up in El Segundo). Further south is one of the area's most charming buildings: the **Point Fermin Lighthouse** (1-310 241 0684, www.pointferminlighthouse.org), a gentle wooden house from 1874 that's unexpectedly topped with a lighthouse tower. It's open from 1pm to 4pm every day except Monday, and admission is free. Look out, too, for the mysterious, haunting 'Sunken City', a formerly wealthy neighbourhood that effectively slid into the ocean during the 1920s and '30s.

Cabrillo Marine Aquarium

3720 Stephen White Drive, at Pacific Avenue, San Pedro (1-310 548 7562/www.cabrilloaq.org). Bus 445, 446/I-110, exit Harbor Boulevard west. **Open** noon-5pm Tue-Fri; 10am-5pm Sat, Sun. **Admission** free; donations requested. *Parking* free-$1/hr. **No credit cards.**
Dedicated to Southern California marine life, this low-key aquarium is home to a jellyfish farm, a hands-on tidal pool exhibit and 30 ocean-life tanks. Special seasonal events include two-hour whale-watching trips, occasional guided walks to the tidal pools at Point Fermin Marine Life Refuge and grunion runs (held during the migrating season of this small, pencil-sized fish).

Los Angeles Maritime Museum

Berth 84, end of W 6th Street, San Pedro (1-310 548 7618/www.lamaritimemuseum.org). Bus 446, 447/I-110, exit Harbor Boulevard west. **Open** 10am-5pm Tue-Sat; noon-5pm Sun. **Admission** $3; $1 discounts. *Parking* free. **No credit cards.**

The largest maritime museum in the state contains a potted history of fishing in California, the story of San Pedro's canning industry, and an array of model boats and ships. Check online for details of temporary shows, which cover related topics. The handsome 1940s Streamline Moderne building that houses the museum once acted as a ferry terminal.

Long Beach

The Long Beach of popular imagination is one of dockers, deadbeats and cops debating what they should do with all the drunken sailors. But since the factories closed and Navy work dwindled in the 1980s, it's changed beyond recognition. The area is smarter than it's ever been, and more cultured. However, those in search of its old edge can still find it: turf wars between rival black, Latino and Cambodian gangs keep up tensions.

Long Beach's metamorphosis from blue-collar grittiness to white-collar tidiness is most tangible along **Ocean Boulevard**. However, the broad, near-waterside sweep of street deserves better than the collection of flat-pack modern skyscrapers that line it. Familiar hotels (Renaissance, Westin) and financial institutions (Wells Fargo, International Credit Bank) sit in familiar-looking buildings; were it not for the aroma of salty sea air, you could be in any middle American city. The '20s-vintage **Ocean Center Building** (110 W Ocean Boulevard) is passably elegant; the **Long Beach Performing Arts Center** (300 E Ocean Boulevard) is anything but. By far the most charismatic building is the unexpected, French Gothic-styled **Villa Riviera** apartment building (800 E Ocean Boulevard), completed just before the Depression and recently spruced up by developers.

Long Beach's two primary tourist attractions sit to the south of Ocean Boulevard, alongside or on the water. The excellent **Aquarium of the Pacific** (*see p138*) is at Rainbow Harbor, while the **Queen Mary** (*see p138*) ocean liner is moored across the Queensway Bay Bridge. North of Ocean Boulevard, commerce is centred on Pine Avenue, though the shops are generally less interesting than the historic buildings that house them: look out, in particular, for the handsome **Farmers & Merchants Bank** at the north-east corner of Pine and 3rd Street, and the old **Press-Telegram Building** at Pine and 6th, now being converted into apartments.

Sunken City, Point Fermin Park, San Pedro Where Donnie's ashes are scattered in *The Big Lebowski*

East of here, at the corner of Alamitos Avenue and 7th Street, sits the resurgent **Museum of Latin American Art** (*see below*).

Heading east away from Downtown Long Beach, Ocean Boulevard turns into E Livingston Drive and then leads into the neighbourhood of **Belmont Shore**. Assuming you can find a parking spot, the stretch of E 2nd Street east of Livingston is worth a look for its interesting shops and restaurants, such as independent record store **Fingerprints** (No.4612; *see p209*) and **Vint's American Grill** (No.4722).

Continue along 2nd and you'll wind up in **Naples** (off 2nd Street, between Bay Shore and Marina Avenues). Set on three islands, this curious residential neighbourhood aims to bring a little Italy to Southern California. However, from the kitschy architecture to the wedding-cake fountain (named, ludicrously, 'La Bella Fontana di Napoli'), it recalls nothing so much as Las Vegas – it lacks the raffish decay that's blighted parts of Venice, but it also lacks its charisma. Gondola rides are offered by **Gondola Getaway** (5437 E Ocean Boulevard, 1-562 433 9595, www.gondolagetawayinc.com, reservations required).

Aquarium of the Pacific

100 Aquarium Way, at Shoreline Drive (1-562 590 3100/www.aquariumofpacific.org). Metro 1st Street/bus 60, 232, 360/I-710, exit Shoreline Drive east. **Open** 9am-6pm daily. **Admission** $20.95; $11.95-$17.95 discounts. *Parking £7.* **Credit** AmEx, DC, MC, V.

Dedicated as much to education as entertainment, this spectacular aquarium more than justifies the drive down to Long Beach, especially if the alternative is the razzle-dazzle of San Diego's considerably pricier SeaWorld. Inevitably, the Shark Lagoon is the most popular exhibit, though the bite of the becalmed residents is presumably worse than their non-existent bark; other highlights include the low-key but fascinating Whales: Voices of the Sea. Much of the rest of the aquarium is divided geographically: loveable sea lions in the Southern California section, all kinds of garish fish in the Tropical Pacific area, a variety of exotic creatures in the new Gulf of California exhibit. If the real thing isn't enough for the little brats, they may enjoy an animated and exaggerated version of same in the shape of *A Fish Story 3-D* ($3).

Long Beach Convention & Visitors Bureau

1 World Trade Center, at E Ocean Boulevard (1-562 436 3645/www.visitlongbeach.com). Metro Transit Mall/bus 60, 232, 360/I-710, exit Shoreline Drive east. **Open** 8am-5pm Mon-Fri.

> **Queen Mary** (*p138*)
> The stricken ocean liner in
> *The Poseidon Adventure*

Long Beach Museum of Art

2300 E Ocean Boulevard, at Kennebec Avenue (1-562 439 2119/www.lbma.org). Bus LBA, LBD/I-405, then I-710 south. **Open** 11am-5pm Tue-Sun. **Admission** $7; $6 discounts; free under-12. Free to all Fri. *Parking* free. **Credit** DC, MC, V.

Though only true connoisseurs will reckon it worth the drive down in itself, the Long Beach Museum of Art nonetheless keeps its locals entertained with a cultured roster of temporary exhibits. The extensive video library is now in the hands of the Getty, but the museum's permanent collection still includes some notable Californian pieces. The building's an intriguing one: completed in 1912, it was designed and originally used as a summer home by philanthropist Elizabeth Milbank Anderson.

Museum of Latin American Art

628 Alamitos Avenue, at E 6th Street, Long Beach (1-562 437 1689/www.molaa.com). Metro 5th Street/bus 60, 232, 360, LB7/I-710, exit Alamitos Avenue north. **Open** 11.30am-7pm Tue-Fri; 11am-7pm Sat; 11am-6pm Sun. **Admission** $7.50; $5 discounts; free under-12s. Free to all Fri. *Parking* free. **Credit** AmEx, DC, MC, V.

MoLAA might be located on land that once housed the Balboa Amusement Producing Company, the most productive silent film studio of its day, but history is conspicuous by its absence: from the building in which it's housed to the art contained within it, this is a forward-thinking enterprise. Founded in 1996, MoLAA was expanded in 2007 by architect Manuel Rosen, whose eye-catching additions to the museum more than doubled its total exhibition space and added a tidy sculpture garden.

The core of the permanent collection is in the Long Gallery, with work by one artist from every Latin American country. A little more captioning detail would be useful, especially since the majority of the artists will be unfamiliar, but plenty of the pieces speak for themselves: look out, in particular, for El Salvadorean artist César Menéndez's slightly mysterious *Canción al Silencio* ('Song to Silence'). A range of temporary shows and a programme of special events provide added interest; as does the Viva Café, which offers Latino interpretations of American classics (chicken caesar salad with black beans and a chipotle-tinged vinaigrette). A nice day out.

Queen Mary

1126 Queens Highway (1-562 435 3511/www.queenmary.com). Metro Transit Mall/I-405, then I-710 south. **Open** 10am-6pm daily. **Admission** $24.95-$32.95; $12.95-$28.95 discounts. *Parking* free 0-30mins; $3 31mins-1hr; $12 more than 1hr. **Credit** AmEx, DC, Disc, MC, V.

This grand old ocean liner disproves F Scott Fitzgerald's contention that there are no second acts in American lives. Constructed by Clydeside shipbuilders John Brown & Company in the '30s, the *Queen Mary* sailed the Atlantic for three decades before easing into a second existence as a partly appealing, partly tacky tourist attraction. Most of

The newly expanded and increasingly impressive **Museum of Latin American Art**.

the appeal comes courtesy of the self-guided tours, which afford porthole views of the ways in which monied guests might once have spent their leisurely weeks crossing the ocean alongside similar glimpses of the life enjoyed by the boat's sizeable crew. Look out, too, for the displays of archive photographs, and be sure to have a drink in the gorgeous Observation Bar, an art deco lounge that's been kept in handsome shape. The Ghosts & Legends attraction plays up to the boat's reputation as a ghoul magnet, but it's ultimately a fairly undignified diversion, not least because it's presumably responsible for the elevated admission prices. Still, if you do really like the place, you can spend the night in one of the cabins: the boat doubles as a hotel (*see p66*).

Orange County

The South Coast

Just south of the LA County border, **Seal Beach** and **Sunset Beach** begin the 50-mile stretch of beach bliss that is coastal Orange County, flanked in its entirety by the Pacific Coast Highway (aka Highway 1, or PCH). Alongside its almost immaculate sandbar, notable sights are few and far between: Seal Beach is notable only for the presence of a

9,000-resident retirement community called Leisure World, while Sunset Beach's sole claim to fame is the epoch-definingly abysmal soap opera of the same name that it inspired in the '90s. It's really all about location, location, location: time your visit right, and you'll see why Sunset Beach got its name.

The real OC action starts south of here in **Huntington Beach**, an altogether livelier pocket of beach-bum culture. Hang out at the pier or on the sand and you'll see how the city got its nickname of 'Surf City'. From dawn to dark, surfers head here in search of the perfect wave, before retreating to a regenerated and slightly anodyne Main Street that's lined with surf-gear stores and buzzing bars with names like the Longboard Café and Sharkeez. There's even a surfing museum here (*see p140*).

South of here, **Newport Beach** is a more intriguing proposition. Southern California's moneyed leisure classes cluster in the lavish homes that overlook **Newport Harbor**, popping over to the upscale **Fashion Island** open-air mall to pick up some treats. However, things are considerably earthier on the stretches of Balboa and Newport Boulevards between 21st and 30th Streets, a mix of smart-ass stores, biker-friendly bars and old-school restaurants such as the **Crab Cooker** (2200 Newport

Boulevard). This is the sunny, mellow and
pedestrian-friendly **Balboa Peninsula**, home
to an iconic Ferris wheel and the **Newport
Harbor Nautical Museum** (600 East Bay
Avenue, 1-949 675 8915, www.nhnm.org).
It's linked to the man-made **Balboa Island**
by a regular ferry service.

Just down the coast, **Laguna Beach** began
as an artists' colony and is now the home of
the admired **Laguna Art Museum** (307 Cliff
Drive, 1-949 494 8971, www.lagunaartmuseum.
org). With its pick-up basketball and volleyball
games, Main Beach offers excellent people-
watching. A little further south, **San Juan
Capistrano** is famous for the swallows that
return to **Mission San Juan Capistrano**
(1-949 234 1300, www.missionsjc.com) each
spring, although the beautifully maintains
structure is worth visiting on its own account.
And at the county's end, **San Clemente** has
all the sun and waves but few of the crowds of
its neighbours. Richard Nixon's western White
House, the Spanish-inspired **Casa Pacifica**,
can be seen from San Clemente State Beach.

International Surfing Museum

*411 Olive Avenue, between Main & 5th Streets,
Huntington Beach (1-714 960 3483/www.surfing
museum.org). Metro 5th Street/bus LB181, LB182/
I-405, exit Beach Boulevard south.* **Open** noon-
5pm Mon-Fri; 11am-6pm Sat, Sun. **Admission**
$2; $1 discounts; free under-6s. *Parking* free.
No credit cards.
This small museum honours Duke Kahanamoku,
the godfather of surfing, and celebrates surf music,
surf life-saving and – of course – surf babes.
Temporary exhibits come and go like the waves, but
there's usually something here to see. The museum
is staffed with volunteers who are full of surfing
stories, some of which may actually be true.

Anaheim & inland

An archetype of both the sunny Southern
Californian lifestyle and the suburban
American dream, the populous city of
Anaheim is dominated by one landmark:
Disneyland (*see below*), open since 1955
and still the engine that drives the area's
economy. Away from the Happiest Place on
Earth, the town holds little of interest for the
visitor, although the two local sports teams –
baseball's **Angels** (*see p269*) and the hockey-
playing **Ducks** (*see p270*) – draw impressively
loyal crowds.

The towns around Anaheim are similarly
short on charisma, although there are some
notable sights amid the miles of featureless
residential and commercial sprawl. North-west
of Anaheim is **Buena Park**, home to the old-
fashioned theme-park attractions of **Knott's
Berry Farm** (*see p142*). To the north is
Fullerton, enlivened by the presence of
California State University. And further east
is Yorba Linda, where you'll find the **Richard
Nixon Library & Birthplace** (*see p142*).

South of Anaheim in Garden Grove stands
the immense **Crystal Cathedral** (12141 Lewis
Street, Garden Grove, 1-714 971 4000, www.
crystalcathedral.org), an all-glass house of
worship visible from miles around. Built in 1980
by architects Philip Johnson and John Burgee for
preacher Dr Robert H Schuller and his ministry,
it's a marvel of hubristic excess. Visitors are
welcome; check online for service times.

Just west of Garden Grove, the town of
Westminster plays up to its name by
rendering its street signs in a mock-Gothic font.
However, it's more notable for the presence of
what's reputed to be the largest Vietnamese
community outside Vietnam. The Little Saigon
neighbourhood has a number of Vietnamese food
shops and restaurants; **S Vietnamese Fine
Dining** (545 Westminster Mall Drive, 1-714 898
5092) is the smartest and probably the best.

Conversely, nearby **Santa Ana** is a distinctly
Latino city. Strolling along busy 4th Street
between French and Ross Streets, with its
colourful storefronts and hum of Spanish, you
could almost believe you were walking through
a small city in Mexico (or, at least, in East LA).
The **Bowers Museum of Cultural Art** (2002
N Main Street, 1-714 567 3600, www.bowers.
org) has a strong Native American collection.

Anaheim/Orange County
Visitor & Convention Bureau

*800 W Katella Avenue, at N Batavia Street (1-714
765 8888/www.anaheimoc.org).* **Open** 8am-5.30pm
Mon-Fri.

Disneyland

*1313 S Harbor Boulevard, between Katella Avenue
& Ball Road, Anaheim (1-714 781 4565/www.disney
land.com). Bus OC205, OC430/I-5, exit Disneyland
Drive.* **Open** Hours vary by day: call or check online
for full details. *Disneyland: Summer* usually 8am-
midnight daily. *Winter* usually 9am-8pm Mon-Thur;
8am-midnight Fri, Sat; 9am-9pm Sun. *California
Adventure: Summer* usually 10am-8pm Mon-Thur;
10am-9pm Fri-Sun. *Winter* usually 10am-6pm
Mon-Thur; 10am-8pm Fri; 10am-9pm Sat, Sun.
Admission *1 park for 1 day* $66; $56 discounts;
free under-3s. *Both parks for 1 day* $91; $81
discounts; free under-3s. Call or check online for
details of multi-day tickets. *Parking* $12. **Credit**
AmEx, DC, Disc, MC, V.

The longstanding Disneyland resort isn't just a set of theme parks: it's a spectacular piece of pop art that's as bright or as dark as you'd like it to be. Incorporating two parks – the 50-year-old, near-mythic Disneyland, plus the younger and less celebrated Disney's California Adventure – the resort calls itself 'The Happiest Place on Earth'. And if you bring the right mood with you, it'll likely live up to its nickname.

Certainly, Disney does all it can to get you in the right mood. Disneyland isn't so much a park as its own separate world; there are even three Disney-operated hotels (see p66) in the resort, so you need not have the illusion shattered at the end of the day. The hotels, though, do bring to attention the main drawback to spending time here: the sheer expense. You can save hundreds of dollars staying at one of the non-Disney hotels just outside the property, and you may need to do so in order to afford the steep prices of food, drink and admission. It's worth noting, though, that ticket prices drop if you visit for multiple days, recommended if you want to get a real feel for the place and enjoy all the rides.

Both parks boast dozens of dining spots, with cuisine ranging from burgers and pizza to pastas and seafood. Still, you may want to dine at Downtown Disney, a pedestrian-only avenue of nightclubs (including a House of Blues) and restaurants between the two parks. It's not that the food is that much better, but if you're going to be paying Disney's high prices, you might need a drink or two in order to soften the blow: liquor sales were banned from Disneyland by Walt himself, citing the undesirable 'carnie atmosphere' booze might have created, and alcohol remains banned from the park itself.

The other main demerit against Disneyland is the crowds: they can be overwhelming, particularly in summer and, unexpectedly, on Christmas Day. (Top tip: few visit on Super Bowl Sunday.) But the crowds can't be helped, and they're unlikely to improve: Disneyland is popular for a reason.

Disneyland

Disneyland is packed with must-do attractions spread over seven 'lands', all immaculately themed in every detail. **Main Street USA** embodies turn-of-the-19th-century America, while **Frontierland** takes on Westward expansion (the John Wayne version) and **New Orleans Square** is just like its namesake, only without the floods, the poverty and the booze. **Adventureland** offers thrills of the jungle variety; **Tomorrowland** is a kitschily charming look into the future; **Critter Country** is the wooded home of Winnie the Pooh and Br'er Rabbit; and **Fantasyland** is where Disney's animated films come to life. As for the iconic mouse, you're most likely to find him scurrying about with his pals in **Mickey's Toontown**.

The secret of Disneyland's charm lies in its special history. Unlike the company's other parks, Disneyland was largely designed by Walt himself, and it's the only one in which he ever set foot. As a result, Disneyland is practically a biography of its creator's life, if you know where to look. Try reading the names in Main Street's upper-level windows; you'll find many of Disney's collaborators and artists listed. The Walt Disney Story features artefacts from Disney's entertainment career. And in Frontierland, you'll find the petrified tree Walt once gave his wife as an anniversary present.

But most people, of course, are here for the rides. Among the best are **Space Mountain** (located in

Crystal Cathedral.

Sightseeing

Tomorrowland), a legitimately thrilling indoor rollercoaster ride through 'deep space'; the epic **Indiana Jones Adventure** (in Adventureland), based on the Spielberg adventure movies; **Pirates of the Caribbean** (in New Orleans Square), the basis for the hit Johnny Depp film franchise and one of the most detail-packed and atmospheric rides in the park; and the **Matterhorn** (in Fantasyland), a breakneck bobsled ride around and through a scaled-down replica of the Swiss peak.

Beyond that, there are dozens of carnival-style 'dark' rides, boat trips, rollercoasters, flume rides and Audio-Animatronics shows, many of them wonderfully charismatic and touchingly old-fashioned. If anything defines Disneyland, it's the human touch that's so obviously been lavished on many of its featured rides and attractions. Certainly, it's difficult to imagine Universal Studios retaining anything as charming as the **It's a Small World** boat ride (you'll be singing the theme song for weeks afterwards, whether you want to or not) or the fabulous **Enchanted Tiki Room**.

Disney's California Adventure

Located in a former car park, this decent little enterprise is no match for Disneyland in terms of size or attention to detail, but it does a decent job of celebrating the geography, culture and history of its namesake state. Also, unlike Disneyland, it serves alcohol, and has done so since opening day with little of Walt's feared carnie interference. In 2007, a $1.1-billion renovation of the park was announced, scheduled for completion in 2012. Disruption will hopefully be minimal, but visitors are advised to check online before heading to the park.

While DCA doesn't have anything as engrossing as Pirates of the Caribbean, it does feature some decent rides. The **Twilight Zone Tower of Terror**, a special effects-packed 'drop'-ride based on the classic TV show and housed in the **Hollywood Pictures Backlot** section of the park, is worth a look, as is **Soarin' over California**, a beautiful flight simulator. Soarin' over California is located in the **Golden State** section, itself split up into separate areas that pay homage to (among other places) San Francisco and Wine Country. The highlight of the **Paradise Pier** section, meanwhile, is the **California Screamin'** rollercoaster, the tallest and fastest coaster ever built in a Disney park. Not every ride is suitable for kids of all ages, but very young children are welcome in **A Bug's Land**.

Knott's Berry Farm

8039 Beach Boulevard, at La Palma Avenue, Buena Park (1-714 220 5200/www.knotts.com). Bus OC29/I-5, exit Beach Boulevard south. **Open** Hours vary by day: call or check online for full details. *Knott's Berry Farm: Jan-Apr, Sept-Dec* 10am-6pm Mon-Fri; 10am-10pm Sat; 10am-7pm Sun. *May* 10am-6pm Mon-Fri; 9am-11pm; 10am-7pm Sun. *June-Aug* 10am-10pm Mon-Fri, Sun; 9am-11pm Sat. *Soak City: May-mid June* usually 10am-6pm daily. *Mid June-Labor*

Day usually 10am-7pm daily. *Labor Day-end Sept* usually 10am-5pm Sat, Sun. **Admission** *Knott's Berry Farm* $49.99; $19.99-$39.99 discounts; free under-3s. *Soak City* $28.99; $17.99-$23.99 discounts; free under-3s. Call or check online for details of multi-day tickets. *Parking* $10. **Credit** AmEx, DC, Disc, MC, V.

Knott's Berry Farm started as a farm selling the home-made preserves of one Mrs Cordelia Knott. Although Ma Knott and her family are long gone, her jams are still on sale. But on the whole, Knott's Berry Farm seems to have realised that it can't get by on nostalgia alone: there seems to have been a concerted effort of late among the park managers to haul this formerly old-fashioned enterprise into the 21st century.

Parts of Knott's Berry Farm aim to portray an idealised, kinder America than you might find at, for example, Universal Studios. Some charming remnants of the park's early years remain: most notably in the **Ghost Town** section, which contains a number of buildings that have been transplanted from old mining towns. The continued presence of Snoopy as the park's mascot is another gentle nod to tradition. Ultimately, though, the thrill-seekers win out over the sentimentalists thanks to a number of water rides, the stomach-churning **Xcelerator** and **Montezooma's Revenge** attractions, and two new rollercoasters: the **Sierra Sidewinder** and the **Pony Express**.

Next door to the Berry Farm sits **Soak City**, a mammoth water park that's open only during the summer months. Combination tickets are available for the two attractions; check online for details.

Richard Nixon Library & Birthplace

18001 Yorba Linda Boulevard, at Imperial Highway, Yorba Linda (1-714 993 3393/www.nixon foundation.org). Bus OC26/Hwy 90, exit Yorba Linda Boulevard west. **Open** 10am-5pm Mon-Sat; 11am-5pm Sun. **Admission** $9.95; $3.75-$6.95 discounts; free under-7s. *Parking* free. **Credit** AmEx, DC, Disc, MC, V.

Consistently ranked by historians as one of the worst American presidents of the 20th century, Tricky Dick is remembered chiefly for two ignominious events: his defeat at the hands of John F Kennedy in 1960, and the Watergate scandal that led to him becoming the only American president to resign his post. Both events are discussed in this museum, housed on the site where Nixon was born in 1913; other interesting exhibits include a rare 1823 facsimile of the Declaration of Independence, and a gallery devoted to America's space programme. Dick and wife Pat are enjoying their after-lives in the gardens.

Old Orange County Courthouse, 211 W Santa Ana Boulevard The site of the murder trial in *Legally Blonde*

Sightseeing

Eat, Drink, Shop

Restaurants	**144**
Coffeehouses	**170**
Bars	**175**
Shops & Services	**187**

Features

The best Restaurants	145
Life is sweets	146
Star power	153
Around the world	158
Vintage vittles	163
The best Coffeehouses	171
Are you looking at me?	172
The best Bars	176
Piano men	179
Top ten Happy hours	182
The best Shops	187
Where to shop	188
Who's on 3rd?	192
It's easy being green	195
Take a letter	204

Lisa Kline. *See p197.*

Restaurants

Eat your way around the world without leaving LA.

Typhoon: come on, you know you've always wanted to try toasted scorpion. *See p147.*

When it comes to restaurants in Los Angeles, nobody knows it all. Indeed, nobody even knows most of it. New York has a reputation as the world's most competitive dining destination, but this is really only true at the top end of the market. In LA, though, natural selection rules at all levels. No restaurateur can afford to rest on his or her laurels: places that don't consistently deliver good food and good service are soon history. The down side is that as soon as a restaurant gets a white-hot reputation, the chef is besieged with offers from investors, and often leaves to open a new place. The result is high staff turnover, with some places trading on the recipes and reputation of a chef who has long since gone.

> ❶ Purple numbers given in this chapter correspond to the location of restaurants on the street maps. *See pp326-331.*

In the admittedly incomplete survey that follows, we've been slightly biased toward chef-owned restaurants that have a proven record of stability in the kitchen, and have included the hot spots that we're betting will still be cooking up a storm when you read this. Happily, we're on more certain ground with the ethnic eateries around town, where the people in the kitchen are more focused on making your dinner than arranging their next TV appearance.

INSIDE INFORMATION

Always book ahead if possible, and be sure to call if you're running late. Many restaurants take reservations via online services such as www.opentable.com, but no restaurant books all its tables in this way: if you call, you might get into a place that the internet claims is booked out. Even with a reservation, there's often a wait: if you have theatre tickets or other time constraints, let the host know when you arrive and advise your server as you order.

Some restaurants that double as nightspots increase the volume of the music and dim the lights at a certain point in the evening, so your dining experience may change part-way through your meal. If you suspect this might happen, ask to be seated in a quiet area. And although the term 'California casual' was invented here, don't push your luck: some of the finer eateries draw the line at shorts and jeans. Smoking is banned in all restaurants, although it is sometimes permitted on patios.

If you're happy with the service, tip at least 15 per cent; anything less is taken as severe criticism. A few restaurants have started to add a service charge, but most are decent enough to inform diners before they total the bill.

Please note that prices given throughout this chapter are for an average main course.

Santa Monica & the beach towns

Malibu

Allegria

22821 Pacific Coast Highway, at Coastline Drive (1-310 456 3132/www.allegriamalibu.com). Bus 534/I-10, exit PCH north. **Open** 11.30am-2.30pm, 5-10pm Mon-Fri; 11.30am-10pm Sat, Sun. **Main courses** *Lunch* $14. *Dinner* $24. **Credit** AmEx, DC, MC, V. **Italian**
Allegria isn't so much a Cal-Italian restaurant as a bastion of traditional Italian cuisine that just happens to be located by the ocean in Malibu. The cooking is excellent and the setting is romantic (ask for a garden view when you book); all in all, it's well worth the 20-minute drive up the coast.

Inn of the Seventh Ray

128 Old Topanga Canyon Road, at Riding Lane, Topanga (1-310 455 1311/www.innoftheseventhray. com). I-10, exit PCH north. **Open** 11.30am-3pm, 5.30-10pm Mon-Fri; 10.30am-3pm, 5.30-10pm Sat; 9.30am-3pm, 5.30-10pm Sun. **Main courses** *Lunch* $15. *Dinner* $30. **Credit** AmEx, DC, MC, V. **Californian**
This famous hippie haven has gone haute cuisine, but it hasn't lost touch with its roots: stylish vegan dishes sit with the likes of pomegranate-lacquered duck breast with maple-scented yams. Sunday brunch is great, especially the wholegrain Belgian waffles, and the romantic garden setting has to be seen to be believed. Allow extra time: the inn is accessible only by a two-lane road that can be slow going.

Moonshadows

20356 Pacific Coast Highway, west of Big Rock Drive (1-310 456 3010/www.moonshadowsmalibu.com). Bus 534/I-10, exit PCH north. **Open** 11.30am-3.30pm, 4.30-10.30pm Mon-Thur; 11.30am-3.30pm, 4.30-11pm Fri; 11am-3.30pm, 4.30pm-11pm Sat; 11am-3.30pm, 4.30-10pm Sun. **Main courses** *Lunch* $17. *Dinner* $27. **Credit** AmEx, DC, MC, V. **Seafood**

Moonshadows has made changes to both its menu and its decor in an attempt to attract a younger crowd, but people head here for the same reason they always have: to dine on good seafood while enjoying unparalleled views of the ocean. The simple dishes are still the best.

Nobu Malibu

Malibu Country Mart, 3835 Cross Creek Road, north of PCH (1-310 317 9140/www.noburestaurants. com). Bus 534/I-10, exit PCH north. **Open** 5.45-10pm Mon-Thur, Sun; 5.45-11pm Fri, Sat. **Main courses** $28. **Credit** AmEx, DC, MC, V. **Japanese**
You can have standard Japanese sushi at Nobu – but why would you? The speciality here is Peruvian-style sushi, made with consummate artistry using citrus marinades and chilli peppers. Try the *tiradito*, ceviche as you've never tasted before, and continue from there. Book early or risk a considerable wait until space clears at the bar.

Santa Monica

Anisette

225 Santa Monica Boulevard, at 2nd Street, Santa Monica (1-310 395 3200/www.anisettebrasserie. com). Bus 4, 20, 534, 704, 720, SM1, SM7, SM8, SM10/I-10, exit 4th-5th street north. **Open** 7.30am-midnight Mon-Thur; 7.30am-1am Fri; 8am-1am Sat; 8am-midnight Sun. **Main courses** $25. **Credit** AmEx, DC, MC, V. **Map** p326 A3 ❶ **French**
See p153 **Star power.**

The best Restaurants

For a classic LA experience
Canter's Deli (*see p159*), El Cholo (*see p161*), Dan Tana's (*see p155*), Philippe the Original (*see p163* Vintage vittles) and Spago of Beverly Hills (*see p155*).

For great food at great prices
Cassell's (*see p160*), Farmers Market (*see p159*) and Chinese food in Monterey Park (*see p158* Around the world).

For a brilliant breakfast
Clementine (*see p152*), the Griddle Café (*see p156*) and Millie's (*see p162*).

For a special occasion
Bastide (*see p155*), Hotel Bel-Air (*see p152*), Mélisse (*see p147*), Patina (*see p165*) and Urasawa (*see p155*).

For a room with a view
Moonshadows (*see p145*), Restaurant at the Getty Center (*see p149*) and Yamashiro (*see p158*).

Eat, Drink, Shop

Life is sweets

There are more than 50 languages spoken across LA's vast sprawl, and alongside each native tongue you'll find a matching sweet tooth. In the city where the hot fudge sundae was invented (by CC Brown in 1906), there are hundreds of strangely wonderful confections waiting to ensnare the willing culinary explorer.

Since it's probably hot outside, it's best to start with the chilly treats, and there are none better than the avant-garde gelato creations dished up at **Scoops** (*see p158*). Tai Kim, a Korean American graduate of both art school and cooking school, dreams up unexpected flavour combinations such as Guinness tiramisu and bacon caramel; varieties change daily and he's happy for you to taste them.

Kim's concoctions aren't the only frozen treats worth a taste. In Little Tokyo's Japanese Village Plaza, try a sour, berry-dotted Korean-style frozen yoghurt at **Ce Fiore** (*see p164*). You'll find delicately perfumed Persian ice-cream in flavours such as rosewater saffron at **Mashti Malone's** (*see p157*); don't miss the bitter lemon and cherry syrups on the tables, meant to be drizzled on top. And if you head into any of LA's Latin neighbourhoods, look out for *paletas*, slick-sided rustic popsicles flavoured with hunks of fresh strawberry or coconut.

The language of sweet fried dough is just as universal. When you're exploring the Mexican marketplace at **Olvera Street** (*see p111*), chomp on a cinnamon-sugared *churro*. At **India Sweets & Spices** (*see p164*), try *gulab jamun*, a rose-flavoured round doughnut fried in clarified butter and soaked in sugar syrup. And if you ever order dim sum, look out for a dish that resembles golden golf balls studded with sesame seeds: this is scrumptious *jin deui*, a chewy rice flour doughnut stuffed with sweet lotus paste.

Thai desserts are also worth the diversion. At weekends outside **LAX-C** (*see p164*), the 'Thai Costco' near Chinatown, vendors set up outdoor kitchens and prepare sweet treats such as *kanom krok*, a round and creamy coconut rice fritter cooked over charcoal. For a full education in the range of Thai sweets, visit the **Bhan Kanom** bakery (*see p156*).

And if you've still got an appetite, take in a trio of Latino comfort foods. The chocolatey spin on goat milk flan offered by chef-owner Robert Berrelleza at **Babita Mexicuisine** (*see p167*) is terrific, as are the green corn tamales served at **El Cholo** (*see p161*). Finally, in winter, look out for *champurrado*, a stick-to-your-ribs Aztec hot chocolate that's thick with corn chunks and spices and is sold by restaurants and street vendors.

Eat, Drink, Shop

Counter

*2901 Ocean Park Boulevard, between 29th Street &
30th Street (1-310 399 8383/www.thecounterburger.
com). Bus SM6, SM8/I-10, exit Centinela Boulevard
south.* **Open** 11am-10pm Mon-Thur; 11am-11pm
Fri, Sat; noon-9pm Sun. **Main courses** $10.
Credit AmEx, DC, MC, V. **Map** p326 D4 **②**
Cafés & diners

This casual and wildly popular burger joint offers
hundreds of possible combinations, served with an
array of sauces and add-ins. Some people delight in
trying the most outlandish options: turkey burger
with olives, grilled pineapple and brie, anyone?
Other pluses include good beer and wine lists plus,
for dessert, delightful apple crumble.

Drago Ristorante

*2628 Wilshire Boulevard, at 26th Street (1-310 828
1585/www.celestinodrago.com). Bus 20, 720, SM2/
I-10, exit Cloverfield Boulevard north/20th Street
north.* **Open** 11.30am-3pm, 5.30-11pm Mon-Fri;
5.30-11pm Sat; 5.30-10.30pm Sun. **Main courses**
Lunch $20. *Dinner* $29. **Credit** AmEx, DC, Disc,
MC, V. **Map** p326 D2 **③** **Italian**

The Drago family's Los Angeles restaurant empire
started out in 1991 at this operation, a celebrity-
friendly hangout that's worth the often rather substantial expense required to dine here. Celestino
Drago remains at the helm and continues to serve
stylishly arranged but mostly traditional renditions
of Italian regional cuisine.

Galley

*2242 Main Street, between Pacific & Strand Streets
(1-310 452 1934/www.thegalleyrestaurant.net).
Bus 33, 333, SM1, SM2, SM8, SM10/I-10, exit 4th-
5th Street south.* **Open** 5pm-10pm Mon-Sat; 1-10pm
Sun. **Main courses** $28. **Credit** AmEx, DC, Disc,
MC, V. **Map** p326 A4 **④** **American**

During the 70-plus years it's been in business, the
oldest restaurant in Santa Monica has accumulated
an amiable clutter of nautical junk lit by garish fairy
lights, not to mention a cluster of jocular local characters at the bar. The steaks and seafood are surprisingly good, and the house special salad dressing
is delicious.

Josie

*2424 Pico Boulevard, at 25th Street (1-310 581
9888/www.josierestaurant.com). Bus SM7/I-10,
exit Cloverfield Boulevard south/20th Street south.*
Open 6-9pm Mon-Thur; 6-10pm Fri, Sat; 5.30-8.30pm
Sun. **Main courses** $32. **Credit** AmEx, DC, MC, V.
Map p326 D4 **⑤** **American**

Josie LeBalch and two other female chefs work in
the kitchen while LeBalch's husband Frank manages front of house at this greatly admired Santa
Monica favourite. Progressive American, French
and Italian influences abound, producing combinations such as buffalo foie burger with truffle fries.

Mélisse

*1104 Wilshire Boulevard, between 11th Street &
12th Street (1-310 395 0881/www.melisse.com).
Bus 20, 720, SM2/I-10, exit Lincoln Boulevard*
north. **Open** 6-9.30pm Tue-Thur; 6-10pm Fri; 5.45-
10pm Sat. **Main courses** $42. **Credit** AmEx, DC,
Disc, MC, V. **Map** p326 B2 **⑥** **French**

Josiah Citrin is one of the best chefs in Los Angeles,
and the long, expensive meals he serves at this
white-tablecloth operation are the stuff of both legend and controversy. Dinner is about $100 per per-
son, but a tasting menu of Provence-meets-Pacific
cooking with fine wines can easily run to $400 and
take three hours.

Monsoon

*1212 Third Street Promenade, at Wilshire Boulevard
(1-310 576-9996/www.globaldiningca.com). Bus 4,
20, 33, 333, 704, 720, SM1, SM5, SM7, SM8,
SM10/I-10, exit 4th-5th Street north.* **Open** 11.30am-
10.30pm Mon-Thur; 11.30am-11.30pm Fri, Sat;
2-9.30pm Sun. **Main courses** $18. **Credit** AmEx,
DC, Disc, MC, V. **Map** p326 A2 **⑦** **Pan-Asian**

Of the several Third Street Promenade restaurants
favoured by locals, this theatrical Asian eaterie is
the most interesting. Dining under garish iron chandeliers amid Victorian Colonial style is like eating
very well in the middle of a movie set. Prepared in
an open kitchen, the food is a mix of Vietnamese,
Chinese and pan-Asian fusion.

Typhoon

*3221 Donald Douglas Loop South, at Santa Monica
Airport (1-310 390 6565/www.typhoon.biz). Bus
SM6, SM8, SM14/I-10, exit Bundy Drive south.*
Open noon-2pm, 5.30-9.30pm Mon-Thur; noon-2pm,
5.30-10pm Fri; 5.30-10pm Sat; 11am-2.30pm, 5-9pm
Sun. **Main courses** *Lunch* $18. *Dinner* $20.
Credit AmEx, DC, Disc, MC, V. **Map** p326 D5 **⑧**
Pan-Asian

This stylish, only-in-LA place serves toasted scorpi-
ons, fried crickets and other unusual dishes alongside
more conventional fare. The pan-Asian food is very
good even if you don't go for any of the strange stuff
(the house drink is a potent mix of alcohol and
Chinese herbal aphrodisiacs), and the view of the vintage aircraft outside adds appeal. Upstairs is the
Hump, which delivers expensive sushi. *Photo p144.*

Warszawa

*1414 Lincoln Boulevard, at Santa Monica Boulevard
(1-310 393 8831/www.warszawarestaurant.com).
Bus 4, 20, 33, 333, 704, 720, SM1, SM5, SM7,
SM8, SM10/I-10, exit Lincoln Boulevard north.*
Open 6-11pm Tue-Sat; 5-10pm Sun. **Main courses**
$17. **Credit** AmEx, DC, Disc, MC, V. **Map** p326 B3
⑨ **Polish**

There are few Polish restaurants in Los Angeles, but
this one has become popular far outside its own community. Although Polish isn't exactly the hip cuisine of the moment, stylish young diners join Polish
expats in this genteel converted cottage to create a

Neptune's Net (42505 PCH,
Malibu) Where Keanu Reeves
meets surfer chick Lori Petty
in *Point Break*

Eat, Drink, Shop

lively ambience. Specialities include crisp-skinned fried duck, the traditional stew called *bigos*, and the addictive ravioli known as *pierogis*.

Venice

Axe
1009 Abbot Kinney Boulevard, at Broadway (1-310 664 9787/www.axerestaurant.com). Bus 33, 333, SM1, SM2/I-10, exit 4th-5th Street south. **Open** 11.30am-3pm, 6-10pm Tue-Thur; 11.30am-3pm, 6-10.30pm Fri; 9am-3pm, 6-10.30pm Sat; 9am-3pm, 5.30-9.30pm Sun. **Main courses** *Lunch* $8. *Dinner* $24. **Credit** AmEx, DC, Disc, MC, V. **Map** p326 A5 ❿ **Californian**
Whether you end up loving it or hating it, Axe (pronounced 'ah-shay') is a fascinating experience – hyper-healthy food served in an elegant minimalist setting. The flavours are rich and satisfying, and brunch is among the best you'll find anywhere in Los Angeles, but the service can be brusque and the dining room is often a little noisy.

Baby Blues
444 Lincoln Boulevard, at Sunset Avenue (1-310 396 7675/www.babybluesbarbq.com). Bus SM2, SM3/I-10, exit Lincoln Boulevard south. **Open** 11.30am-10pm Mon-Thur; 11.30am-11pm Fri, Sat; noon-10pm Sun. **Main courses** $20. **Credit** AmEx, DC, Disc, MC, V. **Map** p326 B5 ⓫ **American**
Though Baby Blues is best known for its succulent barbecued meats, there's a lot more to love on its menu: delicious catfish and shrimp, both corn-topped with Mexican *cotija* cheese, and very good sautéed turnip greens. Vegetarians can dine here quite happily, soaking up the artsy atmosphere and making a meal of sides, while others tuck into massive plates of pork and beef.

Joe's
1023 Abbot Kinney Boulevard, between Broadway & Westminster Avenues (1-310 399 5811/www.joes restaurant.com). Bus 33, 333, SM1, SM2/I-10, exit 4th-5th Street south. **Open** noon-2.30pm, 6-10pm Tue-Thur; noon-2.30pm, 6-11pm Fri; 11am-2.30pm, 6-11pm Sat; 11am-2.30pm, 6-10pm Sun. **Main courses** *Lunch* $15. *Dinner* $28. **Credit** AmEx, DC, Disc, MC, V. **Map** p326 A5 ⓬ **Californian**
When chef Joseph Miller opened this restaurant in 1991, Abbot Kinney was a rough area. However, the gangs have now been replaced by valet parking, and Joe's is now the top dining destination on what's become a very hip street. Brunch and lunch are a bargain, especially the prix fixe; the excellent Cal-French dinners are also fairly priced. Get recommendations from your server or from Miller himself, who's often found out front chatting with diners.

Terrace
7 Washington Boulevard, at Speedway (1-310 578 1530/www.theterracecafe.com). Bus 33, 333, SM1, SM2/I-10, exit 4th-5th Street south. **Open** 8am-2am daily. **Main courses** $20. **Credit** AmEx, DC, Disc, MC, V. **Map** p326 A6 ⓭ **Eclectic**

LA isn't a late-night kind of town (it's too busy working to stay up), so places like the Terrace are prized by locals. This funky café serves very good American and Russian specialities until late: try the fried grouper, the roast duck or just a good burger, and watch the arty crowd from the patio. Alternative late-night eats are offered nearby, until 3am, at vintage Mexican spot **La Cabaña** (738 Rose Avenue, 1-310 392 7973, www.lacabanavenice.com).

Marina del Rey to LAX

Café del Rey
4451 Admiralty Way, between Bali & Promenade Ways (1-310 823 6395/www.cafedelreymarina.com). Bus 108/Hwy 90, exit Mindanao Way. **Open** 11.30am-3pm, 5.30-10pm Mon-Thur; 11.30am-3pm, 5.30-10pm Fri; 11.30am-2.30pm, 5.30-10pm Sat; 10.30am-2.30pm, 5-9.30pm Sun. **Main courses** *Lunch* $18. *Dinner* $34. **Credit** AmEx, DC, Disc, MC, V. **Californian**
By day, the view of the marina from Café del Rey is lovely; by night, though, the whole interior seems to glow. The restaurant's signature is the kitchen's creative use of the freshest vegetables and seafood, cooked using French, Asian and Californian ideas. The servers are pros and the sommelier's an expert, so don't be shy about asking for advice.

Truxton's
8611 Truxton Avenue, at W Manchester Avenue, Westchester (1-310 417 8789/www.truxtons americanbistro.com). Bus 42, 115, 439/I-10, exit La Tijera Boulevard south. **Open** 5.30-10.30pm Mon-Fri; 9am-10pm Sat, Sun. **Main course** $15. **Credit** AmEx, DC, Disc, MC, V. **American**
The hippest place near LAX is this hopping spot on a side street in Westchester. Specialising in comforting American cuisine, Truxton's uses market produce and smokes brisket overnight; not wildly unusual in LA, but unique in this particular culinary desert. The food is comfortably the best in the area.

Brentwood to Beverly Hills

Brentwood

Restaurant at the Getty Center
1200 Getty Center Drive, at I-405 (1-310 440 6810/www.getty.edu). Bus 761/I-405, exit Getty Center Drive. **Open** 11.30am-2.30pm Tue-Thur; 11.30am-3pm, 5-9pm Fri-Sat; 11am-3pm, 5.30-11pm Sun. **Main courses** *Lunch* $16. *Dinner* $25. **Credit** AmEx, DC, MC, V. **American**
The Getty's restaurant operates limited hours; still, no matter how much you need to tweak your schedule, it's worth the effort. Enjoy spectacular views of the city and the coastline, and the vineyard of a private winery, while dining on excellent modern American cuisine. Combinations of fruit and meat are the theme, and the results are marvellous: it turns out that not all the Getty's art is on its walls.

Takao

11656 San Vicente Boulevard, at Darlington Avenue (1-310 207 8636). Bus 20, 720, SM2, SM4/I-10, exit Bundy Drive north. **Open** 11.30am-2.30pm, 5.30-10.30pm Mon-Sat; 5-10pm Sun. **Main courses** $22. **Credit** AmEx, DC, MC, V. **Japanese**

Takao Izumida is famous in LA as an alumnus of celebrity chef Nobu's kitchen. However, at his own restaurant, he serves sushi without the Peruvian embellishments. The quality is very high, and the $100 *omakase* menu is a real highlight: tell the chef your likes and dislikes and then fasten your seatbelt, because things are sure to get interesting.

Culver City

La Dijonaise

8703 Washington Boulevard, at Helms Avenue (1-310 287 2770/www.ladijonaise.com). Bus 33, 220, 333, C1/I-10, exit Robertson Boulevard south. **Open** 7am-9pm Mon-Fri; 8am-9pm Sat; 8am-5pm Sun. **Main courses** $13. **Credit** AmEx, DC, MC, V. **French**

This appealing bistro/bakery is a culinary bargain: the French country cooking is very good and the prices are fair. Don't expect innovation or a high-class atmosphere, but if you want steak Bordelaise, bouillabaisse or (of course) chicken Dijon for under $20 with a glass of wine, this is the place. At breakfast, there are excellent omelettes and pastries.

Double Dutch

9806 W Washington Boulevard, at Culver Boulevard (1-310 280 0991/www.cooksdoubledutch.com). Bus 33, 220, 333, C1/I-10, exit Robertson Boulevard south. **Open** 11am-3.30pm Mon-Thur; 11am-3.30pm, 6-10pm Fri; 6-10pm Sat. **Main courses** *Lunch* $10. *Dinner* $19. **Credit** AmEx, DC, MC, V. **American**

Convenient for both the historic movie studios and Culver City's increasingly interesting blend of galleries and shops, this vegetarian-friendly restaurant offers something for everyone. Jennie Cook prides herself on obtaining the freshest farmers' market ingredients and changes the menu daily, although some favourites are always on offer.

Ford's Filling Station

9531 Culver Boulevard, at Cardiff Avenue (1-310 202 1470/www.fordsfillingstation.net). Bus 33, 220, 333, C1/I-10, exit Robertson Boulevard south. **Open** 11am-11pm Mon-Sat; 10am-10pm Sun. **Main courses** *Lunch* $16. *Dinner* $24. **Credit** AmEx, DC, MC, V. **American**

Chef Benjamin Ford (yes, he's the son of Harrison) is talented, but the staff at his restaurant seem to have trouble keeping up with the crowds: after a deluge of favourable reviews hit the press, the average waiting time before getting a table has risen and there have been many complaints about bad service. And while the kitchen offers decent variations on gastropub favourites such as fish and chips, it's not up to the ambitious standards that Ford set at some of his previous restaurants.

Fraiche

9411 Culver Boulevard, at Main Street (1-310 839 6800/www.fraicherestaurantla.com). Bus 33, 220, 333, C1/I-10, exit Robertson Boulevard south. **Open** 11.30am-2.30pm, 5.30pm-midnight Mon-Fri; 5.30pm-midnight Sat, Sun. **Main courses** *Lunch* $14. *Dinner* $23. **Credit** AmEx, DC, MC, V. **Mediterranean**

This newcomer was doing good business even before the *New York Times* labelled it as one of the ten best new restaurants outside the Big Apple in early 2008. Happily, Jason Travi's cooking, served in a handsome room and priced fairly, deserves the raves.

Leaf Cuisine

11938 W Washington Boulevard, at Inglewood Boulevard (1-310 390 6005/www.leaf cuisine.com). Bus C2, SM14/I-405, exit Washington Boulevard west. **Open** 8am-9pm Mon-Sat; 10am-9pm Sun. **Main courses** $10. **Credit** DC, MC, V. **Eclectic**

You'd think that a town as health-conscious as LA would have more innovative vegetarian restaurants. Still, it's hardly Leaf's fault that they don't have much competition. Ethnic authenticity isn't a priority: pad Thai, for instance, bears only a passing resemblance to anything served in Thailand. Still, if you take the dishes on their own merits, you might like them.

Tender Greens

9523 Culver Boulevard, at Cardiff Avenue (1-310 842 8300/www.tendergreensfood.com). Bus 33, 220, 333, C1/I-10, exit Robertson Boulevard south. **Open** 11.30am-9pm Mon-Thur, Sun; 11.30am-10pm Fri, Sat. **Main courses** $10. **Open** DC, MC, V. **American**

This casual spot has become a locals' favourite, and with good reason: the food is decent and, just as importantly, it's dished up in next to no time from a poshed-up canteen-stylecounter. Choose from something meaty and/or something salady, made from local ingredients, then repair to a nearby table with the food and a glass of wine. Best for lunch.

West LA

Apple Pan

10801 W Pico Boulevard, at Glendon Avenue (1-310 475 3585). Bus C3, SM7, SM8, SM13/I-10, exit Overland Avenue north. **Open** 11am-midnight Tue-Thur, Sun; 11am-1am Fri, Sat. **Main courses** $6. **No credit cards**. **Map** p327 A5 **⑭** **Cafés & diners** *See p163* **Vintage vittles**.

Lemon Moon

12200 W Olympic Boulevard, at S Bundy Drive (1-310 442 9191/www.lemonmoon.com). Bus SM5, SM14/I-10, exit Bundy Drive south. **Open** 8am-3pm Mon-Fri. **Main courses** $11. **Credit** AmEx, DC, Disc, MC, V. **American**

Looking for a quick gourmet breakfast or lunch? Consider the artful fast food served at this restaurant, conceived by Josiah Citrin of Mélisse and JiRaffe's Raphael Lunetta. Top-quality ingredients are used to make sandwiches, salads and omelettes that appear at your table within minutes.

Il Moro

11400 W Olympic Boulevard, at Purdue Avenue
(1-310 575 3530/www.ilmoro.com). Bus SM5/I-405,
exit Santa Monica Boulevard west. **Open** 11.30am-
3pm, 5-10pm Mon-Thur; 11.30am-3pm, 5-10.30pm
Fri; 5-10.30pm Sat; 4.30-9.30pm Sun. **Main courses**
$25. **Credit** AmEx, DC, MC, V. **Italian**
From the sidestreet entrance in Purdue Avenue, Il
Moro looks tiny, but it widens into a modern, comfortable space with a wonderful terrace. Host
Gaetano Foiano sets out the most beautiful happy-
hour appetisers in town, while chef Davide Ghizzoni
delves into more obscure Italian village recipes:
poison ivy berry risotto, for example, or dishes
with wild boar, elk, rabbit and other exotic items.
Although it's tempting, don't eat so much that you
have no room for the showstopping desserts.

Orris

2006 Sawtelle Boulevard, at La Grange Avenue
(1-310 268 2212/www.orrisrestaurant.com). Bus
SM5/I-405, exit Santa Monica Boulevard west.
Open 6-10pm Tue-Fri; 5.30-10.30pm Sat; 5.30-9.30pm
Sun. **Tapas** $11. **Credit** AmEx, Disc, DC, MC, V.
Californian/Asian
They don't take reservations at this comfortable
restaurant, decorated like a stylish living room. The
house speciality is small plates meant for sharing,
and, for the experience, the prices are very reasonable. Japanese and Mediterranean flavours combine
very well, and the fast but friendly service makes
this a good pre-theatre spot. Take to the outdoor
terrace on sunny days.

Tlapazola Grill

11676 Gateway Boulevard, between Barry Avenue
& S Barrington Avenue Boulevard (1-310 477
1577). Bus SM7/I-10, exit Bundy Drive south.
Open 5-10pm Mon; 11am-10pm Tue-Thur, Sun;
11am-11pm Fri, Sat. **Main courses** $14. **Credit**
DC, MC, V. **Mexican**
This is one of the few eateries in LA that offers
innovative versions of Oaxacan food, a cuisine that's
subtler and more interesting than run-of-the-mill
Mexican fare. All right, so the mini-mall location
does serve to lower expectations (little good ever
comes from them), but the menu raises them again
– the likes of salmon in pumpkin seed sauce, trout
in salsa fresca and braised lamb are all unusual
options. The food is exceptional, and the service is
fluent and expert.

Upstairs2

2311 Cotner Avenue, beween W Pico & W Olympic
Boulevards (1-310 231 0316/www.upstairs2.com).
Bus SM5/I-405, exit Santa Monica Boulevard east.
Open 5.30-10pm Wed, Thur; 5.30-11pm Fri, Sat.
Tapas $12. **Credit** AmEx, DC, MC, V.
Mediterranean
When LA's largest wine store decided to open a
restaurant upstairs, they did what you might expect:
created a stellar wine list and paired it with the food.
The prices are surprisingly reasonable, but you can
end up spending serious money if you start explor-
ing the upper reaches of the wine list. Still, if you
really like one of the wines, you can go downstairs
and buy a few bottles to take home.

Eat, Drink, Shop

Double Dutch.

Kate Mantilini (9101 Wilshire
Boulevard, Beverly Hills)
Pacino meets De Niro in *Heat*

Westwood

Gardens on Glendon

*1139 Glendon Avenue, at Lindbrook Drive,
Westwood (1-310 824 1818/www.gardensonglendon.
com). Bus 2, 20, 302, 720/I-405, exit Wilshire
Boulevard east.* **Open** 5-10pm Mon; 11.30am-10pm
Tue-Thur, Sun; 11.30am-11pm Fri, Sat. **Main
courses** *Lunch* $20. *Dinner* $28. **Credit** AmEx,
DC, MC, V. **French/Italian**
Most Westwood restaurants are student hangouts
or noisy hipster joints. Gardens on Glendon is different: this rambling, cottage-like brick building is
a comfortable, old-fashioned place in which to linger
over a meal. The menu draws on French and Italian
ideas but adds a little innovative flair: the Bombay
lamb is a French take on Indian spicing, for instance.
The service is blessedly free of attitude.

Nanbankan

*11330 Santa Monica Boulevard, at Corinth Avenue
(1-310 478 1591). Bus 4, 704/I-405, exit Santa
Monica Boulevard west.* **Open** 5.30-10.30pm daily.
Main courses $22. **Credit** DC, MC, V. **Japanese**
LA's original *robatayaki* restaurant is still one of the
best, in terms of both selection and execution. Diners
line up for a wide variety of meats and vegetables,
grilled with subtle Japanese seasonings and served
with beer, saké or wine. Large parties should steer
clear on the busier nights: the seating policy means
that you may never get a table while smaller groups
are seated ahead of you.

Native Foods

*1110½ Gayley Avenue, at Kinross Avenue (1-310
209 1055/www.nativefoods.com). Bus 2, 20, 302,
720/I-405, exit Wilshire Boulevard east.* **Open** 11am-
10pm daily. **Main courses** $10. **Credit** AmEx, DC,
Disc, MC, V. **Eclectic**
This vegan café has become popular with students
thanks to the healthy food, the fast service and
prices that won't break a budget. The food is good:
even non-vegetarians may be seduced by Moroccan,
Greek or Indian-style rice and veggie bowls.

Bel Air

Hotel Bel-Air

*701 Stone Canyon Road, at Tortuoso Way (1-310
472 5234/www.hotelbelair.com). No bus/I-405, exit
Sunset Boulevard east.* **Open** 7-10.30am, noon-2pm,
6.30-9.30pm Mon-Sat; 7am-10am, 11am-2pm, 6.30-
10pm Sun. **Main courses** *Breakfast* $21. *Lunch* $23.
Dinner $33. **Credit** AmEx, DC, Disc, MC, V.
Californian
It's one of the most famous hotels in the country,
a place of almost legendary Californian refinement,
but somehow many Angelenos never think of eating at the Bel-Air. They're missing a gem: the setting is an unparalleled combination of rustic and
elegant motifs, and the food is first-class. You'll feel
as if you're in a Wine Country spa, but the hustle
and bustle of LA is only a few minutes away.

Century City

La Cachette

*10506 Little Santa Monica Boulevard, at Thayer
Avenue (1-310 470 4992/www.lacachetterestaurant.
com). Bus 4, 16, 704/I-405, exit Santa Monica
Boulevard east.* **Open** noon-2pm, 6-9.30pm Mon-
Thur; 6-10pm Sat, Sun. **Main courses** *Lunch* $32.
Dinner $37. **Credit** AmEx, DC, Disc, MC, V.
Map p327 A4 ⓯ **French**
Jean François Meteigner has some unusual ideas
about French cuisine that fit well with LA ideals –
luxurious but low-fat, with almost no use of butter
and cream. His Provençal-style cottage on a hill is
worth the trip; if you can, schedule your visit around
one of his wine dinners. This is also one of the only
places in LA that serves a tasting menu for lunch:
allow plenty of time and take the rest of the day off.

Clementine

*1751 Ensley Avenue, at Santa Monica Boulevard
(1-310 552 1080/www.clementineonline.com). Bus
4, 16, 704/I-405, exit Santa Monica Boulevard east.*
Open 7am-7.30pm Mon-Fri; 8am-5pm Sat. **Main
courses** *Breakfast* $8. *Lunch* $15. **Credit** AmEx,
DC, MC, V. **Map** p327 B3 ⓰ **American**
Annie Miller's lovely, low-key café-bakery offers
delicious fuel to the neighbourhood's shoppers and
office workers. The food ranges from the deeply
healthy (home-made granola) to the even more pro-
foundly naughty (look out for 'BBQ Fridays'); don't
leave without trying one of the appetising and ever-
changing array of sweet things.

Beverly Hills

Breadbar

*8718 W 3rd Street, between S Hamal Road & Amaz
Drive (1-310 205 0124/www.breadbar.net). Bus 20,
220, 720/I-10, exit La Cienega Boulevard north.*
Open 7am-7pm daily. **Main courses** $12. **Credit**
AmEx, DC, MC, V. **Map** p328 A3 ⓱ **French**
Breadbar started as a gourmet bakery, but its guest-
chef programme was so popular that the restaurant
decided to add a permanent menu. Chef Noriyuki
Sugie got things rolling with the unexpected plate of
crab guacamole and black cod sliders; he's scheduled to leave for San Francisco in late 2008, but his
menu will hopefully remain intact.
Other locations Westfield Century City (*see p190*;
1-310 277 3770).

Cut

*Beverly Wilshire Hotel, 9500 Wilshire Boulevard, at
S Rodeo Drive (1-310 276 8500/www.wolfgangpuck.
com). Bus 4, 14, 16, 20, 316, 704, 720/I-405, exit*

Star power

Gordon Ramsay

It isn't just the entertainment industry that trades on celebrity in Los Angeles. While the city offers an almost unmatched variety of low-key ethnic dining (*see p158* **Around the world**), the other end of the market is increasingly populated by star chefs, who've made their names in other cities or on TV before heading to LA to bolster their reputations still further. The last few years in particular have seen a rush of imports; happily, many of them deliver not just celebrity cachet but excellent food.

Osteria Mozza (*see p157*) was opened in 2007 by a crack team comprising no fewer than three star names: chef Mario Batali, La Brea Bakery founder Nancy Silverton and wine expert Joseph Bastianich. Served tapas-style, the Italian food is exquisite: try the selection of mozzarellas paired with all manner of meats, vegetables and herbs, a one-of-a-kind treat; or the pasta tasting menu, seven courses served family-style for

$69. The same trio are behind **Pizzeria Mozza** (*see p157*), which serves what might be the best pizza in LA.

Opened in 2008 by Jon Shook and Vinny Dotolo, better known as the Two Dudes Catering on the Food Network, **Animal** (*see p159*) offers a crazy-adventurous menu that adds unexpected twists to the cooking of the American South: Johnnycakes with foie gras, for instance. The room is bare and often loud. The food, though, is fantastic.

Paris-born chef Alain Giraud first came to prominence in the late '90s at Santa Monica's Lavande, before moving to Beverly Hills and really making his name at Bastide. In June 2008, Giraud returned to Santa Monica and opened **Anisette** (*see p145*), a bistro at the foot of the old clock tower. Compare and contrast Giraud's traditional Gallic cooking with the more American fare delivered by fellow Frenchman Laurent Tourondel at **BLT** (short for Bistro Laurent Tourondel; *see p155*), another 2008 opening. The steaks (including Kobe beef) and the seafood are both of the highest quality; however, the sides, especially the featherlight popovers, steal the show.

Tourondel's restaurant immediately made a favourable impression. **Gordon Ramsay**, though, got off to a slower start at his restaurant at the London in West Hollywood (*see p155*), where the 2008 opening was dented by reports of chaotic service and uneven food. Still, Ramsay's famous perfectionism will hopefully ensure that the kinks are eradicated before long.

Although the arrival of big names such as Ramsay and Tourondel have made headlines, Wolfgang Puck retains plenty of cachet in LA. Indeed, his celebrity-chef status resulted in a bizarre, only-in-LA legal snafu during 2008. With influential California-cooking eaterie **Spago** (*see p155*), a sister to the now-closed Sunset Strip original, and the newer **Cut** (*see p152*), a high-powered steakhouse, Puck has long retained a presence in Beverly Hills. So when German waiter-made-good Wolfgang Zwiener moved into the area with a restaurant called **Wolfgang's Steakhouse** (*see p155*), Puck sued in the hope of forcing Zwiener to change the restaurant's name, arguing that diners may be fooled into believing it's a Puck operation. The court didn't bite: in June 2008, Zwiener won, and the name remains.

Eat, Drink, Shop

Bastide.

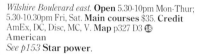

Wilshire Boulevard east. **Open** 5.30-10pm Mon-Thur;
5.30-10.30pm Fri, Sat. **Main courses** $35. **Credit**
AmEx, DC, Disc, MC, V. **Map** p327 D3 🔞
American
See p153 **Star power**.

Fogo de Chao

*133 N La Cienega Boulevard, between Wilshire
Boulevard & Clifton Way (1-310 289 7755/www.
fogodechao.com). Bus 20, 220, 720/I-10, exit La
Cienega Boulevard north.* **Open** 11.30am-2pm, 5-
10pm Mon-Thur; 11.30am-2pm, 5-10.30pm Fri; 4.30-
10.30pm Sat; 4-9.30pm Sun. **Main courses** *Lunch*
$32. *Dinner* $54. **Credit** AmEx, DC, Disc, MC, V.
Map p328 B4 🔞 **Brazilian**
Most Brazilian barbecues supplement good meat
with carelessly prepared side dishes that are an obvious afterthought. Fogo de Chao is different: the beautiful salad bar and the buffet are both full of fine cold
dishes made with premium ingredients. This is the
priciest *churrascaria* in LA but by far the best, aided
by its exceptional South American wine list.

Grill on the Alley

*9560 Dayton Way, at Wilshire Boulevard (1-310
276 0615/www.thegrill.com). Bus 20, 720/I-405, exit
Wilshire Boulevard east.* **Open** 11.30am-11pm Mon-
Thur; 11.30am-midnight Fri, Sat; 5-9pm Sun. **Main
courses** *Lunch* $28. *Dinner* $40. **Credit** AmEx, DC,
Disc, MC, V. **Map** p327 C3 🔞 **American**
The food is good, but that's not actually the reason
why most people come here: along with **Mastro's**

Steakhouse (246 N Canon Drive, 1-310 888 8782,
www.mastrosteakhouse.com) and the fabled **Polo
Lounge** at the Beverly Hills Hotel (*see p54*), this is
Hollywood power-lunch central. Even though the
restaurant has only been here since the 1980s, it
already feels like an old-money hangout. Order a
steak or crab Louie, gawk at the stars, and enjoy
being pampered by consummate professionals who
treat everybody like they're somebody.
Other locations 6801 Hollywood Boulevard,
Hollywood (1-323 856 5530).

Matsuhisa

*129 N La Cienega Boulevard, between Wilshire
Boulevard & Clifton Way (1-310 659 9639/www.
nobumatsuhisa.com). Bus 20, 220, 720/I-10, exit La
Cienega Boulevard north.* **Open** 11.45am-2.15pm,
5.45-10.15pm Mon-Fri; 5.45-10.15pm Sat, Sun. **Main
courses** *Lunch* $20. *Dinner* $24. **Credit** AmEx, DC,
MC, V. **Map** p328 B4 🔞 **Japanese**
Celebrity chef Nobuyuki Matsuhisa's empire began
at this Beverly Hills operation, which continues to
thrive. Matsuhisa's masterful merging of Japanese
and Peruvian cuisines is best experienced at the
omakase dinners of seven courses or more (starting
at $90). Tell the chef your likes and dislikes and then
let him loose on your tastebuds.

Nate 'n Al's

*414 N Beverly Drive, between Santa Monica
Boulevard & Brighton Way (1-310 274 0101/
www.natenal.com). Bus 20, 720/I-405, exit Wilshire*

Boulevard east. **Open** 7am-9pm daily. **Main courses** $15. **Credit** AmEx, DC, MC, V. **Map** p327 C3 ㉒ **Jewish**
Nate 'n Al's isn't the best Jewish deli in greater LA, but 60 years of service have certainly made it an institution. The food is heavy but good, and the servers are seasoned veterans who've seen everything and treat punks, millionaires, families and elderly Jewish matrons exactly the same.

Oliver Café
9601 Wilshire Boulevard, at S Camden Drive (1-310 888 8160/www.olivercafe.com). Bus 20, 720/I-405, exit Wilshire Boulevard east. **Open** 9am-10.30pm daily. **Main courses** $16. **Credit** AmEx, DC, Disc, MC, V. **Map** p327 C3 ㉓ **American**
The Oliver Café is located right next to a gym (you may be able to see people working out from your booth); naturally, then, it has a good selection of healthy dishes. All the food has passed muster with a local dietician, so you can feel virtuous while eating that salmon panino or shrimp salad. Designed by Dodd Mitchell, it's a handsome room.

Spago of Beverly Hills
176 N Canon Drive, between Clifton Way & Wilshire Boulevard (1-310 385 0880/www.wolfgangpuck. com). Bus 4, 14, 16, 704/I-10, exit Robertson Boulevard north. **Open** 11.30am-2.15pm, 5.30-10.30pm Mon-Thur; 11.30am-2.15pm, 5.30-11pm Fri; noon-2.30pm, 5.30-11pm Sat; 5.30-10.30pm Sun. **Main courses** $35. **Credit** AmEx, DC, Disc, MC, V. **Map** p327 D3 ㉔ **Californian**
See p153 **Star power**.

Tokyo Table
50 N La Cienega Boulevard, between Wilshire Boulevard & Clifton Way (1-323 657 9500/www. tokyotable.com). Bus 20, 220, 720/I-10, exit La Cienega Boulevard north. **Open** 11.30am-1am daily. **Main courses** $13. **Credit** AmEx, DC, Disc, MC, V. **Map** p328 B4 ㉕ **Japanese**
Not everything at Tokyo Table is wacky. The fresh tofu salad and crispy flounder, for instance, are traditional and delectable. But why choose them when such creative items as raw fish pizza and French fries dusted with dried seaweed are available, and at such reasonable prices? Save room for the house dessert of toast filled with ice-cream and strawberries and drizzled with honey.

Urasawa
218 N Rodeo Drive, at Wilshire Boulevard (1-310 247 8939). Bus 4, 16, 20, 720/I-10, exit Robertson Boulevard north. **Open** 6-8pm Tue-Sat. **Main courses** *Set menu* $300. **Credit** AmEx, DC, MC, V. **Map** p327 C3 ㉖ **Japanese**
LA is awash with sushi bars, but Urasawa is at the top of the heap. Flown in daily, the fish is prepared by chef Hiroyuki Urasawa and one assistant. Meals stretch to 25 artfully prepared courses; the experience will be amazing and expensive. Booking is imperative (there are no walk-ins), and an early-evening slot is best: if you arrive at 8pm, each course will arrive as soon as you've finished the previous tidbit.

Wolfgang's Steakhouse
445 N Canon Drive, at Santa Monica Boulevard, Beverly Hills (1-310 385 0640/www.wolfgangs steakhouse.com). Bus 4, 14, 16, 704/I-10, exit Robertson Boulevard north. **Open** 11.30am-10.30pm Mon-Thur, Sun; 11.30am-11.30pm Fri, Sat. **Main courses** $35. **Credit** AmEx, DC, Disc, MC, V. **Map** p327 C2 ㉗ **American**
See p153 **Star power**.

West Hollywood, Hollywood & Midtown

West Hollywood

Bastide
8475 Melrose Place, at N La Cienega Boulevard (1-323 874 0377). Bus 10, 105/I-10, exit La Cienega Boulevard north. **Open** noon-2pm Tue-Fri; 6-9pm Tue-Sat. **Main courses** *Prix fixe* $100-$125. **Credit** AmEx, DC, MC, V. **Map** p327 C3 ㉘ **French**
You'll have to make only one choice at this long-standing French favourite – five courses or seven? Chef Paul Shoemaker's food isn't quite as pyrotechnical as some of his predecessors here; however, his cooking is very assured, and sommelier Pieter Verheyde's wine pairings are unerring. It's a lovely room, too. One for a special occasion.

BLT
8720 W Sunset Boulevard, between Palm Avenue & Alta Loma Road, West Hollywood (1-310 360 1950/www.bltsteak.com). Bus 10, 105, 705/I-10, exit La Cienega Boulevard north. **Open** 5.30-11pm Mon-Thur; 5.30-11.30pm Fri, Sat; 5-10pm Sun. **Main courses** $40. **Credit** AmEx, DC, MC, V. **Map** p328 B2 ㉙ **American/French**
See p153 **Star power**.

Dan Tana's
9071 Santa Monica Boulevard, between N Doheny Drive & Nemo Street (1-310 275 9444/www.dan tanasrestaurant.com). Bus 4, 704/I-10, exit Robertson Boulevard north. **Open** 5pm-12.30am daily. **Main courses** $28. **Credit** AmEx, DC, Disc, MC, V. **Map** p328 A2 ㉚ **Italian**
Nobody goes to Dan Tana's for the cooking. It's not that the simple, old-fashioned Italian fare is bad: it's more that the old Hollywood atmosphere is wonderfully thick. The older servers can tell you what LA was like back when this food was cutting-edge, a time when they were much younger but Dan Tana's looked the same. It's favoured by celebs with respect for olde Hollywood (George Clooney, James Woods); younger stars prefer **Foxtail** next door (9077 Santa Monica Boulevard, 1-310 859 8369, www.sbeent.com).

Gordon Ramsay
London West Hollywood, 1020 N San Vicente Boulevard, at Holloway Drive, West Hollywood (1-310 358 7788/www.gordonramsay.com/gratthe londonwh). Bus 4, 105, 220, 305, 550, 704/I-10, exit La Cienega Boulevard north. **Open** 6.30-10.30am,

noon-10.30pm Mon-Fri; 7-11am, noon-10.30pm Sat;
7-11am, noon-10pm Sun. **Main courses** *Small plates*
$18. *Set dinner* $85. **Credit** AmEx, DC, Disc, MC, V.
Map p328 A2 ❸❶ **British**
See p153 **Star power**.

Griddle Café

*7916 W Sunset Boulevard, at N Fairfax Avenue
(1-323 874 0377/www.thegriddlecafe.com). Bus
2, 217, 302/I-10, exit Fairfax Avenue north.*
Open 7am-4pm Mon-Fri; 8am-4pm Sat, Sun.
Main courses $10. **Credit** AmEx, DC, MC, V.
Map p328 C1 ❸❷ **Cafés & diners**
A useful standby in this part of town, this is a greasy
spoon as only West Hollywood knows how, which
is to say that it's not in the least bit greasy. Buff
young hunks and hunkettes chow down on immense
pancakes and lunchtime sandwiches; they're watching your figure, even if you're not.

Lucques

*8474 Melrose Avenue, at N La Cienega Boulevard
(1-323 655 6277/www.lucques.com). Bus 10, 105,
705/I-10, exit La Cienega Boulevard north.* **Open**
6-10pm Mon; noon-2.30pm, 6-10pm Tue; noon-
2.30pm, 6-11pm Wed-Sat; 5-10pm Sun. **Main
courses** *Lunch* $17. *Dinner* $33. **Credit** AmEx,
DC, MC, V. **Map** p328 B2 ❸❸ **French**
To get in the right frame of mind for this modern
French-Mediterranean restaurant, decide that you're
willing to try absolutely anything. Chef Suzanne
Goin is fantastically inventive, using obscure ingredients in exuberant and unlikely combinations. Fill
the centre of your table with appetisers and then
order a main or two: if it's available, try the veal
cheek. The lunch and Sunday-night prix fixe menus
are among the best deals in town.

Il Sole

*8741 W Sunset Boulevard, between N La Cienega
& San Vicente Boulevards (1-310 657 1182). Bus 2,
105, 302, 705/I-10, exit La Cienega Boulevard north.*
Open 6-10pm Mon-Sat; 5.30-9.30pm Sun. **Main
courses** $50. **Credit** AmEx, DC, Disc, MC, V.
Map p328 A1 ❸❹ **Italian**
The food at Il Sole is authentically Tuscan and very
good, but it's served with a dose of attitude – if
you're a celebrity, or easily mistaken for one, you'll
likely get a much better table than the rest of us. To
some, it's worth it for a chance to share a small room
with big stars. For others, the truffle risotto is the
main draw: it's so good that you may not even notice
who's dining at the next table.

Hollywood

Bhan Kanom

*5271 Hollywood Boulevard, at N Hobart Boulevard
(1-323 871 8030/www.bhankanomthai.com). Metro
Hollywood-Western/bus 180, 181, 207, 217, 757,
780, LDH/US 101, exit Western Avenue north.*
Open 10am-2am daily. **Desserts** $4. **Credit** DC,
MC, V. **Map** p329 D1 ❸❺ **Desserts**
See p146 **Life is sweets**.

Citizen Smith

*1600 N Cahuenga Boulevard, at Selma Avenue
(1-323 461 5001/www.citizensmith.com). Metro
Hollywood-Vine/bus 163, 180, 181, 210, 212,
217, 312, 363, 780, LDH/US 101, exit Hollywood
Boulevard west.* **Open** 11am-3pm, 6pm-2am Mon-Fri;
6pm-2am Sat, Sun. **Main courses** *Lunch* $13.
Dinner $25. **Credit** AmEx, DC, Disc, MC, V.
Map p329 B2 ❸❻ **American**
Given the dramatic decor at Citizen Smith, it's a
surprise when the speciality proves not to be some
sort of exotic cuisine but Southern fried chicken.
This sleek eaterie does have some edgy dishes on its
menu, not to mention some decent steaks, but the
Americana-with-an-edge is what pulls in the punters.
Try and visit the elegant bar hidden in the back: it's
sometimes empty even when the front is jammed.

Falcon

*7213 W Sunset Boulevard, between N Poinsettia
Place & N Alta Vista Boulevard (1-323 850 5350/
www.falconslair.com). Bus 2, 302, LDHWD/I-10,
exit La Brea Avenue north.* **Open** 7pm-2am Mon-
Thur; 6pm-2am Fri, Sat. **Main courses** $22.
Credit AmEx, DC, Disc, MC, V. **Map** p328 D1 ❸❼
American
A visually striking, Asian-inspired landscape in
which indoor and outdoor spaces merge, Falcon's
dramatic interior is almost worth a visit in itself. The
formerly Asian-esque menu now has more French
and Italian accents, but the wood oven still turns out
meats crusted with herbs and perfumed by smoke.
The sensuous atmosphere is a draw: as the evening
goes on, this becomes one of LA's livelier bar scenes.

Jitlada

*5233 W Sunset Boulevard, between N Hobart
Boulevard & N Kingsley Drive (1-323 663 3104).
Metro Hollywood-Western/bus 2, 175, 207, 302/US
101, exit Western Avenue north.* **Open** 5-10pm Mon;
11am-11pm Tue-Sun. **Main courses** $14. **Credit**
AmEx, DC, Disc, MC, V. **Map** p329 D2 ❸❽ **Thai**
Jitlada is just outside the borders of LA's Thai
Town, but it's still the most famous Thai restaurant
in the city. Flick through the menu to the back page,
where you'll find the brutally spicy but intensely
flavourful southern Thai specialities. The chef will
tone down the heat on request, but the food is at its
best (and most authentic) when it's at its hottest.

Mario's Peruvian Seafood

*5786 Melrose Avenue, at N Vine Street (1-323 466
4181). Bus 10, 210/I-10, exit La Brea Avenue north.*
Open 11.30am-8.30pm Mon-Thur, Sun; 11.30am-
11pm Fri, Sat. **Main courses** $10. **Credit** AmEx,
DC, Disc, MC, V. **Map** p329 B3 ❸❾ **Peruvian**
Mario's was one of the first restaurants to bring
Peruvian cuisine into the LA mainstream. The place
has the ambience of an old lunch counter and there's
often a queue, but the food keeps people coming
back: seafood fried rice, beef sautéed with potato and
onion, citrusy fish ceviches and so on. The green
sauce on your table is spicier than it looks, but it's
so flavourful that you'll use too much of it anyway.

Mashti Malone's

1525 N La Brea Avenue, at W Sunset Boulevard (1-323 874 0144 6168/www.mashtimalone.com). Metro Hollywood-Highland/bus 163, 180, 181, 210, 212, 217, 312, 363, 780, LDH/US 101, exit Highland Avenue south. **Open** 11.30am-11.30pm Mon-Thur; 11.30am-midnight Fri, Sat. **Desserts** $4. **Credit** AmEx, DC, Disc, MC, V. **Map** p329 A2 **⓵ Desserts**
See p146 **Life is sweets**.

Miceli's

1646 N Las Palmas Avenue, between Hollywood Boulevard & Selma Avenue (1-323 466 3438/www.micelisrestaurant.com). Metro Hollywood-Highland/bus 163, 180, 181, 210, 212, 217, 312, 363, 780, LDH/US 101, exit Hollywood Boulevard west. **Open** 11.30am-11pm Mon-Thur, Sun; 11.30am-midnight Sat-Sun. **Main courses** *Lunch* $11. *Dinner* $15. **Credit** AmEx, DC, Disc, MC, V. **Map** p329 A2 **⓵ Italian**
LA's oldest Italian restaurant is more famous for its singing waiters than for its food. There are better entertainers and better chefs elsewhere, but an evening here is a lot of fun. Locals and tourists come for pizzas and hearty Sicilian pastas, while the servers bellow opera and pop. The NoHo clone offers the same decent food and variable music.
Other locations 3655 Cahuenga Boulevard, North Hollywood (1-323 851 3344).

Musso & Frank Grill

6667 Hollywood Boulevard, at N Cherokee Avenue (1-323 467 5123). Metro Hollywood-Highland/bus 156, 163, 212, 217, 363, 656, 780, LDH/US 101, *exit Highland Avenue north.* **Open** 11am-11pm Tue-Sat. **Main courses** $27. **Credit** AmEx, DC, MC, V. **Map** p329 A2 **⓵ Russian**
See p163 **Vintage vittles**.

Osteria Mozza

6602 Melrose Avenue, at N Highland Avenue (1-323 297 0100/www.mozza-la.com). Bus 10, 210/I-10, exit La Brea Avenue north. **Open** 5.30-11pm Mon-Fri; 5-11pm Sat; 5-10pm Sun. **Main courses** $27. **Credit** AmEx, DC, MC, V. **Map** p329 A3 **⓵ Italian**
See p153 **Star power**.

Pizzeria Mozza

641 N Highland Avenue, at Melrose Avenue (1-323 297 0101/www.mozza-la.com). Bus 10, 210/I-10, exit La Brea Avenue north. **Open** noon-midnight daily. **Main courses** $14. **Credit** AmEx, DC, MC, V. **Map** p329 A3 **⓵ Italian**
See p153 **Star power**.

Providence

5955 Melrose Avenue, between Cole & Wilcox Avenues (1-323 460 4170/www.providencela.com). Bus 10/US 101, exit Melrose Avenue west. **Open** 6-10pm Mon-Thur; noon-2.30pm, 6-10pm Fri; 5.30-10pm Sat; 5.30-9pm Sun. **Main courses** *Lunch* $28. *Dinner* $42. **Credit** AmEx, DC, MC, V. **Map** p329 B3 **⓵ Seafood**
The most talked-about restaurant in Los Angeles is, in fact, a modern but nonetheless cosy place on a rather dull stretch of Melrose Avenue. Chef Michael Cimarusti is most famous for his wizardry with seafood, but the kitchen team works wonders with

Yamashiro. *See p158.*

Around the world

Most big cities have a few neighbourhoods that feel like they've been dropped in from another corner of the planet. LA celebrates its own ethnic enclaves with rare enthusiasm: everyone from expats to chefs head to them in search of authentic foods that are unavailable elsewhere. Here are five areas in which to explore LA's culinary diversity:

Chinese: Monterey Park

LA's Chinatown has several good restaurants, but the best and most authentic Chinese food is to the east near Monterey Park and Alhambra. Try the Shandong beef rolls at **101 Noodle Express** (1408 E Valley Boulevard, Alhambra, 1-626 300 8654), hand-made noodles at **Dumpling Master** (423 N Atlantic Boulevard, Monterey Park, 1-626 458 8689), or dim sum at any of a hundred places: we recommend **Empress Harbor** (*see p167*).

Indian: Little Bombay, Artesia

The best Indian food in LA is served in Artesia along a stretch of Pioneer Boulevard. Try **Jay Bharat** (18701 Pioneer Boulevard, Artesia, 1-562 924 3310) for hearty South Indian vegetarian food; **Woodlands** (11833 Artesia Boulevard, Artesia, 1-562 860 6500) offers a more elegant version of the same cuisine. Spice junkies will find the Hyderabadi chicken at **Shan** (18621 Pioneer Boulevard, Artesia, 1-562 865 3838, www.shanrestaurant.us) to be the hottest Indian dish in LA.

Mexican: Plaza Mexico, Lynwood

Mexican restaurants are everywhere in LA, but Lynwood's Plaza Mexico mall stands out for its diversity. There are eateries specialising in goat stew, seafood from Yucatan and other regional delicacies, but the standout is Generoso Bahena's stylish, exciting **Malverde** (11215 Long Beach Boulevard, Lynwood, 1-310 631 9177).

Thai: Thai Town, Hollywood

Most Thai restaurants in LA serve a mild, Americanised version of the cuisine. The exceptions are in Hollywood's Thai Town, where the largest Thai community in America demands food the way they serve it at home. Try northern Thai cuisine at **Ocha** (various locations) or southern Thai at **Jitlada** (*see p156*). Be brave and tell your server you want your food Thai hot, not *farang* hot.

Vietnamese: Little Saigon, Westminster

The largest Vietnamese community outside Vietnam is in Westminster, Orange County. One of the area's best restaurants is **Pho Thang Long** (15579 Brookhurst Street, 1-714 839 4955), famous for spicy noodle soup and the wok-fried steak called *shaking* beef. Just want a sandwich? Try **Mr Lee's** or **Mr Baguette** (various locations): both specialise in *banh mi*, French-style sandwiches filled with Vietnamese meat and vegetables.

everything. If you've the money, order a tasting menu: it'll cost about $200, but it comes with generous pours of fine wine and the food is excellent.

Roscoe's House of Chicken & Waffles

1514 N Gower Street, at W Sunset Boulevard (1-323 466 7453/www.roscoeschickenandwaffles.com). Metro Hollywood-Vine/bus 2, 302, LDHWI/US 101, exit Sunset Boulevard west. **Open** 8.30am-midnight Mon-Thur, Sun; 8.30am-4am Fri, Sat. **Main courses** $10. **Credit** AmEx, DC, Disc, MC, V. **Map** p329 B2 ㊻ **American**

You can find better chicken in LA, and better waffles – but for both under one roof, Roscoe's is king. The Hollywood branch is the fanciest. **Other locations** throughout LA.

Scoops

712 N Heliotrope Drive, between Melrose Avenue & Monroe Street (1-323 906 2649). Metro Vermont-Santa Monica/bus 10, 204, 754/US 101, exit

Vermont Avenue north. **Open** noon-10pm Mon-Sat. **Desserts** $2. **No credit cards. Map** p330 A4 ㊼ **Desserts**

See p146 **Life is sweets**.

Yamashiro

1999 N Sycamore Avenue, north of Franklin Avenue (1-323 466 5125/www.yamashirorestaurant.com). Metro Hollywood-Highland/bus 163, 180, 181, 210, 212, 217, 312, 363, 780, LDH/US 101, exit Highland Avenue south. **Open** 5.30-10pm Mon-Thur, Sun; 5.30-11pm Fri, Sat. **Main courses** $28. **Credit** AmEx, DC, Disc, MC, V. Map p329 A1 ㊽ **Pan-Asian**

Built as a private art museum in the 1920s, this Japanese palace is a spectacular structure with extraordinary views of Hollywood. For years, it was a beautiful building in which to eat bad food, but Jason Park's new kitchen team has made a major difference: the restaurant is now worth a look even if you don't get a table with a view. Japanese, Korean and Chinese traditional items are presented alongside sensible and occasionally daring fusion ideas. *Photo p157.*

Fairfax District

Animal

435 N Fairfax Avenue, between Oakwood & Rosewood Avenues (1-323 782 9225/www.animal restaurant.com). Bus 14, 217, 218/I-10, exit Fairfax Avenue north. **Open** 6-11pm Mon-Thur, Sun; 6pm-2am Fri, Sat. **Main courses** $25. **Credit** AmEx, DC, Disc, MC, V. **Map** p328 C3 ⑭ **American**
See p153 **Star power.**

AOC

8022 W 3rd Street, at S Laurel Avenue (1-323 653 6359/www.aocwinebar.com). Bus 16, 218/I-10, exit Fairfax Avenue north. **Open** 6-10pm Mon; 6-11pm Tue-Fri; 5.30-11pm Sat; 5.30-10pm Sun. **Main courses** $14. **Credit** AmEx, DC, MC, V.
Map p328 C3 ⑮ **French**
The acronym stands for Appellation d'Origine Contrôlée, the system for certifying the region of origin of food and wine in France and ensuring its quality. AOC might be a long way from France, but the food, served in tapas-like portions, is Gallic in its perfection: dishes might include clams with sherry, or Dungeness crab with sweet-pea pancakes. The wine list is strong, particularly the reds.

Canter's Deli

419 N Fairfax Avenue, at Oakwood Avenue (1-323 651 2030/www.cantersdeli.com). Bus 14, 217, 218/I-10, exit Fairfax Avenue north. **Open** 24hrs daily. **Main courses** $14. **Credit** DC, Disc, MC, V.
Map p328 C3 ⑯ **Jewish**
This reliable piece of local history, still owned by the Canter family after nearly 80 years, is both a fine old-school Jewish deli and one of LA's favourite after-hours places. Come here at 2am, and you're bound to see musicians from all over town who've just got off-stage and want to tuck into some blintzes or a stacked pastrami sandwich. The mural by the parking lot chronicles Jewish history in LA.

Cobras & Matadors

7615 Beverly Boulevard, between N Curson & N Stanley Avenues (1-323 932 6178). Bus 14, 714/I-10, exit Fairfax Avenue north. **Open** 5-11pm Mon-Thur, Sun; 5pm-midnight Fri, Sat. **Main courses** $25. **Credit** AmEx, DC, MC, V. **Map** p328 C3 ⑰ **Spanish**
Few tapas places in LA have a genuinely Spanish feel, but the simple room, open kitchen and wood-burning oven help Cobras pull off the illusion. The tasty tapas are served fairly quickly; there's no wine licence, so you'll have to bring your own. Warning: later in the evening, the volume skyrockets and the restaurant becomes a party palace, so make an early booking if you'd like conversation with your food.

Farmers Market

6333 W 3rd Street, at Fairfax Avenue (1-323 933 9211/www.farmersmarketla.com). Bus 14, 714/I-10, exit Fairfax Avenue north. **Open** 9am-9pm Mon-Fri; 9am-8pm Sat; 10am-7pm Sun. **Main courses** vary. **Credit** varies. **Map** p328 C3 ⑱ **Various**

Back in 1934, local farmers began selling produce at the corner of 3rd and Fairfax. A handful of stalls still sell groceries, but they're outnumbered by 30-plus catering stands offering a culinary round-the-world trip. Alongside the American comfort food served at the historic, 24-hour **Du-Par's** restaurant (1-323 933 8446, www.du-pars.com), you can get everything from Texas barbecue (**Bryan's Pit BBQ**) to Parisian crêpes (**French Crepe Company**), N'awleens po'boys (**Gumbo Pot**) to sunny Mexican fare (**¡Loteria!**). For dessert, you can't beat **Bennett's Old-Fashioned Ice-Cream**.

Joan's on Third

8350 W 3rd Street, between S Kings Road & S Flores Street (1-323 655 2285/www.joansonthird. com). Bus 16, 218, 316, LDF/I-10, exit Fairfax Avenue north. **Open** 8am-8pm Mon-Sat; 8am-6pm Sun. **Main courses** $10. **Credit** AmEx, DC, MC, V.
Map p328 B3 ⑲ **Cafés & diners**
Recently expanded, this friendly deli is a great place at which to stock up on supplies for an impromptu picnic, but it's also a lovely spot for a sit-down breakfast or lunch. The menu doesn't stretch far beyond salads and sandwiches (plus delicious French toast for breakfast), but the food is beautifully prepared.

M Café de Chaya

7119 Melrose Avenue, at N La Brea Avenue (1-323 525 0588/www.mcafedechaya.com). Bus 10, 212, 312/US 101, exit Highland Avenue south. **Open** 9am-10pm Mon-Sat; 9am-9pm Sun. **Main courses** $11. **Credit** AmEx, DC, MC, V. **Map** p328 D2 ⑳ **Eclectic**
Macrobiotic food tends to have rather muted flavours; it's to the kitchen's immense credit that M Café de Chaya has managed to popularise it. The stylish room is, of course, popular with vegetarians and vegans, but it also serves exceptional sushi and a mild but tasty version of *bibimbap*, a Korean rice dish. It's not unusual to see diners taking pictures of the beautifully prepared food.
Other locations 9343 Culver Boulevard, Culver City (1-310 838 4300).

Manis Bakery

519 S Fairfax Avenue, between W 5th Street & Maryland Drive (1-323 938 8800/www.manisbakery. com). Bus 217, 218/I-10, exit Fairfax Avenue north. **Open** 6.30am-11pm Mon-Thur; 6.30am-midnight Fri; 7am-midnight Sat; 7.30am-10pm Sun. **Main courses** $12. **Credit** AmEx, DC, Disc, MC, V. **Map** p328 C4 ㉑ **Cafés & diners**
This expensive but ultra-healthy little bakery-café is famous for its sugar-free desserts, which taste just as good as the sinful stuff. The rest of the food (sandwiches, salads, omelettes and the like) is simple and well prepared, and the long hours mean that you can have whatever you fancy at almost any time.

Ortolan

8338 W 3rd Street, between S Kings Road & Flores Street (1-323 653 3300/www.ortolanrestaurant. com). Bus 16, 218, 316, LDF/I-10, exit Fairfax

Eat, Drink, Shop

Avenue north. **Open** 6-10pm Tue-Sat. **Main courses** $34. **Credit** AmEx, DC, Disc, MC, V. **Map** p328 B3 **⑤** **French**
The chemistry-set cooking style has calmed down a little since this upscale eatery opened in 2005, but chef Christophe Emé is still experimenting; certainly, no one else in town is serving crayfish with rabbit meatballs, seared escargot or monkfish cooked on hot stones. The champagne cart is appealing, but the servers often forget to mention that the high-end vintages can cost as much as $25 a glass.

Miracle Mile & Midtown

Campanile
624 S La Brea Avenue, between W 6th Street & Wilshire Boulevard (1-323 938 1447/www.campanile restaurant.com). Bus 20, 212, 312, 720/I-10, exit La Brea Avenue north. **Open** 11.30am-2.30pm, 6-10pm Mon-Wed; 11.30am-2.30pm, 5.30-11pm Thur, Fri; 9.30am-1.30pm, 5.30-11pm Sat; 9.30am-1.30pm Sun. **Main courses** *Lunch* $24. *Dinner* $34. **Credit** AmEx, DC, Disc, MC, V. **Map** p328 D4 **⑤** **Californian**
Built for Charlie Chaplin in the 1920s and then owned by his first wife after the couple divorced, the building that houses Campanile is famously, historically lovely. Mark Peel's reliable cooking is based on traditional Italian cuisine leavened with modern American ideas. The likes of tapenade-crusted prime rib might sound a little dubious when you see them on the menu, but they work a treat.

Luna Park
672 S La Brea Avenue, between Wilshire Boulevard & W 6th Street (1-323 934 2110/www.lunaparkla. com). Bus 20, 212, 312, 720/I-10, exit La Brea Avenue north. **Open** 11.30am-10.30pm Mon-Thur; 11.30am-11.30pm Fri; 11.30am-3pm, 5.30-11.30pm Sat; 11.30am-3pm, 5.30-10pm Sun. **Main courses** *Lunch* $15. *Dinner* $17. **Credit** AmEx, DC, MC, V. **Map** p328 D4 **⑤** **Italian**
This loud but friendly diner/restaurant is relatively affordable and fairly speedy, making it a good option if you're heading on to a concert at the nearby Wiltern. The cooking is simple and exuberant: pasta with Moroccan-style beef and vegetables is hearty and tasty, as is the Singapore shrimp fried rice. Your enjoyment of the evening may be aided by the lethal cocktails served at the bar.

Ngoma
5358 Wilshire Boulevard, at S Detroit Street (1-323 934 1595/www.ngomarestaurant.com). Bus 20, 212, 312, 720/I-10, exit La Brea Avenue north. **Open** 11am-10pm Tue-Thur; 11am-11pm Fri; noon-11pm Sat; noon-7pm Sun. **Main courses** $15. **Credit** AmEx, DC, MC, V. **Map** p328 D4 **⑥** **African**
Host Dora Asare is an excellent guide to Ngoma's East and West African menus, and she cooks very well. Roast goat, peanut chicken and ginger shrimp are some of the standouts; if you like spicy food, try the pepper soup that explodes in your mouth. Service is friendly but sometimes slow.

Versailles
1415 S La Cienega Boulevard, between W Pico Boulevard & Alcott Street (1-310 289 0392/www. versaillescuban.com). Bus 105/I-10, exit La Cienega Boulevard north. **Open** 11am-10pm daily. **Main courses** $10. **Credit** AmEx, DC, MC, V. **Map** p328 B5 **⑥** **Cuban**
Although this bustling Cuban joint boasts a large menu, head straight for the garlic chicken served with sweet onion, fried plantains and white rice with black beans. Service is brisk but not rude; if you're not ready when your server comes to take your order, he'll dash to another table, then return to you when you've decided what to eat.
Other locations throughout LA.

Koreatown & around

Cassell's
3266 W 6th Street, between S Berendo Street & S New Hampshire Avenue (1-213 480 5000). Metro Wilshire-Vermont/bus 18, 20, 204, 720, 754/I-10, exit Vermont Avenue north. **Open** 10.30am-4pm Mon-Sat. **Main courses** $6. **Credit** DC, MC, V. **Map** p330 A6 **⑥** **Cafés & diners**
The enormous burgers at Cassell's are made from freshly ground meat, and many burger obsessives believe they are the best in the city bar none. The diner itself is a design-free zone, and no one comes here for the overall dining experience – just the burgers, and possibly the zucchini fries, the potato salad and the home-made lemonade.

Upscale Italian at **Little Dom's**. *See p162.*

El Cholo

1121 S Western Avenue, between W Olympic & W Pico Boulevards (1-323 734 2773/www.elcholo.com). Bus 30, 31, 207, 330, 757/I-10, exit Western Avenue north. **Open** 11am-10pm Mon-Sat; 11am-9pm Sun. **Main courses** $13. **Credit** AmEx, DC, Disc, MC, V. **Map** p329 D6 ❸ **Mexican**

Having opened in 1923, El Cholo is Los Angeles' oldest continuously operated Mexican restaurant, and it probably hasn't been at the cutting edge of cuisine for something like 80 years. Still, the Mexican comfort food is decent and the atmosphere is historic in a way very few other LA eateries can manage. Must-have options include guacamole (made tableside), green corn tamales and the margaritas, by which all others are judged. **Other locations** 1025 Wilshire Boulevard, Santa Monica (1-310 899 1106).

Chosun Galbee

3330 W Olympic Boulevard, at S Manhattan Place (1-323 734 3330/www.chosungalbee.com). Bus 30, 31, 207, 330, 757/I-10, exit Western Avenue north. **Open** 11am-11pm daily. **Main courses** $30. **Credit** AmEx, DC, Disc, MC, V. **Map** p329 C6 ❹ **Korean**

If you're new to Korean food but fancy learning a little more about it, this upscale Koreatown spot is a good choice. The food is tasty, authentic and popular with Koreans, but it isn't the spiciest in town, and the servers speak fluent English. The menu includes noodles, rice dishes and casseroles; however, you should try *gal bi*, marinated short ribs grilled at your table and served with a delicately spicy tang.

Guelaguetza

3337½ W 8th Street, at Irolo Street (1-213 427 0601/www.guelaguetzarestaurante.com). Metro Wilshire-Normandie/bus 20, 66, 206, 366, 720/I-10, exit Vermont Avenue north. **Open** 8am-10pm daily. **Main courses** $11. **Credit** AmEx, DC, Disc, MC, V. **Map** p329 ❺ **Mexican**

The *guelaguetza* is an Oaxacan dance; its use as the name of this restaurant serves as a reminder that the food served here differs from classic Mexican. The speciality is meat (chicken, beef or pork) served with richly fragrant and spicy sauces called *moles*, which use fresh-ground herbs and chocolate to create a depth of flavour. Try the oxtail stew or a *tlayuda*, a strange pizza-like corn-cake, with a fresh juice. **Other locations** 3014 W Olympic Boulevard, Koreatown (1-213 427 0608).

Papa Cristo's

2771 W Pico Boulevard, at S Normandie Avenue (1-323 737 2970/www.papacristos.com). Bus 30, 31, 206/I-10, exit Normandie Avenue north. **Open** 9am-8pm Tue-Sat; 9am-4pm Sun. **Main courses** $12. **Credit** AmEx, DC, Disc, MC, V. **Map** p329 D6 ❻ **Greek**

Papa Cristo's sits in the shadow of the Greek Orthodox cathedral in LA's Byzantine-Latino District, one of the more interesting cultural fusions in this very mixed city. The simple grilled meats and seafood are always good, but the best day to visit is on a Thursday, when the restaurant offers complete family-style dinners with wine-tastings and entertainment for $25 per person. Good fun.

Soot Bull Jeep

3136 W 8th Street, between S Berendo & S Catalina Streets (1-213 387 3865). Metro Wilshire-Western/bus 20, 66, 366, 720/I-10, exit Vermont Avenue north. **Open** 11am-11pm daily. **Main courses** $20. **Credit** AmEx, DC, Disc, MC, V. **Map** p330 A6 ❼ **Korean**

Soot Bull Jeep is one of the few Koreatown restaurants that hasn't switched to gas or electric grills, and the smoke from the charcoal fires permeates everything. The side items are good but basic; the real attraction is the excellent meat, which comes with a predictably but pleasingly smoky flavour and spicy sauce.

Taylor's Steak House

3361 W 8th Street, at S Ardmore Avenue (1-213 382 8449/www.taylorssteakhouse.com). Metro Wilshire-Normandie/bus 66, 206, 366/I-10, exit Western Avenue north. **Open** 11.30am-9.30pm Mon-Thur; 11.30am-10.30pm Fri; 4-10.30pm Sat; 4-9.30pm Sun. **Main courses** *Lunch* $16. *Dinner* $25. **Credit** AmEx, DC, Disc, MC, V. **Map** p329 D5 ❻ **American**

In this city of illusions, it should come as no surprise to stumble upon a steakhouse that looks and feels decades older than it actually is. Founded in 1953 but on this site only since 1970, Taylor's cultivates a '30s feel. The old-fashioned atmosphere and hearty food have kept it in business even as the neighbourhood has turned Asian and Latino around it.

Eat, Drink, Shop

La Poubelle (5907 Franklin Avenue, Los Feliz) Where Wilson and Vivian meet at the start of *In Search of a Midnight Kiss*.

Los Feliz to Echo Park

Los Feliz

Fred 62

1850 N Vermont Avenue, at Franklin Avenue (1-323 667 0062/www.fred62.com). Bus 26, 180, 181, 204, 754/US 101, exit Vermont Avenue north. **Open** 24hrs daily. **Main courses** $13. **Credit** AmEx, DC, Disc, MC, V. **Map** p330 A2 ㊳ **Cafés & diners**
Chef Fred Eric was born in 1962, which explains the name of this 24-7 diner on Vermont. The food is a bit erratic, though the breakfasts and the meatloaf are both among the best in the city. Still, even if the cooking doesn't knock you out, the funky decor and the good service should raise your spirits.

Little Dom's

2128 Hillhurst Avenue, at Avocado Street (1-323 661 0055/www.littledoms.com). Bus 180, 181/ I-5, exit Los Feliz Boulevard west. **Open** 8am-3pm, 6-11pm Mon-Thur, Sun; 8am-3pm, 6pm-midnight Fri, Sat. **Main courses** $14. **Credit** AmEx, DC, MC, V. **Map** p330 B1 ㊐ **Italian**
Joining a Japanese eatery (SanSui) and a Mexican joint (Mexico City) on this stretch of Hillhurst, Little Dom's aims to bring to Los Feliz the Italian sophistication that's long characterised Dominick's, its 60-year-old big brother in Hollywood. Early reports were mixed after its 2008 opening; stick to the standards and you'll hopefully be OK. *Photo p160.*

SanSui

2040 Hillhurst Avenue, between Ambrose & Finley Avenues (1-323 660 3868/www.san-sui.com). Bus 180, 181/I-5, exit Los Feliz Boulevard west. **Open** 11.30am-2pm, 5.30-10pm Mon-Fri; 5.30-10pm Sat, Sun. **Main courses** *Lunch* $11. *Dinner* $18. *Sushi* $8. **Credit** AmEx, DC, Disc, MC, V. **Map** p330 B2 ㊑ **Japanese**
Unlike most Japanese restaurants in LA, this tranquil eatery specialises in what it calls 'mountain cuisine'. Bowls of hearty udon soup are available, as is sushi, but why not try one of the rice bowls with burdock or lotus root and mushrooms? A peaceful venue in the middle of a hectic nightlife district.

Tropicalia

1966 Hillhurst Avenue, at Clarissa Avenue (1-323 644 1798/www.tropicaliabraziliangrill.com). Bus 180, 181/I-5, exit Los Feliz Boulevard west. **Open** 11am-11.30pm daily. **Main courses** $13. **Credit** AmEx, DC, Disc, MC, V. **Map** p330 B2 ㊇ **Brazilian**
Most Brazilian restaurants in LA focus on *churrascaria*, essentially a special-occasion barbecue feast.

Tropicalia, though, is more interesting, offering a range of rainforest and coastal recipes mixed with modern ideas about healthy dining (some good seafood and vegetarian dishes). The restaurant's owners are also wine merchants, which helps explain the well-chosen and interesting list.

Silver Lake

Alegria on Sunset

3510 W Sunset Boulevard, at Maltman Avenue (1-323 913 1422/www.milliescafe.net). Bus 2, 4, 302, 704/US 101, exit Silver Lake Boulevard north. **Open** 11am-10pm Mon-Thur; 11am-11pm Fri; 10am-11pm Sat. **Main courses** *Breakfast & lunch* $10. *Dinner* $15. **No credit cards. Map** p330 C3 ㊽ **Mexican**
Located in a seen-better-days strip mall, Alegria transcends its unbecoming location and drab interior with some lively and agreeably messy Mexican food. The dinners are good, but you may have to wait for a table (it doesn't take reservations); breakfast and lunch are perfectly acceptable alternatives.

Café Stella

3932 W Sunset Boulevard, between Sanborn & Hyperion Avenues (1-323 666 0265). Bus 2, 4, 175, 302, 704/US 101, exit Silver Lake Boulevard north. **Open** 6-11pm Mon-Sat; 6-10pm Sun. **Main courses** $25. **Credit** AmEx, DC, MC, V. **Map** p330 B3 ㊓ **French**
Located just near Sunset Junction, Café Stella can get pretty cramped, and the service is sometimes poor when the restaurant is busy. However, on mellower nights, the atmosphere is charming, and the French bistro food is usually very decent: order steak frites, mussels or the famous beet salad.

Edendale Grill

2838 Rowena Avenue, between Hyperion Avenue & Glendale Boulevard (1-323 666 2000/www.edendale grill.com). Bus 92, 201/I-5, exit Hyperion Avenue west. **Open** *Summer* 5.30-10pm Mon-Thur; 5.30pm-midnight Fri, Sat; 10am-3pm, 5.30-10pm Sun. *Winter* 5.30-10pm Wed-Sat; 10am-3pm, 5-10pm Sun. **Main courses** $20. **Credit** AmEx, DC, MC, V. **Map** p330 D2 ㊟ **American**
The building that houses the Edendale Grill spent most of its life as a fire station, but the land on which it sits has long-established ties to the movie industry: cinema buffs will enjoy looking at the old prints on the weathered brick walls. Deals are done in the restaurant over grilled salmon, steaks with anchovy butter and the legendarily good meatloaf; wind down over a drink in adjoining Mixville (see *p184*).

Millie's

3524 W Sunset Boulevard, at Maltman Avenue (1-323 664 0404/www.milliescafe.net). Bus 2, 4, 302, 704/US 101, exit Silver Lake Boulevard north. **Open** 7.30am-4pm daily. **Main courses** $10. **Credit** DC, Disc, MC, V. **Map** p330 C3 ㊗ **Cafés & diners**
This cheerful little breakfast and lunch joint is tiny and often packed, but the inexpensive but generous food is worth the wait and the servers rise to the

Vintage vittles

Musso & Frank Grill.

Although LA tends to look forwards rather than backwards, it's home to a smattering of historic restaurants that have gallantly resisted the urge to modernise. Squint through their windows and it's easy to imagine yourself in the city of red-car trains and starlets on soda-fountain stools. And then look down at the plate: are you sure your 21st-century palate wants to sample *that*? Happily, a few of these evocatively old-fashioned dining destinations serve food you might actually want to eat.

Open since 1919, the **Musso & Frank Grill** (*see p157*) is Hollywood's oldest restaurant, a steak-and-cocktails joint formerly favoured by Charlie Chaplin and Raymond Chandler. With its many obscure dishes and individually priced sides (and salad dressings!), the menu can be daunting. However, some dishes are fail-safes. At breakfast, grab an order of crêpe-thin flannel cakes; later in the day, the grilled meats are excellent. And every table gets a half-loaf of house-made sourdough bread, the perfect accompaniment to a dry martini.

In business since 1908, **Philippe the Original** (*see p165*) is one of two local spots that claims to have invented the French dip sandwich. Savvy customers select the traditional lamb or lighter turkey filling, then

ask the server to double-dip the bread in the meaty juice; a French-dip sandwich is also incomplete without some of the sinus-clearing house mustard. The wines by the glass aren't bad, a concession to the lunch trade from nearby City Hall.

The **Pacific Dining Car** (*see p164*) is an elegant throwback to the early 20th century, when robber barons met over thick steaks and thicker cigar smoke. The bargain-hunter's secret is the breakfast menu (available 24 hours a day): among the wonderful spins on eggy standards is a great Creole benedict.

The Scottish-themed **Tam O'Shanter** (*see p164*) was Walt Disney's favourite restaurant, and remains resolutely old-fashioned. Prime rib with horseradish is a classic; for a more casual option, eat in the bar from the sandwich carving station. For dessert, it's got to be CC Brown's Hot Fudge Sundae, a perfect replica of the late, lamented Hollywood Boulevard original.

Over at West LA's **Apple Pan** (*see p150*), diners ring a U-shaped counter to inhale burgers slathered with hickory sauce. However, the burgers aren't anything to write home about. For a more satisfying experience, stick with the classic tuna or egg salad sandwich, crispy fries and a slice of luscious banana cream pie.

challenge of delivering it quickly to the hungry
hordes. Try the home-made granola or the weird but
alluring hangover cure called the Devil's Mess.

Atwater Village

India Sweets & Spices

*3126 Los Feliz Boulevard, at Edenhurst Avenue
(1-323 345 0360/www.indiasweetsandspices.net).
Bus 180, 181/I-5, exit Los Feliz Boulevard east.*
Open 10am-9.30pm daily. **Desserts** $4. **Credit**
AmEx, DC, MC, V. **Desserts**
See p146 **Life is sweets**.

Tam O'Shanter

*2980 Los Feliz Boulevard, between Revere & Boyce
Avenues (1-323 664 0228/www.lawrysonline.com).
Bus 180, 181/I-5, exit Los Feliz Boulevard east.*
Open 11am-2pm, 5-9pm Mon-Thur; 11am-2pm,
5-10pm Fri; 11am-4pm, 5-10pm Sat; 10.30am-2.30pm,
4-9pm Sun. **Main courses** Lunch $25. Dinner $34.
Credit AmEx, DC, Disc, MC, V. **American**
See p163 **Vintage vittles**.

Downtown

Asian Noodles

*643 N Spring Street, between W César E Chávez
Avenue & Ord Street (1-213 617 1083). Metro
Union Station/bus 33, 40, 42, 68, 70, 71, 78, 79/
US 101, exit Alameda Street north.* **Open** 11.30am-
3pm, 5-9pm Mon-Fri; 11am-9.30pm Sat, Sun. **Main
courses** $9. **Credit** AmEx, DC, Disc, MC, V.
Map p331 C1 ⑦ **Filipino**
Despite the name, this Chinatown spot serves more
than just noodles: the house speciality is the spicy,
slightly sour soup called *sinigang*, and the kitchen is
also known for adobo-marinated pork. If the owner
serves you, the service will be fast but grouchy.

Ce Fiore

*134 Japanese Village Plaza Mall, E 2nd Street & S
San Pedro Street (1-213 626 0806). Metro Union
Station/bus 30, 31, 40, 42/US 101, exit Alameda
Street south.* **Open** 10am-11pm daily. **Desserts**
$5. **Credit** AmEx, DC, Disc, MC, V. **Map**
p331 D2 ⑦ **Desserts**
See p146 **Life is sweets**.

Ciudad

*445 S Figueroa Street, between W 4th & W 5th
Streets (1-213 486 5171/www.ciudad-la.com). Metro
7th Street-Metro Center/bus 16, 18, 55, 62/I-110,
exit 6th Street east.* **Open** 11.30am-9pm Mon, Tue;
11.30am-11pm Wed, Thur; 11.30am-midnight Fri;
5pm-midnight Sat; 5-9pm Sun. **Main courses** Lunch
$16. Dinner $23. **Credit** AmEx, DC, Disc, MC, V.
Map p331 B3 ⑦ **South American**

Chefs Susan Feniger and Mary Sue Milliken became
famous for re-imagining Mexican food at the Border
Grill. Ciudad, though, is more ambitious, offering a
modern take on items from all over Central and
South America. For the timid, there's always an
Argentine or Brazilian barbecue; wilder Peruvian
and Bolivian items await more adventurous diners.
One of the most consistently enjoyable Downtown
restaurants. *See also p182* **Top ten: Happy hours**.

LAX-C

*1100 N Main Street, at W College Street (1-323 343
9000/www.lax-c.com). Metro Chinatown/bus 76, 376/
US 101, exit Main Street north.* **Open** 8am-8pm
Mon-Sat; 8.30am-5pm Sun. **Desserts** $3. **Credit**
DC, MC, V. **Desserts**
See p146 **Life is sweets**.

Mikawaya

*118 Japanese Village Plaza Mall, E 1st Street & S
Central Avenue (1-213 687 6514/www.mikawaya
usa.com). Metro Union Station/bus 30, 31, 40,
42/US 101, exit Alameda Street south.* **Open** 10am-
7pm Mon; 10am-10pm Tue-Thur; 9am-11pm Fri;
9.30am-10pm Sat. **Desserts** $3. **No credit cards.**
Map p331 D2 ⑩ **Desserts**
See p146 **Life is sweets**.

Ocean Seafood

*750 N Hill Street, between Ord & Alpine Streets
(1-213 687 3088/www.oceansf.com). Metro Union
Station/bus 33, 40, 42, 68, 70, 71, 78, 79/US
101, exit Alameda Street north.* **Open** 9am-10pm
Mon-Fri; 8am-10pm Sat, Sun. **Main courses**
$14. **Credit** AmEx, DC, Disc, MC, V. **Map**
p331 C1 ⑪ **Chinese**
The culinary capital of Chinese food in LA is now
Monterey Park, but the restaurants in Chinatown
still have a devoted following. Ocean Seafood is the
best bet in the area for Hong Kong-style dim sum,
and also offers fresh fish every from the tanks. The big
upstairs room is packed every weekend; however, if
you go during the week, you're unlikely to wait.

Original Pantry

*877 S Figueroa Street, at 9th Street (1-213 972
9279/www.pantrycafe.com). Metro 7th Street-Metro
Center/bus 14, 37, 70, 71, 76, 78, 79, 96/I-110,
exit 9th Street east.* **Open** 24hrs daily. **Main
courses** $11. **No credit cards. Map** p331 B4
⑫ **Cafés & diners**
There's no lock on the door, nor does there need to
be: now owned by former mayor Richard Riordan,
this greasy spoon has been open 24-7 since 1934,
with only the briefest of breaks to rework the kitchen
into modern health standards. Expect American
diner favourites in gargantuan portions; nothing is
exceptional, but everything is good.

Pacific Dining Car

*1310 W 6th Street, at Columbia Avenue (1-213 483
6000/www.pacificdiningcar.com). Bus 18/I-110, exit
6th Street west.* **Open** 24hrs daily. **Main courses**
$40. **Credit** AmEx, DC, MC, V. **American**
See p163 **Vintage vittles**.

Patina

Walt Disney Concert Hall, 141 S Grand Avenue, between W 2nd & W 3rd Streets (1-213 972 3331/ www.patinagroup.com). Metro Civic Center/bus 14, 37, 70, 71, 76, 78, 79, 96/I-110, exit 3rd Street east. **Open** 11.30am-1.30pm, 5-11pm Tue-Fri; 5-11pm Sat; 4-10.30pm Sun. **Closed** from 9.30pm on nights when there is no performance. **Main courses** *Lunch* $21. *Dinner* $39. **Credit** AmEx, DC, Disc, MC, V. **Map** p331 B2 ❸ **Italian**

For a while, the Patina Group opened new restaurants at a fearsome pace. The quality suffered, and it took a while for them to regain their previous consistency. This Disney Hall restaurant seems to be the group's new flagship, and is as adventurous as the Patina of old: Joachim Splichal has always been capable of brilliant and occasionally bizarre culinary inventions, and he's on top form with this Italianate menu. Expensive, but worth it.

Philippe the Original

1001 N Alameda Street, at Ord Street (1-213 628 3781/www.philippes.com). Metro Union Station/ bus 33, 40, 42, 68, 70, 71, 78, 79/US 101, exit Alameda Street north. **Open** 6am-10pm daily. **Main courses** $5. **No credit cards**. **Map** p331 D1 ❷ **Cafés & diners**

See p163 **Vintage vittles**.

Spring Street Smokehouse

640 N Spring Street, at E César E Chávez Avenue (1-213 626 0535/www.sssmokehouse.com). Metro Union Station/bus 33, 40, 42, 68, 70, 71, 78, 79/ US 101, exit Alameda Street north. **Open** 10.30am-9pm Mon-Fri; noon-9pm Sat, Sun. **Main courses** $10. **Credit** AmEx, DC, Disc, MC, V. **Map** p331 C1 ❻ **American**

Located on the edge of Chinatown, the Spring Street Smokehouse is a barbecue joint that is owned by the catering service for the nearby county jail. However, never fear, you'll eat better than the prisoners. Served with very spicy sauce, the pork ribs and beef brisket are the standouts, but they kitchen also turns out good sandwiches and, if you call ahead, deep-fried turkey. The place serves a good selection of beers and hosts a comedy club on Fridays.

Traxx

Union Station, 800 N Alameda Street, between US 101 & E César E Chávez Avenue (1-213 625 1999/www.traxxrestaurant.com). Metro Union Station/bus 33, 40, 42, 68, 70, 71, 78, 79/US 101, exit Alameda Street north. **Open** 11.30am-2.30pm, 5.30-9pm Mon-Thur; 11.30am-2.30pm, 5.30-9.30pm Fri; 5-9.30pm Sat. **Main courses** *Lunch* $19. *Dinner* $23. **Credit** AmEx, DC, MC, V. **Map** p331 D1 ❻ **American**

People with no plans to take a train often come to dine at Traxx in Union Station: the food really is that good. It's surprisingly adventurous: tofu steak with pea-shoot tendrils, king salmon with asparagus and violet mustard, house-cured pork chops with fig polenta. The art deco appearance and the excellent people-watching from the terrace add visual appeal.

Water Grill

544 S Grand Avenue, between W 5th & W 6th Streets (1-213 891 0900/www.watergrill.com). Metro 7th Street-Metro Center/bus 14, 37, 70, 71, 76, 78, 79, 96/I-110, exit 6th Street east. **Open** 11.30am-9.30pm Mon-Fri; 5-9.30pm Sat; 4.30-8.30pm Sun. **Main courses** $36. **Credit** AmEx, DC, Disc, MC, V. **Map** p331 B3 ❺ **Seafood**

Chef David LeFevre has taken this famous and expensive seafood restaurant in a different direction. Rather than the defiantly eclectic fare served under predecessor Michael Cimarusti, LeFevre offers more Mediterranean ideas and French presentations. The fish is still the freshest in town, and the service remains exceptional.

East Los Angeles

La Parrilla

2126 E César E Chávez Avenue, between Chicago & St Louis Streets (1-323 262 3434/www.laparrilla restaurant.com). Bus 68, 620/I-10, exit E César E Chávez Avenue east. **Open** 8am-11pm daily. **Main courses** *Breakfast* $8. *Lunch/Dinner* $10. **Credit** AmEx, DC, Disc, MC, V. **Mexican**

It takes something special to lure outsiders to run-down Boyle Heights. Although it has three other restaurants around the city, La Parrilla is that something. Strolling mariachis add entertainment and authenticity, but it's the vast platters of barbecued meat that make it worth the trip. Allow time for a leisurely meal, and don't forget to tip the musicians.

La Parrilla.

Cicada (617 S Olive Street, Downtown) Julia Roberts struggles to eat the snails in *Pretty Woman*

Other locations 3129 Sunset Boulevard, Silver Lake (1-323 661 8055); 1300 Wilshire Boulevard, Downtown (1-213 353 4980).

La Serenata di Garibaldi

1842 E 1st Street, between N State Street & N Boyle Avenue (1-323 265 2887/www.laserenataonline. com). Bus 30, 31, 620/I-10, exit Boyle Avenue north. **Open** 11.30am-10.30pm Mon-Fri; 9am-10.30pm Sat, Sun. **Main courses** *Lunch* $12. *Dinner* $16. **Credit** AmEx, DC, Disc, MC, V. **Mexican**

This elegant restaurant in an otherwise slightly seedy block is a place of pilgrimage for those who appreciate fresh seafood the way it's prepared in Veracruz. This isn't to slight the very good chicken mole, the squash soup or the other items on the menu, but the red snapper is the star of the show. Valet-park at the rear of the building to avoid an endless hunting for a spot on the street.
Other locations 1416 4th Street, Santa Monica (1-310 656 7017); 10924 W Pico Boulevard, West LA (1-310 441 9667).

South Los Angeles

Coley's Caribbean American Cuisine

300 E Florence Avenue, at S La Brea Avenue, Inglewood (1-310 672 7474/www.coleyscuisine.com). Bus 40, 111, 115, 212, 315, 340, 711/I-10, exit La Brea Avenue south. **Open** 8am-9pm Mon-Thur; 8am-10.30pm Fri, Sat; 8am-8pm Sun. **Main courses** *Lunch* $12. *Dinner* $15. **Credit** AmEx, DC, Disc, MC, V. **Jamaican**

This Jamaican success story is run by endlessly hospitable islanders who serve excellent jerk chicken, codfish patties and shrimp St James. Not everything is spicy, but beware of the home-made ginger beer: it's very nice, but its peppery tang won't help cool off your burning mouth.
Other locations 10842 Magnolia Boulevard, North Hollywood (1-818 761 4944).

Harold & Belle's

2920 W Jefferson Boulevard, between Arlington Avenue & Crenshaw Boulevard, Jefferson Park (1-323 735 9023/www.haroldandbellesrestaurant.com). Bus 38, 210, 305, 710/I-10, exit Crenshaw Boulevard south. **Open** 11.30am-10pm Mon-Thur, Sun; 11.30am-11pm Fri, Sat. **Main courses** $28. **Credit** AmEx, DC, Disc, MC, V. **American**

This white-tablecloth restaurant in a paper-plate neighbourhood offers New Orleans-style cooking with a side of jazz. Expect savoury but not explosively hot gumbo and étouffée; finish with the best bread pudding in town. A genteel slice of the old South that's every local's choice for a big night out.

The Valleys

San Fernando Valley

Alcazar

17239 Ventura Boulevard, between Louise & Amestoy Avenues, Encino (1-818 789 0991/ www.al-cazar.com). Bus 150, 240/I-405, exit Ventura Boulevard west. **Open** 11.30am-2.30pm, 5.30-10.30pm Mon-Thur; 11.30am-2.30pm, 5.30-midnight Fri; 11.30am-midnight Sat; 11.30am-9pm Sun. **Main courses** $15. **Credit** AmEx, DC, Disc, MC, V. **Lebanese**

Los Angeles has few high-style Lebanese restaurants, but Alcazar stands out among the not particularly vigorous competition. The oriental opulence of the dining room is a perfect setting for the high-quality Arabic food on the menu: order one of the combination plates or pile the table with appetisers from the list of mezedes.

Art's Deli

12224 Ventura Boulevard, between Laurel Canyon Boulevard & Whitsett Avenue, Studio City (1-818 762 1221/www.artsdeli.com). Bus 150/US 101, exit Laurel Canyon Boulevard south. **Open** 7am-9pm daily. **Main courses** *Breakfast* $13. *Lunch/Dinner* $15. **Credit** AmEx, DC, Disc, MC, V. **Jewish**

Art Ginsburg's 50-year-old deli has built a great reputation and a very loyal following with its menu of hefty sandwiches and excellent chicken noodle and cabbage soups. If you stick to the traditional dishes, you're assured of a good meal.

Calitalia

23536 Calabasas Road, at El Canon Avenue, Calabasas (1-818 223 9600/www.calitaliarestaurant. com). Bus 161/US 101, exit Parkway Calabasas. **Open** 11am-2.30pm, 5-9pm Tue-Fri; 5-11pm Sat, Sun. **Main courses** $28. **Credit** AmEx, DC, Disc, MC, V. **Italian**

Calabasas is a bit of a backwater, but if you have business in Woodland Hills or the West Valley, consider coming here for the exceptional Italian food and seafood. The odd decor is left over from its previous incarnation as a Southwestern restaurant, but the sand dabs in lemon-caper sauce, the bison with port reduction and the pastas taste just as good when you're surrounded by Indian motifs.

Dr Hogly-Wogly's Tyler Texas BBQ

8136 Sepulveda Boulevard, between Roscoe Boulevard & Lanark Street, Panorama City (1-818 780 6701/www.hoglywogly.com). Bus 152, 153, 234/I-405, exit Roscoe Boulevard east. **Open** 11.30am-10pm daily. **Main courses** $13. **Credit** AmEx, DC, Disc, MC, V. **American**

Many people swear that this by the roadside shack is the only authentic Texas barbecue joint in LA; whether that's true or not, it's almost certainly the best. Supplement your slabs of smoky meat and dollops of spicy sauce with potato salad and coleslaw, and try and save room for a slice of pecan pie.

Saddle Peak Lodge

*419 Cold Canyon Road, at Piuma Road, Calabasas
(1-818 222 3888/www.saddlepeaklodge.com).
No bus/PCH, exit Malibu Canyon Road.* **Open**
5-10pm Wed-Fri; 11am-3pm, 5-10pm Sat, Sun.
Main courses $42. **Credit** AmEx, DC, Disc, MC, V.
American
This upscale lodge at the end of a country road was
a Hollywood star retreat in the 1920s, and retains an
Old West feel. The speciality is game: partridge, elk
and venison are favourites, though the specials can
include even more exotic fare. Weekend brunch is
popular with folks out for a day in the country; or
come to view sunset from the upper dining rooms.

Sushi Yotsuya

*18760 Ventura Boulevard, between Burbank
Boulevard & Yolanda Avenue, Tarzana (1-818 708
9675). Bus 150, 240, 750/US 101, exit Reseda
Boulevard south.* **Open** 6-10pm Mon-Sat. **Sushi**
$4-$10. **Credit** AmEx, DC, MC, V. **Japanese**
Ventura Boulevard is known as Sushi Row because
of the number and quality of Japanese restaurants
along its length; Yotsuya is among the most celebrated of them. Chef Masa Matsumoto is a tradition-
alist: there are no novelties, just fresh fish on warm
rice with delicate Japanese seasonings.

San Gabriel Valley

Babita Mexicuisine

*1823 S San Gabriel Boulevard, at Norwood Place,
San Gabriel (1-626 288 7265). Bus 79, 487/I-210, exit
Sierra Madre Boulevard south.* **Open** 11.30am-2.30pm,
5.30-9pm Tue-Fri; 5.30-9pm Sat, Sun. **Desserts** $8.
Credit AmEx, DC, Disc, MC, V. **Desserts**
See p146 **Life is sweets**.

Celestino Ristorante

*141 S Lake Avenue, between E Green & Cordova
Streets, Pasadena (1-626 795 4006/www.celestino
pasadena.com). Metro Lake/bus 180, 181, 485/I-210,
exit Lake Aveune south.* **Open** 11.30am-2.30pm, 5.30-
10pm Mon-Fri; 5.30-10.30pm Sat. **Main courses**
$18. **Credit** AmEx, DC, Disc, MC, V. **Italian**
If you're in the market for uncomplicated but
superbly prepared Sicilian food served in an elegant
setting, Celestino Drago would like to make your
acquaintance. Drago's Pasadena location is famed
for its excellent pastas, among them excellent pumpkin tortelloni with sage, but the menu also takes in
other dishes. Reservations are essential.

Empress Harbor

*111 N Atlantic Boulevard, at W Garvey Avenue,
Monterey Park (1-626 300 8833/www.empress
harbor.com). Bus 20, 260, 361, 370/I-10, exit
Atlantic Boulevard south.* **Open** 9am-10pm daily.
Main courses $15. **Credit** AmEx, DC, MC, V.
Chinese
The city of Monterey Park fills to capacity every
weekend with Chinese families doing their shopping
and eating dim sum. If you're after the latter,
Empress Harbor is a great bet: it's a huge place, but
service is brisk and the food is very decent. The
English-language skills of the servers are only mod-
erate, but that's nonetheless a step above many other
restaurants in the area.

Japon Bistro

*927 E Colorado Avenue, between N Lake & N
Mentor Avenues, Pasadena (1-626 744 1751/
www.japonbistro-pasadena.com). Metro Lake/
bus 180, 181, 485/I-210, exit Lake Avenue south.*
Open 11.30am-2.30pm Mon; 11.30am-2.30pm,
5.30-9.30pm Tue-Thur; 11.30am-2.30pm,

Pig out at **Dr Hogly-Wogly's Tyler Texas BBQ**.

5.30-10.30pm Fri; 5.30-10.30pm Sat; 5.30-9.30pm Sun. **Main courses** *Lunch* $12. *Dinner* $23. **Credit** AmEx, DC, MC, V. **Japanese**

At this Pasadena restaurant, Japanese ideas are modernised with references to other cuisines. Try the fried tofu with *chawan mushi* savoury custard or apple-ginger sauce, but pay close attention to the specials. The saké bar has some limited-release Japanese sakés that can be expensive but that might stretch your definition of perfection.

La Luna Negra

44 W Green Street, between S Fair Oaks & S De Lacey Avenues, Pasadena (1-626 844 4331/www.lalunanegrarestaurant.com). Metro Del Mar/bus 177, 260, 361/Hwy 134, exit Orange Grove Boulevard south. **Open** 11am-2pm, 5-10pm Tue-Thur; 11am-11pm Fri, Sat; 11am-10pm Sun. **Main courses** $25. **Tapas** $11. **Credit** AmEx, DC, MC, V. **Spanish**

La Luna Negra attracts a young, party-hearty crowd every night. The tables are tightly packed and the room is boisterous; on nights when there's a band playing, you can forget conversation. However, the food is worth attention, with standard tapas, paellas and roasts joined by more modern oddities.

Wahib's

910 E Main Street, at S Granada Avenue, Alhambra (1-626 281 1006/www.wahibsmiddleeast.com). Bus 78, 176, 378/I-10, exit Garfield Avenue north. **Open** 9am-10pm Mon-Thur, Sun; 9am-2am Fri, Sat. **Main courses** *Breakfast* $6. *Lunch/Dinner* $14. **Credit** AmEx, DC, Disc, MC, V. **Middle Eastern**

A lunch spot and casual family restaurant during the week, Wahib's morphs into a nightclub with at the weekends. The kitchen bakes its own breads and pastries; the lamb dishes are superb. On Sundays, there's an amazing all-in buffet for only $18.

Yazmin

27 E Main Street, between Garfield Avenue & N Stoneman Avenue, Alhambra (1-626 308 2036). Bus 78, 176, 378/I-10, exit Garfield Avenue north. **Open** 11am-9.30pm Mon, Wed-Fri; 11am-10pm Sat, Sun. **Main courses** $9. **Credit** DC, MC, V. **Malaysian**

LA has few Malaysian and Singaporean restaurants, but the community near the imposing mosque has supported all manner of nearby eateries, among them Yazmin. It's a bright, cheerful and inexpensive place; menu highlights include laksa soup.

Heading south

The South Bay

Chez Melange

Palos Verdes Inn, 1716 Pacific Coast Highway, between Palos Verdes Boulevard & Camino de las Colinas, Redondo Beach (1-310 540 1222/www.chezmelange.com). Bus 130, 232/I-405, exit Artesia Boulevard west. **Open** 11.15am-2.30pm, 5.30-9.30pm Mon-Thur; 11.15am-2.30pm, 5-10pm Fri; 8am-2.30pm, 5-10pm Sat; 8am-2.30pm, 5.30-9pm Sun. **Main courses** *Brunch* $12. *Lunch* $18. *Dinner* $25. **Credit** AmEx, DC, Disc, MC, V. **Californian**

Darren's, a Manhattan Beach classic.

Chez Melange may be stuck with a nondescript location tucked away inside a hotel, but it is one of the best kitchens in a wide radius. It's the restaurant that brought California cuisine to the area as long ago as 1982 – almost prehistoric times for LA. More than 25 years later, it retains relationships with suppliers that ensure that they get the best of everything. Come for adventurous food: house-cured and smoked meats, buttermilk fried chicken salad.

Darren's
1141 Manhattan Avenue, at 12th Street, Manhattan Beach (1-310 802 1973/www.darrensrestaurant. com). Bus 126, 232/I-405, exit Hawthorne Boulevard north. **Open** 5-10.30pm Mon-Sat. **Main courses** $28. **Credit** AmEx, DC, MC, V. **Californian**
Chef Darren Weiss has built a reputation on bright, full-flavoured dishes such as beet and Humboldt Fog cheese salad, rock shrimp ravioli and Thai peanut-crusted salmon. At this elegant salon-like room, he serves all his old favourites and daily specials inspired by the market. By Manhattan Beach standards, it's quiet – the noisy party crowd tends to congregate elsewhere.

Petros Greek Cuisine & Lounge
451 Manhattan Beach Boulevard, between Morningside Drive & N Valley Drive, Manhattan Beach (1-310 545 4100/www.petrosrestaurant.com). Bus 126, 232/I-405, exit Hawthorne Boulevard north. **Open** 5.30-11pm Mon-Thur, Sun; 5pm-midnight Fri, Sat. **Main courses** $28. **Credit** AmEx, DC, Disc, MC, V. **Greek**
Petros Benekos hired the executive chef from the Athens Olympic Village to cook at his Manhattan Beach showplace, and his mother flies in from Epirus once in a while to make sure he's cooking the family recipes the way she would. This is Greek cuisine treated with the seriousness of fine French cooking; it's expensive, sure, but worth it.

Restaurant Christine
24539 Hawthorne Boulevard, at Newton Street, Torrance (1-310 373 1952/www.restaurant christine.com). Bus 444/I-110, exit Hwy 1 west. **Open** 11.30am-2pm, 5-10pm Mon-Fri; 5-10pm Sat, Sun. **Main courses** *Lunch* $15. *Dinner* $25. **Credit** AmEx, DC, Disc, MC, V. **American**
At her eponymous Torrance restaurant, Christine Brown has invented an original fusion of Asian, French and Southwestern dishes. She even sometimes discusses her philosophy of cooking while working at the stove in the centre of her restaurant. The menu changes, but the value and service do not: this is top-class cooking at suburban prices.

Orange County

Jagerhaus
2525 E Ball Road, at S Sunkist Street, Anaheim (1-714 520 9500/www.jagerhaus.net). I-5, exit Ball Road east. **Open** 7am-9pm Mon-Thur; 7am-10pm Fri; 8am-10pm Sat; 8am-9pm Sun. **Main courses** $15. **Credit** AmEx, DC, MC, V. **German**

Anaheim was established by German immigrants in the 1800s, so it makes sense that some of them are still here running restaurants. Jagerhaus is open for breakfast through dinner, and the Austrian raisin pancakes will give you the strength to trek through Disneyland. Come back for a dinner of home-made sausage, braised wild boar or *sauerbraten* (beef marinated and roasted) with great brown bread. Note: the parking lot entry is from Sunkist Street.

El Misti Picanteria Arequeña
3070 W Lincoln Avenue, at Beach Boulevard, Anaheim (1-714 995 5944/www.elmisticuisine.com). I-405, exit Beach Boulevard north. **Open** 11am-9pm daily. **Main courses** $12. **Credit** DC, MC, V. **Peruvian**
El Misti is the best Peruvian restaurant in the region, an unpretentious spot decorated with colourful murals. Come here for inexpensive and tasty seafood dishes, grilled lamb ribs and stir-fry with potatoes, all of them Peruvian mainstays. The lucuma-flavoured ice-cream is a tropical delight.

Napa Rose
Disney's Grand Californian Hotel & Spa, 1600 S Disneyland Drive, at Katella Avenue, Anaheim (1-714 300 7170). I-5, exit Harbor Boulevard south. **Open** 5.30-10pm daily. **Main courses** $30. **Credit** AmEx, DC, Disc, MC, V. **Californian**
Believe it or not, the Napa Rose actually would do well in Napa, or in any other food and wine-crazed town. Duck breast stuffed with wild mushrooms and wrapped in bacon is not what you might expect to find at a Disney hotel, but it's served here and is wonderful. The wine list is amazing and fairly priced for the surroundings, and the service is top-notch.

Sapphire
1200 South Coast Highway, at Brooks Street, Laguna Beach (1-949 715 9888/www.sapphirellc. com). I-405, exit Hwy 133 south. **Open** 11am-10.30pm Mon-Fri; 10am-11pm Sat, Sun. **Main courses** $30. **Credit** AmEx, DC, MC, V. **American**
Chef Azmin Ghahreman claims to cook a truly global cuisine, and he has a better case than most. The food at Sapphire is an incomparable modern blend: everything from chicken pot pie to duck confit with cherry-chocolate mole sauce via Tunisian crab, all of it excellent. The location is lovely and the food extraordinary. Book early and show up on time.

Stonehill Tavern
St Regis Monarch Beach Resort, 1 Monarch Beach Resort, Dana Point (1-949 234 3318/www.stregismb. com). I-5, exit Crown Valley south. **Open** 5.30-10pm Wed-Sun; also Tue in summer. **Main courses** $40. **Credit** AmEx, DC, Disc, MC, V. **American**
Celebrated chef Michael Mina offers up his twist on modern tavern fare (the term is used in its lightest sense), employing seasonal products of the highest quality. Try the seasonal tasting menus and wine pairings for full effect. Set in the deluxe St Regis Resort and kitted out by designer Tony Chi, this is a very welcome addition to the OC.

Eat, Drink, Shop

Coffeehouses

One more cup of coffee for the road.

Many Angelenos like to try and make their hard-earned wealth seem accidental, and there's no better way to cultivate an aura of leisure than to while away a few workday hours in a coffeehouse. From the national chains to low-key local favourites, from shops with galleries to shops for writers, LA has always been blessed with plenty of places to grab a cup of joe, and the variety gets broader by the year.

The most recent trend is for upscale coffeehouses: decadent lunches and pastries on the menu, outrageously expensive equipment churning behind the bar. Still, plenty of relaxed hangouts remain – as, of course, do the major chains. **Starbucks** (www.starbucks.com) is as unavoidable here as in other American cities. However, it's given plenty of competition by the **Coffee Bean & Tea Leaf** (www.coffeebean.com), a California-based chain famous for its 'Ice Blended' drinks – essentially, coffee plus flavourings whipped with ice and non-fat milk to resemble a frothy ice-cream drink.

If you're not fussed about ambience, you could always try McDonald's, which beat Starbucks (and several other chains) in a blind taste-test held in 2007. But Los Angeles has a little more to offer than just golden arches and pungent java. Here are more than 20 of the best coffeehouses, scattered all over the region.

Abbot's Habit.

Santa Monica & the beach towns

Santa Monica

18th Street Coffee House

1725 Broadway, at 18th Street (1-310 264 0662). Bus 4, SM1, SM10/I-10, exit Cloverfield Boulevard north. **Open** 7am-7pm Mon-Fri; 8.30am-6pm Sat. **No credit cards. Map** p326 C3 ❶
Serving high-quality coffees alongside a range of sweets and savouries, the moody-broody 18th Street Coffee House draws a loyal crowd of locals who also happen to be successful screenwriters and/or red-carpet celebrities. There's a no-cellphone policy.

❶ Orange numbers given in this chapter correspond to the location of coffeehouses on the street maps. *See pp326-331.*

Funnel Mill

930 Broadway, at 9th Street (1-310 597 4395/ www.funnelmill.com). Bus 4, 20, 33, 333, 704, 720, SM1, SM5, SM7, SM8, SM10/I-10, exit Lincoln Boulevard north. **Open** 9am-9pm Mon-Fri; 10am-7pm Sat. **Credit** DC, MC, V. **Map** p326 B3 ❷
At this low-key, independent shop, an array of rare coffees is elegantly served on silver trays with milk and sugar on the side. The most notable item on the menu is a $65 cup of coffee, made from beans that have already passed through the digestive system of a creature called the Sumatran Paradoxurus. All the more delicious on your lips.

Venice

Abbot's Habit

1401 Abbot Kinney Boulevard, at California Avenue (1-310 399 1171). Bus 33, 333, SM1, SM2/I-10, exit 4th-5th Street south. **Open** 6am-10pm daily. **Credit** DC, MC, V. **Map** p326 A6 ❸
Venice attracts a mixed crowd; and this café, which arrived on Abbot Kinney long before most of its neighbours, is no exception. Affluent home-owners mix with starving artists; while the coffee's not out-standing, the scene makes this a Venice classic.

Jin Patisserie

1202 Abbot Kinney Boulevard, at San Juan Avenue (1-310 399 8801/www.jinpatisserie.com). Bus 33, 333, SM1, SM2/I-10, exit 4th-5th Street south.

Open 10.30am-7pm Tue-Sun. **Credit** AmEx, DC, Disc, MC, V. **Map** p326 A5 ④
At Jin Patisserie, liquid refreshment comes second to desserts: there's something for every indulgent fancy, from green tea-flavoured treats to chocolate concoctions. The tiny garden is a civilised spot in which to take a break from the low-grade insanity on Abbot Kinney.

Marina del Rey to LAX

Joni's Coffee Roasting Café
552 Washington Boulevard, between Beach & Wilson Avenues (1-310 305 7147/www.joniscoffee.com). Bus 108, C1/I-10, exit Lincoln Boulevard south. **Open** *Summer* 6am-9pm daily. *Winter* 6am-5pm daily. **Credit** AmEx, DC, MC, V. **Map** p326 A6 ⑤
Ancient by LA standards (it's more than 20 years old), this coffeehouse has a nice hippie vibe. They take pride in their coffee: it's all made in a huge antique roaster that only produces small batches of beans, and so only one cup of coffee is brewed at a time. They also make their own granola.

Tanner's Coffee Co
200 Culver Boulevard, at Vista del Mar (1-310 574 2739). Bus 115/I-405, exit Manchester Boulevard west. **Open** 6am-8pm Mon-Fri; 6.30am-8pm Sat; 6.30am-7pm Sun. **Credit** DC, MC, V.
The coffee served at Tanner's is widely regarded as pretty good, but the secret is in the sugar. The shop carries a range of unusual syrups with which to flavour your hot or cold drink, and the range of pastries is laudable. There's Wi-Fi; still, since Tanner's is adjacent to a park and one block from the beach, you'll probably want your caffeine fix to go.

Brentwood to Beverly Hills

Culver City

Teaforest
8686 Washington Boulevard, between Helms & Hutchison Avenues (1-310 815 1723/www. teaforest.com). Bus 33, 333, C1, C3, C5/I-10, exit La Cienega Boulevard south. **Open** 7.30am-6pm Mon-Fri; 9am-2pm Sat. **Credit** AmEx, DC, MC, V.
This pared-down little spot doesn't seem welcoming at first glance (cement flooring and wooden chairs), but the drinks and panini ensure return visitors. The coffee is from Illy, while teas run the gamut from traditional British varieties to soy boba extravaganzas. Located in the heart of Culver City's arts district, it's a good stop-off after a spell spent gallery-hopping.

West LA

Cacao Coffee House
11609 Santa Monica Boulevard, at Federal Avenue (1-310 473 7283/www.cacaocoffeehouse. com). Bus 4/I-405, exit Santa Monica Boulevard west. **Open** 6pm-3am daily. **No credit cards.**

Cacao is all tiki, all the time. OK, so there's also some UFO paraphernalia, but it's mostly an island-themed spot. Plain old coffee is available; however, the proprietors have a love of frappes, mochas and caramel swirls. If you need something to get you through the night, you're in luck: it might not open until 6pm, but it does keep serving until the wee small hours.

Beverly Hills

Caffe Dell'arte
428 N Bedford Drive, at Brighton Way (1-310 271 6842). Bus 20, 720/I-405, exit Wilshire Boulevard east. **Open** 6.30am-6pm Mon-Fri; 7.30am-4pm Sat. **No credit cards.**. **Map** p327 C3 ⑥
This fairly basic and unpretentious little café can get lost amid the flash and glitz of the luxury emporiums around it. However, if you're looking for a cheap pick-me-up after a marathon shopping session, this is the place to do it.

Le Pain Quotidien
9630 Santa Monica Boulevard, between N Bedford & N Camden Drives (1-310 859 1100/www.pain quotidien.com). Bus 4, 14, 16, 704/I-10, exit Robertson Boulevard north. **Open** 7.30am-7pm daily. **Credit** AmEx, DC, MC, V. **Map** p327 C3 ⑦
The main LA branch of this worldwide chain is a favourite among ladies and gentlemen of leisure, who can be found tappling away on their laptops or chatting on their iPhones. The coffee is good and the pastries are delicious, while the full menu means you can stay for a full lunch.

West Hollywood, Hollywood & Midtown

West Hollywood

Urth Caffe
8565 Melrose Avenue, between Westbourne & Westmount Drives, (1-310 659 0628/www.urth caffe.com). Bus 4, 105, 220, 305, 550, 704/I-10, exit La Cienega Boulevard north. **Open** 6.30am-11.30pm daily. **Credit** AmEx, DC, Disc, MC, V. **Map** p328 B2 ⑧

The best **Coffee**

For an early-morning wake-up
Café Tropical. *See p173.*

For a lunchtime treat
Susina Bakery. *See p173.*

For a late-night lift
Cacao Coffee House. *See p171.*

Urth has three locations in Los Angeles, but this one is the starlets' hangout of choice (you may even have seen it on *Entourage*). The focus is on the organic coffees, teas and vegan desserts, but the real point of interest is the collection of minor, medium and occasionally major celebrities who dine here… and the paparazzi parked outside to document their caffeine habits.

Other locations 2327 Main Street, Santa Monica (1-310 314 7040); 267 S Beverly Drive, Beverly Hills (1-310 205 9311)

Hollywood

Bourgeois Pig

5931 Franklin Avenue, between Tamarind & N Bronson Avenues (1-323 464 6008). Bus 26, 180, 181, 207, 217, LDH/US 101, exit Gower Street north. **Open** 8am-2am daily. **Credit** DC, MC, V. **Map** p329 C19 ❾

The dim-lit Bourgeois Pig lives on a stretch of Franklin Avenue in Hollywood that's particularly hip right now, thanks in no small part to the presence nearby of the Upright Citizens Brigade Theatre (*see p226*). Pop in for tea or an espresso before the show, but don't go if you're in a hurry – the service is notoriously slow.

Sabor y Cultura

5625 Hollywood Boulevard, at Gramercy Place (1-323 466 0481/www.saborycultura.com). Metro Hollywood-Western/bus 180, 181, 207, 217, 757, 780, LDH/US 101, exit Western Avenue north.

Open 6.30am-11pm Mon-Thur; 6.30am-midnight Fri; 7.30am-midnight Sat; 7.30am-10pm Sun. **Credit** AmEx, DC, Disc, MC, V. **Map** p329 C1 ❿

The location isn't all that, but Saboy y Cultura is huge and welcoming, and makes a nice setting for the regular Friday-night board-game sessions. The coffee is good, but it's the Mexican hot chocolate that wins the biggest raves. There's free Wi-Fi if you don't want to be chatted up by strangers.

Fairfax District

Insomnia

7286 Beverly Boulevard, at N Poinsettia Place (1-323 931 4943). Bus 14, 212/1-10, exit La Brea Avenue north. **Open** 10am-2am daily. **No credit cards.** **Map** p328 D3 ⓫

This quiet hangout is popular with writers: there's only the scratching of pens and the clacking of keyboards to distract from the classical music. Better still, cellphones are not allowed inside – which causes many patrons to hurry outside with their pants vibrating every 15 minutes.

Susina

7122 Beverly Boulevard, at N La Brea Avenue (1-323 934 7900/www.susinabakery.com). Bus 14, 212/1-10, exit La Brea Avenue north. **Open** 7am-11pm Mon- Fri; 8am-11pm Sat, Sun. **Credit** AmEx, DC, MC, V. **Map** p328 D3 ⓬

Susina is one of the most popular bakeries in town, and with good reason. The café itself is charming, carrying with it a Vienna-at-the-turn-of-the-century

Susina.

vibe, and both coffees and cakes are excellent: in particular, the summer berries cake is the stuff of legend in the city, though a variety of mixed salads are also available. Staff are happy for you to linger with your cuppa for as long as you wish.

Hancock Park

Peet's Coffee & Tea
124 N Larchmont Boulevard, at W 1st Street (1-323 978 1003/www.peets.com). Bus 14, 210, 710/I-10, exit La Brea Avenue north. **Open** 5am-9pm daily. **Credit** AmEx, DC, Disc, MC, V. **Map** p329 B4 ⑬
This small Northern California chain has managed to keep its hippie cred intact since opening in 1966. The coffee is all grown organically; flavoured coffees are conspicuous by their absence, though you're welcome to the cinnamon sticks. This particular location offers lovely people-watching (rich hippies, yummy mummies), particularly when the Sunday farmers' market is in full swing across the street. **Other locations** throughout LA.

Los Feliz to Echo Park

Silver Lake

Café Tropical
2900 W Sunset Boulevard, at Silver Lake Boulevard (1-323 681 8391). Bus 92, 201/I-5, exit Hyperion Avenue west. **Open** 6am-10pm Mon-Fri; 7am-10pm Sat, Sun. **Credit** DC, MC, V. **Map** p330 C2 ⑭

This much-cherished Cuban café in Silver Lake offers coffee, extra-sweet pastries and lovely *empanadas* (meat pies). With its cosy and earnest Cuban American vibe, it's a wonderful change from the chain-store establishments. And the coffee, needless to say, is both strong and excellent.

Coffee Table
2930 Rowena Avenue, between Avenal & Herkimer Streets (1-323 644 8111). Bus 92, 201/I-5, exit Hyperion Avenue west. **Open** 7am-11pm daily. **Credit** AmEx, DC, Disc, MC, V. **Map** p330 C2 ⑮
With its lovely covered outdoor patio, this is a great place in which to while away a few hot afternoon hours. In addition to the regular gamut of coffee drinks, huge tempting cakes and oversized cookies are on display. There's also a full breakfast, lunch and dinner menu; plus, unexpectedly, a full housewares store attached.

Intelligentsia
3922 W Sunset Boulevard, at Sanborn Avenue (1-323 663 6173/www.intelligentsiacoffee.com). Bus 2, 4, 175, 302, 704/US 101, exit Silver Lake Boulevard north. **Open** 6am-8pm Mon-Wed, Sun; 6am-11pm Thur-Sat.* **Credit** AmEx, DC, Disc, MC, V. **Map** p330 B3 ⑯
Intelligentsia's gorgeous tiled patio is always chock-full with beautiful people having very important discussions. Made on machines costing thousands of dollars, the coffee is expensive, but you need only buy one drink to sit outside for hours. On hot days, the overhead misters keep everyone cool at what is the hippest daytime hangout in LA right now.

If you're after an alternative, you're in luck: a few doors along Sunset stands the **Casbah Café** (3900 W Sunset Boulevard, 1-323 664 7000). Housed in a pretty turquoise building, the lovely little French-Moroccan café specialises in strong coffees, fresh mint teas and big, simple salads.

LA Mill
1636 Silver Lake Boulevard, between Berkeley Avenue & Effie Street (1-323 663 4441/www.lamillcoffee.com). Bus 201/US 101, exit Silver Lake Boulevard north. **Open** 7am-10pm Mon-Thur, Sun; 7am-11pm Fri, Sat. **Credit** AmEx, DC, Disc, MC, V. **Map** p330 C4 ⑰
At the only spot in the city with a coffee sommelier, you can choose between 30 beans, and roasts prepared in four different ways; or try the same bean in drip, vacuum, filter and espresso styles to discover how preparation changes the java's flavour. Five-star food is rare in coffeehouses, but it's present here. Still, a large lunch may well be required after trying the coffee that comes pre-flavoured by cigarettes.

Echo Park

Chango Coffee House
1559 Echo Park Avenue, at Morton Avenue (1-213 977 9161/www.myspace.com/changocoffee house). Bus 92/US 101, exit Glendale Boulevard.

Open hours vary; call for details. **No credit cards.**
Map p330 D4 ⑲
Echo Park's dirty hipster crowd congregates at this
popular hangout. The service leaves a lot to be
desired, but no matter: lots of people in bands spend
hours here each day. With galleries (there's even one
in Chango), dress shops, a salon and a custom jeans
store/music studio, the entire block is hipster heaven.

Downtown

Groundwork Coffee Shop

*108 W 2nd Street, at S Main Street (1-213
620 9668/www.lacoffee.com). Metro Pershing
Square/bus 33, 55, 83, 92/US 101, exit Main
Street south.* **Open** 7am-7pm Mon-Fri; 7am-1pm
Sat, Sun. **Credit** AmEx, DC, Disc, MC, V.
Map p331 C2 ⑳
The Groundwork mini-chain is the coffeehouse of
choice among many of the city's coffee snobs, and
this location is popular with the denizens of the arts
district in Downtown. Most coffee shops of this ilk
take great pride in their fancy equipment. However,
Groundwork famously got rid of their $10,000 cof-
fee machine, saying it didn't live up to the hype.

A few doors down is the **Lost Souls Café** (124
W 4th Street, 1-213 617 7006, www.lostsouls.com),
which offers poor food, decent coffee and a roster of
art shows and other evening events.
Other locations throughout LA.

San Gabriel Valley

Buster's Ice Cream & Coffee Shop

*1006 Mission Street, at Meridian Avenue, South
Pasadena (1-626 441 0744). Metro Mission/bus
176/Hwy 110, exit Fair Oaks Avenue south.*
Open 7am-7pm daily. **No credit cards.**
Buster's only adds to the quaint aura of charming
South Pasadena. The menu includes everything
from simple drip coffees to elaborate sundaes (made
with LA's favourite ice cream, Fosselman's), and the
coffeehouse is a perfect place in which to rest after
a day spent ogling Craftsman homes.

Zona Rosa Caffe

*15 S El Molino Avenue, at E Colorado Boulevard,
Pasadena (1-626 793 2334/www.zonarosacaffe.com).
Metro Memorial Park/bus 180, 181, 267, 687/Hwy
110 to Pasadena (hwy ends at Colorado Boulevard).*
Open 7.30am-9pm Mon; 7.30am-11pm Tue-Thur;
7.30am-midnight Fri, Sat; 9am-10pm Sun.
No credit cards.
Carrying with it a funky Latin feel, this café has
injected a little tang into Pasadena. The second floor
houses a gallery, while the first floor is full of goods
imported from Latin America; Mexican holidays are
even celebrated here. Check out the *horchata*, and
the special latte made with Mexican chocolate.

Are you looking at me?

Just as London is irrevocably divided into
north of the river and south of the river, so
the most potent geographical distinction in LA
is between the West Side and the East Side.
Covering everything west of Beverly Hills, the
West Side comes with plenty of wealth and
a sunny disposition. Stretching out from
Hollywood and taking in Silver Lake and Echo
Park, the East Side is scruffier, poorer and
cooler. However, one characteristic shared
by both sides of town is that the locals love
both people-watching and being people-
watched themselves: this is a city built on
exhibitionism. Nowhere is this trend more
visible than in the city's coffeehouses, but
the approaches taken to the art vary depending
on which side of the city you're sipping.

On the West Side, grab a seat either close
to the entrance or at the front on the patio.
You may have to show up early to snag such
prime real estate, but it's worth the effort:
to the locals, such a primo seat is worth its
weight in gold. You'll have a better view of the
talent, and – very important to the average
West Sider – you'll be respected for putting

yourself on display. If you see a local you'd
like to get to know, approach them with
swagger: it reminds them of rock stars and
talent agents, top of the heap in this part of
town. It helps if you have a fancy cellphone
and pricey shades, though knock-offs from
Downtown's Fashion District usually work fine.

Over on the East Side, you'll need to take a
different tack if you want to track the locals in
their natural daytime habitat. Upon entering
the coffeehouse, proceed to the back of the
room: the more hidden your seat, the more
colourful the humanity on display (hipsters
adore exclusivity). Watch when someone's
phone rings: they'll take it outside and
proceed to pace grandly in front of the shop.
This is how the average East Sider lets
everyone else know how popular he/she
is. For your own part, bring a pad and pen
and scribble furiously, retaining a furrowed
brow at all times. And when you're ready to
be hit on, sigh and lean back with a look of
contentment. You'll come off like a serious
struggling artist, and on the East Side,
there's nothing more attractive than that.

Bars

Cabs at the ready...

It's cool. No, really. **Air Conditioned**. *See p176.*

Like its movie industry, LA's bars scene is immensely competitive. New hangouts battle for attention like aspiring actors jostling for that first breakthrough role, and promoters spare no expense in an attempt to make an impression. Lavish interiors, decadent speciality drinks and big-name DJs are just three of the tools used to grab the attention of local drinkers, or at least those who make it past the velvet rope that may guard the entrance to the city's new *bar du jour*.

However, LA's drinking culture is not solely about such extravagance. For every ostentatiously upscale Beverly Hills hotel bar and ludicrously exclusive Hollywood lounge, there are countless casual taverns, divey taprooms and welcoming cocktail bars that pour their drinks for discerning locals. Granted, LA isn't a drinking town in the same way that,

for instance, San Francisco is a drinking town. For that, you can partly blame the reliance on the car. But the variety of bars here is as broad as the city itself. Dress code is rarely an issue, even at the smartest joints, though no one's going to complain if you turn up the style a notch or two.

BOOZE & THE LAW

All bars are subject to California's alcohol laws: you must to be 21 or over to buy and consume alcoholic drinks (take photo ID even if you look much older). Wine, beer or any other spirits can only be sold between 6am and 2am. Almost every bar calls last orders at around 1.45am; technically, staff are obliged to confiscate unconsumed alcohol after 2am.

Regardless of your destination, you'll need to plan ahead by finding a designated driver or mapping your route on public transport. Parts of LA are poorly served by buses or trains, but you're in luck if you're staying in Hollywood or Downtown. Both are served by the Metro's Red line; and both, not coincidentally, have interesting and lively drinking scenes.

> ❶ Pink numbers given in this chapter correspond to the location of each bar on the street maps. *See pp326-331.*

Santa Monica & the beach towns

Some are smart; others are divey. A few boast ocean views; others don't even have windows. However, most bars in **Santa Monica** and **Venice** are linked by one characteristic: inclusivity. While fashion plays its part, there are few velvet ropes in this part of town, and dress codes are refreshingly rare.

Santa Monica

Air Conditioned

2819 Pico Boulevard, between 28th & 29th Streets (1-310 829 3700/www.airconditionedbar.com). Bus SM13/I-10, exit Cloverfield Boulevard south. **Open** 6pm-2am Tue-Fri; 7pm-2am Sat, Sun. **Credit** AmEx, DC, MC, V. **Map** p326 D4 ①

Nightlife fashion tends to run north–south in SoCal, with trends emerging in LA before heading down to San Diego. Air Conditioned is one of those rare bars that's moved in the opposite direction. A handsome, low-lit lounge far from the beachside action, this Santa Monica take on a San Diego hot spot isn't a mould-breaker. However, it does what it does – good wines (there are regular tasting sessions), old-school music, friendly staff – very nicely indeed. *Photo p175.*

Bar Copa

2810 Main Street, at Hill Street (1-310 452 2445/www.barcopa.net). Bus 33, 333, SM1, SM2, SM8, SM10/I-10, exit 4th-5th Street south. **Open** 9am-2am Tue-Sat. **Credit** AmEx, DC, MC, V. **Map** p326 A4 ②

The sexy, scarlet-and-black minimalist vibe and the soul-funk grooves spinning in the background have both proved hits with cool West Side kids in full blown denial of their quarter-life crisis. With tracks from the golden age of hip hop, some soul, funk and

a bit of '80s thrown in alongside the strong speciality drinks, the dancefloor stays good and loose. If it looks too full, then just a little down the street is the Circle Bar (2926 Main Street, 1-310 450 0508, www.thecirclebar.com), another staple for pretty young twenty- and thirtysomethings.

Chez Jay

1657 Ocean Avenue, between Colorado Avenue & Pico Boulevard (1-310 395 1741/www.chezjays.com). Bus 33, 333, SM1, SM7, SM8, SM10/I-10, exit 4th-5th Street south. **Open** 2pm-2am Mon; noon-2am Tue-Fri; 9am-2am Sat, Sun. **Credit** AmEx, DC, MC, V. **Map** p326 A3 ③

This divey but loveable spot close to Santa Monica Pier was a regular haunt for Brian Wilson back in the day. The traces of sawdust on the floor and the coterie of leathery beach locals hanging around the small bar probably haven't changed much since he last swung by. The full dinner menu helps grant the place a constantly ticking trade.

Father's Office

1018 Montana Avenue, at 10th Street (1-310 393 2337/www.fathersoffice.com). Bus SM3/I-10, exit Lincoln Boulevard north. **Open** 5pm-1am Mon-Thur; 4pm-2am Fri; noon-2am Sat; noon-midnight Sun. **Credit** AmEx, DC, MC, V. **Map** p326 B2 ④

A convivial buzz fills this airy place even when there's just a handful of people inside it. Blame, or credit, the 30-plus beers, many from Californian microbreweries; there's also a nice range of wines. Food-wise, forgo the tapas in favour of the fabled Office burger, and be sure to eat it in the way the menu suggests: no additions and no substitutions.

Hideout

112 W Channel Road, at PCH (1-310 429 9920/www.santamonicahideout.com). Bus 534, SM9/I-10, exit PCH north. **Open** 7pm-2am daily. **Credit** AmEx, DC, MC, V. **Map** p326 A1 ⑤

If your ambitions for the evening ahead encompass drinking, a little dancing and perhaps a spot of cosy romantic isolation, this is the place. Tucked away in a residential corner of Santa Monica, this low-key bar is popular with locals and the occasional celeb seeking top-shelf liquor and, more importantly, private nooks that block prying eyes. *See also p182.* **Top ten: Happy hours**.

Renée's Courtyard Café & Bar

522 Wilshire Boulevard, between 5th & 6th Streets (1-310 451 9341). Bus 4, 20, 33, 333, 704, 720, SM1, SM5, SM7, SM8, SM10/I-10, exit 4th-5th Street north. **Open** noon-2.30pm, 5.30pm-2am Mon-Fri; 5.30pm-2am Sat, Sun. **Credit** AmEx, DC, Disc, MC, V. **Map** p326 B2 ⑥

There's food here, but this longtime Santa Monica hangout is really all about the keenly priced drinks and the scene that gets livelier as the evening progresses. Larger than it looks, Renée's is less frou-frou than many other West Side bars, but it's still a looker, each eye-catching room decorated in different fashion. A quirky favourite.

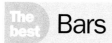

The best Bars

For Hollywood with a grin
Woods. *See p182.*

For olde LA
Formosa Café. *See p180.*

For 21st-century Downtown drinking
Broadway Bar. *See p185.*

For a glimpse of the stars
Hyde Lounge. *See p180.*

For beers and a burger
Father's Office. *See p176.*

Sink in to Russian kitsch at **Bar Lubitsch**. *See p179.*

Venice

Beechwood

822 W Washington Boulevard, at Abbot Kinney Boulevard (1-310 448 8884/www.beechwood restaurant.com). Bus 108, C1/I-10, exit Lincoln Boulevard south. Open 6-11pm Mon, Sun; 6pm-1am Tue-Sat. Credit AmEx, DC, MC, V. Map p326 B6 **❼**
The decor at this bar/restaurant is modern and upmarket, the attitude is relaxed and there isn't a bad seat in the house. But thanks to the fire pits and strategically placed heat lamps, the patio is really the place to be. Temper the booze with an order of the revered sweet potato fries.

Brig

1515 Abbot Kinney Boulevard, at Milwood Avenue (1-310 399 7537/www.thebrig.com). Bus 33, 333/ I-10, exit Lincoln Boulevard south. Open 6pm-2am daily. Credit AmEx, DC, MC, V. Map p326 A6 **❽**
Once a dive bar, the Brig underwent a successful facelift a few years ago. The pool table and the solid jukebox remain as reminders of its seedier past, and the stainless steel fittings are a little less lustrous these days. Still, it remains sleek, although the Brig is more a happy-hour neighbourhood hangout.

Otheroom

1201 Abbot Kinney Boulevard, at San Juan Avenue & Aragon Court, Venice (1-310 396 6230/www.the otheroom.com). Bus 33, 333, SM2/I-10, exit Lincoln Boulevard south; or I-405, exit Marina Freeway. Open 5pm-2am daily. Credit AmEx, DC, Disc, MC, V. Map p326 A5 **❾**
Wide-open windows welcome patrons into this dark, sexy wine bar, which epitomises the best aspects of the newer, slicker Venice. Get there early on weeknights if you're hoping to enjoy a mellow conversation over one of the numerous wines by the glass, or show up after 8pm for some serious mingling.

Brentwood to Beverly Hills

The bars in these West Side regions follow the character of their neighbourhoods. Those in **West LA** and **Culver City** tend to be mellow and unpretentious. However, the bars of **Beverly Hills**, many in hotels, carry an almost unspoken exclusivity: if you need to ask about a dress code, you probably need to go back and change. **Westwood** and **Brentwood** don't offer much of interest for the drinker.

West LA

Irish Times

3267 Motor Avenue, between Irene Street and Rose Avenue (1-310 559 9648/www.theirishtimesla.com). Bus C3/I-10, exit National Boulevard west. Open 2pm-2am Mon-Thur; noon-2am Fri-Sun. Credit DC, Disc, MC, V.

Since LA's actors and models are, to all intents and purposes, forbidden by fashion and overweening ambition to tuck into a portion of fish and chips, they tend to stay away from the basic bar menu and beer-centric vibe at this jovial, unpretentious neighbourhood pub. The hum of conversation is sometimes augmented by live music.

Culver City

Bottle Rock
3847 Main Street, between Venice & Culver Boulevards (1-310 836 9463/www.bottlerock.net). Bus 33, 220, 333, C1/I-10, exit Rosecrans Boulevard south. **Open** 11.30am-11pm Mon-Thur; 11.30am-1am Fri, Sat; 3-11pm Sun. **Credit** AmEx, DC, MC, V.
The first and still the most popular of several wine bars in the area, Bottle Rock performs double-duty as a sophisticated wine bar and an upscale wine store: trying before you buy is encouraged. Small plates of meats, cheeses and salads complement the liquid refreshment, which also stretches to one of the city's best selections of beers.

Buggy Whip
7420 La Tijera Boulevard, at I-405 (1-310 645 7131/www.thebuggywhip.com). Bus 42/I-405, exit La Tijera Boulevard west. **Open** 4-10pm Tue-Thur, Sun; 4-11pm Fri, Sat. **Credit** AmEx, DC, MC, V. *See p179* **Piano men**.

Dear John's
11208 Culver Boulevard, at Sepulveda Boulevard (1-310 397 0276). Bus C7/I-405, exit Culver Boulevard east. **Open** 11am-10pm Mon-Thur, Sun; 11am-11pm Fri, Sat. **Credit** AmEx, DC, MC, V. *See p179* **Piano men**.

Mandrake Bar
2692 S La Cienega Boulevard, between Venice & Washington Boulevards (1-310 837 3297/www. mandrakebar.com). Bus 33, 105, 333, 534, 705/ I-10, exit La Cienega Boulevard south. **Open** 4pm-midnight Tue-Thur; 4pm-1am Fri; noon-1am Sat; 6pm-midnight Sun. **Credit** AmEx, DC, MC, V.
If you're looking to bar-hop around Culver City, the Mandrake won't fall on your radar: it's tucked away from its competitors. However, it's convenient for the emerging local arts district, and even has its own gallery space. The bar itself is a mellow locals' hang-out, with unpretentious service and reasonably priced drinks. The fake-tree-stump patio seating provides a fine setting for smoking and conversation. *See also p182* **Top ten: Happy hours**.

Saints & Sinners
10899 Venice Boulevard, between Kelton & Midvale Avenues (1-310 842 8466). Bus 33, 333, C1, C3, C7/I-10, exit Overland Avenue. **Open** 5pm-2am daily. **Credit** AmEx, DC, Disc, MC, V.
All aglitter with retro '70s gilded splendour, its decor dominated by a circular fireplace complete with groovy glass marbles, this is a likeable, entertaining hangout. The bartenders have zero attitude, the

drinks aren't too expensive, and the capable bar-side DJs spin tunes that encourage movement, though there's nothing remotely close to a dancefloor.

Beverly Hills

Avalon Lounge
Avalon Hotel, 9400 Olympic Boulevard, at S Canon Drive (1-310 277 5221/www.avalonbeverlyhills.com). Bus 28, 328, SM5/I-10, exit Overland Avenue. **Open** 7am-midnight Mon-Sat; 7am-midnight Sun. **Credit** AmEx, DC, Disc, MC, V. **Map** p327 D4 ⑩
Be very, very quiet when entering and departing this retro-'50s hotel (*see p54*), owned and operated by the Kor Group. The bar scene consists largely of white canvas poolside cabanas housing scenes that could come straight from a Hollywood textbook: a little industry schmoozing here, an older fellow with arm-candy there. It's all incredibly civilised.

Bar Nineteen 12
Beverly Hills Hotel & Bungalows, 9641 W Sunset Boulevard, at N Crescent Drive (1-310 273 1912/ www.barnineteen12.com). Bus 2, 302/I-405, exit Sunset Boulevard east. **Open** 5pm-2am daily. **Credit** AmEx, DC, Disc, MC, V. **Map** p327 B2 ⑪
This historic LA hotel (*see p54*) boasts a stylish indoor-outdoor lounge with a tight guest-list policy. However, there's not always a need to wheedle your way in: simply stake your claim before the doorman arrives for the 8pm shift. They won't kick you out if you're already entrenched, and an earlier arrival means more time to hob-nob with the Malibu set.

Nirvana
8689 Wilshire Boulevard, between N Hamel & N Willaman Drives (1-310 657 5040/www. nirvanabeverlyhills.com). Bus 20, 220, 720/I-10, exit Robertson Boulevard north. **Open** 5pm-midnight daily. **Credit** AmEx, DC, Disc, MC, V. **Map** p328 B4 ⑫
Canopies hang cosily over beds, a fireplace lights the bar, a menu of appetisers is headlined 'Foreplay': Nirvana is a very Angeleno attempt to rework *Tales of the Kama Sutra* as a cocktail bar. Thankfully, the neutral colour scheme and subtle lighting combine to ensure that this attempt at seduction doesn't wander into tawdry territory.

Writer's Bar
Raffles L'Ermitage, 9291 Burton Way, between N Foothill Road & N Elm Drive (1-310 278 3344/ www.beverlyhills.raffles.com). Bus 16, 316/I-405, exit Wilshire Boulevard east. **Open** 10.30am-2am daily. **Credit** AmEx, DC, Disc, MC, V. **Map** p327 D2 ⑬
The hotel setting and upscale decor help make this bar into the kind of place in which you can have a conversation without the need to raise your voice. And if that conversation just so happens to be about swinging the financing of your new film, then so much the better: you'll be in good company as this has been an industry haunt for years. The drinks are unsurprisingly pricey: $8 for a beer, anyone?

Piano men

Peter Wagner at the **Buggy Whip**.

Are piano bars making a comeback in LA? Not exactly: in truth, they never really went away. Although fashion moved on several decades ago, a handful of piano-playing showmen (and a few ladies) have continued crooning their hearts out for crowds who are more than happy to toss a few dollars in the piano-top fishbowl as a thank-you. And so while most bars draw their music from a jukebox or a DJ, there are still a number of hangouts at which low-key entertainers sing and play old-school standards and '70s soft-rock guilty pleasures.

The plainly named **Piano Bar** (*see p181*) is a rare find in the heart of Hollywood: a low-key and friendly dive. On any given night, the house piano man generally keeps things lively in this endearingly contrived Brit-themed hangout. It's certainly a world away from the bar at Pasadena's upscale **Langham**

Huntington Hotel & Spa (*see p186*), where a pianist skips the kitsch and plays romantic jazz every Friday and Saturday.

Over in Culver City stands **Dear John's** (*see p178*), a genuinely old-school supper club with a faux brick interior and a piano man at the weekend. The songs tend to be drawn from the hit parades of the '50s, '60s and '70s, and are well received by the bizarre mix of pensionable locals and non-hipster thirtysomething regulars who remember them.

Just a few junctions south of Dear John's, veteran piano man Peter Wagner holds court in the dining lounge of the resolutely retro **Buggy Whip** (*see p178*) every Friday and Saturday. Dinner reservations for the bar area are strongly recommended if you want to secure a front-row seat while Wagner sings the familiar likes of 'You Belong to Me'.

West Hollywood, Hollywood & Midtown

The **Hollywood** bar scene is a Jekyll-and-Hyde experience. On the one hand, the area boasts an array of straightforward boozatoriums: some divey, some smarter and most in business for years. On the other, it's also home to a string of high-concept, high-priced cocktail bars with DJs, clienteles heavy on celebs but heavier on wannabes, and long lines outside the velvet ropes. Which is Jekyll and which is Hyde? That pretty much depends on the drinker.

West Hollywood

For the area's gay bars, *see p244*.

Bar Lubitsch

7702 Santa Monica Boulevard, between N Spaulding & N Stanley Avenues (1-323 654 1234). Bus 4, 217, 218, 704/I-10, exit Fairfax Avenue north. **Open** 6pm-2am Mon-Fri; 7pm-2am Sat; 8pm-2am Sun. **Credit** AmEx, DC, Disc, MC, V. **Map** p328 C2 ⑭ Although there's a pronounced Russian theme at this newcomer, West Hollywood's small and pensionable Russian community have yet to show their faces. This is a modern WeHo archetype: the decor is more kitsch than authentic, and the drinks

Woods. *See p182.*

(inevitably, heavy on the vodka) are strong and expensive. Still, it's a likeable spot, more relaxed and less pretentious than you might expect. *Photo p177*.

Bar Marmont
Chateau Marmont, 8171 Sunset Boulevard, between N Harper Avenue & Havenhurst Drive (1-323 650 0575/www.chateaumarmont.com). Bus 2, 302, LDHWH/I-10, exit La Cienega Boulevard north. **Open** 6pm-2am daily. **Credit** AmEx, DC, Disc, MC, V. **Map** p328 B1 ⑮
Like the hotel in which it's housed (*see p58*), Bar Marmont is both gently exclusive and fabulously elegant. The bar itself is a stately gem, with an air of permanence lacking in so many other LA hangouts; the decor elsewhere is just as beautiful, and the butterflies pinned to the ceiling are a lovely touch. The gastropubby food now comes courtesy of Carolyn Spence, formerly of New York's fabled Spotted Pig, but this otherwise remains a reassuringly old-fashioned presence on the Sunset Strip.

Formosa Café
7156 Santa Monica Boulevard, at Formosa Avenue (1-323 850 9050/www.formosacafe.com). Bus 4, 212, 312, 704/I-10, exit La Brea Avenue north. **Open** 4pm-2am Mon-Fri; 6pm-2am Sat, Sun. **Credit** AmEx, DC, Disc, MC, V. **Map** p328 D2 ⑯
There's a full Asian-influenced menu, but the food comes a poor third to the history and the strong, well-crafted drinks. In business for seven decades, the Formosa was a hangout of the Hollywood aristocracy during the '40s and '50s. The clientele these

days is younger and less famous, but the walls remain lined with images of the stars that once graced the still-atmospheric bar and the dark booths.

Hyde Lounge
8029 W Sunset Boulevard, at N Laurel Avenue (1-323 655 8000/www.sbeent.com). Bus 4, 704, LDHWH/I-10, exit Fairfax Avenue north. **Open** 10pm-2am daily. **Credit** AmEx, DC, Disc, MC, V. **Map** p328 C1 ⑰
Local moguls Sam Nazarian and Brent Bolthouse found the magic formula for success in LA years ago – in a nutshell, exclusivity – and have worked with it ever since. While a guest-list spot granting access to this tiny spot can be tricky to secure, you may have more luck by wading through the paparazzi earlier in the evening if you want to drink in proximity to the young, attractive famous people who keep the gossip rags sizzling.

Hollywood

Beauty Bar
1638 N Cahuenga Boulevard, between Hollywood Boulevard & Selma Avenue (1-323 464 7676/ www.beautybar.com). Metro Hollywood-Vine/bus 163, 180, 181, 210, 212, 217, 312, 363, 780, LDH/US 101, exit Hollywood Boulevard west. **Open** 9pm-2am Mon-Wed, Sun; 6pm-2am Thur-Sat. **Credit** AmEx, DC, MC, V. **Map** p329 B2 ⑱
The Hollywood outpost of this multi-city chain of beauty parlour-styled bars is right at the heart of the nightlife-dominated, velvet rope-heavy Cahuenga

Corridor. With names such as Platinum Blonde and Prell, the drinks are cutesy; you can order them with a slightly sub-par manicure. The whole set-up is, of course, more than a little contrived, but that doesn't seem to dissuade the eclectic crowd.

Blu Monkey Lounge

5521 Hollywood Boulevard, at N Western Avenue (1-323 957 9000). Metro Hollywood-Western/bus 180, 181, 207, 217, 757, 780, LDH/US 101, exit Western Avenue north. **Open** 10pm-2am Tue; 9pm-2am Wed-Sat. **Credit** AmEx, DC, Disc, MC, V. **Map** p329 C1 ⑲

Simian kitsch meets Moroccan culture across a solid walnut bar at this unexpected spot. The Blu Monkey mercifully skips the elitist attitude common to so many Hollywood bars, but the drinks are undeniably upmarket. Couches frame the consistently full dancefloor: once the DJ gets going, trying to hold a conversation is an exercise in futility.

Cat & Fiddle

6530 W Sunset Boulevard, between Seward Street & Wilcox Avenue (1-323 468 3800/www.thecat andfiddle.com). Bus 2, 302/US 101, exit Sunset Boulevard west. **Open** 11.30am-2am daily. **Credit** AmEx, DC, MC, V. **Map** p329 B2 ⑳

We can't claim that the English pub interior is especially authentic, but it was good enough for Morrissey, who was known to favour this place when in his former home town. Good: it's got one of the best patios in Hollywood. Bad: the food, on the whole, is pretty ordinary. Still, happy hour here is great (*see p182* **Top ten: Happy hours**) and the locals are a chummy bunch.

Central

1710 N Las Palmas Avenue, at Hollywood Boulevard (1-323 871 8022). Metro Hollywood-Highland/bus 156, 163, 212, 217, 363, 656, 780, LDH/US 101, exit Hollywood Boulevard west. **Open** 9pm-2am Tue-Sat. **Credit** AmEx, DC, MC, V. **Map** p329 A1 ㉑

Lodge meets luxury in this ultralounge, which offers drinks, expensive appetisers and DJs, who spin from a glass booth on the mezzanine level. Central draws a starry and usually black-clad Hollywood crowd, and is one of the few posh clubs in town owned and run by a woman (Shereen Arazm).

86

6533 Hollywood Boulevard, at Schrader Boulevard (1-323 871 8634/www.86hollywood.com). Metro Hollywood-Highland/bus 156, 163, 212, 217, 363, 656, 780, LDH/US 101, exit Hollywood Boulevard west. **Open** 9.15pm-1.30am Wed; 7.30pm-1.30am Thur-Sat. **Credit** AmEx, DC, Disc, MC, V. **Map** p329 B1 ㉒

You might need to blink a few times to adjust your eyes when you walk in the door. This new restaurant and lounge delivers as much speakeasy glamour as you're likely to find in LA, complete with a jazz soundtrack to match. Burlesque dancers with endless gams put on a show, which looks pretty nice from over the rim of a gin ricky.

Frolic Room

6245 Hollywood Boulevard, at N Argyle Avenue (1-323 462 5890). Metro Hollywood-Vine/bus 163, 180, 181, 210, 212, 217, 312, 363, 780, LDH/US 101, exit Vine Street south. **Open** 11am-2am daily. **Credit** AmEx, DC, Disc, MC, V. **Map** p329 B1 ㉓

In business since the '30s and with one of the finest neon signs in the entire Los Angeles region, the Frolic Room remains what it's always been: a straightforward, friendly little room in which to get loaded with others of a similar mindset, a neighbourhood hangout in a neighbourhood without many of them, and a bar not for dilettantes but drinkers. Look out for the beautiful Al Hirschfeld cartoon mural on the back wall.

Piano Bar

6429 Selma Avenue, at N Cahuenga Boulevard (1-323 466 2750). Metro Hollywood-Vine/bus 163, 180, 181, 210, 212, 217, 312, 363, 780, LDH/US 101, exit Hollywood Boulevard west. **Open** noon-2am Mon-Fri; 11am-2am Sat, Sun. **Credit** AmEx, DC, Disc, MC, V. **Map** p329 B2 ㉔

See p179 **Piano men**.

S Bar

6304 Hollywood Boulevard, at N Vine Street (1-323 957 2279/www.sbeent.com/sbar). Metro Hollywood-Vine/bus 163, 180, 181, 210, 212, 217, 312, 363, 780, LDH/US 101, exit Vine Street south. **Open** 10pm-2am Mon-Thur; 9pm-2am Fri-Sun. **Credit** AmEx, DC, MC, V. **Map** p329 B1 ㉕

This small lounge looks a little like a furniture showroom turned on its ear. Table lamps hang upside down over modern, cross-shaped white tables, while rugs, oil paintings and candelabras add to the hippie vibe. It's a Sam Nazarian operation and you'll need to dress tidily to get in.

Tropicana Bar

Roosevelt Hotel, 7000 Hollywood Boulevard, at La Brea Avenue (1-323 466 7000/www.hollywood roosevelt.com). Metro Hollywood-Highland/bus 163, 180, 181, 210, 212, 217, 312, 363, 780, LDH/US 101, exit Hollywood Boulevard west. **Open** 11am-2am Mon-Sat; 11am-10pm Sun. **Credit** AmEx, DC, Disc, MC, V. **Map** p329 A1 ㉖

The poolside bar at the revitalised Roosevelt (*see p61*) offers a scene that's pure modern Hollywood: stiff and expensive drinks, acres of attitude, a few famous actors and models, a great many more wannabe actors and models, and a pack of attention-seekers who are secretly hoping to be thrown in the pool. In other words, the people-watching is fantastic. Come early (by 6pm) if you hate to queue.

La Velvet Margarita Cantina

1612 Cahuenga Boulevard, between Selma Avenue & Hollywood Boulevard (1-323 469 2000/www.velvet margarita.com). Metro Hollywood-Vine/bus 163,

Frolic Room Kevin Spacey drinks here in *LA Confidential*

Eat, Drink, Shop

Happy hours

Bigfoot Lodge
See p184.
5-8pm Mon-Fri: $1 off all drinks.
5-8pm Sat, Sun: $1 off all drinks, plus $2 tap beers, $3 well drinks and $4 bloody Marys.

Cat & Fiddle
See p181.
4-7pm Mon-Fri (bar only): $3.50 tap beers, house wines and well drinks, plus free food.

Cha Cha Lounge
See p184.
5-9pm daily: $1.50 PBR and $2.50 well drinks, plus (Sat only) $2.50 bloody Marys.

Ciudad
See p164.
4-7pm Mon-Fri: $4 selected drinks, including Pacifico beer and house sangria, plus $4 tacos.

Edison
See p186.
5-8pm Wed-Fri; 6-8pm Saturday: half-price drinks, plus (5-7pm Thur only) 35¢ martinis, a 1910 martini at a 1910 price.

Formosa Café
See p180.
4-7pm Mon-Fri: $3 beers, $4 appetisers and $5 cocktails.

Golden Gopher
See p186.
5-8pm Fri: $1 off beer and $2 off mixed drinks, plus a $3 shot of the day.

Hideout
See p176.
Noon-2pm, 7-9pm Mon-Thur, Sun: half-price drinks.
9pm-1am Tue, Thur (karaoke): $4 beers and $6 well drinks, plus (Thur only) free tacos.

Little Bar
See p183.
5-8pm Mon-Fri, all day Sun: $2 off tap beers, selected wines and well cocktails.

Mandrake Bar
See p178.
5-7pm Tue-Sun: $5 PBR & a shot of whiskey, $5 Tecate & a shot of tequila, plus $2 off house cocktails.

180, 181, 210, 212, 217, 312, 363, 780, LDH/US 101, exit Hollywood Boulevard west. **Open** 11.30am-2am Mon-Fri; 6pm-2am Sat, Sun. **Credit** AmEx, DC, Disc, MC, V. **Map** p329 B2 ㉗
The Mexi-Goth styling may seem a little on the heavy-handed side. But you know what? After the first margarita, all that black velvet will start to feel about right. If you like your Dia de les Muertos on the kitschy side, you're more than ready to order a flaming margarita, and maybe something from the dinner menu: the drinks are not designed to be enjoyed on an empty stomach. Compared to other Cahuenga hangouts (such as Goa, No.1615, 1-323 465 1615, www.goasupperclub.com), this is a lot more fun and a lot less exclusive.

Woods
1533 N La Brea Avenue, between W Sunset Boulevard & Hawthorn Avenue (1-323 876 6612/www.vintagebargroup.com). Metro Hollywood-Highland/bus 156, 163, 212, 217, 363, 656, 780, LDH/US 101, exit Sunset Boulevard west. **Open** 8pm-2am Mon-Thur, Sat, Sun; 7pm-2am Fri. **Credit** AmEx, DC, MC, V. **Map** p329 A2 ㉘
This newish hangout is just far enough from the thick of the Hollywood action to deter the worst of the bar-hopping crowds; as such, it's popular but, happily, not too popular. The forestry theme could have ended up looking terribly kitschy, but it's actually pretty

good fun, and the crowd is nothing like as precious as you'll find in other spots nearby. It's expensive, but then so's everywhere round here. *Photo 180.*

Fairfax District

Canter's Kibitz Room
419 N Fairfax Avenue, at Oakwood Avenue (1-323 651 2030/www.cantersdeli.com). Bus 14, 217, 218/I-10, exit Fairfax Avenue north. **Open** 10am-2am daily. **Credit** DC, Disc, MC, V. **Map** p328 C3 ㉙
This agreeably worse-for-wear little taproom is tucked off to the side of Canter's Deli. The mood is matey and the drinking tends to be pretty focused. It's sometimes quiet, but alt-rocking bands drop in most evenings and liven things a little. Drinks are predictably strong. Across the road is the Dime (442 N Fairfax Avenue), a swanky attempt at mimicking this kind of dive-bar culture.

El Carmen
8138 W 3rd Street, between S La Jolla Avenue & S Crescent Heights Boulevard (1-323 852 1552). Bus 16, 217, 218, 316/I-10, exit La Cienega Boulevard north. **Open** 5pm-2am Mon-Fri; 7pm-2am Sat, Sun. **Credit** AmEx, DC, MC, V. **Map** p328 C3 ㉚
The *lucha libre* theme at this lively spot goes well beyond mere motif: the Mexican-inspired decor is several thousand feet over the top. The healthy

selection of tequilas and 25 different mescals together combine to create innumerable excuses for the inevitable morning-after hangover. The lauded El Perfecto margarita is a highlight.

Miracle Mile & Midtown

Little Bar
757 S La Brea Avenue, between W 8th Street & Wilshire Boulevard (1-323 937 9210/www.littlebar lounge.com). Bus 20, 212, 312, 720/I-10, exit La Brea Boulevard north. **Open** 5pm-2am Mon-Fri; 3pm-2am Sat, Sun. **Credit** AmEx, DC, Disc, MC, V. **Map** p328 D4 ❸❶
You'll probably feel at home at this neighbourhood bar, even if it's not in your neighbourhood: it's a real antidote to the high-end drinking and carousing scene just north in Hollywood, a place to kick off your shoes, figuratively at least. The hospitality even extends to the provision of menus covering an assortment of local food-delivery spots. *See also p182* **Top ten: Happy hours**.

Tom Bergin's Tavern
840 S Fairfax Avenue, between Wilshire & San Vicente Boulevards (1-323 936 7151/www.tom bergins.com). Bus 20, 217, 720, LDF/I-10, exit Fairfax Avenue north. **Open** 11.30am-2am daily. **Credit** AmEx, DC, Disc, MC, V. **Map** p328 C4 ❸❷
Convincingly Irish, this sports pub has been a part of the local scene for more than 70 years, having moved from a nearby site to this building as long ago as 1949. Some of the regulars have earned themselves namesake shamrocks behind the bar; mere mortals can rub elbows with them while trying to get in with the curmudgeonly staff.

Koreatown & around

Brass Monkey
3440 Wilshire Boulevard, at S Mariposa Avenue (1-213 381 7047/www.caffebrassmonkey.com). Metro Wilshire-Normandie/bus 20, 720/I-10, exit Normandie Avenue north. **Open** 11am-2am Mon-Fri; 4pm-2am Sat, Sun. **Credit** AmEx, DC, Disc, MC, V. **Map** p329 D5 ❸❸
Located in the ground floor of a nondescript office building (park and enter at the back), this ski lodge-styled room has one of the most comprehensive karaoke songbooks in the city. Waiting times on weekends routinely hit 45 minutes, so you'll have time to down plenty of liquid courage before you get your shot at the stage.

HMS Bounty
3357 Wilshire Boulevard, at S Kenmore Avenue (1-213 385 7275/www.thehmsbounty.com). Metro Wilshire-Normandie/bus 20, 204, 720/I-10, exit Western Avenue north. **Open** 11am-midnight Mon, Sun; 11am-1am Tue-Sat. **Credit** AmEx, DC, Disc, MC, V. **Map** p329 D5 ❸❹
Naturally enough, LA's best nautical-themed bar sits fully 15 miles from the water. This agreeably

egalitarian bar is famed for the warmth of its welcome and the cheapness of its drinks, characteristics that are embraced by everyone from visiting rockers to residents of the apartment hotel directly above the taproom. Well-seasoned waitresses handle the table service, distributing dishes from a traditional American menu.

Prince
3198 W 7th Street, at S Catalina Street (1-213 389 1586). Metro Wilshire-Vermont/bus 20, 720, LDWCK/I-10, exit Vermont Avenue north. **Open** 4pm-2am daily. **Credit** AmEx, DC, Disc, MC, V. **Map** p330 A6 ❸❺
The management is Korean, as is the music, but the rest of the place resembles a bizarre cross between a bordello and an English gentlemen's club. Drinks aren't cheap, so stick to something simple (bottled Hite, perhaps) and then order the unusual yet delicious fruit platter.

Los Feliz to Echo Park

You won't find too many velvet ropes or guest lists east of Hollywood; nor will you have to take out a second mortgage to order a round of drinks. There's variety here: the bars are smartest in **Los Feliz**, hippest in **Silver Lake** and grungiest in **Echo Park**. However, the whole East Side scene generally hangs together nicely.

Los Feliz

Dresden Room
1760 N Vermont Avenue, between Franklin Avenue & Hollywood Boulevard (1-323 665 4294/www. thedresden.com). Metro Vermont-Sunset/bus 4, 156, 204, 754/US 101, exit Vermont Avenue north. **Open** 4.30pm-2am Mon-Sat; 4.30pm-midnight Sun. **Credit** AmEx, DC, Disc, MC, V. **Map** p330 A2 ❸❻
Retrace key scenes from *Swingers* and you'll end up here, settled in for an evening with inimitable musical duo Marty & Elayne. A beacon of genuine, unironic kitsch, nothing has changed here in umpteen years, from the corkboard walls to the wrought-iron lighting fixtures.

Good Luck Bar
1514 N Hillhurst Avenue, at Hollywood Boulevard (1-323 666 3524). Bus 4, 156, 204, 754/US 101, exit Hollywood Boulevard east. **Open** 7pm-2am Mon-Fri; 8pm-2am Sat, Sun. **Credit** AmEx, DC, MC, V. **Map** p330 B3 ❸❼
Aside from the familiar party-pleasing favourites on its jukebox, the Good Luck Bar is Mandarin-themed to the max: red-soaked, black-lacquered and

Prince Faye Dunaway meets Jack Nicholson here in *Chinatown*

windowless in a way that makes you feel as if you're hiding on a movie set moments before the aerodynamic kung fu scene kicks off. Cocktails come served with borderline-iconic dragon stirrers, but beer and shots are still the best-sellers.

Atwater Village

Bigfoot Lodge
3172 Los Feliz Boulevard, between Edenhurst Avenue & Glenfeliz Boulevard (1-323 662 9227/ www.thebigfootlodge.com). Bus 180, 181/I-5, exit Los Feliz Boulevard east. **Open** 5pm-2am daily. **Credit** AmEx, DC, Disc, MC, V.
Every log cabin winter experience you've ever endured will come flooding back when you step through the doors of this engaging spot. From the fireplace to the signage, rendered in that quaint '50s National Park font, management haven't missed a beat in their bid to rebuild the wilderness in Atwater Village. *See also p182* **Top ten: Happy hours**.

Griffin
3000 Los Feliz Boulevard, at Boyce Avenue (1-323 644 0444). Bus 180, 181/I-5, exit Los Feliz Boulevard east. **Open** 5pm-2am Mon-Fri; 8pm-2am Sat, Sun. **Credit** AmEx, DC, Disc, MC, V.
Smarter than the nearby Roost but still quite casual and cosy, the stylish Griffin is the kind of low-key, hipster-happy lounge you'd like in your neighbourhood. The music is perfectly pitched and the drinks

are decent, but the ambience is key: friendly without being over-friendly, stylish yet unpretentious. A nice addition to the locale.

Silver Lake

Cha Cha Lounge
2375 Glendale Boulevard, at Silver Lake Boulevard (1-323 660 7595/www.chachalounge.com). Bus 92/ I-5, exit Glendale Boulevard south. **Open** 5pm-2am daily. **Credit** AmEx, DC, Disc, MC, V. **Map** p330 D2 ❸
This Tiki-Mex beer bar has a party attitude, with colourful decorations to match. Budget-conscious drinkers opt for PBR, though the bartenders can also mix a decent drink. Cram into the photo booth with a bunch of friends for souvenir shots to commemorate the occasion, so you'll at least be able to remember where you picked up that raging hangover. *See also p182* **Top ten: Happy hours**.

Mixville Bar
Edendale Grill, 2838 Rowena Avenue, between Auburn & Rokeby Streets (1-323 666 2000/www. edendalegrill.com). Bus 92, 201/I-5, exit Hyperion Avenue west. **Open** 5pm-2am daily. **Credit** AmEx, DC, MC, V. **Map** p330 C2 ❸
The bar at this Silver Lake restaurant is a destination drinking-hole in its own right. The tin ceilings and the lengthy dark-wood bar seem redolent of a bygone era; it's a surprise to find that the building

Who's got the power? The **Edison**. *See p186*.

spent most of its past life as a fire station. A small seating area accommodates martini-sipping guests; sociable sorts chat each other up while pinned along the narrow bar-side stretch.

Smog Cutter

864 N Virgil Avenue, between Normal & Burns Avenues (1-323 660 4626). Bus 10, 26/US 101, exit Vermont Avenue north. **Open** 1pm-2am daily. **No credit cards. Map** p330 B4 ⑩

As the sign says, 'Hangovers installed and serviced'. Your hosts will be no-nonsense Korean bartenders who keep the funny business – excesses of alcoholic bravado, arguments with the staff – to a minimum. And your soundtrack will be the karaoke stylings of assorted drunken hipsters: when it gets going, this place is even rowdier than the Brass Monkey.

Tiki-Ti

4427 W Sunset Boulevard, between Sunset Drive & Fountain Avenue (1-213 669 9381/www.tiki-ti.com). Bus 2, 26, 175, 302/US 101, exit Vermont Avenue north. **Open** 4pm-2am Wed-Sat. **No credit cards. Map** p330 B3 ⑪

Enormous and powerful tropical drinks are the raison d'etre at this homage to Polynesian pop culture, a tiki landmark in a city without many such hangouts still standing. It's a must-visit, though perhaps only for one drink: unless you get lucky and snag a seat, you might struggle to get comfortable in what is really a very small room indeed.

Echo Park

Gold Room

1558 W Sunset Boulevard, at Echo Park Avenue (1-213 482 5259). Bus 2, 4, 302, 704/US 101, exit Glendale Boulevard. **Open** noon-2am daily. **Credit** AmEx, DC, MC, V. **Map** p330 D5 ⑫

While the neighbourhood around it gentrifies, this mostly-locals dive keeps thing honest with top-shelf tequilas and Mexican League *futbol*. The crowd these days is mainly made up of thirtysomething males taking a break over cheap drinks in an atmosphere teeming with casino-waitress hospitality. Not the place to flaunt a weird haircut or bust out a lofty attitude: locals and staff have zero tolerance for poseurs.

Short Stop

1455 W Sunset Boulevard, between Sutherland & Portia Streets (1-213 482 4942). Bus 2, 4/I-110, exit Sunset Boulevard. **Open** 5pm-2am daily; also 2hrs before Dodgers home games. **Credit** AmEx, DC, MC, V. **Map** p330 D5 ⑬

A former cop bar that found a new lease of life after it was bought by Afghan Whigs frontman Greg Dulli, the Short Stop helped kickstart the still-ongoing Echo Park renaissance several years ago. The formula is familiar, but the blend of scruffy decor, clued-in music and unfussy, fairly priced drinks still attracts über-fashionable customers. The DJs are alternately lauded and lambasted by locals, but the dancefloor is nearly always full.

Highland Park & Eagle Rock

Johnny's Bar

5006 York Boulevard, at N Avenue 50 (1-323 551 6959). Metro Highland Park/bus 83/I-110, exit Avenue 52 north. **Open** 5pm-2am Mon-Sat; 2pm-2am Sun. **Credit** AmEx, DC, Disc, MC, V.

This old boozer, divey without really being a dive, has been discovered by artsy indie kids, who mix freely with locals and refugees from the York next door. Entertainment from the excellent jukebox is supplemented by semi-regular movie screenings; a pool table provides additional diversion.

York

5018 York Boulevard, betwuen N Avenues 50 & 51 (1-323 255 9675/www.theyorkonyork.com). Metro Highland Park/bus 83/I-110, exit Avenue 52 north. **Open** 5pm-2am Mon-Fri; 10.30am-2am Sat, Sun. **Credit** AmEx, DC, Disc, MC, V.

The grown-up epicentre of Highland Park's social scene, this gastropub offers a carefully edited selection of microbrews and a shortish food menu that's a cut above usual bar fare. The burlap banquettes and exposed brick walls give it a warm boho personality; and you can still hear your own conversation even when the place gets full.

Downtown

The last few years have seen a sea change in Downtown's nightlife, from more or less non-existent to unexpectedly hopping.

Bar 107

107 W 4th Street, at S Main Street (1-213 625 7382/www.myspace.com/bar107). Metro Pershing Square/bus 33, 55, 83, 92/US 101, exit Main Street south. **Open** 3pm-2am daily. **Credit** DC, MC, V. **Map** p331 C3 ⑭

The local hangout of choice for the converted loft community, Bar 107 is painted red and gold all the way up to its 20-foot ceilings. The architectural bones may be fancy but the vibe is that of a mellow dive. Bar 107 prides itself on its no-dance-music policy, instead preferring to soundtrack its evenings with hipster-friendly rock and country.

Broadway Bar

830 S Broadway, between 8th & 9th Streets (1-213 614 9929/www.thebroadwaybar.net). Metro Pershing Square/bus 2, 4, 30, 31, 40, 42, 45, 68/ I-110, exit 9th Street east. **Open** 5pm-2am Tue-Fri; 8pm-2am Sat. **Credit** AmEx, DC, Disc, MC, V. **Map** p331 C4 ⑮

Moneyed, fashionable Downtowners gather nightly around the 50-foot circular bar at this lavish hangout, where the upscale atmosphere is a world away from the bleak stretch of Broadway outside: it's the kind of place in which you can imagine Nick and Nora Charles drinking themselves under the table in sophisticated fashion. On weekends, climb the stairs for some canoodling in the intimate lounge.

Eat, Drink, Shop

Edison

108 W 2nd Street, at S Main Street (1-213 613 0000/www.edisondowntown.com). Metro Pershing Square/bus 33, 55, 83, 92/US 101, exit Main Street south. **Open** 5pm-2am Wed-Fri; 6pm-2am Sat. **Credit** AmEx, DC, Disc, MC, V. **Map** p331 C2 ㊻

Don't let the dress code (no T-shirts, sportswear, sneakers or baggy jeans) scare you off: you'll be thankful you made the effort when you set foot inside this power plant-turned-Downtown hot spot. The names of the party lounges (Tesla, Generator) pay homage to the building's past life; the occasional cabaret shows hint at the era from which it sprang. *See also p182* **Top ten: Happy hours.** *Photo p184.*

Golden Gopher

417 W 8th Street, between Hill & Olive Streets (1-213 614 8001/www.goldengopherbar.com). Metro 7th Street-Metro Center/bus 14, 37, 70, 71, 76, 78, 79, 81, 96/I-110, exit 9th Street east. **Open** 8pm-2am Mon-Thur, Sat, Sun; 5pm-2am Fri. **Credit** AmEx, DC, Disc, MC, V. **Map** p331 C4 ㊼

Although this place boasts one of the oldest liquor licences in LA, it's really a symbol of Downtown's recent resurgence. The bar was revived a couple of years ago with a blend of old-school sturdiness and modern style: chandeliers dangle above *Ms Pac Man* tables, and suits mix easily with college students. *See also p182* **Top ten: Happy hours.**

Hank's Bar

Stillwell Hotel, 840 S Grand Avenue, between W 8th & W 9th Streets (1-213 623 7718). Metro 7th Street-Metro Center/bus 14, 37, 70, 71, 76, 78, 79, 96/ I-110, exit 9th Street east. **Open** 11am-2am daily. **Credit** DC, MC, V. **Map** p331 B4 ㊽

The streets around it are constantly being rebuilt, but this old residential hotel remains unchanged. The same can be said for its ground-floor bar: divey yet approachable, unpredictable and charismatic, it's a little piece of the past in a neighbourhood that's mostly anxious to press on towards the future.

Roof at the Standard

Standard Downtown Hotel, 550 S Flower Street, between W 5th & W 6th Streets (1-213 892 8080/www.standardhotel.com). Metro 7th Street-Metro Center/bus 16, 18, 55, 62/I-110, exit 6th Street east. **Open** noon-2am daily. **Credit** AmEx, DC, Disc, MC, V. **Map** p331 B3 ㊾

Although this rooftop hangout isn't as happening as it once was, the clientele of models, wannabes and admirers hanging out around the pool continue to look, and act, like they've sprung from the pages of *Vice*. It's best on weekend afternoons, with DJs spinning, liquor flowing and terrific views of Downtown.

Royal Claytons

1855 Industrial Street, at Mill Street (1-213 622 0512/www.royalclaytonstavern.com). Bus 60, 62/

I-10, exit Alameda Street north. **Open** 11am-2am Mon-Fri; 10am-2am Sat, Sun. **Credit** DC, MC, V.

One of the first of many new bars to have opened in Downtown's old industrial buildings, this smartish bar/restaurant sits in a slightly isolated 1924 warehouse that's been converted into loft apartments. It seems to be aiming for an ambience halfway between New York tavern and English pub, though the music is livelier than either and the food is good.

Seven Grand

515 W 7th Street, at S Olive Street (1-213 614 0737/www.sevengrand.la). Metro 7th Street-Metro Center/bus 14, 37, 70, 71, 76, 78, 79, 81, 96. **Open** 5pm-2am Mon-Fri; 7pm-2am Sat, Sun. **Credit** AmEx, DC, MC, V. **Map** p331 B4 ㊿

From the neon stag on the sign outside to the impressive selection of whiskies behind the bar (and the impressive staff who pour them), Seven Grand's theme is manliness. Pool tables, plaid wallpaper and mounted game help create an atmosphere influenced by tradition but with a very modern sense of humour.

The Valleys

San Fernando Valley

Blue Room

916 S San Fernando Boulevard, between E Alameda & E Valencia Avenues, Burbank (1-323 849 2779). Bus 94, 96, 183, 394/I-5, exit Alameda Avenue east. **Open** 10am-2am daily. **No credit cards.**

Although it's featured in several movies, this old-school hangout still manages to stay below the radar. The barflies and cheap drinks are a delight; so are the matronly waitresses, who tend to customers like they're extended family. The digital jukebox ensures a broad and varied soundtrack.

San Gabriel Valley

Bodega Wine Bar

260 E Colorado Boulevard, between N Marengo & N Garfield Avenues, Pasadena (1-626 793 4300/www. bodegawinebar.com). Metro Memorial Park/bus 181, 256, 686, 780/I-110, exit Colorado Boulevard east. **Open** 4pm-1am daily. **Credit** AmEx, DC, MC, V.

Fans of the grape can't go too far wrong at the Bodega, a wine bar that doesn't take itself too seriously. The wines by the glass are all $8, so sampling a few varieties is fairly affordable. The long tables encourages the intermixing of parties over plates of tapas, at least until the DJ arrives. There's a sister in Santa Monica (814 Broadway; 1-310 394 3504).

Langham Huntington Bar

1401 S Oak Knoll Avenue, at Wentworth Avenue, Pasadena (1-626 568 3900/http:// pasadena.langhamhotels.com). Bus 485/I-110, exit Glenarm Street east. **Open** 2pm-midnight Mon-Thur; 2pm-2am Fri; noon-2am Sat; noon-midnight Sun. **Credit** AmEx, Disc, MC, V.

See p179 **Piano men.**

Blue Room Ferdy's Bar in *Memento*

Shops & Services

Mall talk, and more besides…

Popular cliché equates shopping in LA with the high-priced, star-studded glamour of Rodeo Drive. The fabled Beverly Hills street lives up to its reputation, but there's more to the city's shopping scene than its super-pricey designer stores. From the independent boutiques of Venice to the chain-packed malls that dot every corner of the region, LA doesn't lack variety; your main concern will be finding the time and beating the traffic. For the city's key shopping districts, *see p188* **Where to shop**.

Shop hours in LA are generally 10am to 6pm, though some stores remain open until 7pm and most malls are open until at least 9pm. Return policies in the big chains are nearly always in the buyer's favour, but some smaller boutiques will go to the end of the world to avoid giving you a refund. A sales tax of 8.25 per cent will be added to the marked price of all merchandise and services in LA County; in Orange County, the sales tax is 7.75 per cent.

General

Department stores

Barneys New York

9570 Wilshire Boulevard, at S Camden Drive, Beverly Hills (1-310 276 4400/www.barneys.com). Bus 4, 16, 20, 720/I-10, exit Robertson Boulevard north. **Open** 10am-7pm Mon-Wed, Fri, Sat; 10am-8pm Thur; noon-6pm Sun. **Credit** AmEx, DC, Disc, MC, V. **Map** p327 C3.

Every fashionista's best friend, the LA outpost of the legendary New York department store offers five floors of cosmetics, jewellery, shoes, designer clothes (for both sexes), lingerie and home accessories; the high-end likes of Prada, Fendi and Marc Jacobs are typical of the fare for sale. Above sits more elegance: Barney Greengrass, a classy rooftop restaurant.

Bloomingdale's

Westfield Century City (p190), Century City (1-310 772 2100/www.bloomingdales.com). Bus 4, 16, 28, 316, 704, 728/I-405, exit Santa Monica Boulevard east. **Open** 10am-9pm Mon-Sat; 11am-7pm Sun. **Credit** AmEx, Disc, MC, V. **Map** p327 B4.

Presenting a range of stock that falls somewhere between middlebrow Macy's and upmarket Neiman Marcus in the pricing stakes, Bloomie's specialises in just-about-affordable designer clothing (Calvin Klein, DKNY, Lucky Brand and others), jewellery,

shoes and accessories: it's strong on handbags and, perhaps inevitably given the location, there's an excellent selection of sunglasses.
Other locations Beverly Center (*see p188*; 1-310 360 7200); Fashion Island (*see p189*; 1-949 729 6600); South Coast Plaza (*see p190*; 1-714 824 4600).

Macy's

Beverly Center (p188), West Hollywood (1-310 854 6655/www.macys.com). Bus 14, 16, 105, 316, LDF, LDHWH/I-10, exit La Cienega Boulevard north. **Open** 10am-9.30pm Mon-Sat; 11am-8pm Sun. **Credit** AmEx, DC, Disc, MC, V. **Map** p328 B3.

Middle-market Macy's has spent the past decade or so expanding from its original New York home right across the nation. Its wares include costly garments from American designers, but also more affordable and casual clothing lines (from the likes of BCBG and Tommy Hilfiger), accessories and cosmetics.
Other locations throughout LA.

Neiman Marcus

9700 Wilshire Boulevard, at S Roxbury Drive, Beverly Hills (1-310 550 5900/www.neimanmarcus.com). Bus 4, 16, 20, 720/I-10, exit Robertson Boulevard north. **Open** 10am-6pm Mon-Fri; 10am-7pm Sat; noon-6pm Sun. **Credit** AmEx. **Map** p327 C3.

Residing at or near the top of the department-store tree, Neiman Marcus is widely nicknamed 'Needless Mark-ups'. However, nothing is really overpriced here: the goods are simply top-of-the-line, and you're paying for the quality and the label: expect to find clothes from the likes of Diane von Furstenberg, Jean Paul Gaultier and Chloë). Good shoe department.
Other locations Fashion Island (*see p189*; 1-949 759 1900).

The best Shops

For a one-stop shop
Grove. *See p189.*

For prehistoric toys
Dinosaur Farm. *See p193.*

For high fashion
Golden Triangle & Rodeo Drive. *See p193.*

For a bite or three
LA's farmers' markets. *See p203.*

For more on LA, and beyond
Traveler's Bookcase. *See p190.*

Where to shop

SANTA MONICA & VENICE

Santa Monica's pedestrianised, chain-packed **Third Street Promenade** is popular, but there's more interesting shopping to be found north on **Montana Avenue**, tidily lined with upscale boutiques. South of Santa Monica, **Main Street** in Ocean Park has a variety of stores selling clothes and gifts. And in Venice, head first to the proudly independent gift, clothing and art stores on **Abbot Kinney Boulevard** before you think of heading to the **Boardwalk** for $2 shades and African masks.

BEVERLY HILLS

A few familiar chains have moved into the **Golden Triangle**, bounded by Santa Monica Boulevard, Wilshire Boulevard and Rexford Drive, but this is still swank central. Chichi boutiques are also in abundance on the stretch of **Robertson Boulevard** south of Beverly Boulevard, where paparazzi regularly snap starlets shopping.

WEST HOLLYWOOD & HOLLYWOOD

The highlight of West Hollywood's shopping is **Sunset Plaza**, on Sunset Boulevard just east of La Cienega. Shopping in Hollywood itself is mixed, but the **Hollywood & Highland** complex does hold some worthwhile stores.

FAIRFAX & MELROSE DISTRICTS

There's plenty of stylish shopping on **Melrose Avenue** between Fairfax Avenue and San Vicente Boulevard. South and east of here, the stretch of **W 3rd Street** between La Cienega and Crescent Heights Boulevards (see p192 **Who's on 3rd?**) is also awash with great independent shops and cafés.

LOS FELIZ & SILVER LAKE

Both these East Side neighbourhoods offer a cultured, alt-slanted selection of stores. In Los Feliz, head to **Vermont Avenue** and **Hillhurst Avenue**; Silver Lake's shopping is concentrated around **Sunset Junction** and along Sunset Boulevard.

DOWNTOWN

Central **Downtown** doesn't offer much, but its edges contain treasures. Both **Chinatown** and **Little Tokyo** have worthwhile multicultural shopping; further south, the **Fashion District** offers bargains galore, not all of them legit.

THE VALLEYS

Shopping in the Valleys is focused around malls, but Old Town in **Pasadena** breaks the mould. Centred around Colorado Boulevard, its old buildings have been modernised to form a handsome, strollable street.

Nordstrom

Westside Pavilion (p190), West LA (1-310 470 6155/www.nordstrom.com). Bus C3, SM7, SM8, SM12, SM13/I-10, exit Overland Boulevard north. **Open** 10am-9pm Mon-Fri; 10am-8pm Sat; 11am-7pm Sun. **Credit** AmEx, DC, Disc, MC, V. **Map** p327 A5.
In the hierarchy of department stores, Nordstrom falls neatly into the middle: not as swish as Neiman Marcus, but smarter than Macy's. Designers range from Betsey Johnson to Diesel via DKNY; the shoe and cosmetics departments are uniformly excellent. **Other locations** throughout LA.

Saks Fifth Avenue

9600 Wilshire Boulevard, at S Peck Drive, Beverly Hills (1-310 275 4211/www.saksfifthavenue.com). Bus 4, 16, 20, 720/I-10, exit Robertson Boulevard north. **Open** 10am-6pm Mon-Wed, Fri; 10am-8pm Thur; 10am-7pm Sat; noon-6pm Sun. **Credit** AmEx, DC, MC, V. **Map** p327 C3.
Saks opened its Beverly Hills branch in 1938 and draws the city's biggest spenders with a carefully glamorous selection of fashion. There's a menswear store at 9634 Wilshire Boulevard (1-310 275 4211). **Other locations** South Coast Plaza (see p190; 1-714 540 3233).

Target

7100 Santa Monica Boulevard, at N La Brea Avenue, West Hollywood (1-323 603 0004/ www.target.com). Bus 4, 212, 312, 704/I-10, exit La Brea Avenue north. **Open** 8am-10pm Mon-Sat; 8am-9pm Sun. **Credit** AmEx, DC, Disc, MC, V. **Map** p328 D2.
Formerly dowdy and prosaic, this hugely successful countrywide chain has reinvented itself over the last few years with the help of designers such as Isaac Mizrahi and Michael Graves; locals jokingly pronounce the name 'Targée'. But for all its aspirations, it's basically still best approached as a reliable supplier of low-cost but wearable clothes, along with cheap appliances and housewares. **Other locations** throughout LA.

Malls

Beverly Center

8500 Beverly Boulevard, at S La Cienega Boulevard, West Hollywood (1-323 603 0004/www.beverly center.com). Bus 14, 16, 105, 316, LDF, LDHWH/ I-10, exit La Cienega Boulevard north. **Open** 10am-9pm Mon-Fri; 10am-8pm Sat; 11am-6pm Sun. **Map** p328 B3.

It won't win any architectural awards, but this hulking, ugly mall is a good one-stop all-rounder. It's anchored by two department stores, Bloomingdale's and Macy's, and a list of fashion retailers that includes Diesel, Calvin Klein, Karen Millen, Dolce e Gabbana and Burberry. Other shops include Aveda, Sephora and a huge Bed, Bath & Beyond; there's also a decent food court and a cineplex.

Fashion Island

401 Newport Center Drive, at San Miguel Drive, Newport Beach (1-949 721 2000/www.shopfashion island.com). I-5 to Hwy 55 south. **Open** 10am-9pm Mon-Fri; 10am-7pm Sat; 11am-6pm Sun.
There's nothing at this vast OC mall that you won't find in LA, but it's a good one-stop shop if you're in the area. There are four department stores (Macy's, Bloomingdale's, Nordstrom and Neiman Marcus), along with an Apple Store, a Barnes & Noble and a selection of fashion stores that are a cut above the usual mall fare (Anthropologie, Betsey Johnson, Trina Turk). It can get hellishly busy on weekends.

Glendale malls

N Central Avenue & W Colorado Street, Glendale. Bus 92, 180, 181, 183, 201/I-5, exit Colorado Street east. **Open** *Americana at Brand* 10am-9pm Mon-Wed; 10am-10pm Thur-Sat; 11am-9pm Sun. *Glendale Galleria* 10am-9pm Mon-Sat; 11am-7pm Sun.
Glendale's two malls are fierce competitors, but they're also next door to each other, and it's easy to drift between the pair.
The larger of the two is the **Glendale Galleria** (1-818 240 9481, www.glendalegalleria.com), an old-fashioned indoor operation which counts its size as its greatest asset. There are more than 200 separate operations here, among them five department stores

(Macy's, Robinsons-May, Nordstrom, JC Penney and a huge branch of Target) as well as a string of mid-market fashion favourites (Abercrombie & Fitch, Gap, Banana Republic, Victoria's Secret and so on).
But as of May 2008, the Galleria has had strong competition from the more fashionable **Americana at Brand** (1-877 897 2097, www.americanaatbrand. com). This immaculate, open-air mall mimics the Grove, its sister operation, with Vegas-esque architecture and a slew of upscale shops. Among the highlights are Cole Haan, Anthropologie, Kate Spade, Kiehl's and Tiffany & Co; there's also a range of restaurants and an 18-screen cineplex.

Grove

189 The Grove Drive, at W 3rd Street, Fairfax District (1-323 900 8080/www.thegrovela.com). Bus 16, 217, 218, 316, LDF/I-10, exit Fairfax Avenue north. **Open** 10am-9pm Mon-Thur; 10am-10pm Fri, Sat; 11am-8pm Sun. **Map** p328 C3.
In a town where most malls are housed inside bland, air-conditioned structures, this upscale open-air centre has been a hit. There are only around 50 retailers, but the selection is strong (an Apple Store, Barneys New York Co-Op, Crate & Barrel, Lucky Brand, the West Coast's flagship Abercrombie & Fitch) and there's also a decent movie theatre. Fears that it would kill the adjacent Farmers Market (*see p203*) have, happily, proven groundless.

Hollywood & Highland

6801 Hollywood Boulevard, at N Highland Avenue, Hollywood (1-323 817 0220/www.hollywoodand highland.com). Metro Hollywood-Highland/bus 156, 163, 212, 217, 363, 656, 780, LDH/US 101, exit Hollywood Boulevard west. **Open** 10am-10pm Mon-Sat; 10am-7pm Sun. **Map** p329 A1.

Fashion District. *See p194.*

Eat, Drink, Shop

It's difficult to say whether Hollywood & Highland has helped drive Hollywood's recent commercial renaissance, or whether it's ridden to success on its coat-tails. Either way, this ambitious mall has become a popular destination after a shaky start. The mall's stores are a jumble of familiar favourites (Gap, American Eagle, LA's only Virgin Megastore) and smaller chains (Bebe, Hot Topic, Swatch); it's designed to appeal to a younger crowd. The mall's layout isn't exactly user-friendly, but you'll find what you're looking for in due course. The parking entrance is on Highland Avenue.

South Coast Plaza

3333 Bristol Street, at I-405, Costa Mesa (1-800 782 8888/www.southcoastplaza.com). I-405, exit Bristol Street north. **Open** 10am-9pm Mon-Fri; 10am-8pm Sat; 11am-6.30pm Sun.
This monster is the third largest mall in the US, and it's not shy when it comes to talking about its size. There are nearly 300 stores here in all. Chains dominate, of course, but whatever you want, the mall probably stocks it somewhere, whether in one of the five department stores (from Sears to Saks Fifth Avenue), the vast array of fashion retailers, or in one of innumerable specialist stores that sell everything from jewellery to sneakers. And if not, then you're very close to the Lab (2930 Bristol Street, 1-714 966 6660, www.thelab.com), which offers a more youth-oriented range of retailers (Urban Outfitters, Buffalo Exchange and the like).

Westfield Century City

10250 Santa Monica Boulevard, between Century Park W & Avenue of the Stars, Century City (1-310 277 3898/www.westfield.com/centurycity). Bus 4, 16, 28, 316, 704, 728/I-405, exit Santa Monica Boulevard east. **Open** 10am-9pm Mon-Sat; noon-7pm Sun. **Map** p327 B4.
Renovated in recent years, this immense mall has also moved slightly upmarket, adding some smarter shops to its roster of main-street perennials. The likes of Gap and Sunglass Hut now rub shoulders with Brooks Brothers, Kate Spade, Thomas Pink and even Swarovski; however, the mall's two department stores remain Bloomingdale's and Macy's. There's also a 15-screen movie theatre here: *see p228.*

Westside Pavilion

10800 W Pico Boulevard, at Westwood Boulevard, West LA (1-310 474 2785/www.westsidepavilion. com). Bus C3, SM7, SM8, SM12, SM13/I-10, exit Overland Boulevard north. **Open** 10am-9pm Mon-Fri; 10am-8pm Sat; 11am-6pm Sun. **Map** p327 A5.
This glass-roofed Westside mall was renovated in recent years; the work added a new cinema (the Landmark; *see p228*), a variety of new stores and a rather tidier appearance. For all the improvements, there aren't too many surprises here – the department stores are Nordstrom and Macy's, and the selection of largely middle-market fashion retailers isn't anything out of the ordinary. Fans of Tom Petty might like to note that he filmed his video for 'Free Fallin'' here while riding the escalators.

Markets

For food markets, *see p203.* For antiques markets and flea markets, *see p207.*

Specialist

Books & magazines

General

There are branches of **Barnes & Noble** and **Borders** all over LA. To get you started, B&N has a shop at the Grove (1-323 525 0270, www. bn.com), and there's a Borders on the Third Street Promenade in Santa Monica (No.1415, 1-310 393 9290, www.borderstores.com). Call one or check online to find your nearest.

Book Soup

8818 Sunset Boulevard, between Larabee Street & Horn Avenue, West Hollywood (1-310 659 3110/ www.booksoup.com). Bus 2, 105, 302/I-10, exit La Cienega Boulevard north. **Open** 9am-9pm Mon-Thur, Sun; 9am-10pm Fri, Sat. **Credit** AmEx, DC, Disc, MC, V. **Map** p328 A2.
The variety of stock at Book Soup is huge and diverse, even if the space itself is a little squeezed, and the newsstand is well stocked with domestic and international papers.

Skylight Books

1818 N Vermont Avenue, at Melbourne Avenue, Los Feliz (1-323 660 1175/www.skylightbooks.com). Metro Vermont-Sunset/bus 4, 156, 204, 754/US 101, exit Vermont Avenue north. **Open** 10am-10pm daily. **Credit** AmEx, DC, Disc, MC, V. **Map** p330 A2.
This much-cherished bookstore in Los Feliz strikes a neat balance between intellectual crowd-pleasers and more unusual fare. Open since the mid '90s, it bucked book-industry trends by expanding into neighbouring premises in 2008.

Small World Books

1407 Ocean Front Walk, at Horizon Avenue, Venice (1-310 399 2360/www.smallworldbooks.com). Bus 33, 333, SM1, SM2/I-10, exit 4th-5th Street south. **Open** 10am-8pm daily. **Credit** AmEx, DC, MC, V. **Map** p326 A5.
Tucked away amid the T-shirt hawkers and jewellery makers on the Venice Boardwalk is this great indie bookseller. The stock carried is an all-round mix, everything from pop fiction to scientific tomes.

Vroman's

695 E Colorado Boulevard, between N El Molino & N Oak Knoll Avenues, Pasadena (1-626 449 5320/ www.vromansbookstore.com). Metro Lake/bus 180, 181, 485/Hwy 110 to Pasadena (hwy ends at Colorado Boulevard). **Open** 9am-9pm Mon-Thur; 9am-10pm Fri, Sat; 10am-9pm Sun. **Credit** AmEx, DC, Disc, MC, V.

The largest independent bookshop in Southern California was founded over a century ago, and continues to provide welcome competition to the big two up in the Valley. The stock is strong and the staff are very helpful. Keep an eye out for the regular readings and the book signings.

Specialist

Aside from the speciality shops below, LA has bookstores devoted to comics (**Meltdown**, 7522 W Sunset Boulevard, Hollywood, 1-323 851 7223, www. meltcomics.com), food (**Cook's Library**, 8373 W 3rd Street, Fairfax District, 1-323 655 3141, www.cookslibrary.com), African American literature (**Eso-Won**, 4331 Degnan Boulevard, Leimert Park, 1-323 290 1048, http://esowon.booksense.com), spirituality (**Bodhi Tree**, 8585 Melrose Avenue, West Hollywood, 1-310 659 1733, www.bodhitree. com) and even children's book art (**Every Picture Tells a Story**, 1311 Montana Avenue, Santa Monica 1-310 451 2700, www. everypicture.com), among other subjects.

Children's Book World

10580½ W Pico Boulevard, between Prosser & Parnell Avenues, West LA (1-310 559 2665/ www.childrensbookworld.com). Bus C3, SM7, SM8, SM12, SM13/I-10, exit Overland Boulevard north. **Open** 10am-5.30pm Mon- Fri; 10am-5pm Sat. **Credit** DC, MC, V. **Map** p327 B5.
This huge children's bookshop offers 80,000 titles and super-knowledgeable staff. There are regular storytelling sessions on Saturdays at 10.30am.

A Different Light

8853 Santa Monica Boulevard, at N San Vicente Boulevard, West Hollywood (1-310 854 6601/www. adlbooks.com). Bus 4, 105, 220, 305, 550, 704/ I-10, exit La Cienega Boulevard north. **Open** 10am-10pm Mon, Wed, Sun; 10am-11pm Tue, Thur; 10am-midnight Fri, Sat. **Credit** DC, MC, V. **Map** p328 A2.
America's most famous gay bookshop, A Different Light opened in 1979. In addition to selling books, videos and mags for gays, lesbians and transgendered people, the shop hosts readings and signings.

Equator Books

1103 Abbot Kinney Boulevard, at Westminster Avenue, Venice (1-310 399 5544/www.equatorbooks. com). Bus 33, 333, SM1, SM2/I-10, exit 4th-5th Street south. **Open** 11am-10pm Tue-Thur; 11am-11pm Fri, Sat; 11am-5pm Sun. **Credit** AmEx, DC, MC, V. **Map** p326 A5.
Equator offers a gloriously esoteric selection of books, from chunky pictorial tomes on modern photography to super-rare music-related tomes. There's art on the walls and rare records at the back.

Samuel French

7623 W Sunset Boulevard, betwen N Stanley Avenue & Courtney Avenue, West Hollywood (1-323 876 0570/www.samuelfrench.com). Bus 2, 302/I-10, exit Fairfax Avenue north. **Open** 10am-6pm Mon-Fri; 10am-5pm Sat. **Credit** AmEx, DC, Disc, MC, V. **Map** p328 C1.
From silver screen to printed page: Samuel French sells just about every film script in print, plus myriad theatre scripts and books about drama and film. **Other locations** 11963 Ventura Boulevard, Studio City (1-818 762 0535).

Traveler's Bookcase

8375 W 3rd Street, at S King's Road, Fairfax District (1-323 655 0575/www.travelbooks.com). Bus 16, 105, 218, 220, 316/I-10, exit La Cienega Boulevard north. **Open** 10am-7pm Mon-Sat; 11am-5pm Sun. **Credit** AmEx, DC, MC, V. **Map** p328 B3.
The best travel bookshop in Southern California offers a broad range of guidebooks and maps, along with an impeccably chosen selection of travel literature. The friendly staff are more than happy to help.

Used & antiquarian

Other fine used bookshops include the funky **Counterpoint Records & Books** in Hollywood (5911 Franklin Avenue, 1-323 957 7965, www.counterpointrecordsandbooks.com) and the musty **Cliff's Books** in Pasadena (630 E Colorado Boulevard, 1-626 449 9541).

Brand Bookshop

231 N Brand Boulevard, between W California & W Wilson Avenues, Glendale (1-818 507 5943/ www.abebooks.com). Bus 92, 180, 181, 183, 201/

Hollywood & Highland. *See p189.*

Who's on 3rd?

Traveler's Bookcase.

LA's two most celebrated shopping malls sit roughly a mile apart, south-east of Beverly Hills. At the corner of Beverly and La Cienega Boulevards is the huge **Beverly Center**; east of here, right by the Farmers Market, is the infinitely prettier, open-air **Grove**. Between them, the malls contain almost every major chain you might want to visit. And yet the best shopping in the area is on the stretch of road that links the two malls: **W 3rd Street**, the most agreeable concentration of boutiques, bookshops, cafés and gift stores in LA.

Start just east of La Cienega at one of the two branches of **Polkadots & Moonbeams** on W 3rd (No.8381; *see p198*); this one sells chic new modern clothes. In between here and its vintage counterpart (No.8367; *see p198*), there are two excellent bookstores: the **Traveler's Bookcase** (No.8375; *see p191*) and the **Cook's Library** (No.8373; *see p191*). If you're hungry, stop at **Who's on Third?** (No.8369, 1-323 651 2928).

It gets even sweeter down the road. The wonderful **Orchid Wrangler** (No.8365, 1-323 655 0855, www.orchidwrangler.com) is just next door to **Puppies & Babies** (No.8363, 1-323 653 3995, www.puppiesandbabies. com), selling gifts for dogs and toddlers, which in turn adjoins foodie-friendly gift store **Fraiche** (No.8361, 1-323 655 2880). Across the road is Meghan Kinney's **Meg** (No.8362, 1-323 653 3972, www.megshops.com),

where the clothes range from old and glamorous to modern and chic. Next to Meg sits **Seaver** (No.8360, 1-323 653 8286, www.seavergifts.com), a delightful gift store. By now, you'll have earned a snack – let **Joan's on Third** (No.8350, 1-323 655 2285, www.joansonthird.com) provide it.

While the girls are browsing the exquisite toiletries in **Palmetto** (No.8321, 1-323 653 2470) on the north side of W 3rd, the boys can rifle through the immaculate shirts at **Douglas Fir** (No.8309, 1-323 651 5445), before both meet up at **OK** (No.8303, 1-323 653 3501, www.okstorela.com), which sells a cultured mix of books, art and housewares. Or continue heading east along the southern side of W 3rd, stopping to browse the luxe furnishings at **Zipper** (No.8316, 1-323 951 0620, www.zippergifts.com) or the clothes for designer waifs at **Kristin Londgren** (No.8308, 1-323 653 9200, www.kristinlondgren.com).

Past a couple more stores, cross the road and pick up some high-style travel goodies from **Flight 001** (No.8235; *see p210*). Just down the street, sample the updated hippy chic at **Avita** (No.8213, 1-323 852 3200, www.avitastyle.com), the space-age furniture of **Plushpod** (No.8211, 1-323 951 0748, www.plushpod.com) and the T-shirts and jeans in **Milk** (No.8209, 1-323 951 0330, www.shopatmilk.com). Hungry again? **Doughboys** (No.8136, 1-323 651 4202).

I-5, exit Colorado Street east. **Open** 10am-9pm Mon-Thur; 10am-10pm Fri, Sat; 11am-7pm Sun. **Credit** AmEx, DC, Disc, MC, V.
Arguably the best reason to visit Glendale, Brand offers upwards of 100,000 used books on more or less every subject imaginable. You're bound to find something you like.

Children

Fashion

There are branches of **Gap Kids** everywhere, including one on the Third Street Promenade in Santa Monica (No.1355, 1-310 393 0719, www.gap.com). Upmarket chains with a presence in LA include **Janie & Jack** (1311B Montana Avenue, Santa Monica, 1-310 458 0167, www.janieandjack.com) and **Pottery Barn Kids** (The Grove, *see p189*; 1-323 549 9344, www.potterybarnkids.com).

Entertaining Elephants

12053½ Ventura Place, at Ventura Boulevard, Studio City (1-818 766 9177/www.entertaining elephants.com). Bus 150, 240, 750/US 101, exit Laurel Canyon Boulevard south. **Open** 10am-6pm Tue-Sat; 8am-2pm Sun. **Credit** DC, MC, V.
Entertaining Elephants offers sophisticated, modern clothes and accessories, plus furniture and toys, from around the globe. There's an emphasis on natural and recycled materials.

Kitson Kids

108 S Robertson Boulevard, at Alden Drive, Beverly Hills (1-310 246 3829/www.shopkitson.com). Bus 14, 16, 220/I-10, exit Robertson Boulevard north. **Open** 10am-7pm Mon-Fri; 9am-7pm Sat; 11am-6pm Sun. **Credit** AmEx, DC, Disc, MC, V. **Map** p328 A3.
Hipsters with families love the goods on offer here, from the likes of Flowers by Zoe, Trunk and Great China Wall. This stretch of Robertson is home to the whole Kitson empire: womenswear is at No.115; menswear is at No.146; and the newer Kitson Studio, stocking accessories, is at No.142.

Paulina Quintana

1519 Griffith Park Boulevard, at Sunset Boulevard, Silver Lake (1-323 662 4010/www.paulinaquintana. com). Bus 2, 4, 175, 302, 704/US 101, exit Silver Lake Boulevard north. **Open** 11am-5.30pm Mon-Fri, Sun; 9.30am-5.30pm Sat. **Credit** AmEx, MC, V. **Map** p330 C3.
Quintana applies stylish modern designs to lounge pants, tank tops, T-shirts, leggings, frocks and shorts, sized for newborns up to six-year-olds.

Toys

Dinosaur Farm

1510 Mission Street, between Fair Oaks Avenue & Fremont Avenue, South Pasadena (1-626 441 2767/www.dinosaurfarm.com). Metro Mission/bus

176/Hwy 110, exit Fair Oaks Avenue south. **Open** 10am-6pm Mon-Sat; 11am-5pm Sun. **Credit** AmEx, DC, Disc, MC, V.
Adored by families throughout the LA area, this award-winning toy shop is a must-visit if your kids have an interest in dinos. The stock includes toy dinosaurs, dinosaur books and dinosaur costumes.

Puzzle Zoo

1413 Third Street Promenade, at Santa Monica Boulevard, Santa Monica (1-310 393 9201/www. puzzlezoo.com). Bus 4, 20, 704, 720/I-10, exit 4th-5th Street north. **Open** 10am-midnight Mon-Thur, Sun; 10am-midnight Fri, Sat. **Credit** AmEx, DC, Disc, MC, V. **Map** p326 A3.
Jigsaws remain a speciality at this friendly favourite, but there are also tons of board games, action figures, dolls and whizz-bang modern goodies.

Electronics & photography

General

There are branches of **Circuit City** and **Best Buy**, the two biggest general electronics chains in the country, all over LA. Circuit City's locations include a store at 4400 W Sunset Boulevard in Los Feliz (1-323 663 6033, www.circuitcity.com), while the most central Best Buy is at 1015 N La Brea Avenue in West Hollywood (1-323 883 0219, www.bestbuy.com).

Specialist

CompUSA sell PCs and other gear in Burbank (761 N San Fernando Boulevard, 1-818 848 8588, www.compusa.com). Mac stalwarts should try the **Apple Store** at the Grove (*see p189*; 1-323 965 8400, www.apple.com). For computer repairs, try **CAM Technologies** (9312 Civic Center Drive, Beverly Hills, 1-310 777 0316), which fixes both Macs and PCs.
The countrywide **Ritz Camera** chain (branches include one at 270 N Beverly Drive, Beverly Hills, 1-310 285 9616, www.ritzcamera. com) is good for photographic basics. And if you're looking to rent a cellphone, try **TripTel** (1-877 874 7835, www.triptel.com) which has a branch at LAX but also delivers across the city.

Fashion

Designer

You'll find every designer label under the sun in Los Angeles: the array of shops rivals those in better-known fashion cities such as New York, London and Paris. Alongside the big names, LA also boasts a growing stable of home-grown designers, who mix Hollywood glitz, hippie chic and beachy sportswear.

Eat, Drink, Shop

The swankiest shopping area is the so-called Golden Triangle in **Beverly Hills** (*see p91*), with Rodeo Drive housing many of fashion's big names. In **Two Rodeo**, an outdoor complex at the corner of Rodeo Drive and Wilshire Boulevard, you'll find **Versace** (No. 248, 1-310 205 3921, www.versace.com); on Rodeo itself, designers include **Christian Dior** (No. 309, 1-310 859 4700, www.dior.com), **Dolce & Gabbana** (No. 312, 1-310 888 8701, www.dolcegabbana.it), **Chanel** (No. 400, 1-310 278 5500, www.chanel.com), **Hermès** (No. 434, 1-310 278 6440, www.hermes.com), **Ralph Lauren** (No. 444, 1-310 281 7200, www.polo.com), **Miu Miu** (No.317, 1-310 247 2227, www.miumiu.com) and **Prada** (No. 343, 1-310 278 8661, www.prada.com).

The British invasion of Los Angeles continues. Among the imports are **Ted Baker** (131 N Robertson Boulevard, 1-310 550 7855, www.tedbaker.com), **Burberry** (9560 Wilshire Boulevard, Beverly Hills, 1-310 550 4500, www.burberry.com), **Paul Smith** (8221 Melrose Avenue, West Hollywood, 1-323 951 4800, www.paulsmith.co.uk), **Stella McCartney** (8823 Beverly Boulevard, West Hollywood, 1-310 273 7051, www.stellamccartney.com) and, since 2008, *enfant terrible* **Alexander McQueen** (8379 Melrose Avenue, West Hollywood, 1-323 782 4983, www.alexandermcqueen.com).

Cabaña

1511 Montana Avenue, between 15th & 16th Streets, Santa Monica (1-310 394 5123). Bus SM3/ I-10, exit Lincoln Boulevard north. **Open** 10am-6pm Mon-Sat; noon-5pm Sun. **Credit** AmEx, DC, MC, V. **Map** p326 C3.
This adorable boutique sells Lilly Pulitzer's preppy-but-wearable collection of summery, candy-coloured outfits for grown-ups and little girls.

Chrome Hearts

600 N Robertson Boulevard, at Melrose Avenue, West Hollywood (1-310 854 9800/www.chromehearts.com). Bus 4, 105, 220, 305, 550, 704/I-10, exit La Cienega Boulevard north. **Open** 11am-7pm Mon-Sat. **Credit** AmEx, DC, MC, V. **Map** p328 A2.
Does spending a lot of money on leather, black jeans and gothic jewellery qualify you as an authentic rock 'n' roll rebel? The shoppers here, who include Cher and P Diddy, think so.

Diane von Furstenberg

8407 Melrose Avenue, at N Orlando Avenue, West Hollywood (1-323 951 1947/www.dvf.com). Bus 10, 105/I-10, exit La Cienega Boulevard north. **Open** 11am-7pm Mon-Sat; noon-6pm Sun. **Credit** AmEx, DC, Disc, MC, V. **Map** p328 C2
Diane von Furstenberg invented the wrap dress, but her LA boutique shows there's much more to her designs. From evening gowns to sports gear, everything is chic yet practical.

James Perse

8914 Melrose Avenue, between N Almont & N La Peer Drives, West Hollywood (1-310 276 7277/www.jamesperse.com). Bus 4, 105, 220, 305, 550, 704/ I-10, exit La Cienega Boulevard north. **Open** 10am-6pm Mon-Sat; noon-5pm Sun. **Credit** AmEx, Disc, MC, V. **Map** p328 A2.
Perse offers casually classic clothes for men, women and children, made from refined fabrics and featuring appropriately seasonal colours.
Other locations 3835 Cross Creek Road, Malibu (1-310 456 0354); 225 26th Street, Santa Monica (1-310 394 9160); 357 N Canon Drive, Beverly Hills (1-310 776 7100).

Marc Jacobs

8400 Melrose Place, between N Orlando & N Croft Avenues, West Hollywood (1-323 653 5100/www.marcjacobs.com). Bus 10, 105/I-10, exit La Cienega Boulevard north. **Open** 11am-7pm Mon-Sat; noon-6pm Sun. **Credit** AmEx, DC, Disc, MC, V. **Map** p328 B2.
More than any other collection, Jacobs' designs epitomise the style of young Hollywood; in 2007, he even picked the then-12-year-old Dakota Fanning as his latest model. From clothing to accessories, everything is gorgeous, but be prepared to spend high – or aim for the more affordable Marc by Marc Jacobs at No. 8409 (1-323 653 0100).

Trina Turk

8008 W 3rd Street, between S Edinburgh & S Laurel Avenues, Fairfax District (1-323 651 1382/ www.trinaturk.com). Bus 16, 217, 218, 316/I-10, exit Fairfax Avenue north. **Open** 11am-7pm Mon-Sat; noon-6pm Sun. **Credit** AmEx, DC, MC, V. **Map** p328 C3.
Turk's striking collections come with a retro Palm Springs feel. Funky shades and bags complete the look, and the friendly staff are happy to help.

Discount

The nearest outlet malls are **Citadel Outlets** south-east of Downtown (100 Citadel Drive, Commerce, 1-323 888 1724, www.citadeloutlets.com), where you'll find the likes of Calvin Klein, Kenneth Cole and Reebok, and **Premium Outlets**, 45 minutes north of LA (740 E Ventura Boulevard, Camarillo, 1-805 445 8520, www.premiumoutlets.com), where Barneys, DKNY and Nike are among the 120 stores.

In Downtown's **Fashion District** (*see p117*), vendors hawk clothing, accessories and fabrics for low prices from 10am to 5pm daily. Still, it's not exactly guilt-free shopping: LA has become an international manufacturing centre for fake designer accessories. For tours, *see p71*.

General

All the major mid-market chains have stores in LA, and some have several. In particular, branches of **Old Navy** (Beverly Connection,

It's easy being green

All Shades of Green.

store does offer adult clothing and some worthwhile green items for the home.

Like Sherman Oaks, Silver Lake hosts a pair of green boutiques. Although it does stock some clothes, **All Shades of Green** (3038 Rowena Avenue, 1-323 665 7454, www.allshadesofgreen.net) is more interested in promoting an overall green lifestyle: the store carries everything from non-toxic cleaning products to beeswax candles. Not far away the likewise coloured **Kelly Green** (4008 Santa Monica Boulevard, 1-323 660 1099, www.kellygreendesign.net) offers an interesting array of homewares, bags and blankets made from recycled products and organic materials, plus an interesting selection of books and some pricey but well-made clothes.

Finally, what would the beach towns be without proper eco representation? A substantial portion of sales at longstanding store **Natural High Lifestyle** (2400 Main Street, Santa Monica, 1-310 450 5837, www.naturalhighlifestyle.com) are wholesale, but the store does carry comfortable, well-designed hemp and bamboo fabric clothing, sustainable yoga mats and homewares.

You'll find your fair share of musty Birkenstocks and tie-dyed T-shirts in Venice. But elsewhere, going green in LA is a more modish pursuit: organic cotton T-shirts, sustainably produced jeans designed by rock stars, hemp flip-flops with recycled rubber soles. Some high-end stores in Beverly Hills have joined the march towards environmental friendliness, but the most stylish clothes can be found in green boutiques such as **Avita** (8213 W 3rd Street, West Hollywood, 1-323 852 3200, www.avitastyle.com). Some specialise in eco-friendly fashions by local designers; others offer clothing alongside green objects for the home.

Calling itself 'eco-chic', **GreenRohini** (13327 Ventura Boulevard, Sherman Oaks, 1-818 981 0023, www.greenrohini.com) stocks plenty of handsome clothes, including some by local designers. Its keenness for greenness even extends to the shop itself, which is designed to meet LEED standards for environmental sustainability. Close by is the similarly prefixed **Green Cradle** (13344 Ventura Boulevard, Sherman Oaks, 1-877 4762 7350, www.greencradle.com). The stock here is largely child-oriented, but the

Eat, Drink, Shop

Lisa Kline.

100 N La Cienega Boulevard, Fairfax District, 1-310 854 0658, www.oldnavy.com), **Gap** (1355 Third Street Promenade, Santa Monica, 1-310 393 0719, www.gap.com) and **Banana Republic** (357 N Beverly Drive, Beverly Hills, 1-310 858 7900, www.bananarepublic.com) abound throughout the city. Based in LA, **American Apparel** also has plenty of stores around town, including one in Little Tokyo (327 E 2nd Street, 1-213 687 0467) and the offshoot California Vintage store in Echo Park (2111 W Sunset Boulevard, 1-213 483 8331).

You also won't have to travel too far to find an outpost of **Abercrombie & Fitch**: the west coast flagship is at The Grove (*see p189*; 1-323 954 1500, www.abercrombie.com). Also at The Grove are branches of **Forever 21** (1-323 934 0018, www.forever21.com), which is great for cheap, Top Shop-style clothes and bags; preppy **J Crew** (1-323 939 1070, www.jcrew.com); and **Lucky Brand Jeans** (1-323 965 8332, www.luckybrandjeans.com). One of the four **Diesel** (www.diesel.com) stores in Los Angeles is at the Third Street Promenade in Santa Monica (No. 1340, 1-310 899 3055), where you'll also find funky **Urban Outfitters** (No. 1440, 1-310 394 1404, www.urbanoutfitters.com), the reliable clothes of **American Eagle** (301 Arizona Avenue, 1-310 255 0223, www.ae.com)

and, for well-priced basics, **Zara** (No. 1338, 1-310 458 0892, www.zara.com).

British chains that have found a home and a market in and around LA include upmarket **Reiss** (145 N Robertson Boulevard, 1-310 276 0060, www.reiss.co.uk), mid-market **Jigsaw** (Paseo Colorado, 340 E Colorado Boulevard, Pasadena, 1-626 577 7300, www.jigsaw-london.com) and downmarket **FCUK** (1338 Third Street Promenade, Santa Monica, 1-310 393 4484, www.frenchconnection.com). Swedish brand **H&M** is at the Beverly Center (*see p188*) and at 8580 Sunset Boulevard, West Hollywood (1-310 855 9683, www.hm.com).

For **Kitson**, *see p193* **Kitson Kids**. *See also p195* **It's easy being green** and *p192* **Who's on 3rd?**.

Alpha

8625 Melrose Avenue, at Huntley Drive, West Hollywood (1-310 855 0775/www.alpha-man.com). Bus 4, 105, 220, 305, 550, 704/I-10, exit La Cienega Boulevard north. **Open** 11am-6pm Mon-Sat; noon-5pm Sun. **Credit** AmEx, DC, Disc, MC, V. **Map** p328 A2.

This metrosexual lifestyle store offers clothes from natives such as Band of Outsiders, Nicole Farhi and Travata, plus the necessary grooming products to supplement the lifestyle, including wallets, books, candles, toiletries, jewellery and luggage.

American Rag

150 S La Brea Avenue, between W 1st & W 2nd Street, Fairfax District (1-323 935 3154/www. amrag.com). Bus 14, 16, 212/I-10, exit La Brea Avenue north. **Open** 10am-9pm Mon-Sat; noon-7pm Sun. **Credit** AmEx, DC, MC, V. **Map** p328 D3.

One of the city's largest collections of designer wear in a relaxed, warehouse setting. New clothing covers a huge array of brands for both men and women, along with accessories, shoes and the 'World Denim Bar', but the vintage section is equally browsable. **Other locations** Fashion Island (*see p189*; 1-949 760 1510).

Anthropologie

1402 Third Street Promenade, at Santa Monica Boulevard, Santa Monica (1-310 393 4763/www. anthropologie.com). Bus 4, 20, 704, 720/I-10, exit 4th-5th Street north. **Open** 10am-9pm Mon-Thur; 10am-10pm Fri, Sat; 11am-9pm Sun. **Credit** AmEx, DC, Disc, MC, V. **Map** p326 A3.

Girly gear designed to get you noticed, including pretty dresses, designer jeans, brightly printed handbags, A-line skirts and must-have shoes. **Other locations** throughout LA.

Atmosphere

1728 N Vermont Avenue, at Hollywood Boulevard, Los Feliz (1-323 666 8420/www.atmospherela.com). Metro Vermont-Sunset/bus 4, 156, 204, 754/US 101, exit Vermont Avenue north. **Open** 11am-7pm Mon-Sat; noon-7pm Sun. **Credit** AmEx, DC, Disc, MC, V. **Map** p330 A2.

Label hounds sniff out this store for its regularly updated racks of upmarket clothing by LA-centric designers, such as Unis and John Varvatos.

Blues Jean Bar

1409 Montana Avenue, at 14th Street, Santa Monica (1-310 656 7898/www.bluesjeanbar.com). Bus SM3/I-10, exit Lincoln Boulevard north. **Open** 11am-6pm Mon-Sat; 11am-5pm Sun. **Credit** AmEx, DC, MC, V. **Map** p326 B2.

Struggling to decide on jeans that fit properly? Fret no more. The Blues Jean Bar offers 'denim on tap', whereby customers browse the jeans at the wooden bar and then enlist the services of the 'bartender' to help choose. The 25-plus brands include Chip & Pepper, Earnest Sewn and William Rast.

Curve

154 N Robertson Boulevard, between Beverly Boulevard & Alden Drive, Beverly Hills (1-310 360 8008). Bus 4, 16, 20, 220, 720/I-10, exit Robertson Boulevard north. **Open** 10am-6pm Mon-Sat; noon-6pm Sun. **Credit** AmEx, MC, V. **Map** p328 A3.

Nevena Borissova's spacious boutique stocks a well-chosen mix of classic and funky fashion and accessories by Burberry, Missoni, Valentino and others of a similar ilk.

Fred Segal

8118 Melrose Avenue, between N Crescent Heights Boulevard & N Kilkea Drive, Fairfax District (1-323 651 1935/www.fredsegal.com). Bus 10/I-10, exit

Fairfax Avenue north. **Open** 10am-7pm Mon-Sat; noon-6pm Sun. **Credit** AmEx, DC, MC, V. **Map** p328 C2.

A number of shops under one roof, Fred Segal sells hip casual clothes and expensive designer gear, plus gifts, furniture and beauty goods. It's a great platform for local designers. The Santa Monica branch also has a state-of-the-art spa and a hair salon. **Other locations** 500 Broadway, Santa Monica (1-310 451 7178).

Jill Roberts

417 N Beverly Drive, between S Santa Monica Boulevard & Brighton Way, Beverly Hills (1-310 860 1617/www.jillroberts.com). Bus 4, 16, 20, 720/I-10, exit Robertson Boulevard north. **Open** 10am-6pm Mon-Sat; noon-5pm Sun. **Credit** AmEx, DC, MC, V. **Map** p327 C3.

A who's who of top designers is offered at this Beverly Hills boutique: Philip Lim to Jenni Kayne, See by Chloé to Seaton (Roberts' own line of casual luxury). Clutches, shoes by Sigerson Morrison and beachwear by Melissa Odabash are further draws. **Other locations** 920 Montana Avenue, Santa Monica (1-310 260 1966); 4724 Admiralty Way, Marina del Rey (1-310 821-2300).

Kids Are Alright

2201 W Sunset Boulevard, between Mohawk Street & Rosemont Avenue, Echo Park (1-213 413 4014/ www.thekidsarealright-shop.com). Bus 2, 200, 603/US 101, exit Alvarado Street north. **Open** noon-7pm Mon-Sat; noon-5pm Sun. **Credit** AmEx, DC, MC, V. **Map** p330 D5.

Clothing by lesser-known designers – the likes of Porridge, Hoss Intropia – is displayed in a schoolroom setting, along with jewellery by Sparkling Sage and leather bags. **Other locations** 3405 E Broadway, Long Beach (1-562 433 5890).

Lisa Kline

136 S Robertson Boulevard, between Alden Drive & W 3rd Street, Beverly Hills (1-310 246 0907/www. lisakline.com). Bus 14, 16, 220/I-10, exit Robertson Boulevard north. **Open** 10am-7pm Mon-Sat; 11am-6pm Sun. **Credit** AmEx, DC, MC, V. **Map** p328 A3.

From humble beginnings, Kline's shop has become a major traffic-stopper in an area full of boutiques: Britney Spears, Reese Witherspoon and Jennifer Aniston have all thumbed its racks. The cute kids' shop is at No. 123; the men's store is at No. 143. **Other locations** 3835 Cross Creek Road, Malibu (1-310 317 9170); 11677 San Vicente Boulevard, Brentwood (1-310 820 2300).

Madison

8115 Melrose Avenue, between N Crescent Heights Boulevard & N Kilkea Drive, Fairfax District (1-323 651 3662/www.madisonlosangeles.com). Bus 10/ I-10, exit Fairfax Avenue north. **Open** 11am-7pm Mon-Sat; non-5pm Sun. **Credit** AmEx, DC, MC, V. **Map** p328 C2.

Beloved by the city's style mavens, this store is a treasure trove of designer wear, shoes and bags,

Eat, Drink, Shop

featuring obscure names in among the well-known likes of Chloé, Marc Jacobs and Paul & Joe. Start browsing here and you may never leave. **Other locations** 3835 Cross Creek Road, Malibu (1-310 317 9170); 11677 San Vicente Boulevard, Brentwood (1-310 820 2300).

oOu

1764 N Vermont Avenue, between Kingswell & Melbourne Avenues, Los Feliz (1-323 665 6263). Metro Vermont-Sunset/bus 4, 156, 204, 754/US 101, exit Vermont Avenue north. **Open** noon-7pm Mon-Fri; 11am-7pm Sat; noon-6pm Sun. **Credit** AmEx, DC, Disc, MC, V. **Map** p330 A2.
This oddly named store is a Los Feliz archetype: hip and contemporary, but with one eye on the past. Downstairs, there's a well-chosen range of local and international designers; upstairs holds lower-priced contemporary items, plus a catwalk displaying vintage pieces. The accessories are fabulous, and the owners are constantly seeking out eco-friendly lines.

Planet Blue

2940 Main Street, betwven Pier Avenue & Kinney Street, Santa Monica (1-310 396 1767/www.shop planetblue.com). Bus 33, 333, SM1, SM2, SM8, SM10/I-10, exit 4th-5th Street south. **Open** 10am-7pm Mon-Sat; 10am-6pm Sun. **Credit** AmEx, DC, MC, V. **Map** p326 A4.
West Side fashionistas head here to stock up on rags by the likes of Diane von Furstenburg, James Perse, Cynthia Vincent and True Religion, plus gorgeous bags by Kooba. This branch and the one in Malibu also sell cult toiletries such as Bliss and Kai. **Other locations** 3835 Cross Creek Road, Malibu (1-310 317 9975); 800 14th Street, Santa Monica (1-310 394 0135); 409 N Beverly Drive, Beverly Hills (1-310 385 0557).

Polkadots & Moonbeams

8367 & 8381 W 3rd Street, between S Kings Road & S Orlando Avenue, Fairfax District (Modern 1-323 655 3880/Vintage 1-323 651 1746/www. polkadotsandmoonbeams.com). Bus 16, 105, 218, 220, 316/I-10, exit La Cienega Boulevard north. **Open** 11am-7pm Mon-Sat; 11am-6pm Sun. **Credit** AmEx, DC, MC, V. **Map** p328 B3.
Two stores close to each other: No.8381 sells new designer pieces (Ella Moss, Corey Lynn Calter) and jewellery by Sheila Fajl, while No.8367 has a mix of vintage clothing and new but vintage-inspired items (Trashy Diva dresses, for example).

Show Pony

1543 Echo Park Avenue, at Grafton Street, Echo Park (1-213 482 7676). Bus 2, 4, 302, 304/US 101, exit Echo Park Avenue north. **Open** noon-6pm Wed-Sat; noon-5pm Sun. **Credit** AmEx, DC, Disc, MC, V. **Map** p330 D4.
Show Pony celebrates soon-to-break designers and avant-garde artists; there are parties showcasing their work on the first Saturday of every month. The clothing, a mix of vintage and new, is cutting edge. Some of the designers are right out of school; some of the jewellery is right out of the workshop upstairs.

Theodore

The Grove (p189), Fairfax District (1-323 935 1636). Bus 16, 217, 218, 316, LDF/I-10, exit Fairfax Avenue north. **Open** 10.30am-7pm Mon-Wed; 10.30am-9am Thur-Sat; 11am-7pm Sun. **Credit** AmEx, Disc, MC, V. **Map** p328 C3.
This publicity-shy, celebrity-friendly outlet for avant-garde designers, including names such as Ann Demeulemeester and People of the Labyrinth, also offers sportswear, from Plein Sud to Theory. **Other locations** throughout LA.

Tracey Ross

8595 Sunset Boulevard, between Alta Loma Road & N La Cienega Boulevard, West Hollywood (1-310 854 1996/www.traceyross.com). Bus 2, 105, 302/ I-10, exit La Cienega Boulevard north. **Open** 10am-7pm Mon-Sat; noon-5pm Sun. **Credit** AmEx, DC, MC, V. **Map** p328 B1.
Adored by celebrities and trust fund kids alike, Tracey Ross's boutique is a West Hollywood classic. The A-Z of designer items is carefully done, with prices naturally set to match.

Used & vintage

At **Buffalo Exchange** (131 N La Brea Avenue, Fairfax District, 1-323 938 8604, www.buffalo exchange.com) and **Crossroads Trading Co** (7409 Melrose Avenue, Fairfax District, 1-323 782 8100, www.crossroadstrading.com), gently used clothes are sold at low prices. Each chain has several LA locations.
See also p197 **American Rag** *and above* **Polkadots & Moonbeams**.

Decades

8214½ Melrose Avenue, between N Harper & N La Jolla Avenues, Fairfax District (1-323 655 0223/ www.decadesinc.com). Bus 10/I-10, exit La Cienega Boulevard north. **Open** 11.30am-6pm Mon-Sat. **Credit** AmEx, DC, MC, V. **Map** p328 B2.
America's most glamorous vintage shop boasts couture classics from the 1960s and '70s, chic outfits by the likes of Hermès, Thierry Mugler and Ossie Clark hand-picked by owner Cameron Silver.

It's a Wrap!

3315 W Magnolia Boulevard, at N California Street, Burbank (1-818 567 7366/www.itsawraphollywood. com). Bus 163, 183/I-5, exit Olive Avenue west. **Open** 11am-8pm Mon-Fri; 11am-6pm Sat, Sun. **Credit** DC, Disc, MC, V.
Dress like a star, literally: this massive shop sells clothes worn by actors and actresses in films and TV shows, from sleek designer clothes to absurd *Star Trek* costumes. Prices are decent. **Other locations** 1164 S Robertson Boulevard, Beverly Hills (1-310 246 9727).

Squaresville

1800 N Vermont Avenue, at Melbourne Avenue, Los Feliz (1-323 669 8464). Metro Vermont-Sunset/bus 4, 156, 204, 754/US 101, exit

Vermont Avenue north. **Open** noon-7pm Mon, Sun; 11am-8pm Tue-Sat. **Credit** AmEx, DC, Disc, MC, V. **Map** p330 A2.

A funky selection of old threads is offered at this Los Feliz favourite: some smart, but most casual and agreeably hipster-friendly. Prices are keen.

Fashion accessories & services

Clothing hire

MW Tux

8621 Wilshire Boulevard, between N Stanley Drive & N Carson Road, Beverly Hills (1-310 659 7296/ www.afterhours.com). Bus 20, 105, 220, 720/I-10, exit La Cienega Boulevard north. **Open** 10am-9pm Mon-Fri; 10am-6pm Sat; 11am-6pm Sun. **Credit** AmEx, DC, Disc, MC, V. **Map** p328 B4.

Nominated for an Oscar and forgotten your jacket? Tuxedos are available here for purchase or rental. **Other locations** throughout LA.

One Night Affair

1726 S Sepulveda Boulevard, at Santa Monica Boulevard, West LA (1-310 474 7808/www. onenightaffair.com). Bus 4, 704, C6, SM1/I-405, exit Santa Monica Boulevard east. **Open** by appt only. **Credit** AmEx, DC, Disc, MC, V.

Rent everything from cocktail dresses to wedding gowns, some by Versace and Badgley Mischka.

Cleaning & repairs

Many strip malls in LA have a dry cleaner: you're never far from one.

Brown's Cleaners

1223 Montana Avenue, between 12th & Euclid Streets, Santa Monica (1-310 451 8531). Bus SM3/ I-10, exit Lincoln Boulevard north. **Open** 7am-6pm Mon-Fri; 7am-noon Sat. **Credit** DC, MC, V. **Map** p326 B2.

It's not exactly cheap, but Brown's, run by the same family since 1939, is a classic of its kind, and the service is excellent. As well as dry-cleaning, there's a tailor available to carry out repairs.

Hats

Goorin Brothers

7627 Melrose Avenue, between N Stanley & N Curson Avenues, Fairfax District (1-323 951 0393/ www.goorin.com). Bus 10, 217, 218, LDF/I-10, exit Fairfax Avenue north. **Open** 11am-7pm Mon-Fri; 11am-8pm Sat; 11am-6pm Sun. **Credit** AmEx, DC, MC, V. **Map** p328 C2.

The hats offered by this longstanding San Francisco firm range from the subtly stylish to the overwhelmingly garish. But with everything from pork-pie titfers to fur-lined ear-warmers on offer, there should be something for most tastes.

Jewellery

There's a huge branch of **Tiffany** at 210 N Rodeo Drive (1-310 273 8880, www.tiffany.com).

Arp

8311½ W 3rd Street, between S Sweetzer & S Flores Avenues, Fairfax District (1-323 653 7764). Bus 16, 105, 218, 220, 316/I-10, exit La Cienega Boulevard north. **Open** noon-6pm Mon-Sat; noon-5pm Sun. **Credit** AmEx, DC, MC, V. **Map** p328 B3.

Beautiful pieces of fine jewellery by Ted Muehling and his protégés; names to look out for include Gabriella Kiss, Nicole Landaw and Lola Brooks. Arp also stocks Muehling's housewares.

Me&Ro

8405 Melrose Place, at Melrose Avenue, West Hollywood (1-323 782 1071/www.meandrojewelry. com). Bus 10, 105/I-10, exit La Cienega Boulevard north. **Open** 11am-7pm Mon-Sat; noon-6pm Sun. **Credit** AmEx, DC, MC, V. **Map** p328 B2.

Me&Ro began when dancer Robin Renzi and model Michele Quan threw in their day jobs and began engraving messages in beautiful Sanskrit, Chinese and Tibetan scripts on platinum, silver and gold. Their fans now include Julia Roberts and Meg Ryan.

Moondance Jewelry Gallery

1530 Montana Avenue, between 15th & 16th Streets, Santa Monica (1-310 395 5516/www.moondance jewelry.com). Bus SM3/I-10, exit Lincoln Boulevard north. **Open** 10am-6pm Mon-Sat; 11am-5pm Sun. **Credit** AmEx, DC, MC, V. **Map** p326 C2.

Bold contemporary jewellery, designed by more than 60 artists and supplemented by the occasional vintage piece, is displayed at this gorgeous gallery.

Lingerie & underwear

Nationwide chain **Victoria's Secret** has shops throughout the LA conurbation, including the Beverly Center (*see p188*; 1-310 657 2958, www.victoriassecret.com).

Agent Provocateur

7961 Melrose Avenue, between N Hayworth & N Edinburgh Avenues, Fairfax District (1-323 653 0229/www.agentprovocateur.com). Bus 10, LDF/ I-10, exit Fairfax Avenue north. **Open** 11am-7pm Mon-Sat. **Credit** AmEx, DC, MC, V. **Map** p328 C2.

Thanks to its saucy window displays and huge star following, Brit chain Agent Provocateur has become the most talked-about lingerie retailer in the world. Signature items include half- and quarter-cup bras, sexy corsets, suspenders and slips.

Trashy Lingerie

402 N La Cienega Boulevard, at Oakwood Avenue, West Hollywood (1-310 652 4543/www.trashy.com). Bus 4, 105, 220, 305, 550, 704/I-10, exit La Cienega Boulevard north. **Open** 10am-7pm Mon-Sat; noon-5pm Sun. **Credit** AmEx, DC, MC, V. **Map** p328 B3.

Not for shrinking violets, Trashy is the byword for racy undies and swimwear, with collections entitled School Girl, Ho Down and Burlesque. You have to become a member to shop here, but it's only $2.

Luggage

See also p210 **Travellers' needs**.

Beverly Hills Luggage

404 N Beverly Drive, at Brighton Way, Beverly Hills (1-310 273 5885/www.beverlyhillsluggage.com). Bus 4, 16, 20, 720/I-10, exit Robertson Boulevard north. **Open** 9.30am-6pm Mon-Fri; 9.30am-5.30pm Sat. **Credit** AmEx, DC, MC, V. **Map** p327 C3.
More than 110 years old, this shop sells all major brands of luggage and also offers repairs.

Luggage 4 Less

12011 Wilshire Boulevard, at S Saltair Avenue, West LA (1-310 268 6698/www.luggage4less.com). Bus 20, 720/I-405, exit Wilshire Boulevard west. **Open** 10am-8pm Mon-Fri; 10am-6pm Sat; 11am-6pm Sun. **Credit** AmEx, DC, Disc, MC, V.
Low prices on brand-name luggage.
Other locations 5144 Lankershim Boulevard, North Hollywood (1-818 760 1360); 19701 Ventura Boulevard, Woodland Hills (1-818 774 0212).

Shoes

Offering discounted contemporary styles, **DSW** (7021 Hollywood Boulevard, Hollywood, 1-323 461 0489, www.dsw.com) and **Shoe Pavilion** (7919 Beverly Boulevard, Fairfax District, 1-323 651 4456, www.shoepavilion. com) have stores around LA.

Belle by Sigerson Morrison

9604 Brighton Way, at N Camden Drive, Beverly Hills (1-310 858 1564, www.sigersonmorrison.com). Bus 4, 16, 20, 720/I-10, exit Robertson Boulevard north. **Open** 10am-6pm Mon-Sat; noon-5pm Sun. **Credit** AmEx, DC, Disc, MC, V. **Map** p327 C3.
This is the first dedicated store on the west coast for Belle, the more affordable sister line of Sigerson Morrison (8307 W 3rd Street, 1-323 655 6133). Expect lots of head-turning shoes, boots and bags.

London Sole

1331 Montana Avenue, between Euclid & 14th Streets, Santa Monica (1-310 255 0937/www. londonsole.com). Bus SM3/I-10, exit Lincoln Boulevard north. **Open** 10am-6.30pm Mon-Sat; noon-6pm Sun. **Credit** AmEx, DC, MC, V. **Map** p326 B2.
Classic ballet flats in all colours and designs are sold at this cutesy boutique. There are solid shades, glittery and leopard print pairs, and they're all comfy.

Re-Mix Shoe Company

7605½ Beverly Boulevard, at N Curson Avenue, Fairfax District (1-323 936 6210/www.remixvintage shoes.com). Bus 14, 217, 218/I-10, exit Fairfax Avenue north. **Open** noon-7pm Mon-Sat; noon-5pm Sun. **Credit** AmEx, DC, Disc, MC, V. **Map** p328 C3.

Galco's Old World Grocery. *See p202.*

Despite its URL, not everything at Re-Mix is old: besides the rows of vintage shoes is its own brand of retro creations, from wingtips to slingbacks.

Undefeated

2654B Main Street, between Ocean Park Boulevard & Hill Street, Santa Monica (1-310 399 4195/ www.undftd.com). Bus 33, 333, SM1, SM2, SM8, SM10/I-10, exit 4th-5th Street south. **Open** 11am-7pm Mon-Sat; 10am-4pm Sun. **Credit** AmEx, DC, MC, V. **Map** p326 A4.
An über-cool hangout for sneaker geeks, Undefeated stocks limited editions from the likes of Vans and Nike, along with its own clothing. Fans should also try Waraku down in Venice (1225 Abbot Kinney Boulevard, 1-310 452 5300, www.warakuusa.com). **Other locations** 112 S La Brea Avenue, Fairfax District (1-323 937 6077); 3827 W Sunset Boulevard, Silver Lake (1-323 668 1315).

Food & drink

Bakeries

See also pp170-174 **Coffeehouses**, especially the excellent **Susina Bakery**.

Boule

413 N Bedford Drive, at Brighton Way, Beverly Hills (1-310 273 4488/www.boulela.com). Bus 4, 16, 20, 720/I-10, exit Robertson Boulevard north. **Open** 9am-6pm Mon-Fri; 10am-6pm Sat; noon-5pm Sun. **Credit** AmEx, DC, Disc, MC, V. **Map** p327 C3.

A little piece of Paris in Beverly Hills, David Myers' pâtisserie will have you torn between cakes, viennoiserie and pastries – not to mention ice-creams and sorbets when it's sweltering outside. Intelligentsia coffees and Mariage Frères teas add appeal; there are also gourmet goodies to take away.
Other locations 408 N La Cienega Boulevard, West Hollywood (1-310 289 9977).

La Brea Bakery

624 S La Brea Avenue, between W 6th Street & Wilshire Boulevard, Miracle Mile (1-323 939 6813, www.labreabakery.com). Bus 20, 212/I-10, exit La Brea Avenue north. **Open** 7.30am-6pm Mon-Sat; 8am-4pm Sun. **Credit** AmEx, DC, Disc, MC, V. **Map** p328 D4.

Nancy Silverton is credited with single-handedly introducing Angelenos to the joys of the fresh, flavoursome loaf. In the two decades since her store opened, she's become a household name and her store has grown into an international operation, supplying restaurants such as Campanile. At the original store, dough reigns supreme – along with tarts, pastries and sandwiches.

Maison du Pain

5373 W Pico Boulevard, between S Ridgeley Drive & S Burnside Avenue, Midtown (1-323 934 5858/www.lamaisondupainla.com). Bus SM5, SM7, SM13/I-10, exit Fairfax Avenue north. **Open** 8am-6pm Mon-Sat. **Credit** AmEx, DC, Disc, MC, V. **Map** p329 A6.

It's hard to believe that two Filipino sisters with no baking experience opened this lovely café in 2005.

They set their sights high, remortgaging their properties in order to fly in kitchen equipment and a young chef from France. The result? The best croissants and cinnamon rolls in the city.

SusieCakes

11708 San Vicente Boulevard, at S Barrington Avenue, Brentwood (1-310 442 2253/www.susie cakesla.com). Bus 20, 720, SM2, SM4/I-10, exit Bundy Drive north. **Open** 10am-7pm Mon-Sat. **Credit** AmEx, DC, Disc, MC, V.

Frosting-filled cupcakes are the order of the day at this self-styled 'all-American home-style bake shop', opened in 2006 by Susan Sarich to showcase her grandmother's recipes. Don't miss the whoopie pies or the banana pudding.
Other locations 2043 Westcliffe Drive, Newport Beach (1-949 646 6881).

Drinks

Du Vin

540 N San Vicente Boulevard, at Rangely Avenue, West Hollywood (1-310 855 1161/www.du-vin.net). Bus 4, 105, 220, 305, 550, 704/I-10, exit La Cienega Boulevard north. **Open** 10am-7pm Mon-Sat. **Credit** AmEx, DC, Disc, MC, V. **Map** p328 A2.

The cobblestone courtyard entrance to Du Vin is more Europe than LA; inside, it's more wine cellar than shop. Californian, Italian and French wines are supplemented by spirits, beers and accessories.

Galco's Old World Grocery

5702 York Boulevard, at N Avenue 57, Highland Park (1-323 255 7115/www.sodapopstop.com). Metro Highland Park/bus 83/I-110, exit Avenue 52 north. **Open** 9am-6.30pm Mon-Sat; 9am-4pm Sun. **Credit** DC, MC, V.

This extraordinary store stocks every kind of soda under the sun. And we mean *every* kind: colas and cherry limeades, sasparillas and root beers, 500 varieties in total. And that's not all: you'll also find a similarly wild variety of candies, plus one of the best beer selections in LA and even a deli counter serving knockout sandwiches. Awesome. *Photo p201.*

Silverlake Wine

2395 Glendale Boulevard, at Brier Avenue, Silver Lake (1-323 662 9024/www.silverlakewine.com). Bus 92/US 101, exit Glendale Boulevard north. **Open** 11am-9pm Mon-Wed, Sun; 11am-10pm Thur; Fri; 10am-10pm Sat.* **Credit** AmEx, DC, Disc, MC, V. **Map** p330 D2.

The owners of this store take pleasure in making their favourite artisanal wines known to customers. Tastings are held three times a week, and boutique beers and sakés round out the careful selection.

General

Supermarket chains include **Ralphs** (www.ralphs.com), **Vons** (www.vons.com) and **Albertsons** (www.albertsons.com). **Trader**

A+R. *See p204.*

Joe's (www.traderjoes.com) is good for gourmet and organic foods, as are the various branches of **Whole Foods Market** (www.wholefoodsmarket.com).

Markets

From Leimert Park to Little Tokyo, Los Angeles is dotted with farmers' markets, at which local producers sell fresh fare (some of it organic) directly to shoppers. But the goods on offer are not limited to just fruit and vegetables, alongside the farmers you'll find other retailers selling flowers, fresh juices, coffee, hot food and knick-knacks.

There are farmers' markets in **West Hollywood** (9am-2pm Mon at Plummer Park, N Vista Street & Fountain Avenue), **Beverly Hills** (9am-1pm Sun at 9300 block of Civic Center Drive), **Hollywood** (8am-1pm Sun at Ivar & Selma Avenues) and **Downtown** (10am-4pm Thur-Sat at 7th & Figueroa Streets; 10am-2pm at City Hall). **Santa Monica** has four: on Wednesday at Arizona Avenue & 3rd Street (9am-2pm); on Saturday at Arizona & 3rd Street (8.30am-1pm) and at Virginia Park (corner of Pico & Cloverfield Boulevards, 8am-1pm); and on Sunday at Main Street & Ocean Park Boulevard (9.30am-1pm). For others, see www.farmernet.com.

The numerous stalls at the **Grand Central Market** in Downtown LA (Broadway, between W 3rd & W 4th Streets, 1-213 624 2378, www.grandcentralsquare.com) offer fruit, veg, meat, fish, herbs, spices and flowers. Here since 1917, it's still open daily, and a visit is a lively way to pass a couple of hours.

Specialist

In addition to the stores listed below, **Joan's on Third** (see p192) offers a wide range of gourmet dry goods.

Cheesestore of Silverlake

3926 W Sunset Boulevard, between Hyperion & Sanborn Avenues, Silver Lake (1-323 644 7511/ www.cheesestoresl.com). Bus 2, 4, 302, 704/US 101, exit Silver Lake Boulevard north. **Open** 10am-6.30pm Mon-Sat; 11am-5am Sun. **Credit** AmEx, DC, Disc, MC, V. **Map** p330 B3.
To go with the fromage from cows, sheep and goats, there's an impressive array of epicurean treats: chocolates, cured meats, olives and teas, for example. A delightful shop.

Erewhon Natural Foods Market

7660 Beverly Boulevard, at The Grove Drive, Fairfax District (1-323 937 0777/www.erewhonmarket.com). Bus 14, 714/I-10, exit Fairfax Avenue north. **Open** 8am-10pm Mon-Sat; 9am-9pm Sun. **Credit** AmEx, DC, Disc, MC, V. **Map** p326 C3.

The best organic supermarket in town sells a range of produce, natural remedies, cosmetics and toiletries. The excellent food counters feature salads, soups, sushi, deli items, fresh juices and coffee.

K Chocolatier/Diane Krön

9606 Little Santa Monica Boulevard, at N Camden Drive, Beverly Hills (1-310 248 2626/www.diane kronchocolates.com). Bus 4, 16, 20, 720/I-10, exit Robertson Boulevard north. **Open** 10am-6pm Mon-Sat; 11am-5pm Sun. **Credit** AmEx, DC, Disc, MC, V. **Map** p327 C3.
The K Sensual line of chocolates is designed to increase your libido, but the more straightforward ranges of truffles and chocolates are just as seductive. Don't miss the signature chocolate teddy bears. **Other locations** 3835 Cross Creek Road, Malibu (1-310 317 0400).

Market Gourmet

1800A Abbot Kinney Boulevard, between Venice Boulevard & Victoria Avenue, Venice (1-877 662 7538/www.marketgourmet.biz). Bus 33, 333, SM1, SM2/I-10, exit 4th-5th Street south. **Open** 9am-7pm Mon-Fri; 10am-7pm Sat; noon-6pm Sun. **Credit** AmEx, DC, Disc, MC, V. **Map** p326 B6.
The shelves of this emporium are full of fine foods from all over the world. If you're unsure about a particular delicacy, the friendly staff may even open it and give you a taste.

Petrossian Paris

321 N Robertson Boulevard, at Beverly Boulevard, West Hollywood (1-310 271 0576/www.petrossian. com). Bus 14, 16, 220/I-10, exit Robertson Boulevard north. **Open** 10am-6pm Mon-Thur 10am-8pm Sat. **Credit** AmEx, DC, Disc, MC, V. **Map** p326 A3.
A French-owned and -run resource for delights beloved by Francophiles: caviar, truffles, smoked salmon and so on. There's also a charming café, and a refreshing lack of pretension throughout.

Surfas

8777 W Washington Boulevard, at National Boulevard, Culver City (1-310 559 4770/www. surfasonline.com). Bus 33, 220, 333, C1/I-10, exit Robertson Boulevard south. **Open** 9am-6.30pm Mon-Sat; 11am-5pm Sun. **Credit** AmEx, DC, MC, V.
This family-run business, a huge gourmet food and restaurant supply emporium, celebrated its 70th birthday in 2007, which makes it virtually prehistoric by LA standards. The food is as fresh and tasty as ever, and there's an upmarket café attached.

Gifts & souvenirs

Museum shops are good for gifts. Try the **Craft & Folk Art Museum** (see p99), the **Getty Center** (see p84), the **Getty Villa** (see p75), the **Japanese American National Museum** (see p113), **LACMA** (see p100) and **MoCA** (see p116). You'll also find souvenirs on Hollywood Boulevard and the Venice Boardwalk. See also p204 **Take a letter** and p192 **Who's on 3rd?**.

Eat, Drink, Shop

A+R

1716 Silver Lake Boulevard, at Effie Street, Silver Lake (1-323 913 9558/www.aplusrstore.com). Bus 201/US 101, exit Silver Lake Boulevard north. **Open** noon-6pm Thur-Sun. **Credit** AmEx, DC, Disc, MC, V. **Map** p330 C3.

Run by and named after British expat Andy Griffith and LA style journalist Rose Apodaca, A+R offers a super-fresh selection of desirable designer goodies: mostly homewares, alongside a few other gift ideas (books, artworks and other chic novelties). Goods are sourced from around the world, making it a good place to find something unusual. The Venice branch is open every day except Monday. *Photo p202.* **Other locations** 1121 Abbot Kinney Boulevard, Venice (1-310 392 9128).

Clover

2756 Rowena Avenue, at Glendale Boulevard, Silver Lake (1-323 661 4142/www.cloversilverlake.com). Bus 92/I-5, exit Glendale Boulevard south. **Open** 10am-7pm Mon-Sat; noon-6pm Sun. **Credit** AmEx, DC, MC, V. **Map** p330 D2.

This Silver Lake favourite is packed with a lovely selection of goodies: clothes and bags, lotions and candles, green teas and household trinkets. There's a little something for everyone here.

Farmacia y Botánica Million Dollar

301 S Broadway, at W 3rd Street, Downtown (1-213 687 3688). Metro Pershing Square/bus 2, 4, 30, 31, 40, 42, 45, 48/I-110, exit 3rd Street east. **Open** 9am-6pm daily. **No credit cards**. **Map** p331 C3.

When witch doctors (*santeros*) go shopping, they head to this *botánica*, which has all the herbs and ingredients they need to make their potions. There's lots of DIY hocus pocus, too: love potions, bath oil that quells gossip, medallions to protect children.

Firefly

1413 Abbot Kinney Boulevard, at California Avenue, Venice (1-310 450 6288/www.shopfirefly.com). Bus 33, 333, SM1, SM2/I-10, exit 4th-5th Street south. **Open** 11am-7pm Mon-Sat; 11am-5pm Sun. **Credit** AmEx, DC, MC, V. **Map** p326 A6.

Take a letter

With Blackberrys in one hand and Macbooks in the other, Angelenos are truly wedded to their technology. Still, even in this tech-savvy city, there are times when a Valentine's Day SMS or an 'It's a boy!!!' email announcement just won't cut the mustard, which is where the city's stationery specialists can help.

South of Hollywood on the edge of Hancock Park, **Pulp** (452 S La Brea Avenue, 1-323 937 3505) supplements its dizzying selection of cards with hand-made, hand-printed and even hand-embroidered papers imported from India, as suitable for framing as they are for gift-wrapping. While you're here, pick up a

Fortune Folio, a die-cut method to preserve your fortune cookie prophesies.

For eco-friendly paper, follow stylish brides-to-be to West Hollywood's **Soolip Paperie & Press** (8646 Melrose Avenue, 1-310 360 0545, www.soolip.com). Loyal locals stock up on the shop's signature tree-free paper (made from cotton remnants) and opulent Japanese Yuzen silkscreens; glass pens and floral-scented inks are for special occasions.

Offering a more traditional take on the art of letter-writing, **Embrey Papers** in Brentwood (11965 San Vicente Boulevard, 1-310 440 2620, www.embreypapers.com) sells elegant

Soolip Paperie & Press.

One of the most charming shops on Abbot Kinney, Firefly offers a catch-all selection of gifts for more or less every occasion (assuming, that is, that you're not buying for a guy): a few clothes, some books, plenty for the bathroom and a nice selection of cards.

Pleasure Chest

7733 Santa Monica Boulevard, at N Genesee Avenue, West Hollywood (1-310 860 9009/www.the pleasurechest.com). Bus 4, 217, 218, 304/I-10, exit Fairfax Avenue north. **Open** 10am-midnight Mon-Wed, Sun; 10am-1am Thur-Sat. **Credit** AmEx, DC, MC, V. **Map** p328 C2.

Vibrators, dildos and all kinds of other things both unmentionable and unimaginable are offered at this longstanding emporium of sauciness.

Skeletons in the Closet

LA County Coroner, 1104 N Mission Road, at Marengo Street, Downtown (1-323 343 0760/ http://lacstores.co.la.ca.us/coroner). I-5, exit E César E Chávez Avenue west. **Open** 8.30am-4.30pm Mon-Fri. **No credit cards.**

brands such as Crane & Co and Vera Wang in a warm, almost library-like setting. Over in Beverly Hills, **William Ernest Brown Paperie** (340 N Beverly Hills Drive, 1-310 278 5620) is the only authorised Cartier personalised-album dealer in the world.

Finally, don't miss Venice's shoebox-sized **Urbanic Paper Boutique** (1644 Abbot Kinney Boulevard, 1-310 401 0427), which stocks a carefully edited selection of letterpress cards and striking gift wrap. There's also a collection of cheeky folders and Post-Its that should liven up any office space.

Gallows humour meets capitalism at this bizarre coroner's department shop. Gifts, 'to die or kill for', include beach towels, doormats and T-shirts emblazoned with corpse outlines.

Soap Plant/Wacko

4633 Hollywood Boulevard, at N Vermont Avenue, Los Feliz (1-323 663 0122/www.soapplant.com). Metro Vermont-Sunset/bus 4, 156, 204, 754/US 101, exit Vermont Avenue north. **Open** 11am-7pm Mon-Wed; 11am-9pm Thur-Sat; noon-6pm Sun. **Credit** AmEx, DC, MC, V. **Map** p330 A2.

This Los Feliz building houses a trio of zany enterprises: two stores, Soap Plant and Wacko, and a gallery, La Luz de Jesus (*see p239*). The stock – tchotchkes, artworks and stocking-stuffers – is a mix of the kitsch, the silly and the just plain bizarre.

Health & beauty

Hairdressers and spas are everywhere in LA; as are nail salons, which don't usually require clients to have made an appointment.

Hairdressers & barbers

Argyle Salon & Spa

Sunset Tower, 8358 Sunset Boulevard, at N Sweetzer Avenue, West Hollywood (1-310 623 9000/www.argylela.com). Bus 2, 302, LDHWH/ I-10, exit La Cienega Boulevard north. **Open** 9am-7pm Tue; 9am-8pm Wed; 9am-9pm Thur-Sat; 10am-7pm Sun. **Credit** AmEx, DC, Disc, MC, V. **Map** p328 B1.

The spa at the Sunset Tower Hotel (*see p61*) offers a full menu of facials, massages and more, but the real reason to visit is the hairdressing. Among the talent on offer is Mauricio: he's famed for his 'Brazilian blowout', designed to leave the frizziest of barnets smooth for weeks. For colour, see Suzy or JJ.

Rudy's Barber Shop

4451 W Sunset Boulevard, at Hollywood Boulevard, Los Feliz (1-323 661 6535/www.rudysbarbershop. com). Metro Vermont-Sunset/bus 2, 4, 26, 302, 704/I-10, exit Vermont Avenue north. **Open** 9am-9pm Mon-Sat; 11am-7pm Sun. **Credit** AmEx, DC, Disc, MC, V. **Map** p330 B3.

Formerly a garage, this salon is now one of the hippest places in LA to get coiffed. Check out the art on the walls while you're being shorn. Rudy's has salons in both Standard hotels (*see p60* and *p63*). **Other locations** throughout LA.

Sol Salon

10115 Washington Boulevard, between Clarington & Jasmine Avenues, Culver City (1-310 836 9166). Bus 33, 220, 333, C1/I-10, exit Robertson Boulevard south. **Open** 9am-7pm Tue-Fri; 9am-5pm Sat. **Credit** DC, MC, V.

At this excellent salon, staff can handle anything from a simple trim to a total overhaul. The prices are low ($50 for a women's cut); as a result, it's very popular, but try to book Cynthia if you can.

Eat, Drink, Shop

Opticians

There are several branches of **Sunglass Hut** in LA, including one at the Beverly Center (*see p188*; 1-310 652 4012, www.sunglasshut.com). You'll find treet vendors hawking cheap shades all over the city; Venice Boardwalk and Downtown's Fashion District both offer a good variety.

LA Eyeworks

7407 Melrose Avenue, at N Martel Avenue, Fairfax District (1-323 653 8255/www.laeyeworks.com). Bus 10/I-10, exit Fairfax Avenue north. **Open** 10am-7pm Mon-Sat. **Credit** AmEx, DC, Disc, MC, V. **Map** p328 D2.
The frames at LA Eyeworks, a local favourite for years, are so hip that people with 20/20 vision have been known to wear them.
Other locations 7386 Beverly Boulevard, Fairfax District (1-323 931 7795); South Coast Plaza 1010, 3333 Bristol Street, Costa Mesa

Oliver Peoples

8642 W Sunset Boulevard, between Sunset Plaza & N Sherbourne Drives, West Hollywood (1-310 657 2553/www.oliverpeoples.com). Bus 2, 105, 302, 705/I-10, exit La Cienega Boulevard north. **Open** 10am-7pm Mon-Fri; 10am-6pm Sun.
Credit AmEx, DC, MC, V. **Map** p328 A1.
Oliver Peoples' fab retro-style sunglasses have been spotted on everyone from Angelina Jolie to Kate Moss. The friendly staff can also help you select prescription glasses.
Other locations 3900 Cross Creek Road, Malibu (1-310 456 1333); South Coast Plaza (*see p190*; 1-714 557 7000).

Pharmacies

There are branches of **Rite Aid** (1130 N La Brea Avenue, West Hollywood, 1-323 463 8539, www.riteaid.com), **Walgreens** (8770 W Pico Boulevard, Beverly Hills, 1-310 275 2117, www.walgreens.com) and **CVS** (8491 W Santa Monica Boulevard, West Hollywood, 1-310 360 7303, www.cvs.com) across LA.

Shops

Excellent national chain **Sephora** has several branches in LA, including one at the Beverly Center (*see p188*; 1-310 657 9670). Beauty-supply stores are everywhere in LA, many offering discounted name brands.

Fresh

1407 Third Street Promenade, at Santa Monica Boulevard, Santa Monica (1-310 451 0302/www. fresh.com). Bus 4, 20, 704, 720/I-10, exit 4th-5th Street north. **Open** 10am-9pm Mon-Thur; 10am-10pm Fri, Sat; 11am-8pm Sun. **Credit** AmEx, DC, MC, V. **Map** p326 A3.

The yummy-smelling products from this Boston-based company come with unexpected ingredients – soy, sugar, milk, vanilla – and unlikely perfume combinations such as cannabis rose. The make-up palettes are also cute.
Other locations The Grove (*see p189*; 1-323 932 2580); South Coast Plaza (*see p190*; 1-714 549 7086).

Larchmont Beauty Center

208 N Larchmont Boulevard, between Beverly Boulevard & W 1st Street, Hancock Park (1-323 461 0162/www.larchmontbeauty.com). Bus 14, 210, 710/I-10, exit La Brea Avenue north. **Open** 8.30am-8pm Mon-Sat; 10.30am-6pm Sun. **Credit** AmEx, DC, Disc, MC, V. **Map** p329 B3.
This small local operation sells all manner of prettifying products (skincare, haircare, makeup) from high-end brands such as Decléor, Dr Hauschka, Fresh, JF Lazartigue and Shiseido.

Lather

17 E Colorado Boulevard, at N Fair Oaks Avenue, Pasadena (1-626 396 9636/www.lather.com). Metro Memorial Park/bus 180, 181, 260, 361/Hwy 110 to Pasadena (hwy ends at Colorado Boulevard). **Open** 11am-9pm Mon-Thur; 11am-10pm Fri, Sat; 11am-7pm Sun. **Credit** AmEx, DC, MC, V.
A clinical-looking place (we mean that in a good way), Lather sells face, body and hair products that eschew synthetic fragrances and colours in favour of natural ingredients such as cranberry, lemon-grass and grapefruit.

Strange Invisible Perfumes

1138 Abbot Kinney Boulevard, at San Juan Avenue, Venice (1-310 314 1505/www.siperfumes.com). Bus 33, 333, SM1, SM2/I-10, exit 4th-5th Street south. **Open** 11am-7pm Tue-Sat; noon-6pm Sun. **Credit** AmEx, DC, Disc, MC, V. **Map** p326 A5.
Alexandra Balahoutis weaves arcane stories into her unique line of handmade organic perfumes, with essences gathered from around the world. Her serene store now also stocks natural products from This Works, Saipua, 100% Pure and Aqua Dessa.

Spas & salons

For **Fred Segal**, *see p197*; for the **Argyle Salon & Spa**, *see p205*; for the **Beauty Bar**, *see p180*. And for a round-up of the best hotel spas, *see p53* **Spa for a day**.

Burke Williams

8000 W Sunset Boulevard, at N Crescent Heights Boulevard, West Hollywood (1-323 822 9007/www. burkewilliamsspa.com). Bus 2, 218, 302/I-10, exit Fairfax Avenue north. **Open** 9am-10pm Mon-Fri; 8am-10apm Sat, Sun. **Credit** AmEx, DC, Disc, MC, V. **Map** p328 C1.
Treatments to uplift your body and spirit, from manicures to exotic herbal wraps. Create your own simple rejuvenation package: warm up in the jacuzzi, cool down in the plunge pool, detox in the sauna.
Other locations throughout LA.

Face Place

8701 Santa Monica Boulevard, at Westbourne Drive, West Hollywood (1-310 855 1150/www.sallyhersh bergerfaceplace.com). Bus 2, 105, 302, 705/I-10, exit La Cienega Boulevard north. **Open** 8.30am-7pm Tue, Wed; 8.30am-5.30pm Thur-Sat. **Credit** AmEx, DC, Disc, MC, V. **Map** p328 B1.

Founded in 1972, the Face Place was one of the first salons in LA to use galvanic current and vitamin C in its results-oriented facial (they offer only one type). Hairdresser-to-the-stars Sally Hershberger, a longtime client, recently launched a skincare line in collaboration with the salon. Great for problem skin.

Kate Somerville

8428 Melrose Place, between N Croft Avenue & N Alfred Street, West Hollywood (1-323 655 7546/ www.katesomerville.com). Bus 10, 105/I-10, exit La Cienega Boulevard north. **Open** 10am-7pm Mon-Sat. **Credit** AmEx, DC, Disc, MC, V. **Map** p328 B2.

Somerville's facials are consistently voted the best in LA. At her expanded salon, luxurious potions and modern equipment combine to ensure great results. The aestheticians are as skilled as they are charming; clients include Debra Messing and Paris Hilton. If you can't make it, you can pick up the products at Nordstrom (*see p188*) and Neiman Marcus (*see p187*).

Ole Henriksen

8622A W Sunset Boulevard, at Sunset Plaza Drive, West Hollywood (1-310 854 7700/www.olehenriksen. com). Bus 2, 105, 302, 705/I-10, exit La Cienega Boulevard north. **Open** 8.30am-5pm Mon; 8am-8pm Tue-Sat; 9.30am-4.30pm Sun. **Credit** AmEx, DC, MC, V. **Map** p328 B1.

Danish-born Henriksen has been making faces glow and bodies gleam for three decades. The spa is a Zen-style retreat, where you can sip green tea as you soak in a candlelit hydrotherapy tub. A magnet for Hollywood stars and ordinary hipsters.

Paint Shop

319½ S Robertson Boulevard, between Olympic Boulevard & Gregory Way, Beverly Hills (1-310 652 5563/www.paintshopbeverlyhills.com). Bus 28, 220/ I-10, exit Robertson Boulevard north. **Open** 10am-6pm Wed, Fri; 10am-7pm Thur, Fri; 9am-6pm Sat; 10am-5pm Sun. **Credit** AmEx, DC, MC, V. **Map** p328 A4.

Another popular spot with celebs, this funky, down-to-earth place isn't just an ordinary nail shop. The menu of services includes the must-have, tequila-themed 'Ritas & rocks' pedicure.

Skin Haven Spa Studio

300 N Crescent Heights Boulevard, at Beverly Boulevard, Fairfax District (1-323 658 7546/www. skinhaven.com). Bus 14/I-10, exit Fairfax Avenue north. **Open** 11.30am-8.30pm Mon, Tue, Thur; 10am-5.30pm Fri; 10am-7pm Sat, Sun. **Credit** AmEx, DC, MC, V. **Map** p328 C3.

This spa is loved by its devotees as much for its massages as for its facials. It's also one of the few places that offer manicures and pedicures that use non-toxic varnishes. Look out for the internet specials.

La Vie L'Orange

638½ N Robertson Boulevard, between Melrose Avenue & Santa Monica Boulevard, West Hollywood (1-310 289 2501/www.lavielorange.com). Bus 4, 105, 220, 305, 550, 704/I-10, exit La Cienega Boulevard north. **Open** 10am-6pm Tue; 10am-9pm Wed, Thur; 10am-8pm Fri; 9am-7pm Sat; 10am-7pm Sun. **Credit** AmEx, DC, MC, V. **Map** p328 A2.

This is one of the city's most luxurious nail spas. Settle back, with a glass of wine or juice by your side, and enjoy one of the myriad manicures and pedicures that are on offer.

Tattoos & piercings

Zulu Tattoo

165 S Crescent Heights Boulevard, between W 1st & W 3rd Streets, Fairfax District (1-323 782 9977/ www.zulutattoo.com). Bus 14, 16/I-10, exit Fairfax Avenue north. **Open** 11am-7pm Mon-Sat; noon-7pm Sun. **Credit** AmEx, DC, Disc, MC, V. **Map** p328 C3.

Zulu offers high-quality tattoo work using organic inks, with professional, friendly service to boot. For eye-catching Polynesian designs, Afa is your man. However, if you want to go home with a permanent souvenir of Los Angeles, you'll need to book an appointment well in advance.

House & home

Antiques

Most of LA's good antique shops are located in West Hollywood, along Robertson and Beverly Boulevards and La Brea Avenue. It's also worth looking near the **Pacific Design Center** (at 8687 Melrose Avenue, West Hollywood, www.pacificdesigncenter.com); on W 3rd Street, east of La Cienega Boulevard (*see p192*); and on Echo Park's **Antique Row**, on the 2200 block of W Sunset Boulevard. The **Pasadena Antique Center & Annex** (444 & 480 S Fair Oaks Avenue, Pasadena, 1-626 449 7706, www.pasadenaantiquecenter.com) hosts around 100 dealers, who set up shop daily.

Several markets merit mention. The biggest is the **Long Beach Outdoor Antique & Collectible Market** (Long Beach Veterans Memorial Stadium, Clark Avenue & E Conant Street, 1-562 655 5703, www.longbeachantique market.com), on the third Sunday of the month from 5.30am. The **Santa Monica Antique & Collectible Market** is held at Santa Monica Airport on the first & fourth Sunday of the month (1-323 933 2511, www.santamonica airportantiquemarket.com). And both the **Pasadena Flea Market** (at the Rose Bowl, 8am-4pm on the first Sunday of the month) & **Fairfax Senior High School Flea Market** (7850 Melrose Avenue, Fairfax District; 8am-3pm every Sunday) also offer bargains.

Blackman Cruz

836 N Highland Avenue, between Waring & Willoughby Avenues, Hollywood (1-310 657 9228/ www.blackmancruz.com). Bus 14, 714/US 101, exit Melrose Avenue west. **Open** 10am-6pm Mon-Fri; noon-5pm Sat. **Credit** AmEx, DC, Disc, MC, V. **Map** p329 A3.

Blackman Cruz moved to these new premises in 2008, but has retained its attachment to rare and peculiar antiques: expect to find all manner of odd furniture, lights and other trinkets.

Liz's Antique Hardware

453 S La Brea Avenue, between W 4th & W 6th Streets, Miracle Mile (1-323 939 4403/www.lahard ware.com). Bus 20, 212/I-10, exit La Brea Avenue north. **Open** 10am-6pm Mon-Sat. **Credit** AmEx, DC, MC, V. **Map** p328 D4.

With more than a million pieces of hardware for doors, windows and furniture in stock, you're sure to find the right vintage handle here. The stock also includes some contemporary wares.

General

See also p195 **It's easy being green** *and p204* **A+R**.

HD Buttercup

3225 Helms Avenue, at Venice Boulevard, Culver City (1-310 558 8900/www.hdbuttercup.com). Bus 33, 220, 333, C1/I-10, exit Robertson Boulevard south. **Open** 10am-7pm Mon-Sat; 11am-6pm Sun. **Credit** AmEx, DC, Disc, MC, V.

The old Helms Bakery in Culver City is now filled with around 15 homewares and design stores, which sell everything from rugs to ceiling fans. Selling goods from more than 50 different manufacturers, HD Buttercup is perhaps the most interesting of the lot; for others, see www.helmsbakerydistrict.com.

Jonathan Adler

8125 Melrose Avenue, at N Kilkea Drive, Fairfax District (1-323 658 8390/www.jonathanadler.com). Bus 10/I-10, exit Fairfax Avenue north. **Open** 10am-6pm Mon-Sat; noon-6pm Sun. **Credit** AmEx, DC, Disc, MC, V. **Map** p328 C2.

Coolly creative pottery, pillows, rugs, chairs, bedding, light and table-top items from the legendary ceramicist turned all-round design guru.

OK

8303 W 3rd Street, at S Sweetzer Avenue, Fairfax District (1-323 653 3501/www.okstore.la). Bus 16, 105, 218, 220, 316/I-10, exit La Cienega Boulevard north. **Open** 11am-6.30pm Mon-Sat; noon-6pm Sun. **Credit** AmEx, DC, Disc, MC, V. **Map** p328 B3.

This store sells beautifully crafted wares: glassware, tableware, jewellery and *noguchi* paper lamps, as well as books on art, architecture and fashion.

Yolk

1626 Silver Lake Boulevard, between Effie Street & Berkeley Avenue, Silver Lake (1-323 660 4315/www. yolk-la.com). Bus 2, 4, 302, 704/US 101, exit Silver

Lake Boulevard north. **Open** 11am-7pm Tue-Fri; 10am-7pm Sat; noon-5pm Sun. **Credit** AmEx, DC, MC, V. **Map** p330 C3.

'Free Range Design' is the tagline at this colourful shop in Silver Lake, at which the products are sourced from around the world. Expect fresh, modern ideas for the home, along with children's furniture and accessories.

Specialist

Surfing Cowboys

1624 Abbot Kinney Boulevard, at N Venice Boulevard, Venice (1-310 450 4891/www.surfing cowboys.com). Bus 33, 333, SM1, SM2/I-10, exit 4th-5th Street south. **Open** Mon by appt only; 11am-7pm Tue-Sat; 11am-6pm Sun. **Credit** AmEx, DC, MC, V. **Map** p326 A6.

Donna and Wayne Gunthers' California-inspired collection of mid-century pieces and collectables covers everything from posters to chaises longues, with surfboards a particular strong point. Jewellery includes eye-catching one-offs by local designers such as Lou Zeldis. Great for browsers.

Tortoise

1208 Abbot Kinney Boulevard, between San Juan & California Avenues, Venice (1-310 314 8448/www. tortoiselife.com). Bus 33, 333, SM1, SM2/I-10, exit 4th-5th Street south. **Open** noon-6pm Wed-Sun or by appt. **Credit** DC, MC, V. **Map** p326 A5.

Eat, Drink, Shop

A symbol of longevity in Japan, the tortoise is the theme for this lovely little store that showcases traditional Japanese crafts and items designed to last. The stock normally includes cast-iron ornaments and recycled glassware. There's a sister store just down the road (No.1342, 1-310 396 7335).

Music & entertainment

CDs & records

As well as the shops below, there's a **Virgin Megastore** in the Hollywood & Highland mall (1-323 769 8520, www.virgin.com). Those in the market for electronica should investigate **Turntable Lab** (424 N Fairfax Avenue, 1-323 782 0173, www.turntablelab.com); hip hop fans should turn to **Fat Beats** (7600 Melrose Avenue, 1-323 655 8997, www.fatbeats.com).

Amoeba Music

6400 W Sunset Boulevard, at N Cahuenga Boulevard, Hollywood (1-323 245 6400/www. amoebamusic.com). Metro Hollywood-Vine/bus 2, 302/US 101, exit Sunset Boulevard west. **Open** 10.30am-11pm Mon-Sat; 11am-9pm Sun. **Credit** DC, Disc, MC, V. **Map** p329 B2.

While the longstanding likes of Rhino in Westwood and House of Records in Venice have fallen by the wayside, the LA branch of SF's Amoeba has gone from strength to strength; indeed, this is the largest independent record store in the US. The variety of stock (CDs and DVDs, new and used) is awesome, the prices are fair and the staff know their onions.

Fingerprints

4612 E 2nd Street, at Roycroft Avenue, Long Beach (1-562 433 4996/www.fingerprintsmusic.com). I-405, exit 7th Street west. **Open** 10am-10pm Mon-Thur, Sun; 10am-11pm Fri, Sat. **Credit** AmEx, DC, Disc, MC, V.

This fine independent store is bigger than it looks from the outside: the premises are unexpectedly capacious, and every shelf is crammed with CDs both new and used.

Record Surplus

11609 W Pico Boulevard, at Federal Avenue, West LA (1-310 478 4217/www.recordsurplusla.com). Bus C3, SM7, SM8, SM12, SM13/I-10, exit Overland Boulevard north. **Open** 11am-9pm Mon-Sat; 11am-7pm Sun. **Credit** AmEx, DC, Disc, MC, V.

One of the last remaining used CD and record stores in the city, Record Surplus lives up to its name: much of the stock here is priced at less than a buck.

Rockaway Records

2395 Glendale Boulevard, at Silver Lake Boulevard, Silver Lake (1-323 664 3232/www.rockaway.com). Bus 92/US 101, exit Silver Lake Boulevard north. **Open** 11am-7pm daily. **Credit** AmEx, DC, MC, V. **Map** p330 D2.

Amoeba Music.

Used CDs, rare vinyl, new alternative and LA-based bands, 1960s memorabilia and videos are the specialities of this unassuming shop. Prices are keen.

DVDs

For **Amoeba Music**, *see p209*. For **CineFile Video**, *see p230*.

Rocket Video

726 N La Brea Avenue, between Melrose & Waring Avenues, Hollywood (1-323 965 1100/www.rocket hollywood.com). Bus 10, 212, 312/I-10, exit La Brea Avenue north. **Open** 10am-11pm daily. **Credit** AmEx, DC, MC, V. **Map** p329 A3.
The cinephile's video shop, Rocket is your best bet for finding that obscure foreign masterpiece. Sales and rental.

Vidiots

302 Pico Boulevard, at 3rd Street, Santa Monica (1-310 392 8508/www.vidiotsvideo.com). Bus 33, 333, SM7, SM8/I-10, exit Lincoln Boulevard north. **Open** 10am-11pm Mon-Thur, Sun; 10am-midnight Fri, Sat. **Credit** AmEx, DC, MC, V. **Map** p326 A3.
This wonderfully named store has all the usual commercial fare and plenty more besides: foreign flicks, art-house videos and rare films, on DVD and video, for sale or rental.

Musical instruments

If you want to make rather than listen to music, visit the **Guitar Center** in Hollywood (7425 W Sunset Boulevard, 1-323 874 1060, www.guitar center.com), which stocks most kinds of musical instruments alongside the axes. Two guitar shops merit mention: the wonderful **McCabe's Guitar Shop** in Santa Monica (3101 Pico Boulevard, 1-310 828 4497, www.mccabes guitar.com) is a favourite of folkies, while the instruments at East LA's **Candelas Guitars** (2427 E Cesar E Chavez Avenue, 1-323 261 2011, www.candelas.com) have been favoured by everyone from Andres Segovia to Ozomatli.

Sports & fitness

Several chains dot LA, all offering a wide range of products. The biggest, appropriately, is **Big 5 Sporting Goods**; one of their many stores is at 3121 Wilshire Boulevard, Santa Monica, 1-310 453 1747, www.big5sportinggoods.com). The most central **Sport Chalet** is at Beverly Connection (100 N La Cienega Boulevard, 1-310 657 3210, www.sportchalet.com); the most central **Sports Authority** is in West LA (1919 S Sepulveda Boulevard, 1-310 312 9600, www.sportsauthority.com). Outdoor specialists **REI** have several stores, including one in Santa Monica (402 Santa Monica Boulevard, 1-310 458 4370, www.rei.com).

Adventure 16

11161 W Pico Boulevard, between S Sepulveda Boulevard & I-405, West LA (1-310 473 4574/ www.adventure16.com). Bus C3, SM7, SM8, SM12, SM13/I-10, exit Overland Boulevard north. **Open** 10am-9pm Mon-Fri; 10am-7pm Sat; 11am-6pm Sun. **Credit** AmEx, DC, MC, V. **Map** p327 A6.
Whether you're off on an extended desert expedition or a little hillside hike, the city's best outward-bound shop will be able to kit you out.

ZJ Boarding House

2619 Main Street, at Ocean Park Boulevard, Santa Monica (1-310 392 5646/www.zjboardinghouse. com). Bus 33, 333, SM1, SM2, SM8, SM10/I-10, exit 4th-5th Street south. **Open** 10am-8pm Mon-Fri; 10am-7pm Sat; 10am-6pm Sun. **Credit** AmEx, DC, Disc, MC, V. **Map** p326 A4.
There are several surf shops in this part of the city, and many others further down the coast in surfer-friendly towns such as Huntington Beach. ZJ is a good bet for travellers for its board rental: $15 for a half-day or $20 for a full day.

Tickets

If you want tickets for a performance or a sporting event in Los Angeles, you'll probably have to go through **Ticketmaster**. The global chain sells tickets on behalf of countless institutions, adding often-high booking fees to the face-value ticket price. Buy online at www.ticketmaster.com, by phone on 1-213 480 3232 or at one of nine ticket windows (the most central is at the Beverly Center; *see p188*). However, always try the venue first.

Travellers' needs

For **Traveler's Bookcase**, *see p191*. For computer repairs and cellphone rentals, *see p193*. For luggage specialists, *see p201*.

Distant Lands

56 S Raymond Avenue, at E Green Street, Pasadena (1-626 449 3220/www.distantlands.com). Metro Memorial Park/bus 180, 181, 260, 361/Hwy 110 to Pasadena (hwy ends at Colorado Boulevard). **Open** 10.30am-8pm Mon-Thur; 10.30am-9pm Fri, Sat; 11am-6pm Sun. **Credit** AmEx, DC, Disc, MC, V.
Maps, guidebooks, luggage, binoculars, electrical adaptors, passport holders… This fine retailer stocks pretty much everything that you need.

Flight 001

8235 W 3rd Street, at S Harper Avenue, Fairfax District (1-323 966 0001/www.flight001.com). Bus 16, 105, 218, 220/I-10, exit La Cienega Boulevard north. **Open** 11am-7pm Mon-Sat; 11am-6pm Sun. **Credit** AmEx, DC, Disc, MC, V. **Map** p328 C3.
The excellent Flight 001 harks back to a time when people travelled in style. Pick up everything from inflatable neck-rests to retro-styled luggage tags.

Arts & Entertainment

Festivals & Events	212
Children	217
Comedy	223
Film & TV	227
Galleries	235
Gay & Lesbian	242
Music	250
Nightclubs	261
Sports & Fitness	268
Theatre & Dance	277

Features

And the winner is...	213
The best Kids' stuff	217
Bob's your uncle	221
The best Comedy	223
The view from the stage	225
The best Cinema	227
Festivals Film	229
Caught on camera	232
Trains of thought	239
Gay beaches	243
Festivals Gay	244
The gay outdoors	246
Surprise!	249
Music for nothing	251
Festivals Rock	252
Mix and match	259
The best Nightclubs	261
High spirits	263
Spinning around	264
Two wheels good	271
Them's the breaks	274
Help the homeless	281
Great Shakes	282

I Dreamed I Could Fly by **Jonathan Borofsky**. *See p239.*

Festivals & Events

What's on when in La-La Land.

To every thing there is a season. And contrary to popular belief, that includes life in LA. Besides Pilot Season, Première Season, Sweeps Season, Awards Season and Allergy Season, LA boasts an impressive year-round array of unusual parades, cultural celebrations, sporting events and other spectacles, from the family-friendly to the truly far-out. For event listings when you're in town, try www.flavorpill.com, the calendar at www.laweekly.com and the *LA Times*' www.calendarlive.com.

Spring

Academy Awards
See p213 **And the winner is....**

Los Angeles Marathon
Starts at Lankershim & Cahuenga Boulevards, Universal City; finishes at S 5th & W Flower Streets, Downtown (1-310 444 5544/www.lamarathon.com). **Date** 1st Sun in Mar.
Every year, more than 23,000 runners and wheelchair racers take to the streets for this 26-mile slog through the city. But it's not a typical marathon: this being LA, the route is dotted with 1,000 cheerleaders, and neighbourhoods from Boyle Heights to Downtown celebrate with street performances.

Blessing of the Animals
El Pueblo de Los Angeles Historical Monument, Olvera Street, between US 101 & E César E Chávez Avenue, Downtown (www.olvera-street.com). Metro Union Station/bus 33, 40, 42, 68, 70, 71, 78, 79/ US 101, exit Alameda Street north. **Map** p331 C1. **Date** Sat before Easter.
Led by a cow festooned with flowers, this procession of farm animals and pets (with their owners), winds its way down LA's oldest street, where each animal is blessed with holy water.

Long Beach Grand Prix
Downtown Long Beach (1-888 827 7333/1-562 981 2600/www.longbeachgp.com). Metro Transit Mall/ bus 60, 232, 360/I-710, follow signs (expect road closures). **Date** mid Apr.
Nicknamed the 'Southern California Official Spring Brake', this high-speed extravaganza features the

▶ For **film festivals**, *see p229*.
▶ For **gay & lesbian festivals**, *see p244*.
▶ For **music festivals**, *see p252*.
▶ For **sporting events**, *see pp268-271*.

cars and stars of the CART Champ Car World Series. The two-mile street circuit includes plenty of straights and curves; spectators should expect to spend the afternoon biting their nails.

LA Times Festival of Books
UCLA campus, Westwood Boulevard & Le Conte Avenue, Westwood (1-213 237 7335/www. latimes.com/fob). Bus 2, 20, 302, 720/I-405, exit Wilshire Boulevard east. **Date** late Apr.
More than 100,000 people flock to the UCLA campus each spring to commune with authors giving readings and doing signings. Alongside the talks and discussions, a variety of booksellers set up stalls so that they can hawk their wares directly to the public.

Santa Clarita Cowboy Festival
Melody Ranch & Motion Picture Studio, just north of Hwy 14 (1-661 286 4021/www.cowboyfestival.org). Hwy 14, exit Santa Clarita. **Date** late Apr.
Dig out your dude-ranch duds for this Western hoedown. Attractions include the Walk of Western Stars gala, horseback rides, a cowboy couture fashion show, a casino and plenty of cowboy comedy, poetry and chow. The festival is the only time that Gene Autry's ranch opens to the public.

Fiesta Broadway/Cinco de Mayo
Around Broadway & Main Street, between E César E Chávez Avenue & 11th Street, Downtown (1-310 914 0015/www.fiestabroadway.la). Various Metro stations & buses/I-110 or US 101, Downtown exits. **Map** p331 C1-C4. **Date** last Sun in Apr.
Covering 36 square blocks and drawing crowds that top 500,000, this free fiesta lives up to its reputation as the largest Cinco de Mayo celebration in the world. The festival commemorates the day in 1862 when Mexicans defeated French invaders, and is a blowout of feasting, piñata-breaking, music and general indulgence.

Summer

Pasadena Chalk Street Painting Festival
Old Town Pasadena (1-626 795 9100/www. pasadenachalkfestival.com). Metro Del Mar/bus 177, 180, 181, 256, 380/I-110, exit Colorado Boulevard east. **Date** mid June.
Hundreds of artists create temporary masterpieces in chalk on the streets of Pasadena, while thousands of onlookers watch where they walk. Eventually, awards are presented in a number of different categories, and then it's all washed away for good.

Arts & Entertainment

Independence Day

Across Los Angeles. **Date** 4 July.
The **Hollywood Bowl** hosts LA's most famous fireworks display, synchronised to music by the LA Philharmonic. However, celebrations aren't limited to the Bowl: **Huntington Beach** stages a parade during the day, capped by fireworks, and there's more patriotic razzle-dazzle at **Venice Beach**, the **Rose Bowl** and **Disneyland**. Note: many fireworks displays take place on the closest weekend to 4 July; check newspapers for schedules.

Pageant of the Masters

Broadway, Laguna Beach (1-949 494 1145/www. foapom.com). Pacific Coast Highway to Laguna Beach. **Date** early July-late Aug.
Life imitates art, literally: classic paintings, statues and murals take on a new dimension, as real people dress and pose to re-create original masterpieces, a trick popularised by vaudeville artiste Lolita Perine at the first festival in 1932. A professional orchestra, a narrator, intricate sets and theatrical lighting now help bring the works to life.

And the winner is…

There are now so many awards shows on the LA calendar that the already shaky concept of prize-giving has become devalued to the point of worthlessness. But from a star-spotting point of view, they're a red-carpet must. Some carry kudos: the **Screen Actors Guild Awards**, staged in January at the Shrine Auditorium, and Film Independent's **Spirit Awards**, held in a specially erected tent on Santa Monica Beach the day before the Oscars. Others, such as the **MTV Movie Awards** (June, at the Gibson Amphitheatre in Universal City), are of no lasting importance. But for the industry mogul and star-spotter alike, there are three that stand well above the pack.

It's hard to exaggerate the importance of the **Academy Awards** to LA. Oscar day is like LA's own Christmas. The ceremony is held on a Sunday in late February at the Kodak Theatre on Hollywood Boulevard (*see p96*); fans queue for days to get places in the stands overlooking the red carpet.

A glimpse of what can be expected in Oscar week, the **Golden Globe Awards** are awarded the month before by the Hollywood Foreign Press Association, comfortably the thing for which it's best known. The event is held at the Beverly Hilton (*see p55*).

Essentially TV's Oscars, the **Emmys** are held in two stages: the Daytime Emmys are dished out at the Kodak Theatre in June, with the Primetime Emmys handed out at LA Live (*see p119*) in September. As with the Oscars, the days when celebs didn't bother to show up are long gone, so you'll be treated to a full raft of stars from the small screen, as well as plenty of film stars acting as presenters for the evening.

Lotus Festival

Echo Park, between Glendale Avenue & Echo Park Boulevard, Echo Park (1-213 485 1310/www.lotus festival.org). Bus 2, 4, 92, 302, 704/US 101, exit Glendale Boulevard north. **Map** p330 D5. **Date** 2nd wknd in July.

Held among the lotus blooms in Echo Park, this low-key festival celebrates the cultures of Asia and the Pacific islands. Highlights include a market, dragon boat races and martial arts demonstrations.

US Open of Surfing

Huntington Beach Pier, at Main Street & Pacific Coast Highway, Huntington Beach, Orange County (www.usopenofsurfing.com). I-405, exit Beach Boulevard south. **Date** end July/start Aug.

America's largest pro surfing competition attracts the world's elite, who compete for big money while wowing 200,000 beach boys and girls with their skill, grace and innovative board designs. Heating up the festivities are live bands, a sports expo and after-parties with the friendly locals.

Festival of the Chariots

Ocean Front Walk, Windward Circle, Venice Beach Boardwalk, Venice (1-310 836 2676/www.festival ofchariots.com). Bus 33, 333, SM1, SM2/I-10, exit 4th-5th Street south. **Map** p326 A5-A6. **Date** first Sun in Aug.

Hosted by the Hare Krishnas, this Indian tradition attracts 50,000 people who chant and cheer for three honoured deities, representations of whom are paraded from the Santa Monica Civic Auditorium to Venice Beach on elaborately decorated chariots. A free Indian feast is held at the end of the route.

X Games

Staples Center, Downtown (listings p269); & Home Depot Center, Carson (listings p271) (www.expn.com). **Date** early Aug.

Competitors from around the world battle for both honour and treasure in extreme sports; thousands of adoring fans risk sunstroke to cheer them on.

Nisei Week Japanese Festival

Little Tokyo, Downtown (1-213 687 7193/www.nisei week.org). Metro Union Station/bus 30, 31, 40, 42/ US 101, exit Alameda Street south. **Map** p331 D2-D3. **Date** mid Aug.

This eight-day event celebrates Japanese culture with displays of martial arts, tea ceremonies, flower arranging and more, and culminates with the coronation of the Nisei Week Queen. 'Nisei' refers to the first generation of Japanese to be born in America.

Watts Summer Festival

African American Unity Center, 944 W 53rd Street, at S Vermont Avenue, Watts (1-323 789 7304/ www.wattsfestival.org). Metro Slauson/bus 204, 206/I-110, exit Slauson Avenue west. **Date** mid Aug.

Conceived in 1966, the year after the Watts Riots, this black pride event is the longest-running African American cultural festival in the US. Besides music, the event includes various other performances, a fashion show, a parade and a child-oriented area.

Sunset Junction Street Fair

3900-4300 blocks of Sunset Boulevard & around, Silver Lake (1-323 661 7771/www.sunsetjunction. org). Bus 2, 4, 302, 704/US 101, exit Silver Lake Boulevard north. **Map** p330 B3-C4. **Date** late Aug.

Here comes Santa Claus: it's the **Hollywood Christmas Parade**. *See p216.*

This historic annual street festival unites the diverse populations of hipsters and immigrants who live in Silver Lake. Despite the recent imposition of an entry fee, the festival's cultural grab-bag of music, food and people-watching attracts more than 200,000 visitors.

LA African Marketplace & Cultural Faire

Rancho Cienega Park, 5001 Rodeo Road, at W Martin Luther King Boulevard, Crenshaw (1-323 293 1612/www.africanmarketplace.org). Bus 102, 105, 212, 312/I-10, exit La Brea Avenue south. **Date** last 3 wknds in Aug.

This much-loved festival blends traditional African and Afro-Caribbean sights, sounds and flavours with contemporary African American culture. To keep the children entertained and to trick them into learning, there are magicians, storytellers and a petting zoo. But there's also good news for adults: the festival's increasingly sophisticated programme features music, dance, sports and an outdoor film series.

Fuck Yeah Fest

Echo & Echoplex (listings p256), Echo Park (www.fuckyeahfest.com). **Date** late Aug.

The enthusiastically named Fuck Yeah Fest rallies rowdy post-punkers, low-brow artists, anarchist skaters, caustic stand-ups and all manner of other virulently anti-establishment types for a weekend of indier-than-thou amp-busting fringe culture.

Autumn

Fiesta Hermosa Arts & Crafts Fair

Hermosa Beach, at Hermosa & Pier Avenues (1-310 376 0951/www.fiestahermosa.com). Bus 130, 439/ I-405, exit Rosecrans Boulevard west. **Date** Labor Day wknd (early Sept).

Wear a swimsuit under your clothes: after roaming the 250 stalls at this arts festival, sampling the fine foods and listening to the music, you may want to take a dip in the nearby ocean. There's another Fiesta over Memorial Day weekend (late May).

LA Greek Festival

St Sophia Cathedral, 1324 S Normandie Avenue, at W Pico Boulevard, Koreatown (www.lagreekfest. com). **Date** wknd after Labor Day (early Sept).

LA isn't known for its large Greek community, but there are enough locals with roots to the islands to merit this weekend-long festival of baklava, moussaka and mandolin music on the grounds of a cathedral in – naturally – Koreatown.

Port of Los Angeles Lobster Festival

Ports o' Call Village, San Pedro (1-310 798 7478/ www.lobsterfest.com). Bus 446, 447/I-110, exit Harbor Boulevard west. **Date** mid Sept.

Bizarre fact: although this weekend-long festival is held in the coastal town of San Pedro, all the lobsters eaten at it are flown in from Maine. There's a fine line-up of bands curated by local rock station Indie 103.1, and Saturday's troubling LobsterDog Parade, when locals dress their pet pooches as sea creatures.

LA County Fair

Pomona County Fairplex, W McKinley & N White Avenues, Pomona (1-909 623 3111/www.lacounty fair.com). I-10, exit Fairplex Avenue. **Date** mid Sept-early Oct.

LA has changed immeasurably since 1921, when this event was first staged as an agricultural fair. However, the perennially popular event still has farm-friendly appeal (livestock beauty contests, locally farmed produce) alongside the more modern acrobats, wine tastings, exhibitions and concerts.

West Hollywood Book Fair

West Hollywood Park, 647 N San Vicente Boulevard, between Santa Monica Boulevard & Melrose Avenue, West Hollywood (www.westhollywoodbookfair.org). Bus 4, 105, 220, 305, 550, 704/I-10, exit La Cienega Boulevard north. **Date** late Sept.

Cruise the vendors at the nearby Pacific Design Center for the new bookshelves that you'll probably need after a visit to the award-winning WeHo Book Fair. Readings, panel discussions, workshops are all among the IQ-elevating activities on the schedule.

Abbot Kinney Boulevard Festival

Abbot Kinney Boulevard, between Main Street & Venice Boulevard, Venice (1-310 396 3772/www. abbotkinney.org). Bus 33, 333, SM1, SM2/I-10, exit 4th-5th Street south. **Map** p330 D5. **Date** late Sept.

Take every artsy street fair you've ever attended, add all the stereotypes about the fun-loving Venice Beach locals you've ever heard, and you've got the general idea. Be sure to hit not only the guest vendors but also the locally owned galleries, shops and salons that line the world's poshest skid row.

Calabasas Pumpkin Festival

Juan Bautista de Anza Park, 3701 Lost Hills Road, at Agoura Road, Calabasas (1-818 222 5680/ www.calabasaspumpkinfestival.com). US 101, exit Parkway Calabasas. **Date** mid-late Oct.

Yes, there's more to pumpkins than Halloween jack-o'-lanterns: pumpkin bowling, pumpkin beer, pumpkin bread and, of course, pumpkin pie. The festival is held in Paramount's Western-themed studio in the Santa Monica mountains, the backdrop for such immortal TV shows as *Dr Quinn, Medicine Woman*.

Halloween

Across Los Angeles. **Date** 31 Oct.

The main action is at the **West Hollywood Halloween Carnival**, held on Santa Monica Boulevard between La Cienega Boulevard and Doheny Drive (www.weho.org). More than 400,000 rowdy revellers are entertained by DJs, bands, costume contests, drag queen competitions and the crowning of the celebrity Honorary Mayor.

Dia de los Muertos (Day of the Dead)

Across Los Angeles. **Date** 1st Sat in Nov.

Self-Help Graphics in East LA (*see p122*) hosts art-oriented workshops and theatre performances, while the historic Downtown paseo of **Olvera Street**

offers a day dancing and piñata-breaking. Meanwhile, the haunting romance of the cinematic Golden Age is celebrated with the elaborate art-altar competition at the **Hollywood Forever Cemetery** (see p97).

Mariachi Festival
Mariachi Plaza, at N Boyle Avenue & E 1st Street, Boyle Heights (1-323 526 3059/www.lacity.org). Metro Mariachi Plaza (open 2009)/bus 30, 31, 330/ US 101, exit 1st Street east. **Date** mid Nov.
Decked out in ruffled, rainbow-coloured splendour, the itinerant musicians at this festival of Latino culture entertain visitors in mariachi styles. Tequila, tacos and other spicy specialities add further appeal.

Winter

Hollywood Christmas Parade
Parade starts at Mann's Chinese Theatre, travels east on Hollywood Boulevard, south on Van Ness Avenue, then east on Sunset Boulevard (1-323 469 2337/www.hollywoodchristmas.com). **Date** Sun after Thanksgiving.
The event that inspired Gene Autry to write 'Here Comes Santa Claus' is a glitzy, star-studded presentation that attracts a million fans. First held in 1928, the parade features elaborate floats, pop stars galore, celebs riding in antique cars, camels, equestrian shows and marching bands giving it the full razzle-dazzle. Even with reserved bleacher seats, early arrival is a must, and parking hideous. *Photo p214*.

Griffith Park Light Festival
Griffith Park, Crystal Springs Drive, between Los Feliz Boulevard & the Ventura Freeway, Los Feliz (1-323 913 4688/www.dwplightfestival.com). Bus 96/ I-5, exit Crystal Springs Drive north. **Map** p330 C1. **Date** late Nov-late Dec.
Brighten up your holiday season with a drive along this mile-long stretch of lights. High points include flamboyant depictions of Hollywood landmarks composed of electric bulbs. Weekend nights can be bumper to bumper; it might be best to park at the nearby LA Zoo and stroll the mile instead.

Marina del Rey Holiday Boat Parade
Main channel, Marina del Rey (1-310 670 7130/ www.mdrboatparade.org). Bus 108, C1, C7/I-405, exit Hwy 90 west. **Date** mid Dec.
It's anchors aweigh at this watery festival, as more than 70 ornamented boats compete for attention and prizes. Watch proceedings from Fisherman's Village or Burton Chace Park.

Hannukah Family Festival
Skirball Cultural Center, 2701 N Sepulveda Boulevard, at I-405, West LA (1-310 440 4500/ www.skirball.org). Bus 761/I-405, exit Skirball Center/Mulholland Drive north. **Date** mid/late Dec.
Enjoy the music, games, tastes and traditions that mark the Jewish festival of lights up at the Skirball Center (see p85). Anyone can participate in the Hanukkah play, complete with costumes and songs.

Las Posadas
Olvera Street, at E César E Chávez Avenue, Downtown (1-213 485 6855/www.olvera-street.com). Metro Union Station/bus 33, 40, 42, 68, 70, 71, 78, 79/US 101, exit Alameda Street north. **Map** p331 C1. **Date** mid-late Dec.
This surprisingly cheerful re-enactment of Mary and Joseph's journey to Bethlehem features a candlelit procession, songs, dancing and piñata-breaking, with free candy for children and adults.

LA County Holiday Celebration
Dorothy Chandler Pavilion, Music Center Plaza, S Grand Avenue & W 1st Street, Downtown (www.lacountyarts.org/holiday.html). Metro Civic Center/bus 14, 37, 70, 71, 76, 78, 79, 96/I-110, exit 3rd Street east. **Map** p331 B2. **Date** 24 Dec.
This day-long festival of art, music and good merriment aims to represent the range of cultural and religious traditions that have put down roots in LA. The event has a worthy commitment to inclusivity, but it's also an entertaining way to spend the last few hours before Christmas.

Tournament of Roses Parade
Parade starts in Pasadena at S Orange Grove Boulevard & Ellis Street, travels east on Colorado Boulevard and north on Sierra Madre Boulevard, ends at Paloma Street (1-626 449 4100/www. tournamentofroses.com). Various Metro stations & buses/I-110 to Pasadena (various exits). **Date** 1 Jan.
The first Rose Parade in 1890 was staged to show off California's sun-kissed climate. The tradition is still going strong, complete with elaborate floral floats, musical performances and marching troupes (not to mention the crowning of the fresh-faced Rose Queen and her court), but the celebration now draws more than a million spectators who line the streets of Pasadena. The Rose Bowl (see p270) follows the parade. Later in the month, the event is spoofed with a day of costumed mayhem at the **Doo Dah Parade** (1-626 205 4029, www.pasadenadoodahparade.info).

Chinese New Year
Parade travels along N Broadway, between E César E Chávez Avenue & Bernard Street, Downtown (1-213 617 0396/www.lagoldendragonparade.com). Metro Chinatown or Union Station/various buses/ US 101, exit Alameda Street north. **Date** early Feb.
The spectacular Golden Dragon Parade through Chinatown is the highlight of this annual two-day street fair, which also includes a carnival, lantern processions, fashion shows, and plenty of food.

Brazilian Carnival
Queen Mary, Queens Highway, Long Beach (www.braziliannites.com). Metro Transit Mall/ bus 60, 232, 360/I-710, exit Shoreline Drive east. **Date** early Feb.
If you can't make it all the way to Rio, you'll have to make do with this over-the-top explosion of feathers, sequins, production numbers and tan lines. It's held each year at the vintage ocean liner that's now permanently docked in Long Beach (see p138).

Children

Los Angeles has it made for your little angels.

Although a city designed around the car might not seem an ideal place for a family holiday, LA is actually great for kids. The climate and the topography both help: you can spend all day on one of the many beaches or up in the mountains, assuming you've brought enough sunscreen. But LA's family-friendliness is also due in part to the demanding nature of many locals, who insist on the best for their children.

The attractions are many and varied, with different neighbourhoods offering all sorts of cultural experiences. Want Johnny to hear a mariachi band? Take him to a park in East LA on a Saturday. Want Janet to ride horses? Head to Griffith Park. Want the true, quintessential American entertainment experience? Welcome to Disneyland. If you're keen to lavish stuff on your kids, a baby boom has spawned a simultaneous flowering of child-oriented shops (see p193). And if you'd like your little cutie to be in the spotlight, LA's the place: the city is predictably brimming with child modelling and acting agencies.

Sightseeing

Attractions & museums

Budget permitting – none is exactly a cheap day out – the various LA-area theme parks are all child-pleasers. For **Disneyland** and **Knott's Berry Farm** in Orange County, see pp141-142; for **Universal Studios** and **Six Flags California** in the San Fernando Valley, see pp130-131. If you're planning on driving to San Diego, there's **California Legoland**, off I-5 in Carlsbad (1-760 918 5346, www.lego.com).

Without doubt the best new attraction for kids in LA is Noah's Ark at the **Skirball Cultural Center** (see p86), up the hill from the Getty Center. Five years in the making, Noah's Ark was inspired by the ancient flood story, and designed to help people of all cultures 'connect with one another, learn the value of community, and help build a better world'. It sounds like a lofty goal, but the reality is a brilliant display of pure imagination: three rooms transformed into a wooden ark and filled with full-sized animals made of found objects, as well as steampunk-style interactive gizmos that create the sensations of a flood. And all without a computer or piece of plastic in sight.

Los Angeles has two large children's museums; or, at least, it will have when the **Children's Museum of Los Angeles** reopens in 2010 at the Hansen Dam Recreation Area in the San Fernando Valley; for more, see www.childrensmuseumla.org. The other is Pasadena's **Kidspace Children's Museum** (see p134), an inside–outside learn-while-you-play environment with climbing towers, a mock bug food kitchen and a fake earthquake zone. To see real bugs, as well as other educational exhibits, visit Exposition Park, home to a pair of kid-friendly museums in the shape of the **Natural History Museum of Los Angeles County** and the **California ScienCenter** (for both, see pp124-125).

Many of the city's art museums offer workshops for children. Among them are **LACMA** (see p100), **MoCA** (see p116), the **Japanese American National Museum** (see p112), the **Getty Center** (see p84) and the newly restored **Getty Villa** (see p75); check the various websites for details. And for kids drawn to the stars, the **Griffith Observatory** (see p106) is a must-visit. Newly reopened after a lengthy restoration, it's considered one of the premier public observatories in the world. If you or your kids aren't interested in stargazing, the site and its spiffy 1930s deco architecture are worth a visit in their own rights.

Animal attractions are a favourite with youngsters, and LA's are no exception. The **Los Angeles Zoo** (see p107) and the **Star Eco Station** (see p87) are supplemented by a string of marine-oriented draws: the **Santa Monica Pier Aquarium** (see p77), the **Cabrillo Marine Aquarium** in San Pedro (see p137) and the **Aquarium of the Pacific**

The best Kids' stuff

For messy meals
Cheesecake Factory. See p220.

For astro-geeks
Griffith Observatory. See p106.

For earth, air and water babies
Noah's Ark at the Skirball. See p217.

in Long Beach (*see p138*). Other kid-friendly diversions include the low-key but delightful **Travel Town Museum** in Griffith Park (*see p105*) and **Ripley's Believe it or Not!** (*see p97*).

At the end of Santa Monica Pier is **Pacific Park** (1-310 260 8744, www.pacpark.com), an amusement park that's as much fun as any you'd find on the English seaside (and with more reliable weather). There's a rollercoaster, a big wheel, some smaller rides for little kids, amusement arcades and a carousel. On Thursday nights in summer, there's a free concert series: bring a picnic.

Outdoors & nature

Beaches

On **Santa Monica Beach** and **Venice Beach**, between Santa Monica Pier to the north and Venice Pier to the south, there's sand, sea, bike and skate paths, with cycles and in-line skates available for hire. Near the bike path are a number of small play-parks; the largest is at the Venice Recreation Center, next door to basketball and racquetball courts for teens and adults. And there are even regular surf camps for over-sevens at Santa Monica Beach and, further south, at **El Segundo Beach**. For more, call 1-310 663 2479 or check www.learntosurfla.com.

If your kids want to swim but are nervous of the ocean's strong currents, big waves and cold temperatures, the city boasts a number of public swimming pools. Two of the most family-friendly are listed below.

AAF Rose Bowl Aquatic Center

360 N Arroyo Boulevard, in Brookside Park, Pasadena (1-626 564 0330/www.rosebowl aquatics.org). Metro Memorial Park/bus 167/ Hwy 134, exit Arroyo Boulevard north. **Open** *Recreational/family swim* 2.30-5.30pm, 7.30-8.30pm Mon-Fri; 3-4.30pm Sat, Sun. **Admission** $2; $1 under-17s. **Credit** DC, MC, V.
This beloved open-air swimming centre has two Olympic-sized pools for serious swimmers, but also provides plenty of access for families and swimming lessons for beginners.

Santa Monica Swim Center

Santa Monica College, 2225 16th Street, at Pacific Street, Santa Monica (1-310 458 8700/www.smgov. net/aquatics). Bus 534, SM6, SM7/I-10, exit Lincoln Boulevard south. **Open** 3-6.30pm Mon-Fri; 11am-7pm Sat, Sun. **Admission** $5; $2 under-18s. **Credit** DC, Disc, MC, V. **Map** p326 C4.
A clean, cheerful, brightly tiled and not overly chlorinated pair of open-air pools. One is competition size; the other is large enough for laps but shallow enough for children. Private and group swimming lessons are available.

Griffith Park. See p105.

Parks

With its picnic areas, miles of hiking and horse-riding trails, 1920s merry-go-round and zoo, the rolling hills of **Griffith Park** (*see p105*) make a great outdoor experience for kids. That said, most of LA's parks are good for families. The best are the **Kenneth Hahn State Recreation Area** (*see p128*) and the **Will Rogers State Historic Park** (*see p75*), though the latter was rumoured in 2008 to be facing closure or a rise in fees due to state budget deficits.

The botanical gardens at the **Huntington Library** (*see p132*) feature a lovely children's garden, containing nine kinetic sculptures that explore the natural elements of earth, light, air and water. Children aged two and older can walk under a rainbow in a circle of mist, vanish into a sea of billowing fog and feel sound waves moving through water in a sonic pool.

TreePeople

12601 Mulholland Drive, at Coldwater Canyon Drive, Beverly Hills (1-818 753 4600/www.treepeople.org). US 101, exit Coldwater Canyon Boulevard south. **Open** *Park* sunrise-sunset daily. **Admission** free.
This non-profit group plants and cares for native and exotic trees, and the environment. The centre is located in the idyllic 45-acre Coldwater Canyon Park, a welcome break from the urban sprawl.

Playgrounds

How times have changed. LA's children no longer spend hours playing in parks that consist only of a slide, a few bars and some battered old swings. Tots today get to develop their muscles in clean and safe neighbourhood play-parks, many of which come with hanging bridges, towers, tubes, slides in multiple wave forms and, on the ground, sand or padded rubber to protect bottoms from bumps. Most of these kids' parks are in bigger parks with football and basketball fields, and many of the better ones are in the relatively more affluent parts of the city.

The best kid-friendly play-parks on the Westside include **Venice Beach** (at Windward Avenue), **Santa Monica Beach** (at Ocean Park Boulevard), **Roxbury Park** in Beverly Hills and the park in the Playa Vista development at the south end of Playa Vista Drive. However, there are plenty of others across LA. For details on all the parks in Los Angeles county, online resources for visitors include a handful of pretty comprehensive websites: there's http://parks.lacounty.gov; for Santa Monica, you should visit www.smgov.net/osm/park_facil.htm; and for Beverly Hills, there's www.beverlyhills.org.

Restaurants & cafés

While many LA restaurants accommodate kids, some actively welcome them: look for paper rather than cloth on the tables, and diversions such as fountains, fish tanks and crayons. Chinese and Mexican restaurants are often a good bet: the service is fast, there's finger food for tiny hands and, in Mexican restaurants especially, the waiters are nuts about children.

Angeli Caffe

7274 Melrose Avenue, between N Alta Vista Boulevard & N Poinsettia Place, West Hollywood (1-323 936 9086/www.angelicaffe.com). Bus 10, 212, 312/I-10, exit La Brea Avenue north. **Open** 11.30am-2.30pm, 5-10pm Tue-Fri; 5-10pm Sat, Sun. **Credit** AmEx, DC, Disc, MC, V. **Map** p328 D2.
The food at this child-friendly operation is fresh, simple Italian and moderately priced, and the setting is modern and comfortable. Crayons are available if the children want to scribble between courses, and the staff are as friendly as can be.

Café 50s

11623 Santa Monica Boulevard, between Barry & Federal Avenues, West LA (1-310 479 1955/www.cafe50s.com). Bus 4, 704, SM1, SM10/I-10, exit Bundy Drive north. **Open** 7am-midnight Mon-Thur, Sun; 7am-1am Fri; 8am-1am Sat; 8am-midnight Sun. **Credit** MC, V.

Color Me Mine.

a proper dessert at **Gill's Old Fashioned Ice Cream** (1-323 936 7986). Also here is **Du-Pars**, a longtime family favourite that serves hearty comfort food and free ice-creams to the children. Aside from its Farmers Market location (1-323 933 8446), it has branches in Studio City and Thousand Oaks.

Newsroom Café

120 N Robertson Boulevard, between W 3rd Street & W Beverly Boulevard, Beverly Hills (1-310 652 4444). Bus 14, 16, 220, LDHWH, LDHWI/I-10, exit Robertson Boulevard north. **Open** 8am-9pm Mon-Thur; 8am-10pm Fri; 9am-10pm Sat; 9am-9pm Sun. **Credit** AmEx, DC, MC, V. **Map** p328 A3.
You won't have to worry about your offspring making too much noise in this big, boisterous restaurant. Set opposite children's bookstore and art gallery Storyopolis (*see p221*), the Newsroom offers healthy and organic food, and has tables outside. Overhead TV screens play news reports or music videos.

Pitfire Pizza Company

5211 Lankershim Boulevard, at Magnolia Boulevard, North Hollywood (1-818 980 2949/www.pitfire pizza.com). Metro North Hollywood/bus 156, 224, 656/Hwy 170, exit Magnolia Boulevard east. **Open** 11am-9pm Mon, Tue; 11am-10pm Wed-Sat; noon-9pm Sun. **Credit** AmEx, DC, Disc, MC, V.
With branches in Westwood and Downtown, Pitfire offers great pizzas, pastas and salads. This branch also has plenty of outside tables.

Wolfgang Puck Express

1315 Third Street Promenade, at Wilshire Boulevard, Santa Monica (1-310 576 4770/www.wolfgangpuck. com). Bus 20, 720, SM2, SM3, SM4, SM5, SM9/I-10, exit 4th-5th Street north. **Open** 11am-9.30pm Mon-Thur, Sun; 11am-10.30pm Fri, Sat. **Credit** AmEx, DC, Disc, MC, V. **Map** p326 A2.
Puck's top-end eateries, such as Spago (*see p155*), are by no means ideal for families. However, this rather cheaper chain is very child-friendly.

Kitschy dining fun for those weary of the Johnny Rockets chain but still craving the occasional old-fashioned burger, milkshake or egg-cream. Mini jukeboxes sit at each table; kids eat for free if they dress in pyjamas on the last Wednesday of the month.

California Pizza Kitchen

Throughout LA (www.cpk.com).
The 15-plus kid-friendly branches of the California Pizza Kitchen are a favourite fallback among LA families. Check online for the operation nearest to you.

Cheesecake Factory

Throughout LA (cheesecakefactory.com).
This is a failsafe destination for many a family who's had it with being embarrassed by screaming children in restaurants. The Cheesecake Factory positively welcomes all-comers, and the eclectic and lengthy menu offers something for every tastebud. You'll find branches all over the city, with portions as large as junior himself.

Farmers Market

See p159.
No restaurant in the city surpasses the energy and variety of edibles on offer at the food court at the Farmers Market. While the children munch on pizza or burgers, adults can try more interesting fare – Brazilian food at the **Pampas Grill** (1-323 931 1928), say, or cajun cooking at the **Gumbo Pot** (1-323 933 0358) – before all the generations reunite for

Arts & entertainment

For details of what's on, check the 'Calendar' section of the Sunday *Los Angeles Times*, the *LA Weekly* and the free monthly *LA Parent*, which can be found in any location that caters for children and is also available online. Also useful is http://gocitykids.parentsconnect.com.

Activities

Allied Model Trains

4411 S Sepulveda Boulevard, between Barman Avenue and Braddock Drive, Culver City (1-310 313 9353/www.alliedmodeltrains.com). Bus 220, C5, C6/ I-405, exit Culver Boulevard east. **Open** 10am-6pm Mon-Sat. **Credit** AmEx, DC, Disc, MC, V.
Housed in a miniature replica of Union Station, this 12,000sq ft (1,115sq m) shop bills itself as the largest model train store in the world. Trains chug around

the enormous displays through meticulously constructed scenes. And even if you can't afford the models, young fans of Thomas the Tank Engine are certain to be entertained.

Color Me Mine
1109 Montana Avenue, between 11th & 12th Streets, Santa Monica (1-310 393 0069/www.color memine.com). Bus 20, 720, SM3/I-10, exit Lincoln Boulevard north. **Open** 11am-9pm daily. Rates $10/session for adults; $6/session under-10s. **Credit** AmEx, DC, Disc, MC, V. **Map** p326 B2.

For a few hours of creative fun, visit one of Color Me Mine's locations. Choose from a selection of ceramic plates, bowls, teapots or animals, which you then paint and have fired. The items cost from $3; but on Wednesdays, kids paint for free without a purchase. **Other locations** throughout LA.

Storyopolis
12348 Ventura Boulevard, between Laurel Canyon Boulevard & Coldwater Canyon Avenue, Studio City (1-818 509 5600/www.storyopolis.com). Bus 150, 218, 240, 750/US 101, exit Laurel Canyon

Bob's your uncle

The entertainment that most kids enjoy today is of the spoon-fed variety, passed through a tiny sieve to remove any taint of weirdness. LA's tykes, then, are lucky to have the merry band of puppeteers led by **Bob Baker**, who's been staging original shows in his own theatre since 1961 (*see p222*). And what shows they are, starring sexy Parisian pussycats and goons from space, buck-toothed hayseeds and singing watermelons, disco maniacs and comely onions, even skeletal burlesque babes with pasties on their ribs.

Baker's whimsical puppets have appeared in dozens of TV shows and films, among them *Bedknobs and Broomsticks* and *Bewitched*. But they're most at home in his own space, tucked away between Downtown and Echo Park. During a typical performance, as many as 100 characters might caper under the able

hands of black-clad young artists trained by the master, supplemented by an occasional showcase performance from Baker himself.

Most Baker shows take a loose theme – in the case of the masterful *Something to Crow About*, a day on the farm – and then string together a story based around vintage songs acted out by the puppets. There's no stage: grown-ups get folding chairs while kids sit in a big U-shape on a rug. The puppets come right up and sit on the kids' laps, which usually results in giggles or shrieks so sincere that the whole room melts. The entertainment ends with a complimentary cup of ice-cream in the attached Party Room, decorated in an explosion of circus stripes and vintage puppet pictures. For birthday parties, call the theatre in advance to order a cake from Hansen's, an old-school, specialist cake bakery.

Arts & Entertainment

Boulevard south. **Open** 10am-6pm Tue-Sat; 11am-4pm Sun. **Credit** AmEx, DC, MC, V.
This Studio City space, part children's bookstore and part gallery, exhibits original artwork from children's books, and hosts numerous family-friendly events (book signings, concerts and weekly storytimes for babies and toddlers).

Bookstores & libraries

Much to the surprise of many visitors, LA is full of bibliophiles, and plenty of literary provision is made for kids. The children's section of the **Richard J Riordan Central Library** (*see p116*) has plenty of kids' books and a strong programme of events: there are regular storytelling sessions, among other family-friendly reading sessions. Elsewhere, the city spent the last decade building new district libraries, all of which feature children's reading areas and special kids' programmes; see www.lapl.org for branches and details of events.

The LA region also boasts a wealth of children's booksellers that offer author and illustrator meet-and-greets, dress-up parties, crafts workshops, singalongs and story times. Listed below are some of the best-loved bookstores; check their websites for special events. For **Children's Book World**, another kids specialist, *see p191*; for **Storyopolis**, *see p221*; and for **Vroman's**, which has special children's events, *see p190*.

Chevalier's Books

126 N Larchmont Boulevard, at W 1st Street, Hancock Park (1-323 465 1334). Bus 10, 720/US 101, exit Melrose Avenue west. **Open** 10am-6pm Mon-Sat; 11am-5pm Sun. **Credit** AmEx, DC, MC, V. **Map** p329 B4.

Once Upon a Story

3740 E 4th Street, between Loma & Grand Avenues, Long Beach (1-562 433 6856/www.onceuponastory books.com). I-405, exit Cherry Avenue south. **Open** 10am-5.30pm Tue-Fri; 9am-5pm Sat; 9am-4pm Sun. **Credit** AmEx, DC, Disc, MC, V.

San Marino Toy & Book Shoppe

2424 Huntington Drive, between San Marino & Del Mar Avenues, San Marino (1-626 309 0222/ www.toysandbooks.com). Bus 79/I-110, exit Atlantic Boulevard north. **Open** 10am-6pm Mon-Sat; 11am-5pm Sun. **Credit** DC, Disc, MC, V.

Music & theatre

On weekdays during July and August, the LA Philharmonic lays on performances and workshops for under-tens in a series called Summer Sounds at the **Hollywood Bowl** (*see p251*). During autumn, winter and spring, take the young 'uns to a youth concert by the LA Philharmonic at the marvellous **Walt Disney Concert Hall** (*see p251*).

During long car journeys (and let's face it, there are going to be plenty of those), tune in to **KDIS** (1110 AM). Disney's 24-hour radio station features music, character voices and call-in contests, and should keep the kids quiet.

Bob Baker Marionette Theater

1345 W 1st Street, at Glendale Boulevard, Echo Park (1-213 250 9995/www.bobbakermarionettes.com). Bus 14/I-110, exit 3rd Street west. **Open** Box office 9am-5pm Tue-Fri. *Shows* 10.30am Tue-Fri; 2.30pm Sat, Sun. **Tickets** $15; free under-2s. **Credit** AmEx, Disc, MC, V. **Map** p330 D6.
Baker has been staging marionette shows for more than 40 years; booking for them is essential. Staff can also cater for children's parties. *See p221* **Bob's your uncle**.

Geffen Playhouse

10886 Le Conte Avenue, between Tiverton Avenue & Westwood Boulevard, Westwood (1-310 208 5454/www.geffenplayhouse.com). Bus 2, 305, 702, C6/I-405, exit Wilshire Boulevard east. **Box office** 10am-6pm Mon-Fri; 11am-6pm Sat, Sun. **Tickets** $15; $10 under-12s. **Credit** AmEx, DC, MC, V.
LA is short on good theatre aimed at children, but this venue is one of the better ones. On Saturdays at 11am, the Geffen hosts Saturday Scene, a popular entertainment programme for children.

Hollywood Bowl

See p251.
One of the most gorgeous attractions in LA, the Bowl offers a programme of children's concerts, plus an outdoor arts studio that's held each weekday morning over a six-week span in July and August. For tickets and information, call 1-323 850 2000.

Pasadena Symphony Musical Circus

Pasadena Civic Auditorium, 300 E Green Street, at Euclid Avenue, Pasadena (1-626 449 7360/Pasadena Symphony 1-626 793 7172/www.pasadena symphony.org/circus). Metro Memorial Park/bus 181, 267, 687/I-110, exit Green Street east. **Open** some Sats; call or check online. **Tickets** free.
Musicians and teachers help under-10s discover the joy of music-making at these monthly Saturday-morning sessions. After a musical petting zoo (8.30am), where children get a close-up look at various instruments, there's a family concert (9am).

Babysitters

Babysitters Guild

1-310 837 1800. **Open** Office 10.30am-4.30pm Mon-Fri. **No credit cards.**
LA's largest and oldest babysitting service serves hotels all over the city for $11/hr (and up) plus travel. There's a four-hour daily minimum except on Saturdays, when it's five hours. Staff require at least 24 hours' notice.

Comedy

How's everybody doin' tonight?

The comedy scene in Los Angeles is arguably one of the strongest in the US, and certainly one of the most varied. From nationally known stand-ups warming up for a *Tonight Show* turn via Chicago-style improv to experimental sketch comedy, you'll find a little of everything.

Long-established laughatoriums such as the **Comedy Store** and the **Improv** keep packing 'em in, but you may pay dearly for the privilege of sitting hip to hip with crowds weaned on poopy humour. Happily, there are alternatives: check out, for starters, the always interesting **Upright Citizens Brigade Theatre** and the unusual programming at the **Steve Allen Theatre**. And keep your eyes peeled for the array of oddball shows staged in coffeehouses and other unexpected locations: take the often amazing nights held in the back room of **Meltdown Comics** (*see p191*), for instance, where even the booze is gratis.

Reservation policies vary by club, but you should try and book ahead if possible. The clubs' individual websites all offer details of upcoming performances; the *LA Weekly* also provides weekly listings.

Comedy clubs

Acme Comedy Theatre
135 N La Brea Avenue, between Beverly Boulevard & W 1st Street, Hollywood (1-323 525 0202/www. acmecomedy.com). Bus 10, 212/I-10, exit La Brea Avenue north. **Shows** 8pm, 9pm, 10pm, 11pm Fri; 8pm Sat; other nights vary. **Admission** *Regular shows* $10 & 1-drink min. *Special shows* $10-$20. *All-evening pass* $15. **Credit** AmEx, DC, MC, V. **Map** p329 A4.
This small and well-kept Hollywood theatre hosts *Saturday Night Live*-quality nights, and you can take that analogy however you please. Sketch comedy is the Acme's speciality; however, there's also improv, some of it in the shape of long-running, soap-style series *Scandal!* (11pm Fri).

Bang
457 N Fairfax Avenue, between Rosewood & Oakwood Avenues, Fairfax District (1-323 653 6886/www.bangstudio.com). Bus 14, 217, 218, LDF/I-10, exit Fairfax Avenue north. **Shows** 8pm Thur-Sat; other nights vary. **Admission** $7-$10. **Credit** DC, MC, V. **Map** p328 C3.
Bang is both a comedy showcase and an improv study centre frequented by novice and experienced comics. On the whole, the shows are original and

cleverly themed: look out for *Piñata*, at which established comedy writers read their humorous essays. Good value, too.

Comedy & Magic Club
1018 Hermosa Avenue, between 10th Street & Pier Avenue, Hermosa Beach (1-310 372 1193/www. comedyandmagicclub.com). Bus 130, 439/I-405, exit Rosecrans Boulevard west. **Shows** 8pm Tue-Thur; 7pm, 9.15pm Sat; 7pm Sun; other nights vary. **Admission** $13.50-$30; 2-drink min. **Credit** AmEx, DC, MC, V.
The biggest names in stand-up come to this hallowed yet funky beach club miles from the Sunset Strip. Jay Leno tries out new material for his talk show every Sunday, at least until he retires from NBC in 2009, and Jerry Seinfeld often plays when he's in town. Up-and-coming comics sometimes play the smaller-scale Live at the Lounge series.

Comedy Central Stage
6539 Santa Monica Boulevard, between Seward Street & Wilcox Avenue, Hollywood (1-323 960 5519/www.comedycentral.com). Bus 4, 156, 704/ US 101, exit Vine Street south. **Shows** 8pm, nights vary. **Admission** free. **Map** p329 B2.
Developing comedians get a chance to hone their skills in front of a live audience at this low-key, always-free theatre run by the Comedy Central TV network. The result is intelligent comedy of all varieties, and booking ahead is a must. If you're lucky, you may see the next Flight of the Conchords. If you're unlucky, don't blame us.

ComedySportz
733 Seward Street, at Melrose Avenue, Hollywood (1-323 856 4796/www.comedysportzla.com). Bus 10/US 101, exit Vine Street south. **Shows** 8pm Thur; 8pm, 10.30pm Fri, Sat; 8pm Sun; other nights vary. **Admission** $15-$17. **Credit** AmEx, DC, Disc, MC, V. **Map** p329 B3.

The best Comedy

For ha-ha headliners
Laugh Factory. See p226.

For indie innovators
Upright Citizens Brigade. See p226.

For improv lunacy
IO West. See p225.

Take a seat for the stand-up at the **Upright Citizens Brigade Theatre**. *See p226.*

At ComedySportz' eponymous flagship show (8pm Fri, 8pm & 10.30pm Sat), teams of improvisers go head-to-head a la *Whose Line is it Anyway?*, complete with a referee, peanuts and even the national anthem. Other shows take a similar improv bent: in the sporadically staged *U-Sical*, an entire musical is improvised around a single audience member.

Comedy Store
8433 W Sunset Boulevard, at N Olive Drive, West Hollywood (1-323 650 6268/www.thecomedystore. com). Bus 2, 302, LDHWH/I-10, exit La Cienega Boulevard north. **Shows** times vary, nightly. **Admission** free-$20; 2-drink min. **Credit** AmEx, DC, MC, V. **Map** p328 B1.
The site that once held notorious Sunset Strip club Ciro's morphed into the Comedy Store in 1972. Three separate stages host a monstrous array of stand-ups more or less every night of the week: check the website for precise times. If Chris Rock doesn't show up, you're bound to see someone who's almost as funny. Probably.

Comedy Union
5040 W Pico Boulevard, between S Sycamore & S La Brea Avenues, Midtown (1-323 934 9300/ www.thecomedyunion.com). Bus 212, 312/I-10, exit La Brea Avenue north. **Shows** 9pm Mon-Thur; 10pm Fri; 8pm, 10.30pm Sat. **Admission** free-$14; 2-drink min. **Credit** DC, MC, V. **Map** p328 D5.
Damon Wayans and DL Hughley are among the comics who've starred at this mid-city club specialising in talented African American stand-ups famous from their appearances on the likes of HBO's *Def Comedy Jam*.

Downtown Comedy Club
Wilshire Grand, 930 Wilshire Boulevard, at S Figueroa Street, Downtown (imformation 1-310 213 3195/tickets 1-213 514 5345/www.downtown comedyclub.com). Metro 7th Street-Metro Center/bus 66, 81, 366, 381/I-110, exit 6th Street east. **Shows** 8pm Fri, Sat. **Admission** $20. **Credit** DC, MC, V. **Map** p331 B3.
Garrett Morris, an original *Saturday Night Live* Not Ready for Prime-Time Player, runs the only regular comedy club in Downtown LA, specialising in savvy stand-up. Morris himself often joins the headliners on stage, and even offers a money-back guarantee.

Fake Gallery
4319 Melrose Avenue, between N Vermont & N Mariposa Avenues, Midtown (www.fakedotcom.com). Metro Vermont-Beverly/bus 10, 204, 754/US 101, exit Vermont Avenue north. **Shows** 8pm Thur-Sat. **Admission** $10-$20. **No credit cards**. **Map** p330 A4.
Experimental themed productions and more straightforward stand-up shows are staged for adventurous audiences at this unusual operation, equal parts art gallery and performance space. Held every month, *Fake Radio* sees comics recreating classic radio plays on stage.

Groundlings Theatre
7307 Melrose Avenue, at N Poinsettia Place, West Hollywood (1-323 934 9700/www.groundlings.com). Bus 10/I-10, exit Fairfax Avenue north. **Shows** 8pm Wed, Thur; 8pm, 10pm Fri, Sat; 7.30pm Sun. **Admission** $15-$21.50. **Credit** AmEx, DC, Disc, MC, V. **Map** p328 D2.

Arts & Entertainment

The holy hall of improvisational and character-based sketch comedy operates a popular theatre alongside their extensive programme of improv classes. Kathy Griffin, Will Ferrell, Phil Hartman and innumerable *Saturday Night Live* cast members have all shot to stardom from here.

Ice House

24 N Mentor Avenue, at E Colorado Boulevard, Pasadena (1-626 577 1894/www.icehousecomedy. com). Metro Lake/bus 180, 181, 256, 485/I-210, exit Lake Avenue south. **Shows** 8pm Tue-Thur; 8.30pm, 10.30pm Fri; 7pm, 9pm, 11pm Sat; other nights vary. **Admission** $5-$17.50; 2-drink min. **Credit** AmEx, DC, Disc, MC, V.

Nationally known touring comics such as Craig 'The Lovemaster' Shoemaker and Gabriel Iglesias are regulars at this stand-up specialist up in Pasadena. The Ice House is also home to Rudy Moreno's popular Latino Comedy Showcase, held every Tuesday.

Improv

8162 Melrose Avenue, between N Kildea Drive & N La Jolla Avenue, West Hollywood (1-323 651 2583/ www.improv.com). Bus 10, LDF/I-10, exit La Cienega Boulevard north. **Shows** 8pm Mon; 5pm, 8pm, 10pm Tue; 8pm, 10pm Wed-Sat; 7.30pm, 9.30pm Sun. **Admission** free-$20. **Credit** AmEx, DC, MC, V. **Map** p328 C2.

The oldest brick wall in town hosts two stand-up shows each night, with an early-evening open-mic on Tuesdays and popular black comedy night Mo' Betta Mondays. Big-name drop-ins are frequent.

IO West

6366 Hollywood Boulevard, at Ivar Avenue, Hollywood (1-323 962 7560/http://west.ioimprov. com). Metro Hollywood-Vine/bus 180, 181, 210, 212, 217, LDH/US 101, exit Vine Street south. **Shows** times vary, daily. **Admission** free-$10. **Credit** DC, MC, V. **Map** p329 B1.

The view from the stage

Ladies and gentlemen: Mr Paul F Tompkins! The 'Mr' is important when introducing LA's hardest-working and, in all likelihood, funniest comic. Whether he's playing an upscale club or a bare-bones stage, Tompkins is always nattily turned out in an immaculate suit, often pinstriped. And turn out he does: a founding member of the LA alternative comedy scene that sprung up in the early '90s and that saw the likes of David Cross, Janeane Garofalo and Margaret Cho performing material that didn't rely on punchlines, the Philadelphia-born stand-up is busier than ever.

Tompkins appears regularly on TV – VH1's *Best Week Ever, Countdown with Keith Olbermann* on MSNBC, the much-missed *Mr Show with Bob & David* – and has even been tapped to appear in a number of movies, among them *Magnolia, Anchorman: The Legend of Ron Burgundy* and *There Will Be Blood.* But even so, he can't stay off the stage. He takes to the spotlight at **Largo** (*see p226*) for The Paul F Tompkins Show on the first Saturday of the month, and also appears regularly at the **M Bar** (*see p226*) and other venues. 'I really should slow down,' he admits.

You won't, though, see him on the stages of chuckle factories like the **Comedy Store** (*see p224*) or the **Improv** (*see p225*) anymore. 'People go to get drunk,' says Tompkins. 'Drunk people are not fun to perform for. You can't hold their attention and they make too much noise.' And he's never even been to the famous **Comedy &**

Magic Club (*see p223*), which charges a cover of up to $30 and a pricey drinks minimum. 'For that price,' gasps Tompkins, 'I hope you get both comedy *and* magic…'

The comic feels very differently about one LA venue at which he's frequently seen. 'I would direct people to the **UCB [Upright Citizens Brigade Theatre**; *see p226*],' he says, when asked to recommend a club. 'There are so many unique and talented people working there. You could go on any night of the week and see a great show.'

The LA outpost of the Chicago-based comedy set-up (formerly ImprovOlympic) offers between three and five shows a night, many featuring the house improv speciality known as 'The Harold'. *Opening Night: The Improvised Musical* (Fridays at 9pm) and *Big News* (Sundays at 10pm) are among the weekly staples; the cover charges and drinks prices are the cheapest on Hollywood Boulevard. If you're here in June, look out for the annual improv festival.

LA Connection

13442 Ventura Boulevard, Sherman Oaks,(1-818 710 1320 ext 2/www.laconnectioncomedy.com). **Shows** *8.30pm Thur; 7pm, 8pm, 9pm, 10.30pm Fri, Sat; 8pm Sun.* **Admission** $7-$12. **Credit** DC, MC, V. **Map** p328 B1.

Dedicated to nurturing comic talent, LA Connection is your best – OK, only – choice for improv, sketch and stand-up comedy in the Valley. If there's available seating, a single cover charge admits you to all three shows on any given night. Kids perform for kids on weekend afternoons.

Largo

For listings, see p257.

Now based in the old Coronet Theater, Largo is chiefly a music venue, but there's also plenty of smart, inventive comedy on the schedule. Major names such as Greg Proops, Sarah Silverman and Patton Oswalt play the 280-seat main space; a cosy 60-seat club hosts the famed Largo Comedy Night on Monday, where drop-ins by the likes of Janeane Garofalo, Eddie Izzard, Flight of the Conchords and Mary Lynn Rajskub keep audiences excited.

Laugh Factory

8001 W Sunset Boulevard, at Laurel Canyon Boulevard, West Hollywood (1-323 656 1336/ www.laughfactory.com). Bus 2, 302, LDHWH/ I-10, exit La Cienega Boulevard north. **Shows** 8pm Mon, Wed; 6.30pm, 10pm Tue; 8pm, 10pm Thur, Sun; 8pm, 10pm, midnight Fri, Sat. **Admission** free-$25; $30-$45 VIP seating; 2-drink min. **Credit** DC, MC, V. **Map** p328 B1.

Jon Lovitz has vowed to get raunchy on this stage every Wednesday until his death. On other nights, this Sunset Strip staple showcases touring stand-ups alongside themed evenings (Latino Night on Mondays, the outrageous urban comedy of Sunday's Chocolate Sundae). You'll need to spring for VIP tickets to guarantee a seat. Dane Cook made it big here, but don't hold that against what is generally a dependable joint.

M Bar

1253 N Vine Street, at Fountain Avenue, Hollywood (1-323 856 0036/www.mbarhollywood.com). Bus 210/US 101, exit Vine Street south. **Shows** 8pm nightly. **Admission** free-$15; $10 food min. **Credit** AmEx, DC, Disc, MC, V. **Map** p329 B2.

Beth Lapides' monthly Un-Cabaret brings thoughtful, personal stand-up by the likes of Taylor Negron, Greg Behrendt and Laura Kightlinger to this Hollywood setting, where you're also expected to dine. The schedule varies weekly: call for details of what's on when you're in town. If you're lucky, you might catch Brentley Heilbron performing R Kelly's 'Trapped in the Closet' on a ukulele.

Second City Studio Theatre

6560 Hollywood Boulevard, at Schrader Boulevard, Hollywood (1-323 464 8542/www.secondcity.com). Metro Hollywood-Vine/bus 180, 181, 210, 212, 217, LDH/US 101, exit Vine Street south. **Shows** times vary, Tue-Thur, Sun; 8pm, 9.30pm Fri; 9.30pm, 11pm Sat; other nights vary. **Admission** free-$15. No **credit cards**. **Map** p329 B1.

Tucked away in an upstairs room on Hollywood Boulevard, this tiny theatre hosts regular improv shows that continue the comedy experimentation made famous by Chicago legends such as John Belushi and Del Close. The joint pays homage to its Windy City origins in the weekly *Ditka*, which claims to offer '1985 Chicago Bears-style improv'.

Steve Allen Theater

Center for Inquiry, 4773 Hollywood Boulevard, at N Berendo Street, Los Feliz (1-323 666 4268/ www.steveallentheater.com). Metro Vermont-Sunset/bus 26, 180, 181, 204, 206, 754/US 101, exit Vermont Avenue north. **Shows** times & days vary. **Admission** $5-$20. **No credit cards**. **Map** p330 A2.

The Tomorrow Show, a bizarre variety performance with music and comedy, runs every Saturday at midnight, hosted by hotshots Craig Anton, Brendon Small and Ron Lynch. The programme also often includes fantastic, oddball shows by former Kids in the Hall, Emo Phillips and Mary Lynn Rajskub, among others. A true gem.

Upright Citizens Brigade Theatre

5919 Franklin Avenue, at N Bronson Avenue, Hollywood (1-323 908 8702/www.ucbtheatre.com/la). Bus 26, 180, 181, 217, LDH/US 101, exit Gower Street north. **Shows** times vary, daily. **Admission** free-$10. **No credit cards**. **Map** p329 C1.

UCB offers three or four shows per night across a variety of disciplines. Highlights include the flagship Asssscat improv show, $8 on Saturdays but free on Sundays, and the consistently star-studded Comedy Death-Ray (Tuesdays, 8pm), where you might find Sarah Silverman, David Cross and Patton Oswalt on the same bill. There's no bar, but you can bring your own from the nearby Gelson's market. *Photo p224.*

Westside Eclectic Comedy Club

1323a Third Street Promenade, at Arizona Avenue, Santa Monica (1-310 451 0850/www.westside eclectic.com). Bus 33, 333, SM1, SM5, SM7, SM8, SM10/I-10, exit 4th-5th Street north. **Shows** times & days vary. **Admission** free-$8. **No credit cards**. **Map** p326 A2.

Upstart improv comedy comes to the beach at the Westside Eclectic, where you'll find fine young performers perfecting their craft in solid troupes such as the Waterbrains and the Transformers. However, if you're over 30, you may not get the joke.

Film & TV

Hooray for Hollywood!

Film

Below the gleaming typographic splendour of the HOLLYWOOD sign stretches the picture-postcard landscape of greater Los Angeles, all palm trees, white beaches and scattered skylines. The world's most photographed megalopolis, LA thrives on the snap-snap fuss that it's attracted ever since it took the movie industry under its wing a century ago. The city's outsized story runs parallel to the parabolic history of American film.

Blue skies and easy living helped make pastoral Los Angeles the film industry's manifest destination. Technicians, artistes and ragtag opportunists traded East Coast stability for West Coast ambition as they went in search of sunshine: Hollywood. LA's rural real estate soon dissolved into a hive of activity, dense with studio lots, movie palaces and other trickledown businesses. The 1927 advent of sound fortified the burgeoning industry.

After the Great Depression, Hollywood began to cement its assembly-line reputation by limiting artistic license and locking major stars-directors-writers into long-term contracts. The town just about retained its power through lean times in the '60s and early '70s, before a renaissance saw audacious movie brats such as Coppola and Bogdanovich shed old modes. Lucas, Spielberg et al quickly reminded moviegoers of the Seventh Art's alchemic essence, and reaffirmed LA's place at the heart of the movie world.

Despite a Tarantino hiccup, the last two decades of cinema's first century mostly adhered to a producer-approved diet of big-budget blockbusters and shoestring independents. Save a strong 2007, recent mainstream cinema has been loaded with cinematic synonyms: sequels, remakes, lacklustre rip-offs. But digital days beckon: new technology (pioneered by the above-mentioned Lucas) and its desktop-auteur operatives hold the promise of an industry facelift in the near future. It'll be interesting to see how Hollywood reacts.

Movie theatres

Cinemas are everywhere in Los Angeles, their varied architecture, artistic slants and client bases approximating *la ciudad*'s multilingual diversity. From Bruckheimer blockbusters to fancies of yesteryear, Bauhaus abstracts to Iranian comedies, all cinematic life is here, assuming you know where to look.

For weekly listings, reviews, and special events, thumb through the tried-and-true 'Calendar' section of the *LA Times* or pick up the *LA Weekly*. The Film Radar website (www.filmradar.com) provides a special focus on the arthouse and repertory movie scenes.

PREMIERES & PREVIEWS

Woody Allen once wisecracked that the only cultural advantage to Los Angeles is that you're able to make a right turn on a red light. Still, moviegoers have at least one other perk: the chance to see new films before anybody else. In areas that attract heavy foot traffic (the Hollywood Walk of Fame, Santa Monica's Third Street Promenade, Universal CityWalk), studio recruiters tempt non-industry passers-by into attending test-the-market preview screenings, at which the latest studio movies are screened well in advance of their release. Tickets are free; payback comes with the expectation that attendees pass comment on what they've just seen by filling out a lengthy form afterwards.

Multiplexes

Most of Los Angeles' ultra-modern, THX-certified cineplexes are located in consumer paradises: malls, shopping centres and the like. Five of the most popular are detailed below; the nicest is probably the new Landmark in Westwood, which rationalises its boastful name

The best Cinema

For the pick of the flicks
ArcLight Hollywood. *See p228.*

For a blast from the past
American Cinematheque. *See p231.*

For a rave from the grave
Cinespia at the Hollywood Forever Cemetery. *See p234.*

Arts & Entertainment

with bourgeois features (deluxe concession stands, a romantic wine bar) and free parking. Show times and tickets are available from individual cinemas, via MovieFone (1-310 777 3456 or 1-323 777 3456) or at www.fandango.com.

AMC Century 15
Westfield Century City, 10250 Santa Monica Boulevard, between Century Park W & Avenue of the Stars, Century City (1-310 289 4262/www.amc theatres.com). Bus 4, 16, 704/I-405, exit Santa Monica Boulevard east. **Screens** 15. **Tickets** $11.50; $6-$10.50 discounts. **Credit** AmEx, DC, Disc, MC, V. **Map** p327 B4.

AMC Citywalk Stadium 19 with IMAX
Universal Citywalk, 100 Universal City Plaza, Universal City (1-818 508 0711/www.amctheatres. com). Metro Universal City/bus 96, 156, 166/US 101, exit Universal Center Drive. **Screens** 19. **Tickets** $12; $6-$9 discounts. **Credit** AmEx, DC, Disc, MC, V.

Bridge: Cinema de Luxe/IMAX
The Promenade at Howard Hughes Center, 6081 Center Drive, at Sepulveda Boulevard, Westchester (1-310 568 3375/www.thebridgecinemas.com). Bus 429/I-405, exit Howard Hughes Parkway west. **Screens** 17. **Tickets** $8.75-$12.75; $8.50-$9 discounts. **Credit** DC, MC, V.

Landmark
10850 W Pico Boulevard, at Westwood Boulevard, Westwood (1-310 281 8233/www.landmark theatres.com). Bus C3, SM7, SM8, SM13, SM16/ I-10, exit Overland Avenue north. **Screens** 12. **Tickets** $12; $8-$9 discounts. **Credit** AmEx, DC, MC, V. **Map** p327 A5.

Pacific Theaters at the Grove
The Grove, 6301 W 3rd Street, between N Fairfax Avenue & N Gardner Street, West Hollywood (1-323 692 0829/www. pacifictheatres.com). Bus 16, LDHWI/I-10, exit Fairfax Avenue north. **Screens** 14. **Tickets** $9.75-$12.75; $7.75-$8.75 discounts. **Credit** AmEx, DC, MC, V. **Map** p328 C3.

Classic picture houses

ArcLight Hollywood
6360 W Sunset Boulevard, between Ivar Avenue & Vine Street, Hollywood (1-323 464 1478/www.arc lightcinemas.com). Bus 180, 181, 210, 212, 217, 310, LDH, LDHWI/US 101, exit Vine Street south. **Screens** 15. **Tickets** $14; $9-$12 discounts. **Credit** AmEx, DC, MC, V. **Map** p329 B2.

A Hollywood favourite since 2002, the ArcLight offers comfortable seats, state-of-the-art sight and sound, fantastic snack bars and, for some Dionysian indulgence, an in-house café-bar. The programming is an astute mix of first-run flicks, indies, foreign fare

ArcLight Hollywood.

Festivals Film

Orpheum Theatre, which features
as part of **Last Remaining Seats**.

Pan African Film Festival

1-323 295 1706/www.paff.org. **Date** Feb.
A slate of African and African American films,
many addressing issues of cultural and racial
tolerance. Screenings are held at the AMC
Magic Johnson 15 multiplex in Crenshaw.

Los Angeles Asian Pacific Film Festival

1-213 680 4462/http://festival.vconline.org.
Date May.
A variety of Asian and Asian American
films, screened in several venues in West
Hollywood and Little Tokyo.

Silver Lake Film Festival

www.silverlakefilmfestival.org. **Date** May.
Hirsute hipsters populate this East Side
event, which supplements independent films
with art, music and partying. Venues stretch
from the Echo to the Egyptian Theatre.

Film Independent's Los Angeles Film Festival

1-866 345 6337/www.lafilmfest.com.
Date June.
With 200-plus features, shorts and music
videos, this prestigious ten-day festival at
various Westwood venues is cardio cinema.

Last Remaining Seats

1-213 623 2489/www.laconservancy.org.
Date May/June.
The LA Conservancy offers a wonderful
time-machine trip by reopening Downtown's
grand old movie palaces for one-night-only
screenings of classic films.

Outfest

1-213 480 7088/www.outfest.org. **Date** July.
A ten-day festival of gay and lesbian shorts
and features, spread across ten venues
dotted around LA.

Downtown Film Festival

*1-213 221 7685/www.downtown
filmfestla.com.* **Date** Aug.
Launched in 2008 by the folks behind the
Silver Lake Film Festival, the DFF aims to
celebrate the resurgence of Downtown LA
across a wide variety of venues.

Los Angeles International Short Film Festival

1-323 461 4400/www.lashortsfest.com.
Date Sept.
The world's largest shorts festival crams 400
entries into a typically dense programme.

Artivist Film Festival

1-310 712 1222/www.artivists.org. **Date** Oct.
This festival, at Hollywood's Egyptian Theatre,
offers a platform for activist artists.

Los Angeles Latino International Film Festival

www.latinofilm.org. **Date** Oct.
Mexican and Latin American filmmakers come
to Hollywood to promote their work.

AFI Los Angeles International Film Festival

1-866 234 3378/www.afifest.com. **Date** Nov.
This ten-day festival shows some 130 films
from 40 countries, along with special events.

Arts & Entertainment

and premieres; unusually, alcohol is allowed in some screenings. It's the most appealing modern multiplex in LA, but it falls under the 'Classic' section for the Cinerama Dome, a fabulous and unique domed movie theatre that opened in 1963. Note that parking is usually a nightmare: allow plenty of time to find a space, and don't expect to escape quickly.

Grauman's Chinese Theatre

6925 Hollywood Boulevard, between N Orange Drive & N McCadden Place, Hollywood (1-323 464 8111/ www.manntheatres.com). Metro Hollywood-Highland/ bus 210, 212, 217, 310, LDHWH/US 101, exit Highland Avenue south. **Screens** 1. **Tickets** $11.25; $8.25-$9 discounts. **Credit** AmEx, Disc, DC, MC, V. **Map** p329 A1.

In terms of both variety and technology, there are better options in Hollywood. However, the famous hand- and footprints outside this iconic theatre (for more, *see p95*) only enhance the experience, and the innumerable galas that pass beneath its renowned pagoda add to its star quality. A six-screen multiplex (also owned by Mann; same website and phone number) adjoins it in the Hollywood & Highland mall. Almost opposite stands the beautiful El Capitan (*see p94*).

Mann Bruin

948 Broxton Avenue, at Weyburn Avenue, Westwood (1-310 208 8998/www.manntheatres. com). Bus 20, 720, SM1, SM2, SM3, SM8/I-405, exit Wilshire Boulevard east. **Screens** 1. **Tickets** $11; $8-$9 discounts. **Credit** AmEx, DC, Disc, MC, V.

Built in 1937, this streamline moderne cinema draws sometimes-rowdy college crowds from nearby UCLA, who gather in front of its single screen to take in the latest mainstream favourites. Westwood is also home to the **Mann Village Theater** (961 Broxton Avenue, 1-310 208 5576), another single-screen, '30s-vintage operation that seats 1,400.

Arthouse & independent

You should also find arthouse and independent movies at some of the cinemas mentioned above, among them the **Landmark** and the **ArcLight Hollywood**.

Nuart Theatre

11272 Santa Monica Boulevard, at Sawtelle Boulevard, West LA (1-310 281 8223/www. landmarktheatres.com). Bus 4, 704, SM4/I-405, exit Santa Monica Boulevard west. **Screens** 1. **Tickets** $9.50; $7.25 discounts. **Credit** AmEx, DC, MC, V.

Exclusive engagements of independent movies, foreign flicks, arthouse curios and restored classics fill the calendar at this longstanding operation. There are midnight screenings on Fridays and Saturdays, with the latter always dedicated to the *Rocky Horror Picture Show.* Just nearby stands CineFile Video (11280 Santa Monica Boulevard, 1-310 312 8836, www.cinefilevideo.com), a cult rental store that specialises in rare, unusual and hard-to-find films.

Handprints and hustlers: it's **Grauman's Chinese Theatre**.

Regent Showcase

614 N La Brea Avenue, between Clinton Street & Melrose Avenue, Hollywood (1-323 934 2944/www. regenttheaters.com). Bus 10, 212, 312/I-10, exit La Brea Avenue north. **Screens** 1. **Tickets** $10; $7 discounts. **Credit** AmEx, DC, MC, V. **Map** p329 A3.
Built during Hollywood's heyday and still going relatively strong today, this 800-seat single-screen art deco theatre offers a mix of independent movies. It's particularly strong for LGBT film.

Sunset 5

8000 W Sunset Boulevard, at N Laurel Avenue, West Hollywood (1-323 848 3500/www.laemmle. com). Bus 2, 217, 218, 302, LDHWH/I-10, exit Fairfax Avenue north. **Screens** 5. **Tickets** $10; $7-$8.50 discounts. **Credit** AmEx, DC, MC, V. **Map** p328 C1.
Located in a glitzy outdoor plaza, this small theatre exhibits a shake-up attitude toward the status quo marquee, screening a slate of new independents and small studio films. The Laemmle group also runs the Monica 4-Plex (1332 2nd Street, Santa Monica, 1-310 394 9741), the Royal (11523 Santa Monica Boulevard, West LA, 1-310 477 5581) and the Music Hall 3 (9036 Wilshire Boulevard, Beverly Hills, 1-310 274 6869).

Repertory & experimental

Raging against wholesale modernity, Los Angeles' standalone repertory cinemas are eureka-evoking resources. In addition to the movie houses detailed below, LA's museums also contribute to the scene: the **Museum of Contemporary Art** (*see p116*) concentrates on avant-garde and experimental offerings; while LACMA (*see p100*) programmes enlightened retrospectives and, on Tuesdays, Hollywood classics for $2 a ticket.

American Cinematheque

Egyptian Theatre *6712 Hollywood Boulevard, between N Highland & N Las Palmas Avenues, Hollywood. Metro Hollywood-Highland/bus 210, 212, 217, 310, LDHWH/US 101, exit Highland Avenue south.* **Map** p329 A1.
Aero Theatre *1328 Montana Avenue, at 14th Street, Santa Monica. Bus SM3/I-10, exit Lincoln Boulevard north.* **Map** p326 B2.
Both *1-323 466 3456/www.americancinematheque. com.* **Screens** 1. **Tickets** $10; $7-$8 discounts. **Credit** AmEx, DC, MC, V.
Its design inspired by King Tutankhamun's sepulchre, the Egyptian Theatre edges its Santa Monica counterpart for sheer dramatic majesty. However, the main attraction at both venues is actually still the programme: the not-for-profit American Cinematheque delivers a wide range of excellent themed mini-festivals and one-off Q&As with legendary figures. On Sundays at the Egyptian Theatre, the LA Filmforum screens experimental films and video art.

Billy Wilder Theatre

UCLA Hammer Museum, 10899 Wilshire Boulevard, at Westwood Boulevard, Westwood (1-310 206 8013/www.cinema.ucla.edu) Bus 20, 720, SM1, SM2, SM3, SM8/I-405, exit Wilshire Boulevard east. **Screens** 1. **Tickets** $10; $7-$9 discounts. **Credit** AmEx, DC, MC, V. **Map** p327 A4.
The Hammer Museum's intimate, state-of-the-art spot boasts '70s game-show decor and 295 pink, stadium-style seats. Programming consists of screenings tied to the museum's exhibition schedule and the excellent UCLA Film & Television Archive.

Cinefamily at the Silent Movie Theatre

611 N Fairfax Avenue, at Clinton Street, Fairfax District (1-323 655 2520/www.cinefamily.org). Bus 10, 217, 218, LDHWI/I-10, exit Fairfax Avenue north. **Screens** 1. **Tickets** $10; $8 discounts. **Credit** AmEx, DC, Disc, MC, V. **Map** p328 C2.
LA's equivalent of the Cinémathèque Française responds to Truffaut's puzzled inquiry – 'Is the cinema more important than life?' – with a wholehearted 'yes'. After a spell in the doledrums, this lovely venue is now curated by the Cinefamily organisation of enthusiasts and no longer limits itself to silent flicks: you'll now find everything from kitschy B-movies to punch-proud masterpieces.

Cinespace

6356 Hollywood Boulevard, at Ivar Avenue, Hollywood (1-323 817 3456/www.cinespace.info). Metro Hollywood-Vine/bus 180, 181, 210, 212, 217, LDH/US 101, exit Hollywood Boulevard west. **Screens** 1. **Tickets** movies free with dinner. **Credit** AmEx, DC, Disc, MC, V. **Map** p329 B1.
This hipster-friendly space offers an indulgent dinner and a movie every Friday and Saturday, with faintly arty recent releases or more straightforward romcoms. The bon chic ambience comes at a price.

Fairfax Regency

7907 Beverly Boulevard, at N Fairfax Avenue, Fairfax District (1-323 655 4010/www.regency movies.com). Bus 14/I-10, exit Fairfax Avenue north. **Screens** 3. **Tickets** $6; $3.50-$4 discounts. **No credit cards. Map** p328 C3.
Not quite a first-run movie house but also not quite a repertory cinema, this mighty triplex receives films a few weeks their after opening weekend, a time-lag that translates to cheap tickets. Cult classics are screened on Fridays at midnight.

New Beverly Cinema

7165 Beverly Boulevard, at N Detroit Street, Fairfax District (1-323 938 4038/www.newbevcinema). Bus

> **Grauman's Chinese Theatre**
> (*p230*) Woman: 'Look, Herman, I'm in Hedy Lamarr's shoes!' Harvey Korman, walking briskly past: '*Hed*-ley...'

Caught on camera

On 24 October 1907, a Chicago judge ruled that 'Colonel' William N Selig's movie equipment, acquired on the black market, infringed Edison Motion Picture patents. Banned from filming in Illinois, Selig read an LA Chamber of Commerce brochure promising '350 days a year of sunshine!', and duly sent Francis Boggs to film a scene for his adaptation of **The Count of Monte Cristo**.

Boggs liked LA so much that he never left. His film **In the Sultan's Power** (1909), shot on a vacant Downtown lot (at 751 S Olive Street, now a parking garage), was the first dramatic film shot wholly in the city, and kicked off LA's 100-year reign as the most filmed town on earth. Since his arrival, the city has been captured in countless movies, playing itself with various degrees of enthusiasm and commitment in everything from surf flicks (John Milius's 1978 flick **Big Wednesday**) to movies about car theft (the original 1974 version of **Gone in 60 Seconds**). Here are some of the best.

CRIME & PUNISHMENT

Just as LA gave birth to noir literature, so Hollywood took up the mantle of filming it. **Double Indemnity** (1944), **Mildred Pierce** (1945) and **The Postman Always Rings Twice** (1946, remade 1981) are steamy tales of hapless schlubs done in by femme fatales. Stephen Frears' rough-and-tumble **The Grifters** (1990) ploughs a similar furrow. And then there are the escapades of Chandler's Philip Marlowe: played by Hollywood smoothie Dick Powell in **Farewell, My Lovely** (1944), urbane tough guy Humphrey Bogart in **The Big Sleep** (1946), restrained grump James Garner in **Marlowe** (1969), crumpled mumbler Elliot Gould in **The Long Goodbye** (1973) and ageing battler Robert Mitchum in another version of **Farewell, My Lovely** (1975).

Other crime films have used LA in opaque ways. Take **DOA** (1949, dismally remade in 1988), whose LA is edgy and artless, or **Heat** (1995) and **Collateral** (2004), Michael Mann's sumptuous travelogues; contrast them with **Memento** (2000), a dizzying puzzle of revenge, and **Training Day** (2001), which offers a vivid tour that hits East LA, Downtown, Echo Park and South Central in a single day. David Lynch demonstrated that LA noir needn't be confined to the detective genre in **Mulholland Dr.** (2001), arguably the best film about LA's incestuous relationship to the Hollywood fantasy machine. And then, of course, there are the crooks and ninnies in the movies of Quentin Tarantino, with the malls, diners and warehouses of Inglewood, Toluca Lake and Torrance taking centre stage in **Reservoir Dogs** (1992) and **Pulp Fiction** (1994).

However, two crime films really stand out from the pack. Roman Polanski's creepy **Chinatown** (1974) follows the tough, well-meaning but ultimately ineffectual PI Jake Gittes (Jack Nicholson) through seedy, sun-kissed pre-war LA as he tries to unravel the mystery of a phoney drought, a doomed mystery woman and her monstrous tycoon father. **LA Confidential** (1997), based on the James Ellroy novel, is a more stylised but no less fascinating recreation of the seedy city in the 1950s. Its release imbued the city itself with a new iconography and cool.

WEALTH & POVERTY

Filmmakers have had plenty of fun detailing the lifestyles of LA's rich and famous. Paul Bartel essays the perversions of the idle rich in **Scenes from the Class Struggle in Beverly Hills** (1989); Hal Ashby's **Shampoo** (1975) follows the romantic travails of a bed-hopping Hollywood hair stylist played by (who else?) Warren Beatty; and **Clueless** (1995) paints a satirical yet winning portrait of LA rich kids and their pampered lives. *Clueless*, indeed, could hardly provide a greater contrast to **Rebel Without a Cause** (1955), shot in part at the Griffith Observatory.

However, filmmakers have also revelled in the city's seedy and deprived subcultures, amplifying the voices of characters whose cries are largely unheard in day-to-day LA. **Barfly** (1987) finds Mickey Rourke mumbling through a part-autobiographical Charles Bukowski script set in LA's fleabag hotels and odiferous dive bars. In John Cassavetes' **The Killing of a Chinese Bookie** (1976), a strip club provides a home for an extended family of lonely dancers. And **Permanent Midnight** (1998) chronicles the heroin addiction of former TV writer Jerry Stahl (Ben Stiller).

Although Charles Burnett's **Killer of Sheep** (1977) was set in Watts, it was another 15 years before South Central LA's poverty-wrecked black communities found a cinematic focus. John Singleton's **Boyz N the Hood** (1991) launched a trend of movies that indicted, glorified and poked fun at black LA culture. The Hughes Brothers' quite terrifying **Menace II Society** (1993) and Carl Franklin's adaptation of Walter Mosley's **Devil in a Blue Dress** (1995) provide alternative perspectives on LA's black communities.

FILM & FAME

Dreams of stardom have been tackled ad nauseam, from **Sullivan's Travels** (1941) via **A Star Is Born** (1937, remade in 1954 and 1976) through to the more modern likes of **Postcards from the Edge** (1990), **Guilty by Suspicion** (1991), **Barton Fink** (1991), **The Player** (1992), **Swimming with Sharks** (1994) and **Get Shorty** (1995). Other movies, though, have imbued the subject with a little more pathos. Tim Burton's **Ed Wood** (1994) links the laughable films of 'the worst director of all time' with the underbelly of Hollywood's has-beens, wannabes and never-weres. Paul Thomas Anderson's **Boogie Nights** (1997) journeys into the heart of the San Fernando Valley's fabled porn industry, while Paul Schrader's **Auto Focus** (2002) tackles the sex addiction that led to the downfall of *Hogan's Heroes* star Bob Crane. The gothic vivisection of Hollywood's self-loathing detailed by Billy Wilder in **Sunset Blvd** (1950) is still horrifying; Edgar G Ulmer's **Detour** (1945) plays like its cancerous brother. And then, of course, there's **Singin' in the Rain** (1952), about stumbling into the Sound Era.

SPRAWL & DECAY

LA has had plenty of affection smothered on to it by its native chroniclers. **LA Story** (1991) is Steve Martin's Left Coast equivalent of Woody Allen's *Manhattan*; **Swingers** (1996) captures the rise of cocktail culture; and in the sleek, silky form of **Pretty Woman** (1990), LA found its *Pygmalion*. Others have appeared ambivalent but ultimately affectionate: witness Robert Altman's **Short Cuts** (1993), Alan Rudolph's earlier **Welcome to LA** (1976) and even, perhaps, Paul Thomas Anderson's **Magnolia** (1999).

However, a handful of other directors have provided a fearsome counterpoint to their affections, depicting the city as smog-choked, monstrous and alienating. As LA entered the 1990s with floods, fires, earthquakes and riots, in film it became almost synonymous with urban fear and paranoia. The New Agey **Grand Canyon** (1991) essays pre-Rodney King white malaise at the turn of the 1990s; Todd Haynes' **Safe** (1995) focuses on a rich LA wife who believes she's being poisoned by the modern world; and **Crash** (2004) updates the city's multi-ethnic tensions post-9/11. Still, the last word on LA's sprawl belongs to **Falling Down** (1992), which tracks an Angry White Man (Michael Douglas) as he cuts a violent swathe from East LA to Venice Beach after getting stuck in rush-hour gridlock. Try not to follow his lead.

The Killing of a Chinese Bookie

14, 212/I-10, exit La Brea Avenue north. **Screens**
1. **Tickets** $7; $4-$6 discounts. **No credit cards.**
Map p328 D3.
Cinephiles study their ABCs at this beloved grind-
house, defined by its bargain prices, shabby charm
and film-for-film's-sake attitude. All the regular repertory presentations are double-features; midnight
screenings help get movie buffs through the night.

Other cinemas

California ScienCenter IMAX

*California ScienCenter, 700 State Drive, between
S Figueroa Street & S Vermont Avenue, Exposition
Park (1-213 744 2014/www.casciencectr.org). Bus
40, 42, 102, 550/I-110, exit Exposition Boulevard
west.* **Screens** 1. **Tickets** $8; $4.75-$5.75 discounts.
Credit AmEx, DC, MC, V.
The ScienCenter's gargantuan screen engenders
wonder with its flora and fauna explorations and
way-of-the-world programming.

Cinespia at the Hollywood Forever Cemetery

*6000 Santa Monica Boulevard, at Gordon Street,
Hollywood (1-323 221 3343/www.cinespia.org). Bus
4, 156, 704/US 101, exit Santa Monica Boulevard
west.* **Screens** 1. **Tickets** $10. **No credit cards.**
Map p327 C2.
A slide show of vintage film posters and a mood-
setting DJ combine to relax the picnicking crowd at
this famous cemetery before the main event: a classic film projected on to a wall of one of the larger
mausoleums. The *carpe diem* ambience enchants,
though the fact that alcohol is permitted also helps.

Echo Park Film Center

*1200 N Alvarado Street, at W Sunset Boulevard,
Echo Park (1-213 484 8846/www.echoparkfilm
center.org). Bus 2, 4, 302, 704/US 101, exit
Glendale Boulevard north.* **Screens** 1. **Tickets**
free-$7. **No credit cards.** **Map** p330 D5.
Aimed at curious locals and aspiring filmmakers,
this community media arts organisation holds a film
school, a rental shop and a 50-seat microcinema that
screens *art brut* alive with DIY aesthetics.

TV

LA's self-appointed role as the centre of the
entertainment industry is given credence by
the massive number of TV shows filmed in the
city. The packed shooting schedule means that
tickets are surprisingly easy to obtain. You can
apply online ahead of time through a specialist
ticketing agency or, in some cases, through the
relevant TV network. However, if you haven't
booked in advance, clipboard-touting agents
can be found at tourist hangouts such as
Grauman's Chinese Theatre, Universal
CityWalk, Santa Monica's Third Street

Promenade and Venice Beach, dispensing tickets
for that week's shows.
Tickets for shows are free, but be warned that
the experience may involve three to four hours
and a lot of sitting around. And check the fine
print: tickets may not guarantee admission (early
arrival is usually required), and shows have age
restrictions. For tours of studios, *see p73.*

Individual shows

Jimmy Kimmel Live

Tickets *1-866 546 6984/www.1iota.com.*
Shows 6.15pm Mon-Thur.
Filmed in Hollywood, Kimmel's show has a relaxed
atmosphere, but still draws top-shelf guests. You
can apply for tickets to sit in the show's studio audience, or for a mini-concert performed by that night's
musical guest. Don't be fooled by the show's name:
it's filmed an hour before it airs out east.

The Price is Right

Tickets *1-323 575 2458/www.cbs.com.*
Shows 1pm & 4pm, days vary.
Tickets for this daytime perennial can be booked
online through CBS's own ticket server, though you
can also call for ticket information. The CBS site contains a shooting schedule.

The Tonight Show

Tickets *3000 W Alameda Avenue, Burbank, CA
91523 (www.nbc.com).* **Shows** 4.30pm Mon-Fri.
Getting in to this late-night staple takes persistence.
Tickets are available at least six weeks in advance
by mail only: check online for details of how to
apply. A limited number of tickets are handed out
for that day's show from 8am. You'll need to arrive
by 2.30pm at the latest to guarantee entry.

Ticket agencies

Audiences Unlimited

1-818 753 3470/www.tvtickets.com.
Audiences Unlimited deals largely with sitcoms,
providing tickets to favourites such as *Two and a
Half Men* and *Rules of Engagement.*

Hollywood Tickets

1-818 688 3974/www.hollywoodtickets.com.
Hollywood Tickets' site is wonderfully straightforward: select the show you want to see, or the dates
you're available, and up will spring a list of options.

On Camera Audiences

1-818 295 2700/www.ocatv.com.
American Idol, Dancing with the Stars and *The Late
Late Show* are among the shows served by OCA.

TV Tix

1-323 653 4105/www.tvtix.com.
Deal or No Deal, Wheel of Fortune, Jeopardy and others are just a few mouse-clicks away. The company
also enlists movie extras.

Galleries

Art in LA means serious business.

LA Louver. *See p236.*

LA's art scene is beginning to give New York a run for its money. A recent Rand Corporation study found that 'the arts' are responsible for more than $4 billion of economic activity in Los Angeles County every year. The burst-bubble troubles of the early 1990s are a distant memory, as is any debate over the viability and longevity of the city's place in the art world.

Indeed, the main drawback is the variety: shows open constantly in all corners of the city. The three key districts are the reinvigorated **Bergamot Station** in Santa Monica; **Culver City**, now stuffed with more than 50 galleries; and Chinatown and Gallery Row in **Downtown LA**. However, there's more elsewhere: the old-school hot spots of **Silver Lake** and **Venice** are holding their own just fine, as are their more upscale counterparts on the **Miracle Mile**.

> ▶ For the **Getty Center**, *see p84.*
> ▶ For **LACMA**, *see p100.*
> ▶ For **MOCA**, *see p116.*
> ▶ For the **UCLA Hammer Museum**, *see p88.*
> ▶ For **Pasadena's art museums**, *see p132.*

INFORMATION

For listings, locals rely on the exhaustive *Art Scene* (www.artscenecal.com) over and above the *Art Now Gallery Guide*. *LA Weekly* has bare-bones listings; the *LA Times*' 'Calendar' has largely been supplanted by online cousin MetroMix (www.metromix.com). Also online, Flavorpill (www.flavorpill.com) provides less comprehensive but more in-depth listings, while Fette's Flog (www.the-flog.com) documents the shows and the scene. Most neighbourhoods also have a dedicated website; see below for details.

Most (but not all) galleries are open from around 11am to 5pm, Tuesday to Saturday. However, always call first to save a wasted trip.

Santa Monica & the beach towns

Santa Monica

The centre of Santa Monica's art scene is **Bergamot Station** (2525 Michigan Avenue, www.bergamotstation.com), a former trolley stop that's now home to 30-plus galleries. The galleries are generally open 10am-6pm Tuesday to Friday and 11am-5.30pm on Saturdays; the Bergamot website has contact details for all tenants. If you head here on a Saturday night, you're likely to find more than one gallery owner uncorking the chardonnay as they launch a new show. And twice a year, the Santa Monica Auctions (www.smauctions.com) are held here, offering deals on A-list art released from private collections in LA.

Among the galleries are **Peter Fetterman**, a sophisticated purveyor of museum-level photography. High-concept abstraction is the mainstay at **Ruth Bachofner**; epic shows and experimental performances draw interested crowds of onlookers at **Track 16**. **Robert Berman** and **William Turner**, two of the standard-bearers for avant-garde West Coast abstraction, are both present; a more British bent inspires the shows at **Mark Moore Gallery**. **Patricia Correia** focuses on the passionate, vibrant and sometimes political traditions of Chicano art in SoCal; **Richard Heller** mounts show of post-illustration art; and **Craig Krull** casts his net wide enough to cover architectural photography by Julius Shulman alongside work by artists who draw inspiration from LA's natural world.

If you leave the Bergamot at the back of the complex and head east up Olympic Boulevard, you'll soon reach the **Griffin Contemporary** (2902 Nebraska Avenue, 1-310 586 6886, www.griffincontemporary.com). Striking an academic tone, it showcases rare modern and post-modern mixed media works from the likes of Joseph Beuys and Leon Golub. A little further east is **GR2** (2062 Sawtelle Boulevard, 1-310 445 9276, www.gr2.net), a gallery spin-off of *Giant Robot* that delivers cutesy-fierce Japanisme. Heading west out of the Berg, meanwhile, it's just a short hop to the galleries, theatre and studios on the 1600 block of 18th Street; try the **18th Street Arts Complex** (www.18thstreet.org), a residential arts centre that stages exhibitions and other events.

Other galleries are scattered throughout Santa Monica. **Christopher Grimes** (916 Colorado Avenue, 1-310 587 3373, www.cgrimes.com), shows cutting-edge painting and video from North and South America; **Terrence Rogers** (1231 5th Street, 1-310 394 4999, www.trogart.com) and **Bill Lowe** (2034 Broadway, 1-310 449 0184, www.lowegallery.com) both favour dynamic contemporary painting; and there's cool wit and edgy aesthetics at **Angles** (2222 & 2230 Main Street, 1-310 396 5019, www.anglesgallery.com).

Venice

For years, Venice has boasted a healthy and prominent community of artists; for first-hand evidence, head to the **Venice Art Walk** in May (www.veniceartwalk.org), which affords unparalleled access to artists' studios in the area. And if you're not around in May, there'll still be something to see. Head first to venerable **LA Louver** (45 N Venice Boulevard, 1-310 822 4955, www.lalouver.com; *picture p235*), which deals in LA's contemporary masters and younger artists from New York, South America and the UK. It's recently been joined on Venice Boulevard by **Commissary Arts** (68 N Venice Boulevard, 1-310 823 0999, www.commissaryarts.com), which runs a big programme of promising local painters and photographers.

Over on Abbot Kinney Boulevard, **Equator Books** (*see p191*) augments its art-heavy library with exhibitions of art and photography with attitude, while nearby **G2** (No.1503, 1-310 452 2842, www.theg2gallery.com) exhibits a range of environmentally conscious art. At the corner of Venice and Abbot Kinney, **Epoxybox** (602 Venice Boulevard, 1-310 578 2100, www.epoxybox.com) is Venice's original alternative materials showcase. And east along Venice Boulevard, you'll pass **Overtones** (12703 Venice Boulevard, 1-310 915 0346, www.overtonesgallery.com) and **Cherry & Martin** (No.12611, 1-310 398 7404, www.cherryandmartin.com), which offer two of the city's most engaging programmes of international contemporary painting, sculpture, video, installation and everything in between.

Brentwood to Beverly Hills

Culver City

Culver City's transformation from forgotten suburb to lively cultural quarter has been one of the more interesting LA turnarounds in recent years, and the artists who helped make it happen haven't yet been priced out of the area. The district is packed with a community of galleries that together showcase a wide variety of art from LA and beyond; there's a guide to the area at www.ccgalleryguide.com. If you're here in late May/early June, look out for the Culver City Art Walk, an annual event at which many of the galleries throw open their doors for special festivities.

The heart of the burgeoning gallery district is the intersection of S La Cienega Boulevard and W Washington Boulevard. On Washington, west of La Cienega, are pioneers such as **Kinsey/Desforges** (No.6009, 1-310 837 1989, www.kinseydesforges.com), heavy on figurative painting and edgy post-graffiti art. The **Indie Collective** (No.6039, 1-310 837 7714, www. indiecollective.com) splices art with fashion; close by, **DEN Contemporary** (No.6023, 1-310 559 3023, www.dencontemporaryart.com) delivers quirky, conceptual takes on painting, drawing and installation. Former WeHo staple **Koplin del Rio** (No.6031, 1-310 836 9055, www.koplindelrio.com) makes good use of its large new space by showcasing figurative painting from an impressively diverse roster.

A few blocks west on Washington lies another cluster of enterprises. Among them are **Corey Helford** (No.8522, 1-310 287 2340, www.coreyhelfordgallery.com), which blends the production values of a mainstream gallery with the edginess of a fringe venue, and party-friendly **Lab 101** (No.8539, 1-310 945 5974, www.thelab101.com), which offers a cheeky blend of photography, fashion, skate culture and music. The **Museum of Design Art & Architecture** (No. 8609, 1-310 558 0902, www.modaagallery.com) focuses its shows on the functional aspects of monumental art. And just off Washington in the Helms Bakery, the **Scion Installation Space** (3521 Helms Avenue, 1-310 815 8840, www.scion.com/space) merges avant-garde no-brow art with brilliant branding through fashionable group shows.

East on Washington from La Cienega sit several galleries with very different aesthetics. **Susanne Vielmetter** (No.5795, 1-323 933 2117, www.vielmetter.com) shows intense figurative work side by side with first-rate minimalist abstractions; **Billy Shire** (No.5790, 1-323 297 0600, www.billyshirefinearts.com) is smartly subversive; and high-profile **Roberts & Tilton** (No.5801, 1-323 549 0223, www. robertsandtilton.com) offer an acclaimed roster of local and European artists.

And there's plenty more on S La Cienega Boulevard. Highlights include **LAXART** (No.2640, 1-310 559 0166, www.laxart.org), a high-profile, non-profit organisation with curatorial input from avant-garde luminaries such as Bettina Korek; and **Taylor de Cordoba** (No.2660, 1-310 559 9156, www. taylordecordoba.com) and **Walter Maciel** (No. 2642, 1-310 839 1840, www.waltermaciel gallery.com), which offer major shows by emerging voices. The northernmost spot on the stretch is Kim Light's aggressively cutting-edge **Lightbox** (No.2656, 1-310 559 1111, www.kimlightgallery.com).

Beverly Hills

Beverly Hills' galleries are among the most prestigious in LA. **Gagosian** (456 N Camden Drive, 1-310 271 9400, www.gagosian.com)

remains the place to head for notable post-war painting, sculpture and star-studded openings, while the Beverly Hills outpost of **ACE** (9430 Wilshire Boulevard, 1-310 858 9090, www. acegallery.net; *see also p239*) is often replete with work by A-listers such as Robert Wilson. At the nearby **Taschen Store** (354 N Beverly Drive, 1-310 274 4300, www.taschen.com), a mix of art and pop culture glamour-pusses are canonised in the pages of high-end tomes and on the walls of the store's gallery.

West Hollywood

WeHo's arts scene is focused on the streets around the intersection of Melrose Avenue and N Robertson Boulevard, where a group of businesses together promote themselves under the umbrella of **Avenues of Art & Design** (www.avenuesartdesign.com). On N Almont Drive sit **Manny Silverman** (No.619, 1-310 659 8256, www.mannysilvermangallery.com), which deals in American abstract expressionism, and **Regen Projects** (No.633, 1-310 276 5424, www.regenprojects.com), which shows hipster darlings who've made it big (Raymond Pettibon, Lari Pittman, Catherine Opie). On N Robertson, **Margo Leavin** (No.812, 1-310 273 0603) offers contemporary drawing, painting and sculpture.

On San Vicente Boulevard, the hard-to-miss **Pacific Design Center** (*see p207*) houses 130-plus showrooms containing architects, dealers and designers, plus a design-oriented annexe of MoCA. Nearby, the north end of N La Cienega Boulevard is home to artist-run **Gallery 825** (No.825, 1-310 652 8272, www.laaa.org). There's more action further east, courtesy of the incomparable **MAK Centre** (*see p94*) and the underground star-makers at **New Image Art** (7908 Santa Monica Boulevard, 1-323 654 2192, www.newimageartgallery.com).

Hollywood

Despite the revival of **LA Contemporary Exhibitions** (6522 Hollywood Boulevard, 1-323 957 1777, www.artleak.org), one of the city's most vital alternative spaces, the scene in Hollywood is pretty small. **Carmichael** (1257 N La Brea Avenue, 1-323 969 0600, www. carmichaelgallery.com) deals in graffiti-based figurative painting; **Circus** (7065 Lexington Avenue, 1-323 962 8506, www.circus-gallery.com) deals in fresh-faced gallows humour. East of La Brea on Melrose Avenue sits hip **Kantor/Feuer** (No.7025, 1-323 933

Arts & Entertainment

6976, www.kantorfeuer.com), which has shown the likes of Haring and Ruscha; and **1988** (No.7020, 1-323 937 7088, www.gallery1988. com), with toy- and comic-based pop art.

Fairfax District

A number of notable galleries are clustered at the corner of N Crescent Heights and Beverly Boulevards. On Crescent Heights, try **DF2** (No.314, 1-323 782 9404, www.df2gallery.com); on Beverly, there's **Michael Kohn** (No.8071, 1-323 658 8088, www.kohngallery.com), a major dealer in representational and abstract art, and the LA branch of New York's influential **Forum** (No.8069, 1-323 655 1550, www.forum gallery.com). All these galleries open through back doors off a shared parking lot.

East along Beverly, close to where it crosses Fuller Avenue, **Stephen Cohen** (No.7358, 1-323 937 5525, www.stephencohengallery.com), shows photography by stars from Viggo Mortensen to Larry Clark; it also runs the **Photo LA** fair in Santa Monica every January. Nearby, **Richard Telles** (No.7380, 1-323 965 5578, www.tellesfineart.com) is devoted to cutting-edge work, and keeps a low profile except among critics and brave collectors.

The stretch of La Brea Avenue between Melrose Avenue and W 3rd Street is also dotted with galleries. **Jack Rutberg** (357 N La Brea Avenue, 1-323 938 5222, www.jackrutbergfine arts.com) deals in the likes of Jerome Witkin and Alexander Calder; **Fahey/Klein** (148 N La Brea Avenue, 1-323 934 2250, www.faheykleingallery. com) shows photography; and the renowned **Merry Karnowsky** (170 S La Brea Avenue, 1-323 933 4408, www.mkgallery.com) welcomes the likes of Shepard Fairey and Dean Karr.

The Miracle Mile & Midtown

The Miracle Mile is home to one of LA's most important art museums (**LACMA**; *see p100*) and a pair of interesting non-profit galleries (the **Craft & Folk Art Museum** and the **A+D Museum**; for both, *see p99*). However, the commercial art world also retains a presence. As has been the case elsewhere in LA, many local galleries have joined together in order to promote themselves. The third Saturday of the month sees the **Miracle Mile Artwalk** (www.midcitywest.org), which often takes in an after-party at LACMA.

Most of the notable galleries are on Wilshire Boulevard, close to the intersection with Fairfax Avenue. The building at **6150 Wilshire Boulevard**, houses a number of enterprises, among them **ACME** (1-323 857 5942, www. acmelosangeles.com), the inscrutably avant-

garde **Marc Foxx** (1-323 857 5571, www. marcfoxx.com) and reticent classicist **Daniel Weinberg** (1-323 954 8425, www.daniel weinberggallery.com). Conceptual painting and avant-garde sculpture shine at **Carl Berg** (No.6018, 1-323 931 6060, www.carlberggallery. com), while **Steve Turner Contemporary** (No.6026, 1-323 931 3721, www.steveturner contemporary.com) exhibits fresh, witty work from Tim Sullivan, Mark Bradford and others.

Heading east from here, **Lawrence Asher** (No.5820, 1-323 935 9100, www.lawrenceasher. com) mounts stylish group shows with a lively, youthful flair. **ACE** (No.5514, 1-323 935 4411, www.acegallery.net; *see also p237*) often fills an entire floor of the landmark Desmond's art deco building with youngsters and modern masters. And just north in Hancock Park, **Karyn Lovegrove** (500 S Hudson Avenue, 1-323 525 1755, www.karynlovegrovegallery. com) programmes darkly whimsical mixed- and multi-media art.

Silver Lake, Los Feliz & Echo Park

Galleries are a mainstay on the funky East Side, none more so than Los Feliz's **La Luz de Jesus** (4633 Hollywood Boulevard, 1-323 666 7667, www.laluzdejesus.com). With Wacko and Soap Plant, it provides a one-stop shopping experience with paintings, books and toys that nod to high art, low art and everything in between. North-east in Atwater Village sit **Black Maria** (3137 Glendale Boulevard, 1-323 660 9393, www.blackmariagallery.com) and **Pounder-Koné Art Space** (3407 Glendale Boulevard, 1-323 913 2247, www.cchpkas.com), which focuses on art of the African (and occasionally Asian) diaspora.

Over in Silver Lake, your first stop should be **Ghettogloss** (2380 Glendale Boulevard, 1-323 912 0008, www.ghettogloss.com; *picture p240*): the premier East Side destination for artists both funky and punky, it also boasts an absolutely fabulous boutique of artsy knickers and rare knicknacks. Also in the neighbourhood is the all-outdoors **Materials & Applications** (1619 Silver Lake Boulevard, 1-323 913 0915, www.emanate.org), which aims to combine art (architecture) and nature (landscape), and the **Found Gallery** (1903 Hyperion Avenue, 1-323 669 1247, www.foundla.com), an ambitious smaller spot that gives a voice to the area's dense population of semi-outsider locals.

In Echo Park, **Echo Curio** (1519 Sunset Boulevard, 1-213 977 1279, www.echocurio.com) is also in the user-generated-content business, but branches out to include underground music

Arts & Entertainment

Trains of thought

LA's public transport system is a babe in arms next to those in New York, Chicago and London, but it boasts one element that other cities can't match: a network-wide collection of great public art. From the tile murals along stations' mezzanine walls to architectural installations above the platforms, there's plenty to see while you're waiting for your train, much of it really impressive. Art tours and printed guides are available from the MTA's website at www.metro.net, but here are a few highlights to get you started.

Even before Roy Nicholson completed *Solar Shift San Bernardino and Santa Monica*, a glass mosaic, the walls and ceiling of **Union Station** were a feast for the eyes. But now that Nicholson has laid the last of approximately 308,000 glass pieces in his homage to the sunset and mountains at the entry portal to the Gold line, there's yet another reason to take a trip to the hub of transit activity in Downtown.

You can connect with other travellers in more ways than one at the end wall of the **Wilshire–Western** station on the Purple line. *People Coming/People Going*, a 52-foot mural by Richard Wyatt, portrays a number of people moving towards and away from the viewer. On the Red line, look out for Jonathan Borofsky's figures suspended above the platform at **Civic Center**. Alternatively, take

a history lesson at the **Universal City** station: artist Margaret Garcia's hand-painted tiles narrate the story of the Campo de Cuhuenga, next to where Mexico relinquished control of California to the US in 1847.

While the underground installations have travellers' eyes all to themselves, the works of art created for the network's above-ground platforms have to compete with a backdrop of buildings and freeways. Some artists have used this open-air forum to create particularly bold sculptures: on the Gold line, check out Jud Fine's copper-bound stone tree at **Highland Park** station, and Michael Stutz's larger-than-life walking man at **Mission**.

At the transfer point between the Green and Blue lines at **Imperial–Wilmington**, artist JoeSam. (sic) has created a series of brightly coloured metal cut-out figures that appear to be playing hide and seek among the columns of the underpass. Further along the Green line, which ends at **Redondo Beach**, artists have taken their cues from the aerospace industries, creating playful representations of humankind's desire for flight.

Public art isn't limited to the rail network. Each stop on the Orange line, a rapid-bus service that travels along its own roadway in the San Fernando Valley, contains slick shelters designed by LA architect Virginia Tanzmann and other works.

Ghettogloss, a staple of the Silver Lake scene. *See p239*.

and performance events. Also in Echo Park, Shepard Fairey's relocated Obey Giant spin-off **Subliminal Projects** (1331 Sunset Boulevard, 1-213 213 0078, www.subliminalprojects.com) shows gritty, fantastical painting with a flair for the dramatic, while **Tropico de Nopal** (1665 Beverly Boulevard, 1-213 481 8112, www.tropicodenopal.com) describes itself, more or less accurately, as a 'swap-meet-church-machine-shop-chemistry-lab installation'.

Mt Washington to Eagle Rock

Several neighbourhoods north-east of Echo Park boast low-key art scenes of their own. The former Capitol Records pressing plant at 2121 N San Fernando Road in Glassell Park is home to **Another Year in LA** (1-323 223 4000, www.anotheryearinla.com), which mixes concept, craft and humour, and **Drkrm** (1-323 223 6867, www.drkrm.com), which focuses on photographs that illuminate once-subversive subcultures. In Highland Park, look out for shows at the **Outpost for Contemporary Art** (6375 N Figueroa Street, 1-323 982 9461, www.outpost-art.org) and the **Avenue 50 Studio** (131 N Avenue 50, 1-323 258 1435, www.avenue50studio.com). And up in Eagle Rock, try the **Eagle Rock Centre for the**

Arts (2225 Colorado Boulevard, 1-323 226 1617, www.centerartseaglerock.org) and the Chicano avant-garde art displayed at **Sea & Space Explorations** (4755 York Boulevard, 1-323 445 4015, www.seaandspace.org).

Some of these galleries, and others in the area, join forces and open late on the second Saturday of the month for **NELAart Gallery Night**. For details, see www.nelaart.org.

Downtown

The gentrification of Downtown LA is continuing apace, but the artists and galleries that moved in when rents were cheap remain in place. Indeed, the scene is stronger than ever, and still united. Many galleries coordinate receptions for their new shows to coincide with the **Downtown Art Walk** on the second Thursday of the month (www.downtownartwalk.com): as part of the event, many venues stay open until 9pm, and there's also live music and other types of performance.

While Chinatown (*see p241*) continues to thrive, the real story is the explosive success of **Gallery Row**, the semi-official nickname for the stretches of Main and Spring Streets between 2nd and 9th Streets. **Bert Green** (102 W 5th Street, 1-213 624 6212, www.bgfa.us)

took the initiative by relocating to the immense shop-window-girdled corner of 5th & Main. He's been followed by an array of first-rate outfits: painters' collective and green-building pioneer **Pharmaka** (No.101 W 5th Street, 1-213 689 7799, www.pharmaka-art.org), installation engineers **Bank** (No.125 W 4th Street, 1-213 621 4055, www.bank-art.com), photography and video specialists **De Soto** (108 W 2nd Street, 1-323-319 6331, www.gallerydesoto.com) and the avant-garde **Morono Kiang** (in the historic Bradbury Building, 218 W 3rd Street, 1-213 628 8208, www.moronokiang.com). For a full guide to the scene, see www.galleryrow.org.

The art world further east in Downtown isn't as well organised, but it offers plenty of interest. **Cirrus** (542 S Alameda Street, 1-213 680 3473, www.cirrusgallery.com) has promoted edgy art and printmaking since 1971, while the **Hangar** (1018 S Santa Fe Avenue, 1-213 239 9060, www.hangar1018.com) and **Dangerous Curve** (500 Molino Street, 1-213 617 8483, www.dangerouscurve.org) mount regular festivals and exhibitions. The queen bee of the interdisciplinary scene is **Create:Fixate** (www.createfixate.org), which runs an energised programme of audio and video lounges, with art and DJs, that draws a hip and energetic party crowd. And then there's the renovated train-depot campus of the **Southern Californian Institute of Architecture** (960 E 3rd Street, 1-213 613 2200, www.sciarc.edu), which stages lectures, screenings and major exhibitions from luminaries such as Greg Lynn.

Chinatown & around

The art community has also taken hold just north of the 101 freeway in Chinatown, where a tenacious and still-expanding concentration of galleries has set up on pedestrianised Chung King Road. Perhaps emboldened by the street's decrepit charm, many tenants chose not to change the names of the import shops formerly in residence: look out for the envelope-pushing **Black Dragon Society** (No.961, 1-213 620 0030, www.black-dragon-society.com) and the **Happy Lion** (No.963, 1-213 625 1360, www.thehappylion.com). Also here are **Mary Goldman** (No.932, 1-213 617 8217, www.marygoldman.com), which deals in established experimental artists; **Telic** (No.975, 1-213 344 6137, www.telic.info), which runs hypnotic multimedia installations; and **Peres Projects** (No.969, 1-213 617 1100, www.peresprojects.com), a kind of clearing house of controversial work by artists such as Beijing-born, New York-based Terence Koh that has a sister gallery in Berlin.

A few more top-notch places sit elsewhere in Chinatown. At 990 Hill Street sit **Sam Lee** (1-323 227 0275, www.samleegallery.com) and **High Energy Constructs** (1-323 227 7920, www.highenergyconstructs.com). **Acuna-Hansen** (427 Bernard Street, 1-323 441 1624, www.ahgallery.com), which shows odd stuff by art fair darlings such as Bart Esposito, and stentorian **David Kordansky** (510 Bernard Street, 1-323 222 1482, www.davidkordansky gallery.com) lure you around the corner; keep going and you'll stumble upon **Farmlab** (1745 N Spring Street, 1-323 226 1158, www.farmlab.org), a public salon exploring the nexus of art, design, environmentalism and social change.

Other Chinatown galleries worth a look include **Sister** (437 Gin Ling Way, 1-213 628 7000, www.sisterla.com), a small space operated in partnership with the ACME team. To the east sits **Jail Gallery** (965 N Vignes Street, 1-213 621 9567, www.thejailgallery.com) a ballsy enterprise that often invites local artists to curate group shows with political themes. And to the north is **La Mano Press** (1749 Main Street, 1-323 227 1275, www.lamanopress.com) a fine gallery and print shop.

Even further north of Downtown, across the Los Angeles River in the shadow of I-5, sits the **Brewery Arts Complex** (2100 N Main Street), a pioneering operation that's home to artists' spaces, rehearsal studios and galleries including **LA Artcore** (1-323 276 9320, www.laartcore.org) and **Abundant Sugar** (www.abundantsugar.com). The galleries are year-round, but the 200-plus artist residents of the complex throw open their doors for the twice-yearly **Brewery Art Walk** (www.breweryartwalk.com).

Elsewhere in LA

The art scenes elsewhere aren't as pronounced or as interesting as the abovementioned hot spots, but several of them are keen to promote their wares. Several outlying towns host artwalk-type events, during which local galleries stay open late and both caterers and performers take to the streets. Among them are **Santa Ana** (first Sat of month; www.santaana artwalk.com), **Riverside** (first Thur of month; www.riversideartmuseum.org) and **Pomona** (second and last Sat of month, www.metro pomona.com/artwalk.php).

Annual events outside the main artistic centres include the **Sound Walk**, a sound art-oriented event held in Long Beach every September (www.soundwalk.org); summer's Dada-esque **Doo-Dah Parade** in Pasadena (www.doodahparade.com); and the **Pageant of the Masters** in Laguna Beach (*see p213*).

Gay & Lesbian

Get out and about.

Beige at the **Falcon**. *See p244.*

A larger-than-life homage to youth, glamour and reinvention, a modern metropolis that brought the world everything from *The Jetsons* to Jeff Stryker, Los Angeles has been a fabulously gay city for decades. It remains one hell of a queer playground, especially in certain focal neighbourhoods. But it's also a very progressive place: in 2008, California became only the second state of the union (after Massachusetts) to recognise same-sex marriage under state law.

Like a protective Peter Pan, the Hollywood sign hangs over LA, watching as yet more wannabes pour into its streets. Beneath the famous Hollywood Hills is the epicentre of this urban gay candy store: **West Hollywood**. Venture just a little east and you'll hit **Hollywood**, cleaning up its once-lost glory as a glamour nightlife hub. Further east sits **Silver Lake**, where the grittier gay scene offers respite from the twinkie turns of WeHo.

For gay and lesbian resources, including the **Los Angeles Gay & Lesbian Center** and health clinics, *see p307*. Admission to all bars and clubs is free unless stated.

Theatre & film

LA's gay theatre scene remains intimate and accessible. The **Celebration Theatre** (7051 Santa Monica Boulevard, West Hollywood, 1-323 957 1884, www.celebrationtheatre.com) is the most renowned LGBT theatre in SoCal, and offers both irreverent and socially conscious works. The two theatres at the **Los Angeles Gay & Lesbian Center** (*see p307*) have staged everything from one-woman musicals about Dusty Springfield to plays by Tennessee Williams. Conversely, the shows at **Highways** (1651 18th Street, Santa Monica, 1-310 315 1459, www.highwaysperformance.org) are edgy for LA, while the **Cavern Club Theater** nights at Silver Lake's Casita del Campo (1920 Hyperion Avenue, 1-323 969 2530, www.cavernclub theater.com) are rawer and camper.

Outfest, LA's gay and lesbian film festival (*see p228*), retains a presence in the city all year. Outfest Wednesdays are held roughly twice a month at the **American Cinematheque**'s Egyptian Theatre (*see p230*), offering new movies and gay- and lesbian-interest classics.

Gay

'All the world's a stage,' reckoned Madonna on 'Take a Bow'. Sure, the quote belongs to Shakespeare, but this is Los Angeles, where literary references are delivered in direct and deadly serious proximity to pop culture. Gay LA is coloured dramatically by the town's entertainment industry: movies and music are the golden breath of Hollywood, and so it's only fitting that a number of gay clubs feel like studio sound-stages. Restaurant, bar and club promoters employ big-name designers to art-direct their businesses as if they were film sets; drinkers and diners aren't shy of performing.

Come shine or come heatwave, LA's glorious gay scene belongs to the great outdoors. Gorgeous, sun-filtered patios are where the gays play: sunbathing, after all, is a Californian art form. Fear not: when temperatures drop below 60°F and local TV anchors deliver stern 'Storm Watch' warnings, the restaurants and bars bring out their gas lamps. Seriously.

INFORMATION
To find out what's on, pick up one of the free magazines found in bars, cafés and shops in West Hollywood. Titles include *Frontiers* (www.frontierspublishing.com), *In Los Angeles* (www.inlamagazine.com) and *Edge* (www.edgelosangeles.com), all are published fortnightly. Online, www.westhollywood.com is a useful guide.

West Hollywood

Despite an influx of straight immigration (blame it on the reality shows immortalising the area), West Hollywood belongs to the gays. A modern experiment in habitation (there's a curious subculture of conservative Russian immigrants who co-exist peacefully with the homos), WeHo has risen from ghetto to upscale gay suburb, but the area retains its edge. Today, it succeeds beautifully as both an elegant residential enclave and an exuberant party town. It's safe, serene and, thankfully, never subtle.

Main Street WeHo is **Santa Monica Boulevard** between N Doheny Drive and N Fairfax Avenue, a notorious stretch of bars, clubs and über-gay coffeehouses. The area's epicentre, though, is **Robertson Boulevard**, where gorgeous gays and lesbians with lipo-sculpted bodies leave little to the imagination. There's more substance on the scenes further east, of course, but you'll want to worship at the WeHo temple for a while.

Order a margarita, the power fuel of Los Angeles, and marvel at the town's remarkable guilt-free hedonism.

Where to stay
San Vicente Inn-Resort
845 N San Vicente Boulevard, between Cynthia Street & Santa Monica Boulevard (1-800 577 6915/ 1-310 854 6915/www.gayresort.com). Bus 4, 105, 220, 305, 550, 704/I-10, exit La Cienega Boulevard north. **Rates** $79-$229. **Credit** AmEx, DC, Disc, MC, V. **Map** p328 A2.
There's excitement on Santa Monica Boulevard, sure, but there's also plenty of action to be had at this steamy oasis with a pool and a jacuzzi, a tropical garden, nude sunbathing and a high sexual temperature. Clothing is optional but rarely encouraged.

Gay beaches

Many of southern California's beaches (*see pp82-83*) are gay-friendly, but those listed below are three of the best. Gay men and lesbians both head here, but the scenes are male-dominated.

Laguna Beach
Laguna Beach: off PCH, 30 miles south of Long Beach. Gay beach: just past the pier; look for the rainbow flag.
It's a long drive from LA on congested Saturdays, but the water is clean and the beach is hot. After the beach, try the **Boom Boom Room** (1401 S Coast Highway, 1-800 653 2697, www.boomboomroom.com), which offers dancing, drinks specials and plenty of guys who've mislaid their shirts.

Venice Beach
Venice: see p79. Gay beach: where Windward Avenue meets the beach, next to the wall, just down from Muscle Beach.
It figures that LA's most Bohemian district should also welcome the gay community. The quasi-legendary Roosterfish (1302 Abbot Kinney Boulevard, 1-310 392 2123, www.roosterfishbar.com) is a must-see for the guys.

Will Rogers State Beach
Will Rogers State Beach: on PCH, two miles north of Santa Monica Pier, in front of the Beach Club.
This cruisey beach is packed on sunny weekends, and it's easy to see why: it's free, it's got tons of guys playing volleyball and it lasts until sunset.

Arts & Entertainment

Bars & nightclubs

In addition to the venues below, **Mustache Mondays** draws a raunchy mix of alterna-gays to Charlie O's (501 S Spring Street, at E 5th Street, Downtown); Tuesdays sees the Falcon (7213 W Sunset Boulevard; *see p156*) host **Beige**, which draws a Hollywood crowd of directors, producers and A-list celebs; and Jeffrey Sanker of White Party fame hosts a monthly Sunday-nighter at **Area** (*see p262*).

East West Lounge

8851 Santa Monica Boulevard, at Larrabee Street, West Hollywood (1-310 360 6186/www.eastwest lounge.com). Bus 4, 105, 220, 305, 550, 704/I-10, exit La Cienega Boulevard north. **Open** 4.30pm-2am Tue-Sun. **Credit** DC, MC, V. **Map** p328 A2.
Martini drinkers mingle to the sound of slinky beats at this upscale bar. The place packs in a well-heeled mix of gays and lesbians most nights, but is all-girl on Thursdays. Come for the weekday happy hour, held from 4.30pm to 7.30pm.

Eleven

8811 Santa Monica Boulevard, at Palm Avenue, West Hollywood (1-310 855 0800/www.eleven.la). Bus 4, 105, 220, 305, 550, 704/I-10, exit La Cienega Boulevard north. **Open** 4pm-2am daily. **Credit** AmEx, DC, Disc, MC, V. **Map** p328 A2.
A relative newcomer to Boys Town, Eleven has robbed the Abbey and Here of their Friday-night crowds. Gorgeous guys, Cirque du Soleil-like stage shows and a formidable lesbian presence are all present on Friday and Saturday nights, but the bar is an excellent early option on any night of the week.

Factory/Ultra Suede

652 N La Peer Drive, between Santa Monica Boulevard & Melrose Avenue (1-310 659 4551/ www.factorynightclub.com). Bus 4, 105, 220, 305, 550, 704/I-10, exit La Cienega Boulevard north. **Open** 9pm-2am Wed, 10am-2am Fri, Sat. **Admission** $3-$10. **Credit** *Bar only* AmEx, DC, MC, V. **Map** p328 A2.
Two venues for the price of one, run by the same team and almost sharing a building. The Factory's

Festivals Gay

June's **LA Gay Pride** (www.lapride.org) is one of the biggest pride events in the US. As many as 400,000 people watch the often raucous three-hour Sunday parade make its way down Santa Monica Boulevard; tens of thousands attend the nearby two-day festival, renowned for its diva headliners, drag starlets and top DJs.

For **Outfest**, LA's gay and lesbian film festival, *see p228* **Festivals**.

line-up is highlighted by Friday's top-40 Popstarz party; on the same night, Ultra Suede offers Girlbar (*see p249*). Saturday nights aren't always gay nights, call ahead to check.

Fiesta Cantina

8865 Santa Monica Boulevard, at Larrabee Street, West Hollywood (1-310 652 8865). Bus 4, 105, 220, 305, 550, 704/I-10, exit La Cienega Boulevard north. **Open** 4pm-2am Mon-Thur; noon-2am Fri-Sun. **Credit** AmEx, DC, Disc, MC, V. **Map** p328 A2.
A West Hollywood oasis, Fiesta Cantina is Club Tropicana for gays and their straight gal-pals, celebrating island life with a slew of festive drinks and loud music. Things pump even harder during the daily happy hour (4-8pm).

Fubar

7994 Santa Monica Boulevard, between N Laurel & N Edinburgh Avenues (1-323 654 0396/www.fubar la.com). Bus 4, 217, 218, 704/I-10, exit Fairfax Avenue north. **Open** 7pm-2am Mon-Thur, Sun; 5pm-2am Fri; 8pm-2am Sat. **Credit** AmEx, DC, Disc, MC, V. **Map** p328 C2.
Fubar is LA's slightly more tepid equivalent of NYC bar the Cock. Wild times abound, particularly at Thursday night's Big Fat Dick soirée: genitalia flashes while the WeHo scene's celebs swarm to California electro-trash.

Here Lounge

696 N Robertson Boulevard, at Santa Monica Boulevard (1-310 360 8455/www.herelounge.com). Bus 4, 105, 220, 305, 550, 704/I-10, exit La Cienega Boulevard north. **Open** 4pm-2am Mon-Sat; 4pm-2am Sun. **Credit** DC, MC, V. **Map** p328 A2.
Located off the Santa Monica Boulevard drag, the minimalist, upscale Here Lounge accommodates a large crowd comprised of the scene's prettiest and cruisiest guys. The Sunday afternoon/early evening Size event is when the locals come out in force.

Motherlode

8944 Santa Monica Boulevard, at N Robertson Boulevard (1-310 659 9700). Bus 4, 105, 220, 305, 550, 704/I-10, exit La Cienega Boulevard north. **Open** 3pm-2am daily. **No credit cards**. **Map** p328 A2.
Everyone's favourite beer bust is held on Sunday afternoons at LA's friendliest gay bar. An unexpectedly straightforward hangout, especially for this part of town.

O-Bar

8279 Santa Monica Boulevard, between N Sweetzer & N Harper Avenues (1-323 822 3300/www.obar restaurant.com). Bus 4, 105, 704, LDHWH/I-10, exit La Cienega Boulevard north. **Open** 6pm-midnight Mon, Wed; noon-2am Tue, Thur-Sat. **Credit** AmEx, DC, Disc, MC, V. **Map** p328 B2.
This restaurant/bar is where clued-in locals kick off the weekend. Tom Whitman's Smack party on Thursdays features a five-minute cocktail free-for-all at 11.15pm and hourly thereafter, but the clientele aren't cheap: the atmosphere is more upscale than at most WeHo bars. Dress the part.

Girls allowed: it's the **East West Lounge**.

Rage

8911 Santa Monica Boulevard, between Hilldale Avenue & N San Vicente Boulevard (1-310 652 7055/www.rageclub.com). Bus 4, 105, 220, 305, 550, 704/I-10, exit La Cienega Boulevard north. **Open** noon-2am daily. **Admission** free-$15. **Credit** *Bar only* AmEx, MC, V. **Map** p328 A2.

The quintessential WeHo gay club hosts a range of themed nights, from its refreshing alternative club on Mondays to techno and diva house at the weekend. A favourite among the younger crowd.

Restaurants & coffeehouses

In addition to the venues detailed below, **Basix Café** (8333 Santa Monica Boulevard, 1-323 848 2460, www.basixcafe.com) does a mean Sunday brunch, while **Marix** (1108 N Flores Avenue, 1-323 656 8800, www.marixtexmex.com; *photo p248*) serves Tex-Mex food and what some swear are the best margaritas in town.

Abbey

692 N Robertson Boulevard, at Santa Monica Boulevard (1-310 289 8410/www.abbeyfoodandbar. com). Bus 4, 105, 220, 305, 550, 704/I-10, exit La Cienega Boulevard north. **Open** 9am-2am daily. **Main courses** $17. **Credit** AmEx, DC, Disc, MC, V. **Map** p328 A2.

This expansive restaurant/cocktail bar is a popular spot, and it more than deserves the crowds it attracts. The large outdoor patio with statues and fairy lights, is pleasant; the food is superb and won't break the bank; and the various martinis on offer are beyond reproach. And unlike the rest of WeHo's scene, it attracts an ethnically diverse crowd.

Benvenuto Caffe

8512 Santa Monica Boulevard, at N La Cienega Boulevard, West Hollywood (1-310 659 8635/www. benvenuto-caffe.com). Bus 4, 105, 220, 305, 550, 704/I-10, exit La Cienega Boulevard north. **Open** 5-10pm Mon-Thur, Sun; 5-11pm Fri- Sat. **Main courses** $15. **Credit** AmEx, DC, Disc, MC, V. **Map** p328 B2.

Recently renovated, Benvenuto offers quality, inexpensive Italian fare in its restaurant, a former recording studio (the Doors recorded *LA Woman* here). The front patio is great for people-watching. After dinner, head upstairs to the cosy cocktail lounge.

Café La Boheme

8400 Santa Monica Boulevard, at N Orlando Avenue, West Hollywood (1-323 848 2360/www. globaldiningca.com). Bus 4, 105, 704/I-10, exit La Cienega Boulevard north. **Open** 5-10pm Mon-Thur, Sun; 5-11pm Fri, Sat. **Main courses** $26. **Credit** AmEx, DC, Disc, MC, V. **Map** p328 B2.

Fine dining goes gay and goth at this sophisticated but unstuffy restaurant. One imagines this is what Cher's dining room looks like: glamorous, OTT and a little tacky. A mix of gays, celebs and industry folk bask under chandeliers and down potent martinis.

The gay outdoors

Los Angeles is renowned for its desire to lead a healthy life, and gay LA is no exception. The city's gym culture has a gay slant (*see p246*), but other gay men and lesbians choose to stay in shape in more novel ways, forming a gay contingency who meet outside the usual cocktail hour.

Take a Hike LA (http://takeahike la.connexion.org), a low-key all-male hiking group, has amassed more than 500 members through little more than word-of-mouth. Between 20 and 50 men meet for an hour-long hike each weekend. Most hikes happen at Runyon Canyon; sign up on the website to be emailed details.

Take a Hike LA's female equivalents are the **Hiking Hunnies** (www.myspace.com/ hikinghunnies), an all-girl hiking group that intersperses aerobic activity with picnicking and pancakes at various locales around LA. Participants communicate via MySpace pages; there's definitely more than power-walking going on.

Naked Yoga (www.nakedyoga.net) doesn't happen outdoors for obvious reasons. Classes incorporate power, partner and contact yoga: while some touching is allowed, the emphasis is on finding your om. Check the website for classes and retreats.

Lost in the woods: **Runyon Canyon**.

Hamburger Mary's

8288 Santa Monica Boulevard, at N Sweetzer Avenue (1-323 654 3800/www.hamburgermarys weho.com). Bus 4, 704/I-10, exit Fairfax Avenue north. **Open** 11am-midnight Mon-Thur; 11am-1am Fri; 10am-1am Sat; 10am-midnight Sun. **Credit** AmEx, DC, Disc, MC, V. **Map** p328 B2.

Burger hounds have a tricky choice. Do you go to this gay-oriented mini-chain (tag line: 'Eat, drink and be Mary'), which hosts popular bingo tourneys on Sunday? Or do you try **Irv's Burgers** (8289 Santa Monica Boulevard, 1-323 650 2456), a tiny mainstay for decades? If you're greedy, you could try both…

Mark's

861 N La Cienega Boulevard, between Santa Monica Boulevard & Melrose Avenue (1-310 652 5252/www. marksrestaurant.com). Bus 4, 105, 220, 305, 550, 704/I-10, exit La Cienega Boulevard north. **Open** 6-10pm Mon-Thur; 6-11pm Fri, Sat; 10am-3pm, 6-10pm Sun. **Main courses** *Dinner* $20. *Brunch* $10. **Credit** AmEx, Disc, MC, V. **Map** p328 B2.

There's never a shortage of eye-candy at Mark's, but one doesn't have to sacrifice gastronomy to guys-tronomy: the food's excellent, a Cal-American jumble of healthy and indulgent dishes. On Mondays, the Dish It Out promotion slashes prices.

Sur

606 N Robertson Boulevard, at Melrose Avenue, West Hollywood (1-310 289 2824/www.sur-restaurant.com). Bus 4, 105, 220, 305, 550, 704/ I-10, exit La Cienega Boulevard north. **Open** 11.30am-3pm, 5.30-10pm Mon-Thur; 11.30am-3pm, 5.30-11pm Fri; 5.30-10pm Sun. **Main courses** *Lunch* $16. *Dinner* $22. **Credit** AmEx, DC, Disc, MC, V. **Map** p328 A2.

Romance and dining go hand in hand at this Southern European-inspired eaterie, a stone's throw from the Abbey. Delicious California/Mediterranean dishes are enjoyed by an upscale mixed crowd: Catherine Zeta-Jones, Meg Ryan and Penelope Cruz have dined here.

Gyms

Gay-friendly gyms include **24-Hour Fitness** (*see p276*), distinguished by its great pool and cruisey atmosphere, and **Gold's Gym** (1016 Cole Avenue, 1-323 462 7012; *see p276*), a fantasyland of porn performers and soap stars.

Crunch

8000 W Sunset Boulevard, at N Laurel Avenue (1-323 654 4550/www.crunch.com). Bus 2, 217, 302/

I-10, exit Fairfax Avenue north. **Open** 5am-11pm
Mon-Thur; 5am-10pm Fri; 8am-8pm Sat, Sun.
Rates $25/day. **Credit** AmEx, DC, Disc, MC, V.
Map p328 C1.
It's hard to know which is more breathtaking: the
views of the Hollywood Hills, or the Adonises who
choose the hills as the backdrop for their exercise.
Crunch classes LA fitness: select from
stripper pole-like classes or hip hop routines.
Flirtation can be part of the workout: wash up in the
oft-discussed 'peek-a-boo' see-through showers.

Bathhouses & sex clubs

Midtowne Melrose Spa
*7269 Melrose Avenue, at N La Brea Boulevard
(1-323 937 2122/www.midtowne.com). Bus 10, 212,
312/I-10, exit La Brea Avenue north.* **Open** 24hrs
daily. **Admission** Per 8hrs $27 room; $18 locker.
Credit AmEx, MC, V. **Map** p328 D2.
This two-storey spa close to WeHo attracts a varied
clientele. Amenities of note include a rooftop patio,
a huge adult movie room and a darkened maze for
anonymous action. In case all of this screws you up,
the spa has its own resident sex therapist.

Shops & services

If you're looking to soak up the LA sunshine
and snap the stars, head to **The Grove** (*see
p189*), the city's mega-popular outdoor mall.
Whether navigating the Studio 54-like circuit
scene of Abercrombie & Fitch or soaking up
Donna Summer's *Last Dance* blaring from
speakers by the Bellagio-inspired water show,
it's the local homos' favourite shopping haunt.
    For **A Different Light**, a fine gay and
lesbian bookstore, *see p191*.

Dorothy's Surrender
*7985 Santa Monica Boulevard, at N Laurel Avenue,
West Hollywood (1-323 650 4111). Bus 4, 217, 218,
704/I-10, exit Santa Monica Avenue north.* **Open** 10am-
10pm daily. **Credit** AmEx, DC, Disc, MC, V. **Map**
p328 C2.
Located inside the flamboyant French Market, this
colourful house of camp seems like a leftover from
Reagan's '80s. It stocks an array of rainbow-themed
paraphernalia, including risqué greeting cards, gay-
themed board games and hilariously OTT toys.

Drake's
*8932 Santa Monica Boulevard, between N Robertson
& N San Vicente Boulevards, West Hollywood (1-310
289 8932/www.drakesusa.com). Bus 4, 105, 220,
305, 550, 704/I-10, exit La Cienega Boulevard north.*
Open 10am-2am daily. **Credit** AmEx, DC, Disc, MC,
V. **Map** p328 A2.
Conveniently located near a slew of bars, Drake's
sells sex to the Santa Monica Boulevard boys – and
beyond. It's a one-stop shopping spot for DVDs,
glossy mags, toys, sex aids and an incredibly large
range of big-brand lubes.

Hollywood

Cleaner and safer than it's been for years,
Hollywood has undergone an urban facelift
of late, with the addition of an upscale mall
and a number of paparazzi-infested clubs. Gay
nightlife revolves around designated nights in
the gymnasium-sized danceplexes.

Bars & nightclubs

Circus Disco and **Arena**, two related clubs
(6655 Santa Monica Boulevard; *see p263*), both
host gay nights: the former has Boys Night Out
on Tuesdays, while the latter runs a Latin night
on Saturdays. On Thursdays, a trendy crowd
heads to **Avalon** (1735 N Vine Street; *see p262*)
for **Tigerheat**; above, in the infamous Heaven
Lounge, it's the more exclusive **Spider Club**.
And look out for **Dragstrip 66** (www.drag
strip66.com), held four times a year at **Safari
Sam's** (5214 Sunset Boulevard; *see p258*).

Spotlight Bar
*1601 N Cahuenga Boulevard, at Selma Avenue (1-
323 467 2425). Metro Hollywood-Vine/bus 163, 180,
181, 210, 212, 217, 312, 363, 780, LDH/US 101,
exit Hollywood Boulevard west.* **Open** 6am-2am daily.
No credit cards. Map p329 B2.
For a drink on the darker side, check out LA's oldest gay bar. Trannies abound midweek, but there's
a diverse clientele most nights and days (including
a few straights and the occasional celeb).

Bathhouses & sex clubs

Hollywood Spa
*1650 N Ivar Avenue, between Hollywood Boulevard
& Selma Avenue (1-323 464 0445/www.hollywood
spa.com). Metro Hollywood-Vine/bus 163, 180, 181,
210, 212, 217, 312, 363, 780, LDH/US 101, exit
Vine Street south.* **Open** 24hrs daily. **Admission**
Per 8hrs $26-$30/room; $16-$19/locker. **Credit**
AmEx, DC, Disc, MC, V. **Map** p329 B2.
The best-known bathhouse in the city has a good
gym, but that's not the main reason why people
come here. At weekends, a live DJ provides a sound-
track to the shenanigans until 6am.
Other locations: 5636 Vineland Avenue, North
Hollywood (1-818 760 6969).

Silver Lake

Locals – or, as some call themselves, Slakers –
proclaim a proud affinity to Silver Lake similar
to the smug love that San Franciscans lavish on
the Bay Area. It's easy to understand their
affection: the area is home to some of the city's
best bars, restaurants and cafés. The gay scene
here is less twink and more kink; after WeHo,
it's the city's best-known homo 'hood.

Arts & Entertainment

Marix. See p245.

MJs

2810 Hyperion Avenue, at Monon Street (1-323 660 1503/www.mjsbar.com). Bus 175/US 101, exit Silver Lake Boulevard east. **Open** 4pm-2am Mon-Thur; 2pm-2am Thur-Sun. **Credit** AmEx, DC, Disc, MC, V. **Map** p330 C2.

This bar is more West Hollywood than Slakers care to enjoy, but an array of outlandish theme nights keeps everyone happy. Tuesday nights belong to Rim Job, a homage to homo sleaze that brings WeHo queers and Silver Lake boys together; arrive before 10pm to beat the long line. Friday nights welcome Mario Diaz's Swallow night.

Other Side

2538 Hyperion Avenue, between Evans & Tracy Streets (1-323 661 0618/www.flyingleapcafe.com). Bus 175/US 101, exit Silver Lake Boulevard east. **Open** noon-2am daily. **Credit** AmEx, DC, Disc, MC, V. **Map** p330 C2.

The average age at the Other Side may be 60-plus, but the talent performing at this classy piano bar is terrific and the atmosphere is always welcoming. LA kitsch at its finest.

Bathhouses & sex clubs

Slammer

3688 Beverly Boulevard, between N Virgil & N Vermont Avenues (1-213 388 8040/www.slammer club.com). Metro Vermont-Beverly/bus 14/US 101, exit Beverly Boulevard west. **Open** 8pm-late Mon-Fri; 2pm-late Sat, Sun. **Admission** $22. **No credit cards.** **Map** p330 B5.

Silver Lake's only sex club caters mostly to the leather crowd. Tuesdays are for gym buffs and Wet Wednesdays attract those into watersports. Don't expect many of Hollywood Spa's pretty guys. Free HIV testing is available.

Lesbian

From bi-curious Paris Hilton smooching for the cameras at Falcon's Sunday soirée or a Melissa sighting at Marix, LA's lesbian scene is nothing if not glamorous. But scratch the surface and you'll discover that lesbian life in the city is more intimate than you might expect. While the boys are out partying like there's no tomorrow, the girls tend to stay behind the scenes, and in doing so provide a backbone for much of the GLBT community. That's not to say there isn't a prolific community: there is, but you'll need to look a little harder for it.

INFORMATION

For information, see free monthly mag *Lesbian News* (www.lesbiannews.com) or *Frontiers* (*see p243*), which covers women's issues alongside its male-oriented content. **A Different Light**

Bars & nightclubs

Eagle LA

4219 Santa Monica Boulevard, at W Sunset Boulevard, Silver Lake (1-323 669 9472/www.eaglela.com). Metro Vermont-Santa Monica/bus 2, 4, 302, 704/US 101, exit Vermont Avenue north. **Open** 4pm-2am Mon-Fri; 2pm-2am Sat, Sun. **Admission** free-$5. **No credit cards.** **Map** p330 B3.

Porn plays alluringly on the monitors as leather daddies get their boots polished at the premier leather and fetish bar in Los Angeles. Throbbing Thursdays are the bar's busiest nights, and host a wet shorts contest; other events come with self-explanatory names such as Boot Camp, Meat Rack and Heavy Equipment.

Faultline

4216 Melrose Avenue, at N Vermont Avenue (1-323 660 0889/www.faultlinebar.com). Metro Vermont-Beverly/bus 10, 204, 754/US 101, exit Vermont Avenue north. **Open** 5pm-2am Wed-Fri; 2pm-2am Sat; 2pm-1am Sun. **Admission** free-$10. **No credit cards.** **Map** p330 A4.

Leather men and their followers hold Faultline in the highest regard, but other fetishes are catered for too: bikers, bodybuilders and body piercers are all regulars. The DJs have a strict 'no divas' music policy, instead spinning an edgy mix of electronica and rock. The weekly beer bust is Silver Lake's most popular Sunday soirée.

(*see p181*) is a good source for lesbian literature. For lesbian resources, *see p307*.

Bars & nightclubs

Few LA bars or clubs devote themselves to lesbians seven days a week, so pick your events carefully. At the **Here Lounge** (*see p244*), Thursdays warm up with Heat (arrive early to beat the long lines) and stay hot over at the **East West Lounge** (*see p244*): it's a popular watering hole for women on any given night, but it's at its liveliest on Thursdays, with a pick-up scene that brings out lipstick femmes, butch queens and a slew of reality-show stars cashing in their 15 minutes.

On Fridays, the Here Lounge hosts the grungier Truckstop; **O-Bar** (*see p244*) offers upscale LUSH (Ladies' Ultra Sexy Hangout); and **Ultra Suede** (*see p244*) welcomes the ever-popular Girlbar, the biggest night of the week. Saturdays belong to **Executive Suite** (3428 E Pacific Coast Highway, Long Beach, 1-562 597 3884, www.executivesuitelb.com), while Sundays at **Falcon** (*see p156*) bring out the L-word gal pals and the ladies who love them.

Jewel's Catch One

4067 W Pico Boulevard, at S Norton Avenue, Midtown (1-323 734 8849/www.jewelscatchone.com). Bus 30, 31, 210/I-10, exit Crenshaw Boulevard north. **Open** 10pm-4am Sat, 9pm-2am Sun. **Admission** $5-$10. **Credit** AmEx, MC, V. **Map** p329 B6.

Opened in 1972 as the first nightclub aimed at the African American gay and lesbian communities, Jewel's Catch One continues to draw a mixed clientele with a variety of theme nights that stretch from hip hop to leftfield rock. Check the website for an up-to-date schedule.

Normandie Room

8737 Santa Monica Boulevard, between Hancock Avenue & Huntley Drive, West Hollywood (1-310 659 6204/www.thenormandieroom.com). Bus 4, 105, 704/I-10, exit La Cienega Boulevard north. **Open** 5pm-2am daily. **Credit** DC, MC, V. **Map** p328 A2.

This popular neighbourhood bar draws an eclectic crowd, but Saturday is the best night for the ladies. The bar's motto reads: 'no homophobes, no heterophobes, no assholes'.

Oil Can Harry's

11502 Ventura Boulevard, between Colfax Avenue & Tujunga Avenue, Studio City (1-818 760 9749/www.oilcanharrysla.com). Bus 150/US 101, exit Tujunga Boulevard south. **Open** 7.30pm-12.30am Tue, Thur; 9pm-2am Fri; 8pm-2am Sat. **Admission** varies. **Credit** AmEx, MC, V.

Bring your cowboy boots and affect your best country twang at this femme-dominated line-dancing

joint. Whether you go solo or with a group, there's always someone with whom to dance. Lessons are held on Tuesdays and Thursdays (7.45-9.15pm).

Palms

8572 Santa Monica Boulevard, between Westbourne Drive & W Knoll Drive, West Hollywood (1-310 652 6188/www.thepalmsbar.com). Bus 4, 105, 220, 305, 550, 704/I-10, exit La Cienega Boulevard north. **Open** 8pm-2am Mon-Fri; 4pm-2am Sat, Sun. **Admission** $5-$15. **Credit** AmEx, DC, MC, V. **Map** p328 B2.

The oldest lesbian bar in LA is still going strong, supplementing its mellower evenings with regular dance nights inside its cosy confines: among them is Club Gloss, held on the second and fourth Fridays of every month. The Sunday-afternoon beer bust remains popular.

Restaurants & coffeehouses

Gay venues popular with lesbians include newcomer **Java Detour** (8948 Santa Monica Boulevard, West Hollywood, 1-310 358 5282), the **Abbey** (*see p245*), **Marix** (*see p245*) and the **Coffee Bean & Tea Leaf** at 8735 Santa Monica Boulevard in West Hollywood. In Silver Lake, try the **Coffee Table** (*see p174*).

Surprise!

Billed as a mix of flash-mob culture and the French Revolution, **Guerrilla Gay Bar** is a hilarious homo institution common to several US cities but particularly enjoyable in LA. The idea came from a gay man bored with what he saw as a segregated queer scene, and it could hardly be simpler or more effective. Once a month, an unsuspecting straight bar – the more uptight the better – is 'targeted' by the GGB website, whereupon dozens of homos descend on the place and add to it all seven colours of the rainbow.

Although it sounds like queer-terrorism, it's actually rather lighter: GGB is more about embracing diversity through humour and colourful crowds than flag-waving. The guerrillas get an unusual but enjoyable night out, while the bars themselves enjoy 15 minutes of gin-soaked stardom. Guerrilla attacks usually take place on the second Friday of the month. For details, sign up to the email list (www.guerrillagaybar.com): you'll receive an email several days ahead of time containing the date, followed by details of the intended target.

Music

The sound of the city… and of other countries, too.

LA is too big to have a single coherent music scene – and that's what brings a perpetual sense of adventure and surprise to its concert halls, arenas and nightclubs. The melding of cultures ensures a rich variety of sounds that bubbles with ideas. At the same time, LA attracts a steady flow of hot-ticket touring acts, from slick pop stars to gritty hip hoppers via a constant turnover of indie buzz bands. And the sheer range of venues, from vast arenas to hole-in-the-wall neighbourhood bars, means your night out could be as immense as the city itself or as intimate as a quiet night at home.

TICKETS & INFORMATION

Big-name concerts, both classical and rock, often sell out; buy tickets in advance if possible. Try to get tickets directly from the venue – by phone, online or in person – to save on fees. Otherwise, you're stuck with the fees charged by Ticketmaster (1-213 480 3232, www.ticket master.com). Even if a show is advertised as 'sold out', it's worth checking with the box office on the day of the show: promoters sometimes release extra seats at the last minute.

The most comprehensive listings appear in the *LA Weekly*. The *LA Times'* 'Calendar' on Sundays and its Thursday supplement, 'The Guide', are good sources, as is online guide *Metromix* (www.losangeles.metromix.com), which also has a print edition. The LA version of cool-kid newsletter flavorpill.net also spotlights the town's hottest tickets.

Classical

LA's classical scene is one of the strongest in the US. The LA Philharmonic has had an excellent reputation for years, but the town's other, smaller ensembles also deliver the goods.

Concert venues

Concerts are held at a number of venues around the LA region: the grand **Pasadena Civic Auditorium** (300 E Green Street, at S Marengo Avenue, Pasadena, 1-626 449 7360, www.the pasadenacivic.com); a handful of churches; museums such as **LACMA** (*see p100*) and the **Skirball Center** (*see p85*); and college venues such as **Schoenberg Hall** and the beautiful **Royce Hall** at UCLA (1-310 825 2101, www. uclalive.org; *see p87*), the **Norris Auditorium** at USC (1-213 740 7111, www.usc.edu; *see p125*) and the **Harriet & Charles Luckman Fine Arts Complex** at Cal State University over in East LA (1-323 343 6600, www.luckmanart.org).

Your best bet is to check the *LA Times* or *LA Weekly* for details of what's on where while you're in town. For the weekly concerts at LACMA's **Leo S Bing Theatre**, *see p251* **Music for nothing**. And it's worth considering a trip out of town to the **Ojai Festival** in June (www.ojaifestival.org), which offers a strong programme that ranges from familiar classics to modern works (the 2008 event offered plenty of Steve Reich).

Gustavo Dudamel at the LA Philharmonic. *See p252.*

Music for nothing

Ticket prices continue to spiral for major shows in Los Angeles, and the booking fees added to them by ticket agencies continue to horrify. However, it's not all bad news: from the clutch of outdoor festivals in summer to the year-round in-store PAs at **Amoeba Music** (*see p209*) and some branches of **Borders** (*see p190*), there are still plenty of places to catch music for free in LA.

The most impressive programme of free music in the city is held not at a concert hall or a nightclub but an art museum: the **Los Angeles County Museum of Art** (*see p100*), which supplements its collections with regular free concerts. On Fridays at 6pm (Apr-Nov only), there's jazz in the museum's central courtyard; on Saturdays from 5pm (May-Sept only), there's Latin music in the Dorothy Collins Brown Amphitheatre; and from 6pm every Sunday in the Leo S Bing Theatre, there's chamber music as part of the year-round Sundays Live series (www.sundayslive.org).

Other museums that stage regular free or near-free concerts include the **Skirball Center** (folk and roots music; *see p85*) and the **Getty Center** (mostly jazz and classical; *see p84*). Some of the Skirball's concerts, much like the excellent, hipster-friendly First Friday shows at the **Natural History Museum of Los Angeles County** (*see p125*), come free with regular museum admission.

The sizeable core of local workers has inspired two separate free concert series in Downtown LA, both of which run from June to September. The **Pershing Square Summer Concert Series** (www.laparks.org) offers a variety of pop- and rock-oriented acts; concerts are usually held noon-2pm on Tuesdays and Thursdays, and 6-8pm on Wednesdays. And up at California Plaza (Grand Avenue & 4th Street), there's all manner of music on offer as part of the **Grand Performances** season (www.grandperformances.org).

Out by the ocean, the **Twilight Dance Series** (7-10pm Thursdays, June-Aug only; www.twilightdance.org) offers a laudably broad range of acts on a stage at Santa Monica Pier: 2008 saw everyone from Toots & the Maytals to Gerry & the Pacemakers. If you don't want to stand with the crowds on the pier, bring a blanket and settle down on the beach. There are also rather more low-key summer concerts at Marina del Rey (www.visitmarina.com).

Dorothy Chandler Pavilion

Music Center, 135 N Grand Avenue, between W 1st & W Temple Streets, Downtown (1-213 972 7211/ www.musiccenter.org). Metro Civic Center/bus 2, 4, 10, 11, 14, 48, 92, 302, 714/I-110, exit 4th Street east. **Box office** *In person* 10am-6pm Mon-Sat. *By phone/online* Via individual companies (eg LA Opera) or Ticketmaster (*p210*). **Tickets** $10-$250. *Parking* $8. **Credit** AmEx, DC, MC, V. **Map** p331 B2.

The arrival of Disney Hall left this '60s-era concert hall in shade, almost taunting its rather dated exterior architecture (the interior is nicer) and, more pertinently, exposing its acoustics as substandard. The music at the 3,200-capacity theatre is now mostly limited to performances by the LA Opera (*see p252*); the sound is best from the upper floors, although the views from the top can be vertiginous.

Hollywood Bowl

2301 N Highland Avenue, at US 101 (1-323 850 2000/www.hollywoodbowl.com). Bus 156/US 101, exit Highland Avenue north. **Box office** *In person* May-Sept noon-6pm Tue-Sun. *By phone/online* Via individual companies (eg LA Philharmonic) or Ticketmaster (*p210*). **Tickets** $14-$30. **Credit** AmEx, DC, Disc, MC, V.

This gorgeous outdoor amphitheatre has been hosting concerts since the LA Philharmonic first played here in 1922. Nestled in an aesthetically blessed fold in the Hollywood Hills, the 18,000-seat venue can bring out the romantic in the terminally cynical, and the glorious setting almost makes up for the somewhat dodgy acoustics. It's the summer home of the LA Philharmonic, but it's hosted everyone from the Beatles to Big Bird, and today mixes classical concerts with all manner of rock and pop.

Walt Disney Concert Hall

111 S Grand Avenue, between W 2nd & W 3rd Streets, Downtown (1-323 850 2000/www.disney concerthall.com). Metro Civic Center/bus 2, 4, 10, 11, 14, 48, 92, 302, 714/I-110, exit 4th Street east. **Box office** *In person* noon-6pm Tue-Sun. *By phone/online* Via individual companies (eg LA Philharmonic) or Ticketmaster (*p210*). **Tickets** $25-$150. *Parking* $8. **Credit** AmEx, DC, Disc, MC, V. **Map** p331 B2.

The $274-million crown jewel of the LA Music Center, Disney Hall opened in 2003 to rave reviews. The novelty hasn't yet worn off: both inside and out, this is a terrific venue. Designed by Frank Gehry, the hall features a 2,265-capacity auditorium with an open platform stage. Chief acoustician Yasuhisa Toyota combined the best aspects of orchestral halls in Tokyo, Berlin, Amsterdam and Boston in a bid to provide aural warmth and clarity; the result of his endeavours is a virtually perfect acoustic that works almost as well for amplified events as for orchestral performances. The hall is the new home of the LA Philharmonic and the LA Master Chorale, but the programme is surprisingly varied throughout the year. The complex also includes the 250-seat Roy and Edna Disney/CalArts Theatre (aka the Redcat; *see p277*), a gallery and a roof garden. For tours of the building, call 1-213 972 4399, or see online for a schedule. *See also p31 and p115*.

Ensembles

In addition to the ensembles below, check out the **Da Camera Society's Chamber Music in Historic Sites** programme (1-213 477 2929, www.dacamera.org), which presents concerts by first-rate ensembles and soloists in some of the city's more interesting buildings.

Elsewhere, the **Pasadena Symphony** (information 1-626 793 7172, tickets 1-626 584 8833, www.pasadenasymphony.org) gives around eight concerts a year at the Pasadena Civic Auditorium. The **Long Beach Symphony** (1-562 436 3203, www.lbso.org) and **Long Beach Opera** (1-562 432 5934, www. longbeachopera.org) both perform semi-regularly in the region, while the **Pacific Symphony** (information 1-714 755 5788, tickets 1-714 755 5799, http://pacificsymphony.entericorp.com) keeps Orange County entertained.

Los Angeles Chamber Orchestra
1-213 622 7001/www.lamc.org.
Celebrating its 40th birthday in 2008-09, the LACO plays seven or eight approachable programmes a year, performing at the Alex Theatre in Glendale and UCLA's Royce Hall with the occasional foray to Disney Hall and elsewhere.

Los Angeles Master Chorale
Information 1-213 972 7282/tickets 1-213 972 7282/www.lamc.org.
Founded in 1964, the 120-voice LA Master Chorale is the largest choir of its kind in the US. Leaning on a crowd-pleasing repertoire, it performs roughly a dozen concerts each year at Disney Hall, some a cappella and others with accompanying musicians (often the LA Chamber Orchestra).

Los Angeles Opera
1-213 972 8001/www.losangelesopera.com.
The LA Opera made its debut in 1986 with an acclaimed production of Verdi's *Otello*. Now led by Plácido Domingo and James Conlon, the company specialises in high-concept stagings of popular favourites (*Fidelio*, *La Bohème*, *Jenufa*) interspersed with the occasional new work. Performances are held at the Dorothy Chandler Pavilion (*see p251*).

Los Angeles Philharmonic
1-323 850 2000/www.laphil.org.
Established in 1919 by tycoon William Andrews Clarke, the LA Philharmonic has long served as proof that the city isn't a cultural wasteland. After the orchestra's 1964 move to the Dorothy Chandler Pavilion, and the concurrent tenure of Zubin Mehta as musical director, the Phil began to attract international attention. But its reputation has really soared since it moved in 2003 to Disney Hall, giving the orchestra the acoustic that its talents deserved.

Under justly acclaimed Finnish conductor Esa-Pekka Salonen, the Phil has introduced a forward-thinking sensibility to its programme, with modern works and rarely-performed pieces supplementing more widely heard selections. UpBeat Live, a series of lectures that precede some concerts, adds insight; there are also events aimed at children. The majority of the concerts are staged at Disney Hall (Oct-May; *see p251*); in summer, the Phil moves outside to the Hollywood Bowl (June-Sept; *see p251*) and concentrates on crowd-pleasers.

The next few years look like being interesting. Salonen is stepping down as music director at the end of the 2008-09 season and will be replaced by dynamic Venezuelan twentysomething Gustavo Dudamel, whose early guest spots with the Phil in 2005 and '07 were well received. Expect these hot tickets to become even hotter when he arrives. *Photo p250*.

Festivals Rock

Southern California's biggest rock festival is held 100 miles east of LA in Indio on the last weekend of April: **Coachella** (www.coachella.com), a three-day wing-ding that mixes buzz-bin alt-rock bands with the headline-grabbing likes of Prince and Madonna. The following weekend, Indio hosts the country-oriented **Stagecoach Festival** (www.stagecoachfestival.com).

LA's festivals are on a smaller scale, but you can expect to find noteworthy alt-rock acts at the **Sunset Junction Street Fair** in Silver Lake (*see p214*) and the **Eagle Rock Music Festival** (www.myspace.com/eagle rockmusicfestival), a day-long conflation of genre-blurring performers held in early October. And look out for **International Pop Overthrow** (www.internationalpopover throw.com), a two-week festival of guitar-pop held at various venues in July/August.

Rock & pop

From the dizzy heights of the Sunset Strip during the '60s to the stagnant waters of the 1990s, LA's music scene has had its highs and lulls. However, since the turn of the millennium, local groups have begun to make an impression once again. Among the highlights: the underground hip hop of Stones Throw Records

Nokia Theatre at LA Live. *See p255.*

acts such as Madlib, breakout indie-rock bands including Rilo Kiley, and such unique products of the city's musical melting pot as Dengue Fever. And although some nightclubs (the Roxy, the Troubadour) will probably be here as long as the city itself, they've been joined by some newer spots in recent years, from the casual Safari Sam's to the vast Nokia Theatre.

Bring photo ID to every venue: some shows are open only to over-18s or over-21s, and you'll need to be 21 or older to get served at the bar. For major festivals, *see p252* **Festivals**; for free events, *see p251* **Music for nothing**.

Arenas, theatres & large clubs

Two traditionally classical venues have seen a recent uptick in the number of rock and pop shows they stage: **Disney Hall** (*see p251*) has welcomed everyone from Grizzly Bear to the Chieftains, while the **Hollywood Bowl** (*see p251*) has featured Radiohead, Gnarls Barkley and Tom Petty. For the 1,200-seat **Avalon**, which stages both club nights and gigs, *see p262*; for the **Pantages Theatre**, which hosts occasional concerts in between its runs of musical theatre, *see p278*.

El Rey Theatre

5515 Wilshire Boulevard, between Burnside & Dunsmuir Avenues, Miracle Mile (information 1-323 936 6400/tickets via Ticketmaster (p210)/www.
theelrey.com). Bus 20, 21, 720, LDF/I-10, exit La Brea Avenue north. **Admission** $10-$40. **Credit** *Ticketmaster* AmEx, DC, Disc, MC, V. **Map** p328 D4.
It might be a gorgeous art deco relic, but the 900-capacity El Rey runs a roster that's decidedly dust-free. From MSTRKRFT to the Raveonettes, Dizzee Rascal to Autolux, the schedule is full of acts *du jour*, with the older but still-interesting likes of Roky Erickson and Nick Lowe also appearing. Sound and sightlines are both excellent.

Forum

3900 Manchester Boulevard, at S Prairie Avenue, Inglewood (1-310 330 7300/www.thelaforum.com). Bus 115, 211, 212, 315, 442/I-405, exit Manchester Boulevard east. **Box office** *In person* show days only. *By phone/online* Ticketmaster (*p210*). **Tickets** $25-$200. **Parking** $22. **Credit** *Ticketmaster* AmEx, DC, Disc, MC, V.
It's been a while since this 18,000-seat, acoustically challenged space was the city's go-to arena: the venue housed some of Guns n' Roses' most infamous concerts, but the Staples Center gets all the glory these days. Still, big acts still play here, anyone from LA rockers Foo Fighters to R&B star R Kelly.

Greek Theatre

2700 N Vermont Avenue, in Griffith Park (1-323 665 5857/www.greektheatrela.com). Bus 180, 181/ US 101, exit Vermont Avenue north. **Box office** *In person* noon-6pm Mon-Fri; 10am-4pm Sat, Sun. *By phone/online* Ticketmaster (*p210*). **Tickets** $25-$150. **Parking** $15. **Credit** AmEx, DC, MC, V. **Map** p330 A1.

Arts & Entertainment

Hotel Café. *See p256.*

This pleasant, open-air, 6,000-seat theatre stages big summer shows by acts such as the Kings of Leon and Norah Jones. The 'stacked' parking means getting out of the car park often takes longer than the show; VIP 'Quick Parking' is a ludicrous $50.

Gibson Amphitheatre

Universal CityWalk, 100 Universal City Plaza, Universal City (1-818 622 4440/www.hob.com). Metro Universal City/bus 96, 156, 166/US 101, exit Universal Center Drive. **Box office** *In person* 1-9pm Mon-Sat. *By phone/online* Ticketmaster *(p210).* **Tickets** $25-$150. *Parking* $10-$20. **Credit** AmEx, DC, Disc, MC, V.

This slick, semi-circular mid-sized room serves a wide array of major pop, R&B and Latin acts, from mellow to loud. The sterile setting and sometimes frigid air-conditioning are downsides, but clean sight lines and good sonics make this a popular spot. Parking is both inconvenient and dear.

Hollywood Palladium

6215 W Sunset Boulevard, between N Argyle & N El Centro Avenues, Hollywood (1-323 962 7600). Metro Hollywood-Vine/bus 2, 212, 217, 302, LDHWI/US 101, exit Vine Street south. **Box office** *In person* show days only. *By phone/online* Ticketmaster *(p210).* **Tickets** Call for details. **Credit** *Ticketmaster* AmEx, DC, Disc, MC, V. **Map** p329 B2.

Once ruled by the big band sounds of Glenn Miller and Tommy Dorsey, this vintage ballroom later hosted hip hop shows, punk bands and indie faves such as Interpol. It's closed for renovations until late 2008.

House of Blues

8430 W Sunset Boulevard, at N Olive Drive, West Hollywood (1-323 848 5100/www.hob.com). Bus 2, 302, LDHWH/I-10, exit La Cienega Boulevard north. **Box office** *In person* show days only. *By phone/ online* Ticketmaster *(p210).* **Admission** $10-$50. **Credit** AmEx, DC, Disc, MC, V. **Map** p328 B1.

This club's faux blues-shack exterior stands in odd contrast to the major-to-rising rock, punk and rap acts that fill its calendar. The cramped conditions and surly staff are annoying, but the food is good (come for Gospel Brunch on Sundays) and the sound is above average, except under the balcony.

Music Box at the Henry Fonda Theater

6126 Hollywood Boulevard, between N El Centro Avenue & N Gower Street, Hollywood (1-323 930 7100/www.henryfondatheater.com). Metro Hollywood-Highland/bus 212, 217, LDHWH/US 101, exit Hollywood Boulevard west. **Box office** *In person* show days only. *By phone/online* Ticketmaster *(p210).* **Admission** $15-$40. **Credit** *Ticketmaster* AmEx, DC, Disc, MC, V. **Map** p329 B1.

Although it's named after a Hollywood legend, the Fonda Theater now concentrates on music, hosting alt-rock favourites such as the Magnetic Fields and the Hold Steady. It's a handsome room and the sound is decent enough, but parking in the neighbourhood can be a real trial at weekends.

Nokia Theatre at LA Live

777 Chick Hearn Court, 11th & Figueroa Streets, Downtown (1-213 763 6030/www.nokiatheatrelive. com). Metro Pico/bus 81, 381, 442, 444, 445, 446, 447, 460/I-110, exit Olympic Boulevard east. **Box office** *In person* from Staples Center (*below*); otherwise show days only. *By phone/online* Ticketmaster (*p210*). **Tickets** $30-$50. **Parking** $25. **Credit** AmEx, DC, Disc, MC, V. **Map** p331 A5.
Part of the corporate regeneration of Downtown, this slick, 7,100-capacity hall opened in late 2007. The sound system is fantastic and the seating is plush; offerings range from dinosaur rock (the Eagles, Neil Young, Rush) and R&B (Kanye West, Mary J Blige) to comedy and kids' shows. The drinks are pricey and parking can be tough if there's an event at the Staples Center (*see below*) next door: it's quicker to park further away and walk, or to take public transport. And smokers: you can't even light up outside. *Photo p253.*

Orpheum

842 S Broadway, between 8th & 9th Streets (1-877 677 4386/www.laorpheum.com). Metro Pershing Square/bus 2, 4, 30, 31, 40, 42, 45, 48/I-110, exit 9th Street east. **Box office** *In person* show days only. *By phone/online* Ticketmaster (*p210*). **Tickets** $30-$100. **Credit** Ticketmaster AmEx, DC, Disc, MC, V. **Map** p331 C4.
Judy Garland once graced the stage of this landmark, which opened in 1926. Nowadays, it prefers more rock and pop acts such as Ben Harper, Joe Jackson and Ani DiFranco, alongside the occasional comic. The sound, especially from under the balcony on the main floor, is fine, and the space is wonderfully grand. Unfortunately, the seats have to be the most knee-crunchingly close-set in town, and parking can be a chore.

Staples Center

1111 S Figueroa Street, at 11th Street, Downtown (1-213 742 7340/www.staplescenter.com). Metro Pico/bus 81, 381, 442, 444, 445, 446, 447, 460/ I-110, exit Olympic Boulevard east. **Box office** *In person* 9am-6pm Mon-Sat. *By phone/online* Ticketmaster (*p210*). **Tickets** $30-$150. **Parking** $15-$25. **Credit** AmEx, DC, MC, V. **Map** p331 A5.
Downtown's sports shrine (*see p269*) also hosts big musical acts, such as Kanye West, U2 and the reunited Spice Girls. Though it's plush and modern, the sound quality in the 20,000-capacity arena is surprisingly variable. At the concession stand, don't miss the nachos camachos, an LA favourite.

Wiltern

3790 Wilshire Boulevard, at S Western Avenue, Koreatown (1-213 388 1400/www.livenation.com). Metro Wilshire-Western/bus 20, 21, 207, 209, 720,
LDHWI/I-10, exit Western Avenue north. **Box office** *In person* show days only. *By phone/online* Ticketmaster (*p210*). **Tickets** $20-$50. **Credit** MC, V. **Map** p329 D5.
This classy art deco gem packs 'em in for shows from the alt-rock likes of the Pretenders, the Killers and Eddie Vedder, as well as the odd comic act such as Ron White or Tenacious D. Concerts are seated or standing-room-only, depending on the act. The sight lines are a plus, but elbow room in the best spots can be at a premium.

Bar & club venues

In addition to the clubs below, other venues in the city stage live music. The **Key Club** (9039 W Sunset Boulevard, West Hollywood, 1-310 274 5800, www.keyclub.com) offers occasional shows alongside its club programming. **Crash Mansion LA** (*see p265*) brings in touring acts like the Bravery, the Donnas and the Coup to supplement its club nights. The programme at **El Cid** (4212 Sunset Boulevard, Los Feliz, 1-323 668 0318, www.elcidla.com) is mostly made up of flamenco and burlesque, but local indie groups play from time to time, and Ronnie Mack's venerable country Barn Dance concert happens on the first Tuesday of every month.
Club shows in LA generally start between 8pm and 9pm and finish between 11pm and midnight, though there are exceptions. Tickets for club shows are usually available on the door, though some venues do sell tickets in advance; check venue websites for details of individual ticketing policies.

Bordello

901 E 1st Street, at Vignes Street (1-213 687 3766/www.bordellobar.com). Metro Union Station-Gateway Transit Center/bus 30, 31, 330/US 101, exit Alameda Street south. **Admission** free-$15. **Credit** AmEx, DC, Disc, MC, V.
This baroque spot trades on the legend of its past as (it says) the oldest bar and brothel in Downtown LA. The ladies of the night have long since departed but the vibe lives on, with a scarlet interior and dressed-to-impress bartenders. Along with dance nights such as the '60s-themed Satisfaction Club, local underground acts including Very Be Careful and Xu Xu Fang play here semi-regularly.

Café-Club Fais Do-Do

5257 W Adams Boulevard, at Cloverdale Avenue, West LA (1-323 931 4636/www.faisdodo.com). Bus 37/I-10, exit La Brea Avenue south. **Admission** $5-$8. **Credit** MC, V.
Once mostly the province of blues and zydeco acts, Fais Do-Do (Cajun dialect for 'dance party') now stages a variety of events, anything from rockabilly and Brazilian bands to hip hop turntablists. The faded opulent interior and desolate West Side location add to the exotic vibe.

Cinema Bar

3967 Sepulveda Boulevard, between Washington Place & Venice Boulevard, Culver City (1-310 390 1328/www.myspace.com/thecinemabar). Bus C1, C6/I-405, exit Washington Boulevard east. **Admission** free. **Credit** AmEx, DC, Disc, MC, V.

This tiny, rustic spot, the oldest bar in Culver City, draws a Bohemian crowd to its nightly shows. You'll find a high percentage of fine local acts, such as singer-songwriters Randy Weeks and Duane Jarvis, retro-rocker Ben Vaughn and country-jazz artist Lisa Finnie. Drinks are cheap and street parking is usually plentiful.

Dragonfly

6510 Santa Monica Boulevard, at Wilcox Avenue, Hollywood (1-323 466 6111/www.thedragonfly.com). Bus 4, 156, 304/I-10, exit La Brea Avenue north. **Admission** $5-$15. **Credit** AmEx, DC, MC, V. **Map** p329 B2.

Its programme packed with local hard-rock and alternative acts, this glam throwback draws an attractive, tattooed clientele that includes the occasional slumming celeb. New-wave tribute act the Spazmatics play every Sunday and consistently pack the place. However, while the spacious smoking patio at the back is a real boon, some locals are put off by the sketchy door policy and too-cool-for-school crowds.

Echo

1822 W Sunset Boulevard, at Glendale Boulevard, Echo Park (1-213 413 8200/www.attheecho.com). Bus 2, 4, 96, 302, 304/US 101, exit Glendale Boulevard north. **Admission** free-$25. **Credit** AmEx, DC, MC, V. **Map** p330 D4.

A recent remodel expanded and spiffed up this often-jammed club, where hipsters flock for all flavours of indie, dub reggae and electronica. The temperature can still rise to uncomfortable levels when it's crowded (management's reluctance to turn on the A/C doesn't help), although the back patio offers some relief. This may be the East Side, but you'll be paying Hollywood prices for the drinks.

Echoplex

1154 Glendale Boulevard, at W Sunset Boulevard, Echo Park (1-213 413 8200/www.attheecho.com). Bus 2, 4, 96, 302, 304/US 101, exit Glendale Boulevard north. **Admission** $5-$25. **Credit** AmEx, DC, MC, V. **Map** p330 D5.

This big, low-slung space is situated under the Echo, but it's a separate venue with a different entrance. The fare is similar to that offered at the Echo: local indie acts, the occasional residency by LA luminaries, and touring artists who draw bigger crowds (Ed Harcourt, Built to Spill). Like the Echo, it can be sweltering when crowded.

14 Below

1348 14th Street, at Santa Monica Boulevard, Santa Monica (1-310 451 5040/www.14below.com). Bus 4, 304, SM1, SM10, SM11/I-10, exit 26th Street north. **Admission** free-$20. **Credit** AmEx, DC, MC, V. **Map** p326 B3.

Wannabes, washed-up '80s acts and tributes to major stadium-fillers from days of yore make up the bill at this Santa Monica venue. The volume is often deafening; to save your ears, watch the show on TV from the pool room.

Hotel Café

1623½ N Cahuenga Boulevard, between Hollywood Boulevard & Selma Avenue, Hollywood (1-323 461 2040/www.hotelcafe.com). Metro Hollywood-Vine/

Smell. *See p258*.

bus 156, 210, 212, 217, 710, LDH/US 101, exit
Hollywood Boulevard west. **Admission** $8-$15.
Credit MC, V. **Map** p329 B1.
This intimate haven hosts local singer-songwriters,
from incubating newbies such as folk-popper Meiko
to veterans like Gus Black, as well as touring acts of
the calibre of Brooklyn psych-folk group Salt &
Samovar and Peter Morén of Peter Björn & John.
However, when the place is packed, and it often is,
sightlines aren't great, and the bar chatter sometimes overwhelms the music. *Photo p254.*

Joint
*8771 W Pico Boulevard, at S Robertson Boulevard,
Beverly Hills (1-310 275 2619/www.myspace.com/
thejoint). Bus 28, 220/I-10, exit Robertson Avenue
north.* **Admission** free. **Credit** AmEx, MC, V.
Map p328 A5.
Joint has a chaotic booking policy, encompassing
everything from hip hop DJs to folk singers and local
wannabe bands. Check out the club's jam sessions,
where you might catch some major stars let rip.

Knitting Factory
*7021 Hollywood Boulevard, at N Sycamore Avenue,
Hollywood (1-323 463 0204/www.knittingfactory.
com). Metro Hollywood-Highland/bus 212, 217,
LDHWH/US 101, exit Hollywood Boulevard west.*
Admission $5-$25. **Credit** AmEx, MC, V. **Map**
p329 A1.
The West Coast version of the famed New York club
isn't the hippest place in town, and the industrial
setting can feel both cold and claustrophobic. But
the three stages do offer a wide variety of local and
touring acts: indie groups such as Girl in a Coma,
lots of LA ska- and rockabilly-punk, and occasional
hit-makers like Gavin DeGraw.

Largo
*366 N La Cienega Boulevard, at Oakwood Avenue,
West Hollywood (1-310 855 0350/www.largo-la.com).
Bus 4, 105, 220, 305, 550, 704/I-10, exit La
Cienega Boulevard north.* **Admission** $10-$20.
Credit AmEx, DC, MC, V. **Map** p328 C3.
The address has changed and the dinner menu has
gone (it's now snacks only), but the performers
remain the same at LA's home for cultured, bankable
singer-songwriters, relocated to a '40s theatre. The
likes of Aimee Mann, John Doe, Jill Sobule and perennial hot-ticket artist-in-residence Jon Brion ply their
trade in the 280-seat theatre.

Mint
*6010 W Pico Boulevard, at Stearns Drive, Midtown
(1-323 954 9400/www.themintla.com). Bus 217/
I-10, exit Fairfax Avenue north.* **Admission** $7-$15.
Credit AmEx, DC, MC, V. **Map** p328 C5.
Having expanded its space and upgraded its sound,
the 70-year-old Mint is now a pretty comfortable
room. The schedule of roots- and blues-oriented acts
includes notable touring acts (Alejandro Escovedo,
the Dirty Dozen Brass Band) and fine local stalwarts
(Café R&B, Leo Nocentelli) along with more unremarkable fare. Excellent food, though.

Mr T's Bowl
*5621 N Figueroa Avenue, between Avenue 56 &
Avenue 57, Highland Park (1-323 256 7561/http://
mrtsbowl.tripod.com). Metro Highland Park/bus
83/Highway 110, exit Avenue 52.* **Admission**
free-$5. **Credit** AmEx, DC, MC, V.
An unlikely amalgam of young punks and old locals
mix happily together at a former bowling alley in a
tough Highland Park neighbourhood. Despite the
edgy surroundings, the food is delicious.

Arts & Entertainment

Roxy

9009 W Sunset Boulevard, between San Vincente Boulevard & Doheny Drive, West Hollywood (1-310 276 2222/www.theroxyonsunset.com). Bus 2, 105, 302/I-10, exit La Cienega Boulevard north. **Credit** AmEx, DC, Disc, MC, V. **Map** p328 A2.

In its 30-plus years as a Sunset Strip stalwart, the Roxy has been both a major player (hosting early Springsteen and Guns n' Roses shows) and a disappointing has-been (insert name of horrible '80s hair band here). Now that the Roxy has settled comfortably into middle age, the club offers metal, punk, indie rock, singer-songwriters and the occasional local up-and-comer. The tables offer the best views, but the sightlines from the standing risers are fine – and closer to the bar.

Safari Sam's

5214 W Sunset Boulevard, at N Kingsley Drive, Hollywood (1-323 666 7267/www.safari-sams.com). Metro Hollywood-Western/bus 2, 302/US 101, exit Western Avenue north. **Credit** *Restaurant/bar only* AmEx, DC, MC, V. **Map** p329 D1.

A 1980s Huntington Beach punk institution, Safari Sam's moved to Hollywood in 2006. It's retained its old-school punk streak, but it also features touring acts (Black Francis, the Kooks), some artier sounds, a few tribute bands and even an Americana brunch on Sundays. It's an all-ages venue.

Silverlake Lounge

2906 W Sunset Boulevard, at Parkman Avenue, Silver Lake (1-323 663 9636/www.foldsilverlake. com). Bus 2, 4, 302, 304/US 101, exit Silver Lake Boulevard north. **Admission** $7-$10. **No credit cards**. **Map** p330 C4.

Depending on the night, this hangout is either a grungy watering hole favoured by transvestites or a grungy rock club favoured by indie bands. The sound is dire, the sightlines are impossible and the smell of beer is fierce, but ascendant out-of-towners (XYZ Affair, Ari Hest) and local acts (Weather Underground, Hello Dragon) usually deliver.

Smell

247 S Main Street, between 2nd & 3rd Streets, Downtown (www.thesmell.org). Metro Pershing Square/bus 16, 316/I-110, exit 4th Street east. **Admission** $5. **Credit** AmEx, DC, MC, V. **Map** p331 C3.

The closest thing to a European squat-style venue in Los Angeles, this stark, hard-to-find warehouse-like space near Skid Row hosts the latest in indie-noise, political art-punk and the like. The Smell doesn't serve booze, and thus attracts an all-ages crowd skewed towards the younger end of the range. Veggie-friendly snacks are available. *Photo p256.*

Spaceland

1717 Silver Lake Boulevard, at Effie Street, Silver Lake (1-323 661 4380/www.clubspaceland.com). Bus 201/US 101, exit Silver Lake Boulevard north. **Admission** $7-$20. **Credit** AmEx, DC, MC, V. **Map** p330 C3.

This sprawling dive celebrated its 13th anniversary in 2008, and it remains the leading LA shrine to all things indie. The sound isn't great and parking is a combat sport, but at least there's an area for smokers. The Monday-night programme, which features free monthly residencies for local buzz bands on their way up, is always worth a look.

Tangier

2138 Hillhurst Avenue, at Avocado Street, Los Feliz (1-323 666 2407/www.foldsilverlake.com). Bus 180, 181/US 101, exit Hollywood Boulevard east. **Admission** $5-$10.**Credit** AmEx, DC, MC, V. **Map** p330 B1.

Despite the North African name, this intimate boîte in Los Feliz area favours genre-defying chamber-indie sounds such as Colorforms, Quazar and the Bamboozled and local favourite Eleni Mandell, a smokily eccentric songstress with elastic pipes. The venue draws a typically cool East Side crowd.

Troubadour

9081 Santa Monica Boulevard, at N Doheny Drive, West Hollywood (1-310 276 6168/www.troubadour. com). Bus 4, 304/I-405, exit Santa Monica Boulevard east. **Admission** free-$30. **Credit** AmEx, MC, V. **Map** p328 A2.

Still one of LA's best clubs, the Troubadour has a rich musical history: Randy Newman got his start here, and Elton John made his US debut on its stage in 1970. Still, the place hasn't lapsed into irrelevance in the time since: Interpol, Joss Stone and Franz Ferdinand all played early US shows here in the last few years. The sound is great and the views are decent from almost anywhere in the room – just stay out from under the balcony.

Viper Room

8852 W Sunset Boulevard, at Larrabee Street, West Hollywood (1-310 358 1880/www.viperroom.com). Bus 2, 105, 302/I-10, exit La Cienega Boulevard east. **Admission** free-$20. **Credit** AmEx, MC, V. **Map** p328 A2.

Clumsy punk acts, actors' bands and Hollywood detritus of varying vintages play this faux-deco hole on the Sunset Strip. It also offers the occasional solid singer-songwriter, and showcases by radio favourite Indie 103.1 FM have brought it a dash of contemporary cool. You may remember it from the fact that River Phoenix keeled over and died here.

Whisky A Go-Go

8901 W Sunset Boulevard, at N San Vicente Boulevard, West Hollywood (1-310 652 4202/www. whiskyagogo.com). Bus 2, 105, 302/I-10, exit La Cienega Boulevard north. **Admission** $10-$15. **Credit** MC, V. **Map** p328 A2.

The Doors were once the house band at the Whisky, until the owner objected to the lyrics of 'The End' and banned the group. Its place in Sunset Strip lore can't be denied, but these days the music comes mostly from classic-rock tribute acts (Led Zepagain, anyone?) and young bands of the punk/metal variety, few of whom you'll ever hear of again.

Mix and match

LA's many musical cultures often bump up against each other and merge into something new. Imported sounds are fused with native arrangements, pop melodies are wedded to exotic rhythms. And from the Latino-rock party music of Ozomatli to the mind-boggling Dakah Hip Hop Orchestra, a 60-piece aggregation of orchestral scoring with rap aesthetics, the results are often thrilling.

Perhaps the best known of LA's newer melting-pot bands is Cambodian-inspired psychedelic-rock sextet **Dengue Fever**. Moved by the music he heard after visiting Cambodia, leader Ethan Holtzman first fired up his Farfisa in 2001; along with brother Zac and three other pals, he recruited singer Chhom Nimol, who croons only in Khmer, and started doing mostly covers of Cambodian rock tunes. Released in 2008, Dengue Fever's third album *Venus on Earth*, which features mostly original material, has taken them far beyond LA's borders.

The city is full of variations on this world-fusion theme, all of which attract a cool but friendly array of fans. The **Entrance Band** combines classic rock with Indian and Arabic influences to create a head-crushingly psychedelic experience that's also somehow danceable. **Very Be Careful** offers an irresistible sound, that's drawn from traditional Colombian music called Vallenato, a blend of lively vocals, squeezebox, bass, cajón drum and cowbell. Gypsy-folk group **Fishtank Ensemble** swirls flamenco and swing into its sparkling Eastern European brew, while dub-punks **Future Pigeon** meld psychedelia, Afrobeat and electro into a Lee-'Scratch'-Perry-meets-the-Clash kind of thing.

There's more genteel fare on offer, too. **Jessica Fichot** melts vocals (in French, Chinese and Spanish) into a mixture of gypsy jazz, chanson, and Latin and Chinese folk. Guitarist Alex de Grassi, bassist Michael Manring and percussionist Chris Garcia combine more than their names in instrumental group **De Mania**: they also blend Appalachian folk, Indian raga, Latin and blues in compositions both mellow and grooving. Garcia also plays with **Quarteto Nuevo** (actually a quintet), which puts together jazz and Latin styles with Andean folk and Indian classical sounds.

Roots & blues

Country, folk and – yes – Irish music join imported beers on the menu at **Molly Malone's** (575 S Fairfax Avenue, Miracle Mile, 1-323 935 1577, www.mollymalonesla.com). **The Derby** (4500 Los Feliz Boulevard, Los Feliz, 1-323 663 8979, www.clubderby.com) offers swing bands every Sunday.

Babe's & Ricky's Inn

4339 Leimert Boulevard, at 43rd Street, Leimert Park (1-323 295 9112/www.bluesbar.com). Bus 42, 210, 305, 608, 710/I-10, exit Crenshaw Boulevard south. **Admission** $5-$10. **Credit** AmEx, MC, V.
One of LA's oldest blues clubs, Babe's & Ricky's was founded in the '60s but moved to the heart of Leimert Park a decade ago. Smokin' veteran artists such as Mickey Champion (here every Monday) are well worth a look, as is house band Bill Clark & the Mighty Balls of Fire. Club owner Laura Mae Gross is now in her eighties, but still works the room.

Harvelle's

1432 4th Street, between Broadway & Santa Monica Boulevard, Santa Monica (1-310 395 1676/www. harvelles.com). Bus 4, 304, SM1, SM2, SM3, SM4, SM10/I-10, exit 4th-5th Street north. **Admission** $3-$10; 2-drink min. **No credit cards**. **Map** p326 A3.

A surprisingly sleek place four blocks from the Pacific, Santa Monica's self-styled home of the blues also offers a little funk and jazz. The comfortable bar/lounge setting is often packed at weekends, and it pays to show up early.

McCabe's

3101 Pico Boulevard, at 31st Street, Santa Monica (1-310 828 4497/www.mccabesguitar.com). Bus SM7/ I-10, exit Centinela Avenue south. **Admission** $5-$30. **Credit** AmEx, DC, Disc, MC, V. **Map** p326 D4.
By day a revered guitar shop, McCabe's doubles as an intimate performance space. The roster has included rootsy singers such as Odetta and Chris Hillman, but also indie perennials such as Kristin Hersh and Peter Case, and more unexpected acts including Nels Cline and Eugene Chadbourne. Gigs are usually held on Fridays, Saturdays and Sundays.

Jazz

The city's jazz circuit is scattered from pillar to post. Aside from the venues that are listed below, you'll find all manner of bars, hotels and restaurants hosting jazz acts, many of them top-notch sessioneers playing as much for pleasure as for pay.

In addition to the venues detailed below, a few club nights feature prime talent from the

Arts & Entertainment

Spud U Like: the **Baked Potato**.

avant-garde jazz scene. Among them is **Rocco** (www.roccoinla.com), which sets up shop Downtown at Café Metropol (923 E 3rd Street, 1-213 614 1357, www.cafemetropol.com). Festivals include the one-day JVC Jazz Festival, held at the Hollywood Bowl in June.

Baked Potato

3787 N Cahuenga Boulevard, at Lankershim Boulevard, North Hollywood (1-818 980 1615/ www.thebakedpotato.com). Bus 96, 150, 156, 240, 750/US 101, exit Lankershim Boulevard south. **Admission** $10-$30; 2-drink min. **Credit** AmEx, Disc, MC, V.

Don Randi's pint-sized room spawned the LA jazz fusion sound in the 1970s. It's still the site of synth-driven romps, though nowadays Latin jazz acts appear too. Famous session sidemen show up incessantly – if you've always wanted to see the guitar player from Toto solo on into the night, this is your joint. The menu is full of – yes! – potatoes.

Catalina Bar & Grill

6725 W Sunset Boulevard, between N Highland & N Las Palmas Avenues, Hollywood (1-323 466 2210/ www.catalinajazzclub.com). Bus 2, 302/US 101, exit Sunset Boulevard west. **Admission** $10-$30; 2-drink min except for diners. **Credit** AmEx, DC, Disc, MC, V. **Map** p329 A2.

Catalina Popescu pulls some of jazz's heaviest hitters to her civilised Hollywood establishment: old-timers such as McCoy Tyner and Pharoah Sanders, plus younger stars of the calibre of Joshua Redman and a good proportion of dinner jazz-friendly vocalists. However, it's worth pointing out that the food isn't as good as the music.

Charlie O's

13725 Victory Boulevard, at Woodman Avenue, Valley Glen (1-818 994 3058/www.charlieos.com). Bus 158, 164/I-405, exit Victory Boulevard east. **Admission** free-$20. **Credit** DC, MC, V.

There's good jazz nightly at this friendly, unpretentious hangout up in Valley Glen, with local stalwarts such as saxophonist Pete Christlieb appearing on a regular basis. Monday is always big-band night, a rare treat in a venue this intimate and a city otherwise dominated by small-group jazz. The other six nights of the week, admission is free.

Jazz Bakery

3233 Helms Avenue, at Venice Boulevard, Culver City (1-310 271 9039/www.jazzbakery.org). Bus 33, 333, C1, C3, C5/I-10, exit La Cienega Boulevard south. **Admission** $10-$35. **Credit** DC, MC, V.

Housed in the old Helms Bakery, this not-for-profit enterprise offers an interesting programme of young and often forward-thinking jazz acts balanced with the occasional big name. Done out with rather austere theatre-style seating, the room lacks a little atmosphere; conversely, though, there's nothing to detract from the music.

La Ve Lee

12514 Ventura Boulevard, at Whitsett Avenue, Studio City (1-818 980 8158/www.laveleejazz club.com). Bus 150, 240, 750/US 101, exit Laurel Canyon Boulevard south. **Admission** $10-$20; 2-drink min. **Credit** AmEx, DC, MC, V.

A Studio City institution, La Ve Lee stages a fair mix of music in its handsome room, but the emphasis is on Latin music of both super-smooth and toe-tapping varieties. It's not necessarily a place for big names, but standards are usually high. And the Mediterranean food ain't bad, either.

Vibrato

2940 Beverly Glen Circle, at Beverly Glen Boulevard, Bel Air (1-310 474 9400/www.vibratogrilljazz.com). I-405, exit Sunset Boulevard east. **Admission** free. **Credit** AmEx, MC, V.

Co-owned by Herb Alpert, this high-end steakhouse books better talent; and, while the food and drinks are very expensive, there's rarely a cover charge and a drinks minimum. The food is actually terrific, and you might catch Will Smith or LAPD Police Chief William Bratton nodding their heads to the likes of Bobby Hutcherson, Kenny Barron and local bass legend John Heard. Reservations are recommended.

World Stage

4344 Degnan Boulevard, between 43rd Street & 43rd Place, Leimert Park (1-323 293 2451/www. theworldstage.org). Bus 40, 105, 210, 305, 710/ I-10, exit Crenshaw Boulevard north. **Admission** free-$10. **No credit cards**.

Strictly for the hardcore jazzer, this Leimert Park space is where local cats come to hone their chops. It really is all about the music here: there's no food, no booze and no dancefloor. Big names sometimes sit in, but it's the young unknowns who'll knock you out.

Arts & Entertainment

Nightclubs

Starry, starry night...

LA's mainstream dance venues aren't likely to stun anyone who's been clubbing in the likes of London, New York and Miami. You're not going to find many ultra-modern architectural monuments to DJ culture: most of the money that's invested in LA clubland fuels the creation of intimate and velvet-roped lounges *du jour* that cater chiefly to celebrity brats. And in many of these upscale rooms, the music emanating from the speakers couldn't be more middle of the road if it arrived with white lines painted across it.

Beneath the surface, though, LA nightlife gets a lot more interesting. There are myriad entrenched and enthused culture tribes flourishing outside the *TMZ* zone, from the dance-'til-you-drop after-hours crowds at Avalon Hollywood to the American Apparel-wearing cool kids who frequent the Echo and Echoplex. DJ culture has had a huge following in LA since the dawn of the '90s, and thousands of revellers hit the city's superclubs each weekend. The city's techno renaissance echoes that of Berlin and Detroit, and there are few places in the world pushing the neon flavour of dance-punk as much as LA.

The scene is also varied, if you know where to look. Care to witness the electro resurgence at first hand, complete with original artists such as Egyptian Lover or Arabian Prince on the turntables? Word up! How about hipsters dancing to rootsy, Columbian *vallenato* music? *Aquí, en LA*. If you want to join some of the sexiest Asian American partiers in the world, you've come to the right place. This is perhaps the most diverse city in the United States, and clubland reflects the ethnic variety.

Since the '80s, when East Side Latinos turned backyard parties into DJ-driven massives and British expats introduced the city to a rave-like underworld, LA has had a thriving dance scene below the surface. Today's standout one-offs come in the form of Doc Martin's house music hoedowns (www.sublevelcalifornia.com), DJ Harvey's dub-disco affairs (www.harvey sarcasticdisco.com), Droid Behavior's techno throwdowns (www.droidbehavior.com) and Hipgenesis' hippie-trance dances (www. hipgenesis.com). Some of these underground events are held in legit locales, but many others skirt the line of legality: LA boasts various warehouse districts with few neighbours to complain and even fewer police to respond. However, don't expect anarchy: most of these gigs are offered with pre-sale tickets, 21-and-up bars (from licenced caterers) and plenty of security guards. It's the music, not the punters, that provides the edginess.

Contrast these underground scenes to the city's starstruck mini-clubs, where you might not be made to feel welcome unless you're rocking gold or platinum plastic and are willing to rack up a fat bar tab that might top your air fare. That's all well and good if you're in the market for once-in-a-lifetime actor-spotting (in which case, get in line behind the 'paps'). However, the experience will fill your ears with top-40 fluff and then expose your eyes to the ugliest pretty people you've ever seen. And after you've added valet parking ($10 and up) and either bottle-service fees (*see p263* **High spirits**) or cocktails (as much as $30 each) to your cover charge, your wallet will be lighter than Nicole Richie. The gentrified nightlife of new Hollywood is just like old Vegas: the odds favour the house. Many of the stars are there for open-bar charity events or organised parties; in some cases, they're even being paid by the management simply to add a little kudos to their nightclub. These ventures are counting on you to subsidise their clientele's *Entourage* lifestyle – and their own profits. Invest wisely.

PRACTICAL INFORMATION

You must be 21 or over to drink, and no amount of over-tipping will buy you a brew if you're any younger. If you want refreshment after 2am, you'd better have stashed some alcohol at your room because you won't get a drop more from the bartender. Whether clubbing or shopping for spirits, be prepared to prove your

The best Nightclubs

For imported DJs
Avalon. See p262.

For relentless techno
King King. See p265.

For a night of star-spotting
Area. See p262.

Avalon.

up a copy of *LA Weekly* or logging on to Metromix (www.losangeles.metromix.com). Venues crank different sounds and attract different crowds from night to night, thanks to out-of-house promoters who slice up the city's musical demographics like a chef at Benihana. Tickets for most of the larger events can be purchased in advance at www.wanttickets.com and www.grooovetickets.com, both of which are also good resources for information on what's coming soon in the City of Angels.

Area

643 N La Cienega Boulevard, at Melrose Avenue, West Hollywood (1-310 652 2012/www.sbeent.com/area). Bus 4, 105, 220, 305, 550, 704/I-10, exit La Cienega Boulevard north. **Open** 10pm-2am Mon-Thur, Sat; 9.30pm-2am Fri. **Admission** free-$50. **Credit** AmEx, DC, MC, V. **Map** p328 B2.
Cresting the latest wave of celeb-crazed nightspots, Area is an ultra-exclusive and ultra-expensive lounge that's part of Sam Nazarian's nightlife empire. As with many similarly upscale venues, the easiest way for non-SAG cardholders to get in is to fork out for a table with pricey bottle service. If you want to be part of the region's biggest reality show, it might just be worth the expense, but don't expect anything edgier than Timbaland productions coming through the sound system.

Avalon

1735 N Vine Street, at Hollywood Boulevard, Hollywood (1-323 462 8900/www.avalonhollywood.com). Metro Hollywood-Vine/bus 163, 180, 181, 210, 212, 217, 312, 363, 780, LDH/US 101, exit Vine Street south. **Open** 10pm-6am Sat. **Admission** $15-$60. **Credit** AmEx, DC, MC, V. **Map** p329 B1.
Completed in 1927, this cavernous theatre remains LA's pre-eminent superclub. Avalon's Saturday-night bookings have embraced Europe's techno renaissance and aim for a Fabric-like critical edge. There's nary any trance, so leave the glow-sticks at home. And bring earplugs: the venue boasts the best sound system in the city, a floorshaking EAW Avalon Series set-up that cost a cool $1 million.

Boulevard3

6523 Sunset Boulevard, at Wilcox Avenue, Hollywood (1-323 466 2144/www.boulevard3.com). Metro Hollywood-Vine/bus 163, 180, 181, 210, 212, 217, 312, 363, 780, LDH/US 101, exit Sunset Boulevard west. **Open** 9.30pm-2am Fri, Sat. **Admission** $20. **Credit** AmEx, DC, MC, V. **Map** p329 B2.
A ripple in the tidal wave of new Hollywood venues, this indoor-outdoor expanse (in the space that once housed the Hollywood Athletic Club) arrives courtesy of the folks behind Skybar at the Mondrian (*see p58*), and nobly attempts to bring a little dignity to a tipsy and often crass community of celebutantes and actors. Dress up, bring your wallet and try to behave yourself. Hip hop is the weekend soundtrack, but DJs sometimes venture into house on off-nights.

age with a passport or driver's licence. Some venues scan IDs for extra assurance, but beware that these electromagnetic card readers can also grab personal information such as your date of birth and home address.

Many men at clubs in LA dress like slobs at a car show; if they didn't, they'd run the risk of being mistaken for the better-dressed staff. Women, meanwhile, suffer in heels, dresses and $300 jeans. But, hey, flaunt it if you got it. Whatever your gender, travel light: many larger venues ban gum, pens, cameras and even cigarettes (although some crowded outdoor smoking patios seem to be 420-friendly). And if you stash anything resembling a weapon, a pill or a powder in your pockets, you can expect delays and loss of property. If you come face to face with the LAPD, do as they say: officers have a low tolerance for clubland hi-jinks.

If you can bear the extra expense, always try and tip your bartender or server well: if you look after them, they'll look after you. It's not strange to hear Koreans speaking Spanish or to see Mexicans making sushi. Similarly, many LA clubbers tend to turn up their noses at the valets, busboys and security personnel; however, a buck or two, a smile and maybe even a little Spanish (the majority of these staff are Latino) will go a long way.

The currents of clubland change like Britney's hair, so stay up-to-date by picking

Cabana Club
1439 Ivar Avenue, at Sunset Boulevard, Hollywood (1-323 463 0005/www.cabanaclubhollywood.com). Metro Hollywood-Vine/bus 163, 180, 181, 210, 212, 217, 312, 363, 780, LDH/US 101, exit Sunset Boulevard west. **Open** 9pm-2am Fri, Sat. **Admission** free-$20. **Credit** AmEx, DC, MC, V. **Map** p329 B2.

In the warmer months, this resort-themed, indoor-outdoor nightspot buzzes with pretty young people lounging in cabanas near the reflecting pool, while everyone else soaks up mainstream sounds inside (hip hop, rock, pop). No cultural ground is being broken, and it can be expensive, but the casual and sexy LA vibe is certainly in full bloom.

Cinespace
6356 Hollywood Boulevard, at Ivar Avenue, Hollywood (1-323 817 3456/www.cinespace.info). Metro Hollywood-Vine/bus 163, 180, 181, 210, 212, 217, 312, 363, 780, LDH/US 101, exit Hollywood Boulevard west. **Open** 6pm-2am daily. **Admission** free-$50. **Credit** AmEx, DC, MC, V. **Map** p329 B1.

One of the rare Hollywood hot spots that doesn't require guests to book a table through their publicist or shell out something like a week's wages for bottle service, Cinespace has evolved into a crossroads of celebrity heaven and edgier musical nightlife. The roster features everything from the well-received residency of indie-rock king Steve Aoki, and the celebutantes who mix for him, to the occasional progressive and tech-house parties thrown by promoter Giant.

Circus Disco
6655 Santa Monica Boulevard, at N Las Palmas Avenue, Hollywood (1-323 462 5508/www.circus disco.com). Bus 4, 210, 704/US 101, exit Vine Street south. **Open** 9am-2pm Mon, Tue, Fri, Sun; 9pm-4am Sat. **Admission** $15-$40. **No credit cards**. **Map** p329 A2.

Happily, the plans that called for the redevelopment of this legendary 3,300-capacity club into shops and condos have been shelved. One of the city's oldest clubs, Circus is a gay mecca on most evenings, but Saturdays are home to DJ-centric electronic music nights aimed chiefly at straight audiences.

Conga Room
LA Live, 800 W Olympic Boulevard, at S Figueroa Street, Downtown (1-213 749 0445/www.conga room.com). Metro 7th Street-Metro Center/bus 28, 66, 81/I-110, exit Olympic Boulevard east. **Open** 6pm-2am Thur-Sat. **Admission** varies. **Credit** AmEx, DC, Disc, MC, V. **Map** p331 B4.

Co-owned by Latino stars Jimmy Smits, Jennifer Lopez and Sheila E, among others, this fabled and fabulous showcase of Latin music and musicians recently moved from Wilshire Boulevard to the new LA Live complex. The 1,100-capacity venue also features dining alongside the music: electronica is beamed in on Tuesdays, while an 'all-star' salsa band rules on Thursdays and Saturdays.

High spirits

Popularised in Miami, notorious in New York and turned into something approaching an art form in Las Vegas, bottle service is now increasingly common in the bars and nightclubs of Los Angeles. In order to reserve a table at many upscale bars and clubs, especially in Hollywood, you'll need to buy an entire bottle of booze at an outrageous mark-up that could top 1,000 per cent. A bottle of vodka might cost as much as $300 (including mixers but excluding service), and some venues even operate a two-bottle minimum for large groups.

There are 300 green-backed reasons why bottle service is an unappealing trend. However, it does have its advantages if you've got the cash to splash and the overwhelming desire to experience the Hollywood high life. Chief among them is that you'll be guaranteed not only entry but your own table; contrast this to the experience of common-or-garden bar-hoppers, who are often kept waiting in line outside Hollywood hot spots for as much as three or four hours. You might also be excused the venue's cover charge, which makes the proposition slightly more financially appealing. And, with any luck, the bouncer won't treat you with the withering contempt he reserves for the proles waiting in line.

But, it probably goes without saying, bottle service isn't for everyone. It's expensive, of course, and what's more it doesn't even guarantee good service once you've finally made it inside the bar of your dreams. In fact, what you and your friends are purchasing with your $300 isn't so much a bottle of spirits as the idea that you're one of the in-crowd, a mover and a shaker, and part of Hollywood's fashionable elite. Celebrity helps when trying to make it through the bouncer-guarded front door, and a little beauty can go a long way. But for the rest of us, such status is essentially built on the fact that money talks. If you want to join the hallowed throngs beyond the velvet rope, supping half-assed cosmopolitans in the same room as Lindsey Lohan, Mandy Moore and someone who used to be in *The Bold and the Beautiful*, you'd better be prepared to hold yours up to the mic.

Arts & Entertainment

Spinning around

Los Angeles' status as a global crossroads of electronic dance music currents means that it's difficult to define the LA sound in the way that, for instance, Berlin has become the capital of techno, or Miami is the hub of tribal house. Many superclubs import DJs for their Saturday-night parties, while the intimate-but-havin'-it Monday Social soirées at Nacional (*see p266*), organised by DJs **Mick Cole** and **Freddy Be**, feature a who's who of world house, prog and breakbeat spinners that's as international as they are Angeleno.

However, although LA draws plenty of DJs from abroad, there's also plenty of home-grown talent working the scene in a variety of genres. Chief among them is Avalon (*see p262*), which has taken a chance on an up-and-coming trio of locals plugged into the world's minimal techno surge: three-man tag team **Droog**, which performs on the club's terrace monthly. Another regular at Avalon is Manchester transplant **Kazell**, who's known for his sublime, rock-steady tech-house sets on the terrace.

LA's techno revival has been spearheaded by **John Tejada** at Compression (bi-monthly Fridays at **King King**; *see p265*). Further underground, the roving Droid Behavior party (www.droidbehavior.com) supplements its international techno bookings with local live acts such as **Acid Circus** and **Drumcell**. And also on the down-low, look out for one-offs from house legend **Doc Martin** (www.sublevelcalifornia.com) and British-expat **DJ Harvey** (www.harveysarcasticdisco.com).

The city's indie DJ scene is thronged by cool kids in tights and mullets. Young celebs often join the party when **Cinespace**; *see p263*) is on the decks, and some of them – **Danny Masterson** from *That '70s Show* (aka DJ Momjeans), **Efren Ramirez** from *Napoleon Dynamite* – seem keen to follow in Aoki's pop-leaning footsteps. One celeb-pulling spinner who has the skills to pay the bills is Adam Goldstein: as **DJ AM**, Goldstein can be found blasting hip hop and rock at the club he co-owns, **LAX** (*see p265*).

Away from the paparazzi strobes, the **Echo** and adjacent **Echoplex** (*see p256*) together comprise ground zero of LA's dance-punk scene. Regular nights include Bootie LA's mash-up parties featuring **Party Ben** as well as the **Check Yo Ponytail** events that highlight '80s-flavoured e-music. And look out for local acts that embody this new meeting place of guitars, synths and drum machines: **Guns 'n' Bombs**, **Ima Robot** and Australia-born, LA-based **Sam Sparro**.

Crash Mansion

1024 S Grand Avenue, at W Olympic Boulevard, Downtown (1-213 747 0999/www.crashmansionla. com). Metro 7th Street-Metro Center/bus 14, 37, 70, 71, 76, 78, 79, 96/I-110, exit Olympic Boulevard east. **Open** varies. **Admission** $10-$50. **Credit** AmEx, DC, Disc, MC, V. **Map** p331 B4.

New York-born rock venue Crash Mansion recently established an LA outpost that doubles as a dance emporium. The multi-room complex has space for 1,200 and runs an inclusive 18-and-up door policy (over-21s can split off from the bar). The DJ booking policy has been off-the-beaten path, with the unexpected likes of Tommy Lee performing dance music sets for a Vegas-esque crowd. One of the reasons Downtown's nightlife renaissance has more edge than Hollywood's own after-dark revival.

Element

1642 N Las Palmas Avenue, at Hollywood Boulevard, Hollywood (1-323 460 4632/www.element hollywood.com). Metro Hollywood-Highland/bus 163, 180, 181, 210, 212, 217, 312, 363, 780, LDH/US 101, exit Hollywood Boulevard west. **Open** 10pm-2am nightly. **Admission** free-$50. **Credit** AmEx, DC, Disc, MC, V. **Map** p329 A1.

While other starry spots blur the lines between lounge and bar, or between restaurant and disco, Element is built for partying: this is twentysomething Hollywood's main dancefloor, the place where you're most likely to find Justin Timberlake rocking his body to his own tunes through a serious sound system. Although it's not without its velvet ropes and men-in-black-guarded VIP nooks, Element is still more democratic than much of new Hollywood.

Façade Hollywood

6356 Hollywood Boulevard, at Ivar Avenue, Hollywood (1-323 465 4827). Metro Hollywood-Vine/bus 163, 180, 181, 210, 212, 217, 312, 363, 780, LDH/US 101, exit Hollywood Boulevard west. **Open** varies Mon-Thur; 9.30pm-2am Fri-Sun. **Admission** $20. **Credit** AmEx, DC, Disc, MC, V. **Map** p329 B1.

Formerly Ivar, this mid-sized dance club has had trouble finding its place in the Hollywood nightlife renaissance. It's neither an exclusive lounge nor a come-one-come-all superclub but something in between: sleek, modern and DJ-centric, with high ceilings, a glorious outdoor area, a tried-and-true sound system and a minimalist vibe. It's already one of Hollywood's most promising venues; now it just needs to find its musical footing.

Highlands

6801 Hollywood Boulevard, at N Highland Avenue, Hollywood (1-323 461 9800/www.thehighlands hollywood.com). Metro Hollywood-Highland/bus 163, 180, 181, 210, 212, 217, 312, 363, 780, LDH/US 101, exit Hollywood Boulevard west. **Open** 10pm-3am Fri, Sat. **Admission** free-$50. **Credit** AmEx, DC, Disc, MC, V. **Map** p329 A1.

Right at the centre of Hollywood's tourist zone, perched above the Hollywood Walk of Fame in the Hollywood & Highland complex, this modern super-club is probably the most tourist-friendly dance venue in LA. However, that's not necessarily a bad thing. The music policy is mainstream, but you won't find much more local flavour than at Friday's Asian nights, fuelled by big-name hip hop performances and eye-candy extraordinaire.

King King

6555 Hollywood Boulevard, at N Schrader Boulevard, Hollywood (1-323 960 5765/www. kingkinghollywood.com). Metro Hollywood-Highland/ bus 163, 180, 181, 210, 212, 217, 312, 363, 780, LDH/US 101, exit Hollywood Boulevard west. **Open** varies. **Admission** free-$30. **Credit** DC, MC, V. **Map** p329 B1.

King King descends from a legendary, smoke-filled venue on S La Brea Avenue that used to host MC battles, acid jazz bands and DJ-driven parties that felt as illicit as they were artistic. The red-lit Hollywood reincarnation is larger and more mainstream, but you can still find adventure here, with house music, techno, cabaret and salsa offered on different nights. The door policy is inclusive, and there's room for 300 of your pals.

La Cita

336 S Hill Street, between 3rd & 4th Streets, Downtown (1-213 687 7111/www.myspace.com/ lacitabar). Metro Pershing Square/bus 2, 4, 30, 31, 40, 42, 45, 48/I-110, exit 3rd Street east. **Open** 10am-2am daily. **Admission** free-$10. **Credit** AmEx, DC, MC, V. **Map** p331 C3.

One of a handful of old-school Mexican watering holes in the inner city that have been taken over by new-school hipsters, La Cita serves as a bar, a restaurant and a club, complete with a dancefloor and an outdoor patio. Edgy dance-punks and big-name artist-DJs (Shepard Fairey, to name one) have called the red-velvet-adorned venue home in recent times, but you can still find Downtown throwbacks, including many Latinos, sipping Modelos at happy hour.

LAX

1714 N Las Palmas Avenue, at Hollywood Boulevard, Hollywood (1-323 464 0171/www.lax hollywood.com). Metro Hollywood-Vine/bus 163, 180, 181, 210, 212, 217, 312, 363, 780, LDH/US 101, exit Hollywood Boulevard west. **Open** 10pm-2am Wed, Fri, Sat. **Admission** free-$30. **Credit** AmEx, DC, MC, V. **Map** p329 A1.

On a scene where DJs are known more for their tabloid exploits than their skills, DJ AM, aka Adam Goldstein, is the real deal. Goldstein's deft hip hop and rock juggling create quite a lift-off at LAX, which he co-owns, and the long wait behind the velvet ropes should be worth it. This airport-themed venue is where the young and body-conscious blast off, and it's no place for a quiet nightcap.

Little Temple

4519 Santa Monica Boulevard, at Virgil Avenue, Silver Lake (1-323 660 4540/www.littletemple.com). Metro Vermont-Santa Monica/bus 4, 26, 704/US

101, exit Vermont Avenue north. **Open** 9pm-2am Tue-Sun. **Admission** free-$10. **Credit** AmEx, DC, MC, V. **Map** p330 B3.

The crowd at this Silver Lake venue, owned by the folks behind Temple Bar and Zanzibar (*see p267*) in Santa Monica, has a more-underground-than-thou feel; you'll get extra credit for wearing and trainspotting rare kicks. But it's mostly a welcoming club with a range of soul, funk, salsa and, especially, left-field hip hop artists such as Nu Mark and Breakestra appearing on various nights.

Mayan

1038 S Hill Street, at W Olympic Boulevard, Downtown (1-213 746 4287/www.clubmayan.com). Metro Pershing Square/bus 2, 4, 30, 31, 40, 42, 45, 48/I-110, exit 9th Street east. **Open** varies. **Admission** $10-$50. **Credit** AmEx, DC, MC, V. **Map** p331 B4.

In recent decades, this Downtown landmark has been the backdrop for many televised music performances, hosted some of the region's biggest salsa parties, and provided good vibes for spin sessions from the likes of John Digweed and Paul Van Dyk. Unfortunately, while its architecture is amazing, it hasn't been renovated since 1990 and could use a little nip-tuck. Security is hands-on and about as friendly as a New York City sanitation worker.

Mood

6623 Hollywood Boulevard, at Cherokee Avenue, Hollywood (1-323 464 6663). Metro Hollywood-Highland/bus 163, 180, 181, 210, 212, 217, 312, 363, 780, LDH/US 101, exit Hollywood Boulevard west. **Open** 9pm-2am Tue-Sun. **Admission** $20. **Credit** AmEx, DC, MC, V. **Map** p329 A1.

Back when you could still enter most Hollywood clubs for $5 and score any number of pharmaceuticals for not much more, David Judaken brought romance and glamour back to the area at the late, great Garden of Eden. Mood, his second-generation club, offers a Balinese-themed interior, a steady clientele of starlets and a mainstream soundtrack. It's not the latest or greatest A-list venue, but it still has verve, exclusivity and even a little edge in the form of BoJesse Christopher's electronic-flavoured Hot Lava on Saturdays.

Nacional

1645 Wilcox Avenue, at Hollywood Boulevard, Hollywood (1-323 962 7712/www.nacional.cc). Metro Hollywood-Vine/bus 163, 180, 181, 210, 212, 217, 312, 363, 780, LDH/US 101, exit Hollywood Boulevard west. **Open** 10pm-2am daily. **Admission** free-$20. **Credit** AmEx, DC, MC, V. **Map** p329 B1.

While it's no longer the belle of the celebrity ball, Cuban-flavoured Nacional has at least aged gracefully. One of the first paparazzi-encamped venues along Hollywood Boulevard, the two-level venue still gleams, particularly when the often imported DJs of Monday Social (Sander Kleinenberg, MANDY et al) are rocking the decks. A rare 'new Hollywood' club that feels far more like the real LA than the tabloid version on display at the clubs down the street.

Ritual

1743 N Cahuenga Boulevard, at Hollywood Boulevard, Hollywood (1-323 463 0060/www. ritualsupperclub.com). Metro Hollywood-Vine/bus 163, 180, 181, 210, 212, 217, 312, 363, 780, LDH/US 101, exit Hollywood Boulevard west. **Open** varies. **Admission** free-$30. **Credit** *Bar & restaurant only* AmEx, DC, MC, V. **Map** p329 B2.

A few years ago, the all-but legendary White Lotus helped kickstart celebrities' love affair with new Hollywood. Since taking over its location, the owners of the Zen-inspired supper club Ritual have kicked it up several notches, adding a banana tree-lined patio, Asian-fusion dining and a serious dancefloor driven by a hip hop and rock soundtrack. When the Cahuenga corridor lights up at night, it's one of the more exclusive spots to spend an evening, but even extras will be allowed in if they first sit down for dinner (reservations recommended).

740

740 S Broadway, at W 7th Street, Downtown (1-213 627 6277/www.740la.com). Metro Pershing Square/bus 2, 4, 30, 31, 40, 42, 45, 48/I-110, exit 9th Street east. **Open** varies Mon-Thur; 9pm-3am Fri-Sun. **Admission** $20. **Credit** AmEx, DC, MC, V. **Map** p331 C4.

Housed in a 1913 Beaux Arts building that's been restored and re-imagined on a magnificent scale, 740 is a three-level, glass-walled danceteria that offers bottle service, VIP rooms, a dress-to-impress clientele, solid EAW sound but, despite all of this, one of the area's more inclusive door policies. Although its owners experimented with superstar DJs when it first opened, 740 has gone on to become a mostly hip hop-driven venue for LA's own version of New York's bridge-and-tunnel crowd.

Spider Club

1735 N Vine Street, at Hollywood Boulevard, Hollywood (1-323 462 8900/www.avalonhollywood. com). Metro Hollywood-Vine/bus 163, 180, 181, 210, 212, 217, 312, 363, 780, LDH/US 101, exit Hollywood Boulevard west. **Open** varies. **Admission** free-$40. **Credit** AmEx, DC, MC, V. **Map** p329 B2.

If the Spider Club was a celebrity it would be Nicky to Avalon's Paris: less accessible, more reserved but just as hot – and, like, totally related. Joined to the larger Avalon, the intimate, upper-level venue (enter on the north side of the building) hosts many invite-only events but opens up for the headstrong masses on Fridays. Well, sort of: the bangin' after-hours soirée called Spider after Dark actually begins at 3am on Saturdays. Alcohol is a no-no at LA clubs after 2am, but at that time you really should be drinking Red Bull anyway.

Tatou

333 S Boylston Street, at W 3rd Street, Downtown (1-213 482 2000/www.tatoullc.com). Bus 16, 18, 53, 62, 316/I-110, exit 3rd Street west. **Open** 9pm-2am Fri, Sat. **Admission** $20. **Credit** AmEx, DC, Disc, MC, V. **Map** p331 A2.

Zanzibar, the hottest hot spot on the West Side circuit.

Clubbing at 333 S Boylston Street has been a sport since the '80s: the cavernous locale was even owned by Prince for a while. However, the venue's always had trouble getting a foothold in the local nightlife market, unsure of whether it's a Downtown-revival spot for hipsters, a DJ-driven warehouse or an exclusive supper club. Now, as Tatou, it's all three, with a swanky makeover and a blingy schedule of hip hop nights, *Playboy*-sponsored parties and private events. The jury's out as to whether this address has finally got its hooks into late-night LA, but this is certainly one of the biggest, nicest clubs in town.

Vanguard
6021 Hollywood Boulevard, at N Bronson Avenue, Hollywood (1-323 463 3331/www.vanguardla.com). Metro Hollywood-Vine/bus 163, 180, 181, 210, 212, 217, 312, 363, 780, LDH/US 101, exit Hollywood Boulevard west. **Open** 9pm-2am Mon-Fri; 9pm-4am Sat. **Admission** $10-$40. **Credit** AmEx, DC, MC, V. **Map** p329 C1.
This former warehouse has been reborn as a sanctum for superstar DJs, complete with a kicking, UK-built Funktion One sound system, three dance areas and a waterfall-adorned patio big enough for hundreds of your closest friends. Giant brought its best-in-town vibe when it moved its Saturday-night, electronic-music parties from Avalon to Vanguard. Unfortunately, glowsticks still show up, but not on Sundays, when Marques Wyatt's Deep gets down with global house stars such as Louie Vega.

V20
81 Aquarium Way, at West Shoreline Drive, Long Beach (1-562 216 2060/www.v2olongbeach.com). Metro 1st Street/bus 60, 232, 360/I-710, exit Shoreline Drive east. **Open** 9pm-2am Thur-Sat. **Admission** $10-$20. **Credit** AmEx, DC, Disc, MC, V.
This 30,000sq ft megaclub held some promise when it opened and booked a few electronic-music stars. The owners boasted that they put $10 million into building the place. Too bad they haven't invested much in DJs: V20 has lost the plot. Long Beach has a sizeable South-east Asian community, and the Asian-themed nights here go off. But otherwise, it's hard to justify the drive down to the LBC when you can find just as much cheese on Hollywood Boulevard.

Zanzibar
1301 5th Street, at Arizona Avenue, Santa Monica (1-310 451 2221/www.zanzibarlive.com). Bus 4, 20, 33, 333, SM1, SM5, SM7, SM8, SM10/I-10, exit 4th-5th Street north. **Open** 9pm-2am daily. **Admission** free-$15. **Credit** AmEx, DC, MC, V. **Map** p326 B2.
This African-themed hangout is a West Side institution, and boasts some of the region's most eclectic and forward-thinking DJs. With KCRW kingpin Jason Bentley taking early retirement from the decks, a new generation of soul, indie-hip hop and world-beat spinners has taken over, spinning for a well-heeled, international crowd. Groove on the small dancefloor, order a Chimay at the bar or grab a pillow and relax on the benches at the back.

Arts & Entertainment

Sports & Fitness

Hiking to biking, soccer to surfing, LA's climate is perfect for outdoor exertion.

Opening Day with the **Los Angeles Angels of Anaheim**.

Blessed with a climate that simply demands outdoor activities, Southern Californians are legendary for indulging in everything under the gorgeous Californian sun when it comes to getting physical. Sure, people spend hours each week in their cars, the air quality challenges even the hardiest lungs and there's not much of a pedestrian culture, but don't be fooled: this is still one of the healthiest cities in America.

For sporting goods stores, see p210.

Spectator sports

The second-largest sports market in the US (after New York), LA features an abundance of athletic franchises, most of which have devoted fans. Six of them – including a hockey team, an arena football outfit and all three of LA's basketball franchises – are based at the Staples Center in Downtown LA, which hosts everything from concerts (see p255) to political conventions.

INFORMATION AND TICKETS

The sports section in the *LA Times* lists the teams' games and broadcast schedules each day. If you want to look further ahead, check each team's individual websites, or the comprehensive and easy-to-navigate site run by sports TV network ESPN at www.espn.com.

It's best to approach teams' box offices for tickets, but prepare to be disappointed. LA Lakers games routinely sell out, while the very best seats at Dodgers games are sold as part of season-ticket packages. If you get no luck at the team's own box office, contact the ubiquitous Ticketmaster (see p250). And if a baseball game you'd like to attend has sold out, try StubHub (www.stubhub.com): fans resell tickets to other fans here, with StubHub taking a cut as the middle man. The site guarantees the authenticity of all tickets sold through it, so you can be sure your purchase is legitimate.

A riskier approach is to buy tickets from unauthorised touts – aka scalpers – who wait outside the venues before the game. If you do decide to buy from them, be sure to double-check the date before you hand over your money: selling tickets for games that have already happened is the oldest trick in the scalper's book.

Baseball

The Major League Baseball (MLB) season runs from April until late September/early October, whereupon the top four teams from each of the two leagues (the American and the National) begin four weeks of play-off games that end with the World Series.

Los Angeles Angels of Anaheim

Angel Stadium of Anaheim, 2000 Gene Autry Way, between Katella & Orangewood Avenues, Anaheim (information 1-888 796 4256/tickets 1-714 663 9000/http://angels.mlb.com). I-5, exit Katella Avenue east. **Tickets** *$5-$200. Parking $8.* **Credit** *AmEx, DC, MC, V.*

Having muddled through the '90s, the Angels have spent the early 21st century as the team to beat in the American League West division. The turnaround began in 2002, when manager Mike Scioscia led the team to their first World Series. Aside from a blip in 2003, they've been contenders ever since. With outfielder Vlad Guerrero and closer Francisco Rodriquez both out of contract at the end of 2008, and recent signings Torii Hunter and Gary Matthews, Jr not living up to their inadvisably large contracts, there could be tough times ahead. But Scioscia's track record is so strong, and the team's rivals are so inconsistent, that it's difficult to bet against them.

The Angels' ballpark lacks character in comparison to Dodger Stadium. However, it's still a pleasant place to take in a game, and the fans are more enthusiastic than the notoriously blasé Dodger fans. Indeed, the only real problem with the team is that absurd name, changed (from the Anaheim Angels) in 2004 by owner Arte Moreno despite the fact that the team isn't in either the city or the county of Los Angeles, and despite the fact that it translates, tautologously, as 'The the Angels Angels of Anaheim'.

Los Angeles Dodgers

Dodger Stadium, 1000 Elysian Park, at Stadium Way, Echo Park (1-866 363 4377/http://losangeles. dodgers.mlb.com). Bus 2, 4, 302, 704/I-110, exit Dodger Stadium north. **Tickets** *$4-$130. Parking $15.* **Credit** *AmEx, DC, Disc, MC, V.*

Criticism of the Dodgers in recent years has been focused on owner Frank McCourt, whose plans to redevelop parts of much-cherished Dodger Stadium have been widely lambasted. Still, it could be worse: the rows over McCourt's plans for the ballpark have at least distracted some fans from the team, perennial underachievers in the National League West division. For the first time in a while, the future looks bright: the Dodgers currently have a stack of promising young players, among them first baseman James Loney and outfielder Andre Ethier. Hopefully, general manager Ned Colletti won't follow his past form and sign lots of overpaid, underperforming veterans to replace them.

Despite the on-field problems, the fans keep coming. Understandably so, too, since Dodger Stadium is one of the nicest ballparks in the country. If you can't make a game, at least tune in to hear veteran broadcaster Vin Scully call one on TV or radio.

Basketball

The National Basketball Association (NBA) season starts in late October/early November and runs until mid April. At this point, the league's best teams enter the playoffs, which end in mid June.

When the regular season is finished, the WNBA hoves into view, beginning in May and wrapping up in September. Led by hometown hero Lisa Leslie, the **Los Angeles Sparks** draw pretty good crowds to their games at the Staples Center; for tickets, call 1-877 447 7275 or see www.wnba.com/sparks.

Los Angeles Clippers

Staples Center, 1111 S Figueroa Street, at 11th Street, Downtown (1-888 895 8662/www.nba.com/ clippers). Metro Pico/bus 81, 381, 442, 444, 445, 446, 447, 460/I-110, exit Olympic Boulevard east. **Tickets** *$15-$1,100. Parking $15-$25.* **Credit** *AmEx, DC, Disc, MC, V.* **Map** *p331 A5.*

When the Los Angeles Clippers made it into the NBA play-offs in 2005-06, just the third time in 30 years that the team ended the regular season with a winning record, many pundits heralded the team's turnaround and predicted good times ahead. No such luck. If the following year was a disappointment, then the 2007-08 season was a catastrophe. The team won 23 games while losing 59, and the only cause for optimism is the return after injury of point guard Shaun Livingston. Indeed, perhaps the most attractive thing about the Clippers is that it's generally easier to score tickets for a game than it is for the Lakers.

Los Angeles Lakers

Staples Center, 1111 S Figueroa Street, at 11th Street, Downtown (information 1-310 426 6000/ tickets 1-213 480 3232/www.nba.com/lakers). Metro Pico/bus 81, 381, 442, 444, 445, 446, 447, 460/I-110, exit Olympic Boulevard east. **Tickets** *$10-$230. Parking $15-$25.* **Credit** *AmEx, DC, Disc, MC, V.* **Map** *p331 A5.*

While baseball has the New York Yankees and soccer has Manchester United, the Los Angeles Lakers are the NBA team everybody loves to hate. For 'hate', read 'beat': there's not a player in the league who doesn't enjoy putting one over on the most glamorous team in American sports. In recent years, the Lakers haven't been the force they were at the turn of the millennium, when they won the NBA Finals three years in succession. However, the 2007-08 season saw the team's resurgence: led by coach Phil Jackson and superstar guard Kobe Bryant, the Lakers made it all the way to the finals for the first time since 2004.

Like the Clippers, the team play at the Staples Center. Unlike the Clippers, they draw a crowd

Arts & Entertainment

packed with Hollywood stars – including, courtside, a permanently sunglassed Jack Nicholson.

Football

Los Angeles has been without an NFL team since the Raiders returned to Oakland in 1996. And despite a variety of plans being put forward for discussion in recent years, with the Coliseum, the Rose Bowl, Anaheim and even the Dodger Stadium parking lot all suggested as possible locations for a new NFL team in the city, there's no sign of progress on the horizon.

In the absence of the NFL, football fans have a few choices. The **Los Angeles Avengers** (1-888 263 6437, www.laavengers.com) bring a little rough and tumble to the Staples Center between February and June in the Arena Football League (AFL). However, interest is greater in the college game, which runs from September to November before the bevy of bowl games played across the country around New Year's Day. The most famous of these, and the most prestigious, is the Rose Bowl game, held at the stadium of the same name.

Under head coach Pete Carroll, the storied **USC Trojans** (1-213 740 4672, http://usc trojans.cstv.com) have once again become a college football powerhouse, winning the Rose Bowl game in 2007 and 2008. The Trojans play their regular-season games at the Los Angeles Coliseum (3911 S Figueroa Street). The **UCLA Bruins** (1-310 825 2101, http://uclabruins. cstv.com), who play their homes games at the Rose Bowl, struggle by comparison, but still draw passionate crowds.

Horse racing

There are three racetracks in the LA area, all of which feature flat racing. Call or check online for post times.

Hollywood Park Race Track & Casino

1050 S Prairie Avenue, between 90th Street & Century Boulevard, Inglewood (1-310 419 1500/ www.hollywoodpark.com). Bus 117, 211, 212/I-405, exit Manchester Boulevard east. **Admission** $7-$20; $4 discounts; under-17s free. *Parking* $3.

Los Alamitos Race Course

4961 Katella Avenue, at Walker Street, Los Alamitos (1-714 820 2800/www.losalamitos.com). I-5, exit Katella Avenue west. **Admission** $3-$10; $2 discounts. Free to all Thur. *Parking* $3-$8.

Santa Anita Park

285 W Huntington Drive, between Baldwin & Santa Anita Avenues, Arcadia (1-626 574 7223/www. santaanita.com). Bus 79, 264/I-210, exit Baldwin Avenue south. **Admission** $5-$20. *Parking* $4-$6.

Hockey

The National Hockey League (NHL) regular season runs from October to early April, and is followed by two months of playoffs.

Anaheim Ducks

Honda Center, 2695 Katella Avenue, at Douglass Road, Anaheim (information 1-877 945 3946/tickets 1-714 703 2545/http://ducks.nhl.com). I-5, exit Disney Way. **Tickets** $20-$313. *Parking* $15-$25. **Credit** AmEx, DC, MC, V.
The Mighty Ducks of Anaheim changed their name to the more restrained Anaheim Ducks before the 2006-07 season, but their might remained intact: the team won the Stanley Cup for the first time at the end of a gruelling season. The 2007-08 season proved less successful, but the team remains competitive and the fans are just as enthusiastic as ever.

Los Angeles Kings

Staples Center, 1111 S Figueroa Street, at 11th Street, Downtown (1-888 546 4752/http://kings.nhl. com). Metro Pico/bus 81, 381, 442, 444, 445, 446, 447, 460/I-110, exit Olympic Boulevard east. **Tickets** $20-$120. *Parking* $15-$25. **Credit** AmEx, DC, Disc, MC, V. **Map** p331 A5.
Ice hockey in SoCal may seem ridiculous, but the Kings try to get the locals interested. The crowds they draw to the Staples Center are surprisingly enthusiastic; it's just a pity the team, which hasn't made the playoffs since 2001-02, is pretty poor.

Motor racing

The annual glamour event is the **Long Beach Grand Prix**, held on a street circuit in April (www.gplb.com). The **California Speedway** in Fontana (1-909 429 5000, www.california speedway.com), 90 minutes east of LA just off I-10, hosts an assortment of events between April and October.

Irwindale Speedway

13300 E Live Oak Avenue, at I-605, Irwindale (1-626 358 1100/www.toyotaspeedwayatirwindale.com). I-605 north, exit E Live Oak Avenue west. **Tickets** prices vary. **Credit** DC, MC, V.
This half-mile paved oval in the San Gabriel Valley, which opened in 1999, is California's first new short track for 20 years. The 6,500-seat venue features a variety of racing from Feb to Nov.

Soccer

Thanks to the arrival of David Beckham at the **LA Galaxy** (*see below*) and a significant Latino population, soccer is catching on as a spectator sport in the city. Numerous bars and cafés show overseas matches on satellite TV – if you want to catch up on the English Premier League, try the **Cock & Bull** in Santa Monica (2947 Lincoln Boulevard, 1-310 399 9696). There

Arts & Entertainment

Two wheels good

Orange 20 Bikes.

Believe it or not, Los Angeles does have a contingent of cyclists who navigate the city on two wheels. Despite the overwhelming freeway configurations and miles of congested boulevards, groups such as the **Los Angeles County Bicycle Coalition** (LACBC, www.la-bike.org) are determined to convince Angelenos that cyclists deserve to move as freely and safely through the city as their motorised counterparts.

Formed in 1994, the LACBC is the largest and most vocal bicycle advocacy group in Southern California. Working in tandem (sorry) with the LA County Metropolitan Transportation Authority, the coalition has been the driving force behind improved bike paths along several bus lines and thoroughfares, an increase in the number of bike racks on buses, and improved bike access on public transport.

Although it's less politically and more socially active, **CICLE** (Cyclists Inciting Change through Live Exchange; www.cicle. org) has a broadly similar mission. The highlight of its website is the 'Back Roads' section: hardcore cyclists detail their favoured routes through the city, listing the streets, landmarks, specific turns and hazards that will take a cyclist from one side of the city to the other.

LA cyclists will tell you that despite aggressive drivers, wormhole storm-drains and a lack of proper bike lanes, traversing the city can be quite simple and fairly enjoyable. The attitude of these optimistic souls is reinforced at places such as the **Bicycle Kitchen** (706 N Heliotrope Drive, just north of Melrose Avenue, 1-323 662 2776, www.bicyclekitchen.com), a volunteer-run organisation that offers neophytes courses on bike repair. Along with **Orange 20 Bikes** just opposite (713 N Heliotrope Drive, 1-323 662 4537, www.orange20bikes.com), it's at the heart of LA bike culture and is a great place to meet like-minded riders.

Between the LACBC, the Bicycle Kitchen and a number of other bike clubs and shops, there's a wide range of events held throughout the year. Bicycle Kitchen events tend to attract an assortment of hipster bike messengers and adrenalin junkies, while LACBC affairs bring out the gamut of cyclists. The festive **Los Angeles River Ride** is the LACBC's premier fundraiser, held each year in June, and offers five different bike rides of varying lengths. And then there are the **Midnight Ridazz** (www.midnightridazz.com), a very loose collective of cyclists that organises highly informal night rides around LA.

Cyclists visiting LA should do their homework in advance, sourcing routes and perhaps contacting the LACBC. LA remains a drivers' city, but the gracious, enthusiastic cycling community is more than happy to welcome visitors to their side of the road.

are also a huge number of amateur teams and leagues, many of them organised according to the native country of their participants.

LA Galaxy

Home Depot Center, 18400 Avalon Boulevard, Carson (1-877 342 5299/www.lagalaxy.com). I-110, exit 190th Street east. **Tickets** *$25-$275.* **Parking** *$15-$30.* **Credit** *AmEx, DC, Disc, MC, V.*

Without wishing to insult the other members of the LA Galaxy squad, not to mention the team's esteemed Dutch coach Ruud Gullit, the recent spike in the Galaxy's popularity is due in large part to just one man: former Manchester United and Real Madrid midfielder David Beckham, who joined the team in 2007 and arrived to the kind of fanfare normally reserved for major movie stars and world-conquering rock musicians. The team

Arts & Entertainment

Los Angeles Equestrian Center.

faces stiff opposition from local rivals **Chivas USA** (1-877 344 8271, www.cdchivasusa.com), with which it shares the stadium. The season runs from March to November.

A second LA location is due to open at LA Live in Downtown (*see p119*) towards the end of 2008.

Participation sports

Bowling

AMF Bay Shore Lanes

234 Pico Boulevard, between Main & 3rd Streets, Santa Monica (1-310 399 7731/www.amf.com). Bus 33, 333, SM1, SM2, SM8, SM10/I-10, exit 4th-5th Street south. **Open** 9am-midnight Mon-Thur, Sun; 9am-2am Fri, Sat. **Rates** $7/person; $4.75 shoe rental. **Credit** AmEx, DC, Disc, MC V. **Map** p326 A3.

Santa Monica's main bowling alley can get pretty busy on weekends.

Lucky Strike Lanes

Hollywood & Highland, 6801 Hollywood Boulevard, at N Highland Avenue, Hollywood (1-323 467 7776/www.bowlluckystrike.com). Metro Hollywood-Highland/bus 163, 180, 181, 210, 212, 217, 312, 363, 780, LDH/US 101, exit Hollywood Boulevard west. **Open** noon-2am daily. **Rates** $4.95-$7.95/person; $4.25 shoe rental. **Credit** AmEx, DC, Disc, MC, V. **Map** p329 A1.

This slick, party-friendly 12-lane alley is a retro homage to bowling alleys of the 1960s, though it's unlikely that alleys back then operated such strict dress codes (no baggy clothes, no plain white T-shirts, no hats). It's also over-21s only after 7pm.

Cycling

If you don't feel quite brave enough to cycle around the LA streets (*see p271* **Two wheels good**), there are plenty of other alternatives. The most appealing bike trails in the city run along the beaches: the **South Bay Bicycle Trail**, also known as the Strand, runs 22 miles from Will Rogers State Beach to Torrance, while the **Huntington Beach Bicycle Trail** extends eight miles south from Sunset Beach. Many oceanfront stalls in Santa Monica and Venice rent beach bikes, usually with one gear and pedal brakes.

Riding off-road isn't legal, but not much effort has been made to stop the cyclists that weave through the Santa Monica Mountains, home to the most popular and accessible mountain biking areas: numerous fire trails jut off Mulholland Boulevard from Beverly Hills to Topanga and Malibu. You may have to squeeze under a gate or two, but keep pedalling until you reach the peaks. Further inland, Griffith Park has more than 14 miles of bike trails, but some are MTB-accessible only and many are quite hilly.

Fishing

Public fishing is popular at the piers of many local beaches, in part because you do not need a permit when fishing from public piers into ocean waters. In particular, try Santa Monica Pier, Redondo Beach and Manhattan Beach. However, if you're lucky enough to catch a fish, current pollution levels suggest that you might be better off throwing it back than preparing it for dinner.

If you're fishing anywhere else, you'll need a licence. Available from Big 5 Sporting Goods, K Mart and a variety of other locations, licences cost $12.60 for a single day, $19.45 for two days pass and $38.85 for ten days. For full details on licensing, including details on other locations that sell licences, see the California Department of Fish & Game's website at www.dfg.ca.gov or call 1-916 928 5805.

For freshwater fishing in LA, try **Echo Park Lake** in Echo Park (see p108; 1-213 847 3281) and **Lincoln Park Lake** in Lincoln Heights (1-213 237 1726); information on both is available at www.laparks.org.

Alternatively, several companies in the region ferry fishers out into the Pacific on fishing boats. Try **Marina del Rey Sportfishing** (1-310 822 3625, www.marinadelreysport fishing.com) or **Redondo Sportfishing** (1-310 372 2111, www.redondosportfishing. com); expect to pay around $35 for a half-day trip or $50-$60 for a full day's fishing.

Golf

The Department of Recreation & Parks runs 13 municipal courses around the city: seven 18-hole courses, three nine-hole circuits and a trio of par-three set-ups (one 18-holer, two nine-holers). In order to book a tee time, you'll need a registration card, available at any course, from 1-818 291 9980 and at www.laparks.org. It costs $40 for non-residents, but you might get lucky by simply turning up. Always call ahead to find out your chances before setting out.

For a full list of municipal courses, see www. laparks.org. Among them are a nine-hole, par-three course in **Los Feliz** (reservations not required; 3207 Los Feliz Boulevard, 1-323 663 7758); a popular complex containing a 18-hole course and a nine-hole, par-three course in **Rancho Park** (10460 W Pico Boulevard, 18-hole: 1-310 838 7373, nine-hole: 1-310 838 7561); a 36-hole set-up in **Encino** (16821 Burbank Boulevard, 1-818 995 1170); and the Harding and Wilson courses in **Griffith Park** (4730 Crystal Springs Drive, 1-323 663 2555). Rates run from $13.50 ($17 weekends) for nine-hole courses to $24 ($31 weekends) for 18-holers.

LA also offers a number of excellent private courses, although green fees will be rather steeper. Highlights include **Oak Quarry** in Riverside (1-951 685 1440, www.oakquarry. com, $65-$95, twilight $30-$65).

Hiking

There's lots of great hiking around LA: **Griffith Park**, the **Santa Monica Mountains** (including the Hollywood Hills) and the **San Gabriel Mountains** all offer plenty of variety, and are easily accessible by car. Other very popular locations include **Runyon Canyon**, **Temescal Canyon** and **Topanga Canyon**, where you'll also find the Treepeople environmental group (see p218).

The local chapter of the **Sierra Club** (1-213 387 4287, http://angeles.sierraclub.org) runs an astonishing 4,000 outings each year in the area. Particularly noteworthy are the evening hikes in Griffith Park, which depart from the upper merry-go-round car park at 7pm every Tuesday, Wednesday and Thursday – they're wonderful on winter nights, when the park is lit by the moon. The Griffith Park evening hikes are suitable for all levels of fitness, and booking isn't required: just turn up on the night.

Horse riding

LA still taps into the Old West archetype of the cowboy, and horse riding is concomitantly popular. In Griffith Park, you can rent horses at the **Los Angeles Equestrian Center** (480 Riverside Drive, Burbank, 1-818 840 9063, www.la-equestriancenter.com); for riding in the Hollywood Hills, try **Sunset Ranch** (3400 Beachwood Drive, 1-323 469 5450, www.sunset ranchhollywood.com). Expect to pay around $20-$30 an hour at both. Both offer lessons.

Pool & billiards

Hollywood Billiards
5750 Hollywood Boulevard, at N Wilton Place, Hollywood (1-323 465 0115/www.hollywoodbilliards. com). Metro Hollywood-Western/bus 180, 181, 207, 217, 757, 780, LDH/US 101, exit Western Avenue north. **Open** *4pm-2am Mon-Fri; noon-2am Sat, Sun (9.30am-2am Sun in NFL season).* **Rates** *4-8pm* $4/hr. *8pm-2am* $12-$15/hr. **Credit** AmEx, DC, MC, V. **Map** p329 C1.
There are roughly as many draft beers as pool tables in this smart Hollywood fixture: 30 of the former, 28 of the latter. You can even hire a private room.

Rock climbing

Some of the best rock-climbing in the LA region can be found at Malibu Creek State Park (1-818 880 0367, www.parks.ca.gov). Further out, there's also good climbing in **Joshua Tree National Park** (see p292), where the **Joshua Tree Rock Climbing**

Arts & Entertainment

School (1-760 366 4745, www.joshautree
rockclimbing.com) offers a variety of lessons.

Rockreation

*11866 La Grange Avenue, at S Westgate Avenue,
West LA (1-310 207 7199/www.rockreation.com). I-
10, exit Bundy Drive north.* **Open** noon-11pm Mon,
Wed; 6am-11pm Tue, Thur; noon-10pm Fri; 10am-
6pm Sat, Sun. **Credit** AmEx, DC, MC, V.
Use of the facilities here, at one of LA's better indoor
climbing walls, costs $17 a day. There are classes
available for everyone from beginners to experts.

Rollerskating & in-lane skating

For in-line skaters, there's no place like
the **Strand**, an immaculate paved path that
stretches along the coast and is open to cyclists
and skaters. Public parks along the beach
also serve as gathering points for quality
skaters who like to rehearse their tricks
before an audience. Other tranquil spots
include **Griffith Park**, Ocean Front Walk
in **Venice Beach** and the **Sepulveda Dam**

Them's the breaks

Although the beach breaks in LA are often
given low marks by well-travelled surfers,
the below-average reputation isn't always
deserved, and the water is surprisingly clean
outside the hit-or-miss rainy season that runs
from November to April. However, the northern
currents of the Pacific here are cold (58-66˚F
from October to June), so bring or rent a
full wetsuit, and chilly onshore winds are
relentless most afternoons. Working north
to south, here are some of LA's best breaks.

Four decades after the throngs first
descended on **Malibu's Surfrider Beach**
(23200 Pacific Coast Highway; roadside
and pay-lot parking; *see also p83*), it's still
a world-class, right-breaking wave shaped by
an alluvial stone bottom. And it's still over-

populated. 'First Point', closest to the pier,
is where newcomers, longboarders and
beginners go to fight for surf. Water quality
is an issue at Surfrider, so think twice if you
have health conditions. Attempt to avoid the
crowds (and the murk) by heading to County
Line Beach, across from Neptune's Net
restaurant (42505 PCH; roadside parking).

In Santa Monica, **Bay Street** (at the foot of
Bay; pay-lot parking) can have a strong west
swell. There are several great surf stores
here. Stop by Horizons West (2011 Main
Street, Santa Monica, 1-310 392 1122), a
great place for boards, wetsuits, wax and pro
advice from owner Randy Wright. If you need
to rent a stick or rubber, ZJ Boarding House
(*see p210*) has the hard and soft goods.

A few miles south, Venice's surf-meets-the-
streets allure has been buried under million-
dollar condos. When the cold-weather swells
are tasty, surly locals rule the **Breakwater** (at
the foot of Windward Avenue; pay-lot parking)
and **Venice Pier** (at the foot of Washington
Boulevard; pay-lot parking); the rest of the
time, though, it's usually a free-for-all. You
can rent gear at Ocean Echo Sportswear
(23 Washington Boulevard, Venice; 1-310
823 5850). Be sure to lock your car tight
and keep valuables out of sight: Venice
is the home of the smash-and-grab.

Further south, **Dockweiler State Beach**
(Vista Del Mar and Imperial Highway; pay-lot
parking) is a three-mile strip of uncrowded
waves beneath the deafening flight path of
LAX. Cross into Manhattan Beach and you're
at the beloved **El Porto** (on the Strand, at the
foot of 45th Street, Manhattan Beach; pay-lot
parking). Underwater contours give the waves
focus and organisation, even when other
spots are shutting down like inner-city
storefronts at dusk. It gets mobbed, so
remember the golden rule: respect the locals.

Recreation Center just west of Encino in the San Fernando Valley.

Pick-up games of roller hockey take place on open stretches of pavement across LA. If you've come with rollerskates and are looking for some action, good places to look include the beach parking lot just north of Ocean Park in Santa Monica.

Moonlight Rollerway

5110 San Fernando Road, at Hawthorne Street, Glendale (1-818 241 3630/www.moonlightrollerway. com). Bus 94, 394/US 134, exit San Fernando Road south. **Open** times vary. **Admission** $6.50-$8; $3.25 skate rental. **No credit cards.**
This Glendale rink holds a variety of events and classes: Saturday mornings, for example, are for children only, while Sunday nights are only open to over-21s. Moonlight has rollerskates for hire, but not blades or inline skates.

Skateboarding

SkateLab Skate Park

4226 Valley Fair Street, between Vanessa & Winifred Streets, Simi Valley (1-805 578 0040/ www.skatelab.com). US 118, exit Stearns Street south. **Open** times vary. **Admission** $4-$10. **No credit cards.**
Owned by former Dodgers pitcher and Simi Valley native Scott Radinsky, SkateLab is a mecca for boarders and BMXers, with two half-pipes and numerous smaller ramps and obstacles. You'll need to sign a waiver form to skate; under-18s will need a parent's signature. If you've time, check the Skateboarding Hall of Fame.

Scuba-diving

The best places to dive are off **Leo Carillo State Beach**, **Laguna Beach**, **Redondo Beach** and **Palos Verdes**, but if you're really serious, head to **Santa Catalina Island** (*see p295*) or the **Channel Islands** (*see p285*). The LA coastline consists of miles of sloping sand, but the coastal islands have rocky shores with plenty of kelp beds and shipwrecks to explore.

Surfing

Those miles of golden sand that make up Southern California's world-famous beaches are used for more than just sunbathing and posing. If you really want to hook into the California lifestyle, you need to get on a surfboard. But don't expect to ride a wave quickly: it can take weeks just to learn to sit on the board properly, let alone negotiate the whitewash standing up. Most novice surfers opt for the easier-to-learn alternatives: boogie-boards (aka bodyboards), body surfing and skim-boarding.

If you're learning to surf, choose a wide-open beach break such as **Zuma Beach** (*see p83*) or **Will Rogers State Beach** (*see p74 and p232* **Gay beaches**; the surfing is best where Sunset Boulevard meets the PCH). Alternatively, sign up for surfing lessons with one of many surf schools in the LA region: **Surf Academy** (1-310 372 2790, www.surfacademy. org) runs classes for beginners in Santa Monica; and the **Santa Monica Surf School** (1-310 526 3346, www.santamonicasurfschool.com) runs a summer day camp for children and private lessons for adults. Experienced surfers, meanwhile, should check the rundown of the best breaks along the coast; *see p274* **Them's the breaks**.

For surfing and beach conditions, call the Surfing Conditions Hotline on 1-310 578 0478, check with the Department of Beaches & Harbors on 1-310 305 9503 or see http:// beaches. co.la.ca.us. For information on conditions, plus a full listing of surf shops and surf schools, check the excellent website www.surfline.com. And for a round-up of the best beaches in Los Angeles, *see p82* **LA's best beaches**.

Swimming

For the best beaches for swimming, *see p82* **LA's best beaches**. The majority of the city's YMCAs (*see p276*) also contain swimming pools, as do many hotels (*see pp44-66*). For kid-friendly swimming, *see p218*.

Tennis

There are tennis courts in many LA parks; for a full list, see www.laparks.org. **Griffith Park** has courts ($5-$8/hr) at two sites: 12 lit courts at Griffith/Riverside (1-323 661 5318), and 12 courts ones at Griffith/Vermont Canyon (1-323 664 3521). On weekdays before 4pm, the courts are available on a walk-up basis; after 4pm, you can only book with a registration card, which cost $30 for non-residents.

Alternatively, try one of several tennis centres around LA. The most central is the 16-court **La Cienega Tennis Center** (325 N La Cienega Boulevard, West Hollywood, 1-310 550 4765); further north, the **Burbank Tennis Center** (1515 N Glenoaks Boulevard, Burbank, 1-818 843 4105, www.burbanktenniscenter.com) is also open to the public.

Whale-watching

Whale-watching provides California's most extraordinary wildlife experience. The annual season, off the Southern California coastline, is in winter (December to March), following the migratory habits of the gray and wright whales, the two most common species. In Santa Barbara (*see p286*), whale-watching reaches its peak in summer, ending in mid-September. Most marinas have numerous boats offering whale-watching trips and many operate on a 'sightings guaranteed' basis: if you don't see any whales, your money is refunded, or you're given a pass to go free on a subsequent trip.

Condor Express

Santa Barbara Harbor, off Harbor Way, Santa Barbara (1-805 882 0088/www.condorcruises.com). US 101 to Santa Barbara (see p286). **Rates** $48-$94; $28-$50 discounts; free under-5s. **Credit** DC, Disc, MC, V.
Board the Condor to view the whales feeding off Santa Barbara. The company also runs kayaking expeditions into the Painted Cave.

Fitness

Gyms

There are gyms all over LA; the following are open to non-members. YMCAs often have gyms. For gay-friendly gyms, *see p232.*

Gold's Gym

360 Hampton Drive, at Rose Avenue, Venice (1-310 392 6004/www.goldsgym.com). Bus 33, 333, SM1, SM2/I-10, exit Lincoln Boulevard south. **Open** 4am-midnight Mon-Fri; 5am-11pm Sat, Sun. **Rates** *Non-members* $20/day; $70/wk. **Credit** AmEx, DC, Disc, MC, V. **Map** p326 A5.
Gold's bills itself as 'the mecca of bodybuilding', and perhaps with some justification: this is where the Governor of California honed and toned his body. **Other locations** throughout the city.

24-Hour Fitness

8612 Santa Monica Boulevard, at N La Cienega Boulevard, West Hollywood (1-310 652 7440/ www.24hourfitness.com). Bus 4, 105, 220, 305, 550, 704/I-10, exit La Cienega Boulevard north. **Open** 5am-midnight Mon-Thur; 6am-11pm Fri-Sun. **Rates** *Non-members* $20/day. **Credit** AmEx, DC, Disc, MC, V. **Map** p328 B2.
Right in the heart of West Hollywood, this branch offers a pool, sauna, weight, aerobics and even car-dio kick-boxing. **Other locations** throughout the city.

Santa Monica Family YMCA

1332 6th Street, between Santa Monica Boulevard & Arizona Avenue, Santa Monica (1-310 393 2721/ www.ymcasm.org). Bus 4, 20, 33, 333, 704, 720, SM1, SM5, SM7, SM8, SM10/I-10, exit 4th-5th Street north. **Open** 6am-10pm Mon-Fri; 7am-8pm Sat; 8am-8pm Sun. **Rates** *Non-members* $15/day. **Credit** AmEx, DC, Disc, MC, V. **Map** p326 B3.
The Santa Monica YMCA offers racquetball and handball, weights, a lap pool, a spa, aerobics, yoga

and volleyball, among other classes. For other YMCA centres in LA, see www.ymcala.org. **Other locations** throughout the city.

Yoga

YAS

1101 Abbot Kinney Boulevard, at Westminster Avenue, Venice (1-310 396 6993/www.go2yas.com). Bus 33, 333, SM1, SM2/I-10, exit 4th-5th Street south. **Open** 6am-1.30pm, 3-8pm Mon-Fri; 7am-1.30pm, 3-8pm Sat; 8am-1.30pm, 3-8pm Sun. **Map** p326 A5.
Classes $16. **Credit** AmEx, DC, MC, V.
Kimberly Fowler's Venice operation offers the rather unexpected combination of yoga and spinning. It sounds strange but it clearly works: Fowler has plans to expand to Silver Lake and Culver City.

YogaWorks

230 N Larchmont Boulevard, between Beverly Boulevard & 3rd Street, Larchmont Village (1-323 464 1276/www.yogaworks.com). Bus 14, 210, 714/I-10, exit La Brea Avenue north. **Open** 6.30am-9.30pm Mon, Wed; 6.30am-10pm Tue, Thur; 6.30am-8pm Fri; 7.45am-7pm Sat; 8.30am-8.45pm Sun. **Classes** $20. **Credit** AmEx, DC, MC, V. **Map** p327 B4.
With more than a dozen locations throughout LA and Orange County, YogaWorks is a local favourite. Classes are varied, and beginners are welcome. **Other locations** throughout LA.

Theatre & Dance

Back off, Hollywood: *all* the world's a stage.

Casey Nicholaw directs *The Drowsy Chaperone* at **Music Center**.

Theatre

The theatrical landscape in Los Angeles is enormous and far-flung. Between 1,200 and 1,500 professional productions are staged in LA and its surrounding counties each year, the majority in small theatres without large marketing budgets. Still, although LA theatre can be elusive, it can also be a cultural bonanza for savvy and dedicated theatregoers.

Many actors and writers who earn a living in film and TV here find greater creative satisfaction on stage, albeit for far less money. Bad for them, but good for the customer: tickets are generally cheaper than in London or New York. Most seats in small and mid-sized theatres offer excellent sightlines and a remarkable sense of intimacy. And although Mondays to Wednesdays can be thin, weekends overflow with dozens of options.

For schedules, see http://theguide.latimes.com, www.laweekly.com/stage, www.lacity beat.com, www.experiencela.com and www.lastagealliance.com, which also offers half-price tickets (click on 'LAStageTix'). Another half-price ticket source is www.goldstar.com.

Major venues

Music Center theatres

135 N Grand Avenue, between W 1st & W Temple Streets, Downtown (1-213 628 2772/ www.musiccenter.org). Metro Civic Center/bus 2, 4, 10, 11, 14, 48, 92, 302, 714/I-110, exit 4th Street east. **Box office** *In person* noon-9pm Tue-Sat; 11am-7pm Sun. *By phone* 10am-6pm Mon; 10am-8pm Tue-Fri; noon-8pm Sat; 11am-7pm Sun. **Tickets** $10-$250. *Parking* $8. **Credit** AmEx, DC, Disc, MC, V. **Map** p331 B2.

The Center Theatre Group programmes two of the halls that make up LA's primary cultural complex. At the north end, the Ahmanson Theatre presents pre- or post-Broadway fare, with seating capacities ranging from 1,600 to 2,100. And in the Center's centre, the 745-seat Mark Taper Forum has staged a wide range of new plays over the last 40 years and was scheduled to reopen in 2008 after a renovation.

Also part of the Music Center, the Dorothy Chandler Pavilion (*see p251*) offers occasional dance events. And on the south side of the Music Center's Walt Disney Concert Hall (*see p251*), the forward-thinking REDCAT (aka the Roy & Edna Disney/CalArts Theater; www.redcat.org) includes theatre among its many cutting-edge offerings.

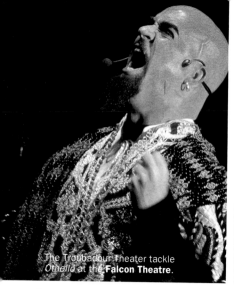

The Troubadour Theater tackle *Othello* at the **Falcon Theatre**.

Pantages Theatre

6233 Hollywood Boulevard, between Argyle Avenue & Vine Street, Hollywood (information 1-323 468 1770/tickets 1-213 365 3500/www.broadwayla.org). Metro Hollywood-Vine/bus 163, 180, 181, 210, 212, 217, 312, 363, 780, LDH/US 101, exit Hollywood Boulevard west. **Box office** 10am-6pm daily. **Tickets** $20-$200. **Credit** AmEx, DC, Disc, MC, V. **Map** p329 B1.

This vintage entertainment palace is the headquarters of Broadway/LA, which specialises in big-budget musicals. When the Pantages is occupied by a long-running show such as *Wicked*, Broadway/LA's shorter runs are booked into other spaces, such as the Wilshire Theatre in Beverly Hills.

Pasadena Playhouse

39 S El Molino Avenue, at E Green Street, Pasadena (information 1-626 792 8672/tickets 1-626 356 7529/www.pasadenaplayhouse.org). Metro Lake/bus 180, 181, 485/I-210, exit Lake Avenue south. **Box office** noon-6pm daily. **Tickets** $25-$100. **Credit** AmEx, DC, Disc, MC, V.

Built in the '20s and revived in the '80s, this gracious 672-seat venue offers mostly new plays and musicals. Upstairs, in the smaller Carrie Hamilton Theatre, is the brash young Furious Theatre Company (www.furioustheatre.org).

Other large theatres

A quartet of theatres south of LA stages regular large-scale productions. **La Mirada Theatre** presents staid but polished fare under husband-and-wife team Tom McCoy and Cathy Rigby. The **Orange County Performing Arts Centre** offers professional-quality musicals, mostly familiar titles; it's a similar story at the **Redondo Beach Performing Arts Centre**,

where musicals are staged by Civic Light Opera of South Bay Cities (www.civiclightopera.com) and the **Richard & Karen Carpenter Performing Arts Centres**, courtesy of Musical Theatre West (www.musical.org).

La Mirada Theatre *14900 La Mirada Boulevard, between Excelsior Drive & Rosecrans Avenue, La Mirada (1-562 944 9801/www.lamiradatheatre.com). I-5, exit Rosecrans Boulevard east.* **Box office** 11am-5.30pm Mon-Fri; noon-4pm Sat. **Tickets** $15-$48. **Credit** AmEx, DC, MC, V.

Orange County Performing Arts Center *600 Town Center Drive, Costa Mesa (1-714 556 2787/www.ocpac.org). I-405, exit Bristol Street.* **Box office** 10am-9pm daily. **Tickets** $20-$100. **Credit** AmEx, DC, MC, V.

Redondo Beach Performing Arts Center *1935 Manhattan Beach Boulevard, at Aviation Boulevard, Redondo Beach (1-310 937 6607/ www.rbpac.com). Bus 126/I-405, exit Inglewood Avenue south.* **Box office** from 1hr before show. **Tickets** $40-$60. **Credit** AmEx, DC, MC, V.

Richard & Karen Carpenter Performing Arts Center *California State University, 6200 Atherton Street, at Palo Verde Avenue, Long Beach (1-562 985 7000/www.carpenterarts.org). I-405, exit Palo Verde Avenue south.* **Box office** 11am-6pm Mon-Fri; noon-4pm Sat. **Tickets** $20-$68. **Credit** AmEx, DC, MC, V.

Mid-sized theatres

In addition, look out for the ancient Greek or Roman play staged each September at the **Getty Villa**'s outdoor amphitheatre (*see p75*).

Colony Theatre

555 N 3rd Street, between E San Jose Drive & E Cypress Avenue, Burbank (1-818 558 7000/ www.colonytheatre.org). Bus 92, 96, 183, 394/

I-5, exit Burbank Boulevard east. **Box office** 2-6pm
Mon-Fri. **Tickets** $37-$42; $32-$37 discounts.
Credit AmEx, DC, Disc, MC, V.
A mix of new plays and recent revivals, reliably sat-
isfying but seldom cheeky, is presented to a loyal
audience in a warm Burbank theatre.

East West Players

*120 N Judge John Aiso Street, between E 1st &
Temple Streets, Downtown (1-213 625 7000/www.
eastwestplayers.org). Metro Union Station/bus 30,
31, 40, 42/US 101, exit Alameda Street south.* **Box
office** 11am-5pm Mon-Fri. **Tickets** $45-$50; $40-$45
discounts. **Credit** AmEx, DC, MC, V. **Map** p331 D2.
EWP specialises in Asian American plays and musicals, and Asian-flavoured revivals of non-Asian
shows. A former church, the company's 240-seat
David Henry Hwang Theatre lacks the wraparound
intimacy you might expect from a theatre of this size.

El Portal Theatre

*11206 Weddington Street, at Lankershim
Boulevard, North Hollywood (1-818 508 4200/
www.elportaltheatre.com). Bus 156, 224/Hwy 170, exit Magnolia Boulevard
east.* **Box office** hrs vary. **Tickets** $39-$60.
Credit AmEx, DC, Disc, MC, V.
The 360-seat main theatre at this inviting former cinema is used by a variety of tenants, but the building
also houses two sub-100-seat theatres. One of them
is the home of Theatre Tribe (www.theatretribe.com).

Falcon Theatre

*4252 Riverside Drive, at N Rose Street, Burbank
(1-818 955 8101/www.falcontheatre.com). Hwy
134, exit Buena Vista Street.* **Box office** noon-4pm
Mon; noon-6pm Tue-Fri; 10am-4pm Sat, Sun.
Tickets $27-$50. **Credit** DC, MC, V.
Hollywood director Garry Marshall (*Pretty Woman,
Beaches*) built this small, inviting venue in the
mid '90s. Its most successful shows are by the deli-
ciously rowdy Troubadour Theater (www.troubie.
com), whose mastermind Matt Walker incorporates
pop music into seemingly incongruous contexts
(*A Charlie James Brown Christmas*, for instance).

Geffen Playhouse

*10886 Le Conte Avenue, between Tiverton Avenue &
Westwood Boulevard, Westwood (1-310 208 5454/
www.geffenplayhouse.com). Bus 2, 302, 305/I-405,
exit Wilshire Boulevard east.* **Box office** 10am-6pm
Mon-Fri; 11am-6pm Sat, Sun. **Tickets** $24-$46.
Credit AmEx, DC, MC, V.
The West Side's most glittery theatrical venue is
home to a good-sized main stage and the cosier
Skirball Kenis Theatre. The company offers a mix
of new work and local premieres, frequently with
big-name (OK, second-tier) Hollywood talent.

International City Theatre

*300 E Ocean Boulevard, at Long Beach Boulevard,
Long Beach (1-562 436 4610/www.ictlongbeach.org).
Metro 1st Street/bus 60, 232, 360/I-710, exit
Shoreline Drive east.* **Box office** 9am-5pm Mon-Fri.
Tickets $32-$42. **Credit** AmEx, DC, MC, V.

Long Beach's ICT offers a well-executed mix of
plays and musicals, including some local premieres.
It's an 825-seat facility, but for the sake of economy
and intimacy, only 289 of the seats are used. Perched
between a massive convention centre and a 3,000-
seat hall, it's hard to find.

Kirk Douglas Theatre

*9820 W Washington Boulevard, at Culver
Boulevard, Culver City (1-213 628 2772/www.
centertheatregroup.org). Bus 33, 220, 333, C1/
I-10, exit Robertson Boulevard south.* **Box office**
By phone 10am-6pm Mon; 10am-8pm Tue-Fri;
noon-8pm Sat, Sun. **Tickets** $20-$40. **Credit**
AmEx, DC, MC, V.
The West Side branch of the Center Theatre Group
(*see p277*) offers the company's most adventurous
fare, along with intermittent collaborations with
some of LA's smaller troupes. The theatre itself was
originally built as a cinema and retains its iconic old
neon sign out front.

Laguna Playhouse

*Moulton Theater, 606 Laguna Canyon Road,
Laguna Beach (1-949 497 2787/www.lagunaplay
house.com). I-405, exit Hwy 133 south.* **Box office**
10am-8pm daily. **Tickets** $25-$70. **Credit** AmEx,
DC, Disc, MC, V.
Located a few blocks from an enticing beach, the
enterprising Laguna Playhouse produces many
American or West Coast premieres in its appealing
420-seat theatre. Ireland's Bernard Farrell is a
favourite writer here.

Los Angeles Theatre Center

*514 S Spring Street, between W 5th & W 6th
Streets, Downtown (1-213 489 0994/www.newlatc.
com). Metro Pershing Square/bus 33, 55, 83, 92/
US 101, exit Main Street south.* **Box office** from
2hrs before show. **Tickets** $15; $12 discounts.
Credit AmEx, DC, MC, V. **Map** p331 C3.
This city-owned, four-theatre complex is housed in
a former bank close to Skid Row in Downtown, and
can be one of the city's most exciting venues. The
Latino Theater Company (www.latinotheater.com)
has operated from here since 2006.

A Noise Within

*234 S Brand Boulevard, between E Colorado & E
Harvard Streets, Glendale (1-818 240 0910/www.
anoisewithin.org). Bus 92/I-5, exit Colorado Street
east.* **Box office** 2-6pm Tue-Fri. **Tickets** $20-$40.
Credit MC, V.
The LA region's leading classical theatre company
presents two annual seasons, each containing three
productions in repertory. The troupe is currently
based in a former masonic temple, but plans to move
to larger quarters in Pasadena in 2009 or 2010.

Rubicon Theatre

*1006 E Main Street, at N Laurel Street, Ventura
(1-805 667 2900/www.rubicontheatre.org). US
101 to Ventura.* **Box office** 10am-5pm Mon-Fri;
11am-5pm Sat; 11am-1pm Sun. **Tickets** $42; $37
discounts. **Credit** AmEx, DC, Disc, MC, V.

Arts & Entertainment

The most consistently impressive company in LA's north-western suburbs offers an interesting and unusual mix of productions, including plenty of new work. The company is behind a new summer theatre festival, scheduled to debut in 2009 at a variety of seaside venues around Ventura.

South Coast Repertory

655 Town Center Drive, at Park Center Drive, Costa Mesa (1-714 708 5555/www.scr.org). I-405, exit Bristol Street north. **Box office** 10am-6pm Mon-Sat; noon-6pm Sun. **Tickets** $28-$62. **Credit** AmEx, DC, MC, V.

One of America's outstanding resident theatre companies, the South Coast Repertory has long been acclaimed for its development of new work. However, it also stages glossy classics, sometimes with an innovative streak. The theatre's modernist façade is warmed up by the cosy interiors of the halls.

UCLA theatres

Sunset Boulevard & Hilgard Avenue, Westwood (1-310 825 2101/www.uclalive.org). Bus 2, 302, 305/I-405, exit Wilshire Boulevard east. **Box office** 10am-4pm Mon-Fri. **Tickets** $18-$88. **Credit** AmEx, DC, Disc, MC, V.

The wide-angled Freud Playhouse on the north-east side of the UCLA campus is home to a pair of contrasting companies: Reprise! (www.reprise.org), which presents polished revivals of rather obscure American musicals under the direction of former *Seinfeld* star Jason Alexander, and UCLA Live's International Theatre Festival, which imports a variety of mostly European companies each autumn.

Will Geer Theatricum Botanicum

1419 N Topanga Canyon Boulevard, at Cheney Drive, Topanga (1-310 455 3723/www.theatricum.com). Bus 534/I-10, exit PCH north. **Box office** noon-6pm Wed-Fri; 11am-7.30pm Sat, Sun. **Tickets** $15-$25; $12-$15 discounts; free under-6s. **Credit** DC, MC, V.

Located in a seductive, rustic setting in the heart of the Santa Monica Mountains, this under-the-stars theatre offers Shakespeare works, other classics and occasional new plays in a repertory season that runs from June until October.

Small theatres

In addition to the enterprises listed below, two sections of town hold an unusually large number of theatres. In **Hollywood**, more than a dozen small venues are clustered around a seven-block stretch of Santa Monica Boulevard in what's become known as **Theatre Row**. Several of LA's more audacious and accomplished groups are based here, among them Unknown Theatre, the Blank Theatre Company, Elephant Stageworks and Open Fist. For links to all the theatres and a map of the district, see www.theaterrowhollywood.com.

On the other side of the Hollywood Hills, more than 20 small theatres sit within a half-mile of the intersection of Magnolia and Lankershim Boulevards in **North Hollywood**. The list includes the Road Theatre Company, the classically-minded **Antaeus Company** and Deaf West, where the productions are in sign language as well as vocalised speech. For more, see www.nohoartsdistrict.com.

Actors Co-op

Crossley Theatre, 1760 N Gower Street, at Carlos Avenue, Hollywood (1-323 462 8460/www.actorsco-op.org). Metro Hollywood-Vine/bus 163, 180, 181, 210, 212, 217, 312, 363, 780, LDH/US 101, exit Hollywood Boulevard west. **Box office** 11am-2pm Mon-Thur; 11am-5pm Fri. **Tickets** $30-$35. **Credit** DC, MC, V. **Map** p329 B1.

Unsurprising material is interspersed with the occasional premiere on the Actors Co-op schedules, and is staged with professional aplomb in two adjacent spaces on a Presbyterian Church campus.

Actors' Gang Theatre

9070 Venice Boulevard, between Culver & Robertson Boulevards, Culver City (1-323 838 4264/www.theactorsgang.com). Bus 33, 333, C1/I-10, exit Robertson Boulevard south. **Box office** show nights only. **Tickets** $6-$25. **Credit** AmEx, DC, MC, V.

Tim Robbins remains in charge of the Actors' Gang, the company he co-founded in the '80s. Productions remain hard-edged and presentational, and often rely on politically charged material. Performances take place in a century-old electricity substation.

Boston Court

70 N Mentor Avenue, at Boston Court, Pasadena (1-626 683 6883/www.bostoncourt.com). Metro Lake/bus 180, 181, 485/I-210, exit Lake Avenue south. **Box office** noon-6pm Tue-Sat. **Tickets** $32; $27 discounts. **Credit** AmEx, DC, MC, V.

Exciting new plays and revivals are staged by this well-regarded group in the most lavishly appointed sub-100-seat venue in the LA area.

Fountain Theatre

5060 Fountain Avenue, between N Normandie & N Mariposa Avenues, Hollywood (1-323 663 1525/www.fountaintheatre.com). Metro Vermont-Sunset/bus 175, 206/US 101, exit Santa Monica Boulevard east. **Box office** 11am-5pm Mon-Fri; 2-5pm Sat; noon-5pm Sun. **Tickets** $15-$30. **Credit** AmEx, DC, MC, V. **Map** p329 D2.

This widely acclaimed company generally concentrates on masters of 20th-century realism, but it recently introduced two 21st-century plays by Athol Fugard to America. Unexpectedly, it also produces a flamenco series.

Hayworth Theatre

2511 Wilshire Boulevard, between Coronado & Carondelet Streets, Westlake (1-213 389 9860/www.thehayworth.com). Metro Westlake-MacArthur Park/bus 66, 366/I-10, exit Vermont Avenue north. **Box office** 10am-6pm Mon-Fri; from 1hr before show Sat, Sun. **Tickets** $15-$30. **Credit** AmEx, DC, MC, V. **Map** p330 B6.

Help the homeless

Cornerstone Theater's *Los Illegals.*

While many theatre groups dream of one day owning their own theatre, others are content to roam from venue to venue around LA. Among such groups are the **Playwrights' Arena** (www.playwrightsarena.org), which produces only new plays by LA writers; **Padua Playwrights** (www.paduaplaywrights. net), which grew out of a summer play-writing workshop; and the unnamed group that coalesces periodically to produce fast-talking comedies by **Justin Tanner**, among the city's best quasi-underground treats. However, one company has turned its itinerant status into a major selling point, specialising in site-specific works that explore the city's cultural and sociological diversity. Most productions from the **Cornerstone Theater** (www.corner stonetheater.org; pictured) begin with the team interviewing members of an identified community: sometimes people linked by geography, sometimes people linked by a common interest. When this process is complete, the group's actors work with a playwright, a director and volunteers to create a play addressing that group's particular issues, before staging the finished piece in an unexpected venue.

In 2007, Cornerstone launched a five-play cycle addressing the theme of justice. The cycle began with *Los Illegals*, a piece about immigration that was staged in a Pasadena parking lot with dialogue that switched between English and Spanish. Subsequent plays will be held in a variety of different locations until the end of 2009; check the company's website for details.

Built as a cinema in 1926 (it was known for decades as the Vagabond), this old spot was renovated and converted for use as a theatre in 2006. It now includes a 99-seat space and two smaller auditoriums upstairs, one of which houses the often-notable Circus Theatricals (www.circustheatricals.com).

[Inside] the Ford
2580 Cahuenga Boulevard, north of Cahuenga Terrace, Hollywood (1-323 461 3673/www.ford amphitheater.org). Bus 156/US 101, exit Cahuenga Boulevard north. **Box office** noon-6pm Wed-Sun. **Tickets** $10-$25. **Credit** AmEx, DC, Disc, MC, V.
Benefiting from local subsidies, daring small companies without permanent homes feature regularly at this county-owned indoor space under the larger, alfresco John Anson Ford Amphitheatre. Among them are Circle X (www.circlextheatre.org), Ziggurat Theatre (www.ziggurattheatre.org) and Zoo District (www.zoodistrict.org). Note the entrance garden.

Odyssey Theatre Ensemble
2055 S Sepulveda Boulevard, between La Grange & Mississippi Avenues, West LA (1-310 477 2055/ www.odysseytheatre.com). I-405, exit Santa Monica Boulevard east. **Box office** 1-6pm Tue, Sun; 1-8pm Wed-Sat. **Tickets** $20-$25. **Credit** AmEx, DC, MC, V.
For four decades, Ron Sossi's three stages have stimulated and entertained West Siders and others, often

Great Shakes

Shakespeare plays crop up from time to time around LA theatres, but two troupes specialise in alfresco productions of the Bard's finest works. Each summer, **Shakespeare Festival/LA** (www. shakespearefestivalla.org) performs an often LA-spiced production in two contrasting settings: one urban (usually in Downtown LA), the other sylvan (the South Coast Botanic Garden in Palos Verde; *see p136*). Admission to the former is free but should be booked ahead. Meanwhile, the **Independent Shakespeare Company** (1-323 836 0288, www.independent shakespeare.com) stages a rep season of three more traditional interpretations in Barnsdall Park (*see p104*) between June and August. Tickets are free, but reservations are recommended.

with politically minded or metaphysically themed work. The OTE is the main attraction, but other companies also appear here.

Pacific Resident Theatre

703-707 Venice Boulevard, at Oakwood Avenue, Venice (1-310 822 8392/www.pacificresidenttheatre. com). Bus 33, 333/I-10, exit 4th-5th Street south. **Box office** 3-7pm Tue-Sat; noon-2pm Sun. **Tickets** $25-$34. **Credit** DC, MC, V. **Map** p331 A6. The productions turned out by this theatrical co-op, which frequently include lesser-known works from 20th-century European and American writers, often become critical favourites. There are three stages.

Theatre Banshee

3435 W Magnolia Boulevard, between N Avon & N Lima Streets, Burbank (1-818 846 5323/ www.theatrebanshee.org). Bus 163, 183/Hwy 134, exit Buena Vista Street north. **Box office** show nights only. **Tickets** $18-$20. **No credit cards.** This Burbank theatre is the LA area's most frequent producer of Irish plays, though it also offers a sprinkling of British and American work: the 2007-08 season included everything from Joe Orton's *What the Butler Saw* to an adaptation of John Steinbeck's *Of Mice and Men*.

Theatre 40

Reuben Cordova Theatre, Beverly Hills High School, 241 S Moreno Drive, between Robbins & Durant Drives, Beverly Hills (information 1-310 364 0535/box office 1-310 364 3606/www.theatre 40.org). Bus 16, 316/I-10, exit Overland Avenue north. **Box office** show nights only. **Tickets** $25. **No credit cards.** Based at a high school, Theatre 40 mixes revivals of well-known pieces with premieres on its varied production schedule. It also frequently heads to Greystone Mansion (*see p90*) to revive *The Manor*, a site-specific play about the tragedies that befell the family that built the house in the '20s.

Victory Theatre

3324-3326 W Victory Boulevard, between N Avon & N Lima Streets, Burbank (1-818 841 5422/ www.thevictorytheatrecenter.org). Bus 163/Hwy 134, exit Buena Vista Street north. **Box office** 1-6pm Mon-Fri. **Tickets** $28-$34. **Credit** DC, MC, V. For several decades now, the Victory has been one of the most consistently active smaller theatres in LA. It frequently produces new plays in its two side-by-side venues, the Big Vic and the Little Vic.

Dance & performance art

Dance performances are held in the LA area on most weekends. However, they aren't nearly as widespread as plays and musicals, and fans may need to put in some diligent research in order to locate them. The best resource is http://theguide.latimes.com: click 'Performing Arts' at the top, then click 'Dance'.

Major national and international ballet companies appear at the Music Center's **Dorothy Chandler Pavilion** (*see p251*) and Segerstrom Hall at the **Orange County Performing Arts Center** (*see p278*). The **Richard & Karen Carpenter Performing Arts Centre** (*see p278*) also offers dance.

The region's most daring dance programmes are staged by **UCLA** in Royce Hall (*see p250*) and at **REDCAT** in the Music Center (*see p277*). However, fans of modern dance should also investigate the **Diavolo Dance Theatre** (www.diavolo.org), in the Brewery Arts Complex north of Downtown. Aside from hosting the resident Diavolo company, it also welcomes modern groups such as the **Los Angeles Contemporary Dance Company** (www.lacontemporarydance.org), **Brockus Project** (www.brockusprojectcontemporary dance.org) and **Ledges & Bones** (www. ledgesandbones.org).

During summer, there's dance at the open-air **Ford Amphitheatre** (*see p281* **[Inside] the Ford**) and at the **Grand Performances** in Downtown LA (*see p251* **Music for nothing**). Smaller theatres with worthwhile dance programmes include **Unknown Theater** on Theatre Row in Hollywood (*see p280*); gay-oriented **Highways Performance Space** in Santa Monica (*see p242*); and the lively, solar-powered **Electric Lodge** (1416 Electric Avenue, Venice, 1-310 306 1854, www.electriclodge.org). And the list of local companies is led by the new **Los Angeles Ballet** (www.losangelesballet.org), which performs at several venues around the region.

Trips Out of Town

Getting Started   284
North to Santa Barbara   285
The Deserts   287
South to San Diego   295

Features

Back to the future   290
Mountain high   293
Hollywood and vines   297
Over the border   299

Map

Trips Out of Town   284

Salvation Mountain. *See p293.*

Getting Started

Along the coast or into the desert? Your call...

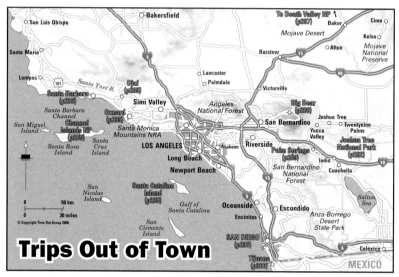

Trips Out of Town

As you've doubtless realised by now, the Los Angeles urban area has an overwhelming quantity and variety of attractions. But LA is also the gateway to some stunning sights and scenery elsewhere in California and even beyond it. Leave early to beat the traffic, and you'll be away from the smog before you can say 'Hit the road, Jack'.

From LA, you've got three main options, a fact reflected in the way we've divided this section of the book. Travelling north up the coast will lead you to the undervalued **Channel Islands National Park** and the well-dressed but easygoing town of **Santa Barbara** (*pp285-286*). Taking the coast road in the opposite direction will bring you to sunbleached **San Diego** and, across the border, the infamous Mexican town of **Tijuana** (*pp295-300*). And if you head east, you'll soon be in the desert, whether isolated in **Joshua Tree** or **Death Valley National Parks**, or crammed into **Palm Springs** and the **Coachella Valley** (*pp287-294*).

The easiest – and sometimes the only – way to get to the places listed in this chapter is by car. On some trips, such as those up US 101 towards Santa Barbara or through the desert

towards Death Valley, the scenery is so jaw-dropping that the drive itself is as notable as the destination. Reaching all the destinations involves a drive of at least an hour and a half and usually more, depending on whether or not you stick to the speed limit. For information on car hire and tips on driving, *see pp302-305*. It's also possible to travel by plane, train or bus to larger destinations such as Palm Springs and San Diego.

Further gems sit even further from LA. To the north are the natural glories of Big Sur and the buzzing town of San Francisco, LA's polar opposite in so many ways. To the north-east lie the photogenic wonders of Sequoia National Park and Yosemite National Park, not to mention the delightful B&Bs of the Gold Country. And north-east – nearly 300 miles away, makeable in less than four hours if you're lucky with both traffic and police – is the incomparable Nevadan city of Las Vegas. All are featured in the 416-page *Time Out California* (UK: Ebury, £13.99; US: PGW, $19.95), a full guide to the state; also available are *Time Out San Francisco* and *Time Out Las Vegas*, a pair of comprehensive city guides (both – UK: Ebury, £12.99; US: PGW, $19.95).

North to Santa Barbara

The coast road to riches.

Join the moneyed classes at the harbour in **Santa Barbara**. *See p286.*

Los Angeles to Ojai

The drive north from LA is lovely, however you choose to begin it. If you take US 101 from Hollywood, cut through the untamed Santa Monica Mountains. Taking route N1 (aka Las Virgenes Road) will bring you down via the start of the **Las Virgenes View Trail**, a two-and-a-half-mile uphill hike that begins at the intersection of N1 and the Mulholland Highway. But it's the coastal road that really appeals. The stretch of Highway 1 north from Malibu to the small town of **Oxnard** is dotted with surfer-friendly beaches: **Leo Carillo State Park** is popular, as are the beaches that form rugged **Point Mugu State Park** (for both: 1-818 880 0350, www.parks.ca.gov).

Close by sits **Ventura**, a largely unspoiled piece of Middle America by the sea and the jumping-off point for the **Channel Islands National Park** (1-805 658 5730, www.nps.gov/chis). Diving, hiking, fishing, kayaking and simple wildlife observation are on offer at this sanctuary, set across a five-island archipelago. Boat transport from Ventura to the islands is organised by Island Packers Cruises (1-805 642 1393, www.islandpackers.com): for details on how to reach the islands, see the park's website.

Located a dozen miles north of Ventura, **Ojai** is a sweet village in a gorgeous setting with a disarming preponderance of wide-eyed hippy residents. The town has long been a magnet for those of a spiritual bent, a fact borne witness by the art galleries of Ojai Avenue and the esoteric businesses on the fringes of the town (the Krotona Institute of Theosophy, for instance). If you've already found yourself, content yourself with a search for bargains at fabulously chaotic **Bart's Books** (302 W Matilija Street, 1-805 646 3755, www.bartsbooks ojai.com); also worth a look, if you're here in June, is the **Ojai Music Festival** (*see p250*).

Where to eat & drink

In Ventura, **71 Palm** (71 N Palm Street, 1-805 653 7222, www.71palm.com, closed Sun & lunch Sat, mains $20) offers fine French cuisine; the **Anacapa Brewing Company** (472 E Main Street, 1-805 643 0350, www.anacapa brewing.com, mains $15) offers smart bar food to go with its own brews. And in Ojai, try the

French-American fare at **Suzanne's Cuisine** (No.502, 1-805 640 1961, www.suzannescuisine. com, closed Tue, mains $25) or the high-class Californian cooking at the **Ranch House** (S Lomita Avenue, 1-805 646 2360, www.the ranchhouse.com, closed Mon, mains $27).

Tourist information

Oxnard *California Welcome Center, 1000 Town Center Drive (1-800 269 6273/1-805 385 7545/ www.visitoxnard.com).* **Open** 9am-5.30pm Mon-Thur; 9am-6pm Fri, Sat; 9am-5pm Sun.
Ventura *Ventura Visitors & Convention Bureau, 101 S California Street (1-800 483 6214/1-805 648 2075/www.ventura-usa.com).* **Open** 8.30am-5pm Mon-Fri; 9am-5pm Sat; 10am-4pm Sun.

Santa Barbara

When a number of senior staffers at the *Santa Barbara News-Press* dramatically resigned in June 2006 over what they alleged to be unwelcome interference from the newspaper's ownership, Santa Barbara bit its collective tongue. This wealthy town had spent decades buffing its image as a postcard-perfect coastal city, and the international headlines that resulted from the long-running controversy were a shock to the local system.

But while the locals lick their wounds as the arguments rumble on (a documentary about the affair premiered in 2008), the rest of Santa Barbara remains unchanged. And this status quo is, one suspects, just how longtime locals like it. A well-heeled, conservation-minded coterie works hard to keep Santa Barbara handsome, almost immaculate. You don't come here for urban thrills, but for history, culture, top-end eating and an old-world aesthetic.

Sheltered between towering green mountains and deep blue ocean, this has long been sought-after land. The local Chumash Indians lived here for 5,000 years, before the Spanish arrived in 1786 and set about building the **Santa Barbara Mission** (2201 Laguna Street, 1-805 682 4149, www.sbmission.org, $4), one of the loveliest in the state. The current building dates from 1870 and is still an active Catholic Church, although parts of it are run as a museum.

For a different historical perspective on the region, try the **Museum of Natural History** (2559 Puesta del Sol Road, 1-805 682 4711, www.sbnature.org, $6-$10), or go Downtown to the **Santa Barbara Historical Society Museum** (100 E De La Guerra Street, 1-805 966 1601, www.santabarbaramuseum.com, closed Mon). Just down De la Guerra Street from here is historic De la Guerra Plaza, flanked by City Hall and the site of the raucous **Old Spanish Days Fiesta** (first weekend in August;

www.oldspanishdays-fiesta.org). Nearby is what's left of the **Presidio** (123 E Canon Perdido, 1-805 965 0095, www.sbthp.org): now a state park, it's currently being restored, though it remains open to the public.

Perhaps the finest example of the town's Spanish-Moorish colonial architectural heritage is the **Santa Barbara County Courthouse** (11 Anacapa Street), complete with lofty towers, an interior covered with murals and sprawling grounds. It's worth taking the elevator up to the top to breathe in the billion-dollar views, from the 4,000-foot tips of the Santa Ynez Mountains to the beach: not for nothing has Santa Barbara been nicknamed the American Riviera.

Two blocks away is the main drag of State Street, a strip of uppity boutiques, decent restaurants and upscale bars. Near the top of the Downtown core is the **Santa Barbara Museum of Art** (1130 State Street, 1-805 963 4364, www.sbmuseart.org), a worthwhile display of ancient creativity and modern-day pretenders. In the other direction, State Street ends at Pacific-side **Stearns Wharf** (www. stearnswharf.org). Up the coast, soft waves make **Leadbetter Beach** the perfect littoral playground; down the coast is the sweet, sandy **East Beach**. Alternatively, head back inland and take in the altogether mellower **Santa Barbara Botanic Garden** (1212 Mission Canyon Road, 1-805 682 4726, www.sbbg.org).

Where to eat & drink

There's plenty of variety here, and plenty of quality. **Bouchon** (9 W Victoria Street, 1-805 730 1160, www.bouchonsantabarbara.com, mains $28) and **Downey's** (1305 State Street, 1-805 966 5006, www.downeyssb.com, mains $32) both serve upscale menus of Californian cuisine with local wines; **Ca'Dario** (37 E Victoria Street, 1-884 9419, www.cadario.net, mains $23) offers traditional Italian cooking. At the harbour, long-time fave **Brophy Bros** (119 Harbor Way, 1-805 966 4418, http://brophybros. com, mains $12) turns out fresh fish and justly celebrated bowls of clam chowder. More affordable fare can be found at the **Sojourner** (134 E Canon Perdido Street, 1-805 965 7922, www.sojournercafe.com, mains $10), the organic old-timers' favourite, and renowned low-budget Mexican spot **La Super-Rica** (No.622, 1-805 963 4940, mains $6). The city's bar scene is busy but not especially interesting.

Tourist information

Santa Barbara *Santa Barbara Visitor Center, 1 Garden Street (1-805 965 3021/ www.sbchamber.org).*

The Deserts

Sun, sand and... well, more sun.

Nature played a cruel trick on the early Western pioneers. Just where the barrier of the Sierra Mountains peters out in the south, a great desert swathe cuts across to the coast. Technically, much of southern California is desert, receiving less than ten inches of rain a year. Were it not for irrigation, air-conditioning and the automobile, large areas would be nigh on uninhabitable for modern man.

Inhospitable, perhaps, but also spectacular. **Death Valley** and **Joshua Tree National Parks** are both breathtaking; the drive to the former is one of the state's most undervalued road trips. In the middle of this alien landscape, in what's known as the Coachella Valley, sit a cluster of sunbleached resort towns, of which **Palm Springs** is easily the most notable. Despite the heat, however, there's skiing close by at **Big Bear Lake** and **Lake Arrowhead**.

The desert is beautiful when seen from behind the wheel of a car – the drive to Death Valley from LA via **Mojave** and **Red Rock Canyon State Park**, having picked up Highway 14 at Santa Clarita, is desert driving at its most beguiling. However, engaging with the environment more closely, preferably on foot, pays large dividends. Go on an interpreted or ranger-led trail to familiarise yourself with some of the basics of geology, flora and fauna. For more, see www.desertusa.com.

Death Valley National Park

Enlarged and redesignated a national park under the 1994 Desert Protection Act, Death Valley is now the largest national park outside Alaska, covering roughly 5,200 square miles. It's also, famously, one of the hottest places on the planet. The park's website calmly offers that 'Death Valley is generally sunny, dry and clear throughout the year'. True, but the word 'generally' masks a multitude of curiosities. Air temperatures regularly top 120°F (49°C) in July and August, and are 50 per cent higher on the ground; fearsome by anyone's standards.

Although you'll pass several points of interest on your way into the park, regardless of whether you enter from the west (via Mojave) or the east (via Death Valley Junction), it's a good idea to head directly to the **Death Valley Visitor Center** (*see p288*) at **Furnace Creek** in order to get your bearings. Here, you'll find an excellent bookshop, decent exhibits, a useful orientation film and helpful staff. Stop in for advice on current weather and road conditions (some tracks are only accessible to 4WD vehicles), pay your fee of $20 per car and take the opportunity to fill up at one of the park's three expensive gas stations.

After you've been to the visitor centre, take the road heading east. Roughly 13 miles off the main road and standing 5,475 feet (1,669 metres) above sea level, **Dante's View** is a wonderful place from which to first survey the park's otherworldly landscape. And just three miles south of Furnace Creek lies ragged, rumpled **Zabriskie Point**.

Further south of Furnace Creek, there's more to see. At **Golden Canyon**, there's a simple two-mile round-trip hike that's best walked in the late afternoon sunlight, when you'll see how the canyon got its name. Continuing south, the landscape gets plainer. Nine miles down the road is the **Devil's Golf Course**, a striking, scrappy landscape formed by salt crystallising and expanding; a few miles further is bleak, eerie **Badwater**, just two miles as the crow flies from Dante's View but more than 5,000 feet (1,524 metres) lower. Indeed, this is the lowest point in the Western Hemisphere, 282 feet (86 metres) below sea level. Unexpectedly, it's only 85 miles from the highest point in the US, the 14,494-foot (4,420-metre) Mount Whitney in the Sierra Nevada. An annual 'ultramarathon' race is held between the two (www.badwater.com), although it no longer extends all the way to Whitney's summit.

Driving north from Furnace Creek offers a greater variety of sights. The remains of the **Harmony Borax Works** have been casually converted into a short trail; there's a similarly simple walk, less historic but more aesthetically pleasing, at nearby **Salt Creek** (look for desert pupfish in the stream in spring). Following the road around to the left will lead you past the eerie **Devil's Cornfield** and the frolic-friendly **Sand Dunes**, which rise and dip in 100-foot (30-metre) increments, and on to the small settlement at **Stovepipe Wells**. Taking a right and driving 36 miles will lead you to the luxurious **Scotty's Castle**; built in the 1920s for Chicago millionaire Albert Johnson, it was named after Walter Scott, his eccentric chancer of a friend. Rangers tell the story on 50-minute tours (usually hourly, 9am-5pm, $11).

It's often too hot to hike, but there are plenty of trails in Death Valley, short and long. The options include the 14-mile round trip to the 11,000-foot (3,300-metre) summit of **Telescope Peak**, a good summer hike (the higher you climb, the cooler it gets). Starting at Mahogany Flat campground, you climb 3,000 feet (900 metres) for some spectacular views of Mount Whitney. In winter, only experienced climbers with ice axes and crampons should attempt it.

Where to eat, drink & stay

Set into the hillside above Furnace Creek Wash, the **Furnace Creek Inn** (reservations 1-800 236 7916, hotel/same-day reservations 1-760 786 2345, www.furnacecreekresort.com, closed mid May-mid Oct, double $305-$410) was built in the 1930s, and retains a cultured dignity reminiscent of the era from which it emerged. The rooms are charming and well equipped, the landscaped gardens are a refined delight, and the inn's upscale Californian food is far better than you might expect.

Elsewhere, the **Furnace Creek Ranch** (same phone & URL, $119-$189) has 200 motel-style rooms and cabins, as well as a pool, tennis courts and the world's lowest golf course, plus a pretty basic bar and restaurant. The 83-room **Stovepipe Wells Village** (1-760 786 2837, www.stovepipewells.com, double $75-$115) also has food on offer, but few other amenities. Four of the park's nine campgrounds are free, with the others costing

between $12 and $18 a night. The most central, and the only one for which reservations are taken, is at Furnace Creek (1-877 444 6777, www.recreation.gov).

Tourist information

Death Valley *Death Valley Visitor Center, Furnace Creek (1-760 786 3200/www.nps.gov/deva).* **Open** 9am-5pm daily.

Getting there

By car

To reach Death Valley, take I-10 west to Ontario, follow I-15 north-east to Baker, drive on Highway 127 to Death Valley Junction and then take Highway 190 west into the park. Alternatively, leave LA to the north-west and, at Sylmar, pick up Highway 14. This eventually turns into Highway 395; from here, take Highway 190 west into the park. Both journeys are around 300 miles; allow 5-6hrs.

Lake Arrowhead & Big Bear Lake

Lake Arrowhead

Nestled on top of one of Southern California's few mountain ranges, two small towns and a handful of scattered neighbourhoods make up the community of Lake Arrowhead. **Blue Jay**, at the west side of the region, is made up of a number of small, forgettable shops, while **Lake Arrowhead Village** offers gift and outlet shops on a water-ringed peninsula.

Death Valley. *See p287.*

Although the boat tours on the **Arrowhead Queen** (1-909 336 6992) offer a little history, sightseeing is largely usurped by the sports and activities: **McKenzie's Water Ski School** in Arrowhead Village (1-909 337 3814, http://mckenziewaterskischool.com), the oldest water-ski school in the United States. The main disappointment, apart from the plethora of speedboats, is the lack of swimming: the lake is privately owned.

Winter sees skiers from the LA conurbation descend on the area. The Arrowhead Ranger Station (1-909 337 2444) can offer guidance on current conditions for cross-country skiing and snow-shoeing. About ten miles up from Lake Arrowhead on US 18 sits the **Snow Valley Resort** (information 1-909 867 2751, snow report 1-800 680 7669, www.snow-valley.com), where you can buy a range of ski and snowboarding passes. The resort is located at a low altitude, but makes its own snow to ensure that the slopes are always in service.

Where to eat, drink & stay

The underwhelming range of eating and lodging options in the array has recently been given a boost with the renovation of the large, handsome **Lake Arrowhead Resort** (27984 Hwy 189, 1-909 336 1511, www.laresort.com, double $179-$349) and the arrival within it of smart eaterie **Bin 189** (1-909 337 4189). European-influenced B&Bs in the area include the **Fleur du Lac** (185 Hwy 173, 1-909 337 8178, www.fleurdelac.com, double $139-$229), itself the subject of a recent remodel.

Tourist information

Lake Arrowhead *Lake Arrowhead Chamber of Commerce, 28200 Hwy 189 (1-909 337 3715/ www.lakearrowhead.net).* **Open** 9am-5pm daily.

Big Bear Lake

Big Bear Lake offers a less charming and more rugged experience than its near-neighbour. But there's also a greater variety of activities available here all year round, with no need to rely on the fake snow that's often required at Lake Arrowhead. Visitors can even swim in the lake here, which is also a first-rate fishery. And many hiking trailheads are easily accessible, with most providing fine views.

During the winter, **Snow Summit** (1-800 232 7686, www.bigbearmountainresorts.com) is one of the most popular ski/snowboard resorts in Southern California. In summer, its East Mountain Express high-speed chairlift is converted into the Scenic Sky Chair (1-800 232

> **Stovepipe Wells sand dunes, Death Valley National Park**
> (*p287*) C-3PO lands here in *Star Wars*

7686): running to an 8,200-foot (2,500-metre) summit, it offers magnificent views of the San Gorgonio Mountains. There are also golfing, hiking and biking opportunities, while families may enjoy careening down the bobsleigh-esque **Alpine Slide** or the summer-only **Alpine Water Slide** (800 Wildrose Lane, 1-909 866 4626, www.alpineslidebigbear.com).

Where to eat, drink & stay

The restaurants along Big Bear Boulevard include the **Old Country Inn** (No.41126, 1-909 866 5600, www.oldcountryinn.net), which specialises in Mexican seafood. B&Bs around the lake include the **Windy Point Inn** (39015 North Shore Drive, 1-909 866 2746, www.windypointinn.com, double $145-$265).

Tourist information

Big Bear Lake *Big Bear Lake Visitor Center, 630 Bartlett Road (1-800 424 4232/www.bigbear.com).* **Open** 9am-5pm daily.

Getting there

By car

Take I-10 and then I-215 to San Bernardino. Pick up Highway 30 eastbound for a mile and then head north on Highway 18; the Lake Arrowhead turn-off is around 30-40mins before Big Bear Lake. The journey from LA should take around 2hrs.

Coachella Valley

Palm Springs

Tucked into an abutment of the San Jacinto and Santa Rosa mountain ranges, Palm Springs first found fame as a destination for the infirm and the tubercular, who were able to soothe their aches and pains at the town's eponymous natural springs. However, after Hollywood began filming silent westerns and Arabian-themed romances in the deserts during the 1920s, the town transformed itself into a winter playground for the Hollywood elite. By the 1950s and '60s, nearly every major American entertainer owned a home in Palm Springs.

Back to the future

What art deco did for Miami Beach in the 1980s, modernism has done for Palm Springs in recent years. Although many of the city's great structures have been razed or changed, invariably in pseudo-Spanish style, beyond recognition, you can still find gems by such modernist architects as William Cody, Richard Neutra, John Lautner, Donald Wexler, E Stuart Williams and Albert Frey in the area. Indeed, Frey's classic 1963 **Tramway Gas Station**, a dramatically angled structure at the town entrance that came perilously close to demolition, has been renovated to serve as a tourist information centre.

It's far from the only must-see modernist site. The upside-down arches of E Stewart Williams' **Washington Mutual Bank** (499 S Palm Canyon Drive; pictured) were built in 1961 across the street from Rudy Baumfeld's blue-tiled 1959 **Bank of America Building** (588 S Palm Canyon Drive). William Cody's

sensually curved **St Theresa's Church** (2800 E Ramon Road), built in 1968, is a quick drive from the equally fantastic **Palm Springs City Hall** at 3200 E Taqhuitz Canyon Way (Albert Frey, 1952) and the nearby **Palm Springs International Airport** (Donald Wexler, 1965).

A map to more than 50 significant structures is available at the visitor centre (*see p292*). It's also fun to get lost in the winding streets of the Las Palmas and Little Tuscany locales west of Palm Canyon Drive at the foot of Mount San Jacinto, where hundreds of ranch-style modern mansions have been preserved in all of their space-age glory. Famous homes include Frank Sinatra's **Twin Palms** (1148 E Alejo Road), where Ol' Blue Eyes lived with Ava Gardner; Liberace's **Casa de Liberace** (501 N Belardo Road), still adorned with the pianist's trademark 'L' logo; and two John Lautner buildings on Southridge Drive, the **Elrod House** and Bob Hope's **Flying Saucer House**.

When the same stars moved on to more lavish spreads elsewhere in the Valley, the town itself metamorphosed into a tawdry tourist trap. However, it's turned itself around once more. Though late mayor Sonny Bono is given most of the credit, the town's resurgence is really down to the combination of a solid economy and an active, town-proud gay community. Renewed interest in mid-century

modernist architecture and the opulent trappings of the leisure-obsessed Rat Pack era have also proved welcome shots in the arm.

Still, the future of the city remains somewhat cloudy. Under the tenure of current mayor Ron Oden, the council has signed off one housing development after another, spoiling many of Palm Springs' scenic vistas. Thankfully, the non-profit Palm Springs Modern Committee (www.psmodcom.com) seems determined to preserve Palm Springs' architectural aesthetic and keep the city from mutating into another ugly Riverside Country exurb.

The city consists simply of a commercial spine: **N Palm Canyon Drive**, home to most of the town's eating, drinking and shopping options. Mid-century antiques shops abound on Palm Canyon and the parallel **N Indian Canyon Drive**; bargains are no longer easy to find, but you can score a lucite table for less than on LA's Beverly Boulevard. On Thursday nights, a mile-long stretch of Palm Canyon is closed to traffic for **Villagefest** (www.palm springsvillagefest.com), when shops open late and stalls line the road.

Though it takes less than an hour to traverse the lengths of Palm Canyon and Indian Canyon by car, don't keep driving in a straight line. Nearly every turn opens up yet another eye-popping mountain view, as well as striking examples of mid-century modern architecture, from simple tract homes to Jetsonian structures. The aforementioned Palm Springs Modern Committee publishes a map, available for $5 online or from the visitor centre (*see p292*), that details the most notable buildings in the city; for more, *see p290* **Back to the future**.

The town is dotted with small attractions. In the heart of Palm Springs sits the impressive **Palm Springs Art Museum** (101 Museum Drive, 1-760 322 4800, www.psmuseum.org, $12.50), which supplements selections from its permanent collection with temporary shows. Across from the airport, the **Palm Springs Air Museum** (1-760 778 6262 ext 222, www.palmspringsairmuseum.org, $10) boasts a collection of propeller-driven World War II aircraft, many still in flying condition. South of town sits the wilfully eccentric **Moorten Botanical Garden & Cactarium** (1701 S Palm Canyon Drive, 1-760 327 6555, $3), a living museum with nature trails, sculpture, rusted-out cars, dinosaur footprints and 3,000 varieties of cacti, succulents and flowers.

Outdoor types are well served. There are hundreds of hiking trails throughout the San Jacintos and Santa Rosas, but the **Indian Canyons** (1-760 323 6018, www.indian-canyons.com, $8), located five miles south of Downtown on S Palm Canyon Drive, are a must-see. Owned and preserved by the Agua Caliente Indians, the Canyons contain miles of hiking trails that wind through an unspoiled wilderness of palm groves, barrel cacti, waterfalls and dramatic rock formations.

For a change of ecosystem, take the **Palm Springs Aerial Tramway** (1-760 325 1391, www.pstramway.com, $22) to the crest of San Jacinto. The rotating tram cars lift you 5,873

feet (1,791 metres) through four different 'life zones' into a lush pine forest that's typically 30°F to 40°F (18°C to 24°C) cooler than on the desert floor. It's worth the journey just to enjoy a drink or a meal at E Stewart William's Tramway Mountain Station.

Where to eat & drink

While Palm Springs offers plenty of culinary variety, top-quality cooking is harder to find. Too many restaurants coast by comfortably on location alone, and plenty of mediocre eateries attach eye-catchingly high prices to dishes that should be retailing for considerably less. Bewar, in particular, of a lot of ordinary Mexican and Italian food.

By and large, you're on safest ground at the lower end of the market. **Tyler's** (149 S Indian Canyon Drive, 1-760 325 2990) is a genuine local favourite, a cute little porch on which residents and weekenders chomp on uncomplicated burgers. There's excellent sushi at **Wasabi** (333 S Indian Canyon Drive, 1-760 416 7788), unexpectedly good Belgian food at **Pomme Frite** (256 S Palm Canyon Drive, 1-760 778 3727, www.pomme-frite.com) and reasonable Mexican food **El Mirasol** (140 E Palm Canyon Drive, 1-760 323 0721). **Manhattan in the Desert** (2665 E Palm Canyon Drive, 1-760 322 3354) is the closest thing to a New York-esque Jewish deli that you're likely to find out here; dropped into the middle of the Coachella Valley Seek out **John Henry's** (1785 E Tahquitz Canyon Way, 1-760 327 7667) for solid American comfort cooking far from the madding crowd. And if you want to push the boat out, consider **Melvyn's** (200 W Ramon Road, 1-760 325 2323, www.inglesideinn.com), a high-priced relic where the food takes second billing to the old-school Palm Springs ambience. The lounge is a real beauty.

Where to stay

Most of the impressive hotels in Palm Springs are housed in classic mid-century buildings. Some have even been decorated in space-age fashion: take the mid-century **Orbit In** (562 W Arenas Road, 1-760 323 3585, www.orbitin.com, double $169-$259), funkily appointed with furniture by Eames et al, or the tiki-on-a-budget theme at the **Caliente Tropics** (411 E Palm

Elrod House, 2175 Southridge Drive, Palm Springs (*p290*)
Designed by John Lautner, it doubles as Willard Whyte's house in *Diamonds are Forever*

Trips Out of Town

Canyon Drive, 1-888 277 0999, www.caliente tropics. com, double $45-$120).

Other local hotels, meanwhile, have been ushered gently into the 21st century. The best of them is the beautiful **Movie Colony** (726 N Indian Canyon Drive, 1-760 320 6340, www.moviecolonyhotel.com, double $119-$249), an Albert Frey-designed construction with a lovely pool area; alternatives include the understated **Horizon** (1050 E Palm Canyon Drive, 1-760 323 1858, www.thehorizonhotel. com, double $95-$250) and the sublime **Parker** (4200 E Palm Canyon Drive, 1-760 770 5000, www.theparkerpalmsprings.com, double $139- $695). Gay lodgings include the smart **East Canyon Hotel** (288 E Camino Monte Vista, 1-760 320 1928, www.eastcanyonhotel. com, rates $119-$219), the only gay hotel with a full-service spa.

The waters that lend their name to the neighbouring town of **Desert Hot Springs** have been exploited by several hotels in the town, each with their own natural mineral pools. The **Desert Hot Springs Spa Hotel** (10805 Palm Drive, 1-760 329 6000, www. dhsspa.com, rates $89-$139) offers good value, but **Hope Springs** (68075 Club Circle Drive, 1-760 329 4003, www.hopespringsresort.com, rates $160-$250) is more stylish. For a full list, see the Desert Hot Springs Chamber of Commerce site at www.deserthotsprings.com.

Tourist information

Palm Springs *Palm Springs Visitors Center, 2901 N Palm Canyon Drive (1-800 347 7746/1-760 778 8418/www.palm-springs.org).* **Open** 9am-5pm daily.

Other Coachella towns

The climate remains just as delicious around the Coachella Valley. However, outside the recuperative waters of **Desert Hot Springs** (*see above*), there's not much of interest. **Cathedral City** is notable only as the last resting place of Frank Sinatra (at the Desert Memorial Park cemetery); **Rancho Mirage**'s sole claim to fame is the Betty Ford Clinic.

Palm Desert's appeal rests on the **Living Desert Zoo & Gardens** (47-900 Portola Avenue, 1-760 346 5694, www.livingdesert.org, $5-$12), a 1,200-acre wildlife and botanical park with animals from local and African deserts. Nearby **Indio** is home to the annual Coachella (www.coachella.com) and Stagecoach (www. stagecoachfestival.com) each spring, and a date industry that thrives all year. The **Shields Date Gardens** (80-225 Highway 111, 1-760 347 7768, free) is one of the area's oldest tourist traditions: stop by for a date shake.

Getting there

By bus

Greyhound (1-800 231 2222, www.greyhound.com) runs up to 4 buses a day. The 3hr trip from LA costs around $55 (round-trip).

By car

To reach Palm Springs from LA, take I-10 eastbound for just over 100 miles. The journey can take anywhere between 2hrs and 3hrs, depending on the traffic and your starting location.

Joshua Tree

Whether you're approaching from LA or Palm Springs, Joshua Tree National Park is best entered from the north via Highway 62: many of the park's highlights are in this northern section. En route, you'll pass **Yucca Valley**, the gateway to **Pioneertown** (www.pioneer town.com). Originally a set for movies and TV shows (*The Cisco Kid*, among many others), this better-than-average tourist trap retains an Old West feel; its dirt roads make you realise why so many cowboys were called Dusty.

Those who prefer their nature unmediated should head to the **Pipes Canyon Preserve**, owned by a private conservation group and every bit as wild as a national park. Ask at the visitor centre (*see p294*) for information about cougars, bears and bobcats, petroglyphs and active springs. Admission is free.

East of Yucca Valley are two smaller settlements, both of which offer entrances into Joshua Tree National Park. The towns of **Joshua Tree** itself and, around 16 miles further along Highway 62, **Twentynine Palms** are both small, rather plain towns with a few hotels and restaurants but not much else.

Joshua Tree National Park

North of Palm Springs, the desert valley gives way to massive granite monoliths and strange, jagged trees with spiky blooms. These are Joshua trees, a form of cactus named by early Mormon settlers after the prophet Joshua, which they believed pointed the way to the Promised Land. The trees lend their name to the 794,000-acre Joshua Tree National Park, a mecca for modern-day explorers that's home to 17 different types of cactus, palm-studded oases, ancient petroglyphs, spectacular rock formations and all manner of wildlife. The park straddles two desert ecosystems, the Mojave and Colorado. The remote eastern half is dominated by cholla cactus, small creosote bushes and

Mountain high

Deep in the California desert, not far from the town of Niland, the snowbird landing pad of Slab City and the environmental disaster that is the Salton Sea, an incredible visionary monument has risen up out of the dry sand. Over the past two decades, it's been shaped in gentle curves to take in terraces, paths and steps, then covered with tens of thousands of gallons of coloured house paint around one central message: 'God is love'. Creator Leonard Knight calls it **Salvation Mountain**.

When Knight came to this spot in the 1980s, he planned to use it as a launch pad for a hot air balloon inscribed with spiritual messages. The balloon rotted in the desert sun; Knight, though, stayed put, and soon started sculpting soil and pouring paint. Now in his seventies, he lives in its shadow in a cabin on the back of an old truck.

Unless he's ridden into town on his scooter to get some lunch, Knight greets visitors warmly. You're encouraged to follow the yellow paint road straight up the side of the mountain to its peak, which offers views over the installation and out into the colourless desert. The mountain's Biblical quotes, funky painted flower beds and waterfalls are all picked out with rivers of donated paint, which led some local politicians to try and have the remote site declared as a toxic hazard. But California Senator Barbara Boxer called the spot a national treasure, and Salvation Mountain is now a protected site.

Knight still works on the site: he recently learned hay bail construction, then built the impressive igloo shrine and museum to the side of the main structure. Inside the museum, artificial trees made from brightly painted telephone poles soar 40 feet to the roof, and sunlight filters in from inset car windows. It's like a desert rat cathedral, and an awesome example of one man's dreams made real. *Salvation Mountain is located north of I-8, south of I-10 and five miles east of Hwy 111 at Niland. Take Main Street east to Salvation Mountain.*

Joshua Tree National Park. *See p292.*

some adrenaline-pumping 4WD routes. The cooler and wetter western section is what the Joshua Tree tourists come to see.

Entering via the West Entrance at the town of Joshua Tree (the $15/car fee is valid for seven days), you'll soon come to Hidden Valley, a collection of climbs, hikes and picnic spots stretching as far as the eye can see. There's walking, too, with more than a dozen trails revisiting remnants of the gold mining era. The **Hidden Valley** mile-long loop winds around a dramatic, rock-enclosed valley, while the nearby **Barker Dam Trail** leads to a lake built by early ranchers; at dusk, it's possible to spot bighorn sheep taking a sip. Try to take at least one of the trails during your visit.

Keys View, due south of Hidden Valley, is worth a side trip; on a clear day, you can see all the way to Mexico. You can also pick up 18-mile **Geology Tour Road** (high clearance vehicles are a must) showing off some of Joshua Tree's most dramatic landscapes. Off-road adventures continue on **Berdoo Canyon Road**, which intersects Geology Tour Road and passes the ruins of a camp constructed in the '30s by builders of the California Aqueduct.

Where to eat, drink & stay

Once a cantina set for numerous westerns, **Pappy & Harriet's Pioneertown Palace** (53688 Pioneertown Road, Yucca Valley, 1-760 365 5956, www.pappyandharriets.com) is now a popular local hangout serving heaped portions of mesquite BBQ and all manner of live music. In Joshua Tree, locals swear by the home cooking at the **Crossroads Café** (61715 Twentynine Palms Highway, 1-760 366 5414, www.crossroadscafeandtavern.com), a hippy-ish eatery that serves sandwiches, salads and the like. The best of a so-so bunch of restaurants in Twentynine Palms is the **Twentynine Palms Inn** (*see below*), which serves steaks, chops and veggies from its own garden (yes, in the desert).

Lodgings are cheap and characterful. Yucca Valley's **Pioneertown Motel** (5040 Curtis Road, 1-760 365 4879, www.pioneer townmotel.com, double $75-$95) hosted actors, such as Barbara Stanwyck, when they filmed in the area. In Joshua Tree, try the hacienda-style **Joshua Tree Inn** (61259 Twentynine Palms Highway, Joshua Tree, 1-760 366 1188, www.joshuatreeinn.com, double $85-$105). Built in the 1950s as a getaway for movie stars, it then drew rock star guests such as the Rolling Stones and the Eagles during the 1960s; Gram Parsons spent his final hours in room 8. Over in Twentynine Palms, skip the vanilla motels on Highway 62 in favour of funky, old-school **Twentynine Palms Inn** (73950 Inn Avenue, 1-760 367 3505, www. 29palmsinn.com, double $70-$155), or the 1950s-style **Harmony Motel** (711661 Twentynine Palms Highway, 1-760 367 3351, www.harmonymotel.com, double $62-$72), where U2 stayed while recording *The Joshua Tree*. In the park, there are nine campsites (see www.nps.gov/jotr), but only two have water. Remember to drink two litres a day.

Tourist information

Joshua Tree National Park *Oasis of Mara, Twentynine Palms (1-760 367 5500/www.nps.gov/jotr).* **Open** 8am-5pm daily.
Joshua Tree National Park *Cottonwood Spring, Joshua Tree National Park (1-760 367 5500/www.nps.gov/jotr).* **Open** 9am-3pm daily.
Joshua Tree National Park *Park Boulevard, Joshua Tree (www.nps.gov).* **Open** 8am-5pm daily.

Getting there

By car

Joshua Tree National Park can be reached from the south via I-10, or from the north via Highway 62 in the towns of Joshua Tree and Twentynine Palms.

South to San Diego

LA a bit too frantic for you? We know just the place…

Santa Catalina Island

The most Mediterranean island in North America, Santa Catalina Island juts more than 2,000 feet (600 metres) above the Pacific Ocean at its highest point, 22 miles off Long Beach. Privately owned for two centuries and now 86 per cent owned and run by the **Santa Catalina Island Conservancy** (125 Claressa Avenue, 1-310 510 2595, www.catalinaconservancy.org), it's protected from overdevelopment.

The first street you walk will be Crescent Avenue, in the tiny town of **Avalon**. Lined with shops and restaurants, the street curves along a postcard-perfect harbour towards the art deco Casino building, home to a theatre and the **Catalina Island Museum** (1 Casino Way, Avalon, 1-310 510 2414, www.catalinamuseum. org, $1-$4, closed Thur Jan-Mar). Busy, wave-free **Crescent Beach** is a big draw, though the **Descanso Beach Club** (closed Nov-Apr), a ten-minute walk along Via Casino from Avalon, is a quieter alternative and is open to the public for a small fee. From the north end of Crescent Avenue, it's a half-hour stroll on Avalon Canyon to the **Wrigley Memorial & Botanical Gardens** (1400 Avalon Canyon Road, $5). The 1934 memorial recognises gum magnate William Wrigley Jr, who bought the island in 1915. The harbour views are beautiful.

You'll need a permit from the Conservancy to either hike (free) or bike ($20/day) outside Avalon or Two Harbours, the rustic settlement at the island's northern isthmus. There's good scuba diving; try **Catalina Divers Supply** (1-310 510 0330, www.catalinadiverssupply. com). The less adventurous can enjoy one of a variety of boat trips; call **Discovery Tours** (1-310 510 8687, www.visitcatalinaisland.com).

Where to eat, drink & stay

Most eateries are in Avalon. For fairly priced fish, try **Armstong's Seafood** (306 Crescent Avenue, 1-310 510 0113, www.armstrong seafood.com, mains $19) on the harbour; those seeking elegant dining should opt for the **Channel House** (205 Crescent Avenue, 1-310 510 1617, mains $25). Want to know where everyone is scoring those saliva-inducing, ice-cream-packed waffle cones? **Big Olaf's** (220 Crescent Avenue, 1-310 510 0798).

It's no wonder most visitors are day-trippers: lodging is scarce and dear. You'll pay to be in the thick of things, but the casual elegance of **Hotel Vista del Mar** (1-800 601 3836, www. hotel-vistadelmar.com, $145-$265), steps from the beach, and the plainer but still handsome **Metropole** (1-310 510 1884, www.hotel-metropole.com, $199-$399) is worth it. **Hermit Gulch** is one of five campsites near Avalon (reservations required; 1-310 510 8368, $12); for others, such as the stunning seaside hike-in at Little Harbour, see ww.visitcatalinaisland.com.

Tourist information

Avalon *Catalina Island Chamber of Commerce & Visitors Bureau, 1 Green Pleasure Pier, Avalon (1-310 510 1520/www.catalina.com).* **Open** 8am-5pm Mon-Sat; 9am-4pm Sun.

Getting there

By boat

Long Beach (1hr) and San Pedro (75mins) are served by Catalina Express (1-800 481 3470, www.catalina express.com, $64.50 round-trip). For the 75-minute trip from Newport Beach, use the less regular Catalina Flyer (1-800 830 7744, www.catalinainfo.com, $68 round-trip). And for the 90min-2hr ride from Marina del Rey, try Catalina Ferries (1-310 305 7250, www. catalinaferries.com, $75 round-trip). Reservations are recommended but not always necessary.

San Diego

To the casual visitor, San Diego might come across as a little bland. It lacks the bohemian earthiness that defines San Francisco (despite an active gay community). It lacks the cascade of competing cultures that makes up LA's urban sprawl. It lacks a little charisma.

Of course, one man's charisma is another man's freak show, which explains how San Diego has grown into America's sixth largest city. Once known for its naval base and its climate, it's blossomed into a cheery centre of business and tourism. It's unashamedly nice: as sunny as the day is long, Californian conservatism at its most approachable. The

Trips Out of Town

Beautiful **Balboa Park**.

and brick sidewalks; conversely, many of the buildings are original. A walking tour of the area departs every Saturday at 11am from the **William Davis Heath House** (410 Island Avenue, 1-619 233 4692, www.gaslampquarter. org), which was built in 1850 and is the city's oldest building. Tour tickets cost $10.

West on Broadway, just a stone's throw from the waterfront stands one of San Diego's most recognisable landmarks, the **Santa Fe Depot** (1050 Kettner Boulevard). Constructed in 1915, the Spanish Mission-Colonial Revival building is still an important travel hub under its modern name of **Union Station**. Across the street is the futuristic, two-storey **Museum of Contemporary Art** (1001 Kettner Boulevard, 1-858 454 3541, www.mcasd.org), the sister to the original venue in La Jolla (*see p298*).

Continue west, and you'll reach the tree-lined **Embarcadero**, which affords panoramic views of the city and numerous reminders of San Diego's naval history: the excellent **Maritime Museum** (1492 N Harbor Drive, 1-619 234 9153, www.sdmaritime.com, $8-$14) sits close to the **USS Midway Museum** (910 N Harbor Drive, 1-619 544 9600, www.midway.org, $9-$17), the longest-serving aircraft carrier in US naval history. Some visitors choose to experience San Diego's water at closer quarters: **San Diego Harbor Excursions** (1050 N Harbor Drive, 1-619 234 4111, www.sdhe.com) offers a variety of tours from Broadway Pier.

Mexican and gay communities have shaken the town out of its woozy stasis, but you don't really come here for an edgy urban experience. Indeed, you don't really come here for an urban experience at all: you come here to find Middle America under Southern Californian skies.

DOWNTOWN SAN DIEGO

The heart of San Diego is its well-scrubbed, thriving **Downtown**, which combines a high-rise business district with a popular commercial core. The area, like Downtowns in many major US cities, had become moribund, but has been revived by a combination of commercial development and high-quality in-fill urban housing. Start at **Horton Plaza**, a complex of shops and restaurants on six open-air levels now run by the national Westfield chain.

Surrounding Horton Plaza is the historic, 16-block **Gaslamp Quarter**. Built in the 19th century, the area has been polished into a busy entertainment district, home to a number of neat, tidy and rather predictable restaurants and bars. Much of the street furniture is modern, including the mock-Victorian street lamps (powered not by gas but electricity)

BALBOA PARK

Like Central Park in New York, 1,200-acre Balboa Park occupies a prominent piece of real estate. But, unlike its Manhattan equivalent, San Diego's city park is dotted with around two dozen fine cultural institutions. Stop by the **Visitor Centre** (1549 El Prado, 1-619 239 0512, www.balboapark.org) for a map and other orientation aids. If you're planning on visiting a number of attractions, ask about the Balboa Park Passport, which entitles the bearer to entry to many of the park's attractions. If $39 is too dear, come on Tuesday, when some of the museums are free on a rotating basis.

Where to start? With the park itself: it's a gorgeous place, handsomely landscaped and smartly kept. Though most tourists just swing by and whistle-stop through a handful of the museums, it's worth taking a time-out to wander away from the crowds.

Culture vultures will want to take in the temporary exhibitions and permanent displays in the decent **San Diego Museum of Art** (1-619 232 7931, www.sdmart.com, $4-$10); the regularly changing exhibits in the modern **Museum of Photographic Arts** (1-619 238 7559, www.mopa.org, $4-$6); and the Dutch

Trips Out of Town

paintings and ancient Italian religious works in the **Timken Museum of Art** (1-619 239 5548, www.timkenmuseum.org, free), a modernist building compared to its neighbours; all three are closed on Mondays. Families are better served by the interactive, kid-friendly exhibits in the **Reuben H Fleet Science Center** (1-619 238 1233, www.rhfleet.org, $6.75-$16.50), the **Natural History Museum** (1-619 232 3821, www.sdnhm.org, $7-$13) and the **San Diego Air & Space Museum** (1-619 234 8291, www.sandiegoairandspace.org, $6-$15).

However, the park's real highlight is the 100-acre **San Diego Zoo** (1-619 234 3153, www.sandiego zoo.org, $16.50-$24.50 or with CityPass; *see pp69-71*). Start by taking a 35-minute bus tour of the highlights, or riding the aerial Skyfari air tram across the park. The pandas and tigers are very popular, as are the polar bears; the hummingbird exhibit is the best place to avoid the crowds. And do notice the fabulous plant life: the site is a botanical garden of no little repute. (The zoo also runs the safari-style Wild Animal Park in the otherwise uninteresting town of Escondido, 30 miles north of San Diego. Check the zoo's website for more.)

HILLCREST AND OLD TOWN

San Diego's two most famous neighbourhoods have little in common save their interest for the casual visitor. A short drive north of Downtown sits **Hillcrest**, a few handsome streets lined with vintage shops, old-fashioned cafés and gay bars. The main drag is University Avenue; if you continue east along it for ten minutes, you'll reach **North Park**, a fast-rising district dotted with interesting bars and restaurants.

A little to the west of Hillcrest, meanwhile, is **Old Town**, the first Spanish settlement in California and the original centre of San Diego. The two dozen original buildings now comprise a State Historic Park, albeit one dotted with a number of rather ordinary restaurants. The visitor centre in the Robinson-Rose building offers further information (1-619 220 5422, www.parks.ca.gov); tours leave from here at 11am and 2pm every day of the year.

CORONADO

You can get a sense of the might of the US Navy driving across the two-mile **Coronado Bay Bridge**, which swoops over the harbour from Downtown to the 'island' (actually a peninsula)

Hollywood and vines

Napa and Sonoma may grab the headlines, but there's a long tradition of winemaking around LA. And, indeed, in LA: the **San Antonio Winery** (737 Lamar Sreet, 1-323 223 1401, www.sanantoniowinery.com) has been making wine less than a mile from the centre of Downtown since 1917. It's not the only working winery in the city, but it's the only one that's open to the public. For others, you'll have to head out – north, east or south.

North of LA, it's 90 minutes to the **Ojai Valley**, where there are more than 15 small wineries. The most interesting is **Casa Barranca** (1350 Foothill Road, Ojai, 1-805 640 1334, www.organic-wine.com), where you can taste organic and biodynamic wines in a spectacular craftsman-style mansion.

Another easy day trip from LA is the 45-minute ride north to the **Antelope Valley**, where the prettiest winery is **Agua Dulce** (9640 Sierra Highway, Agua Dulce, 1-661 268 7402, www.aguadulcevineyards.com). Stop in for a meal at **Le Chene** (12625 W Sierra Highway, 1-661 251 4315, www.lechene.com), where chef and winemaker Juan Alonso has transformed an old cottage into a fine dining destination. Continue a few miles down the Antelope Valley Highway and

you'll be in Lancaster, where you'll find the **Antelope Valley Winery** (42041 20th Street W, 1-661 722 0145, www.avwinery.com). The owners are friendly, and the winemaker is happy to chat when time allows.

Just under an hour east of Downtown, **Rancho Cucamonga** boasts two noteworthy wineries. **Galleano Winery** (4231 Wineville Road, Mira Loma, 1-951 685 5376, www. galleanowinery.com) and **Joseph Filippi** (12467 Base Line Road, Rancho Cucamonga, 1-909 899 5755, www.josephfilippiwinery. com) both produce from old vines. Both also make Angelica, the fortified wine of the Spanish missions that's the only wine style native to Southern California.

Those with time for a weekend getaway should consider a trip to Temecula, about two hours south-west from LA. While there are dozens of hotels, wineries, and restaurants in the area, only one place combines all three – the **South Coast Winery Resort & Spa** (34843 Rancho California Road, Temecula, 1-951 587 9463, www.wineresort.com). This luxurious complex of rambling villas is a perfect base for exploring the area, taking a hot air balloon ride (call in advance) or tasting around the valley.

Trips Out of Town

of Coronado: it yields a dramatic view of the cruisers, destroyers and other vessels anchored in the bay. Most of Coronado is military, but it's also home to a comfortable downtown area and the 1888 **Hotel del Coronado** (*see p300*), one of the US's largest all-wood structures. The hotel overlooks a lovely beach, tying together the sum total of Coronado's other attractions.

HEADING NORTH
The Pacific Ocean sits a ten-minute drive from Old Town, and facing it are a number of beaches and resorts. The stretch of coastline covering shambling **Ocean Beach**, tidier **Mission Beach** and happy-go-lucky **Pacific Beach** is one long blur of mellowed-out beach bummery. The summer never ends around here – weatherbeaten men, old and young, ease through the mellow days with nothing more than a beer, a fish taco, a surfboard, the sun and each other for company. The perennial human quest for life's deeper meaning appears to have ground to a standstill on these shores.

Aside from the weather and the waves, this stretch holds two notable attractions. In Mission Beach, **Belmont Park** (1-858 228 9283, www.belmontpark.com) offers old-fashioned beachside entertainments, including a rollercoaster built in 1925. It's harmless fun, but it's rather overshadowed by the wildly popular aquatic-themed family attractions at **SeaWorld** (1720 South Shores Drive, 1-619 226 3901, www.seaworld.com, $51-$61),.

A ten-minute drive north of here, **La Jolla** ('La Hoy-a') is a very different town. You'll see the occasional bum and surf dog loitering around on its street corners, but this is an altogether wealthier and grander part of the world, prim and precious to the last. The shops along Girard Avenue are a mix of familiar chains and unique boutiques; few of the latter are anything other than upscale.

The **Museum of Contemporary Art, San Diego** (700 Prospect Street, 1-858 454 3541, www.mcasd.org, $5-$10) features more than 4,000 post-1950 works, including impressive collections of pop art and Latin American art, and there are some elegant modern buildings scattered amid plenty of architectural mediocrity: in particular, seek out Louis Kahn's **Salk Institute for Biological Studies** (10010 N Torrey Pines Road) and the **Scripps Institute of Oceanography** (2300 Expedition Way, 1-858 534 3474, www.aquarium.ucsd.edu, $7.50-$11), parts of which were designed by early California Modernist Irving Gill. The Birch Aquarium at the Scripps is an excellent place at which to get acquainted with the local marine life. However, the main attraction of La Jolla is its location. Perched above the Pacific and fronted by a swooping coastline, the town could hardly have been blessed with a more impressive aspect. It's little wonder that the real estate here is the most expensive in San Diego.

Where to eat & drink

Downtown San Diego is packed with bars and restaurants, although the quality, especially in the Gaslamp Quarter, is spotty. For comfort cooking, try the excellent burgers and beers at airy **Neighborhood** (777 G Street, 1-619 446

Over the border

On the northern side of the westernmost US-Mexico border crossing, you'll see a massive parking lot, usually filled with newish cars owned by American day-trippers who've crossed over in search of a little fun and games. On the southern side, meanwhile, is a massive breaker's yard filled with the remains of now-useless Mexican cars. Between them, these two lots provide a useful metaphor for the vast differences in attitudes, aspirations and wealth between nice, middle-class Southern California and earthy, dirty **Tijuana**, the most famous border town on earth.

After squeaky-clean San Diego, Tijuana smacks you upside the head like the third Margarita of the evening. A classic untamed border town, it's messy, edgy and loud, a vibrant reminder of the ongoing tensions between the mutually dependent gringo north and the impoverished south. Prostitutes walk the streets as sharks offer discount drinks; mariachi musicians roam the streets in search of employment and tips, hunting in packs like wolves. Mexicans do the selling; Americans are doing the buying.

It's all about commerce: get your picture taken with a donkey, buy three tacos for a buck, stock up on discount drugs (mostly for depression and erectile dysfunction, two conditions in which the US seems to be a world leader). On Avenida Revolución, shops and street vendors hawk religious kitsch and cheap cigarettes; several big US chains (Burger King et al) cater to astonishingly

unadventurous tourists. Nightfall brings boozy exuberance (the legal drinking age is 18, which is why the town is popular with San Diego students) and an increase in crime, with locals preying on drunk visitors.

Some visitors grumble that Tijuana isn't authentically Mexican. Certainly, the country is different the further south you travel. But, in truth, this Americanised border town is no less authentic than Downtown San Diego, with its airbrushed industrial buildings and electricity-powered ersatz gaslamps. The rip-offs are different on either side of the border – fake Zoloft in Tijuana, $30 parking in San Diego – but they're all cut from the same fiercely capitalist cloth.

To reach Tijuana, drive south on I-5 or I-805 from San Diego for 25 miles to the San Ysidro International Border. You're best off parking here, then walking across the border into Tijuana. Alternatively, from Downtown San Diego, take the San Ysidro trolley ($5 return; 1-619 233 3004, www.sdcommute. com), which runs until 1am daily and until 2am on Saturdays; it connects with various stations in Downtown, including 5th Avenue (at C Street), Civic Center (C Street between 2nd & 3rd Avenues) and Santa Fe Depot. There's a tourist information office just over the border, but the maps it distributes are pretty useless. Travellers can stay without a visa for up to 72 hours, but non-US or Canadian citizens will need a passport and US citizens should carry a driver's licence.

0002, mains $10); down the street, **Zanzibar** (707 G Street, 1-619 230 0125, www.zanzibar cafe.com, mains $13) has sandwiches, salads and coffees. The French cooking at cosy **Café Chloe** (721 9th Avenue, 1-619 232 3242, www.cafechloe.com, mains $20) is solid but pricey, much like the Californian fusion food at **Chive** (558 4th Avenue, 1-619 232 4483, www. chiverestaurant.com, mains $20). There are expensive steaks at **Donovan's** (570 K Street, 1-619 237 9700, www.donovanssteakhouse.com, mains $40) and cheap, agreeably jolly breakfasts at **Café 222** (222 Laurel Street, 1-619 236 9902, www.cafe222.com, mains $8).

Heading north, there are several worthwhile options in Bankers Hill en route to Hillcrest. There's bright, European-influenced Californian cooking at **Bertrand at Mister A's** (2550 5th Avenue, 1-619 239 1377, www.bertrandatmister as.com, mains $33), which affords great views of the city, and some extraordinary desserts at, er, **Extraordinary Desserts** (2929 5th Avenue, 1-619 294 2132, www.extraordinary desserts.com, desserts $8). And in Balboa Park, the Latin-inflected American cuisine served at **Prado** (1549 El Prado, 1-619 557 9441, www.pradobalboa.com, mains $20) is far better than it needs to be given the touristy location.

Up in Hillcrest, try the diner staples at the **Crest Café** (425 Robinson Avenue, 1-619 295 2510, www.crestcafe.net, mains $11) or **Kemo Sabe** (3958 5th Avenue, 1-619 220 6802, www. cohnrestaurants.com, mains $22), where the Southwest meets south-east Asian. Further east in fast-gentrifying North Park, your best bets are the sleek, welcoming **Hawthorns** (2985 University Avenue, 1-619 295 1688, www. hawthornssd.com, mains $20) or the cheap Mexican basics served at **Super Cocina** (3627 University Avenue, 1-619 584 6244, mains $7). On Prospect Street in La Jolla, the recently upgraded **Georges at the Cove** (No.1250, 1-858 454 4244, www.georgesatthecove.com, mains $34) sets the standards for California cuisine. And out in Pacific Beach, try the lively and likeable comfort cooking at relaxed, affordable **Café 976** (976 Felpar Street, 1-858 272 0976, www.cafe976.com, mains $8).

Where to stay

The last ten years or so have seen a sea-change in Downtown's accommodation options, with a slew of modish hotels arriving on the scene. Handsome but blighted by poor service, the **W** (421 W B Street, 1-619 398 3100, www.starwood hotels.com/whotels, $270-$409) has been joined by the gracious **Sofia**, 150 W Broadway, 1-800 826 0009, www.thesofiahotel.com, $205-$225) and the **Hotel Solamar** (435 6th Avenue, 1-877

230 0300, www.hotelsolamar.com, $269-$354), a sunny Kimpton property. For old-school luxury, try the **US Grant** (326 Broadway, 1-866 837 4270, www.usgrant.net, $209-$319 double). Budget travellers should head, instead, for **HI-San Diego** (521 Market Street, 1-619 223 4778, www.sandiegohostels.org, $20-$80).

Outside Downtown, the landmark property is the immaculate **Hotel del Coronado** (1500 Orange Avenue, Coronado, 1-619 435 6611, www.hoteldel.com, $305-$610 double), now with a revamped spa. In Point Loma, not far from Downtown, you'll find the stylish **Pearl** (1410 Rosecrans Street, 1-877 732 7573, www.the pearlsd.com, $164-$230). Pacific Beach offers the glamorous **Tower 23**, (723 Felspar Street, 1-866 869 3723, www.tower23hotel.com, $309-$489). And north in La Jolla, the boutiquey **Hotel Parisi** (1111 Prospect Street, 1-858 454 1511, www.hotelparisi.com, $325-$545) offers a little modish East Coast style.

Tourist information

Balboa Park Visitors Center *House of Hospitality, 1549 El Prado (1-619 239 0512/ www.balboapark.org).* **Open** 9.30am-4.30pm daily.
San Diego Convention & Visitors Bureau *1040 W Broadway, at Harbor Drive (1-619 236 1212/www.sandiego.org).* **Open** *June-Sept* 9am-5pm daily. *Oct-May* 9am-4pm daily.

Getting there

By car
From Downtown LA, take the I-5 south. From West LA, take the I-405 south and then join the I-5. From LA, it takes about 2hrs with no traffic.

By bus
Greyhound (1-800 231 2222, www.greyhound.com) runs up to 20 buses a day. The fare is $35 and the journey takes 2-3hrs.

By train
Amtrak (1-800 872 7245, www.amtrak.com) runs about ten trains per day between Union Station and San Diego. A round trip costs about $68; journey time is around 2hrs 40mins.

Getting around

You can navigate your way around much of metropolitan San Diego on San Diego Transit Corporation buses, or use the San Diego Trolley between Downtown and Old Town (to the north) or Tijuana (to the south). For details on public transport, visit the **San Diego Transit Store** (102 Broadway, 1-619 234 1060, www.sdcommute.com). For route information, call 511 (within San Diego only) and select 'public transportation' or call 1-619 233 3004.

o Union Station   Wilshire/Western

Directory

Getting Around   302
Resources A-Z   306
Further Reference   313
Index   315
Advertisers' Index   322

Features

Travel advice   306
Climate   312

People Coming/People Going
by Richard Wyatt. *See p239*.

Directory

Getting Around

By air

Los Angeles International Airport (LAX)

1-310 646 5252/www.lawa.org/lax.
LAX is situated on the West Side and has nine terminals. Flying in or out of here is rarely enjoyable: signage is poor and the staff are brusque at best. Most flights from Europe arrive at the Tom Bradley International Terminal, currently being renovated; Virgin Atlantic, based at Terminal 2, is the main exception.

The cheapest and most time-consuming way to reach your hotel from LAX is by **public transport**. From the airport, take either the C or G shuttle buses, both free. The C will ferry you to the MTA Bus Center at Vicksburg Avenue and 96th Street, from where you can take a bus; the G heads to the Aviation station on the Metro's Green line (*see p305*). This route, though, isn't recommended.

A fleet of **shuttles** flits between LAX and every neighbourhood in LA. Most services are able to drop you at your hotel; fares start at $20. You can pick up a shuttle outside the arrival terminals from **Prime Time** (1-800 733 8267, www.primetime shuttle.com) and **SuperShuttle** (1-800 258 3826, www.supershuttle. com). Both firms can also pick you up from your hotel and take you back to LAX, given 24 hours' notice.

Taxis can be found outside arrivals. Fares from LAX come with a $2.50 surcharge. If you're staying on the West Side, a taxi from LAX will cost $20-$25 plus tip; it'll be twice that to Hollywood or beyond. There's a flat rate of $44.50 (incl surcharge) between LAX and Downtown. For details of local taxi firms, *see p305*.

Burbank–Glendale–Pasadena Airport

1-818 840 8840/www.burbank airport.com.
If you're flying from a US airport, you may land at Burbank. As with its larger competitor, there are many ways to travel from Burbank to your hotel: by **public transport** (a free shuttle will take you to the MTA bus stop at Hollywood Way and

Thornton Avenue; the airport is also served by Metrolink rail), by **shuttle** (firms are numerous) and by **taxi**.

Major airlines

Air Canada *1-888 247 2262/ www.aircanada.com.*
Air New Zealand *1-800 262 1234/ www.airnewzealand.com.*
Alaska Air *1-800 252 7522/ www.alaskaair.com.*
America West *1-800 428 4322/ www.americawest.com.*
American Airlines *1-800 433 7300/www.aa.com.*
British Airways *1-800 247 9297/ www.britishairways.com.*
Continental Airlines *domestic 1-800 523 3273/international 1-800 231 0856/www.continental.com.*
Delta *domestic 1-800 221 1212/ international 1-800 241 4141/ www.delta.com.*
Lufthansa *1-800 399 5838/ www.lufthansa.com.*
Northwest *1-800 225 2525/ www.nwa.com.*
Southwest Airlines *1-800 435 9792/www.iflyswa.com.*
United Airlines *domestic 1-800 864 8331/international 1-800 538 2929/www.united.com.*
US Air *domestic 1-800 428 4322/ international 1-800 622 1015/ www.usair.com.*
Virgin Atlantic *1-800 821 5438/ www.virgin-atlantic.com.*

By bus

LA's main **Greyhound** station is Downtown, at 1716 E 7th Street. However, Greyhound buses arriving in LA stop at several smaller stations around town. For more on Greyhound, call 1-800 231 2222 or check www.greyhound.com.

By rail

Trains to LA terminate at **Union Station**, at 800 N Alameda Street in Downtown. From here, you can take the Red or Gold Metro lines to your destination, or connect with any number of buses. For

more on **Amtrak**, which runs services from LA to all corners of the US, call 1-800 872 7245 or see www.amtrak.com.

Although public transport in LA is improving, it's a brave soul who chooses to tackle the town without a car. LA's sprawl is best negotiated from behind the wheel.

Driving in LA presents its own challenges. Those used to driving in towns or smaller cities may blanche at the five-lane freeways. However, LA is less terrifying for drivers than, say, New York, in part because the traffic often moves at a snail's pace. Traffic is often atrocious during the morning and evening rush hours, which can run to 7-10am and 3-7pm. For traffic information, call the **CalTrans Traffic Hotline** on 1-800 427 7623, or see www.dot.ca.gov/hq/roadinfo. Radio station KNX (1070 AM) has traffic reports every six minutes during the day; KFWB (980 AM) gives traffic reports every ten minutes, 24-7.

Freeways in LA are referred to by numbers (10, 110, 405, etc) but also by nicknames: west of Downtown, the I-10 ('I' for Interstate), for example, is the Santa Monica Freeway. For more on the system, *see p71* **Street talk**. There's a limit of 65mph on the freeways, but you'll see cars going much faster. Don't expect people to indicate when they change lanes. The outside lanes are the fast lanes, though it's normal to overtake on the inside. It's best to stay in the middle lanes until you need to exit.

Many freeways have a carpool lane, which only cars carrying at least two or three people (depending on the signs) can use. This is not a members-only scheme – if you fit the criterion, you can use the lane, but make sure you get out of it well before your exit. On your own? Keep out of carpool lanes. Fines are steep.

All non-freeways are known as surface streets. When you merge on to a freeway from a surface street, accelerate to freeway speed; similarly, be prepared to brake sharply when exiting. Freeway exits are marked by the name of the surface street with which they link; for all businesses in this guide, we've included a convenient freeway route and exit. However, always plan your route before you leave. If you don't know your entrance and exit and the direction you need to go when you find it (north, south, east or west), you may find yourself being forced off at the wrong intersection.

On surface streets, you can turn right on a red light if your way is clear, and the speed limit is 35mph. At four-way stop signs, 'courtesy driving' is expected: cars cross in the order they arrive at the junction. Seatbelts are compulsory. If you break down, look for yellow call boxes on the sides of major freeways and some roads in LA County, but a cellphone provides more security. However, note that using a non-hands-free cellphone while driving is now illegal. And, staying with the law for a moment, the drink-driving laws across LA are strict and not to be tested.

Large and potentially dangerous intersections, where you should take special care, include the following:

West LA Santa Monica Boulevard at Westwood Avenue; Bundy Drive at Pico Boulevard; Sepulveda Boulevard at National Avenue.
Westwood Wilshire Boulevard at Westwood Avenue.

Beverly Hills Wilshire Boulevard at Santa Monica Boulevard.
West Hollywood W Sunset Boulevard at N Crescent Heights Boulevard, N Harper Avenue, N Gardner Avenue.
Downtown S Alvarado Street at W 3rd Street; S Broadway at W 7th Street; Aliso at N Los Angeles Street; S Hill Street at W Jefferson Boulevard; S Main Street at E 2nd Street.

The American Automobile Association (or 'Triple A') offers maps and guides, free if you're a member or belong to an affiliated club (such as the British AA). Many hotels offer discounts to AAA members. There are offices all over LA; check online for more.

American Automobile Association (AAA) *2601 S Figueroa Street, at W Adams Boulevard, Downtown (1-213 741 3686/www.aaa-calif.com). I-110, exit Adams Boulevard west.* **Open** 9am-5pm Mon-Fri.

Car hire

To rent a car, you'll need a credit card and a driver's licence (British licences are valid). Most firms won't rent to anyone under 25; those that do often add a surcharge. The national rental firms, which tend to offer the best deals, have 1-800 numbers and offer online booking (*see below*).

Rates seesaw wildly. It can pay to book weeks ahead: you can put a hold on a car without committing yourself to pay for it. You may qualify for a discount: members of the AAA and affiliated foreign clubs are eligible, and corporate deals are often available. As a rule, you won't be allowed to take a rental car into Mexico.

All quotes from US websites will exclude insurance. US travellers may be covered by your car rental insurance at home; always check before setting out. If not, you'll have to take out liability insurance (SLI) and collision damage waiver (CDW) with the rental firm, which together usually total around $25-$30 a day.

Travellers from outside the US have several choices. The simplest is to book via the firm's US website and pay the expensive insurance premiums. UK residents should try the car hire firms' dedicated UK sites, where quotes include insurance. UK travellers who regularly travel in the US should consider www.insurance4carhire.com, where the comprehensive annual policies can save drivers a fortune over the rates levied by the rental firms themselves.

Car rental companies

Alamo *US: 1-800 462 5266/ www.goalamo.com. UK: 0870 400 4562/www.alamo.co.uk.*
Avis *US: 1-800 331 1212/ www.avis.com. UK: 0844 581 0147/ www.avis.co.uk.*
Budget *US: 1-800 527 0700/ www.budget.com. UK: 0844 581 2231/www.budget.co.uk.*
Dollar *US: 1-800 800 3665/ www.dollar.com. UK: 0800 085 4578/www.dollar.co.uk.*
Enterprise *US: 1-800 261 7331/ www.enterprise.com. UK: 0870 350 3000/www.enterprise.com/uk.*
Hertz *US: 1-800 654 3131/ www.hertz.com. UK: 0870 844 8844/ www.hertz.co.uk.*
National *US: 1-800 227 7368. UK: 0116 217 3884. Both: www.nationalcar.com.*
Rent-a-Wreck *1-800 944 7501/ www.rent-a-wreck.com.*
Thrifty *US: 1-800 847 4389/ www.thrifty.com. UK: 01494 751540/www.thrifty.co.uk.*

Parking

Parking restrictions vary by street, and the signs detailing them are far from clear. Don't block driveways or fire hydrants, and pay attention to kerb markings: if they're red, you're risking a big fine or, worse, getting towed. Check signs on your side of the block, which should detail parking laws. Most streets have street-cleaning days when parking is illegal; others allow permit parking only after 6pm and at weekends. All parking tickets accrued while in a rented vehicle are your responsibility.

Parking meters and free or cheap car parks are plentiful.

Directory

Most parking meters take quarters (25¢), dimes (10¢) and nickels (5¢). In some bars and restaurants, you can use valet parking; you'll need to tip the valet ($2-$5) on top of the parking fee, but it's cheaper than paying a fine. If you do get nabbed, call the number listed on the ticket; you can usually pay with a credit card.

The LAPD suggests you keep your rental agreement with you at all times in case your car gets towed or stolen (most people stick it in the glove compartment – bad idea). If you do get towed, call the nearest police precinct to find out where the car has been taken. To reclaim it, you'll need your rental papers, the car's licence number, your passport or driving licence and cash to pay the parking ticket, anywhere from $100 and up.

Public transport

LA's public transport system is run by the **Metropolitan Transportation Authority** (MTA). For information on the network, see **www.metro.net**, where you'll find timetables, maps, fare information and an interactive journey planner. If you can't get online, a journey-planner service is available by calling 1-800 266 6883.

We've listed a variety of bus routes for almost every venue featured in this book. Note, though, that Downtown is served by innumerable buses. We've listed a variety of buses for these venues, but if you catch any bus that passes through central Downtown and your destination is also in central Downtown, you'll be no more than a 15-minute walk from your destination.

Buses in LA run every 5-10 minutes on the main routes, less often at night. On main crosstown routes, the service is 24-hour, but there's only one bus an hour after 11pm. For lost property, see p308.

MTA Customer Centres
Miracle Mile *5301 Wilshire Boulevard, at S La Brea Avenue, Miracle Mile. Bus 20, 212, 312/I-10, exit La Brea Avenue north.* **Open** 9am-5pm Mon-Fri. **Map** p328 D4.
Union Station *800 N Alameda Street, at Los Angeles Street. Metro Union Station/bus 33, 40, 42, 68, 70, 71, 78, 79/US 101, exit Alameda Street north.* **Open** 6am-6.30pm Mon-Fri. **Map** p331 D1.
East LA *4501B Whittier Boulevard, at S Ford Boulevard. Bus 18, 256, 720/I-5, exit Olympic Boulevard east.* **Open** 10am-6pm Tue-Sat.
Baldwin Hills *3650 Martin Luther King Boulevard, at Crenshaw Boulevard. Bus 40, 42, 210, 710, 740/I-10, exit Crenshaw Boulevard south.* **Open** 10am-6pm Tue-Sat.

MTA buses

The MTA's 2,000-plus white-and-orange MTA buses cover more than 180 routes across LA. Red 'Rapid' buses cover many of the major routes but make fewer stops.

The fare on all MTA bus routes is $1.25; a further 30¢ is required for a transfer to a bus run by a separate agency (for example, Culver City buses; *see p305*). An all-day pass is $5; weekly ($17) and monthly ($62) passes are also available.

All MTA bus routes in LA are given a number according to the areas they cover:

1-99 Local services to and from Downtown
100-199 Local east–west services that don't pass through Downtown
200-299 Local north–south services that don't pass through Downtown
300-399 Limited-stop services, usually on routes also served by local services; for example, the 302, which takes the same route along Sunset Boulevard as the 2 but makes fewer stops
400-499 Express services to and from Downtown
500-599 Express services in other areas
600-699 Special services (such as the 605, a shuttle bus to the LA County/USC Medical Center)
700-799 Rapid bus services (similar to limited-stop services detailed above)

The following are among LA's more useful crosstown bus services. For full details on routes and services, download maps from www.metro.net.

2 Runs along Sunset Boulevard from its junction with the PCH to Westwood. From here, it runs along the southern border of the UCLA and then follows Sunset through Hollywood, Silver Lake and Echo Park to Downtown, where it follows Hill Street south to Venice Boulevard. The return route is identical save for the fact that it heads north through Downtown on Broadway rather than Hill, and that at Pacific Palisades, it takes a left on to Temescal Avenue to the PCH. The 302 takes an identical route as far as the northern edge of Downtown, but makes fewer stops.
4 Runs along Santa Monica Boulevard from Santa Monica to the junction with Sunset Boulevard in Silver Lake, whereupon it follows the same route as the 2. The 704 is the limited-stop version.
16 Runs between Century City and Downtown LA, following 3rd Street for almost its entire length. The main exception is between Beverly Hills and Century City, where it runs along Santa Monica Boulevard, and within Downtown, where it runs along either 5th Street (westbound) or 6th Street (eastbound). The 316 is its limited-stop alternative.
20 Runs the length of Wilshire Boulevard from Santa Monica to Downtown, whereupon it takes 6th Street (east) or 7th Street (west). The 720 offers a limited-stop alternative.
212 Runs between the Hollywood-Vine Metro station and Inglewood, along Hollywood Boulevard and La Brea Avenue.
217 Runs between the Vermont-Sunset Metro station and the West LA Transit Center, along Hollywood Boulevard and Fairfax Avenue.

LA DASH buses

DASH stands for Downtown Area Short Hop; its six express shuttles (A, B, C, D, E and F) run every 5-20 minutes and serve many of Downtown's important sites, including the Convention Center, City Hall and Union Station.

Despite its name, there are a number of DASH shuttles in other areas of LA. Fares on all DASH routes are 25¢. For more, see www.ladottransit.com, or call 1-213 808 2273, 1-310 808 2273 or 1-323 808 2273. The following are among the most useful routes:

Fairfax (abbreviated in our listings to LDF) Links the Beverly Center with the Melrose District, the Fairfax District and the Miracle Mile.
Hollywood (LDH) Loops around Hollywood, chiefly (but not exclusively) on Highland, Franklin, Fountain and Vermont Avenues.
Hollywood-West Hollywood (LDHWH) Runs between the Beverly Center and the Hollywood-Highland Metro station, via La Cienega and Sunset Boulevards.
Hollywood-Wilshire (LDHWI) Runs between the Hollywood-Vine and Wilshire-Western Metro stations, via Vine Street, Sunset Boulevard, Gower Street, Melrose Avenue and Western Avenue.

Municipal buses

Some areas have their own municipal bus services that complement the MTA services. Among them are the following:

Santa Monica (denoted with prefix 'SM' in this book; SM1, SM2, etc) The Big Blue Bus company serves Santa Monica, Venice and parts of West LA. The fare on all routes is 75¢, with a 50¢ inter-agency transfer. For more, call 1-310 451 5444 or see www.bigbluebus.com.
Culver City (denoted with prefix 'C') Fares on all Culver City's bus routes are 75¢, with inter-agency transfers costing 25¢. Call 1-310 253 6500 or see www.culvercity.org/bus for details.
West Hollywood Cityline is a shuttle service in West Hollywood. The service runs only 9am-6pm Mon-Fri, 10am-6pm Sat. The fare is 25¢. For more, call 1-800 447 2189.
San Gabriel Valley The Foothill Transit service mostly serves the San Gabriel and Pomona Valleys. Fares are $1-$4.40. For details, call 1-626 967 3147 or see www.foothilltransit.org.
Orange County (denoted with prefix 'OC') For details, call 1-714 636 7433 or see www.octa.net. Most fares are $1.25.

Trains

LA's **Metro** system covers only a limited area of the city at present. However, it is expanding, and it can be a very convenient way to get around, especially to and from Downtown. The fare structure is identical to that on the MTA buses; daily, weekly and monthly passes can be used on both trains and buses. Trains run approximately 5am to 12.30am daily. For a map of the network, see p336; below is a summary of its four lines.

Red line The most useful line for visitors, the Red line links Downtown, Westlake, Hollywood, Universal Studios and North Hollywood. At North Hollywood, travellers can connect to the Orange line: it's a bus service that looks and acts like a train line, running in its own dedicated busway between North Hollywood and Canoga Park. At the other end of the line, the Red line connects with Union Station and the Gold line.
Purple line The Purple line follows the Red line route from Union Station to Wilshire-Vermont, then continues along Wilshire for two further stops before terminating at Wilshire-Western. The MTA hopes to extend the line all the way west to UCLA, but such work is a long way off.
Gold line The newest of the Metro lines, the Gold line begins at Union Station, where it connects with the Red line, and heads north-east through Chinatown, Highland Park and Pasadena to Sierra Madre. Due to open in late 2009, an extension to the Gold line will run south through Little Tokyo and out through Boyle Heights and into East LA.
Blue line Starting at the Red line station at 7th and Figueroa, the Blue Line heads south through South Central all the way to Long Beach.
Green line This overground route links the area around LAX (there's no station at the airport) with South Central and Norwalk to the east.
Expo line Currently under construction, this new line will run south from the 7th-Figueroa station to Exposition Park, before heading west to Culver City. The line is due for completion in June 2010.

Taxis & limos

Because of the city's size, taxis aren't a cheap way of getting around LA. Nor are they convenient (there are some taxi ranks, but you can't hail taxis on the street) or especially straightforward (you may even have to give the driver directions). The basic fare is $2.65; each additional one-seventh of a mile (or 47.5 seconds of waiting time) will cost you a further 35¢. There's a $2.50 surcharge on all fares leaving LAX. Large, licensed firms include **Bell Cab** (1-888 235 5222, www.bellcab.com), **Checker Cab** (1-800 300 5007), **Independent Taxi** (1-800 521 8294, www.taxi4u.com), **United Independent** (1-800 822 8294, www.united taxi.com) and **Yellow Cab Co** (1-877 733 3305, www.layellow cab.com). For more details, see www.taxicabsla.org. For lost property, see p308.

If you're really flush, you might want to consider hiring a limousine. The cost of hiring one starts at around $50-$60 an hour, usually with a three- to four-hour minimum; on top of this, the driver will expect a decent tip. Companies include **Alliance** (1-800 679 5466, www.alliancelimo.net) and **Everest** (1-866 308 8089, www.everestla.com).

Cycling

There are bike paths down the coast through Santa Monica and Venice, and there are bike lanes in other parts of LA; you can also mountain-bike in Griffith Park and Topanga Canyon. Otherwise, though, the volume of traffic and distances involved make cycling tough. For more on bikes, see p271.

Walking

Certain sections of LA – Santa Monica and Venice, Beverly Hills, parts of West Hollywood, central Hollywood, the centres of Los Feliz and Silver Lake, pretty much all of Downtown – are easily covered on foot. Jaywalking – crossing the street anywhere except at a designated pedestrian crossing – can get you a $100 ticket; police don't generally enforce the penalty on tourists, but it's best to be on the safe side.

Resources A-Z

Addresses

Written addresses follow the standard US format. Where applicable, the apartment or suite number usually appears after the street address, followed on the next line by the city name and the zip code. For more on street-numbering, *see p71* **Street talk**.

Age restrictions

Buying alcohol 21.
Drinking alcohol 21.
Driving 16.
Sex (heterosexual couples) 18.
Sex (homosexual couples) 18.
Smoking 18.

Attitude & etiquette

California is famously casual, but there are distinct codes within that bracket in LA. If you're here on business, make it expensive, stylish casual; if you're here to go out, dress up – even in a casual way – rather than down. Few restaurants operate a specific dress code, but nor do the posher places approve of torn jeans and scruffy sneakers. Pay attention to social pleasantries.

Business

Angelenos work hard. The city's working day starts early and finishes late, and ambition fuels overtime. Long commutes mean little drinking; business is generally done over still or sparkling, not red or white.

The LA affliction of 'flaking' (making and then rescheduling appointments) occurs both in business and socially – it's nothing personal. That said, if you're here with cap in hand, don't do the flaking yourself: ensure you know your route and leave time to park. And be upfront: don't be shy about name-dropping, and don't be ashamed to talk money.

Conventions & conferences

The **LA Convention Center** (1201 S Figueroa Street, at W Pico Boulevard, Downtown, 11-213 741 1151, www.lacclink. com) is a giant complex at the intersection of I-10 and I-110. The facilities are good, but until LA Live is completed in 2010 (*see p119*), the only hotel nearby is the Figueroa. Allow a ten-minute wait for parking.

Couriers & shippers

DHL *1-800 225 5345/www.dhl.com.* **Credit** AmEx, DC, Disc, MC, V. **FedEx** *1-800 463 3339/www.fedex. com.* **Credit** AmEx, DC, Disc, MC, V. **UPS** *1-800 742 5877/www.ups.com.* **Credit** AmEx, DC, MC, V.

Office services

Kinko's *5500 Wilshire Boulevard, at S Dunsmuir Avenue (1-323 937 0126/www.lacc.com). I-10, exit La Brea Avenue north.* **Open** 24hrs daily. **Credit** AmEx, DC, Disc, MC, V. **Map** p328 D4. **Other locations** throughout LA.
Mail Boxes Etc *1-800 789 4623/ www.mbe.com.* **Open** hrs vary. **Credit** AmEx, DC, Disc, MC, V. Mail forwarding services.
Office Depot *2020 Figueroa Street, at 20th Street, Downtown (1-213 741 0576/www.officedepot.com). Metro Grand/bus 81, 381/I-110, exit Adams Boulevard west.* **Open** 8am-8pm Mon-Fri; 9am-7pm Sat; 10am-7pm Sun. **Credit** AmEx, DC, Disc, MC, V. **Other locations** throughout LA.

Useful organisations

Los Angeles Area Chamber of Commerce *350 S Bixel Street, at W 3rd Street, Downtown, CA 90017 (1-213 580 7500/www.lachamber. org). Bus 14, 16/I-110, exit 3rd Street west.* **Open** 8am-5pm Mon-Fri.

Consumer

Department of Consumer Affairs *1-800 952 5210/deaf callers 1-800 326 2297/www.dca.ca.gov.* Investigates complaints.
Better Business Bureau of the Southland *1-310 945 3166/ www.bbbsouthland.org.* Useful if you need to file a complaint.

Customs

International travellers go through US Customs directly after Immigration. Give the official the white form you were given, and should have completed, on the plane.

Foreign visitors can import the following items duty-free: 200 cigarettes or 50 cigars (not Cuban; over-18s) or 2kg of smoking tobacco; one litre of

---

Travel advice

For up-to-date information on travel to a specific country – including the latest news on safety and security, health issues, local laws and customs – contact your home country government's department of foreign affairs. Most have websites packed with useful advice for would-be travellers.

Australia
www.smartraveller.gov.au

Canada
www.voyage.gc.ca

New Zealand
www.safetravel.govt.nz

Republic of Ireland
foreignaffairs.gov.ie

UK
www.fco.gov.uk/travel

USA
www.state.gov/travel

wine or spirits (over-21s); and up to $100 in gifts ($800 for returning Americans). You must declare and maybe forfeit plants or foodstuffs. See the **US Customs** site (www.cbp. gov/xp/cgov/travel) for more.

HM Revenue & Customs allows travellers returning to the UK to bring in £145 worth of goods tax-free.

Disabled

California's strict building codes ensure equal access to all city facilities, businesses, parking lots, restaurants, hotels and other public places. Only older buildings are likely to present problems, and many of those have been retrofitted. All MTA buses have wheelchair lifts, and Metro provides large-type and Braille-encoded 'Flash Books' for signalling the correct bus. For more, call the **Disabled Riders** line on 1-800 621 7828 or 1-213 922 7023.

Access Services *1-800 827 0829/ www.asila.org.* Refers mobility-impaired people and seniors to door-to-door transportation services.
Department on Disability *1-213 485 6334/www.lacity.org/dod.* Information and resources.
Society for the Advancement of Travel for the Handicapped *1-212 447 7284/www.sath.org.* Advice and referrals for disabled travellers planning trips to the US.

Drugs

Drugs are not uncommon on LA's nightlife scene, but the local authorities take a zero-tolerance approach to drug use and trafficking. Be careful.

Electricity

The US uses a 110-120V, 60-cycle AC voltage. Except for dual-voltage flat-pin shavers, most foreign visitors will need to run appliances through an adaptor. Note that DVDs purchased here will only work in DVD players equipped with multi-region capabilities.

Embassies & consulates

Australia *2029 Century Park East, Suite 3150, at W Olympic Boulevard, Century City CA 90067 (1-310 229 2300/www.losangeles.consulate.gov. au). I-405, exit Olympic Boulevard.*
Canada *550 S Hope Street, between W 5th & W 6th Streets, Los Angeles, CA 90071 (1-213 346 2700/http:// geo.international.gc.ca/can-am/los_ angeles). I-110, exit 6th Street east.*
New Zealand *2425 Olympic Boulevard, Suite 600E, Santa Monica, CA 90404 (1-310 566 6555/www.nzcgla.com). I-10, exit Cloverfield Boulevard north.*
Republic of Ireland *100 Pine Street, San Francisco, CA 94111 (1-415 392 4214/www.irelandemb.org).* This office covers the western states.
UK *11766 Wilshire Boulevard, Suite 1200, at Granville Avenue, Los Angeles, CA 90025 (1-310 481 0031/www.britainusa.com/la). I-405, exit Wilshire Boulevard west.*

Emergencies

For hospitals, *see below*; for helplines, *see p308*; for the police, *see p310*.

Police, fire, ambulance *911.*
Coast Guard *1-310 215 2112.*
Poison Information Center *1-800 222 1222/1-323 222 3212.*

Gay & lesbian

LA Gay & Lesbian Center *1625 N Schrader Boulevard, between Hollywood Boulevard & Selma Avenue, Hollywood (1-323 993 7400/www.lagaycenter.org). Metro Hollywood-Vine/bus 163, 180, 181, 210, 212, 217, 312, 363, 780, LDH/US 101, exit Vine Street south.* **Open** 9am-9pm Mon-Fri; 9am-1pm Sat (pharmacy only). **Map** p329 B2. Myriad resources for LGBT locals.
Progressive Health Services *8235 Santa Monica Boulevard, between N Harper & N La Jolla Avenues, West Hollywood (1-323 650 1508/www.progressivehealth. org). Bus 4, 218/I-10, exit La Cienega Boulevard north.* **Open** appointment only. **Map** p328 B2. A wide range of medical services, with a number of clinics devoted to the LGBT communities.

Health

Ensure you have full medical insurance, preferably the kind that pays upfront. Emergency

rooms are obliged by law to treat emergencies, though they will try to make you pay.

If your problem is not an emergency and you don't have insurance, try the **Saban Free Clinic**, which offers free medical and dental care. However, don't abuse the service – it's there to provide care to locals who can't afford insurance – and don't expect an immediate appointment.

Saban Free Clinic *8405 Beverly Boulevard, at N Orlando Avenue, West Hollywood (1-323 653 1990/ www.lafreeclinic.org). Bus 14/I-10, exit La Cienega Boulevard north.* **Open** *Medical* 8am-8pm Mon-Thur; noon-4.30pm Fri. *Dental* 7.45am-9pm Mon, Tue, Thur; 8.45am-9pm Wed; 7.30am-5pm Fri. **Map** p328 B3. **Other locations** 6043 Hollywood Boulevard, Hollywood; 5205 Melrose Avenue, Fairfax District.

Accident & emergency

The hospitals below have 24-hour emergency rooms.

Cedars-Sinai Medical Center *8700 Beverly Boulevard, at George Burns Road, West Hollywood (1-310 423 3277/www.csmc.edu). Bus 14, 105, 305/I-10, exit La Cienega Boulevard north.* **Map** p328 A3.
Century City Doctors' Hospital *2070 Century Park E, between Constellation & Olympic Boulevards, Century City (1-310 772 4000/ www.ccdoctorshospital.com). Bus 16, 28/I-405, exit Santa Monica Boulevard east.* **Map** p327 C4.
Children's Hospital of Los Angeles *4650 W Sunset Boulevard, at N Vermont Avenue, Los Feliz (1-323 660 2450/www.chla.org). Metro Vermont-Sunset/bus 2, 204, 702, 754/US 101, exit Vermont Avenue north.* **Map** p330 A3.
St John's Health Center *1328 22nd Street, at Santa Monica Boulevard, Santa Monica (310 829 5511/www.stjohns.org). Bus 4, SM1, SM10/I-10, exit 26th Street north.* **Map** p326 C3.

Contraception & abortion

Family Planning Associates Medical Group *12304 Santa Monica Boulevard, at Wellesley Avenue, West LA (1-800 492 3764/ 1-310 820 8084/www.fpamg.net). Bus 4, SM1, SM10/I-405, exit Santa Monica Boulevard west.* **Open** 8am-4.30pm Mon-Fri; 7am-2pm Sat.

Directory

Dentists

The **LADS** offers referrals to approved practices. For the **Saban Free Clinic**, see p307.

LA Dental Society 1-213 380 7669/www.ladentalsociety.com. **Open** 8.30am-4.30pm Mon-Thur; 8.30am-4pm Fri.

Hospitals

See p307.

Opticians

See p206.

Pharmacies

See p206.

STDs, HIV & AIDS

There are also HIV/AIDs clinics at the **LA Gay & Lesbian Center** (the Jeffrey Goodman Special Care Clinic) and **Progressive Health Services**. For both, see p307.

AIDS Healthcare Foundation 99 S La Cienega Boulevard, at S San Vicente Boulevard, West Hollywood (24hr hotline 1-800 797 1717/1-310 657 9353/www.aidshealth.org). Bus 16, 105/I-10, exit La Cienega Boulevard north. **Open** 8.30am-5.30pm Mon-Fri. **Map** p328 B3. Quality care, regardless of the patient's ability to pay.

Helplines

Alcoholics Anonymous 1-323 936 4343/www.alcoholics-anonymous.org. **Child Abuse Hotline** 1-800 540 4000. **Gamblers Anonymous** 1-877 423 6752/www.gamblersanonymous.org. **Peace over Violence: Rape & Battering Hotline** 1-310 392 8381/www.peaceoverviolence.org. **LA Suicide Prevention Hotline** 1-877 727 4747/ www.suicidepreventioncenter.org. **Narcotics Anonymous** 1-800 863 2962/www.todayna.org. **CDC STD & AIDS Hotline** 1-800 232 4636/www.cdc.gov/hiv.

ID

Even if you look 30, you may need a photo ID – preferably a driver's licence with a photograph included – in order to get served in many of the city's bars.

Insurance

Non-nationals should arrange comprehensive baggage, trip-cancellation and medical insurance before they leave home. Medical centres will ask for details of your insurance company and your policy number if you require treatment; keep the details with you at all times.

Internet

Getting online in LA is a cinch. Almost all hotels offer some form of in-room, high-speed access for travellers, either via cable or (increasingly) via a wireless network; many also have a communal computer on which guests can get online. Many cafés (see pp170-174) also offer wireless access, often for free. And free Wi-Fi zones have been set up in parts of Culver City, Hermosa Beach and Long Beach, and Pershing Square in Downtown.

If you don't have your own laptop, a number of locations have open terminals. Chief among them are the numerous branches of the LA Public Library system (see below).

Left luggage

The **LAX International Baggage Service**, while unrelated to LAX itself, offers storage of baggage outside the airport. For details, call 1-310 863 4109. There are no lockers at Union Station.

Legal help

If you get sued, or if you think you have a claim against someone, there are hundreds of attorneys listed in the *Yellow Pages*, but you're best off getting a recommendation. If you're arrested and held in custody, call your insurer's emergency number or contact your consulate (see p307).

Libraries

The main branch of the LA Public Library network is the **Richard J Riordan Central Library** in Downtown LA (see p116), where facilities include free internet access. For details of other libraries, see www.lapl.org.

Lost property

If you've lost something at **LAX**, try your airline, then the general lost property number (1-310 417 0440). For goods lost on **MTA buses or trains**, call 1-323 937 8920. For items left in **taxis**, call the firm in question (see p287).

Media

Newspapers

The **Los Angeles Times** (www.latimes.com, 50¢) has been the only big newspaper in town for years. Its news coverage can be impressive, but the future looks cloudy: the paper announced plans to cut 17 per cent of its newsgathering staff, and reduce the paper's size by 15 per cent. Other strengths include arts (check out the 'Calendar' section on Sundays) and the entertainment industry; weaknesses include spotty business coverage and a below-par sports section.

Magazines

The monthly **Los Angeles Magazine** (www.lamag.com, $4.95) is an enjoyable blend of fawning celebrity profiles, insider enthusiasms and long-form reporting. Two dailies, the **Hollywood Reporter** (www.hollywoodreporter.com) and **Daily Variety** (www. variety.com) have the scoop on industry deals; both are $1.50.

The biggest of the city's free weeklies, **LA Weekly** (www.laweekly.com) is a mix of solid but sometimes over-long reportage, criticism that ranges from the excellent (food critic Jonathan Gold) to the abysmal; and listings that are laudably comprehensive but presented in such a fashion as to render them more or less impenetrable. Since 2008, it's had competition from the *Tribune*-owned **Metromix** (http://losangeles.metromix.com); the small but worthwhile **LA Citybeat** (www.lacitybeat.com) has been snipping at its heels for longer. All three are available in bars and clubs, and from distribution boxes on streetcorners.

Radio

Thanks to the car culture, radio plays a crucial role in LA life. As such, it's a shock to find the airwaves are awash with rubbish: blustery phone-ins, drab classic rock, over-familiar hits. Getting a hire car with satellite radio is a smart idea.

COMMERCIAL MUSIC RADIO

LA's major hip hop station is **Power 106** (KPWR, 105.9 FM, www.power106.fm). **Hot 92.3** (KHHT, 92.3 FM, www.hot923.com) serves up old-school R&B; alt-rock comes courtesy of **Indie 103.1** (KDLD, 103.1 FM, www.indie1031.fm) and **KROQ** (106.7 FM, www.kroq.com). **KLOS** (95.5 FM, www.955klos.com) mixes soft and classic rock.

PUBLIC & COLLEGE RADIO

The best station in LA, and one of the most influential stations in the US, is the NPR-affiliated **KCRW** (89.9 FM, www.kcrw.com), which mixes intelligent news and talk with approachable but slightly off-radar music. Elsewhere on the dial, Loyola

Marymount's **KXLU** (88.9 FM, www.kxlu.com) provides noisy and nice indie sounds, while USC's **KUSC** (91.5 FM, www.kusc.org) mixes classical music and talk. Classical fans should also try Cal State's **KCSN** (88.5 FM, www.kcsn.org); jazz radio is limited to Long Beach State's **KKJZ** (89.9 FM, www.jazzandblues.org).

TALK RADIO

All talk, all the time. **KFI** (640 AM, www.kfi640.com) hosts Rush Limbaugh (9am-noon Mon-Fri) and pop psychologist Dr Laura (noon-3pm Mon-Fri). **KABC** (790 AM, www.kabc.com) offers the outspoken likes of Bill O'Reilly (9-11am Mon-Fri) and Sean Hannity (noon-3pm Mon-Fri); liberals have KCRW's Warren Olney, whose 'Which Way LA?' (7-7.30pm Mon-Thur) and national 'To the Point' (noon-1pm Mon-Fri) are the best issues-forum radio shows in California.

For news, **KNX** (1070 AM, www.knx1070.com), **KFWB** (980 AM, www.kfwb.com) and **KNNZ** (540 AM) offer 24-hour, up-to-the-minute coverage.

Television

LA has affiliates of the three major networks: CBS (**KCBS**, channel 2), NBC (**KNBC**, channel 4) and ABC (**KABC**, channel 7). Competition comes from Fox (**KTTV**, channel 11), WB (**KTLA**, channel 5) and UPN (**KCOP**, channel 13). **KWHY** (channel 22), **KMEX** (channel 34) and **KVEA** (channel 52) serve the city's Latino population, while **KSCI** (channel 18) and **KDOC** (channel 56) offer a mix of Japanese, Korean, Chinese and Armenian programming.

Money

The US dollar ($) is divided into 100 cents (¢). Coins run from the copper penny (1¢) to the silver nickel (5¢), dime

(10¢), quarter (25¢), the less common half-dollar (50¢) and the rarely seen dollar (silver and gold). Notes or 'bills' are all the same green colour and size; they come in denominations of $1, $5, $10, $20, $50 and $100.

Credit cards are accepted almost everywhere in LA. **MasterCard** (abbreviated as MC throughout this book) and **Visa** (V) are the most popular, with **American Express** (AmEx) also common. Thanks to a 2004 agreement between MC and **Diners Club** (DC), all businesses that accept MC can now accept DC. In practice, though, many businesses seem unaware of the agreement – don't be surprised if your card is rejected by staff. In 2008, the **Discover** network purchased DC; it remains to be seen what affect this will have on the acceptance of either card. If you've lost your card, *see p310* for a list of emergency contacts.

Travellers' cheques are still accepted in some shops and restaurants, albeit with some proof of identity (such as a passport). Draw the cheques in US dollars before your trip.

Banks & ATMs

Banks in LA are usually open from 9am or 10am to 4.30pm Monday to Thursday; until 6pm on Friday; and from 9am or 10am until 2pm or 3pm on Saturday. Some, but not all, have bureaux de change. Call the numbers below to locate your nearest bank branch.

There are ATMs all over LA: in banks, in some stores and even in the occasional bar. ATMs accept AmEx, MC and V, as well as some debit cards. However, you may be charged a fee each time you make a withdrawal.

Bank of America 1-213 312 9000/ *www.bankofamerica.com.*
Citibank 1-800 374 9700/ *www.citibank.com.*
Wells Fargo 1-800 869 3557/ *www.wellsfargo.com.*

Directory

Bureaux de change

There are a number of bureaux de change at LAX. However, you may get a better rate away from the airport.

If you need money wired to you, **Western Union** (1-800 325 6000, www.westernunion. com) can receive funds from anywhere in the world; high commission fees underscores their 'emergency' status.

American Express Travel Services *327 N Beverly Drive, between Brighton & Dayton Ways, Beverly Hills (1-310 274 8277/http:// travel.americanexpress.com). Bus 20, 720/I-10, exit Robertson north.* **Open** *10am-6pm Mon-Fri; 10am-3pm Sat.* **Map** *p327 C3.* **Other locations** *8493 W 3rd Street, West Hollywood (1-310 659 1682); 269 S Lake Avenue, Pasadena (1-626 449 2281).*

Lost/stolen credit cards

American Express *1-800 528 4800/www.americanexpress.com.*
Diners Club *1-800 234 6377/ www.dinersclub.com.*
Discover *1-800 347 2683/ www.discovercard.com.*
MasterCard *1-800 622 7747/ www.mastercard.com.*
Visa *1-800 847 2911/www.visa.com.*

Tax

Sales tax in Los Angeles County is 8.25%; food purchased as groceries is exempt. Hotel room tax is a terrifying 14%. In Orange County, sales tax is 7.75%.

Opening hours

Though many establishments in the LA region open at 8am or 9am, the magic hour for shoppers is 10am, when most businesses open. Shops are usually open until 6pm, with malls open until 9pm or later. Museums generally welcome visitors until 6pm, though many are open later on one or two days during the week. Bars must stop serving alcohol by 2am.

Police

For emergencies, *see p307*. For non-emergencies, use the police stations below; www.lapd online.org has details of others.

Beverly Hills *464 N Rexford Drive, at Santa Monica Boulevard (1-310 281 2100/www.beverlyhills.org). Bus 4, 14, 16, 20, 316, 704, 720/ I-405, exit Wilshire Boulevard east.*
Downtown *251 E 6th Street, at Maple Avenue (1-213 485 3294/ www.lapdonline.org). Metro Pershing Square/bus 16, 18, 28, 53, 62/I-110, exit 6th Street east.*
Hollywood *1358 N Wilcox Avenue, between De Longpre & Fountain Avenues (1-213 972 2971/www.lapd online.org). Metro Hollywood-Vine/ bus 1180, 181, 210, 212, 217/US 101, exit Hollywood Boulevard west.*
Santa Monica *333 Olympic Drive, between Main & 4th Streets (1-310 395 9931/www.santamonicapd.org). Bus 33, 333, SM1, SM2, SM8, SM10/I-10, exit 4th-5th Street south.*
West Hollywood *780 N San Vicente Boulevard, at Santa Monica Boulevard (1-310 855 8850/www. wehosheriff.com). Bus 4, 105, 305/I-10, exit La Cienega Boulevard north.*

Postal services

Post offices are usually open 9am to 5pm, but often have last collections at 6pm. Many are open on Saturdays from 9am to 1pm or 2pm. Stamps for postcards within the US cost 27¢ or, for large postcards, 42¢; for Europe, the charge is 94¢. Below are listed several post offices around the city; for others, dial 1-800 275 8777 or check www.usps.com.

Beverly Hills *325 N Maple Drive, between Burton Way & W 3rd Street. Bus 16/I-10, exit Robertson Boulevard north.* **Open** *9am-5pm Mon-Fri; 9am-1pm Sat.* **Map** *p327 D2.*
Downtown *505 S Flower Street, at W 5th Street. Metro 7th Street-Metro Center/bus 16, 18, 55, 62/I-110, exit 6th Street east.* **Open** *8.30am-5.30pm Mon-Fri.* **Map** *p331 B3.*
Santa Monica *1248 5th Street, at Arizona Avenue. Bus 4, 304, SM2, SM3, SM4/I-10, exit 4th-5th Street north.* **Open** *9am-5pm Mon-Fri; 9am-3pm Sat.* **Map** *p326 B2.*
West Hollywood *1125 N Fairfax Avenue, at Santa Monica Boulevard. Bus 4, 217, 218, 704/I-10, exit Fairfax Avenue north.* **Open** *8.30am-5pm Mon-Fri; 8.30am-3pm Sat.* **Map** *p328 C2.*

Poste restante

If you need to receive mail but don't know what your address will be, have it sent to: [your name], General Delivery, 1055 N Vignes Street, Los Angeles, CA 90012, USA. You can collect the parcel from this address, which is in Downtown LA (10am-2pm Mon-Fri).

Religion

Whether established religion or cult – if it exists, it's here.

Aatzei Chaim Synagogue *8018 W 3rd Street, at S Laurel Avenue, Fairfax District (1-323 782 1321). Bus 16, 217, 218, 316/I-10, exit Fairfax Avenue north.* **Map** *p328 C3.*
All Saints Episcopal Church *504 N Camden Drive, at Santa Monica Boulevard, Beverly Hills (1-310 275 0123/www.allsaintsbh.org). Bus 4, 16, 20,720/I-10, exit Robertson Boulevard north.* **Map** *p327 C3.*
Beth Israel Synagogue *8056 Beverly Boulevard, at S Crescent Heights Boulevard, West Hollywood (1-323 651 4022). Bus 14, 217, 218/I-10, exit La Cienega Boulevard north.* **Map** *p328 C3.*
Beverly Hills Presbyterian Church *505 N Rodeo Drive, at Santa Monica Boulevard, Beverly Hills (1-310 271 5194/www.bhpc.org). Bus 4, 16, 20, 316/I-10, exit Robertson Boulevard north.* **Map** *p327 C3.*
First Baptist Church of Hollywood *6682 Selma Avenue, at Las Palmas Avenue, Hollywood (1-323 464 7343). Metro Hollywood-Highland/bus 156, 163, 212, 217, 363, 656/US 101, exit Hollywood Boulevard west.* **Map** *p329 A2.*
Hope Lutheran Church of Hollywood *6720 Melrose Avenue, at N Citrus Avenue, Hollywood (1-323 938 9135/www.hopelutheran church.net). Bus 10, 210/I-10, exit La Brea Avenue north.* **Map** *p329 A3.*
Islamic Cultural Centre *434 S Vermont Avenue, between W 4th & W 5th Streets, Koreatown (1-213 382 9200/www.islamctr.org). Metro Wilshire-Vermont/bus 204, 754/I-10, exit Vermont Avenue north.*
St Mary of the Angels Anglican Church *4510 Finley Avenue, at Hillhurst Avenue, Los Feliz (1-323 660 3700/www.stmaryoftheangels. org). Bus 26, 180, 181/I-5, exit Los Feliz Boulevard east.* **Map** *p330 B2.*
St Monica Roman Catholic Church *725 California Avenue, at Lincoln Boulevard, Santa Monica (1-310 566 1500/www.stmonica.net). Bus 20, 720, SM2/I-10, exit Lincoln Boulevard north.* **Map** *p326 B2.*

Wat Thai Buddhist Temple
8225 Coldwater Canyon Avenue, at Roscoe Boulevard, North Hollywood (1-818 785 9552/www.watthaiusa.org). Bus 167/I-405, exit Roscoe Boulevard east.
Westwood United Methodist Church *10497 Wilshire Boulevard, at Warner Avenue, Westwood (1-310 474 4511). Bus 20/I-405, exit Wilshire Boulevard.* **Map** p327 A3.

Safety & security

LA is pretty safe, but it pays to be cautious: don't fumble with your wallet or a map in public; avoid walking alone at night; keep your doors locked while driving; and avoid parking in questionable areas. On foot, walk with confidence. As a motorist, avoid coming off the freeway in unfamiliar areas, never drive too slowly or too fast, and always carry a map and a phone. Areas in which to take particular care include parts of Venice, Koreatown, Silver Lake, Echo Park, Highland Park, Downtown, Watts and Compton.

Smoking

Smoking is banned in all enclosed public areas: shops, restaurants, cinemas, hotels (except some private rooms) and bars. Some bars and restaurants have terraces where smoking is allowed.

Study

Aside from the universities detailed below, there are numerous colleges devoted to film and TV. USC's **School of Cinematic Arts** (1-213 740 2235, www-cntv.usc.edu) has a great reputation, as does UCLA's **School of Theater, Film & Television** (1-310 825 5761, www.tft.ucla.edu).

California Institute of Technology *1200 E California University, Pasadena, CA 91125 (1-626 395 6811/www.caltech.edu).*
California State University *LA-area campuses in Alhambra, Fullerton Long Beach and Northridge (www.calstate.edu).*

Loyola Marymount University *1 LMU Drive, Los Angeles, CA 90045 (1-310 338 2700/www.lmu.edu).*
Pepperdine University *24255 Pacific Coast Highway, Malibu, CA 90263 (1-310 506 4000/www.pepperdine.edu).*
UCLA *See p88 **Walk**.*
USC *See p125.*

Telephones

Dialling & codes

LA is covered by a number of different area codes. Calling outside your area code from your hotel can be very costly – you're generally better off using a payphone or your cellphone (*see below*). Calls to numbers prefixed 1-800, 1-866, 1-877 or 1-888 are free.

Recent changes to the phone network mean that you must always dial **1 + area code + seven-digit number**, even if you're calling from a phone in the same code as the number you're dialling. All numbers in this book have been listed in this 11-digit format.

For international calls, dial 011 (the international access code), followed by the country code, followed by the number.

Local area codes
213 Downtown
310 Malibu, Santa Monica, Venice, Culver City, West LA, Westwood, Beverly Hills, parts of West Hollywood, Inglewood
323 parts of West Hollywood, Hollywood, East LA, South Central
562 Long Beach
626 San Gabriel Valley
714 Anaheim (northern Orange County)
818 San Fernando Valley
949 Laguna & Newport Beaches

International country codes
61 Australia
81 Japan
64 New Zealand
44 UK

Mobile phones

LA operates on the 1900mHz GSM frequency. Travellers with tri-band handsets should be able to connect to one of

the networks, assuming their service provider at home has an arrangement with a local network; the majority do, but it's worth checking before you depart. European visitors with only dual-band phones will need to rent a handset on arrival from a company such as **TripTel** (*see p210*).

Check the price of calls with your home service provider before you arrive. Rates may be hefty and, unlike in the UK, you'll be charged for receiving as well as making calls.

Operator services
Collect/reverse-charge calls *0.*
Local directory enquiries *411.*
National directory enquiries *1 + [area code] + 555 1212 (if you don't know the area code, dial 0 for the operator).*
International operator *00.*
Police, fire or medical emergencies *911.*

Public phones

Following a trend that's seen the number of payphones in the US halved since 1999, payphones are less common in LA than they once were, and many seem permanently broken. If you do find one, pick up the receiver, listen for a dialling tone and feed it change (50¢ for a local call; the cost increases with distance).

To make long-distance or international calls from a payphone, buy a phonecard from large stores such as Walgreens. The card will give you a fixed amount of talk-time to your chosen destination.

Time

California operates on **Pacific Standard Time**, eight hours behind GMT (London) and three hours behind Eastern Standard Time (New York). Clocks go forward by an hour on the second Sunday in March, and back on the first Sunday in November.

Directory

Climate

	Average high	Average low	Average rain
Jan	68°F (20°C)	48°F (9°C)	3.3in (8.5cm)
Feb	70°F (21°C)	50°F (10°C)	3.7in (9.4cm)
Mar	70°F (21°C)	52°F (11°C)	3.1in (8.0cm)
Apr	73°F (23°C)	54°F (12°C)	0.8in (2.1cm)
May	75°F (24°C)	58°F (14°C)	0.3in (0.8cm)
June	80°F (27°C)	61°F (16°C)	0.1in (0.2cm)
July	84°F (29°C)	65°F (18°C)	0.0in (0.1cm)
Aug	85°F (29°C)	66°F (19°C)	0.1in (0.3cm)
Sept	83°F (28°C)	65°F (18°C)	0.3in (0.8cm)
Oct	79°F (26°C)	60°F (16°C)	0.4in (0.9cm)
Nov	73°F (23°C)	53°F (12°C)	1.1in (2.7cm)
Dec	69°F (21°C)	48°F (9°C)	1.9in (4.9cm)

Tipping

Unlike in Europe, tipping is a way of life in the US, and workers in service industries rely on gratuities. Tip bellhops and baggage handlers $1-$3 a bag; cab drivers, wait staff and food delivery agents 15-20 per cent; parking valets $3-$5; bartenders $1 a drink; and housekeepers $2-$5 a night.

Toilets

There are virtually no public restrooms in LA. If you get caught short, duck into a mall, a department store, a hotel or a chain coffeehouse (eg Starbucks) to use their facilities.

Tourist information

LA Inc, the local CVB, has a wealth of information online (www.discoverlosangeles.com) and at its information centres. For local tourist offices in the likes of Santa Monica, see the relevant Sightseeing chapter (*pp68-142*).

LA Inc Downtown *685 S Figueroa Street, at Wilshire Boulevard (1-213 689 8822). Metro 7th Street-Metro Center/bus 16, 18, 55, 62/I-110, exit 6th Street east.* **Open** *8.30am-5pm Mon-Fri.* **Map** *p331 B3.*
LA Inc Hollywood *Hollywood & Highland, 6801 Hollywood Boulevard, at N Highland Avenue (1-323 467*

6412). Metro Hollywood-Highland/bus 156, 163, 212, 217, 363, 656, 780/ US 101, exit Hollywood Boulevard west. **Open** *10am-10pm Mon-Sat; 10am-7pm Sun.* **Map** *p329 A1.*

Visas & immigration

Under the **Visa Waiver Program**, citizens of 27 countries – including the UK, Ireland, Australia and New Zealand – do not need a visa for stays in the US of less than 90 days (business or pleasure). Visitors are required to have a return ticket and a machine-readable passport that's valid for six months beyond the planned departure date. If the traveller's passport was issued after 26 October 2006, it must have a biometric chip; newly-issued UK passports contain this as standard. Passports issued before this date do not need a biometric chip. Canadians and Mexicans do not need visas but must have legal proof of residency. All other travellers need visas.

However, all travellers are advised to check current requirements in advance of their trip. If you need to apply for a visa, allow plenty of time for your application to be processed. For details on visas, see http://travel.state.gov. UK

citizens can find information at www.usembassy.org.uk, or by calling the embassy's Visa Information Hotline on 09042 450100; calls cost £1.20 a minute from BT landlines.

When to go

Climate

With an annual average of 300 clear days, LA offers generally idyllic weather. However, the smog can be awful, especially when combined with the summer heat and the Santa Ana winds (*see p40*).

The best times to visit are between March and May, and from September to November, and when temperatures are cooler and the air is nicer. June and July are best avoided: the coastal cities are swathed in sea mist, referred to as 'June gloom', and temperatures inland soar. In comparison to the averages in the chart above, summer temperatures are 5-8°F (3-5°C) warmer in the Valleys, and 3-5°F (2-3°C) cooler on the coast.

For 24-hour smog and air-quality checks, contact the **South Coast Air Quality Management District** (1-800 288 7664, www.aqmd.gov).

Public holidays

New Year's Day 1 Jan.
Martin Luther King, Jr Day 3rd Mon in Jan.
Presidents Day 3rd Mon in Feb.
Memorial Day last Mon in May.
Independence Day 4 July.
Labor Day 1st Mon in Sept.
Columbus Day 2nd Mon in Oct.
Veterans Day 11 Nov.
Thanksgiving Day 4th Thur in Nov.
Christmas Day 25 Dec.

Working in LA

Contact the US embassy in your home country for details on visas. With US immigration now clamping down on illegal immigrants, working in Los Angeles without a visa is a bad idea.

Further Reference

Non-fiction

Kenneth Anger *Hollywood Babylon*
The dark side of Tinseltown.
Reyner Banham *Los Angeles:*
The Architecture of Four Ecologies
Architectural history, and a paean to
life in the fast lanes.
Leon Bing *Do or Die*
LA gang culture uncovered.
Carolyn Cole & Kathy
Kobayashi *Shades of LA:*
Pictures from Ethnic Family Albums
A beautifully rendered scrapbook
of the ethnic family in LA.
Mike Davis *City of Quartz;*
Ecology of Fear; Magical Urbanism:
Latinos Reinvent the US City
An exhilarating Marxist critique
of LA's city 'planning'; more
apocalyptic LA-bashing, this time
focusing on LA's precarious ecology;
Davis's view of Latino influence on
modern cities.
Douglas Flamming
Bound for Freedom
The history of African-Americans
in LA from its birth to Jim Crow.
Otto Friedrich *City of Nets*
A fascinating portrait of Hollywood
in the '40s.
Barney Hoskyns *Waiting for*
the Sun; Hotel California
Hoskyns surveys Californian music
in the 1960s.
Steven L Isoardi *The Dark Tree:*
Jazz and the Community Arts in LA
A history of the South Central arts
movement of the 1960s and '70s.
Norman Klein
The History of Forgetting: Los
Angeles and the Erasure of Memory
A part-factual, part-fictional analysis
of LA's myth creation by an always-
readable cultural critic.
Chris Kraus, Jan Tumlir &
Jane McFadden *LA Artland*
A contemporary update of the city's
art scenes.
Mötley Crüe with Neil Strauss
The Dirt: Confessions of the World's
Most Notorious Rock Band
Sunset Strip's 'hair metal' days, from
those who survived.
Carey McWilliams *Southern*
California: An Island on the Land;
North From Mexico: The Spanish-
Speaking People of Los Angeles
A history of LA's sinfulness and
scandals; a pioneering celebration
of the Mexican heritage in the
Southwest (written in 1948).
Leonard Pitt & Dale Pitt
Los Angeles A-Z
An interesting and occasionally
invaluable encyclopaedia of LA's
people, places and institutions.

Domenic Priore
Riot on Sunset Strip
The Southern California music scene
in the '60s.
Kevin Roderick *Wilshire Boulevard:*
Grand Concourse of Los Angeles
The Miracle Mile and beyond.
Josh Sides *LA City Limits*
A history of African-Americans in
LA from the Depression to today.
Kevin Starr *California*
Starr has chronicled the state's
history in a number of books down
the years; this abbreviated history
is a good place to start.
Paul Theroux *Translating LA*
Around the neighbourhoods.
David Thomson
The Whole Equation
An engaging history of Hollywood.
DJ Waldie *Holy Land*
'A suburban memoir' set in Waldie's
home town of Lakewood.

Fiction

Charles Bukowski *Hollywood*
The drunk poet's incisive musings on
making a movie in Tinseltown.
James M Cain *Double*
Indemnity, Mildred Pierce
Classic 1930s/'40s noir.
Raymond Chandler
The Big Sleep; Farewell, My Lovely;
The Long Goodbye
Philip Marlowe in the classic hard-
boiled detective novels.
Joan Didion *Play It as It Lays*
Despair and breakdown in LA.
A big influence on…
Bret Easton Ellis *Less Than Zero*
The classic 1980s coke-spoon-chic
novel about being young and fast
on both coasts.
James Ellroy *The Black*
Dahlia, The Big Nowhere,
LA Confidential, White Jazz
Ellroy's LA Quartet is a masterpiece
of contemporary noir; the black and
compelling *My Dark Places* recounts
his search for his mother's killer.
John Fante *Ask the Dust*
Depression-era Los Angeles as seen
by an Italian emigré.
David Fine (ed)
Los Angeles in Fiction
This fine anthology includes work
by, among others, Walter Mosely,
Norman Mailer, Thomas Pynchon
and James M Cain.
F Scott Fitzgerald
The Pat Hobby Stories
Short stories about Hollywood from
a writer who died there.
Elmore Leonard *Get Shorty*
A Miami loan shark turns movie
producer in this gutsy thriller, later
made into a movie starring John
Travolta and Danny DeVito.

John Miller (ed)
Los Angeles Stories
Fiction and essays by Henry Miller,
Fitzgerald, Chandler et al.
Walter Mosely
The Easy Rawlins Mystery Series
Mosely's Easy Rawlins is an African
American PI in LA. See also *Always*
Outnumbered, Always Outgunned.
Budd Schulberg
What Makes Sammy Run?
A furious attack on the studio system
by one of its employees.
Bruce Wagner *I'm Losing You;*
I'll Let You Go; Still Holding
Biting Hollywood satire.
Evelyn Waugh *The Loved One*
Waugh's hilarious and accurate
satire on the American way of death.
Nathaniel West
The Day of the Locust
A classic, apocalyptic raspberry
blown at the movie industry.

The Aviator (2004)
The glory days of Old Hollywood
and Howard Hughes.
Barfly (1987)
Anti-hero meets anti-hero, as Mickey
Rourke takes a Bukowski script and
runs with it. Or, to be more accurate,
stumbles drunkenly.
The Big Lebowski (1998)
John Goodman. Jeff Bridges. Dude.
Boogie Nights (1997)
The 1970s and '80s San Fernando
Valley porn industry uncovered.
Boyz N the Hood (1991)
Can a right-thinking father stop his
son falling prey to the culture of
gang violence in South Central LA?
Bulworth (1998)
This political satire starred and was
co-written by Warren Beatty, who
plays a rapping Democrat senator.
Chinatown (1974)
Roman Polanski's dark portrait of
corruption in 1940s LA.
City of Angels (1998)
LA has never looked more dreamily
beautiful than in this remake of Wim
Wenders' *Wings of Desire.*
Clueless (1995)
A satirical portrait of LA rich kids
and their lives at Beverly Hills
High School.
Collateral (2004)
Jamie Foxx gives Tom Cruise the
runaround in this after-dark thriller.
Colors (1988)
Gritty locations, plausible dialogue
and a laudable lack of sensationalism
define Dennis Hopper's take on cops
versus LA's murderous gangs.
Crash (2005)
An Altmanian, Oscar-winning run
around 48 hours in LA.

Directory

Double Indemnity (1944)
Billy Wilder's sexy, sweaty, classic film noir, with dialogue by Raymond Chandler.

The End of Violence (1997)
The Griffith Observatory has a starring role in Wim Wenders' love-hate letter to Hollywood.

Falling Down (1992)
Michael Douglas turns vigilante terrorist in a hellish LA.

Get Shorty (1995)
John Travolta stars as a Miami loan shark who ends up in Hollywood.

Heat (1995)
Michae Mann's sprawling, intense crime drama, starring Pacino and De Niro.

The Hours (2002)
Julianne Moore struggles to cope in 1950s suburban LA.

In Search of a Midnight Kiss (2008)
Hipsters struggle to find love in Los Feliz and Downtown.

Jackie Brown (1997)
Quentin Tarantino's mature adaptation of Elmore Leonard's *Rum Punch* features Pam Grier in sterling form.

LA Confidential (1997)
The film version of Ellroy's novel.

LA Story (1991)
Steve Martin's love letter to LA is a sentimental but sweet look at a group of affluent Angelenos.

The Limey (1999)
Terence Stamp heads to LA in a vengeful state of mind.

The Long Goodbye (1973)
Robert Altman's superb homage to Chandler is held together by Elliott Gould playing Marlowe as a shambling slob.

Los Angeles Plays Itself (2003)
This epic bootleg history of the world's most filmed city is well worth seeking out.

Million Dollar Baby (2004)
A nice pastiche of the city's gritty Downtown boxing world.

Mulholland Dr. (2001)
David Lynch's compelling *noir*.

The People vs Larry Flynt (1996)
An engaging portrayal of LA's very own porn king.

The Player (1992)
Robert Altman's semi-affectionate evisceration of the Hollywood world he worked to hard to avoid.

Pretty Woman (1990)
Richard Gere and Julia Roberts in an unlikely Hollywood love story.

Pulp Fiction (1994)
Tarantino's witty, vivid, violent interweaving of three LA stories.

Shampoo (1975)
In which Warren Beatty single-handedly takes on womankind and almost wins.

Short Cuts (1993)
More Altman, this time a epic series of interconnected lives, adapted from stories by Raymond Carver.

Singin' in the Rain (1952)
The greatest movie about Hollywood.

Strange Days (1995)
Kathryn Bigelow's dystopian view of Los Angeles on the eve of 2000.

Sunset Boulevard (1950)
Gloria Swanson and William Holden star in a tale of faded fame, creative ambition and ego in Hollywood.

Swingers (1996)
An out-of-work actor and his pals trawl the town looking for honeys.

The Take (2008)
Armoured-truck driver John Leguizamo goes in search of the thugs who hijacked him in East LA.

Timecode (2000)
Mike Figgis's inventive, four-screen piece of LA realism.

Training Day (2001)
Denzel Washington plays bad cop to Ethan Hawke's rookie.

Music

Bad Religion *Suffer*
SoCal punks. More than 20 years later, they're still plugging away.

Dengue Fever
Escape from Dragon House
Cambodian pop meets indie-rock in an instantly classic piece of Angeleno fusion.

Dr Dre *The Chronic*
Released in 1992, *The Chronic* flipped hip hop on its head. Snoop Doggy Dogg has never been on better form.

The Doors *LA Woman*
The last album from the Los Angeles quartet.

The Eagles *Hotel California*
The defining album of the 1970s, for better or worse.

Elliott Smith
From a Basement on a Hill
Echo Park hermit Elliott Smith's haunting ode to himself.

Hole *Celebrity Skin*
'This album is dedicated to all the stolen water of Los Angeles.'

Mötley Crüe *Girls, Girls, Girls*
The girls! The guitars! The spandex! The haircuts!

Nels Cline with Devin Sarno
Buried on Bunker Hill
Avant-garde paean to a vanished Downtown neighbourhood.

Randy Newman
Trouble in Paradise
The closest LA's finest songwriter has come to making an LA album.

NWA *Straight Outta Compton*
The moment at which gangsta rap went mainstream. Tough to overestimate its influence.

Ozomatli *Ozomatli*
They're best experienced live, but this isn't a bad representation of East LA's genre-busting Latino-rock outfit.

Tom Waits *Small Change*
Streetcorner balladry from the longtime resident of the Tropicana.

X *Los Angeles*
A punk classic, still fresh.

Websites

1947 Project
http://1947project.com
LA's hidden history uncovered, year by year. The same folks are now digging for treasure in Downtown over at www.onbunkerhill.org.

Blog Downtown
http://blogdowntown.com
The most useful of the many blogs chronicling Downtown's resurgence.

City of Los Angeles
www.ci.la.ca.us
The LA government's home page.

Curbed LA
http://la.curbed.com
Architecture, construction and real estate in LA.

Defamer *www.defamer.com*
'The LA gossip rag', runs the subtitle, but it's better written than that description might suggest.

Discover LA
www.discoverlosangeles.com
The LACVB's official tourist-industry resource.

Eater LA *http://la.eater.com*
Restaurants, bars and clubs in the city, brought to you by the folks behind Curbed. The shopping equivalent is at http://la.racked.com.

LA Cowboy
http://lacowboy.blogspot.com
The blog of influential Downtown booster Brady Westwater.

LA Observed *www.laobserved.com*
Politics and the politics of media in Los Angeles.

LA Times *www.latimes.com*
Not the most easily navigable of sites, but it's all up here somewhere. For arts and restaurants, go straight to http://theguide.latimes.com.

LA Weekly *www.laweekly.com*
Listings information for bars, clubs, music venues and so on.

LA.com *www.la.com*
Bars, shops, restaurants and after-hours culture.

Metromix
http://losangeles.metromix.com
The Tribune group have imported their Metromix online magazine to LA, with features, previews, reviews and venue listings.

MTA *www.metro.net*
Public transportation information, including maps and timetables.

Public Art in LA
www.publicartinla.com
An excellent guide to public works in all corners of the city.

Seeing Stars
www.seeing-stars.com
Not the best-looking site on the net, by any means, but there's some good celeb-related stuff buried here.

Traffic News *http://cad.chp.ca.gov*
The latest incidents on the road.

Index

Note: Page numbers in
bold indicate section(s)
giving key information
on a topic; *italics* indicate
photographs.

A+D Museum 99
Abbot Kinney Boulevard
  Festival 215
abortion 307
Academy Awards 213
accident & emergency 307
Accommodation 44-66
  best hotels 45
  by price:
    budget 49-50, 50, 57-58,
      61, 62, 62-63, 64
    expensive 45, 45-48,
      50-51, 53, 54, 54-57,
      58-59 65, 66
    moderate 45-47, 48-49,
      51, 53-54, 54, 57,
      59-61, 61-62, 62,
      3-64, 64, 65 66, 66
  camping 57
  chain hotels 47
  gay & lesbian 243
  hotel spas 53
Adamson House 74, *75*
addresses & street-
  numbering 71, 306
AFI Los Angeles
  International Film
  Festival 229
African-American
  community 123,
    124, 126, 127
age restrictions 175, 261, 306
airports & airlines 302
Alhambra 135
Alisal, El 109
Allied Model Trains 220
American Cinematheque
  230, 231, 242
American football 270
amusement parks
  see theme parks
Anaheim 140
Anaheim Ducks 270
Anaheim/Orange County
  Visitor & Convention
  Bureau 140
Angels baseball team
  140, **269**
Angels Flight 115
Angels Gate Lighthouse 137
Angels Gate Park 137
Angels of Anaheim
  see Los Angeles
  Angels of Anaheim

Angelus Plaza 116
antiques shopping 207-208
Aquarium of the Pacific 137,
  138, 217-218
aquariums see
  zoos & aquariums
arboretum 135
Architecture 25-33
  Downtown 31
  early 25
  Gehry, Frank 32
  Googie 27, 28
  hotels 30
  inter-war 26
  post-war 28
  residential 33
  schools 33
  Spanish Revival 29
ArcLight cinemas
  97, 288, *288*
art see galleries;
  museums; public art
arthouse cinemas 230-231
Artivist Film Festival 229
ATMs 309
automobiles see
  driving & cars
Autry National Center 105
Avalon 262, *262*, 264
Avila Adobe 112
award shows 213

b

Babe's & Ricky's Inn 259
babysitters 222
Baked Potato 260, *260*
bakeries 201-202
Balboa Island 140
Balboa Park 296-297, *296*
Balboa Peninsula 140
Baldwin Hills Crenshaw
  Plaza 124
Ballerina Clown 80, *80*
ballet 282
Ballona Wetlands 81
Bank of America
  Building 290
banks 309
barbers 205
Barnsdall Art Park 104-105
Bars 175-186
  best 176
  gay & lesbian 244, 247,
    248, 249
  happy hours, top ten 182
  piano bars 179
baseball 269
basketball 269
Baxter Steps 109
beaches 82-83
  gay 243

Beckham, David 270, 271
beauty shops 205-207
Bel Air 89
  see also Brentwood
    to Beverly Hills
Belmont Shore 138
Benvenuto Caffe 245
Bergamot Station 78
Betty Ford Clinic 292
Beverly Center 92, 188
Beverly Hills see Brentwood
  to Beverly Hills
Bicycle Rack 114
Big Bear Lake 289
bikes see cycling & bikes
Biscuit Company Lofts 31
Blessing of the Animals 212
Bob Baker Marionette
  Theater 221, 222
books on/set in LA 313
bookshops & book fairs
  190-193, 212, 215, 222
botanical gardens 89,
  132-133, 135, 136, 218
Bowers Museum of
  Cultural Art 140
bowling 272
Boyle Heights 120-122
Bradbury Building 26,
  26, **117**
Brazilian Carnival 216
**Brentwood to Beverly
  Hills 84-91**, 236-237
  accommodation 53-58
  bars 177-178
  Bel Air 89
  Beverly Hills 90-91
  Brentwood 84-86
  Century City 89
  coffeehouses 171-172
  Culver City 86-87
  restaurants 149-155
  Westwood & around
    87-89
Broad Contemporary Art
  Museum (BCAM) 30
Broadway 117, 118-119
Buena Park 140
Bullocks Wilshire 27, 103
Bunker Hill 115
Burbank 129
Burbank-Glendale-Pasadena
  Airport 302
bureaux de change 310
buses 302, 304-305
business 306

c

Cabrillo Beach 137
Cabrillo Marine Aquarium
  137, 217

cabs 305
Café La Boheme 245
cafés see coffeehouses
Calabasas Pumpkin
  Festival 215
California Heritage
  Museum 78
California Legoland 217
California Market Center
  118
California ScienCenter 123,
  124-125, *124*, *125*, 217
California Speedway 270
Californian African
  American Museum
  123, 124
Caltrans District 7
  Headquarters *30*, 33, 114
Calvary Cemetery 121,
  121, 122
camping 57
canals, Venice 80
Capitan Theatre, El 26, 94
Capitol Records Building
  28, 95
cars & car hire see
  driving & cars
Casa de Liberace 290
Casa Italiana 111
Casa Pacifica 140
Casa Romantica 290
Catalina Island 295
Cathedral of Our Lady of
  Angels 31, **115**, *115*
CBS Television City 98
CDs & records 209-210
Celebration Theatre 242
celebrity 37-39
  deaths 102
cellular phones 311
cemeteries 121
Central Avenue Jazz
  Festival 127
Central Plaza 110-111
Century City 89-90
Channel Islands National
  Park 285
chemists 205
Chemosphere 28
Children 217-222
  arts & entertainment
    220-222
  best kids' stuff 217
  outdoors & nature
    218-219
  restaurants & cafés
    219-220
  shops 193
  sightseeing 217-218
Children's Museum
  of Los Angeles 217
Chinatown 110-111, *111*

Chinese American Museum 110, 112
Chinese Historical Society 111
Chinese New Year 110, 216
Chrysalis Music Group 92
churches & cathedrals 115, 128, 129, 140, **310-311**
Cinco de Mayo 212
cinemas 227-234
  drive-in 129
City Hall 25, 27, *112*, **114**
Civic Center 91, 113-114
Claremont 29, **135**
classical & opera music 250-252
cleaning & repairs 200
climate & weather 41, 312
climbing *see* rock climbing
Clippers *see* Los Angeles Clippers
clothing hire 200
Coachella festival **252**, 292
Coachella Valley 289-292
Coca-Cola Bottling Plant 27
Coca-Cola Building 119
Coffeehouses 170-174
  best 171
  for children 219-220
  gay & lesbian 245-246, 249
  people-watching 172
Colorado Court 33
Colour Me Mine 220, *221*
Comedy 223-226
  best, the 223
  Tompkins, Mr Paul F 225, *225*
conferences 306
consulates 307
consumer services 306
contraception 307
conventions 306
couriers 306
Craft & Folk Art Museum 99
credit cards 309, 310
Crenshaw 127
Crossroads of the World 28, 97
Crystal Cathedral 140, *141*
Culver City 86-87
customs 306-307
cycling & bikes 218, **271**, **272**, 305

Da Camera Society 252
dance & performance art 282
Danziger Studio/Residence 32
Day of the Dead 122, **215**
Death Valley National Park 287, *288*
dentists 308
Department of Water & Power Building 115

department stores 187-188
Descanso Gardens 132
Desert Hot Springs 292
Deserts, The 287-294
  Coachella Valley 289-292
  Death Valley National Park 287, *288*
  Joshua Tree 292-294
  Lake Arrowhead & Big Bear Lake 288-289
designer clothes shops 193-194
Dia de los Muertos 122, **215**
dialling codes 311
Diavolo Dance Theatre 282
Directors Guild of America 92
Directory 302-314
disabled travellers 307
discount shops 194
Disney Hall 31, 32
Disney Ice Arena 32
Disney's California Adventure 142
Disneyland 140-142
  hotels 66
Dockweiler State Beach 274
doctors 307
Dodger Stadium 108, 269
Dodgers *see* Los Angeles Dodgers
Doheny Memorial Library 125
Doo-Dah Parade 241
Dorothy Chandler Pavilion 251
Downtown 110-119
  accommodation 63-64
  architecture 31
  bars 185-186
  Broadway 117
  Chinatown 110-111
  Civic Center & around 113-115
  coffeehouses 174
  Fashion District & the Flower District 117-119
  Financial District & Bunker Hill 115-117
  galleries 240-241
  Little Tokyo to Skid Row 112-113
  Olvera Street & the Plaza 111-112
  restaurants 164-165
  South Park & LA Live 119
Downtown Art Walk 240
Downtown Film Festival 229
drinking 175
  see also bars; coffeehouses; food & drink; wine & wineries
drive-in cinemas 129
driving & cars 23, 34-36, 302-304
drugs 307

Ducks hockey team 140, **270**
Duke Ellington Memorial 89
DVD shops/hire 210

Eagle Rock 109
Eagle Rock Music Festival 252
Eames House 28, 74
earthquakes 42
East Los Angeles 120-122
  restaurants 165-166
Eastern Columbia Building 31, 117
Echo Park 108-109
Echo Park Film Center 108, 234
Edgemar Center for the Arts 32
Edward R Roybal Federal Building 114
Egyptian Theatre 26, 94, **231**
El Matador State Beach 82
El Segundo 136
El Segundo Beach 218
Electric Fountain 90
electricity 307
electronics shops 193
Elrod House 28, 290
Elysian Park 108
embassies 307
emergencies 307
Emmys 213
Ennis-Brown House 27, **104**
environmental issues 23
Eternal Fame 37-39
Evergreen Cemetery 121
Exposition Park 123

Fairfax District 98
fairgrounds *see* theme parks
Falcon Theatre *278*, 279
fame 37-39
Farmers & Merchants Bank 137
Farmers Market 98, **159**, 220
farmers' markets 78, 98, 123, 159, 220
Fashion District 118
Fashion Island 139
fashion shops 193-201
  green 195
fauna 42
Festival of the Chariots 214
Festivals & Events 212-216
  autumn 215-216
  film 229
  gay & lesbian 244
  rock music 252
  spring 212
  summer 212-215
  winter 216

Fiesta Broadway 212
Fiesta Hermosa Arts & Crafts Fair 215
Film & TV 227-234
  best cinemas 227
  cinemas/movie theatres 227-234
  festivals 229
  film 227-234
  LA in film 232-233, 313-314
  TV 234
Film Independent's Los Angeles Film Festival 229
fires 41
First Lutheran Church of Northridge 129
Fisher Museum of Art 125
fishing 81, **272-273**
fitness 276
flea markets 207
floods & mudslides 41
Flower District 117-118
Flying Saucer House 290
food & drink
  markets 203
  shops 201-203
  see also coffeehouses; restaurants; wine
football 270
  see also soccer
Ford Amphitheatre 282
Forest Lawn Memorial Park 129
Fort McArthur 137
Forum 253
Fowler Museum of Cultural History 88
Franklin D Murphy Sculpture Garden 88
freeways 34-35
Friendship Bell 137
Friendship Knot 114
Fuck Yeah Fest 215
Fullerton 140
furniture shops 207-209

Galleries 235-241
  see also Museums
Gamble House 26, **132**
Garden of Oz 93
gardens *see* parks & gardens
Gardner 1050 33
Gay & Lesbian 242-249
  Hollywood 247
  organisations 307
  outdoor activity 245
  restaurants & coffeehouses 249
  Silver Lake 247-249
  theatre & film 242-243
  West Hollywood 243-247
Gay Pride *see* LA Gay Pride
Geffen Contemporary 31, **112**, **116**

Geffen Playhouse 222
Gehry, Frank 31, **32**, 79, 112, 116
General Petroleum Building 31
Getty Center 30, **84-85**, *85*, 217, 251
Getty Museum 30
Getty Villa 74, **75**, 217
Gibson Amphitheatre 254
gift shops 203-205
Glass-Simons Memorial 108, *109*
Glendale 129
Golden Globe Awards 213
golf 273
Googie 27, 28, 99
graffiti 239
Grammy Museum 119
Grand Avenue Project 31
Grand Performances 251
Grauman's Chinese Theatre 26, **94**, **95**, *95*, **230**, *230*
graveyards 121
Great Western Forum 128
Greek Theatre 105, **253-254**
Grier Musser Museum 103
Griffith Observatory **105**, *105*, **106**, 217
Griffith Park 98, **105**, 218, *218-219*, 273
Griffith Park Light Festival 216
Grunion Run 81
Guerrilla Gay Bar 249
guided tours 71-73, 119
gyms 276
   gay & lesbian 246-247

Habitat 825 33
hairdressers 205
Halloween 215
Hamburger Mary's 246
Hammering Man 114, 118
Hancock Park 102-103
Hannah Carter Japanese Garden **89**, 93
Hannukah Family Festival 216
hardware shops 207-208
Harriet & Charles Luckman Fine Arts Complex 250
hat shops 200
Hayden Tract 28, 87
Heading South 136-142
   accommodation 65-66
   Orange County 139-142
   restaurants 168-169
   South Bay & Long Beach, The 136-139
health 307
   shops 205-207
Helms Bakery 87
helplines 308
Heritage Square 109
Hermosa Beach 136

Higashi Honganji Buddhist Temple 113
Highland Park 109
Highways Performance Space **242**, 282
hiking 245, **273**, 285
Hills, The 127-128
HIV & AIDS 308
hockey 270
Hollyhock House 27, **104-105**
Hollywood *see* Film & TV; West Hollywood, Hollywood & Midtown
Hollywood & Highland 94
Hollywood Boulevard 94
Hollywood Bowl 33, 222, **251**
Hollywood Bowl Museum 98
Hollywood Christmas Parade *214*, 216
Hollywood Forever Cemetery 97, *98*, 215
Hollywood Hills 97
Hollywood Museum 94, 96
Hollywood Palladium 254
Hollywood Park Race Track & Casino 128
Hollywood Pop Academy 94
Hollywood Reservoir & Dog Park 98
Hollywood Roosevelt **61**, 94
Hollywood sign 18, 97
Hollywood Walk of Fame 96
Hollywood Wax Museum 95
Home of Peace 121
horse racing 270
horse riding 273
hospitals 307
Hotel Café *254*, 256
hotels *see* accommodation
House of Blues 254
household shops 207-209
housing 23, 24
Huntington Beach Bicycle Trail 272
Huntington Library, Art Collections & Botanical Gardens *130*, **132-133**, 218
Huntington Park 127
Huntington State Beach 83, 139

ID 175, 262
IMAX cinema 234
immigration 24, 312
Independence Day 213
Independent Shakespeare Company 282
Inglewood 128
in-line skating 218, **274-275**
Inner-City Arts 28
insurance 308
International Pop Overthrow 252

International Surfing Museum 140
internet access 308
Irwindale Speedway 270

James Irvine Garden 113
Japanese American Cultural & Community Center 113
Japanese American National Museum **112**, **113**, 217
Japanese Village Plaza 113
Jet Propulsion Laboratory 132, 133
jewellery shops 200
Jewelry District 116
Joshua Tree National Park 287, 292-294, *293*

Kenneth Hahn State Recreation Area **128**, 218
Kidspace Children's Museum 132, **134**, 217
Killing of a Chinese Bookie, The 232, *233*
Kings *see* Los Angeles Kings
Kirk Douglas Theatre 86, 279
Knott's Berry Farm 140, 142
Kodak Theatre 96-97
Koreatown 103

LA African Marketplace & Cultural Faire 215
La Cañada Flintridge 132
LA Contemporary Exhibitions 237
LA County Fair 135, **215**
LA County Holiday Celebration 216
LA DASH buses 304-305
LA Galaxy 270, 271-272
LA Gay Pride 244
LA Live 31, **119**
LA Louver *235*, 236
La Mirada Theatre 278
LA Philharmonic *250*, 252
LA Riots (1992) 123
LA Times Festival of Books 212
LA Today 22-24
La Ve Lee 260
LACMA *see* Los Angeles County Museum of Art
Lafayette Park 103
Laguna Art Museum 140
Laguna Beach 140, 243
Lake Arrowhead 288-289
Lakers *see* Los Angeles Lakers
LAPD Headquarters 114
Larchmont Village 103
Las Posadas 216
Last Remaining Seats 229

Latino population 24, 120, 123, 140
Lautner, John 27
left luggage 308
legal help 308
Leimert Park 127
Leo Carillo State Park 285
lesbian scene 248-249
Lexton-MacCarthy House 33
libraries 130, 116, 222, 308
limos 305
lingerie shops 200
Little Joe's 111
Little Tokyo 112-113
Lloyd Wright, Frank 27, 32, 84, 94, 104
Lloyd Wright Home & Studio 94
Long Beach 137
Long Beach Convention & Visitors Bureau 138
Long Beach Grand Prix 212, 270
Long Beach Museum of Art 138
Long Beach Opera 252
Long Beach Symphony 252
Los Angeles Angels of Anaheim 268, 269
Los Angeles Asian Pacific Film Festival 229
Los Angeles Avengers 270
Los Angeles Ballet 282
Los Angeles Chamber Orchestra 252
Los Angeles Clippers 269
Los Angeles Convention Center 31, **119**, 306
Los Angeles County Arboretum & Botanical Garden 135
Los Angeles County Museum of Art (LACMA) 99, 100-101, *100-101*, 217, 250, 251
Los Angeles Dodgers 269
Los Angeles Equestrian Center *272*, 273
Los Angeles Flower Market 117-118
Los Angeles Gay & Lesbian Center 242, **307**
Los Angeles Herald-Examiner Building 33, 119
Los Angeles International Airport (LAX) 302
Los Angeles International Short Film Festival 229
Los Angeles Kings 270
Los Angeles Lakers 269-270
Los Angeles Latino International Film Festival 229
Los Angeles Live Steamers 105
Los Angeles Marathon 212
Los Angeles Maritime Museum 137

Los Angeles Master
Chorale 252
Los Angeles Philharmonic
252
Los Angeles Police
Academy 108
Los Angeles Sparks 269
Los Angeles Zoo **105**,
106, **107**, 217
Los Angles Opera 252
Los Feliz to Echo Park
104-109
bars 183-185
coffeehouses 173-174
Echo Park 108-109
galleries 238-240
Los Feliz 104-107
Mt Washington to
Eagle Rock 109
restaurants 162-164
Silver Lake 108
lost property 308
Lotus Festival 108, **214**
Lovell House 27, **104**
Loyola Law School 32
luggage shops 201

MacArthur Park 103
magazines 308-309
Magic Johnson Theaters 128
MAK Center for Art &
Architecture 27, **94**
Malibu 74
Malibu Beach 83
malls 188-190, 194
Manhattan Beach 83, 136
Mariachi Festival 216
Mariachi Plaza 120, *122*
Marina del Rey 80-81
Marina del Rey Holiday
Boat Parade 216
markets 190
Mark's 246
Mayan Theatre 119
McKinley Residence 33
media 308-309
medical services 307
Melrose Avenue 98
Metlofts 31
Metropolitan Detention
Center 114
Metropolitan
Transportation Authority
(MTA) 304
Mexico 299
Midtown *see* West
Hollywood, Hollywood
& Midtown
Mildred E Mathias
Botanical Garden 89
Million Dollar Theatre
117, 118
Mind, Body and Spirit
sculpture 114
Mineo, Sal 102
Miracle Mile 99

Miriam Matthews
Branch Library 33
Mission San Fernando
Rey de España 129
Mission San Juan
Capistrano 140
mobile phones 311
MoCA 92, **116**, 217
modernism 32, **290**
Mojave 287
money 309-310
Monterey Park 135
Mormon Temple 88
motor racing 270
Mount Wilson Observatory
132, 134
Mt Washington 109
MTA *see* Metropolitan
Transportation Authority
MTV Movie Awards 213
Mulholland Drive 97
murals 239
murders, celebrity 102
Museum of Contemporary
Art 31, **112**, **115**, **116**
Museum of Flying 78
Museum of Jurassic
Technology 87
Museum of Latin American
Art 138, *139*
Museum of Neon Art 113
Museum of the American
West 105
Museum of Tolerance 91
Music 250-260
albums from LA 314
classical 250-253
for children 222
free concerts 251
fusion 259
jazz 259-260
rock & pop 252-259
roots & blues 259
shops 209-210
tickets & information
210, 250
for electronic dance music,
see nightclubs
Music Box at the Henry
Fonda Theater 254-255
Music Center theatres 115,
277, *277*, 282
musical instruments 210
Musso & Frank Grill 95,
157, 163, *163*

Naples 138
National Center for the
Preservation of
Democracy 112-113
national parks 287, 292
Natural History Museum
of Los Angeles County
123, **125**, 217, 251
Natural History Museum,
San Diego 297

Natural World, The
40-42
NBC Studios 73, 129
Nethercutt Collection 129
Newport Beach 139
Newport Harbor 139
Newport Harbor Nautical
Museum 140
newspapers 308
Ngor, Haing S 102
Niemeyer, Oscar 76
Nightclubs 261-267
best 261
bottle service 263
DJs 264
gay & lesbian 244, 247,
248, 249
Nisei Week Japanese
Festival 214
Nixon, Richard 130
Noah's Ark *see* Skirball
Cultural Center
Nokia Theatre at LA Live
253, 255
Norris Auditorium 250
North to Santa Barbara
285-286
Los Angeles to Ojai
285-286
Santa Barbara 286
Northridge 129
Norton Simon Museum
132, *133*, 134

observatories 132, 217
Ocean Boulevard 137
office services 306
off-licences 202
Ojai 285
Ojai Music Festival
250, 285
Old Town Music Hall 136
Olvera Street district 25-26,
112
On the Road 34-36
opening hours 310
opera & classical music
250-252
opticians 205
Orange County 139-142
Orange County Performing
Arts Center 278
Orpheum 118, *118*, *229*, 255
Oscars *see* Academy
Awards
Outfest **228**, 242
outlet malls 194
Oviatt Building 116
Oxnard 285

Pacific Asia Museum
32, 135
Pacific Design Center 92
Pacific Palisades 74-75

Pacific Park 77, 218
Pacific Symphony 252
Page Museum at the La
Brea Tar Pits *99*, 101
Pageant of the Masters
213, 241
Paley Center for Media
30, 91
Palm Spring International
Airport 290
Palm Springs 289-292
Palm Spring's City Hall 290
palm trees 42
Palos Verdes 136
Pan African Film Festival
229
Pantages Theatre 26, 95,
278
Paramount Ranch 129
Paramount Studios 73, 97
parking 303-304
parks & gardens **93**, 105,
132, 133, 135, **218**
Pasadena 26, **131**
Pasadena Chalk Street
Painting Festival 212
Pasadena Civic Auditorium
250
Pasadena Convention &
Visitors Bureau 135
Pasadena Museum of
California Art 132, *134*,
135
Pasadena Playhouse 278
Pasadena Symphony 252
Pasadena Symphony
Musical Circus 222
Pershing Square 116
Pershing Square Summer
Concert Series 251
Petersen Automotive
Museum 99, 101-102
pharmacies 205
photography shops 193
Piano, Renzo 30-31, 100
Pico House 26
piercing shops 207
Pioneertown 292
Pipes Canyon Preserve 292
Placita, La 112
Playa del Rey 81
Playa Vista 81
playgrounds 219
Plaza 112
Poet's Walk 116
Point Fermin Lighthouse
137
Point Mugu State Park 285
police 310
Pomona 135
pool & billiards 273
Port of Los Angeles Lobster
Festival 215
postal services 310
premières & previews 227
Press-Telegram Building
137
Prospect Park 122

public art 105, **114**, **239**
public holidays 312
public transport 23, 302, 304-305
Pueblo de Los Angeles Historical Monument, El 111
puppet shows 221, *221*, 222

Queen Mary ocean liner 137, 138-139

race courses 270
radio 309
Ramirez Canyon Park 74
Ramsay, Gordon 153, *153*, 155-156
Rancho de los Quiotes 29
Randy's Donuts 27, 128
Reagan, Ronald 130
real estate 23, 24
records & CDs 209-210
Red Rock Canyon State Park 287-288
Redondo Beach 136
Redondo Beach Performing Arts Center 278
religion 310-311
repairs & cleaning 200
repertory movie theatres 231-234
Restaurants 144-169
best 146
ethnic dining 158
for children 219-220
gay & lesbian 245-246, 249
historic restaurants 163
Ramsay, Gordon 153, *153*, 155-156
reservations 144
sweet treats 146
tipping 145
Reuben H Fleet Science Center 297
Rey Theatre, El 253
Richard & Karen Carpenter Peforming Arts Center **278**, 282
Richard J Riordan Central Library 27, **116-117**, 222
Richard Nixon Library & Birthplace 140, 142
Ripley's Believe it or Not! 95, 97, 218
Robert F Maguire Gardens 116
rock & pop music 252-259
rock climbing 273-274
Rodeo Drive 187
rollerblading *see* in-line skating
Ronald W Reagan Presidential Library & Museum 129, 130

Rose Garden 123
Roxbury Park 219
Royce Hall at UCLA 250
Runyon Canyon Park 97, 273

safety & security 311
St Peter's Church 111
St Theresa's Church 290
Salazar Park 122
Salvation Mountain 293, *293*
San Clemente 140
San Diego Air & Space Museum 297
San Diego Zoo 297
San Fernando Valley 129-131
San Fernando Valley Conference & Visitors Bureau 130
San Gabriel **135**, 273
San Gabriel Valley 131-135
San Diego *see* South to San Diego
San Juan Capistrano 140
San Marino 26, **132**
San Pedro 136
Santa Ana 140
Santa Ana winds 40-41
Santa Anita Park 135, 270
Santa Barbara *285*, 286
Santa Catalina Island 295
Santa Clarita Cowboy Festival 212
Santa Monica & the beach towns 74-83
accommodation 45-53
bars 176-177
coffeehouses 170-171
galleries 235-236
Malibu 74
Marina del Rey & around 80-81
Pacific Palisades 74-75
restaurants 145-149
Santa Monica 76-79
Venice 79-80
Santa Monica Airport 78
Santa Monica Beach 77, 218, 219
Santa Monica Historical Society Museum 76
Santa Monica Mountains 74, **129**, 273
Santa Monica Museum of Art 78, 79
Santa Monica Pier 77, *77-78*
Santa Monica Pier Aquarium 77-78, 217
Santa Monica Place 32
Santa Monica State Beach 83
Schoenberg Hall 250
Schwarzenegger, Arnold 23, *24*

Science Center School 33
Scotty's Castle 287-288
Screen Actors Guild Awards 213
Scripps College 29
scuba-diving 275
secondhand shops 198-200
Seal Beach 139
Self-Realization Fellowship Lake Shrine 74, 75, 93, *93*
Sepulveda House 111
sex clubs 247, 248
Shakespeare Festival/LA 282
Sherman Oaks 129
shippers 306
shoe shops 201
Shops & Services 187-210
best 187
gay & lesbian 247
W 3rd Street 192
where to shop 188
Shrine Auditorium 125
Sierra Club 105, 273
sightseeing 68-73
best attractions 69
Silver Lake 108
Silver Lake Film Festival 229
Simpson, OJ 84, 102
Sinatra, Frank 290
Six Flags California 129, 130-131
skateboarding 275
Skid Row 113
skiing 289
Skirball Center **85-86**, *86*, 250, 251
Skirball Cultural Center **86**, 217
Smalls, Biggie 102
Smell *256-257*, 258
smoking 311
soccer 270-271
Solar Umbrella House 33
Sony Pictures Studios 73, 86
Sound Walk 241
Source Figure 114
South Bay 136
South Bay Bicycle trail 272
South Central Farm 128
South Coast Botanic Garden 136, *136*
South Los Angeles 123-128
Central Avenue 127
Crenshaw & around 127-128
Exposition Park & around 123-125
Leimert Park 127
restaurants 166
Watts 127
South Park 119
South to San Diego 295-300

San Diego 295-300
accommodation 300
Balboa Park 296-297, *296*
Coronado 297-298
Downtown San Diego 296
eating & drinking 298-300
Heading north 298
Hillcrest & Old Town 297-298
tourist information 300
transport 300
Southwest Museum of the American Indian 109
souvenir shops 203-205
Spaceland 258
Spadena House 26, 90
Spanish revival 29
spas & salons 206-207
Spector, Phil 102
Spirit Awards 213
Sports & Fitness 268-276
participation sports 272-276
shops 210
spectator sports 268-272
Stagecoach Festival **252**, 292
Staples Center 119, 255
Star Eco Station **87**, 217
stationery shops 204-205
STDs, HIV & AIDS 308
Stealth Building 87
Stick House 76
Storyopolis 221-222
Stovepipe Wells 287
Strathmore Apartments 27
streets *see* addresses & street-numbering
studio tours 73
study 311
Sturges House 28, 84
Sunset Beach 139
Sunset Boulevard 97
Sunset Junction Street Fair 108, **214**, 252
Sunset Plaza Drive 92
Sunset Strip 92
supermarkets 202-203
Sur 246
surfing 140, 214, **274**, **275**, 285
Surfrider Beach 274
swimming & swimming pools 82, 218, 275

Tarzana 129
Tate, Sharon 102
tax 187, 310
taxis 305
TBWA Chiat/Day office 32
Team Disney building 32
telephones 311
television 234, 309
Temescal Canyon 273
tennis 275

Theatre & Dance 277-282
  dance & performance
    art 282
  for children 222
  Shakespeare 282
  theatre 277-282
  theatre groups 281
  theme & water parks
    69, 77, 130-131, 131, 218
  tickets & ticket booths 210,
    234, 250, 268
Tijuana 299, *299*
time 311
Times-Mirror Building 114
Timken Museum of Art 297
tipping 145, 312
toilets 312
Tompkins, Mr Paul F
  225, 225
Topanga Canyon & State
  Park 99, 273
Topanga Days 99
Topanga Film Festival 99
tourist information 312
Tournament House 132, 305
Tournament of Roses
  Parade 131, 135, **216**
tours 71-73
Toy Factory apartment
  complex 31
toy shops 193
traffic 23
trains 302, 305
Tramway Gas Station 290
travel advice 306
Travel Town Museum **107**,
  218
travellers' shops 210
TreePeople 218
trees 42
Troubadour 258
TV shows 234
Twentynine Palms 292
Twilight Dance Series 251
Twin Palms 290

UCLA 87, **88-89**
UCLA Bruins 270
UCLA Hammer
  Museum 87, 88
UCLA performance
  centers 282
Umbrella 87
underwear shops 200
Union Station 27, 29, 112
Universal Studios &
  CityWalk 28, 131
universities 88, 125, 311
University of Southern
  California (USC) 125
Upright Citizens Brigade
  Theatre 223, *224*, **226**
urban planning 23
US Bank Tower 116
US Open of Surfing 214
USC Trojans 270

Valleys, The 129-135
  accommodation 64-65
  bars 186
  coffeehouses 174
  restaurants 166-168
  San Fernando Valley
    129-131
  San Gabriel Valley
    131-135
Venice 79-80
Venice Artwalk 79, 236
Venice Beach **80**, 83, 218,
  219, 243
Ventura 28
Vernon 127
Vertical House 33
Villa Aurora 29, *29*
Villa Riviera 137
Villaraigosa, Antonio 23
Vincent Price Art Museum
  122
vineyards 297
vintage shops 198-200
Virgenes View Trail,
  Las 285
visas 312

W 3rd Street 98, 192
walking 305
  see also hiking
walking tours 71, 73
Walt Disney Concert Hall
  32, *32*, 93, **115**, *117*,
  222, **251-252**
Warner Brothers Studios
  73, 129
Warner Grand Theatre 137
Washington Mutual Bank
  290
water parks *see* theme
  & water parks
Watts 127
Watts Summer Festival 214
Watts Towers 26, **126**,
  126, **127**
Wayfarer's Chapel 136
weather & climate 41, 312
websites 314
Wells Fargo Center 115
Wells Fargo History
  Museum 115
West Adams 128
West Angeles Church of
  God in Christ 128
West Hollywood,
  Hollywood &
  Midtown 92-103
  accommodation 58-63
  bars 179-183
  coffeehouses 172-173
  Fairfax District 98
  galleries 237-238
  Hancock Park 102-103
  Hollywood 94-98

  Koreatown & around 103
  Miracle Mile & Midtown
    99-102
  restaurants 155-161
West Hollywood 92-94
Westlake 103
West Hollywood Book Fair
  215
West Hollywood Convention
  & Visitors Bureau 94
Westfield Century City mall
  89, 190
Westlake 103
Westminster 140
Westside Pavilion 88
Westwood 87
Westwood Memorial Park
  87
whale-watching 81,
  275-276
Whisky A Go-Go 92, **258**
wildlife 42
Will Geer Theatricum
  Botanicum 99, 280
Will Rogers Memorial Park
  90
Will Rogers State Beach
  74, **243**, 275
Will Rogers State Historic
  Park 74, 75, 218
Wiltern 103, 255
wine & wineries 202, 297
working 312
Wrigley Gardens 132, 135

X Games 214

yoga 245, 276
Yucca Valley 292

Zanzibar 267, *267*
zoos & aquariums 77-78,
  107, 137, 138, 297
Zuma Beach **83**, 275

Accommodation
Ambrose 48
Angeleno 53
Avalon 54
Banana Bungalow
  Hollywood 62
Banana Bungalow West
  Hollywood 62
Bayside Hotel 49
Beverly Hills Hotel &
  Bungalows 54
Beverly Hilton 55
Beverly Laurel 62
Beverly Wilshire 55
Cadillac Hotel 50
Casa del Mar 45

Casa Malibu Inn
  on the Beach 45
Chamberlain *56*, 58
Chateau Marmont 58
Crescent 57
Custom Hotel *50-51*, 51
Disney's Grand Californian
  Hotel & Spa 66
Disney's Paradise
  Pier Hotel 66
Disneyland Hotel 66
Elan 59
Fairmont Miramar 47
Farmer's Daughter 62
Four Seasons Los Angeles
  at Beverly Hills 55
Georgian Hotel 49
Grafton on Sunset 59
Highland Gardens Hotel 62
HI-Santa Monica 49
Hollywood Roosevelt 61
Hotel Bel-Air 54
Hotel Beverly Terrace 57
Hotel California 49
Hotel Carmel 50
Hotel Figueroa 64, *65*
Hotel Oceana 47
Hotel Palomar 53
Hotel Shangri-La 49
Huntley Hotel 47, *48*
Hyatt Regency Century
  Plaza 54
Inn at 657 64
Inn at Playa del Rey 51
Langham Huntington Hotel
  & Spa Pasadena 65
Loews Santa Monica Beach
  Hotel 47
London West Hollywood 58
Luxe Hotel Rodeo Drive 56
Magic Castle Hotel 61
Maison 140 57
Malibu Beach Inn 45
Merigot, Le 48
Millennium Biltmore 63
Mondrian 58
Montage Laguna Beach 66
Montrose Suite Hotel, Le 60
Mosaic 56
O *62-63*, 63
Omni Los Angeles 63
Orlando 60
Peninsula Beverly Hills 56
Queen Mary 66
Renaissance Hollywood
  60, 61
Ritz Milner 64
Ritz-Carlton, Marina del Rey
  50
Secret Garden B&B 61
Shade 65
Sheraton Delfina 49
Sheraton Gateway 51
Shutters on the Beach
  44, 48
SLS Los Angeles 56
Sofitel Los Angeles 58
Sportsmen's Lodge 64

St Regis Monarch Beach Resort 66
Standard Downtown 63
Standard Hollywood 60
Sunset Marquis Hotel & Villas 59
Sunset Tower 59, 61
Thompson Beverly Hills 55, 57
Venice Beach House 50
Viceroy 48
W 53
Westin Bonaventure 64

Bars
86 181
Air Conditioned 175, 176
Avalon Lounge 178
Bar 107 185
Bar Copa 176
Bar Lubitsch 177, 179
Bar Marmont 180
Bar Nineteen 12 178
Beauty Bar 180
Beechwood 177
Bigfoot Lodge 184
Blu Monkey Lounge 181
Blue Room 186
Bodega Wine Bar 186
Bottle Rock 178
Brass Monkey 183
Brig 177
Broadway Bar 185
Buggy Whip 178
Canter's Kibitz Room 182
Carmen, El 182
Cat & Fiddle 181
Central 181
Cha Cha Lounge 184
Chez Jay 176
Dear John's 178
Dresden Room 183
Edison 184, 186
Father's Office 176
Formosa Café 180
Frolic Room 181
Gold Room 185
Golden Gopher 186
Good Luck Bar 183
Griffin 184
Hank's Bar 186
Hideout 176
HMS Bounty 183
Hyde Lounge 180
Irish Times 177
Johnny's Bar 185
Langham Huntington Bar 186
Little Bar 183
Mandrake Bar 178
Mixville Bar 184
Nirvana 178
Otheroom 177
Piano Bar 181
Prince 183
Renée's Courtyard Café & Bar 176

Roof at the Standard 186
Royal Claytons 186
S Bar 181
Saints & Sinners 178
Seven Grand 186
Short Stop 185
Smog Cutter 185
Tiki-Ti 185
Tom Bergin's Tavern 183
Tropicana Bar 181
Velvet Margarita Cantina, La 181
Woods 180, 182
Writer's Bar 178
York 185

Restaurants & coffeehouses
18th Street Coffee House 170
Abbey 245
Abbot's Habit 171
Alcazar 166
Alegria on Sunset 162
Allegria 145
Angeli Caffe 219
Animal 159
Anisette 145
Apple Pan 150
Art's Deli 166
Asian Noodles 164
Axe 149
Babita Mexicuisine 167
Baby Blues 149
Bastide 154, 155
Bhan Kanom 156
BLT 155
Bourgeois Pig 172
Breadbar 152
Buster's Ice Cream & Coffee Shop 174
Cacao Coffee House 171
Cachette, La 152
Café 50s 219
Café del Rey 149
Café Stella 162
Café Tropical 173
Caffe Dell'arte 171
California Pizza Kitchen 220
Calitalia 166
Campanile 160
Canter's Deli 159
Cassell's 160
Ce Fiori 164
Celestino Ristorante 167
Chango Coffee House 174
Cheesecake Factory 220
Chez Melange 168
Cholo, El 161
Chosun Galbee 161
Citizen Smith 156
Ciudad 164
Clementine 152
Cobras & Matadors 159
Coffee Table 174
Coley's Caribbean American Cuisine 166
Counter 147

Cut 152
Dan Tana's 155
Darren's 168, 169
Dijonaise, La 150
Double Dutch 150, 151
Dr Hogly-Wogly's Tyler Texas BBQ 166, 167
Drago Ristorante 147
Edendale Grill 162
Empress Harbor 167
Falcon 156
Farmers Market 159, 220
Fogo de Chao 154
Ford's Filling Station 150
Fraiche 150
Fred 62 162
Funnel Mill 170
Galley 147
Gardens on Glendon 152
Gordon Ramsay 155
Griddle Café 156
Grill on the Alley 154
Groundwork Coffee Shop 174
Guelaguetza 161
Harold & Belle's 166
Hotel Bel-Air 152
India Sweets & Spices 164
Inn of the Seventh Ray 145
Insomnia 173
Intelligentsia 174
Jagerhaus 169
Japon Bistro 167
Jin Patisserie 171
Jitlada 156
Joan's on Third 159
Joe's 149
Joni's Coffee Roasting Café 171
Josie 147
LA Mill 174
LAX-C 164
Leaf Cuisine 150
Lemon Moon 150
Little Dom's 160, 162
Lucques 156
Luna Negra, La 168
Luna Park 160
M Café de Chaya 159
Manis Bakery 159
Mario's Peruvian Seafood 156
Mashti Malone's 157
Matsuhisa 154
Mélisse 147
Miceli's 157
Mikawaya 164
Millie's 162
Misti Picanteria Arequipeña, El 169
Monsoon 147
Moonshadows 145
Moro, Il 151
Musso & Frank Grill 157
Nanbankan 152
Napa Rose 169
Nate 'n Al's 154
Native Foods 152

Newsroom Café 220
Ngoma 160
Nobu Malibu 145
Ocean Seafood 164
Oliver Café 155
Original Pantry 164
Orris 151
Ortolan 159
Osteria Mozza 157
Pacific Dining Car 164
Pain Quotidien, Le 172
Papa Cristo's 161
Parrilla, La 165, 165
Patina 165
Peet's Coffee & Tea 173
Petros Greek Cuisine & Lounge 169
Philippe the Original 165
Pitfire Pizza Company 220
Pizzeria Mozza 157
Providence 157
Restaurant Christine 169
Restaurants at the Getty Center 149
Roscoe's House of Chicken & Waffles 158
Sabor y Cultura 172
Saddle Peak Lodge 167
SanSui 162
Sapphire 169
Scoops 158
Serenata di Garibaldi, La 166
Sole, Il 156
Soot Bull Jeep 161
Spago of Beverly Hills 155
Spring Street Smokehouse 165
Stonehill Tavern 169
Sushi Yotsuya 167
Susina 173, 173
Takao 150
Tam O'Shanter 164
Tanner's Coffee Co 171
Taylor's Steak House 161
Teaforest 171
Tender Greens 150
Terrace 149
Tlapazola Grill 151
Tokyo Table 155
Traxx 165
Tropicalia 162
Truxton's 149
Typhoon 144, 147
Upstairs2 151
Urasawa 155
Urth Caffe 172
Versailles 160
Wahib's 168
Warszawa 147
Water Grill 165
Wolfgang Puck Express 220
Wolfgang's Steakhouse 155
Yamashiro 157, 158
Yazmin 168
Zona Rosa Caffe 174

Index

Advertisers' Index

Please refer to the relevant pages for contact details

Air France	IFC

In Context

Alamo	8
The Grove	12
The Americana at Brand	13

Sightseeing

| City Pass | 70 |
| Carbon Neutral | 72 |

Eat, Drink, Shop

Hard Rock Café	148
Virgin Megastore	IBC

Place of interest and/or entertainment	▨
Hospital or college	▨
Railway station	▨
Parks	▨
River	▨
Interstate highway	🛡110
US highway	🛡101
State or provincial highway	①1
Main road	
Airport	✈
Metro stop	Ⓜ Ⓜ
Area name	VENICE
Hotel	❶
Restaurant	❶
Coffeehouse	❶
Bar	❶

Maps

LA Overview	324
Santa Monica & Venice	326
Beverly Hills	327
West Hollywood	328
Hollywood & Midtown	329
East of Hollywood	330
Downtown	331
Street Index	332
Metro Rail Network	335
LA by Area	336

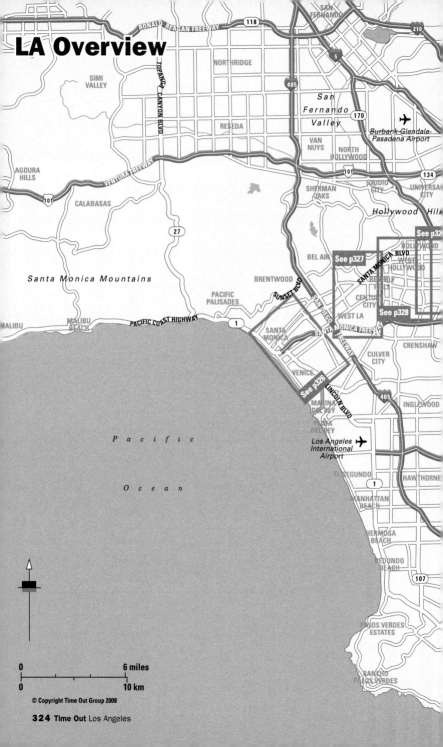

LA Overview

SIMI VALLEY

RONALD REAGAN FREEWAY

118

SAN FERNANDO

5

210

NORTHRIDGE

405

170

San Fernando Valley

RESEDA

VAN NUYS

BURBANK-GLENDALE-PASADENA AIRPORT

Burbank-Glendale-Pasadena Airport

134

AGOURA HILLS

101

VENTURA FREEWAY

NORTH HOLLYWOOD

101

SHERMAN OAKS

STUDIO CITY

UNIVERSAL CITY

CALABASAS

TOPANGA CANYON BLVD

27

Hollywood Hil

See p32

BEL AIR

HOLLYWOOD BLVD

WEST HOLLYWOOD

Santa Monica Mountains

BRENTWOOD

See p327

BEVERLY HILLS

SANTA MONICA

SUNSET BLVD

SAN DIEGO

CENTURY CITY

See p328

WEST LA

PACIFIC PALISADES

PACIFIC COAST HIGHWAY

MALIBU

MALIBU BEACH

1

SANTA MONICA

SANTA MONICA FREEWAY

CRENSHAW

CULVER CITY

VENICE

See p326

LINCOLN BLVD

MARINA DEL REY

405

INGLEWOOD

PLAYA DEL REY

Los Angeles International Airport

Pacific

EL SEGUNDO

HAWTHORNE

1

Ocean

MANHATTAN BEACH

HERMOSA BEACH

REDONDO BEACH

107

PALOS VERDES ESTATES

0 ___ 6 miles
0 ___ 10 km

© Copyright Time Out Group 2008

RANCHO PALOS VERDES

ANGELES CREST HWY
2

FOOTHILL FREEWAY
LA CANADA
FLINTRIDGE

San Gabriel Mountains

BURBANK

GLENDALE
210

PASADENA
SIERRA
MADRE
MONROVIA

VENTURA FREEWAY
210
BRADBURY
AZUSA

ATWATER
VILLAGE
EAGLE ROCK
San Gabriel Valley
ARCADIA

LOS
FELIZ
See p330

SILVER
LAKE
MT
WASHINGTON
SOUTH
PASADENA
19
BALDWIN
PARK

PASADENA FREEWAY

SAN
GABRIEL
605
COVINA

ECHO
PARK
HOLLYWOOD FREEWAY

CHINATOWN

SAN BERNARDINO FREEWAY
EL
MONTE
10

110
MONTEREY
PARK

10
DOWNTOWN
See p331
MONTEBELLO
60
POMONA FREEWAY

WHITTIER BLVD

HUNTINGTON
PARK
710
5
72
WHITTIER

WHITTIER BLVD

FIRESTONE BLVD
DOWNEY

WATTS
LYNWOOD
LA HABRA

105
IMPERIAL HWY
5

GARDENA
COMPTON
PARAMOUNT
FULLERTON

ARTESIA FREEWAY

19

SANTA ANA FREEWAY

TORRANCE
605
CYPRESS
ANAHEIM
5

110
CARSON
405
Municipal
Airport
BEACH BLVD

SAN DIEGO FREEWAY
LOS ALAMITOS
GARDEN GROVE

103
710
22
GARDEN GROVE FREEWAY

213
LONG BEACH
WESTMINSTER
SANTA ANA

SEAL
BEACH
HUNTINGTON
BEACH
405

SAN
PEDRO
Long Beach Harbour
PACIFIC COAST HIGHWAY

SUNSET
BEACH
Time Out Los Angeles 325

Santa Monica & Venice

© Copyright Time Out Group 2008

Brentwood Country Club

Memorial Park

Bergamot Station/Santa Monica Museum of Art

St John's Hospital

Santa Monica Public Library

Post Office

3rd St Promenade

Visitor Center

Santa Monica Municipal Pier

Santa Monica Pier Aquarium

California Heritage Museum

Woodlawn Cemetery

Clover Park

Santa Monica Airport

Penmar Golf Course

OCEAN PARK

VENICE

SANTA MONICA

Symbol	Legend
❶	Hotels pp44-66
❷	Restaurants pp144-169
❸	Coffeehouses pp170-174
❹	Bars pp175-186

Beverly Hills

Legend:
- Hotels pp44-66
- Restaurants pp144-169
- Coffeehouses pp170-174
- Bars pp175-186

© Copyright Time Out Group 2008

900 m
900 yds

Map labels include:

Greystone Park

BEVERLY HILLS

Beverly Hills Hotel & Bungalows
Will Rogers Memorial Park

Los Angeles Country Club

Paley Center for Media

Beverly Gardens

Spadena House

Visitor Center

Westfield Century City

CENTURY CITY

Roxbury Park

20th Century Fox Studios

Museum of Tolerance

Hillcrest Country Club

UCLA Hammer Museum

RANCHO PARK

Rancho Park Golf Course

WEST LA

Westside Pavilion

CHEVIOT HILLS

Street names include:
N BEVERLY DR, W SUNSET BLVD, ELEVADO AVE, N DOHENY DR, FOOTHILL RD, SANTA MONICA BLVD, N BEVERLY BLVD, W 3RD ST, BURTON WAY, N CANON DR, WILSHIRE BLVD, OLYMPIC BLVD, PICO BLVD, LITTLE SANTA MONICA BLVD, CENTURY PARK E, CENTURY PARK W, AVE OF THE STARS, S BEVERLY GLEN BLVD, SANTA MONICA BLVD, OVERLAND AVE, WESTWOOD BLVD, VETERAN AVE, SEPULVEDA BLVD, MANNING AVE, MOTOR AVE, CASTLE HEIGHTS AVE, CATTARAUGUS AVE, NATIONAL BLVD, SANTA MONICA FREEWAY, SAN DIEGO FREEWAY, NATIONAL PL, BEVERLY GLEN BLVD, BENEDICT CANYON DR

West Hollywood

A

B

C

D

SUNSET PLAZA DRIVE

AVE

HOLLYWOOD BLVD 7200

© Copyright Time Out Group 2008

0   900 m
0   900 yds

SUNSET BLVD (SUNSET STRIP)

Chateau Marmont

WEST HOLLYWOOD

Post Office

SUNSET

SANTA MONICA BLVD

Schindler House/ MAK Center

Pacific Design Center

West Hollywood Park

MELROSE AVE

Beverly Center

N LA CIENEGA BLVD

SAN VICENTE BLVD

CRESCENT HEIGHTS BLVD

N FAIRFAX AVE

SANTA MONICA BLVD

Warner Studios

MELROSE AVE

N GARDNER ST

BEVERLY BLVD

N LA BREA AVE

See p329

BEVERLY BLVD

CBS Television City

Pan Pacific Park

FAIRFAX DISTRICT

Farmers Market

The Grove

S FAIRFAX AVE

W 3RD ST

S LA BREA AVE

W 3RD ST

BURTON WAY

WILSHIRE BLVD

BEVERLY HILLS

W 5TH ST

MIRACLE MILE

Hancock Park

LA County Museum of Art

Page Museum at the La Brea Tar Pits

Petersen Automotive Museum

Craft & Folk Art Museum

WILSHIRE BLVD (MIRACLE MILE)

La Cienega Park

OLYMPIC BLVD

OLYMPIC BLVD

W PICO BLVD

S ROBERTSON BLVD

SAN VICENTE BLVD

W PICO BLVD

VENICE BLVD

S LA BREA AVE

W 18TH ST

S FAIRFAX AVE

VENICE BLVD

S REDONDO BLVD

HAUSER BLVD

1	Hotels pp44-66
1	Restaurants pp144-169
1	Coffeehouses pp170-174
1	Bars pp175-186

CADILLAC AVE

S LA CIENEGA BLVD

VENICE BLVD

W WASHINGTON BLVD

SANTA MONICA FREEWAY

328 Time Out Los Angeles

10

Hollywood & Midtown

A B C D

HOLLYWOOD HILLS
Hollywood Bowl

Grauman's Chinese Theater

Hollywood & Highland

LOS FELIZ

HOLLYWOOD

Hollywood Forever Cemetery

Paramount Studios

Wilshire Country Club

LARCHMONT VILLAGE

HANCOCK PARK

KOREATOWN

Wiltern Theater

❶	Hotels pp44-66
❶	Restaurants pp144-169
❶	Coffeehouses pp170-174
❶	Bars pp175-186

0   900 m
0   900 yds

© Copyright Time Out Group 2008

See p330
See p328

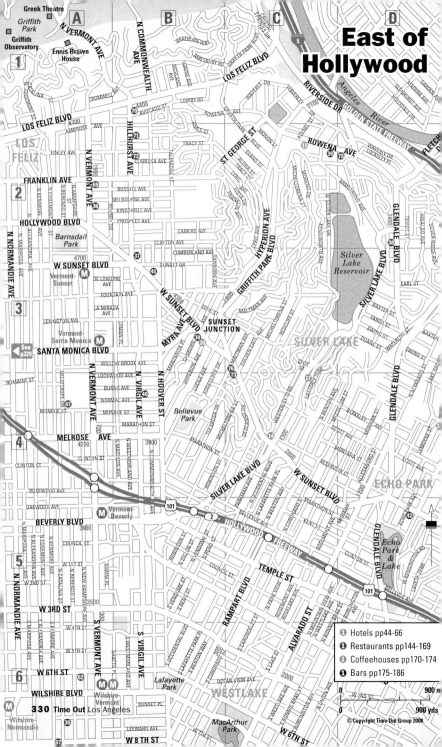

East of Hollywood

Greek Theatre
Griffith Park
Griffith Observatory
Ennis Brown House

Silver Lake Reservoir

SILVER LAKE

ECHO PARK

Echo Park & Lake

LOS FELIZ

WESTLAKE

MacArthur Park

Wilshire-Normandie

❶ Hotels pp44-66
❶ Restaurants pp144-169
❶ Coffeehouses pp170-174
❶ Bars pp175-186

0   900 m
0   900 yds

© Copyright Time Out Group 2008

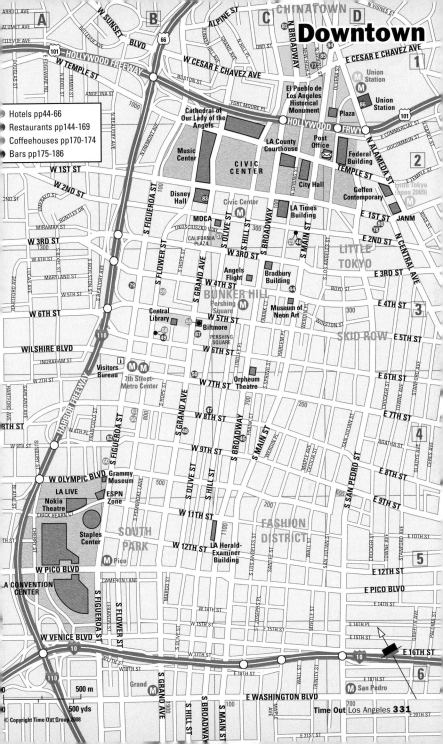

Downtown

- Hotels pp44-66
- Restaurants pp144-169
- Coffeehouses pp170-174
- Bars pp175-186

Street Index

Note: the numbered streets
in Santa Monica (2nd St,
3rd St, and so on) have
been differentiated from the
numbered streets elsewhere
in LA with the label 'SM'.

1st Ct (SM) - p326 A2
E 1st St - p331 C2/D2
W 1st St - p328 B3/C3/D3,
   p329 A4/B4/C4/D4, p330
   A5/B5, p331 A2/B2/C2
2nd Ct (SM) - p326 A2
2nd St (SM) - p326 A2
E 2nd St - p331 C2/D2/3
W 2nd St - p328 D3, p329 A4/
   B4/C4/D4, p329 A5/D6,
   p331 A2/B2/C2
3rd Ave - p329 C5/6
3rd St (SM) - p326 A2-5
E 3rd St - p331 C3/D3
W 3rd St - p327 D2, p328 A3/
   B3/C3/D3, p329 A4/B4/
   C4/D4, p330 A5/B5/6/
   C6/D6, p331 A2/B3/C3
4th Ave (SM) - p326 A4/5
4th Ct (SM) - p326 B2
4th St (SM) - p326 A2
E 4th St - p331 C3/D3
W 4th St - p328 B3/C3, p330
   A6/B6, p331 A3/B3/C3
5th Ave - p329 C5/6
5th Ave (SM) - p326 A5
5th Ct (SM) - p326 B2
5th St (SM) - p326 B2
E 5th St - p331 C3/D3
W 5th St - p328 B3/C4, p330
   A6/B6, p331 A3/B3/C3
6th Ct (SM) - p326 B2
6th St (SM) - p326 B2
E 6th St - p331 C3/D3/4
W 6th St - p328 C4/D4, p329
   A5/B5/C5/D5, p330 A6/
   B6/C6, p331 A3/B3/C3
7th St (SM) - p326 B1-3
E 7th St - p331 C4/D4
W 7th St - p329 C5/D5, p330
   B6, p331 A4/B4/C4
W 8th Pl - p331 A4
E 8th St - p331 C4/D4
W 8th St - p328 C4/D4, p329
   A5/B5/C5/D5, p330 B6,
   p331 A4/B4/C4
9th Ct (SM) - p326 B2
9th St (SM) - p326 B1/2
E 9th St - p331 C4/D4/5
W 9th St - p328 D4, p329 A5/
   B5/C5/D5, p331 A4/B4/C4
10th St (SM) - p326 B1-3
E 10th St - p331 D5
W 10th St - p331 A4
11th Ct (SM) - p326 B2
11th St (SM) - p326 B1-3
W 11th St - p329 C6/D6,
   p331 A5/B5/C5
12th Ct (SM) - p326 B2
12th St (SM) - p326 B1/2
E 12th St - p331 C5/D5
W 12th St - p328 D5, p329 A6/
   B6/C6/D6, p329 A5/B5/C5
14th St (SM) - p326 B1-3
E 14th Pl - p331 D6
E 14th St - p331 D5
W 14th St - p331 B5/C5
15th St (SM) - p326 C1-3
E 15th St - p331 C6/D6
W 15th St - p329 C6/D6,
   p331 B6/C6
16th St (SM) - p326 C1-4
E 16th St - p331 C6/D6
17th St (SM) - p326 C1-4
W 17th St - p331 A6/B6/C6

18th St (SM) - p326 C1-3
E 18th St - p331 C6/D6
W 18th St - p328 A5/B6,
   p331 B6
19th St (SM) - p326 C1-3
20th St (SM) - p326 C1-4
E 20th St - p331 D6
21st Ct (SM) - p326 C2
21st Pl (SM) - p326 C1/2
21st St (SM) - p326 C1-4
E 21st St - p331 C6/D6
22nd St (SM) - p326 C1-4
23rd St (SM) - p326 C1-5
W 23rd St - p328 D6
24th St (SM) - p326 C2/D1/2
W 24th St - p328 A6
25th St (SM) - p326 D1/2
W 25th St - p328 A6
26th St (SM) - p326 D1-3
28th Ave (SM) - p326 A6
28th St (SM) - p326 D4
29th St (SM) - p326 D4
31st St (SM) - p326 D4
33rd St (SM) - p326 D4

**Abbot Kinney Blvd -
p326 A5/6/B6**
Adelaide Dr - p326 A1/B1
Agatha St - p331 D4
Airdrome St - p327 D4, p328
   A5/B5/C5/6
Airport Ave - p326 C5/D5
N Alameda St - p331 D1/2
Albany St - p331 A5/6
Alcott St - p327 D4,
   p328 A5/B5
Alden Dr - p327 D2, p328 A3
N Alexandria Ave - p329 D1-3,
   p330 A2-5
S Alexandria Ave - p329 D4/5
S Alfred St - p328 B4/5
Allesandro St - p330 D3/4
Almayo Ave - p327 B5
N Almont Dr - p327 C1/2/D2/3
S Almont Dr - p328 A4/5
Aloha St - p330 C2
Alpine St - p331 B1/C1
Alta Ave - p326 A1/B1/C1/D1
N Alta Dr - p327 D1/2
Alta Loma Rd - p328 B1/2
N Alta Vista Blvd - p328 D1-3
Alvarado St - p330 C5/6/D3/4
Alvira St - p328 B4/5
Ambrose Ave - p330 A2
Ames St - p330 B1/2
Amesbury Rd - p330 B1
Amoroso Pl - p326 B6
Anchor Ave - p327 D5
Angelina St - p331 A1/B1
Angelo Dr - p327 A1/B1
Appleton Way - p326 C5
N Arden Blvd - p329 B3/4
S Arden Blvd - p329 B5/6
N Arden Dr - p327 D2
N Ardmore Ave - p329 D3
S Ardmore Ave - p329 D5/6
N Argyle Ave - p329 B1/2
Arizona Ave - p326 A2/B1/
   C2/D2
Armstrong Ave - p330 C2/D2
N Arnaz Dr - p328 A3/4
Ashcroft Ave - p328 A3
Ashland Ave - p326 A4/B4/C4
Ashton Ave - p327 A4
Ashwood Ave - p326 C5/6
Ave of the Stars - p327 B4/C4
Avenel St - p330 C1/2
Avocado St - p330 B1
Ayres Ave - p327 B5

Bagley Ave - p327 D5/6
Bangor St - p328 D6

Barbydell Dr - p327 C6
Barton Ave - p329 A3/B3
Baxter St - p330 D3
Bay St - p326 A3/B3
Beachwood Dr - p329 B1/C3/4
N Beaudry Ave - p331 B1/2
S Beaudry Ave - p331 A3/B3
N Bedford Dr - p327 B2/C2/3
S Bedford Dr - p327 C3/4
S Bedford St - p328 B5
Beethoven St - p326 C6
Bellevue Ave - p329 B4/C5/
   D5, p331 A1/B1
Belmont Ave - p330 D6
Benecia Blvd - p327 B4
Benedict Canyon Dr - p327 A1/
   B1/2
S Bentley Blvd - p327 A6
N Benton Ave - p330 C4
N Benton Way - p330 C4/5
S Benton Way - p330 B5
Benvenue St - p326 D1
N Berendo St - p330 A2-5
Berkeley Ave - p330 C4/D4
Berkeley St - p326 D2/3
Beverleywood St - p328 A6
Beverly Blvd - p327 D2, p328
   A3/B3/C3/D3, p329 A4/
   B4/C4/D4, p330 A5/B5/
   C5/6/D6
N Beverly Dr - p327 C1-3
S Beverly Dr - p327 D3-6
Beverly Glen Blvd - p327 A2/3/
   B4/5
Beverlywood St - p327 D5
Beverwil Dr - p327 D4-6
Bicknell St - p326 A4
Bimini Pl - p330 A5
N Bixel St - p331 A1/A2
S Bixel St - p331 A4/5
Blackburn Ave - p328 B3/C3
Blaine St - p331 A4/5
Blythe Ave - p327 B5
Boise Ave - p326 D6
Bonita Ave - p328 C5
N Bonnie Brae St - p330 C6/D5
S Bonnie Brae St - p330 C6
Boston St - p331 B1
Boyd St - p331 D3
N Boylston St - p331 A1/2
S Boylston St - p331 A3
Bradbury Rd - p327 B5/6
Braeburn Way - p330 B1
Brighton Way - p327 C3
Broadway - p326 A3/B3/C3/D3
N Broadway - p331 C1/2
S Broadway - p331 B5/6/C2-4
N Bronson Ave - p329 C1-4
S Bronson Ave - p329 B6/C5/6
Brooks Ave - p326 A5/B5
Bunker Hill Ave - p331 B1/C1
Burlingame Ave - p326 D1
N Burlington Ave - p330 D5
S Burlington Ave - p330 D6
Burns Ave - p330 A4/B4
S Burnside Ave - p328 D4/5
Burton Way - p327 D2,
   p328 A3/B3
Butterfield Rd - p327 B5/6

Cabrillo Ave - p326 A5/6
Cadillac Ave - p328 A6/B6
N Cahuenga Blvd - p329 B1-3
California Ave - p326 A2/B2/
   C2, p326 B5/6
California Plaza - p331 B2/C2
Calle Vista Dr - p327 C1
Calumet Ave - p331 A1
N Camden Dr - p327 B2/C2
S Camden Dr - p327 C3/4
Camerford Ave - p329 B3
Camero Ave - p330 B2

Cameron Lane - p331 B5
Canal St - p326 A6
S Canfield Ave - p327 D5/6
N Canon Dr - p327 C2/3/D3
S Canon Dr - p327 D3/4
Cardiff Ave - p327 D6, p328 A5
Carlos Ave - p329 B1/C1
Carlton Way - p329 C2
Carlyle Ave - p326 B1/C1/D1
Carmelina Ave - p326 D2/3
Carmelita Ave - p327 D2
Carmona Ave - p328 C5
N Carolwood Dr - p327
   A1/2/B2
S Carondelet St - p330 C5/6
Carroll Ave - p331 A1
N Carson Rd - p328 B3/4
Cashio St - p327 D4, p328
   A5/B5
Castle Heights Ave - p327 D5/6
Catalina St - p330 A1
Cattaraugus Ave - p327 D6
Cavendish Dr - p327 C5/6
Cecilia St - p331 C4
Cedar St - p326 B4
Centinela Ave - p326 D2-6
N Central Ave - p331 D2/3
Century Park E - p327 B3/C4
Century Park W - p327 B4
Ceres Ave - p331 D4
César E Chávez Ave - p331
   B1/C1/D1
Chalmers Dr - p328 B4
Channel Rd - p326 A1/B1
Chariton St - p328 B6
Charleville Blvd - p327 C3,
   p328 A4/B4
Chelsea Ave - p326 C2/3
N Cherokee Ave - p329 A2/3
Cherry St - p331 A5
Cheviot Dr - p327 B6/C5/6
Citrus Ave - p329 A3/4
S Citrus Ave - p329 A5/6
Clarissa Ave - p330 B2
S Clark Dr - p328 A4/5
Clayton Ave - p330 B2
Clifton Way - p327 D3, p328
   A3/B3
Clinton St - p328 C2/D2, p329
   A3/B3, p330 A4/B4/C4/D5
Cloverdale Ave - p328 D4/5
Cloverfield Blvd - p326 C4
Club Dr - p327 C6
Club View Dr - p327 B3
S Cochran Ave - p328 D4/5
Colgate Ave - p328 B3/C3
Cologne St - p328 C6
Colorado Ave - p326 A3/B3/
   C3/D3
Colorado Pl - p326 D3
E Commercial St - p331 D1/2
N Commonwealth Ave - p330
   B1/4/5
Comstock Ave - p327 A2/3/B3
Constellation Blvd - p327 B4
Conway Ave - p327 A2
Copley Pl - p327 B2
S Corning St - p328 B4/5
N Coronado St - p330 C4/5
S Coronado St - p330 B6/C6
Council St - p330 A5/B5/C5,
   p331 A2
Country Club Dr - p329 C6
Court St - p330 D6, p331 A1
Courtney Ave - p328 C1
Crenshaw Blvd - p329 B6/C5
N Crescent Dr - p327 B1/C2
S Crescent Dr - p327 D3/4
Crescent Heights Blvd - p328
   B5/6/C2-4
Cresta Dr - p327 C5/D5,
   p328 A5

Crocker St - p331 D3-5
N Croft Ave - p328 B1/2
Cromwell Ave - p330 A1/B1
Crystal Springs Dr - p330 C1
Cumberland Ave - p330 B3
N Curson Ave - p328 C2/3
S Curson Ave - p328 C5
Cushdon Ave - p327 B5
Cynthia St - p328 A2

David Ave - p328 A6
Dawson St - p330 D6
Dayton Way - p327 D3, p328 A3/B3
De Longpre Ave - p329 C2/D2, p330 A3/B3
Delaware Ave - p326 C3/D3/4
Delfern Dr - p327 A1/2
Descanso Dr - p330 C4
N Detroit St - p328 D1-3, p329 A3/4
S Detroit St - p328 D4/5
Devon Ave - p327 A2/3
Dewey St - p326 A5/B5/C5/D5
N Dillon St - p330 B5
Dockweiler St - p329 A6/B6
N Doheny Dr - p327 D1/2, p328 A2/3
S Doheny Dr - p327 D3/4, p328 A4/5
Doheny Rd - p327 C1/D1
Donald Douglas Loop - p326 D5
Doreen Pl - p326 B5
Dorrington Ave - p328 A3
Douglas St - p331 A1
Drexel Ave - p328 B3/C3
Dryad Rd - p326 B1
Duane St - p330 D3
Ducommun St - p331 D2
Dudley Ave - p326 A5
Dunleer Dr - p327 C6
S Dunsmuir Ave - p328 D4/5
Duxbury Rd - p327 D5

Earl St - p330 D3
Earlmar Dr - p327 C5/6
Eastborne Ave - p327 A4
Easterly Terr - p330 C3/4
Echo Park Ave - p330 D4/5
Edgecliffe Dr - p330 B3/4/C3
N Edgemont Ave - p330 A1-5
E Edgeware Rd - p331 A1
Edgewood Pl - p329 A5/6
N Edinburgh Ave - p328 C2/3
Effie St - p330 B3/C3
S El Camino Dr - p327 D3/4
El Centro Ave - p329 B2/3
Eleanor Ave - p329 B2
Electric Ave - p326 A5/6
Elevado Ave - p327 B2/3/C2
N Elm Dr - p327 D2/3
S Elm Dr - p327 D3/4
Emerald St - p331 A2
Ensley Ave - p327 B3
Entrada Dr - p326 B1
Esther Ave - p327 B5
Euclid Ct - p326 B2
Euclid St - p326 B1-3
Evans St - p330 C2
Ewing St - p330 D3
Exposition Blvd - p326 D3/4, p327 A6

Fairburn Ave - p327 A4
N Fairfax Ave - p328 C1/2
S Fairfax Ave - p328 B6/C3-5
Fargo St - p330 D3
Figueroa St - p331 A5/6/B2-4
Finley Ave - p330 A2/B2
Firmin St - p331 A1
Fletcher Dr - p330 D2
N Flores St - p328 B1
Flower Ave - p326 B5
N Flower St - p331 B2
S Flower St - p331 B2-6
Foothill Rd - p327 C1/2/D2/3
N Formosa Ave - p328 D1-3, p329 A2/3
S Formosa Ave - p328 D3
Forrester Dr - p327 C5

Fountain Ave - p328 C1/D1, p329 A2/B2/C2/D2, p330 A2/3/B2/3/C2
Fox Hills Dr - p327 B4
Francis Ave - p329 B5
Francisco St - p331 A4
Frank Ct - p331 C3/C4
Franklin Ave - p329 A1/B1/C1/D1
Franklin St - p326 D3
Franklin St - p326 D2/3
N Fremont Ave - p331 B1/2
N Fuller Ave - p328 D1/2
S Fuller Ave - p328 D3

Garden Ave - p330 D1
N Gardner St - p328 D1-3
Garfield Ave - p326 B6
Garfield Pl - p329 C1
Garland Ave - 315 A4
S Garth Ave - p328 B5
N Genesee Ave - p328 C1-3
S Genesee Ave - p328 C5
Georgia St - p331 A4/5
Georgina Ave - p326 A1/B1
Gibson St - p328 A6
Gladys Ave - p331 D4
Glencoe Ave - p326 C6
Glendale Blvd - p330 D2-6, p331 A2
Glendon Ave - p327 A5/B6
Glenhurst Ave - p330 D1
Glenville Dr - p328 A5
Glyndon Ave - p326 C6
Golden Gate Ave - p330 C3
N Gower St - p329 B1-3
Gramercy Pl - p329 C1-6
Grand Ave - p331 B2-6/C1
Grand Blvd - p326 A6
Grand Canal Ct - p326 A6
Grange Ave - p327 A5
Grant St - p326 B4
Greenfield Ave - p327 A6/B6
Greenwood Ave - p326 C6
Gregory Ave - p329 B3
Gregory Way - p327 D3/3, p328 A4/B4
Griffith Ave - p331 D5/6
Griffith Park Blvd - p330 C1-3
The Grove Dr - p328 C3
Guthrie St - p328 A6/B6

N Hamel Rd - p328 A3/4
Hamilton Dr - p328 B4
Hammond St - p328 A2
N Hampshire St - p330 A2
Hampton Ave - p328 C1/D1
Hampton Dr - p326 A5
Hancock Ave - p328 A2
Harbor St - p326 A6
Hargis St - p327 D6
Harlem Pl - p331 C3
Harold Way - p329 C2
N Harper Ave - p328 B2/3
Hartford Ave - p331 A3/A4
Harvard Ave - p326 D2/3
N Harvard Blvd - p329 D1-4
Harvard Ct - p326 D2
Hauser Blvd - p328 C5/6/D3-5
Havenhurst Dr - p328 B1/C1
Hawthorn Ave - p328 C1/D1, p329 A2
N Hayworth Ave - p328 C1-3
S Hayworth Ave - p328 B5/6
Heliotrope Dr - p330 A3/4
Hidalgo Ave - p330 D2/3
N Highland Ave - p329 A2/3
S Highland Ave - p328 D5/6, p329 A4/5
N Hill Pl - p331 C1
Hill Pl N - p326 B4/C4
Hill St - p331 B4-6/C2/3
Hill St (SM) - p326 A4/B4/C4
Hillcrest Rd - p327 D2
Hillhurst Ave - p330 B1/2
Hillsboro Ave - p327 D5
Hillside Ave - p328 C1
Hobart Blvd - p329 D1-6
Hollister Ave - p326 A4/B4
Holloway Dr - p328 A2/B2

Hollydale Dr - p330 D1/2
Hollywood Blvd - p328 C1/D1, p329 A1/B1/C1/D1, p330 A2
Holman Ave - p327 A4
Holmby Ave - p327 A3/4
S Holt Ave - p328 B4/5
N Hoover St - p330 B3/4
S Hope St - p331 B2-5
Horn Ave - p328 A1/2
Horner St - p328 B5
Hudson Ave - p329 A6/B4/5
Huntley Dr - p328 B2/3, p331 A2
Hyperion Ave - p330 B3/4/C2/3

Idaho Ave - p326 A2/B2/C2
Ilona Ave - p327 B4/5
Indiana Ave - p326 A5/B5
Ingraham St - p329 C5, p331 A3
Iowa Ave - p326 D3
Irolo St - p329 D5/6
N Irving Blvd - p329 C3/4
S Irving Blvd - p329 C4/5
Ivar Ave - p329 B2

N June St - p329 B3

Kansas Ave - p326 C4/D4
Keith Ave - p328 A2
Kelton Ave - p327 A5/6/B6
Kenilworth Ave - p330 C2/3
Keniston Ave - p329 A5/6
N Kenmore Ave - p330 A2-5, p329 D1-3
S Kenmore Ave - p330 A6
W Kensington Rd - p330 D5
Kent St - p330 C5
Kerwood Ave - p327 B4
Keswick Ave - p327 A3
N Kilkea Dr - p328 C2/3
Kingman Ave - p326 B1
N Kingsley Dr - p329 D1-3
S Kingsley Dr - p329 D4/5
N Kings Rd - p328 B1-3
Kingswell Ave - p330 A2/B2
Kinnard Ave - p327 A4
Kirkside Rd - p327 D5
W Knoll Dr - p328 B2

N La Brea Ave - p328 D1/2, p329 A2/3
S La Brea Ave - p328 D3-6
N La Cienega Blvd - p328 B2/3
S La Cienega Blvd - p328 B5/6
N Lafayette Park Pl - p330 C4/5
S Lafayette Park Pl - p330 B5/6
N La Jolla Ave - p328 B2/3
S La Jolla Ave - p328 B2-5
La Mirada Ave - p329 B2/C2/D2, p330 A3/B3
Lake Ave - p326 B5/C5
Lake Shore Ave - p330 D3/4
Lake St - p326 C5
S Lake St - p330 C5/6
Lake View Ave - p330 D2/3
Lanewood Ave - p329 A2
N La Peer Dr - p328 A2
S La Peer Dr - p328 A4/5
N Larchmont Blvd - p329 B3/4
Larrabee St - p328 A2
N Las Palmas Ave - p329 A2/3
S Lasky Dr - p327 C3
N Laurel Ave - p328 C1-3
Laurel Way - p327 B1
Laveta Terr - p330 D5
N Le Doux Rd - p328 B3/4
Lebanon St - p331 B5/6
Leeward Ave - p329 C5, p330 B6
Leland Way - p329 A2/B2
Lemon Grove Ave - p329 D3
Lemoyne St - p330 D4
Lexington Ave - p328 C1/D1, p329 A2/B2/C2/D2, p330 A3/B3
Lexington Rd - p327 B1
Lillian Way - p329 B2/3
Lincoln Blvd - p326 B6

Lincoln Ct - p326 B2
Lindbrook Dr - p327 A3
N Linden Dr - p327 B2/C3
S Linden Dr - p327 C3
Lindley Pl - p331 C3/4
Linnington Ave - p327 B4/5
Locksley Pl - p330 D2
Lockwood Ave - p330 A4/B4
Loma Vista Dr - p327 C1/D1
Lomitas Ave - p327 B2/C1/2
Longpre Ave - p328 C1/D1
S Longwood Pl - p329 A5/6
Loring Ave - p327 A2/3
Lorraine Blvd - p329 C4/5
S Los Angeles St - p331 C2-6/D1/2
Los Feliz Blvd - p330 A1/2/B1/C1
Lovella Ave - p326 C6
Lowry Rd - p330 B1
Lucas Ave - p331 A3
N Lucerne Blvd - p329 B3/4
S Lucerne Blvd - p329 B4/5
Lucille Ave - p326 C6
Lyman Pl - p329 B3
Lyric Ave - p330 C2

Mabery Rd - p326 A1
Madera Ave - p330 D1
N Madison Ave - p330 B4
Main St - p326 A5
N Main St - p331 D1/C2
S Main St - p331 C2-6
Malcolm Ave - p327 A5
Maltman Ave - p330 B4/C3
Manning Ave - p327 A4/B5/6/C6
Mansfield Ave - p329 A2/3
Manzanita Pl - p330 B3
Maple Ave - p331 C4-6
N Maple Dr - p327 C1/D2/3
S Maple Dr - p327 D3/4, p328 A4/5
Maple St - p326 B4
Mapleton Dr - p327 A2
Maplewood Ave - p326 C5/6
Marathon St - p329 C3, p330 A4/B4/C4/5
Marco Pl - p326 B6
Margo St - p331 B5
Marguerita Ave - p326 A1/B1/C1/D1
Marine St - p326 A4/B5/C5
N Mariposa Ave - p329 D1-3, p330 A2-5
S Mariposa Ave - p329 D4-6, p330 A6
Market St - p326 A5
N Martel Ave - p328 D2/3
Maryland Dr - p328 B4/C4
Maryland St - p331 A3
Massachusetts Ave - p327 A4
S Masselin Ave - p328 C5
May St - p326 D6
N McCadden Place - p329 A2/3
S McCarty Dr - p327 C3
McCollum St - p330 C4/D4
McConnell Pl - p327 C5
Meier St - p326 C6/D6
Melbourne Ave - p330 A2/B2
Melrose Ave - p328 B2/C2/D2, p329 A3/B3/C3/D3, p330 A4/B4
Micheltorena St - p330 B4/C2-4
Michigan Ave - p326 B3/C3
Midvale Ave - p327 A5/6/B6
Mildred Ave - p326 A6
Military Ave - p327 A5
Milwood Ave - p326 B6
Miramar St - p331 A2
Mississippi Ave - p327 A5
Mohawk St - p330 D4/5
Monon St - p330 C2
Monroe St - p330 A4/B4
Montana Ave - p326 A2/B2/C2/D2
Montana Pl - p326 D2
Montana St - p330 C4/D4
Monte Mar - p327 D4

Moore St - p326 C6/D6
Moreno Ave - p326 D1
Moreno Dr - p327 C3, p330 C2
Morningside Way - p326 C5
N Morton Ave - p329 C3/4
Motor Ave - p327 C5/6
Mountain Dr - p327 C1
N Mountain View Ave - p330 C5/6
S Muirfield Rd - p329 B5
S Mullen Ave - p329 B5
Myra Ave - p329 B3
Myrtle St - p331 C5/6

National Blvd - p327 A6/B6/C6/D6
National Pl - p327 B6/C6
Navy St - p326 C5
Nebraska Ave - p326 D3, p327 A4
Neilson St - p326 A3-5
N New Hampshire Ave - p330 A4/5
New High St - p331 C1
Normal Ave - p330 A4/B4
N Normandie Ave - p329 D1-3, p330 A2-6
S Normandie Ave - p329 D4-6
Northvale Rd - p327 B6/C6
Norton Ave - p328 C1/D1
S Norton Ave - p329 B6/C5/6
Norwich Dr - p328 A2/B3
Nowita Ct - p326 B6

Oak St - p326 B4/C4
Oakhurst Ave - p327 D6
Oakhurst Dr - p327 D2/3, p328 A2-5
Oakmore Rd - p327 D5
Oakwood Ave - p328 B3/C3/D3, p329 A3/4, p330 A5/B5
N Occidental Blvd - p330 C4/5
S Occidental Blvd - p330 B5/6
Ocean Ave - p326 A1-6
Ocean Front Walk - p326 A5
Ocean Park Blvd - p326 A4/B4/C4/D4
Ocean Park Pl S - p326 B4/C4
Ocean View Ave - p330 B6/C6
Ocean Way - p326 A1
Ogden Dr - p328 C1/2/4/5
Ohio Ave - p327 A4
Olive Ave - p326 A6
S Olive St - p331 B3-5/C2/3
Olvera St - p331 D1
Olympic Blvd - p326 B3/C3/D3, p327 A5/B4/5/C4/D4, p328 A4/B4/C4/D4, p329 A5/B5/6/C6/D6, p331 A4/B4/C4
Orange Dr - p328 D1-3, p329 A2-5
Orange Grove Ave - p328 C1-5
Ord St - p331 C1
N Orlando Ave - p328 B2/3
S Orlando Ave - p328 B3-5
Overland Ave - p327 A4/5/B5/6
N Oxford Ave - p329 D3/4

Pacific Ave - p326 A5/6
Pacific St - p326 B4
Packard St - p328 B5/C5/D5
Palisades Ave - p326 A1/B1
Palisades Beach Rd - p326 A1-3
N Palm Dr - p327 D1-3, p328 A3/4
S Palm Dr - p327 D3/4, p328 A4/5
Palms Blvd - p326 B6/C6/D6, p327 C6
Paloma St - p331 D5/6
Pandora Ave - p327 B4
Parkman Ave - p330 C4/5
N Park View - p330 C5
Parnell Ave - p327 A4/5/B5
Patrick Ave - p327 B5
Patton St - p331 A1
Pearl St - p326 B4/C4

S Peck Dr - p327 C3/4
Pelham Ave - p327 A4/5
S Pembroke Lane - p331 B4/5
Penmar Ave - p326 B6/C5/6
Penn Ave - p326 D3
Pershing Sq - p331 C3
Pickford St - p328 A5/B5/C5/D6
Pico Blvd - p326 C4/D4, p327 A5/6/B5/C4/D4, p328 A5/B5/C5/D5, p329 A6/B6/C6/D6, p331 A5/B5/C5/D5
Pier Ave - p326 A4/B4
Pine St - p326 B4
N Plymouth Blvd - p329 C3/4
S Plymouth Blvd - p329 B4/5
Poinsettia Dr - p328 D1
N Poinsetta Pl - p328 D1/2
S Point View St - p328 B5
Preston Way - p326 C5
S Preuss Rd - p328 A5/6
Princeton Ave - p326 D2/3
Prospect Ave - p330 A2/B2
Prosser Ave - p327 A4/B5
Putney Rd - p327 B5

Queen Anne Pl - p329 B6
Queensbury Dr - p327 C5/6

Rampart Blvd - p330 B6/C5
Rangely Ave - p328 A3
Raymond Ave - p326 A4/B4
Redcliff St - p330 C13
S Redondo Blvd - p328 D5/6
Redwood Ave - p326 C5/6
S Reeves Dr - p327 D3/4
Reeves St - p327 D4
Reno St - p330 B5
Reservoir St - p330 C4/D4
N Rexford Dr - p327 C1/2
S Rexford Dr - p327 D3/4, p328 A4/5
Richland Ave - p330 B1
S Ridgeley Dr - p328 D4/5
N Ridgewood Pl - p329 C4
Rimpau Blvd - p329 B5
Riverside Dr - p330 C1/D1/2
Riviera Ave - p326 A6
N Robertson Blvd - p328 A3/4
S Robertson Blvd - p328 A4-6
Robinson St - p330 B4/5
Rochester Ave - p327 A4
N Rodeo Dr - p327 B2/C2
S Rodeo Dr - p327 C2
Rodney Dr - p330 A2
Romaine St - p328 B2/C2/D2, p329 A3/B3/C3/D3, p330 A4
Rose Ave - p326 A5/B5/C5, p327 C6
Rose St - p331 D2
Roselake Ave - p330 C5
Rosemont Ave - p330 C5
Rosewood Ave - p326 C5/6, p328 A3/B2/C1/D2, p329 A3/B3, p330 A4
S Rossmore Ave - p329 B4/5
Roundtree Rd - p327 B5/6
Rowena Ave - p330 B1/C1/2/D2
Roxbury Dr - p327 B2/C2-5/D4
Rugby Dr - p328 B2
Russell Ave - p329 D1, p330 A2/B2

St Andrews Pl - p329 C1-5
St George St - p330 B2/C2
St Josephs Pl - p331 C5/6
San Juan Ave - p326 A5/B5
San Julian St - p331 C5/D4/5
San Lorenzo St - p326 B1
S San Pedro St - p331 D2-6
San Vicente Blvd - p326 A1/B1/C1/D1, p328 A2/3/B3/4/C4/D5
San Ysidro Dr - p327 B1
Sanborn Ave - p329 B3
Santa Monica Blvd - p326 A3/B3/C3/D3, p327 A4/B3/4/C2/3/D2, p328 A2/B2/C2/

D2, p329 A2/B2/C2/D2, p330 A3/B3
Little Santa Monica Blvd - p327 A4/B3/4/C3/2/D2
Santee St - p331 C4-6
Saturn St - p328 B5/C5
Sawtelle Blvd - p327 A6
Sawyer St - p327 D5, p328 A6/B6
Schrader Blvd - p329 B2
Scott Ave - p330 C4/D4
Selby Ave - p327 A4/5/B6
Selma Ave - p328 C1, p329 A2/B2
Sepulveda Blvd - p327 A5/6
N Serrano Ave - p329 D1/2
N Serrano Blvd - p329 D3/4
Seward St - p329 B2/3
Shatto Pl - p330 A6/B6
Shelby Dr - p327 D6
S Shenandoah St - p328 A5/6
Sherbourne Dr - p328 A1
N Sierra Bonita Ave - p328 D2/3
N Sierra Dr - p327 D1/2
Silver Lake Blvd - p330 B4/5/C4/D2/3
W Silver Lake Dr - p330 C2/3
Silver Ridge Ave - p330 D2/3
N Spaulding Ave - p328 C2/3
S Spaulding Ave - p328 C5
S Spalding Dr - p327 C3
Speedway - p326 A5
N Spring St - p331 C1-3
S Spring St - p331 C3/4
Stanford Ave - p331 D3-6
N Stanley Ave - p328 C1-3
S Stanley Ave - p328 C5
S Stanley Dr - p328 B3/4
Stearns Dr - p328 B5/6
Stewart Ave - p326 D5/6
Stewart St - p326 D4
Strand St - p326 A4/B4
Summit Dr - p327 B1
Sunbury St - p331 A4
Sunset Ave - p326 A5/B4/5
W Sunset Blvd - p327 A2/B2/C1/D1, p328 A1/B1/C1/D1, p329 A2/B2/C2/D2, p330 A3/B3/C3/4, p331 B1
Sunset Dr - p329 B3
Sunset Pl - p330 B6
Sunset Plaza Drive - p328 A1/B1
Superba Ave - p326 B6
S Swall Dr - p328 A4/5
Sweetzer Ave - p328 B1-3
Sycamore Ave - p328 C1-3, p329 A1-5

Taft Ave - p329 C1
Temple St - p330 B5/C5/D5, p331 A1/B1/C2/D2
Tikosciuszko Way - p331 B2/C2
Tilden Ave - p327 A6
N Toluca St - p331 A2
Towne Ave - p331 D3-5
Tracy St - p330 B2/C2
Trinity St - p331 C6
Troon Ave - p327 B5/C5
Tularosa Dr - p329 B4
Talmadge St - p330 B2/3
Teviot St - p330 D2/3
Thayer Ave - p327 A3/4/B4
Tennessee Ave - p327 A5/B4/5
S Tremaine Ave - p329 A5/6

N Union Ave - p330 C6/D6
Urban Ave - p326 D4

Valita St - p326 B5
N Van Ness Ave - p329 C1-4
N Vendome St - p330 B5
S Vendome St - p330 B5
Venezia Ave - p326 B6
Venice Blvd - p326 A6/B6/C6/D6, p327 D6, p328 B6/C6/D5, p329 A6/B6, p331 A5/B5/C6

N Vermont Ave - p330 A1-4
S Vermont Ave - p330 A4-6
Vernon Ave - p326 A5/B5
Veteran Ave - p327 A5/6/B6
S Victoria Ave - p329 B5/6
Vidor Dr - p327 C4
N Vignes St - p331 D1
Vine St - p329 B2/3
N Virgil Ave - p330 B3/4
S Virgil Ave - p330 B6
Virginia Ave - p326 C4/D4
Virginia Ave - p329 C2
Vista Del Mar - p329 B1
Vista Dr - p330 C2
Vista St - p328 D1-3

Wade St - p326 D6
Walden Dr - p327 B3/C3
Walgrove Ave - p326 C5/6
Wall St - p331 C4-6
Walnut Ave - p326 C6
Warden Ave - p326 B5
Waring Ave - p328 B2/C2/D2
Waring Ave - p329 A3/B3
Warnall Ave - p327 B3
Warner Ave - p327 A3/4
Warren Ave - p326 C5/D5/6
Washington Ave - p326 A2/B2/C2/D2
E Washington Blvd - p331 C6/D6
W Washington Blvd - p326 A6/B6, p328 C6/D6
Waterloo St - p330 D3
Waverley Dr - p330 C1
Waverly Dr - p330 C1/D2
Wayne Ave - p330 B1
Welcome St - p330 D6
Wellworth Ave - p327 A4
Werdin Pl - p331 C3/C4
Westbourne Dr - p328 B2
Westchester Pl - p329 C5/6
Westerley Terr - p330 C1/2/3
N Western Ave - p329 C1-3
S Western Ave - p329 D5/6
Westholme Ave - p327 A4
N Westlake Ave - p330 C5/6
S Westlake Ave - p330 C6
Westminster Ave - p326 A5/B5, p329 C4/5
N Westmorland Ave - p330 B4
S Westmorland Ave - p330 B6
Westmount Dr - p328 B2
Westwood Blvd - p327 A5/B6
N Wetherby Dr - p327 D2/3
N Wetherly Dr - p328 A3/4
Whiteley Ave - p329 B1
Whittier Dr - p327 B2/3
Whitworth Dr - p327 D4, p328 A4/B4/C4/D4/5
Wilcox Ave - p329 B1/2
Wilkins Ave - p327 A4
N Willaman Dr - p328 B3/4
Willoughby Ave - p328 B2/C2/D2, p329 A3/B2/C3/D3
Willow Brook Ave - p330 A2/B3
Wilshire Blvd - p326 A2/B2/C2/D2, p327 A3/B3/C3/D3, p328 A4/B4/C4/D4, p329 A5/B5/C5/D5, p330 A6/B6, p331 A3/B3
N Wilton Pl - p329 C1-3
S Wilton Pl - p329 C5/6
N Windsor Blvd - p329 C3/4
S Windsor Blvd - p329 B5/6/C4/5
Windward Ave - p326 A5
Winona Blvd - p329 D1/2
Winston St - p331 C3/D3
Witmer St - p331 A3
Woodbine St - p327 C6
Woodland Dr - p327 C1
Woodruff Ave - p327 A3/A4
S Wooster St - p328 A5/6

Yale Ave - p326 D2/3
Yucca St - p329 A1/B1

Zanja St - p326 B6/C6

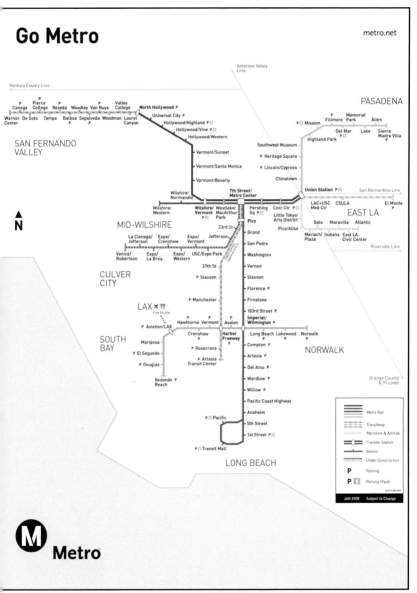

Los Angeles County Metropolitan Transportation Authority 2008.

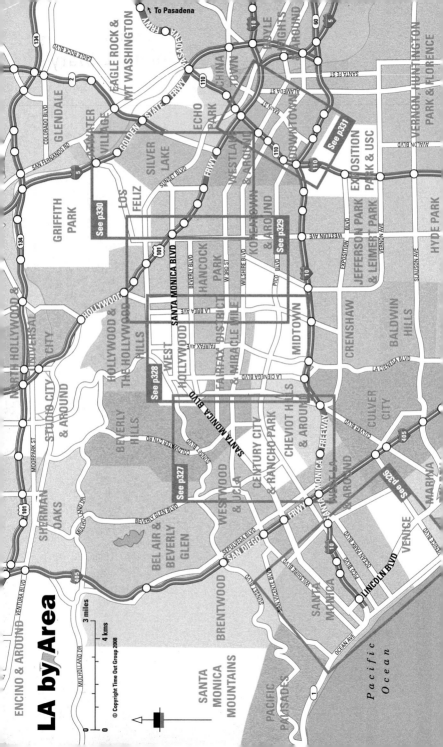